Rome, the Greek World,
and the East

Studies in the History of Greece and Rome

Robin Osborne, P. J. Rhodes, and Richard J. A. Talbert, editors

Rome, the Greek World, and the East

VOLUME 2

Government, Society, and Culture in the Roman Empire

Fergus Millar

Edited by Hannah M. Cotton and Guy M. Rogers

The University of North Carolina Press
Chapel Hill and London

Set in Bembo
by Tseng Information Systems, Inc.
Manufactured in the United States of America

⊚ The paper in this book meets the guidelines
for permanence and durability of the Committee on
Production Guidelines for Book Longevity
of the Council on Library Resources.

Library of Congress Cataloging-in-Publication Data
Millar, Fergus.
Rome, the Greek world, and the East / Fergus Millar;
edited by Hannah M. Cotton and Guy M. Rogers.
p.   cm. — (Studies in the history of Greece and Rome)
Includes bibliographical references and index.
Contents: v. 2. Government, society, and culture in the
Roman Empire
ISBN 0-8078-2852-1 (cloth: alk. paper)
ISBN 0-8078-5520-0 (pbk.: alk. paper)
1. Greece—Civilization. 2. Rome—Civilization.
I. Title. II. Series.
DE3 .M52   2002
938—dc21   2001027500

Cloth 08 07 06 05 04   5 4 3 2 1
Paper 08 07 06 05 04   5 4 3 2 1

Contents

Preface

Fergus Millar, Camden Professor of Ancient History in the University of Oxford emeritus, is one of the most influential ancient historians of the twentieth century. Since the publication of *A Study of Cassius Dio* by Oxford University Press in 1964, Millar has published eight books, including two monumental studies, *The Emperor in the Roman World* (Duckworth, 1977) and *The Roman Near East, 31 B.C.–A.D. 337* (Harvard, 1993). These books have transformed the study of ancient history.

In his study of the role of the emperor in the Roman world Millar argued that the reign of Augustus inaugurated almost three centuries of relatively passive and inert government, in which the central power pursued few policies and was largely content to respond to pressures and demands from below. After more than twenty years of scholarly reaction, *The Emperor in the Roman World* is now the dominant scholarly model of how the Roman Empire worked in practice.

Reviewers immediately hailed Millar's magisterial study of the Roman Near East as a "grand book on a grand topic" (*TLS*, 15 April 1994). In this grand book, displaying an unrivaled mastery of ancient literary, epigraphic, papyrological, and archaeological sources in Greek, Latin, Hebrew, Aramaic, and other Semitic languages, Millar made the indigenous peoples of the Roman Near East, especially the Jews, central to our understanding of how and why the three great religions of the book, Rabbinic Judaism, Christianity, and Islam, evolved in a cultural context that was neither "eastern" nor "western." There can be no doubt that *The Roman Near East, 31 B.C.–A.D. 337* will be the standard work on the subject for a long time to come.

More recently, Millar has published two books, *The Crowd in Rome in the Late Republic* (Michigan, 1998) and *The Roman Republic in Political Thought* (New England, 2002), on the politics of the Roman Republic and how those politics have been understood or misunderstood by political thinkers from the ancient world to the present. These books have challenged widely held notions about the supposed oligarchic political character of the Roman Republic. In the future Millar intends to return to the Roman Near East for a study to be entitled *Society and Religion in the Roman Near East from Constantine to Mahomet*. In this study Millar will bring the story of Greco-Roman culture in the Near East from the early fourth century up to the Islamic invasions of the seventh century A.D.

During the same period when he has produced these ground-breaking books, Millar also has published over seventy essays on aspects of Greco-Roman history, from the Hellenistic period until the middle of the fifth century A.D. These essays have laid the foundations for or supplemented the ideas and arguments presented in Millar's very well known books. Some of these essays, such as "The Emperor, the Senate and the Provinces" (*Journal of Roman Studies* 56 [1966]: 156–66), or "Emperors, Frontiers and Foreign Relations, 31 B.C.–A.D. 378" (*Britannia* 13 [1982]: 1–23), have appeared in hitherto accessible journals and are widely regarded as classics of scholarship. But other outstanding essays, such as Millar's study, "Polybius between Greece and Rome" (published in *Greek Connections: Essays on Culture and Diplomacy* [1987], 1–18), have been more difficult to locate, even for professional historians doing research in the field.

Therefore, the primary goal of our collection, *Rome, the Greek World, and the East*, is to bring together into three volumes the most significant of Millar's essays published since 1961 for the widest audience possible. The collection includes many articles that clearly will be of great intellectual interest and pedagogical use to scholars doing research and teaching in the different fields of the volume headings: Volume 1, *The Roman Republic and the Augustan Revolution*; Volume 2, *Government, Society, and Culture in the Roman Empire*; and Volume 3, *The Greek World, the Jews, and the East*.

At the same time, we have conceived and organized the three volumes of *Rome, the Greek World, and the East* especially in order to make Millar's most significant articles readily available to a new generation of students, who increasingly may not have access to the specialty journals or edited volumes in which many of Millar's more recent articles have appeared.

The principle of arrangement of the essays in each of the three volumes is broadly chronological by subject matter treated within the ancient world. We believe that this chronological arrangement of essays (rather than by publication date of the essays) gives intellectual coherence to each volume on its own and to the collection as a whole. Overall, as Millar himself has defined it, the subject of this collection is "the communal culture and civil government of the Graeco-Roman world, essentially from the Hellenistic period to the fifth century A.D." ("Author's Prologue," volume 1, p. 11).

Publication of a three-volume collection of essays, drawn from a wide variety of journals and edited volumes, over nearly four decades of scholarly production, presents editors with some major stylistic challenges. Our collection contains more than fifty essays. Most of these essays originally were published in learned journals or books, each of which had its own house style. Some learned journals also have changed their house styles over the time when Millar has published in them. For these reasons we have not attempted to bring all of the citations in the texts or notes of the articles in the collection into perfect stylistic conformity. Conformity for the sake of conformity makes no sense; moreover, to achieve such conformity would delay publication of the collection for years.

Rather, the stylistic goal of our collection has been to inform readers clearly and consistently where they can find the sources cited by Millar in his essays. To help achieve that goal we have included a list of frequently cited works (with abbreviations for those works) at the beginning of each volume. Thus, in the text or notes of the essays, readers will find abbreviations for frequently cited journals or books, which are fully cited in our lists at the beginning of each volume. For example, references in the notes to the abbreviation *JRS* refer to the *Journal of Roman Studies*. For the abbreviations themselves we have relied upon the standard list provided in *L'Année Philologique*. In certain cases, where there have been individual citations in the original texts or notes to more obscure collections of inscriptions or papyri, we have expanded the citations themselves in situ, rather than endlessly expanding our list of frequently cited works.

In accordance with Fergus Millar's wishes, for the sake of readers who do not know Latin or Greek, we have provided English translations of most of the extended Greek and Latin passages and some of the technical terms cited by Millar in the text and notes of the original essays. In doing so, we have followed the practice Fergus Millar himself adopted in *The Emperor in the Roman World* in 1977. We believe that providing these translations will help to make Millar's essays more widely accessible, which is the essential goal of the collection. Readers who wish to consult the original Greek and Latin passages or technical terms that we have translated in the collection can look up those passages or technical terms in the original, published versions of the essays.

The editors would like to thank the many friends and colleagues who have helped us in the process of collecting these essays and preparing them for publication. We are indebted first of all to Lewis Bateman, formerly senior editor at the University of North Carolina Press, who suggested the basic arrangement of the essays into three volumes. We are also grateful to David Perry, editor-in-chief, and Pamela Upton, assistant managing editor at the

University of North Carolina Press, for their flexibility, advice, and support of the project.

Gabriela Sara, Ori Shapir, Amir Marmor, and Andrea Rothstein in Israel and Dr. Nancy Thompson of The Metropolitan Museum of Art in New York provided editorial assistance. Our thanks also to Mark Rogers for his help with the maps. We continue to owe a great debt to Priscilla Lange for her helpfulness and kindness to us in Oxford. We also would like to express our gratitude to the Fellows of Brasenose College Oxford and All Souls College Oxford for their hospitality while we were working on this project.

Above all, however, the editors would like to thank Fergus Millar, for his scholarship, his generosity, and his friendship over more than two decades.

Hannah M. Cotton   Guy M. Rogers
The Hebrew University   Wellesley College
Jerusalem   Wellesley

Introduction

Those who study and teach the history of the ancient world suffer from a great disadvantage, which we find difficult to admit even to ourselves: in a perfectly literal sense we do not know what we are talking about. Of course, we can dispose of a vast range of accumulated knowledge *about* what we are talking about. We can compile lists of office-holders in the Roman Empire, without our evidence revealing how government worked or even whether it made any impact at all on the ordinary person; we can discuss the statuses of cities and look at the archaeological remains of some of them (or rather some parts of some of them) without having any notion of their social and economic functions, or of whether it made any real difference whether an inhabitant of the Roman provinces lived in a small city or a large village. We can study the remains of temples, the iconography of gods and goddesses, the nature of myth, ritual and sacrifice; but how and in what way did all this provide an important or intelligible context for a peasant in the fields? In the case of religion in particular our attention turns persistently to the exceptional rather than the ordinary, to those aspects which were novel, imported, mystical, or the subject of philosophical speculation.

—Fergus Millar, "The World of the *Golden Ass*"

So begins one of the articles in this volume, setting out the preoccupation of a lifetime—How did it really work? What did it feel like to be an inhabitant of a Roman province?—and at the same time revealing Fergus Millar's keen awareness of the limits of our knowledge and perception. This declaration of ignorance and *aporia* should not deceive us, nor give us any comfort; it is based on enormous familiarity with the ancient sources and the vast modern commentary on them. Each and every article in the present collection is a variation on the theme of "how did it work and what did it feel like?"—the stubborn and relentless struggle to find out the truth, not to fall into familiar traps, to reread the old texts with a fresh eye and force out something new, informative, and meaningful.

The new reading of the familiar ancient sources was masterfully deployed in the two parts of the first volume (*Rome, the Greek World, and the East: Volume 1, The Roman Republic and the Augustan Revolution*) in order to vindicate the application of the term "democracy" to the Republic, and "monarchy" to the principate right from its inception. The present volume goes one step further in relying heavily on the direct and fresh evidence of documentary texts, inscriptions and papyri, rather than losing itself in the barren study of the Rome-centered ancient texts. The change of emphasis was dictated by the change of subject, as already observed at the end of chapter 11 of the first volume, "The Emperor, the Senate, and the Provinces"—a study of the provincial system that foreshadows some of the issues presented in the present volume:

> The Republic, it may be, can be seen from Rome outwards. To take this standpoint for the Empire is to lose contact with reality. Not only the pattern of the literary evidence, or the existence of an immense mass of local documents, but the very nature of the Empire itself, means that it can only be understood by starting from the provinces and looking inward. (p. 291)

Indeed, the city of Rome, the protagonist of the republican part of the first volume and of Millar's recent book *The Crowd in Rome in the Late Republic*,[1] gradually recedes from our horizon in this volume, to make room for the provinces and the provincials. The two focal points of the present volume are the Empire as a system of government (even if the word "government" suffers from anachronistic overtones), which is the subject of the first part, and the culture and society of the Empire, to which the second part is devoted.

The first part includes papers exploring (and expanding) some of the themes of Millar's monumental *The Emperor in the Roman World (31 B.C.–A.D. 337)*,[2] whose chronological scope corresponds roughly to that of the present volume, the first three centuries A.D. under the Empire, when relative stability allows one to speak of a system of government. Other papers in the first part were written after the publication of that book, covering new ground, but using the same model of the working of imperial government.

The main theme of the first chapter, "Emperors at Work" (1967), rightly

---

1. Jerome Lectures, Ann Arbor, Michigan, Autumn 1993, and American Academy in Rome, 1994. Michigan University Press, 1998.

2. Duckworth and Cornell University Press, 1977; 2nd ed. with Afterword, 1992.

described as a "true classic," lies at the very heart of *The Emperor in the Roman World* and was in fact the most complete statement of Millar's new interpretation of the nature of imperial rule before the book's publication. Its cogent, and at times belligerent, tone is to be explained by the fact that "the hardest thing is precisely to drop anachronistic presuppositions and believe what one reads."[3] On a much smaller scale than *The Emperor in the Roman World*, "Emperors at Work" describes and interprets the role of the emperor in the Roman world through "words issued by, or in the name of, the Emperor, in response to words addressed to him by others."[4] Its message could be summed up in what is often regarded as Millar's personal *credo*: "The emperor was what the emperor did,"[5] that is, the impact of imperial rule was felt to the extent that it was exercised, and "its essential passivity" meant that it was exercised "in response to an initiative from below."[6] The clue to what the emperor did lies first and foremost in the imperial correspondence whose characteristics are best illustrated in the Younger Pliny's correspondence with the emperor Trajan, the subject of chapter 2: "Trajan: Government by Correspondence" (1998).

The fact that Rome remained a republic in theory, and sovereignty was retained by the Senate and People of Rome (*senatus populusque Romanus*), meant that the public treasury, the *aerarium*, like other republican institutions, continued to operate as before (chapter 4: "The Aerarium and Its Officials under the Empire," 1964) alongside the imperial private treasury (better called "estate"), the *fiscus*, which slowly and gradually came to absorb the main functions of the former, thereby losing its private character (chapter 3: "The Fiscus in the First Two Centuries," 1963). Millar's later discussion of the imperial financial and monetary system, chapter 5: "Cash Distributions in Rome and Imperial Minting" (translated here from the French "Les congiaires à Rome et la monnaie," 1991), is perhaps the best example of what I referred to before as Millar's *aporia*: in no other article do we encounter so many unanswered questions, but the sheer value of posing them cannot be overestimated.

We are told in the postscript of chapter 6, "Epictetus and the Imperial Court" (1965), that its genesis lay in "the collection of material for a book on the imperial court from Augustus to Constantine," but its unique theme, a

---

3. "Emperors at Work," text following n. 6.

4. Afterword, *ERW*², 637.

5. *ERW*, 6.

6. This last quotation is taken from chapter 11, "The Emperor, the Senate, and the Provinces," in Fergus Millar, *Rome, the Greek World, and the East* I: *The Roman Republic and the Augustan Revolution*, ed. H. M. Cotton and G. M. Rogers (North Carolina, 2002), 291.

counterpoint to "the values of status and ambition" on which the imperial court and imperial society as a whole were based, was not in fact integrated into *The Emperor in the Roman World*.

The gruesome subject of penal punishment in the Roman Empire is fully explored by Millar for the first time in chapter 7: "Condemnation to Hard Labour in the Roman Empire, from the Julio-Claudians to Constantine" (1984). The dual-penalty system introduced into the Roman legal system in the second century A.D. meant that the various forms of physical punishment, incarceration and hard labour, meticulously described here, were reserved for "lower-class" persons—and also for Christians.

Another classic piece is "The Equestrian Career under the Empire" (chapter 8), which contains the first part of Millar's review from 1963 of H.-G. Pflaum, *Les carrières procuratoriennes équestres sous le Haut-Empire romain* I–III (Paris, 1960–61), and also takes on board Pflaum's *Procurateurs équestres sous le Haut-Empire romain* (Paris, 1950). For Millar Pflaum's reconstruction of the equestrian career not only antedates the evolution of a fully fledged equestrian civil service with a highly regulated career, with rules of promotion and fixed grades of pay. Like other interpretations that rest largely on prosopographical data, it does not pay enough attention to the broader picture, to the sociopolitical and cultural framework which clearly resisted such a development.

Triggered off by E. N. Luttwak's *The Grand Strategy of the Roman Empire from the First Century A.D. to the Third* (Baltimore and London, 1976), chapter 9, "Emperors, Frontiers, and Foreign Relations, 31 B.C.–A.D. 378" (1982), analyzes "the conditions under which the external policy of the Empire was formulated and put into effect."[7] It explores the interplay between the emperor as the commander in chief and the restraining factors of time, distance, and availability of information in shaping foreign policy and expansion. In modern perception diplomatic activity is characteristic of relations with foreign powers beyond the borders of the state. This view proves itself inadequate in the case of the Roman Empire, where the very concept of borders did not exist. Here "most of the evidence for exchanges which have the *form* of diplomatic dealings in fact comes from . . . dealings with cities and communities unambiguously subject to the Roman Empire, which paid tribute to it, and which were in every sense within its borders," as demonstrated in chapter 10: "Government and Diplomacy in the Roman Empire during the First Three Centuries" (1988). The same is true of relations with the so-called client kings whose ambiguous status within the Roman world is revealed in

7. Text following n. 12.

chapter 11: "Emperors, Kings, and Subjects: The Politics of Two-Level Sovereignty" (1996).

The second part of this volume opens with an essay on the survival of local cultures under Roman aegis in a single province (chapter 12). At the time of its first publication "Local Cultures in the Roman Empire: Libyan, Punic, and Latin in Roman Africa" (1968) was a pioneer study in the true sense of the word. Millar's warning at the opening that the results and conclusions reached in such studies "may be falsified by new evidence" should not blind us to the enduring value of the methods employed and the questions asked here for the first time in dealing with the intricate and complex issue of "survival." This is the first expression in print of what became one of Millar's main preoccupations, explored in many of the articles to be included in volume 3 of *Rome, the Greek World, and the East: The Greek World, the Jews, and the East* and in *The Roman Near East, 31 B.C.–A.D. 337*.[8]

Survival is also the subject of chapter 13, "P. Herennius Dexippus: The Greek World and the Third-Century Invasions" (1969), which takes its cue from the resistance put up by the Athenians headed by the historian Dexippus in the face of the Herulian invasion and sack of Athens in 267/8 A.D. This is Fergus Millar at his best, with complete mastery of the ancient sources, the documentary evidence, and the prosopographical data—a lesson indeed in how to use prosopography profitably. There is enough material here for the writing of a new "War and Peace" aiming to explain, in the words of the last paragraph, why "the Byzantine world survived against repeated attack in a way that the Latin world did not; and that a profound attachment to the classical Greek past remained fundamental to Byzantine culture. . . . what we find in the third century is not merely that fuller literary evidence happens to reveal more about popular resistance in the Greek East; but rather that the Greek society of the Empire gained self-confidence and coherence precisely from its vigorous literary and intellectual tradition, and its intimate connection with a heroic past."

The role of the imperial cult in the various phases of the persecution of the Christians is an occasion to explore and nuance the nature of the cult itself in chapter 14 ("The Imperial Cult and the Persecutions," 1973). The racy style of chapter 15, "The World of the *Golden Ass*" (1981), turning Apuleius' fiction into a treasure trove for the depiction of real life in the Roman provincial countryside, gives way to the slowly mounting tension between imperial government and the self-governing cities of the empire

8. Carl Newell Jackson Lectures, Harvard, 1987. Harvard University Press, 1993; paperback 1995.

in chapter 16: "Empire and City, Augustus to Julian: Obligations, Excuses, and Status" (1983). The vitality of city life was sapped by the multiplication of exemptions and immunities from performing municipal duties granted as rewards for employment in the growing imperial civil service. The interplay between private initiative and imperial helplessness or inconsistency encouraged the emergence of status distinctions, which left their mark on the honorific language of the inscriptions even before they received legal sanction. The process by which Italy, which until Domitian had occupied an abnormal status in the framework of the Empire, was provincialized is the subject of chapter 17: "Italy and the Roman Empire: Augustus to Constantine" (1986).

Chapter 18, "Style Abides" (1981), should be read together with the more personal notes about Millar's teacher (and an earlier holder of the Camden chair), the late Sir Ronald Syme, in the prologue to volume 1 (pp. 12–16). Both statements contain important insights into Syme's work, interests, intentions, and personality. No less, however, do they reveal to us by comparison Millar's own road as a historian of Rome. Millar certainly shared Syme's impatience with the German constitutional school. In speaking about Syme he is clearly expressing his own feeling, familiar to all of us who were his students and who found the temptation of exploring such notions as "The imperium of Augustus" irresistible; whereas for Millar Syme's "Imperator Caesar: A Study in Nomenclature"[9] represents "his finest single article" — precisely because the elucidation of the title is taken from the political reality of the time rather than from the Roman law books.

Not that Millar is oblivious to the enormous value of the writings of the Roman jurists for imperial history, as is made abundantly clear in the two chapters that conclude this volume (chapter 19: "A New Approach to the Roman Jurists," 1986; and chapter 20: "The Greek East and Roman Law: The Dossier of M. Cn. Licinius Rufinus," 1999). Lamentably, the juristic texts have not received "the textual attention almost guaranteed to anyone who had the sense to write in verse," and their invaluable contribution to our understanding of "the complex cultural landscape of the Empire" has been sorely missed. The career of the Greek jurist M. Cn. Licinius Rufinus takes us back some thirty-five years to *A Study of Cassius Dio* (Oxford, 1964),[10] where for the first time Millar analyzes "the complex, and in historical terms extremely important, process by which the upper classes of the Greek East 'became Roman' while 'staying Greek.'"

9. *Historia* 7 (1958): 172–88 (= *Roman Papers* I, ed. E. Badian [Oxford, 1979], 361–77.

10. The role of Greeks in the development of Roman law intrigued Millar already then; see *A Study of Cassius Dio*, 188–89.

The Greek historian, Cassius Dio, and the Greek jurist, M. Cn. Licinius Rufinus, embody that process in their careers in the service of the Roman emperors as well as in their writings. Both represent "the fusion of Greek civilization and Roman government"; for both "to be a Roman . . . was to have a certain attitude to history, to identify oneself with an historical tradition going back to the Republic and beyond, and to look at history from Rome outwards . . . while retaining unimpaired the cultural outlook of the Greek world in which [they] were born." Both—but also P. Herennius Dexippus— could be regarded as "a symbol of the process that brought about a Roman Empire ruled from Byzantium, which survived for a thousand years after the western part had passed away" (*A Study of Cassius Dio*, 191–92).

Hannah M. Cotton
Jerusalem
11 December 2002

Abbreviations

Abbot and Johnson, *Municipal Administration*
  F. F. Abbott and A. C. Johnson, *Municipal Administration in the Roman Empire* (1926)
AC
  L'Antiquité Classique
Acta Ant. Acad. Sc. Hung.
  Acta Antiqua Academiae Scientiarum Hungaricae
AE
  L'Année Épigraphique
AJA
  American Journal of Archaeology
AJAH
  American Journal of Ancient History
AJPh
  American Journal of Philology
Amer. Hist. Rev.
  American Historical Review
Ann. Arch. Arab. Syr.
  Annales Archéologiques Arabes Syriennes
Ann. Épig.
  L'Année Épigraphique
Ann. Sc. N. Sup. Pisa
  Annali della Scuola Normale Superiore di Pisa
ANRW
  Aufstieg und Niedergang der römischen Welt. Geschichte und Kultur Roms im Spiegel der neueren Forschung
Ant. Class.
  L'Antiquité Classique

Anz. Öst. Akad.
   Anzeiger für die Altertumswissenschaft, hrsg. von der Österreichischen Humanistischen Gesellschaft
Arch. Esp. de Arqu.
   Archivo Español de Arqueología
Arctos
   Arctos. Acta philologica Fennica
Ath. Mitt.
   Mitteilungen des Deutschen Archäologischen Instituts, Athenische Abteilung
Athenaeum
   Athenaeum. Studi periodici di Letteratura e Storia dell'Antichità
BAA
   Bulletin d'archéologie algérienne
BAR Int. Ser.
   British Archaeological Reports, International Series
BAR Supp.
   British Archaeological Reports, Supplements
BCH
   Bulletin de Correspondance Hellénique
BE
   Bulletin Épigraphique, published in *Revue des Études Grecques*
Ber. Röm-Germ. Kom.
   Bericht der Römisch-Germanischer Kommission
BGU
   Aegyptische Urkunden aus den Königlichen (Staatlichen) Museen zu Berlin, Griechische Urkunden
BICS
   Bulletin of the Institute of Classical Studies of the University of London
BMC
   Catalogue of the Greek Coins in the British Museum
Bonn. Jahrb.
   Bonner Jahrbücher des Rheinischen Landesmuseums in Bonn und des Vereins von Altertumsfreunden im Rheinlande
Brit. Journ. Sociol.
   British Journal of Sociology
BSR
   See *PBSR*
Bull. Épig
   Bulletin Épigraphique, published in *Revue des Études Grecques*

Bull. Ét. Or. Inst. Fr. Damas
   Bulletin des Études Orientales, Institut Français de Damas
Bull. Inst. Cl. Stud.
   Bulletin of the Institute of Classical Studies of the University of London
CAH, CAH²
   Cambridge Ancient History
Cavenaille, *Corp. Pap. Lat.*
   R. Cavenaille, *Corpus Papyrorum Latinarum*
Charlesworth, *Documents*
   M. P. Charlesworth, *Documents Illustrating the Reigns of Claudius and Nero*
Chron. d'Ég.
   Chronique d'Égypte
CIL
   Corpus Inscriptionum Latinarum
CIRB
   Corpus Inscriptionum Regni Bosporani
CJ
   Classical Journal
Class. Phil.
   Classical Philology
Coll.
   Mosaicarum et Romanarum Legum Collatio (FIRA² I, 541–89)
Coll. Int. du CNRS
   Colloques Internationaux du Centre National de Recherche Scientifique
Corpus Gloss. Lat.
   Corpus Glossariorum Latinorum
CPh
   Classical Philology
CQ
   Classical Quarterly
CR
   Classical Review
CRAI
   Comptes-rendus de l'Académie des Inscriptions
Daremberg and Saglio
   Ch. Daremberg and E. Saglio, *Dictionnaire des Antiquités Grecques et Romaines* (1877–1919)
Dial. d'hist. anc.
   Dialogues d'Histoire Ancienne

Dial. di Arch.
  Dialoghi di Archeologia
Diz. Epig.
  Dizionario Epigrafico
Econ. Hist. Rev.
  Economic History Review
EE
  Ephemeris Epigraphica
Ehrenberg and Jones
  V. Ehrenberg and A. H. M. Jones, *Documents Illustrating the Reigns of Augustus and Tiberius*[2] (1955; repr. with addenda 1976, 1979)
ERW
  The Emperor in the Roman World (F. Millar, 1977, 2nd ed. 1992)
ESAR
  T. Frank, ed., *An Economic Survey of Ancient Rome*
FGrH
  F. Jacoby, *Die Fragmente der griechischen Historiker*
FHG
  C. Müller, Th. Müller, et al., *Fragmenta Historicorum Graecorum I–V* (1853–70)
FIRA[2]
  S. Riccobono, J. Baviera, C. Ferrini, J. Furlani, and V. Arangio-Ruiz, *Fontes Iuris Romani Anteiustiniani*[2] I–III (1940–43)
Fontes[7]
  Fontes Iuris Romani Anteiustiniani[7]
Frag. Vat.
  Fragmenta Vaticana (see *FIRA*[2] II)
G&R
  Greece and Rome
GCS
  Griechische Christliche Schriftsteller
Geog. Gr. Min.
  Geographi Graeci Minores
Gesch. d. byz. Lit.
  Geschichte der byzantinischen Literatur
Gesch. d. röm. Lit.[4]
  Geschichte der römischen Literatur
GRBS
  Greek, Roman and Byzantine Studies

Harv. Stud. Class. Phil.
    Harvard Studies in Classical Philology
HSCP, HSCPh
    Harvard Studies in Classical Philology
HThR
    Harvard Theological Review
IBM
    Inscriptions from the British Museum
IEJ
    Israel Exploration Journal
IG
    Inscriptiones Graecae
IGBulg.
    Inscriptiones Graecae in Bulgaria repertae
IGLS
    Inscriptions greques et latins de la Syrie
IGR
    Inscriptiones Graecae ad Res Romanas Pertinentes
IGUR
    Inscriptiones Graecae Urbis Romae
I. K. Eph., I. K. Ephesos
    Inschriften griechischer Städte aus Kleinasien: Ephesos
I. K. Kyme
    Inschriften griechischer Städte aus Kleinasien: Kyme
I. K. Prusa ad Olympum
    Inschriften griechischer Städte aus Kleinasien: Prusa ad Olympum
ILAlg.
    Inscriptions Latines de l'Algérie
ILLRP²
    Inscriptiones Latinae Liberae Reipublicae
ILS
    Inscriptiones Latinae Selectae I–III
Inscr. Cret.
    Inscriptiones Creticae
Ins. Didyma
    A. Rehm and R. Harder, eds., *Didyma II: Die Inschriften*
Ins. Gr. Urb. Rom.
    Inscriptiones Graecae Urbis Romae
Ins. lat. d'Alg.
    Inscriptions Latines d'Algérie

Ins. v. Pergamon
  Die Inschriften von Pergamon
Int. Hist. Rev.
  International History Review
IRT
  Inscriptions of Roman Tripolitana
Ist. Mitt.
  Mitteilungen des Deutschen Archäologischen Instituts, Istanbuler Abteilung
Itin. Ant.
  Itinerarium Antonini
Iura
  Iura. Revista internazionale di Diritto romano e antico
Jahreshefte Öst. Arch. Inst.
  Jahreshefte des Österreichischen Archäologischen Instituts
JEA
  Journal of Egyptian Archaeology
JHS
  Journal of Hellenic Studies
JJS
  Journal of Jewish Studies
JÖAI
  Jahreshefte des Österreichischen Archäologischen Instituts
Journ. Theol. Stud.
  Journal of Theological Studies
JRA
  Journal of Roman Archaeology
JRS
  Journal of Roman Studies
JThS
  Journal of Theological Studies
LRE
  A. M. H. Jones, *The Later Roman Empire* (1964)
LTUR
  E. M. Steinby, *Lexicon Topographicum Urbis Romae* I–VI (1993–2000)
McCrum and Woodhead, *Select Documents*
  M. McCrum and A. G. Woodhead, *Select Documents of the Principates of the Flavian Emperors* (1961)
MAMA
  Monumenta Asiae Minoris Antiqua

MDAI(A)

   Mitteilungen des Deutschen Archäologischen Instituts, Athenische Abteilung

MEFRA and *MEFR*

   Mélanges d'Archéologie et d'Histoire de l'école française de Rome

Mém. Soc. Nat. Ant. Fr.

   Mémoires de la société nationale des antiquaires de France

Migne, *PG*

   J.-P. Migne, *Patrologia Graeca*

Migne, *PL*

   J.-P. Migne, *Patrologia Latina*

MRR

   T. R. S. Broughton, *The Magistrates of the Roman Republic*

Mus. Helv.

   Museum Helveticum

NC

   Numismatic Chronicle

Numis. Chron.

   Numismatic Chronicle

OGIS

   W. Dittenberger, *Orientis Graeci Inscriptiones Selectae* I–II (1903–5)

ORF[3]

   H. Malcovati, *Oratorum Romanorum Fragmenta*[3]

P. Abinn.

   The Abinnaeus Archive: Papers of a Roman Officer in the Reign of Constantius

P. Amh.

   The Amherst Papyri

P. CairIsidor

   The Archive of Aurelius Isidorus in the Egyptian Museum, Cairo, and the University of Michigan (1960)

P. Col.

   Columbia Papyri

P. Dura

   C. B. Welles, R. O. Fink, and Y. F. Gilliam, *The Excavations at Dura-Europus, Final Report* V.1: *The Parchments and Papyri* (1959)

P. Giss.

   Griechische Papyri im Museum des oberhessischen Geschichtsvereins zu Giessen

P. Lips

   Die griechischen Papyri der Leipziger Universitätsbibliothek

P. Mich.

   Michigan Papyri

P. Oxy.
　B. P. Grenfell, A. S. Hunt, et al., eds., *The Oxyrhynchus Papyri* (1898–)
P. Ryl.
　Catalogue of the Greek papyri in the John Rylands Library at Manchester
P. Stras.
　Griechische Papyrus der kaiserlichen Universitäts- und Landesbibliothek zu Strassburg
Pan., Pan. Lat.
　Panegyrici Latini
Pap. Brit. Sch. Athens
　Papers of the British School at Athens
Pap. Brit. Sch. Rome
　Papers of the British School at Rome
PBSA
　Papers of the British School at Athens
PBSR
　Papers of the British School at Rome
PCPS, PCPhS
　Proceedings of the Cambridge Philological Society
Peter, *HRR*
　H. Peter, *Historicorum Romanorum Reliquiae*
Pflaum, *Carrières*
　H.-G. Pflaum, *Les carrières procuratoriennes équestres sous le Haut-Empire romain* I–III (1960–61)
PG
　J.-P. Migne, *Patrologia Graeca*
Philol.
　Philologus
PIR¹, PIR²
　Prosopographia Imperii Romani (1897–98 and 1933–)
PL
　J.-P. Migne, *Patrologia Latina*
Platner and Ashby, *Topographical Dictionary*
　S. Platner and T. Ashby, *Topographical Dictionary of Ancient Rome* (1929)
PLRE
　Prosopography of the Later Roman Empire
Proc. Brit. Acad.
　Proceedings of the British Academy
Proc. Camb. Philol. Soc.
　Proceedings of the Cambridge Philological Society

Proc. Roy. Irish Acad.
　Proceedings of the Royal Irish Academy
Proc. XII. Int. Cong. Pap.
　D. H. Samuel, ed., *Proceedings of the Twelfth International Congress of Papyrology, Ann Arbor, Michigan, 12–17 August 1968* (1970)
PSI
　Papiri greci e latini. Pubblicazioni della Società Italiana per la ricerca dei papiri greci e latini in Egitto
P-W
　Pauly-Wissowa, *Realencyclopädie der klassischen Altertumswissenchaft*
Quad. di arch. della Libia
　Quaderni di archeologia della Libia
RAC
　Reallexikon für Antike und Christentum
RE
　Pauly-Wissowa, *Realencyclopädie der klassischen Altertumswissenschaft*
REA
　Revue des études anciennes
REG
　Revue des études Grecques
Rend. Acc. Naz. Lincei
　Rendiconti dell'Accademia dei Lincei, Classe di scienze morali, storiche e filologiche
Rev. Arch.
　Revue Archéologique
Rev. Belge de Phil. et d'Hist.
　Revue Belge de Philologie et d'Histoire
Rev. Hist.
　Revue Historique
Rev. Hist. Dr. Fr.
　Revue Historique du Droit Français et Étranger
Rev. Hist. Relig.
　Revue de l'Histoire des Religions
Rev. Phil.
　Revue Philologique
RFIC
　Rivista di Filologia e di Istruzione Classica
RG
　Res Gestae Divi Augusti
Rh. Mus., RhM
　Rheinisches Museum

R.I.C.

H. Mattingly and E. A. Sydenham, eds., *Roman Imperial Coinage*
I– (1923–)

RIDA

Revue Internationale des Droits de l'Antiquité

RIL

J.-B. Chabot, ed., *Recueil des inscriptions libyques* I (1940–41)

Riv. di Stor. e Lett. Religiosa

Rivista di Storia e Letteratura Religiosa

Röm.-Germ. Kom.

See *Ber. Röm-Germ. Kom.*

Röm. Mitt.

Mitteilungen des Deutschen Archäologischen Instituts, Römische Abteilung

Rostovtzeff, *SEHRE*²

M. Rostovtzeff, *Social and Economic History of the Roman Empire*², ed.
P. M. Fraser (1957)

RP

R. Syme, *Roman Papers*

RRC I

M. Crawford, *Roman Republican Coinage* I (1974)

Sardis VII.1

W. H. Buckler and D. M. Robinson, *Sardis* VII.1: *Greek and Latin
Inscriptions* (1932)

SB

Sammelbuch griechischer Urkunden aus Aegypten (1915–)

S-B Deutsche Ak. Wiss.

Sitzungsberichte der deutsche Akademie der Wissenschaften

SC

Sources Chrétiennes

Schanz-Hosius

M. von Schanz, *Geschichte der römischen Literatur bis zum
Gesetzgebungswerk des Kaisers Justinian*, 4th ed. by C. Hosius

SCI

Scripta Classica Israelica

SEG

Supplementum Epigraphicum Graecum (1923–)

Sel. Pap.

A. S. Hunt and C. C. Edgar, *Select Papyri* I–III. Loeb Classical Library
(1932–42)

SIG³

Sylloge Inscriptionum Graecarum³ I–IV (1915–24)

St. It. Fil. Class.

Studi Italiani di Filologia Classica

Staatsrecht

Th. Mommsen, Römischer Staatsrecht

Stud. Class. e Or.

Studi Classici e Orientali

Stud. et Doc. Hist. et Iur.

Studia et Documenta Historiae et Iuris

Syll.³

Sylloge Inscriptionum Graecarum³ I–IV (1915–24)

Syr.

Syria

TAM

Tituli Asiae Minoris

TAPA, TAPhA

Transactions of the American Philological Association

Tijdschr. v. Rechtsg.

Tijdschrift voor Rechtsgeschiedenis (= Revue d'Histoire du Droit)

TLL

Thesaurus Linguae Latinae

TLS

Times Literary Supplement

VDI

Vestnik Drevnei Istorii (Moscow)

Wilcken, Chrestomathie

L. Mitteis and U. Wilcken, Grundzüge und Chrestomathie der Papyruskunde I

YCS, Yale Class. Stud.

Yale Classical Studies

ZDPV

Zeitschrift des Deutschen Palästina-Vereins

Zeitschr. f. Pap. u. Epig

Zeitschrift für Papyrologie und Epigraphik

ZPE

Zeitschrift für Papyrologie und Epigraphik

ZSS, ZRG

Zeitschrift der Savigny-Stiftung für Rechtsgeschichte. Romanistische Abteilung

Rome, the Greek World,
and the East

York
Chester
BRITANNIA
Tamesis Camulodunum
(Thames)
Londinium

CHERUSCI

Colonia
Bonna Agrippiniensis
**GERMANIA
INFERIOR**
BELGICA Moguntiacum
**GERMANIA
SUPERIOR**

CHATTI

Rhenus (Rhine)

MARCOMANNI QUADI

Danuvius (Danube)

ATLANTIC
OCEAN

LUGDUNENSIS
Liger (Loire)

Lugdunum
Rhodanus
(Rhône)
AQUITANIA
Burdigala

RAETIA

NORICUM

**PANNO
SUPERI**

Carnuntum
Dravus

**PANNON
INFERI**

TRANSPADANA *Alpes*

ALPES
NARBONENSIS COTTIAE
Arausio ALPES
Nemausus **MARITIMAE**
Tolosa Narbo Arelate
Martius
Massilia

Mediolanum
Padus (Po)
LIGURIANS

Aquileia

Savus

Sirmium

DALMATIA

Apenninus M.
Ariminum

Carunna (Garonne)
Iberus (Ebro)
Pyrenaei M.

Legio

Numantia

Emporiae

LUSITANIA

HISPANIA CITERIOR
Tagus

Emerita

Saguntum

Tarraco

Corduba
Baetis
BAETICA

Gades
Carteia

Carthago Nova

Caesarea

Volubilis

**MAURITANIA
TINGITANA**

**MAURITANIA
CAESARIENSIS**

Balearic Is.

CORSICA

Aleria

SARDINIA

Cirta
Lambaesis
Bulla
Regia

NUMIDIA

Carthago

AFRICA

Tiberis
Rome

Neapolis

Dyrrhachium

Brundisium

Apollo

SICILIA

Agrigentum
Syracusae

MEDITERRANEAN

Lepcis Magna

0   300 mi.

The Roman Empire, ca. 160 A.D.

PART I

The Imperial Government

CHAPTER ONE

*Emperors at Work**

One of the most revealing single items of evidence on the political character of the Empire is an anecdote told by Dio about Hadrian; a woman approached the Emperor on a journey and demanded his attention; Hadrian
said he had no time and moved on—"then stop being Emperor" shouted the
woman after him.[1] The point is clear; the ideology—and the practice—of
the Empire was that the emperor was *personally* accessible to his subjects in
a way which now seems incredible, and which most books on the Empire
tend to ignore, or regard as trivial. One may recall, for instance, Maecenas
struggling to get through the crowd surrounding Augustus as he gave judgement,[2] the *advocati* trying to hold Claudius by physical force on the tribunal
to hear their pleas,[3] or the story of how a muleteer of Vespasian was bribed
to stop and shoe a mule, giving time for a litigant to approach.[4]

Such examples are intended merely as the setting for a discussion of two
specific problems, raised in particular by A. N. Sherwin-White in analysing

---

*First published in *JRS* 57 (1967): 9–19. This chapter was read to the Oxford Philological
Society on 1 November 1963. I intended to leave it unpublished, as being merely a first
essay at a subject which would be an element in a larger work, eventually published as *The
Emperor in the Roman World, 31 B.C.–A.D. 337* (1977), 2nd edition with Afterword (1992). On
reflection it seemed better to make these ideas public and provoke criticism where necessary. I kept the original largely unaltered, though making a number of additions. I was
very grateful for discussion with Mr. A. J. Holladay and Mr. T. D. Barnes, who also provided
some extra material.

1. Dio 69, 6, 3.
2. Dio 55, 7, 2.
3. Suet., *Div. Claud.* 15; cf. *Div. Aug.* 97.
4. Suet., *Div. Vesp.* 23.

the correspondence of Pliny and Trajan.[5] "Did emperors personally read letters sent to them?" "Did they write the replies?" "And if they did not, who did?" It is only by asking specific questions like these that we can get valid answers to questions about the nature of the Empire as a political institution—was it a bureaucracy in which executive decisions could be made anonymously at secretarial levels? What range of decisions did the emperor himself actually make?

Administrative history has peculiar dangers of its own. We all know that we do not understand Roman religion. Administration seems easier, more readily comprehensible in present-day terms. Hence the evidence can be confidently distorted to fit entirely anachronistic conceptions. Our sources say that Claudius was dominated by his freedmen; the first edition of *CAH* reproduced this as "Claudius . . . took the decisive step of creating special departments of what may be termed a Civil Service, each department being controlled by a freedman."[6] But talk about bureaux, offices of state, secretariats, and so forth is mere slogan writing. What we must do is to look again and try to see exactly what the sources say about how things worked at the centre of power. The hardest thing is precisely to drop anachronistic presuppositions and believe what one reads.

I began with the theme of the emperor's personal contact with his subjects. That contact took place in many contexts, as for instance when emperors appeared at the circus or theatre and answered the shouts of the people by gestures, by word of mouth, or through a herald,[7] when they accepted gifts on 1 January,[8] or distributed cash to the people (*congiarium*).[9] But it was true also in the exercise of business—and this gives the link with imperial correspondence. The evidence shows indisputably that it was normal for emperors not only to confront litigants and defendants, petitioners and delegations personally, but to deal with their business personally and make the required decisions themselves. For the ideology one might note especially

5. A. N. Sherwin-White, "Trajan's Replies to Pliny: Authorship and Necessity," *JRS* 52 (1962): 114–15 = (with very slight additions) *The Letters of Pliny* (1966), 536–57.

6. *CAH* X (1934), 686–87.

7. See, e.g., Suet., *Div. Aug.* 42; Dio 54, 11, 7; 59, 13, 5–7; Suet., *Cal.* 30; Jos., *Ant. Jud.* 19, 24–26; Martial, *de spec.* 20; Suet., *Div. Tit.* 8; *Dom.* 13; Dio 69, 6, 1; 16, 3; 71, 29, 4.

8. See Dio 54, 35, 2 (Suet., *Div. Aug.* 57; *CIL* VI, 456 = *ILS* 99, in absence); 57, 8, 6 (Suet., *Tib.* 34—Tiberius out of Rome on 1 January to avoid gifts); 57, 17, 1 (Tiberius, A.D. 17, refuses); 59, 24, 4 (A.D. 40, gifts given symbolically to chair of absent Gaius). It seems to have been this custom which Claudius abolished: Dio 60, 6, 3.

9. See D. Van Berchem, *Les distributions de blé et d'argent à la plèbe romaine* (1939), 164–65.

Augustus' written answer to Tiberius, who had asked the citizenship for a Greek client—"he would not grant it unless the man appeared in person and persuaded him that he had good grounds for his request."[10] For many matters, Crook's *Consilium Principis* makes it unnecessary to cite much of the evidence. Two points, however, need emphasis. Firstly, it is sometimes stated that when a delegation arrived to see the emperor, they first gave in their decree to the bureau *a legationibus* (dealing with embassies), that is, that some preparations were made before the formal hearing.[11] But, for instance, when Philo's delegation arrived, it was Gaius whom they first saw and greeted; nothing could be achieved further, however, until they could actually present the petition and speak before him.[12] Then there is the case of the Bithynian embassy which came to accuse Junius Cilo before Claudius. Admitted to his presence, they gave vent to a confused roar of complaint, so that Claudius had to ask Narcissus, who was standing next to him, what they had said; being a friend of Cilo he said that they had been uttering his praises—"So he will be procurator for two more years," announced Claudius.[13] It is clear that there were as yet *no* papers of the case—and never were, since the embassy was then dismissed. The implications of these stories are confirmed by instructions of Menander the rhetorician about the *presbeutikos logos* (ambassadors' oration): it accompanied the actual handing over of the *psephisma* (decree) to the emperor.[14] This is the procedure in the Oxyrhynchus papyrus reporting an Alexandrian delegation before Augustus in A.D. 13: a delegate called Alexander hands over the decrees of the city and begins the first speech.[15] It is also envisaged in the decree passed in A.D. 4 by the *decuriones* (city councillors) and *coloni* of Pisa on hearing of the death of Gaius: "[I]n the meantime T. Statulenus Iuncus . . . should be asked along with envoys, when the *libellus* had been handed over, to excuse the present difficulty of the colony and to make known this devotion of ours and the goodwill of all to Imperator Caesar Augustus."[16] So when an emperor writes, as Augustus to Cnidos, "Your ambassadors . . . presented themselves to me in Rome and, handing over the

10. Suet., *Div. Aug.* 40. Compare Hadrian's description of his procedure in conducting cases, *Dig.* 22, 5, 3, 3.

11. E.g., Daremberg and Saglio, s.v. "legatio," 1035; *CAH* X, 687.

12. Philo, *Legatio* 179–83.

13. Dio 60, 33, 5. On Cilo, see D. Magie, *Roman Rule in Asia Minor* (1950), chap. 23, n. 4.

14. Spengel, *Rhetores Graeci* III, 423–24. The section ends, "then you will request him to assent to receive the decree."

15. *P. Oxy.* 2435, lines 40–41: "Alexander handed over the decrees and said . . ."; cf. line 44.

16. *ILS* 140 = Ehrenberg and Jones, 69, lines 42–47.

decree, made their accusation,"[17] he means just that. In one of the Alexandrian reports of proceedings we find an emperor (Trajan or Hadrian) reading a letter presented by a delegation—and then summoning his "friends."[18] Thus when Gaius says in a letter to the Panhellenes, "having read the decree given to me by your ambassadors . . . ,"[19] we may take it that he means what he says.

Secondly, the role of advisers: it was in the nature of the *consilium* that the emperor's advisers gave their *sententiae* (opinions), and then the decision was pronounced independently by the magistrate or emperor himself. Nero would have the *sententiae* written down and then retire to consider them.[20] But even in the second and third centuries, when lawyers as such were brought into the *consilium*, emperors would follow this same procedure, even in legal business. Marcellus describes a *cognitio* (trial) conducted by Marcus Aurelius in which he took part; various opinions were put; then the Emperor dismissed the court, meditated, and called them back to hear his decision.[21] Similarly, Paulus describes himself giving his opinion, on a case before Severus; the Emperor considers it but makes up his own mind.[22] Yet if there were any cases of qualified officials making decisions for the emperor it should have been the lawyers.

With that we can come one stage nearer the question of official correspondence and look at the handling of *libelli*—for the moment just *libelli* brought to the emperor by their authors, not ones sent on by officials such as Pliny. *Libelli* in this context divide into two types—ones containing information against third parties and ones containing petitions or requests for legal decisions. Here again we find the informant or petitioner giving the *libellus* direct to the emperor himself—as witness the anecdote of Augustus saying to a man who proffered his *libellus* with excessive timidity. "You are like a man giving a coin to an elephant";[23] compare the case in Suetonius of a man giving Claudius a *libellus* during the *salutatio* (the morning reception),[24] or Martial's line "while the multitude gives you plaintive *libelli*, Augustus," and

17. *Syll.*³ 780 = Abbott and Johnson, *Municipal Administration*, no. 36 = Ehrenberg and Jones, 312.

18. *P. Oxy.* 2177; H. Musurillo, *Acts of the Pagan Martyrs* (1954), 10, fr. 2, col. ii, 1, 59–60.

19. *IG* VII 2711 = *ILS* 8792.

20. Suet., *Nero* 15.

21. *Dig.* 28, 4, 3 *praef.*

22. *Dig.* 4, 4, 38.

23. Told with varying details by Quintilian, *Inst.* 6, 3, 59; Suet., *Div. Aug.* 53; and Macrobius, *Sat.* 2, 4, 3.

24. Suet., *Div. Claud.* 37.

his reference to the man who had come from his *patria* to ask the Emperor for the privileges granted to parents of three children—"But stop wearying our lord with supplicating *libelli*." [25] Then there is the incident in Philostratus when the philosopher Euphrates hands Vespasian a letter with requests for gifts, expecting him to read it in private—but Vespasian puts him to shame by reading it out aloud there and then. [26] Similarly, the plan for the murder of Domitian was that Stephanus should hand him a *libellus* and *while he was reading it* strike him down. [27] The text called *Sententiae et Epistulae* of Hadrian also contains two instances of petitions *per libellum* with the spoken answers of the Emperor. [28] But the classic instance of the emperor's reception of *libelli* is Constantine at the Council of Nicaea. Tired of the mutual accusations made by the bishops in *libelli*, he appointed a special time for this: "[W]hen he had taken his seat, he received *libelli* from each separately, all of which he held in his lap, not revealing what was in them." [29]

Then there were letters sent to the emperor by officials. The best procedure is to start with a few clear examples of emperors reading such letters themselves, and then come finally to the most difficult question, the handling of imperial paperwork and the composition of letters and rescripts.

Firstly then, Suetonius and Dio record that Augustus removed a consular legate from his post on grounds of illiteracy—"because he noticed that he had written *ixi* instead of *ipsi*." [30] We can hardly escape the inference that the legate had written the letter with his own hand and that Augustus read it himself. Then in Philo we find Petronius the legate of Syria sending a letter to Gaius: "When (the messengers) arrived they delivered the letter. Gaius got red in the face before he had finished reading and was filled with anger as he noted each point." [31] Later we find him reading a letter from King Agrippa—"and getting angry at each of the points." [32] Similarly, Philo describes Tiberius reading a letter of complaint from the Jews about Pilate and breaking into

---

25. 8, 82, 1; 8, 31.

26. Philost., *V. Apoll. Tyan.* 5, 38.

27. Suet., *Dom.* 17.

28. *Corpus Gloss. Lat.* III, 31, 34. Cf. Justin, *Apol.* 2, 2 (a woman giving a *libellus—biblidion*—to the Emperor).

29. Rufinus, *EH* 10, 2; Sozomenus, *EH* 1, 16, 3–5; Socrates, *EH* 1, 8, 18–19.

30. Suet., *Div. Aug.* 88; cf. Dio, ed. Boissevain, II, 557. This in one of a number of items which Dio may have taken direct from Suetonius; see F. Millar, *A Study of Cassius Dio* (1964), 85–86.

31. *Legatio* 254, trans. Smallwood.

32. Ibid., 331.

a violent expression of rage.[33] The accounts of the events leading up to the
murder of Caracalla give further evidence, somewhat in conflict. Herodian
tells of messengers from Rome bringing a bundle of official letters to Caracalla in Syria; they arrive to find him just setting off for some chariot racing,
so he tells Macrinus, the praetorian prefect, to look through the letters for
him. Among them Macrinus finds information against himself.[34] Dio's version is less dramatic and clearly preferable. As he had recorded earlier, Caracalla had entrusted the handling of routine *libelli* and letters to his mother,
Iulia Domna;[35] his statement is strikingly confirmed by the publication of
a letter from Iulia to Ephesus, the only known example of a letter from an
empress to a city.[36] Macrinus, according to Dio, was warned privately, while
the official letters, which were delayed, went to Iulia Domna at Antioch—
for she was instructed "to sort out all [communications] that arrived."[37] The
two accounts, though different, have the same bearing on this subject. Then,
to take an example of a semi-official letter, there is the one written by Aelius
Aristides to Marcus Aurelius after the earthquake at Smyrna, which is extant
among his orations (*Or.* 19 Keil). It contained a moving appeal for aid and,
according to Philostratus, when the Emperor came to the words, "the winds
blow through the deserted city," his tears fell on the page.[38] One may presume that he was not looking over the shoulder of the the official in charge
of imperial correspondence at the time.

Then there are some more general references to emperors reading official communications. Julius Caesar had incurred public displeasure "because
during the performance he spent his time reading or answering letters and
libelli"; Augustus was careful to avoid this mistake,[39] but Marcus Aurelius was
not—"It was Marcus' habit to read, listen to, and subscribe [documents] during the circus games."[40] Suetonius describes Vespasian's *ordo vitae* (way of life):

---

33. Ibid., 304. Compare Jos., *Ant. Jud.* 18, 163–64: Tiberius reading a letter from the procurator at Jamnia, Herennius Capito—"having read this letter, the Emperor was deeply
pained."

34. 4, 12, 6–7.

35. 77, 18, 2.

36. *Jahreshefte Öst. Arch. Inst.* 45 (1960): Beiblatt, cols. 80–82, no. 7.

37. Dio 78, 4, 2–3.

38. Philost., *Vit. Soph.* II, 9. Compare Constantine's reply to a letter from Eusebius,
bishop of Antioch, Euseb., *Vita Const.* 3, 61, 1: "I have read with the greatest pleasure the
letter which your sagacity composed."

39. Suet., *Div. Aug.* 45.

40. *HA, Marc. Aur.* 15. Compare *HA, Had.* 20, 11, "He wrote, dictated, listened, and,
incredible as it seems, conversed with his friends, all at one and the same time."

in the morning "after reading his letters and the reports of all the officials, he admitted his friends."[41] So with the two letters in which Trajan tells Pliny that he has read ("legi") *libelli*—in one of which he goes on "having been moved by his prayers"[42]—we may believe what he says; there is no need to imagine that a chief secretary might have read them and advised Trajan.[43] One might note in passing some different types of cases in which emperors are directly or very closely involved with official documents: in the *Sententiae* Hadrian says to a petitioner, "sine videam commentarios," or "let me look up the *commentarii* (records)—and then come back."[44] Similarly, Suetonius records an anecdote when Vespasian was asked by a *dispensator* (steward) how to make an entry in the accounts;[45] and the *Historia Augusta* says that Severus Alexander kept full records of the troops' pay and service in his bedroom and would study them constantly.[46]

With the more complicated question of the composition of imperial correspondence, the only thing is to take the matter schematically and start from the extreme possibility: did emperors write their letters with their own hands?

Firstly, it is worth noting that there *are* cases of official documents written by emperors: Augustus left the "the arrangements for the assemblies" (*ordinatio comitiorum*) "written in his own hand";[47] the accounts of the finances of the Empire, "all of which he had written in his own hand";[48] and his will, "written . . . partly in his own hand, partly in that of his freedmen."[49] Tiberius left two copies of his will, one written out by himself, the other by a freedman.[50] Aurelian was betrayed by a slave who forged a list of names for execution *by imitating his handwriting* and then showed it to the supposed victims.[51]

Actual official letters written by emperors are rare (though it was common for them to write *personal* letters in their own hand).[52] But there are cases of semi-official autograph letters; Tiberius used to write such to Cossus, the

41. Suet., *Div. Vesp.* 21; cf. Philost., *Vit. Apoll. Tyan.* 5, 31.

42. Pliny, *Ep.* 10, 60, 107.

43. So Sherwin-White (n. 5), 120; *The Letters of Pliny*, 546.

44. *Corpus Gloss. Lat.* III, 33, line 32–33.

45. Suet., *Div. Vesp.* 22.

46. *HA, Sev. Alex.* 21, 6–8.

47. Vell. Pat. 2, 124.

48. Tac., *Ann.* 1, 11, 7.

49. Suet., *Div. Aug.* 101.

50. Suet., *Tib.* 76.

51. Eutrop. 9, 15, 2; Zosimus I, 62.

52. E.g., Suet., *Div. Aug.* 71, 87; *vita Horat.*, p. 45 Reiff.; Dio 71, 36, 2; *HA, Clod. Alb.*

urban prefect (*praefectus urbi*): "To him, however, Tiberius wrote much with his own hand; that which he thought should not be entrusted even to his assistants."[53] Then we have Nerva writing "in his own hand" to Trajan on adopting him, and Trajan writing "in his own hand" to the Senate on his accession.[54] Eusebius records that Constantine wrote a letter in his own hand to Sapor II (309–79) on the persecution of Christians in Persia.[55]

These are, of course, specifically exceptional cases. But there were two types of missive which, probably in one case and certainly in the other, emperors often wrote with their own hand. These are *codicilli* (letters of appointment) and *subscriptiones*. We happen to have two texts of codicils, one from Domitian to L. Laberius Maximus, the prefect of Egypt,[56] the other from Marcus Aurelius to a procurator named Domitius Marsianus;[57] both are couched in warm and personal terms—as, evidently, were the *codicilli* of Tiberius to his drinking companions, L. Piso and Pomponius Flaccus, "declaring in their letters of appointment that they were the most agreeable of friends, and at all times."[58] They certainly give the impression of personal messages, dictated if not written by the emperor. Similarly Epictetus represents a *corrector* or *curator civitatium* (a commissioner in charge of city finances) as saying "Caesar wrote me a letter of appointment."[59] Such impressions are no proof; but then we have Caligula at dinner during a show rewarding a senator for the greed with which he ate by sending him codicils, appointing him praetor,[60] and, better, Suetonius' account of how the freedmen arranged appointments under Claudius—"substituting false letters of appointment, or even openly changing those which he had issued."[61] The implication, it is clear, is that the codicils emanated directly from Claudius—what the freedmen did was to alter the documents themselves or substitute others. There

---

2, 2. For other evidence on imperial private correspondence, see, e.g., Nepos, *Att.* 20, 1–2; Quint., *Inst.* 1, 6, 19; Marcus Aurelius, *Med.* I, 7.

53. Sen., *Ep.* 83, 15.

54. Dio 68, 3, 4; 5, 2.

55. Euseb., *Vit. Const.* 4, 8, text in 9–13; cf. Sozom., *EH* 2, 15, 1–5; Theodoret, *EH* 1, 24, 13–25, 11. Cf. H. Dörries, *Das Selbstzeugnis Kaiser Konstantins* (1954), 125–26.

56. Cavenaille, *Corp. Pap. Lat.* 238, with bibliography; cf. Syme, *Tacitus*, app. 7.

57. *AE* 1962, 183. Note the subscription of greeting at the end, "farewell, my Marsianus, very dear to me" (*vale mi Marsiane, karissime mihi*).

58. Suet., *Tib.* 42.

59. Epictetus 3, 7, 30. For the setting, see *JRS* 55 (1965): 142, 145, and Sherwin-White, *Letters of Pliny*, 477–78.

60. Suet., *Cal.* 18.

61. Suet., *Div. Claud.* 29.

is certainly no room in the story for a "bureau," headed by a freedman, by which the documents were produced.

A considerable amount of an emperor's time was taken up with *libelli* which went to him with requests for *beneficia* (favours) or legal guidance. The essential element of the procedure was for the emperor to write on the *libellus* a *subscriptio* (a brief answer to the question, literally "written under" the petition), in his own hand. I have noted already the passages showing Iulius Caesar and Marcus Aurelius busy with this at the shows.

It is quite clear that the *subscriptio* (which means not a signature but a statement or verdict appended by someone) was the work of the emperor's own hand: one may note a case, not a *libellus* this time, related by Suetonius of Nero,[62] "when he was asked according to custom to sign the warrant for the execution of a man who had been condemned to death, he said: 'How I wish I had never learnt to write!'" The story is told in greater detail by Seneca addressing Nero himself, "Burrus, your prefect . . . , about to execute two robbers, pressed you to write their names and your reasons for wanting them executed. That had often been put off, but he insisted that it should be done. Reluctantly he held out the document and handed it to you who were reluctant too; and you exclaimed: 'I wish I had never learnt how to write!'"[63] Or one might note that subscription was part of the work of the prefects of the Aerarium, on Pliny's evidence, "I give jurisdiction, subscribe petitions, make up the records";[64] similarly with the praetor—"he should return [the letter] to the praetor to subscribe in his own hand as he wishes."[65] But such parallels are unnecessary, for we have the rescript of Diocletian and Maximian dating to 292, "we ordain that our authentic and original rescripts themselves, subscribed in our own hand, not copies of them, be entered on the record."[66] Then we have Commodus: "[H]e was so lazy and careless in subscribing that he answered many *libelli* with the same formula."[67] The *Historia Augusta* also records that Carinus "had such an aversion for subscribing [*libelli*] that he appointed for subscribing them a certain filthy fellow . . . whom he generally reviled because he could imitate his handwriting so well."[68] It is certainly surprising to find emperors answering the often fairly insignificant requests and enquiries of communities or individuals in their own hand; but the sur-

62. Suet., *Nero* 10.
63. Sen., *de clem.* 2, 1, 2.
64. Pliny, *Ep.* 1, 10, 9.
65. *Frag. Vat.* 163.
66. *CJ* 1, 23, 3.
67. *HA, Com.* 13, 7.
68. *HA, Carus* 16, 8.

prise may be lessened when it is realized that the *subscriptio* (or *rescriptum*) very often consisted of the address and a single brief sentence—as does that of Antoninus Pius to Smyrna,[69] of Commodus to the *coloni* of the saltus Burunitanus,[70] or of Philip and his son to the Aragueni.[71] Commodus' *subscriptio* is followed by the words, "and in a different hand: 'I have written, I have checked [*scripsi, recognovi*].'" The evidence on the procedure with imperial letters cited below, in particular that of Salvius Julianus, might suggest that the *subscriptio* was in fact dictated, and then *scripsi, recognovi* written on by the Emperor.

For ordinary imperial letters, to cities or officials, dictation was normal. Caligula, after reading the letter of Petronius, dictated his reply to an *ab epistulis*.[72] Titus, according to Suetonius, used to dictate letters for Vespasian in his old age,[73] and Suetonius also describes Domitian dictating an official letter, "when dictating a model letter in the name of his procurators, he began thus: 'Our Lord and God orders that this be done.'"[74] One may also mention Marcus Aurelius' letter written while "Caesar" in the 140s or early 150s, in which he tells Fronto: "At last the messenger is off, and at last I can send you a report of what I have done in the last three days. I cannot say anything; to such an extent I have exhausted my spirits by dictating nearly thirty letters."[75] These might of course have been private letters.

But even when an official letter was dictated, an emperor might add something, possibly in his own hand: later in Philo's narrative Caligula orders another letter to be written to Petronius and then adds a threatening final sentence.[76] I would suggest that this means that he wrote the last sentence on to the letter.

The notion of dictation followed, if necessary, by additions in the emperor's own hand is clearly expressed in the *Historia Augusta*'s account of Severus Alexander's method of dealing with paper work: "The afternoon

69. *CIL* III, 411 = *ILS* 338 = *FIRA*² I, 82.

70. *ILS* 6870 = Abbott and Johnson, no. 111 = *FIRA*² I, 103.

71. *OGIS* 519 = *IGR* IV, 598 = *CIL* III, 14191 = Abbott and Johnson, no. 141. See in general U. Wilcken, "Zu den Kaiserreskripten," *Hermes* 55 (1920): 1.

72. Philo, *Leg.* 258–60. Smallwood translates *hypebale* "dictated." The Loeb translation gives, "gave one of his secretaries instructions about answering Petronius."

73. Suet., *Div. Tit.* 6.

74. Suet., *Dom.* 13. For imperial dictation of a letter, cf. *HA*, *Max.* 12, 5. Lact., *de mort. pers.* 46, 5, records Licinius dictating to a *notarius* (stenographer).

75. Fronto, *Ad. M. Caes.* 4, 7 (Naber 70; Loeb I, 184; Van Den Hout 64).

76. *Legatio* 333–34.

hours he always devoted to subscribing and reading letters, while the officials in charge of the correspondence [*ab epistulis*], the petitions [*a libellis*], and records [*a memoria*] were always in attendance . . . with the clerks and those handling the record office [*scrinium*] re-reading everything to him, in such a way that Alexander would add with his own hand whatever was to be added, adopting the opinion [*sententia*] of the man who was regarded as the most expert."[77] As regards additions by the emperor's hand to the actual substance of a letter we do not seem to have any unambiguous evidence to support this obviously dubious source. But as regards a sentence of greeting written on at the end of a letter we have the clear testimony of the inscription from Brigetio with the letter written by Constantine and Licinius in 311 to Dalmatius on the *privilegia* of soldiers, which ends "and in the divine hand: 'Farewell, Dalmatius, dearest to us'" (*et manu divina: Vale Dalmati carissime nobis*).[78] Imperial letters normally indeed end with a phrase of greeting, often just "be well" or "good luck" or "I wish you well" but sometimes a little longer, as in Caracalla's letter of 213 to Aurelius Julianus of Philadelphia: "Be well, Iulianus, most esteemed, and dearest to me."[79] The addition of a whole sentence rather than a single word or brief phrase seems to have been normal in the fourth century. Constantine's letters end with sentences like, "God will protect you, beloved brother,"[80] or "Farewell my dearest brothers by the common prayer, God ordaining through the ages."[81] None of these added sentences carries any explicit indication that they are written by the emperor; though a letter of Constantine to Arius and his followers in 333 ends, "and in a different hand: 'God will protect you, beloved brothers.'"[82] But the supposition that they were written by the emperors, combined with the fact of their increase in length, would enable us to understand a puzzling phrase used by the *Historia Augusta* of Commodus: "[I]n many of his letters he merely wrote the word 'farewell.'"[83] The implied criticism would thus be a misunderstanding.

Such a *subscriptio* is also presumably what is meant when Dio gives the evidence for the death of Trajan before adopting Hadrian: "This was shown

77. *HA, Sev. Alex.* 31, 1.

78. *FIRA*[2] I, 93.

79. *IGR* IV, 1619b = *Syll.*[3] 883.

80. Euseb., *Vit. Const.* 2, 46, 3; similar phrases appear in the numerous other letters quoted in this work.

81. Optatus., *App.* IX, ad fin.

82. Opitz, *Athanasius Werke* III, 1, doc. 34, ad fin. (p. 75).

83. *HA, Com.* 13, 7.

also by Trajan's letters to the Senate, for they were subscribed, not by him, but by Plotina, although she had not done this in any previous instance."[84]

So much, for the moment, for the role of the emperor. I have deliberately avoided certain complexities about copies of letters or rescripts, their transmission, publication, and so forth. I have simply given such clear evidence as there is about the part played by the emperor himself. The evidence is scattered but it does, I think, suffice to prove that communications, like individuals, could and did get the personal attention of the emperor. The question now arises—what did the freedmen, and later equestrian, "secretaries" actually do? Were they there either to take executive decisions, to prepare substantive drafts for approval by the emperor, or to give technical advice, for instance on legal matters in the Greek provinces? If neither of these, why were they important at all?

Here some principles need to be established. The first is that we cannot deduce a man's function from his title. The title will indicate the area of business with which the post was (or had originally been) concerned; it will tell us nothing about what its holder at any given moment actually did. Secondly, from the fact that some holders of a particular post exercised power and influence it does not follow that their importance arose from the exercise of the specific functions of the post. The evidence on Pallas, which is extensive, contains only a single, retrospective, reference to *rationes* (accounts).[85] Narcissus was *ab epistulis*; the evidence shows him urging condemnations by Claudius, getting Vespasian a post as legionary legate, addressing the mutinous troops of the British expedition, taking a leading part in dealing with Messalina and Silius and in the debate on Claudius' second marriage, attending Claudius at the hearing of an embassy, supervising the draining of a lake, and finally being killed by Agrippina whose marriage to Nero he had opposed.[86] We shall come in a moment to the one reference which illustrates his formal functions. Similarly with Callistus, *a libellis* under Claudius; again with a single exception, the evidence illustrates not his functions but his power: his support of Claudius and participation in the conspiracy against Gaius, his participation also in the affair of Messalina and Silius and in the debate on Claudius' remarriage, his role in saving Domitius Afer, and otherwise his wealth and social prominence.[87]

84. Dio 69, I, 4. The Loeb translation "signed" will not do, because ancient letters were not signed in this sense.

85. See S. I. Oost, "The Career of M. Antonius Pallas," *AJPh* 79 (1958): 113.

86. Evidence in *PIR*[1] N 18.

87. Evidence in *PIR*[2] I 229.

We might say that this pattern of evidence just reflects the interests of our sources. But the key to the situation is given by the fact that the career equestrians who later came to hold these secretarial posts never exercised a comparable degree of personal influence. The *éminences grises* of the second century and after were not *ab epistulis* or *a libellis* but *cubicularii* (chamberlains), like Saoterus and Cleander under Commodus.[88] In other words the exercise of power, at least as it is reflected in our sources, is a function of imperial favour—extended equally on occasion to doctors or dancers—and was chiefly attained by long propinquity. That is shown nowhere better than in Philo's account of Helicon, the *cubicularius* of Caligula.[89]

That said, we are left with the specific task of finding evidence showing the holders of "secretarial" posts actually at work. First, the *ab epistulis*: Suetonius records that Augustus punished Thallus, his *a manu*, "for divulging the contents of a letter"[90]—that unfortunately leaves the actual role of Thallus unclear. Then we have Gaius, as noted before, dictating (or giving instructions for) a letter to an *ab epistulis*. After that, however, we have the one bit of evidence about Narcissus at work in his capacities as *ab epistulis*; he had charge of the secret *grammata* of Claudius against Agrippina and others. Exactly what these were is not really clear—indeed they sound rather like *libelli* of accusation. At any rate he burnt them after the murder of Claudius.[91]

More illuminating is the case of Beryllus, the *ab epistulis graecis* of Nero, "entrusted with the management [*taxis*] of the Greek correspondence." Some ambassadors from Caesarea in Judaea bribed him to beg from Nero a letter invalidating the rights of the Jews in the city. Beryllus went to the Emperor and obtained permission for the letter to be written. Here Nero does not seem to have written the letter himself; but equally Beryllus had no authority of his own and could only make a request to Nero.[92] In one passage alone do we find something approaching a clear statement of the *ab epistulis'* duties, the words of Statius addressed to Abascantus.[93] These show him sending off *mandata* (instructions)—"to send far and wide into the great world the *mandata* of the Emperor, Romulus' descendant" (*magnum late dimittere in orbem / Romulei mandata ducis*)—and also receiving news of events and, apparently, reports on individuals and making them known (*pandere*). But, unfortunately for the questions discussed here, Statius concentrates on the extent and nature

88. See F. Grosso, *La lotta politica al tempo di Commodo* (1964), esp. 113–14, 197–98.
89. Philo, *Legatio* 166–77.
90. Suet., *Div. Aug.* 67.
91. Dio 60, 34, 5.
92. Jos., *Ant. Jud.* 20, 183–84.
93. Statius, *Silvae* 5, 1, 86–87.

of the correspondence passing through the *ab epistulis'* hands, and does not illuminate his precise role, or its relation to that of the Emperor.

It is significant, however, that Beryllus for instance had been the *paidagogos* (tutor) of Nero, and a considerable number of *ab epistulis* in the next century and a half had primarily literary qualifications, for instance, Secundus, a rhetor, who was *ab epistulis* of Otho.[94] It is particularly noteworthy that a number of characters in Philostratus' *Lives of the Sophists* occupied this post—for instance, Alexander of Seleucia (2, 5) or Hadrianos, who was offered it by Commodus when holding the chair of rhetoric in Rome (2, 10).[95] Were they there, as is often thought, to give expert advice on Greek affairs? That is not the implication of our sources. Philostratus says of Aelius Antipater, *ab epistulis graecis* under Severus, "Though there were many men who both declaimed and wrote historical narrative better than Antipater, yet no one composed letters better than he, but like a brilliant tragic actor . . . his utterances were always in accordance with the imperial role. For what he said was always clear, the sentiments were elevated, the style was always well adapted to the occasion, and he secured a pleasing effect by the use of asyndeton."[96] Philostratus also mentions that his relation, Philostratus of Lemnos, wrote a work "How to Write Letters" criticizing the *ab epistulis* Aspasius (also a rhetor) for writing in too obscure and rhetorical a style: "On being appointed *ab epistulis* to the Emperor he wrote certain letters in a style more controversial than is suitable; and others he wrote in obscure language, though neither of these qualities is becoming to an emperor. For the emperor when he writes a letter ought not to use rhetorical syllogisms or trains of reasoning, but ought to express only his own will; nor again should he be obscure, since he is the voice of the law, and lucidity is the interpreter of the law."[97] These passages of course make quite clear that in this period the *ab epistulis graecis* actually wrote the letters. The main emphasis (at least on the part of Philostratus) lies on the style. But the second passage in particular makes clear that the *ab epistulis graecis'* responsibilities extended to the whole form of the letters, and hence inevitably to their effective contents. Much the same impression is given in the passage where Phrynichus talks of the responsibilities of the *ab epistulis graecis* under Marcus Aurelius, Cornelianus, to whom he addressed his work on Attic usage: after describing Cornelianus as "Giving the imperial

94. Plut., *Otho* 9.

95. See in general G. B. Townend, "The Post *ab epistulis* in the Second Century," *Historia* 10 (1961): 375.

96. *VS* 2, 24.

97. *VS* 2, 33.

law court a Greek and an Attic style" he continues, "For the Roman emperors, deeming you worthy of the greatest things, laid upon you the management of all the affairs of the Greeks, setting you up as a guard to themselves,
ostensibly appointing you *ab epistulis* (*epistulae*), but in truth taking you as a
partner in kingship."[98] Phrynichus certainly implies, though here one must
make allowance for flattery of the addressee, that Cornelianus influenced the
content as well as the working of imperial letters.

More specific evidence is not available. The interpretation of these passages, furthermore, is made more difficult by the fact that the numerous imperial letters in Greek known from inscriptions show no trace of a "literary"
style. The contradiction cannot as yet be resolved.[99]

We have even less evidence on the *ab epistulis latinis*. Indeed the only one
we catch a glimpse of at work is Tarruttienus Paternus under Marcus Aurelius — he was sent on a mission to a tribe across the Danube. He was later
praetorian prefect and also left a legal work, *de re militari*.[100] His legal knowledge (if he acquired it first) may have helped him to obtain the post; but
the role of lawyers as assistants to the emperor belongs to the next subject,
the functions of the *a libellis*. Before that one may note the equally unhelpful evidence of Dio that Marcius Agrippa, *a cognitionibus* and *ab epistulis* of
Caracalla, was dismissed for drafting "immature lads" into the army.[101]

The question of the functions of the *a libellis* presents a major difficulty.
The standard passage quoted is Seneca, *ad Polybium* 6, 5: "You must give audience to countless number of men, countless petitions [*libelli*] must be dealt
with; so great is the pile of business, accumulated from every part of the
world, that must be carefully weighed in order that it may be brought to
the attention of the most illustrious princeps in the proper order. You, I say,
are not allowed to weep; in order that you may be able to listen to the many
who weep — in order that you may dry the tears of those who are in peril and
desire to obtain mercy from Caesar's clemency, it is your own tears that you

98. Phrynichus, *Ecloga* 379 (Lobeck ccclvi; Rutherford).

99. There are, however, significant indications that the style of imperial letters became
more discursive and "literary" from about the middle of the third century. Even if one disregards the long letter of Decius to Philippopolis "quoted" by Dexippus (*FGrH* 100 F 26),
one may note the sentiments discursively aired by Valerian and Gallienus writing to Philadelphia in 255, *Anz. öst. Akad. Phil.-hist. Kl.* 93 (1956): 226, no. 8, and further developments
in later Latin letters, the imperial letter to Tymanda (Abbott and Johnson, no. 151), the letter
of Constantine to Ablabius about Orcistus (no. 154) or his rescript to the Umbri (no. 155).

100. See W. Kunkel, *Herkunft und soziale Stellung der römischen Juristen* (1952), 219–20;
Pflaum, *Carrières*, no. 172.

101. Dio 78, 13, 4.

must dry." Suetonius, however, says that Polybius was *a studiis*,[102] and none
of the other references to him mentions his post. Elsewhere in the *Consola-
tio* Seneca mentions Polybius' literary distinction (8, 2–3; 11, 5) and says that
this helped his rise to prominence—"long ago the love of Caesar lifted you
to a higher rank, and your literary pursuits have elevated you" (6, 2); he also
mentions Polybius' occupations, "that is, *studium* et Caesar" (5, 2). Can we
take it, as is normally assumed,[103] that Polybius was both *a libellis* and *a studiis*,
being succeeded in the former post by Callistus, whom Zonaras (before mentioning the death of Polybius) calls "in charge of the *libelli* of petitions"?[104]
If the external evidence gives no indication that Polybius was *a libellis*, what
of the passage of Seneca? The mere mention of *libelli* is not decisive, for all
officials (not to speak of landowners like Pliny, from their *coloni*)[105] were presented with these, though the only unambiguous first-century evidence of
an imperial attendant reading *libelli* relates to Parthenius, the *cubicularius* of
Domitian—"he does not read books [*libri*] but petitions [*libelli*]."[106] The passage shows clearly at least, both from its first phrase and the last sentence,
that Polybius had actually to listen to the entreaties of individuals. Were the
libelli which he was to "disponere" (deal with) intended for the Emperor?
If the conclusion is probable, it is made so by the following clause, making
clear that he arranged matters for the Emperor's attention. If so, were these
the *libelli* handed direct to the Emperor, like those mentioned above, and
then laid aside to be dealt with later? Or did they reach the Emperor only
via an official? The latter interpretation conflicts with the other known evidence, though is not for that reason necessarily wrong. But at any rate it is
certain that even this passage, intended to flatter its addressee, does not give
the slightest hint that an official dealt with the *libelli* in the first instance, in
the sense of producing a "draft reply," or something like it, for the emperor
to approve.

   If this passage is evidence for the functions of the *a libellis* (rather than the
a studiis, about whose functions we have no other evidence),[107] then it is the

102. Suet., *Div. Claud.* 28.

103. P-W, s.v. "Polybius" (5).

104. Zonaras 11, 9–10 = Dio (Boiss.) 60, 30, 6b.

105. Pliny, *Ep.* 9, 15, 1.

106. Martial 11, 1, 5.

107. The normal supposition (e.g., O. Hirschfeld, *Die kaiserlichen Verwaltungsbeamten bis
auf Diocletian*² [1905], 332–33; L. Friedländer, *Sittengeschichte Roms*⁹ [1919–21], 55; A. M. Duff,
*Freedmen in the Early Roman Empire*² [1958], 157) is that the *a studiis* was some kind of "director of research" for the emperor. This is no more than a deduction from the common sense
of *studia*. One might wonder whether the meaning is not better understood by taking it as
a simple plural of *studium* in the sense of "favour" or "support."

only concrete evidence we have. It is noteworthy, however, that in the second and third centuries the post was often held by jurists, first Volusius Maecianus,[108] then Aurelius Papirius Dionysius under Commodus,[109] Papinian,[110] and possibly Ulpian.[111] A. M. Honoré has based a brilliant article on the assumption that the *a libellis* wrote the imperial answers himself[112]—and indeed finds some correlations between the verbal style of each lawyer in his own works and that of the rescripts in the period when he is thought to have held office. But the thing is too vague for real proof (and for lack of evidence on careers the argument is sometimes circular); moreover, what makes it more difficult, none of the works of any of these jurists belongs indisputably to a period before he held office. Here again we just do not know. Who actually wrote the immense number of rescripts in the Codex of Justinian remains a major topic of debate.[113]

The evidence is thus very sparse. But if we use for instance the analogy of the *ad legationes* or *a cognitionibus*, we should be careful about taking too elevated a view of the formal functions of these officials. The *ad legationes* of Gaius, Homilus, as he appears in Philo, attends the emperor and is sent to tell the Jewish delegation that they will be heard soon.[114] The *a cognitionibus* appears in Dio and Philostratus with the job of arranging the order of cases before the emperor and summoning litigants into the *auditorium* (audience hall).[115] Such functions could still give a man status, influence, and wealth. Lucian gives this description of the comparable post which he occupied in the court of the prefect of Egypt: "the initiation of court cases and their arrangement, the recording of all that is done and said, guiding counsels in their speeches, keeping the clearest and most accurate copy of the governor's [*archōn*] decisions in all faithfulness and putting them on public record to be preserved for all time."[116] Moreover Philo describes in considerable detail how a prominent Alexandrian, called Lampon, "would stand beside the pre-

---

108. Kunkel, *Herkunft*, 174–75; Pflaum, *Carrières*, no. 141.

109. Pflaum, *Carrières*, no. 181.

110. Kunkel, *Herkunft*, 224–25; Pflaum, *Carrières*, no. 220.

111. *HA*, *Pesc. Nig.* 7, 4.

112. "The Severan Lawyers: A Preliminary Survey," *Stud. et Doc. Hist. et Iur.* 28 (1962): 162.

113. I have left this paragraph as originally written, while of course wanting to mention here T. Honoré, *Emperors and Lawyers* (1981) and the revised edition (1994), as well as referring to chapter 19 in this volume (review article on Honoré's work).

114. Philo, *Legatio* 181.

115. Dio 75, 15, 5; Philost., *VS* 2, 30 (both of which show that the *a cognitionibus* normally acted on the emperor's instructions); *VS* 2, 32. Cf. Hirschfeld, *Verwaltungsbeamten*[2], 331.

116. Lucian, *Apology* 12.

fects when they were giving judgement and took the minutes of the cases which he introduced in virtue of his position," and amassed a fortune by altering the records of the cases, receiving substantial bribes for his pains.[117] This passage is of particular value in that it shows that the importance and influence of the subordinates of the great men were entirely compatible with the original decision or verdict having been made by the great men themselves, uninfluenced. What happened subsequently to that stage might be equally important.

What is argued here is, in essence, that if the evidence does not allow us to see administrative processes in concrete terms then it does not allow us to understand them at all. Administration is merely one facet of a social system. Where, as here, we are dealing with a social system totally foreign to our own experience, common sense, "judgement," the making of reasonable assumptions about what "must have" happened, are all equally irrelevant, indeed positively misleading. One may make valid deductions from comparable procedures in other parts of the same social system, but no others.

However, some conclusions are possible. The imperial regime was the product of a society where decisions were reached, and authority exercised, by the unaided judgement of members of the ruling class. When one member of that class was elevated above the rest, the *res publica* gave him at first no assistants beyond the lictors and soldiers from the praetorian guard. He dealt directly, in person or by letter, with individuals of all classes and with the communities of the Empire. It took a long time for *officia* to form round him—and thus, so to speak, to reduce his political "exposure." The gradual seclusion of the emperor had entirely intelligible causes. Until that happened, his personal employees performed functions which were in themselves relatively humble: they kept accounts, arranged and kept documents, called litigants into the audience hall, and either wrote letters to dictation or expressed a reply or decision in correct language. If, as some of them certainly did, they exercised power and influence, that was something which they shared with people of all social grades who happened to be close to the emperor. Maecenas,[118] Sejanus,[119] Narcissus the *ab epistulis*,[120] and Paris the dancer[121] could all equally influence the promotion of senators. Influence and fortune lay open to anyone who enjoyed imperial favour; to give only one example, Aelius

117. Philo, *In Flaccum* 130–34 (the text is not certain).
118. Dio. 55, 7, 4.
119. Tac., *Ann.* 4, 68, 2; Juvenal, *Sat.* 10, 78–79.
120. Suet., *Div. Vesp.* 4.
121. Juvenal, *Sat.* 7, 88–90.

Aristides praises the grammarian Alexander of Cotiecum, teacher of the children of Marcus Aurelius, for using his position to shower benefits on cities and individuals—and never asking for cash in return.[122]

It may seem incredible that emperors could have dealt personally with all the business that came to them. Those who were conscientious did indeed work very hard. They might, like Augustus or Hadrian or Marcus Aurelius, go on giving judgement through the night;[123] they continued to hold *cognitiones*, to receive embassies and write letters when at their villas,[124] on journeys, and on campaign. On the other hand, if they did not wish to do business, it was not done. The cases of Tiberius on Capri and of Philo's long pursuit of, and vain confrontation with, Caligula are well known. On hearing the news of Vindex's revolt Nero issued no orders or rescripts for eight days;[125] about that time Vespasian advised Agrippa II to send a man to Nero for judgement—but when the prisoner got there he found the Emperor preoccupied, so he simply returned.[126] Trajan (so the *Historia Augusta* alleges) never answered *libelli* on principle;[127] Commodus gave almost no legal rulings; Caracalla was lazy about holding *cognitiones*, and when he proposed to do so, he might keep his senatorial *amici* waiting at the door from dawn till dusk.[128]

It is possible, of course, that the picture our sources provide of the emperor dealing personally with people and communications is, while true in itself, ultimately totally misleading, in that vast ranges of imperial business were handled by the bureaux, in private, systematically concealed from the view of our literary sources. In the nature of the case no such proposition can ever be conclusively refuted. It can only be stated, firstly, that all the evidence we have points in the same direction; and, secondly, that there is evidence that it was not merely an observable fact but a principle that emperors should compose their own pronouncements, whether written or verbal. For we find Fronto writing to Lucius Verus about the Julio-Claudian emperors: "Which of them could address the people or the Senate in a speech of his own? Which could draw up an edict or a letter in his own words?"[129] As regards speeches

122. Aelius Aristides, *Or.* 12 (Dindorf 32 = Keil, 15–16).

123. Suet., *Div. Aug.* 33; Dio 69, 18, 2–4; 71, 6, 1.

124. See esp. Fronto, *de feriis Alsiensibus* 3 (Naber 224–25; Loeb II, 4–5; Van Den Hout 212–13).

125. Suet., *Nero* 40.

126. Jos., *Vita* 408–9. Cf. *JRS* 56 (1966): 159 (= chapter 11 in volume I).

127. *HA, Macrinus* 13, 1.

128. *Dio* 77, 17.

129. Fronto, *ad Verum* 3, 7 (Naber 124; Loeb II, 138; Van Den Hout 117).

this is in fact inaccurate, for Tacitus comments that Nero on his accession was the first emperor to need "borrowed eloquence" (*aliena facundia*)—Seneca's, as Dio states.[130] (Suetonius, however, records that a speech for delivery to the populace was found in Nero's *scrinium* [writing desk] after his death; the implication seems to be that he had written it himself).[131] Seneca also wrote the letter which Nero sent to the Senate after the murder of Agrippina.[132] Nero was clearly an exceptional case, as was Maximin the Thracian, for whom his friends wrote a speech.[133] So was Domitian, for it is in the chapter devoted to demonstrating his total lack of literary culture that Suetonius writes, "he composed letters, orations, and edicts, with the aid of the talents of others."[134] In the context this may mean no more than that others put his pronouncements into correct style (*formare*). But even if it means more than that, this, like the other evidence just quoted, is specifically an exception to a rule—and it is the rule which is significant.

130. Tac., *Ann.* 13, 3, 3; Dio 61, 3, 1.

131. Suet., *Nero* 47: "Afterwards a speech composed for this purpose was found in his writing desk; but it was thought that he did not dare to deliver it for fear of being torn to pieces before he could reach the Forum."

132. Tac., *Ann.* 14, 11, 4; cf. Quint., *Inst.* 8, 5, 18: "As is the letter written by Seneca to be sent by Nero to the Senate on the occasion of his mother's death."

133. Herodian 7, 8, 3.

134. Suet., *Dom.* 20. Cf. *HA, Ael. Ver.* 4, 7: "and had finished composing, either by his own efforts or with the help of the rhetoricians, a very pretty speech."

CHAPTER TWO

Trajan: Government by Correspondence[*]

Introduction

One way in which it might be useful to think about the Roman Empire is to use the analogy of a living organism. To survive, the organism must do two things: firstly, it must take in enough food, water, and oxygen; and, secondly, it must receive, absorb, and respond to information. This chapter will not be concerned with the first task, that is to say, in the case of the Roman Empire, how it extracted enough resources either from its own subject population, or from foreign enemies, to maintain its governmental structure and its military forces, or to indulge in conspicuous expenditure at the centre. The reign of Trajan is of some interest in this connection, for the conquest of Dacia is the last in the history of Rome of which our sources claim that vast moveable spoils (*manubiae*) were removed from the conquered zone and brought to Rome; and we know that inscriptions on Trajan's magnificent new Forum proclaimed that it had been built *ex manubiis*.[1] Major conquests aside, in spite of all the excellent scholarly work devoted to taxation in cash or kind, in my view we have still not grasped the problems which are involved if we try to envisage, in practical and concrete terms, by what means vast quantities of coin were collected, and then either transported to Rome, re-distributed within the same province, or transferred to other provinces.[2] The minting of

---

[*]First published in J. Gonzalez, ed., *Trajano Emperador de Roma* (Madrid, 2000), 363–88.

1. For a late report of vast spoils removed from Dacia, Lyd., *Mag.* 2.28; see A. C. Bandy, *Ioannes Lydus on Powers* (Philadelphia, 1982), 126, and notes on pp. 299–300. For the inscriptions on the Forum Traianum, see Gell. 13, 25, 1. See now the major work by James E. Packer, *The Forum of Trajan in Rome* I–III (Berkeley, 1997).

2. For some brief observations, F. Millar, "Les congiaires à Rome et la monnaie," in A. Giovannini, ed., *Nourrir la plèbe: hommage à D. van Berchem* (Basel, 1991), 143–59 (for a translation into English, see chapter 5 in this volume). For the wider issue of the diffusion

new coins (or the re-minting of old coins), to which so much attention has been devoted, is one aspect of this empire-wide exchange of value between the Roman state and its subjects. But it is only one aspect. How was it ensured that enough coin reached each of the legions, and each of the auxiliary units, scattered very unevenly across the Empire?

I leave that question there, because my topic relates to the second necessity for the functioning of the Empire, the gathering of information, its processing, the formulation of responses to it, and the sending out of the consequential instructions or decisions. I will be concerned almost entirely with internal communications, that is the flow of information or requests or problems from provincial communities or provincial governors, or other officials, to the emperor, and how and in what forms he responded. The question of reports and information coming from outside the Empire will not be considered here.[3]

In this context too, it seems to me, we have not paid enough attention to the basic physical realities of communication and travel in the imperial period. Firstly, all the evidence which we have tends to show that it was normal for information to take several weeks, perhaps as much as two months, to travel from the frontiers of the Empire to the centre.[4] If the Empire had really set up a signalling system, capable of carrying complex messages, along the main lines of communication, the speed of the flow of information and decisions might theoretically have been much faster. But the truth is that it had no such system.

Nor, in spite of occasional hints in the sources, did it have relays of messengers who were permanently organised and were able to pass messages and documents on from one to another.[5] All our evidence for the first three cen-

---

of value through taxation and expenditure, see K. Hopkins, "Taxes and Trade in the Roman Empire (200 BC–AD 400)," *JRS* 70 (1980): 101–25, and C. Howgego, "The Supply and Use of Money in the Roman World, 200 BC to AD 300," *JRS* 82 (1992): 1–31.

3. See F. Millar, "Emperors, Frontiers and Foreign Relations, 31 BC–AD 378," *Britannia* 13 (1982): 1–23 (chapter 9 in this volume), and "Government and Diplomacy in the Roman Empire during the First Three Centuries," *International History Review* 10 (1988): 345–77 (chapter 10 in this volume), along with A. D. Lee, *Information and Frontiers: Roman Foreign Relations in Late Antiquity* (Cambridge, 1993).

4. See, e.g., R. Duncan-Jones, *Structure and Scale in the Roman Economy* (Cambridge, 1990), chap. 1: "Communication-Speed and Contact by Sea in the Roman Empire."

5. The most concrete reference to such a system is provided by Suet., *Aug.* 49.3: "[I]n order for him [Augustus] to be more speedily informed of what was happening in each and every province he had at first relays of young men stationed along military roads at short intervals, and later on of vehicles."

turies shows that the Empire also did not have at its disposal an organised transport system for official travellers or messengers: the term *cursus publicus* in fact only appears in the fourth century. What the imperial state deployed was something very different, namely a set of rights on the part of official travellers to requisition vehicles, animals, and guides and a corresponding set of obligations on the part of local communities to supply them. This network of rights and obligations was known in Latin as *vehiculatio*, and in Greek often as *angareia*, and was one of the most common sources of tension between the agents of the state and its subjects.[6]

The corollary of the very limited degree to which the state as such arranged for the transference of messages, requests, or complaints was that any material which was thought to require the emperor's attention had physically to be brought to wherever he was, either by groups of interested parties or by individual messengers. "Groups of interested parties" refers most obviously to embassies from provincial communities, bringing decrees passed by cities or provincial councils, delivering them to the emperor with an accompanying oration, and carrying back a reply which might be read out before a city council (*boulē*), or even a whole popular assembly (*ekklēsia*), when they returned. Individual messengers were concerned primarily when provincial governors, or other officials, sent letters to the emperor and received replies from him (or, in certain cases, did not receive any reply).

It is clear, as we will see, that not only persons actually holding office but also individuals of high status could write letters to the emperor and might hope to receive replies. Lower-status individuals were forced either to present petitions (*libelli*) to the emperor, in the hope of his making a brief written reply, or, if they were at a distance, to have their petition (*libellus*) sent on with a letter despatched by an office-holder. As we will see, this latter procedure happens to be particularly well attested for Trajan's reign.

Three accidental circumstances give the reign of Trajan an exceptional significance for us, in looking at the evolution of imperial government by correspondence. One of these is of course the preservation of Pliny's correspondence with Trajan. But here, while it is the exchange of letters between Pliny, in Pontus and Bithynia, and Trajan which has always attracted the most attention, there is at least as much significance in the letters which Pliny sent to Trajan earlier, all of them in fact from quite early in his reign. They all, it seems, belong to periods when Trajan was out of Rome on the frontiers.

---

6. The best collection and discussion of the evidence remains S. Mitchell, "Requisitioned Transport in the Roman Empire: A New Inscription from Pisidia," *JRS* 66 (1976): 106–31. The subject would deserve a comprehensive treatment.

That brings in the second very significant feature of the reign. For a considerable proportion of his 19- to 20-year reign Trajan was absent from Rome and Italy. As Halfmann's invaluable study of imperial journeys shows,[7] Trajan was absent, in Germany and Pannonia, from his accession as sole Emperor in January 98 to about October 99; from March 101 to the end of 102, for the first Dacian war; from June 105 to the winter 106/7 for the second Dacian war; and for the four years from October 113 to his death in Cilicia in 117. Approximately, therefore, some 9 out of the 19–20 years of his reign were spent away from Rome and Italy. As we will see, two documents happen to show also how letters could be written by the Emperor from places in Italy, but outside Rome: in this case both were written from Antium.

In the immediate context of Trajan's reign, that meant, firstly, that those who needed to send messages to him must have had to instruct their messengers to go either to Rome or wherever the Emperor was. Whether this information was necessarily available in advance, we do not know. At any rate we can find parties to a law-suit writing to Trajan in Dacia to ask him to take a case, which he duly does on his return;[8] and, in Dio's well-known report, we hear of the earthquake which struck Antioch when Trajan was wintering there in 115/16 and caught embassies from all over the Empire which had gathered there.[9] It follows from the Emperor's repeated preoccupation with frontier campaigns that whatever governmental apparatus, or staff, he required for the performance of his imperial functions must systematically have travelled with him.

In that sense, Trajan foreshadows the pattern which became clearly established in the middle of the second century, and which continued unbroken up to the end of the fourth, whereby emperors conducted major military campaigns in person. Trajan's attempt to expand the Empire in the East, abortive as it was, also foreshadowed a preoccupation which was to dominate the discharge of their functions by the emperors until the same period.[10] That meant that a particularly significant element now entered the imperial correspondence, namely the letter sent by the emperor on the frontier to the Senate in Rome. There is a neat symmetry in the fact that, in Trajan's case,

7. H. Halfmann, *Itinera Principum: Geschichte und Typologie der Kaiserreisen im Römischen Reich* (Stuttgart, 1986), 184–88.

8. Plin., *epist.* 6, 31, 8–9; see further below.

9. Dio 68, 24–25.

10. C. S. Lightfoot, "Trajan's Parthian War and the Fourth-Century Perspective," *JRS* 80 (1990): 115–26; F. Millar, *The Roman Near East, 31 BC–AD 337* (Cambridge, Mass., 1993), 99–100.

the reign opened with his letter to the Senate, written (so Dio says) "in his own hand" from Germania Inferior;[11] while it ended, or came near to its end, with a stream of letters in 116, some written from Babylonia, in which he reported to the Senate on the conquest of peoples of whom those back in Rome had hardly heard. Dio narrates this as follows, just after he has recorded the famous moment at which the Emperor had reached the shore of the Persian Gulf:[12]

> Yet he would declare that he himself had advanced further than Alexander, and would so write to the Senate, although he was unable to preserve even the territory which he had subdued. For this achievement he obtained among other honours the privilege of celebrating a triumph for as many nations as he pleased; for by reason of the large number of the peoples of whom he was constantly writing to them they were unable in some cases to follow him intelligently or even to use the names correctly.

Dio states clearly that a succession of letters reached the Senate from Trajan in the East. One of them, presumably announcing victories gained in the previous campaigning season, arrived in Rome in February 116. For it is recorded in the *Fasti Ostienses* that nine or ten days before the Kalends of March "laurelled letters" (*laureatae*) were sent to the Senate, causing Trajan to be voted the name *Parthicus*, thankgivings and offerings to the gods (*supplicationes*) to be voted, and public games (*ludi*) to be held. In early May, the fragmentary text records the arrival of another letter from Trajan.[13]

The third significant element in our conception of government by correspondence is that Trajan's reign is the earliest for which our legal sources provide a substantial number of quotations of, or references to, legal pronouncements by the emperor. Thanks to the magnificent collection by G. Gualandi, *Legislazione imperiale e giurisprudenza*, which deserves to be much more fully used than it has been,[14] these quotations and allusions are easily accessible. Though they are of course less numerous than those preserved for Hadrian, the Antonines, or the Severi, they still represent a significant body of text: to be precise forty-four individual citations (amounting to seven pages in Gualandi), of which four contain what are presented as verbatim quotations

---

11. Dio 68, 5, 2.

12. Dio 68, 29, 2–3.

13. See L. Vidman, ed., *Fasti Ostienses*² (Prague, 1982), 48.

14. G. Gualandi, *Legislazione imperiale e giurisprudenza* I–II (Milan, 1963). The pronouncements of Trajan preserved in legal sources are to be found in vol. I, 17–23.

(two of these, however, repeat each other). Two aspects of the Emperor's ful-filment of his role stand out in this material: the prominence of replies to consultations by provincial governors (which are thus exactly analogous to, and contemporary with, Trajan's replies to Pliny in Pontus and Bithynia); and the deliberate expression of the imperial will through the formulation of the *mandata* (codes of instructions) given to governors (an aspect of the Em-peror's role which also plays an important part in the exchanges with Pliny).

In this chapter I will look at three aspects of Trajan's correspondence as a vital aspect of his role as Emperor. The three aspects relate to, but are not quite identical with, the three distinctive features of the reign, and of our knowledge of it, which I have outlined: Trajan's very prolonged absences on the frontier; the two quite distinct bodies of material provided by Pliny's *Letters*; and the very important evidence from juristic sources.

I will deal first with communications with Trajan while on campaign; then with the juristic material, as a background to the correspondence be-tween Pliny, as *legatus* (the governor of an imperial province) of Pontus and Bithynia, and Trajan, who at that period was in Rome; and finally with the nature of the exchanges between Pliny, as governor, and Trajan.

Trajan's Correspondence from the Frontier

As is well known, Trajan's reign as sole emperor began with the death of his adoptive father, Nerva, in January 98, while Trajan himself was *legatus* of Germania Inferior. The news of Nerva's death will obviously have reached Germania Superior first, and we learn from the *Historia Augusta* that Hadrian, who was then in Germania Superior as tribune of *legio XXII*, made every effort to be the first to carry the news north to Trajan. Iulius Servianus, as *legatus* of the province, tried to keep him back, apparently unsuccessfully. Hadrian was further delayed by the breakdown of his *vehiculum* (wagon) but continued on foot, and did succeed in getting there before the *beneficiarius* sent by Servianus.[15] The story is in fact of some real significance, firstly for the implied role (which is otherwise little attested) of *beneficiarii* as messen-gers,[16] and secondly for the hazards of travel. It is not entirely clear whether

---

15. *Hist. Aug., v. Had.* 2.5–6.

16. See most recently J. Ott, *Die Beneficiarier: Untersuchungen zu ihrer Stellung innerhalb der Rangordnung des römischen Heeres und zu ihrer Funktion* (Stuttgart, 1995), which however does not note this passage, and J. Nelis-Clément, *Les* Beneficiarii: *militaires et administrateurs au service de l'Empire (Ier siècle a.c.–VIe siècle p.c.)* (Paris, 2000), 71–73. For communications from emperors, consuls, or Senate to governors and communities in the provinces, and for the types of messenger employed, see now W. Eck, "I sistemi di trasmissione delle

Hadrian will have been using a single official *vehiculum* for the journey from Moguntiacum, where the *legio XXII* was stationed, to the Colonia Agrippinensis, where we are told that Trajan heard the news.[17] The distance is some 150 kilometres in a direct line, therefore surely at least three days' journey. It is perhaps more likely, if the story is true at all, that the reference is to the last of a series of *wagons* which he obtained under the system of *vehiculatio*, and that the journey which was completed on foot was the last stage. In either case, we are vividly reminded that the Empire had no long-distance signalling system, and that the flow of information, on which literally everything depended, was itself dependent on the hazards of movement by humans and animals.

As we have already seen, Trajan reacted appropriately, expressing his respect for the Senate by sending it a letter written in his own hand.[18] He did not come to Rome itself, however, for more than a year and a half, first visiting Pannonia and the Danubian legions. It is into this quite prolonged period that we can fit quite a significant number of items of evidence, which show how long-distance correspondence, carried by messengers or ambassadors, played a vital role in the government and diplomacy of the Empire.

It is of considerable importance that, as Sherwin-White showed in his excellent *Commentary*, the majority of Pliny's personal letters to Trajan fall into this period.[19] At this stage Pliny was prefect of the Treasury of Saturn (*Praefectus Aerarii Saturni*), having been appointed by Nerva and Trajan during their joint reign. In 100 he would be suffect consul, nominated by Trajan. Did each and every one of the 600 senators now write a personal letter of congratulation to Trajan and presumably have it carried to the Colonia Agrippinensis by a messenger? Or was this required only of the more senior? At any rate, since the beginning of Trajan's sole reign resulted from the death of his adoptive father, tact was required in congratulating him and welcoming his rule (*epist.* 10.1):

> It had indeed been the wish of your filial feelings [*pietas*], most sacred
> Emperor, that you would succeed as late as possible to your father. But
> the immortal gods have hastened to apply your virtues [*virtutes*] to the

---

communicazioni d'ufficio in età altoimperiale," in M. Pani, ed., *Epigrafia e territorio: Politica e società. Temi de antichità romane IV* (Rome, 1996), 331. I am grateful to Dr. B. Rankov for discussion of the evidence relating to *beneficiarii*.

17. Eutr. 10, 2, 1.

18. See n. 11.

19. A. N. Sherwin-White, *The Letters of Pliny: A Historical and Social Commentary* (Oxford, 1966), 556–80. There is no discussion of the character of the private letters as such.

reins of the state [*res publica*] which you had taken up. I pray therefore that for you, and through you for the human race, all things may turn out prosperous, that is worthy of your era [*saeculum*]. In both my private and my public capacity, I wish you, best of emperors, to be brave and confident.

How many individuals enjoyed a status which required them to send comparable letters to the distant Emperor, we do not know. No answer was required in this case. But it is quite clear that it was normal for provincial cities, or at least Greek ones, to send embassies of congratulation to a new emperor, and very often to ask at the same time for the confirmation of existing privileges, or to raise controversial matters.[20] The evidence is of course erratic and subject to chance. But we have two clear examples of embassies from Greek cities to which Trajan sent replies while he was consul for the second time and was holding the tribunician power (*tribunicia potestas*) for the second time. Both therefore date to before December 98. The two embassies of this year for which we have documentary evidence therefore made the journey, the one from Delphi and the other from Alexandria, either to Germania or to Pannonia (or, of course, they may have caught up with the Emperor on his journey between the two). Both of them involved the Emperor in composing replies to the city concerned, and also in sending letters to the relevant governors. In the case of Delphi, Trajan writes that he has confirmed the rights and the autonomy (*autonomia*) granted by previous emperors, and records that he has written (or sent orders) to his friend (*amicus*), the *proconsul* (governor of a public province) Herennius Saturninus, and to the *procurator* (financial officer).[21] In the case of the Alexandrians, he also confirms their privileges and says that he has recommended them both to himself and to the prefect of Egypt, and his friend (*amicus*), Pompeius Planta.[22] These two embassies, accidentally recorded, out of the hundreds which must have made the journey, therefore called between them for five imperial letters in response. The letters to cities were brought back by the embassies; those sent to officials were presumably carried by messengers.

We can certainly put in the same category the embassy from Prusa ad Olympum which Dio of Prusa discusses in his *Oration* 40, delivered before his fellow citizens (that is, in the popular assembly), "On Concord with the Apameans." This embassy too had resulted in a letter from the Emperor, which

20. See F. Millar, *The Emperor in the Roman World (31 BC–AD 337)*[2] (London, 1992), 410–20.

21. *Fouilles de Delphes* III.4 (Paris, 1970), no. 287; J. H. Oliver, *Greek Constitutions of Early Roman Emperors from Inscriptions and Papyri* (Philadelphia, 1989), no. 44.

22. *P. Oxy.*, no. 3022; Oliver, no. 46.

had been "read out" when it arrived (either in the city council or the popular assembly). Dio states explicitly that the embassy had been sent to congratulate the Emperor and also implies clearly that they had asked for benefits: but rumours circulated that they had not been favourably received, and that other cities had received actual gifts and had been granted improved rights.[23] Dio's sarcastic reference to the imputed idea that the Emperor might have been eagerly awaiting the arrival of their particular embassy perfectly fits a context in which literally hundreds of embassies will have been making the journey north to appear before him. As always, whether the cities of Italy and the Latin West will also have sent embassies to join this procession remains unclear.

The traffic from Greek cities certainly continued in the following year. In 99 Trajan confirmed the privileges of a synod based at the Isthmus of Corinth,[24] and in the same year wrote again to Delphi. By the time that he replied it was the first half of November 99, and he was able to write from an imperial villa at Antium.[25] The embassy must have started considerably earlier than that and will either have followed him on his journey back to Rome or have had the foresight to wait for him there. It was also from Antium that Trajan wrote the first of two letters to a man called Claudianus, who was resident at Pessinus in Asia Minor and was evidently of high social status. The date must either be autumn 99 to March 101; or early 107 to October 113.[26]

It seems to have been either in the previous year (98), or more probably in the following year (100), that Trajan gave a response to the Smyrneans in a concise form without complete titles or the normal formulae of address and farewell.[27] The form of the document, inscribed at Aphrodisias, strongly suggests that this was a subscription (*subscriptio*), that is to say, a reply to a petition (*libellus*). Greek cities normally addressed the emperor in letters, carried by embassies, and received replies from him in the form of letters from him. So this case is an anomaly; but it may be explained by the analogy of the petitions from the cities of Apamea, Nicaea, and Amisus which Pliny was later to attach to various letters of his to Trajan (see text to n. 53 below). The subject of this subscription was a claim by Smyrna on the services of a citizen of Aphrodisias, and in some way which is not made clear a "testimony" from Aphrodisias had also reached Trajan. But if the communication from

23. Dio Chrys., *Or.* 40, 13–15.

24. Oliver, no. 47.

25. *Fouilles de Delphes* III.4, no. 288; Oliver, no. 45.

26. Oliver, no. 50. The idea that this letter might date to the last few years of Trajan's reign is not tenable.

27. J. M. Reynolds, *Aphrodisias and Rome* (London, 1982), no. 14; Oliver, no. 48.

Smyrna had been a petition attached to the proconsul's letter, that would explain all the more easily why Trajan says in his reply that he has written also to Iulius Balbus, "my *amicus* [friend] and *proconsul*." Both documents will have been carried back to the proconsul by a messenger. The date of Balbus' proconsulship is unfortunately uncertain as between 98 and 100, or even a year or two later.[28]

The Emperor's reception of embassies during 99 and (almost certainly) during the first few days of his third consulate in 100 is also illustrated by the recently published fragments of two letters of his from Miletus.[29] The letters were almost certainly stimulated by a single embassy from Miletus, heard by the Emperor on probably more than one occasion, after his return to Rome in about October 99. At any rate the letter which was inscribed second dates to the period when Trajan was consul II, and designated III (so in the second half of 99); and that which was inscribed first was dated "Eight days before the Ides of January, from Rome," 6 January 100. Just enough survives of this letter to indicate that the context is the familiar competition for privilege among the cities of Asia.

If our evidence for imperial correspondence with Greek cities in the early years of Trajan's reign is slight, it is still extremely indicative. But, because of its uniqueness, there is much greater significance in the dossier of letters which Pliny sent to Trajan in this period, and which sometimes received replies, and sometimes did not. For a start, however successfully Trajan lived up to the model of the *civilis princeps* (a princeps who behaves like a citizen), as he clearly did,[30] it is very striking, as Hannah Cotton pointed out, that almost every one of Pliny's letters uses the words "to indulge" (*indulgere*) or "indulgence" (*indulgentia*).[31] That is to say, vis-à-vis the Emperor, even a high-placed senator like Pliny adopted the rhetorical posture of a humble petitioner. These letters from the first part of *epist.* 10, which are familiar to all, yet are strangely neglected, will be worth a brief look. In *epist.* 2 Pliny is apparently referring to a favourable reply (*rescriptum*) which Trajan had sent to Iulius Servianus, in answer to his petition (*preces*) that Pliny, who was in fact childless, should receive the privileges granted to a parent of three chil-

28. See *PIR*² I 199; B. Thomasson, *Laterculi Praesidum* I (Göteborg, 1984), 220.

29. N. Ehrhardt and P. Weiss, "Trajan, Didyma und Milet. Neue Fragmente von Kaiserbriefen und ihr Kontext," *Chiron* 25 (1995): 315–53; *AE* 1995, nos. 1498–1500. A small fragment of another letter is also included.

30. A. Wallace-Hadrill, "Civilis Princeps: Between Citizen and King," *JRS* 72 (1982): 32–48.

31. H. Cotton, "The Concept of *indulgentia* under Trajan," *Chiron* 14 (1984): 245–66.

dren and more (*ius trium liberorum*); the moment was "at the opening of your auspicious reign." In *epist.* 3a Pliny asks for permission to act as the prosecutor of Marius Priscus during the prefecture of the Treasury of Saturn, to which he had been appointed jointly by Nerva's and Trajan's indulgence (*indulgentia vestra*); Trajan replies positively in a two-sentence letter (*epist.* 3b). We are certainly still in the period of his absence on the frontier. In *epist.* 4 Pliny begins again with the word *indulgentia*, and asks for senatorial status for Voconius Romanus; Trajan does not reply.

In *epist.* 5 and 6 Pliny asks, once again using the word *indulgentia*, for the Roman citizenship for Harpocras, who needs the Alexandrian citizenship also as a precondition. Trajan replies positively in *epist.* 7 but asks to be informed as to which district in Egypt Harpocras came from "so that I may send on your behalf a letter [*epistula*] to Pompeius Planta, prefect of Egypt, my friend [*amicus meus*]." The transaction therefore involved three letters from Pliny and two from Trajan. The date is between mid-98 and mid-99, when Trajan was still on the northern frontier. Pliny's letter (*epist.* 10) duly giving Harpocras' district of origin was written when Trajan's arrival (*adventus*) in Rome was imminently expected, so in the second half of 99. It seems to have been before this, and in anticipation of freedom during September from his duties at the treasury, that Pliny asked leave for that month to go to his estates in Umbria and received a favourable reply (*epist.* 8–9). Trajan was certainly still absent from Rome.

Sherwin-White seems to me to have been correct in deducing from a passage in the *Annales* that in Tacitus' and Pliny's time letters were written to the emperor only when the latter was absent from Rome.[32] If so, it is very likely, as Sherwin-White further suggested, that the last four of the private letters to Trajan all belong in the period of the first Dacian war (101–2). In *epist.* 11 Pliny asks for the citizenship for some dependents; in 12 he asks for a praetorship for Accius Sura; and in 13 he asks for the augurate or the septemvirate for himself. None of the letters received any reply, and we should take it that all three requests were unsuccessful. When Pliny did finally receive the augurate (as we know from *epist.* 4.8) it was probably some three to four years later. In this connection it may be noted that in 101, after his departure on campaign, Trajan is recorded in the *Acts of the Arval Brothers* as writing a letter, with his seal on it, to his colleagues in the priesthood, apparently about the appointment of a public slave to their service.[33]

---

32. Sherwin-White (n. 19), 578, on Tac., *Ann.* 4.39.1: "[I]t was customary at that time to address him in writing even when he was present."

33. H. Henzen, *Acta Fratrum Arvalium* (Berlin, 1874), cxliii–cxliv; J. Scheid, *Recherches*

Finally, in *epist.* 14 Pliny writes to Trajan to congratulate him on his victory in the Dacian war; if it is the first war, as it seems, the date will be 102,
and the immediate occasion will be some time before Trajan's return and his
celebration of a triumph in December.

Far less evidence survives to illuminate the exchange of communications
with the Emperor during either the second Dacian war of 105–6, from which
he may not have returned to Rome until spring 107, or the Parthian war, for
which he left Rome in October 113, never to return. From the Dacian war,
however, we may note the very striking report in Pliny's letters that the heirs
in a case involving a disputed will, which pitted them against both an equestrian (*eques*) and a freedman and procurator of the Emperor, had written to
Trajan in Dacia asking him to take the case, and he on his return had done so.[34]
The context positively implies that the heirs were not people of the highest
social status. Finally, as the only instance which we have (other than letters
to the Senate, already mentioned) from the Parthian war, we may note the
complex exchanges with Pergamum over setting up of a new "iselastic" *agon*,
which date somewhere in the years 114–16.[35] Trajan had arrived in Syria in
December 113.

The conduct of the Emperor's correspondence while he was on journeys
through the provinces, or while he was staying in provincial cities or while
on campaign, is a special case; for, firstly, it must have been conducted in
the context of constant uncertainty as to where the Emperor actually was, or
would be next. Secondly, it implies on the Emperor's part an extraordinary
diversion of time and energy, plus the presence at all times of the necessary
secretarial staff. But in other respects government at a distance, by means of
letters, was simply the standard mechanism through which the Roman Empire worked. In particular, the governor of a province could communicate
with the emperor only by letter, whether the latter was currently in Rome
or on campaign.

Provincial Governors and the Emperor: The Legal Sources

Time and space are the essential elements which we have always to bear in
mind if we are to understand the workings of the Empire. As we will see, a
provincial governor received a code of instructions (*mandata*) from the Em-

---

*archéologiques. Les copies épigraphiques des protocoles annuels de la confrére arvale (21 av.–304 ap.
J-C)* (Rome, 1998), 180, Trajan b fr. 1.

34. Plin., *epist.* 6, 31, 8.

35. *Ins. v. Pergamon* II, 1895, no. 269; *IGR* IV, no. 336; Oliver, no. 49.

peror before leaving (whether this code was handed over in person, or was sent in the manner of a letter, seems uncertain). But once he had set out, and while he was in his province, he could only receive further instructions, send information, or raise problems through the medium of letters carried by messengers, who might take several weeks in either direction (what, if any, escort a messenger had, and what happened if he died, deserted, or was killed by bandits is entirely obscure). We also need to recall that a governor was systematically, by the nature of his office, on the move between the major cities of his province.[36] The Emperor, for his part, might be absent on campaign, or might for extended periods be resident in Rome. Both parties, therefore, were potentially moving targets, whom the messenger might have to find, at the end of a journey whose length might be quite indeterminate.

Pliny's correspondence with Trajan from Pontus and Bithynia of course represents our best evidence for exchanges between a governor and an emperor. But one central purpose of this chapter is to put that correspondence in the context of the important parallel evidence from Trajan's reign, mainly from legal sources.

Some of the evidence, however, in fact comes from Pliny himself, and some from inscriptions. Thus Pliny records two cases in which he participated in Trajan's council (*consilium*), both of which were prompted by letters written to the Emperor by provincial governors: in the one the governor had detected one of his companions (*comites*) in many improprieties (*flagitia*) and "wrote to Caesar."[37] In the other, the issue concerned the wife of a military tribune of senatorial status, who had committed adultery with a centurion. The husband wrote to the consular governor (*legatus consularis*) of the province, and he then wrote to Caesar.[38] Both cases will have been heard near the beginning of the only extended period which Trajan spent in Rome as Emperor, from 107 to 113.

By contrast, the case between the Delphians and the Ambrossians, which was heard by Avidius Nigrinus as (probably) a *legatus* in Achaea, seems to belong to the very end of the reign, when Trajan was engaged on the Parthian war. Trajan had at some earlier point heard the issue himself ("cognoscens"), and had instructed ("iussit") Nigrinus to determine the dispute over boundaries in person, on the site.[39] Neither the sequence of events preceding Nigri-

36. For the best discussion, see still G. P. Burton, "Proconsuls, Assizes and the Administration of Justice under the Empire," *JRS* 65 (1975): 92–106.

37. Plin., *epist.* 6.22.2: "Caesari scripsit." The reference to wrongdoing on the part of "his companion" (*comes suus*) makes it safe to assume that the writer was a provincial governor.

38. *Epist.* 6, 31, 4–6.

39. *Fouilles de Delphes* III.4, no. 292.

nus' judgement nor the nature of the communications involved can be re-constructed. What is evident from the inscription, however, is the way in which the distant Emperor's decision forms the framework for the hearing of the case in Achaea.

The quite extensive legal evidence from Trajan's reign provides very clear parallels for that, as well as offering evidence for other mediums for imperial decision making, which will not be discussed here. The most prominent is the laying down of legal rules by the issuing of edicts (*edicta*).[40] There is also one report which seems to reflect a trial (*cognitio*) held by Trajan, along with advisers.[41] Ulpian also quotes verbatim the clause (*caput*) which Trajan caused to be inserted in the *mandata* which were given to provincial governors, con-cerning the much more liberal rules which were to apply to the drawing-up of valid wills by soldiers: "Following the benevolence of my disposition as regards my most excellent and most loyal fellow soldiers, I have thought it right that consideration should be exercised in regard to their lack of knowl-edge [*simplicitas*]."[42] Though, as I have suggested before, a systematic treat-ment of the *mandata* would be invaluable,[43] the topic will not be pursued further here.

Instead, we can move directly to Trajan's rescripts (*rescripta*) addressed to recipients who are evidently provincial governors, and who in each case will (like Pliny) have taken the initiative in writing to consult him. The jurist Florentinus, for instance, quotes the extensive rescript (which is as long as the fullest of Trajan's replies to Pliny) in which the Emperor tries to explain to Statilius Severus exactly under what conditions a soldier's will, under the terms of the privilege (*privilegium*) given in the *mandata*, can be regarded as valid. There is no doubt that the explanation arises from a case before Severus: "therefore the soldier [*miles*], about whose property a question has been raised before you . . ."[44] The question of military discipline, and the need to keep soldiers at their duties, is also conspicuous, just as it is in the exchanges with Pliny. Thus Trajan replied ("rescripsit") to Minicius Natalis that "festivals [*feriae*] give a holiday only from legal transactions, but those

40. As noted above, the evidence is presented by Gualandi (n. 14). *Edicta* of Trajan: *Frag. de iure fisci* 6; *Inst.* 3, 7, 4; *Dig.* 34, 9, 5, 20; 47, 11, 6, 1; 49, 14, 13 *pr.*-1, with further references to the favour (*beneficium*) conferred by Trajan (evidently in this same *edictum*) in 49, 14, 13, 6 and 8; 15, 3; 16; 42 *pr.* ("according to the enactment of the divine Trajan"); 49.

41. *Dig.* 37, 12, 5 (mentioning the advice of Neratius Priscus and Aristo).

42. *Dig.* 29, 1, 1 *pr.*

43. Millar (n. 20), 641–43.

44. *Inst.* 2, 11, 1.

duties which pertain to military discipline must be carried out even on festal days: among which the inspection of the prisoners [*custodiae*] is also included." The occasion might have been either when Natalis was *legatus* in Numidia in 103–5 or when he was *legatus* of Pannonia Superior in 113 onwards.[45] Other rescripts concerned the physical and other qualifications for military service, especially where deliberate mutilation to avoid service had occurred,[46] while a whole series of rescripts addressed to named individuals who were evidently governors laid down rules for the conduct of criminal jurisdiction — for instance, whether a slave belonging to a husband could be tortured in a case relating to his wife.[47]

But the closest and most vivid parallel to the self-expression of Trajan, as it is visible in his replies to Pliny, is certainly what he says in a rescript addressed to Didius Secundus on the proper handling of the goods of persons who had suffered the relatively mild form of exile known as *relegatio*. The second-century jurist Pomponius, in his fourth book *Ad Sabinum*, quotes the following clause (*caput*) from the rescript:[48]

> I am aware that, by the greed [*avaritia*] of previous times [the reign of Domitian], the property [*bona*] of persons relegated has been claimed for the imperial treasury [*fiscus*]. But different principle accords with my clemency [*clementia*], and I, among the other steps by which the purity [*innocentia*] of my times [is demonstrated], have cancelled this practice also.

It is only rarely that (as with Minicius Natalis) any contemporary documentary evidence allows even a hypothetical identification of an addressee named in a legal source, or of his current post. Moreover, in some other cases of rescripts attributed to Trajan, no addressee is named at all. Alternatively, a provision which may well in fact have been embodied in a rescript sent in reply to an enquiry from a provincial governor may be described neutrally as an enactment (*constitutio*). Thus we come very close again to the world of Pliny's exchanges with Trajan when we read the following extract from Pomponius' sixth book of *Epistulae et Variae Lectiones*, preserved in the *Digest*:[49] "If anyone, in consideration of his own or anyone else's magistracy, has promised that he will construct a public building in any city, by the enactment of the

45. *Dig.* 2, 12, 9; see *PIR²* M 619.
46. *Dig.* 49, 16, 4 *pr.*; 4, 5; 4, 12.
47. *Dig.* 48, 18, 1, 11 (on the torture of a husband's slave *in caput uxoris*); 12; 19; 21; 19, 5 *pr.*
48. *Dig.* 48, 22, 1.
49. *Dig.* 50, 12, 14.

divine Trajan there is an obligation on both him and his heir to complete it."
The imperial rescripts sent to provincial governors were absolutely typical
of the form of the contribution made by the emperors to the evolution of
Roman law, in arising from individual cases but as expressing general principles. Thus, in spite of their specific origins, they could be, and often were,
quoted by juristic writers, and thus came subsequently to be embodied in the
Digest or *Institutes* of Justinian. But if we go back to the original contexts and
problems which gave rise to these rescripts, we are immediately in the same
world as that in which Pliny functioned as *legatus* of Pontus and Bithynia.

Pliny and Trajan

The correspondence between Pliny and Trajan has been discussed many
times, above all by Sherwin-White in his major *Commentary*, and more recently by W. Williams.[50] It therefore need not be treated in detail here. Instead, I have produced a chart (see the appendix), which sets out the pattern
of the correspondence in time and place. Firstly, as regards time, I am convinced by Sherwin-White's argument that the third year of Pliny's governorship must be 111: in reporting the vows (*vota*) of the army and the provincials in *epist*. 100, Pliny could surely not have ignored Trajan's assumption
of his sixth consulship on 1 January 112.[51] Secondly, the correspondence belongs in the one extended period when we know that Trajan was in Rome.
Pliny was constantly on the move, but Trajan (even if he retired from time to
time to villas in Italy) was continuously in Rome. This is not therefore one of
those instances, which must have become increasingly common, when both
emperor and governor presented moving targets for whoever was carrying
messages between them. Thirdly, all the exchanges in the correspondence
were initiated by Pliny. He had received *mandata* from Trajan, which related
among other things to military discipline, and to the rights—or absence of
rights—of association on the part of the provincials: the latter clause had
been embodied in the edict (*edictum*) which Pliny issued, and in response
to which Christian groups had disbanded.[52] But no further instructions or

50. W. Williams, *Pliny the Younger, Correspondence with Trajan from Bithynia (Epistles X)*
(Warminster, 1990).

51. Sherwin-White (n. 19), 81.

52. Pliny's *mandata*: *epist*. 10, 22, 1 (disposition of soldiers); 30, 1 (levying of recruits); 56,
3 (non-restitution of those exiled by *relegatio*); 96, 7 ("since the promulgation of my own
edictum, in which, following your *edicta*, I forbade the forming of associations [*hetaeriae*]");
110–11 (prevention of donations from city funds).

items of information are recorded as having reached Pliny from the Emperor (none the less, it is certain that there will have been some such communications; see Eck in n. 16 above). Fourthly, not all of the letters which Pliny sent received an answer. Fifthly, a conspicuous feature of Pliny's letters is that they quite often had attached to them petitions (*libelli*) submitted by interested parties; some came from private persons, but there were also, as we have noted earlier, others originating from cities: the colony of Apamea, the city of Nicaea, and the free city (*civitas libera*) of Amisus.[53]

Sixthly, Pliny was permanently on the move. The question of the "capital cities" of provinces has been much discussed recently, notably in the massive and scholarly volume by Rudolf Haensch, *Capita Provinciarum*.[54] In this instance it turns out to be impossible to identify a capital city (*caput*) of the province from Pliny's letters. But in any case this particular province was a double one, composed of the bulk of one former Hellenistic royal territory, Bithynia, and of a truncated section, the north-western coastal region only, of another, Pontus. The major recent works by Stephen Mitchell and Christian Marek have set out the extraordinarily complex successive boundary changes which finally left Pontus, the eastern part of Pliny's province, as no more than an extended coastal strip reaching as far as Amisus, and one which was considerably smaller in area than the Pompeian province of Pontus had been.[55] Functionally, it seems from Pliny's letters that this Pontic zone was treated as a mere adjunct to the Bithynian part of the province. The chart shows that for the whole of his first year Pliny did not visit it at all. But it was, beyond all question, in Pontus, and not in Bithynia, that he encountered the problem of the Christians.

The letters forming the correspondence are grouped in the original text, as they are in the chart, by topic, with Trajan's reply, if there was one, following the letter to which it relates. One function of the chart is to illumi-

53. Petitions from individuals: *epist.* 10, 59 (petitions of Flavius Archippus and his accuser, Furia Prima); 81 (petition of Cocceianus Dion); 106–7 (petition of P. Accius Aquila, centurion of the sixth mounted cohors). Petitions from cities: 47–48 (petition of the people of Apamea); 83 (petition of the people of Nicaea); 92–03 (petition of the people of Amisus).

54. R. Haensch, *Capita Provinciarum: Statthaltersitze und Provinzialverwaltung in der römischen Kaiserzeit* (Mainz, 1997). For the assize system (*conventus*), see the discussion on pp. 18–19. For Pontus and Bithynia, see the detailed treatment on pp. 282–90, rightly leaving the question of a "capital" of the province open.

55. See S. Mitchell, *Anatolia* I (Oxford, 1993), 61–62, with map 3 opposite p. 40; C. Marek, *Stadt, Ära und Territorium in Pontus-Bithynia und Nord-Galatia* (Istanbuler Forschungen 39, Tübingen, 1993).

nate what proportion of Pliny's letters received no reply. Some but not all of those which received no reply were requests for favours, of a type which Pliny could have written (and indeed had written) earlier, while holding no office. One clear example is *epist.* 26, a request for preferment to be granted to Pliny's former quaestor, Rosianus Geminus. Trajan does not reply. Some of the requests, however, though of the same type, related specifically to persons who were under Pliny's command as *legatus*. A conspicuous case is *epist.* 106, the request for a grant of the Roman citizenship for the daughter of an auxiliary centurion. This one received a positive reply (107).

The grouping by letter-and-reply obscures the real chronology of the correspondence, as it will have presented itself to Pliny. The exchange of letters depended entirely on the movement of messengers; but none of these is ever explicitly referred to, except for two messengers (*tabellarii*), one sent by King Sauromates of the Bosporan kingdom and one by an imperial freedman named Lycormas. Both are despatched on to Trajan (*epist.* 63–64). If we assume a journey of six or eight weeks in each direction for a messenger, then none of the replies listed under year one will actually have reached Pliny until year two. Equally, if we think of the letters (35, 37, 39, 41, 43, 45, 47, 49) which Pliny sent off in January of year two, none of the replies will have arrived until long after *epist.* 52, written to mark Trajan's day of accession (*dies imperii*) on 28 January, had been despatched. Similarly, Trajan's brief acknowledgment (*epist.* 36) of the vows of 1 January in year two (35) will almost certainly not have arrived in Bithynia until about April.

Equally, it looks as if Pliny's tour of the cities of Pontus began after he had sent off his first letter of year two congratulating Trajan on his birthday (*natalis*) on 18 October (*epist.* 88). It would thus seem very likely that when the messenger returned with Trajan's reply (84) on the right of Nicaea to claim the property of citizens who died intestate (*vindicatio bonorum*), Pliny will already have been in Pontus. A messenger who had assumed that when he got back he might find the *legatus* giving judgement in Prusa or Nicaea would thus have been faced with an extra journey of some 500 kilometres in order to catch up with him in the area of Sinope or Amisus. Even within the boundaries of the double province, therefore, a messenger moving at a reasonable speed will have needed some ten days to travel from the main cities of Bithynia to those of Pontus. We do have to keep these considerable distances constantly in mind. When Pliny was considering the water supply of the colony of Sinope (*epist.* 90), he was some 2,400 kilometres distant from Trajan as the crow flies. No one in the modern world seems to have asked what route to Rome and back the messenger will have taken, or what part of the journey, if any, will have been made by sea. Pliny, for his part, when he was travelling to the province, had made a sea voyage round Cape Malea, presumably starting from Brundisium, and had landed at Ephesus, continuing by land through Pergamum, and then (rather surprisingly) reverting to coastal shipping until he reached Bithynia (*epist.* 10.15–17b). A messenger travelling west from Sinope towards Rome could have made the first part of the journey either by land or sea. After that, he might perhaps have followed Pliny's route in reverse, or more probably have taken the Via Egnatia, or alternatively the major route by land from Byzantium via Philippopolis, Naissus, and Sirmium to northern Italy and Rome. In this instance, even sixty days, or two months, for the journey in each direction, by whatever route, might well seem an underestimate.

Conclusion

The letters which Pliny sent to Trajan from Pontus and Bithynia, and Trajan's replies, have always attracted interest. But I suggest that if we see them in perspective, against a wider background, they actually become not less but more interesting. One sense of the word "background" in this context is what we know of all the other forms of correspondence which pursued the Emperor wherever he was, including those letters which Pliny himself had written to Trajan in the early part of his reign. But a more important sense of "background" is that of the vast spaces of the Roman Empire, across which messengers and ambassadors had to travel, if words intended for the Emperor were ever to reach him. Those distances themselves imposed delays in time which it is genuinely hard now to comprehend, and to take into account. It is not easy for us to grasp the constant flow of messages, complaints, and documents involving complex local issues emanating from the provinces, and of replies embodying the ideology, the propaganda, the values, and the preferences of the imperial will, or the fact that these had to be carried slowly either by ambassadors or by couriers on horseback using wagons (*vehicula*), and travelling backwards and forwards across literally thousands of kilometres, between the provinces and wherever the Emperor was, whether in Rome or in another province, or (on occasion) beyond the frontiers of the Empire. But they were so carried, and there is a real sense in which it was the writing and transmission of these letters which made the Roman Empire what it was.

Appendix

Pliny and Trajan: Time and Place
Epistulae book X

Time	Letter	Author	Subject	Place
Year I (A.D. 109?)				
	15	P	Journey	
	16	T		
17–18 October	17a	P	Arrival. Trajan's birthday. Finances of Prusa	Prusa
	17b	P	Land surveyor	
	18	T		
	19	P	Prisoners	
	20	T		
	21	P	Gavius Bassus, prefect of the Pontic shore ("he replied that he will write to you")	
	22	T	("Gavius Bassus wrote to me as well")	
	23	P	Public bath	Prusa
	24	T		
24 November	25	P	Servilius Pudens, Pliny's *legatus*	Nicomedia
	26	P	Rosianus Geminus (recommendation)	
	27	P	Maximus, freedman procurator, request for *beneficiarii*	
	28	T		
	29	P	Recruits	
	30	T	("following my own instructions")	
	31	P	People sentenced to capital punishments in the cities	
	32	T		
	33	P	Fire at Nicomedia	Another part of the province
	34	T		

Time	Letter	Author	Subject	Place
Year II (A.D. 110?)				
1 January	35	P	Vows	
	36	T		
	37	P	Aqueduct	Nicomedia
	38	T		
	39	P	Building projects	(Nicaea, Claudiopolis)
	40	T		
	41	P	Canal project	Nicomedia
	42	T		
	43	P	City expenditures	Byzantium
	44	T		
	45	P	Travel permits	
	46	T		
	47	P	Accounts of the colony (with the Apameans' petition)	Apamea
	48	T		
	49	P	Temple of Magna Mater	Nicomedia
	50	T		
	51	P	Caelius Clemens (appointment to Bithynia)	
28 January	52	P	Anniversary of Trajan's accession	
	53	T		
	54	P	Public funds (of cities)	
	55	T		
	56	P	Criminal cases	
	57	T		
	58	P	Assizes. Flavius Archippus	Prusa?
	59	P	Flavius Archippus (with petition of Archippus)	
	60	T	(Mentioning petitions of Archippus and of Furia Prima, accuser)	
	61	P	Canal project	(Nicomedia)
	62	T		
	63	P	Messenger of King Sauromates	

Time	Letter	Author	Subject	Place
	64	P	Messenger (Sauromates' letter to Trajan)	
	65	P	Foundlings	
	66	T		
	67	P	Ambassador of Sauromates	Nicomedia
	68	P	Transfer of human remains	
	69	T		
	70	P	Building projects	Prusa
	71	T		
	72	P	Status of children	
	73	T		
	74	P	Callidromus, runaway slave	
	75	P	Iulius Largus, from Pontus	(Heraclea, Tium)
	76	T		
	77	P	Need for centurion on police duty? (reference to instructions to Calpurnius Macer, *legatus* of Moesia Inferior)	(Iuliopolis)
	78	T		
	79	P	Councils of Bithynian cities. Lex Pompeia	
	80	T		
	81	P	Cocceianus Dion (81, 3: "I replied that I would hear the case in Nicaea") (81, 7: Petition of Dion attached)	Prusa
	82	T		
	83	P	Cover letter with attached petition of the people of Nicaea	
	84	T		
	85	P	Maximus, a freedman	
	86a	P	Gavius Bassus	
	86b	P	Fabius Valens	
	87	P	Request on behalf of son of Nymphidius Lupus (87, 3: testimonials of Iulius Ferox and Iulius Salinator)	

Time	Letter	Author	Subject	Place
18 September	88	P	Trajan's birthday	
	89	T		
Tour to Pontus				
	90	P	Aqueduct	Sinope
	91	T		
	92	P	Rights of a free city (petition attached)	Amisus
	93	T		
	94	P	Privileges of a parent of three children for Suetonius	
	95	T		
	96	P	Christians	(Pontus)
	97	T		
	98	P	Drainage	Amastris
	99	T		
Year III (A.D. 111?)				
1 January	100	P	Vows	
	101	T		
28 January	102	P	Anniversary of Trajan's accession	
	103	T		
	104	P	Request for full citizen rights for Latin freedmen	
	105	T		
	106	P	Request for citizenship for daughter of centurion (petition attached)	
	107	T	("I have sent you the subscribed petition which you are to forward to him")	
	108	P	Exaction of money by cities	
	109	T		
	110	P	Recovery of money from Iulius Piso	Amisus
	111	T		
	112	P	Lex Pompeia and city councils	
	113	T		

Time	*Letter*	*Author*	*Subject*	*Place*
	114	P	Lex Pompeia and conferment a city's citizenship on outsiders	
	115	T		
	116	P	Cash distributions in cities	
	117	T		
	118	P	Rewards of athletes	
	119	T		
	120	P	Travel permits	
	121	T		

CHAPTER THREE

The Fiscus in the First Two Centuries[*]

The early Principate tends to be interpreted in terms of the constitutional forms in which it was clothed and the administrative innovations which it brought, to the neglect of those, largely unchanged, social and economic factors which shaped the actual working of Roman politics. In no area has this tendency been more obvious than in works dealing with the Fiscus, which has thus been seen as an alternative "state treasury" created at a given moment, by Augustus, perhaps in 21 or 20 B.C.,[1] by Tiberius,[2] or by Claudius,[3] which absorbed the revenues of the imperial provinces,[4] and some indirect taxes.[5] It is also seen as an administrative unit (like a treasury, or a university chest) concerned with the handling of an area of public finance.[6]

None of these views is fully supported by the evidence. The proper histori-

*First published in *JRS* 53 (1963): 29–42. I should like to thank Mr. P. M. Fraser and Dr. W. A. J. Watson for their help in the preparation of this chapter and Professor A. H. M. Jones, Mr. P. A. Brunt, and Mr. A. J. Holladay for discussing a draft of it with me. None of them is responsible for the views expressed.

1. S. Bolla, *Die Entwicklung des Fiskus zum privatrechtssubjekt mit Beiträgen zur Lehre vom Aerarium* (Prague, 1938), 19–20.

2. S. J. de Laet, *Portorium* (Bruges, 1949), 364–65.

3. *CAH* X, 687 esp.; H. Last, "The Fiscus: A Note," *JRS* 34 (1944): 51, on p. 59; A. Garzetti, "*Aerarium* e *Fiscus* sotto Augusto; storia di una questione in parte di nomi," *Athenaeum* 31 (1953): 298, esp. p. 327.

4. E.g., Last (n. 3) 52; A. Berger, *Encyclopedic Dictionary of Roman Law* (*TAPhA* 43, 2, 1953), 472–73; H. F. Jolowicz, *An Historical Introduction to the Study of Roman Law*[2] (Cambridge, 1952), 339.

5. E.g., O. Hirschfeld, *Die kaiserlichen Verwaltungsbeamten*[2] (Berlin, 1905), 82; de Laet (n. 2).

6. Last (n. 3), 51; A. H. M. Jones, "The *Aerarium* and the *Fiscus*," *JRS* 40 (1950): 22, esp. on p. 25.

cal standpoint for the understanding of the development of the Fiscus in the first two centuries of the Empire has never, to my knowledge, been clearly understood.[7] The significant factor is the importance of the emperor's private wealth in the running of the state. In the way in which that wealth was used for public ends, the Empire, as in all things, shows the practice of republican magnates writ large. Thus Augustus' huge expenditure on public needs, detailed in the *Res Gestae*, was at once the culmination of one aspect of republican politics and the foundation of a permanent element in the structure of imperial finance. It is to these imperial funds that the word "fiscus" refers— and it is normally best translated as "the imperial estate." There was no moment at which an institution called "the Fiscus" was created. The strictly correct way of describing what took place is to say that "fiscus" gradually became the predominant technical term used in speaking of the imperial wealth— and it is only in legal sources that it is used invariably. In literary sources, papyri, and inscriptions, other terms, *res familiaris, res dominica, patrimonium*— or just *pecunia sua* or *mea*—*to basilikon, to (ierōtaton) tameion, ta auktoratorika chrēmata* are often used in contexts where "fiscus," or, *o phiskos* in Greek, or cognate expressions, might have appeared.

The following discussion of the known uses of "fiscus" in the early imperial period will therefore be at the same time a sketch, though necessarily no more than a sketch, of the various sources of income of the imperial estate, and of its role in public finance and in the life of the Empire. The subject, as will appear, has no immediate connection with the question of how the Aerarium ("state treasury") was controlled or how the emperor administered the public revenues in his own provinces.

Imperial Properties

The starting point must of course be the well-known passage of Seneca: "Caesar disposes of everything; his *fiscus*, however, contains only private property [*privata*], his own [*sua*]: everything is subject to his rule [*imperium*] but only his own property [*propria*] is subject to the patrimony [*patrimonium*]."[8] Seneca thus makes a formal correspondence between "fiscus" and

7. C. H. V. Sutherland, "*Aerarium* and *Fiscus* during the early Empire," *AJPh* 66 (1945): 151, gives the full emphasis to the role of the emperor's private wealth in the early Principate but then relates the theme too closely to the separate subject of the emperor's control of the Aerarium—and claims that the latter had been reduced to insignificance by the reign of Trajan.

8. *de benef.* 7, 6, 3: "Caesar omnia habet, fiscus eius privata tantum ac sua: et universa in imperio eius sunt, in patrimonio propria."

"patrimonium"; attempts to explain away the plain meaning of the sentence cannot be accepted.[9] Following on this, it is noteworthy how many other uses of "fiscus" illustrate the private-law position of the princeps as an owner of slaves and properties, a patron (*patronus*) of freedmen, and a party to ordinary commercial and legal transactions.

Like other citizens, the emperor received (subject to various modifications and exceptions) the savings (*peculia*) of his slaves on their death and half the savings of his freedmen; the enormous revenue which will thus have accrued must be responsible for the appearance of the *fiscus libertatis et peculiorum*.[10] Suetonius relates how a freedman of Vespasian, Cerylus, attempted to evade the claims of the Fiscus by changing his name and claiming to be freeborn,[11] while the tombstone of another imperial freedman bears the words "nor does the *fiscus* have a claim to half a share"[12]—this portion of his property at least was to be free of the *fiscus'* demands. A number of sections in the *Fragmenta de iure fisci* illustrate in detail the rights of the Fiscus to the property of imperial slaves and freedmen.[13]

A *familia* of slaves could be a source of expense as well as of income. Agrippa had his own gang of slaves for work on the Roman aqueducts and, when he died, left it to Augustus. On his death Augustus left this *familia* to the state, while Claudius formed another, twice the size, which remained imperial property. Caesar's *familia* was supported "by the *fiscus*," and the Fiscus also supplied the materials used by both.[14] The Fiscus' control of building materials is further illustrated by an inscription from the reign of Commodus which shows the issue of materials at the price paid by the Fiscus to an imperial freedman, Adrastus.[15] Some years later, in 211, one P. Aelius Chrestus is found buying part of a building in Rome from the Fiscus and having his ownership certified by a freedman financial official.[16]

9. E.g., Last (n. 3), 55–56.

10. I.e., the *fiscus* into which sums with which imperial slaves bought their liberty went, and into which, in the event of their death, their savings were absorbed. See, e.g., *CIL* VI, 772, 8450, 8450a. This point was made by Jones (n. 6), 26. It is not necessary to assume that *all* the various "fisci" were sub-divisions of "the Fiscus."

11. Suet., *Div. Vesp.* 23, 1.

12. *CIL* VI, 10876. This is the earliest Roman inscription (from the reign of Hadrian or soon after) in which the word "fiscus," unqualified and in the singular, occurs.

13. *Fragmenta de iure fisci* (*FIRA*[2] II, 627–28), 1, 6 *ad fin.*, 2, 10, 11, 12, 13 (?).

14. Frontinus, *de aquae ductu urbis Romae*, 116ff.

15. *ILS* 5920. For related inscriptions, see R. Macmullen, "Roman Imperial Building in the Provinces," *Harv. Stud. Class. Phil.* 64 (1959): 207, n. 21.

16. *CIL* VI, 10233.

The word "fiscus" appears frequently in connection with the ownership or tenancy of landed properties by the emperor. Pliny the Elder says that Augustus paid the city of Naples 20,000 sesterces per year "from his own *fiscus*" for the Collis Leucogaeus[17] and also mentions that in his time the Fiscus ran the balsam plantations near Jericho and sold the crops.[18] These plantations had an interesting history, described by Pliny as "royal lands" (presumably of the Seleucids); they were presented by Antonius to Cleopatra and rented from her by Herod.[19] With the death of Cleopatra they probably fell to Octavian as booty and were retained as his private property.[20] A similar fate befell the Cyprus copper mines, which had been restored to Cleopatra by Antonius, became Augustus' private property, of which he gave a half share to Herod,[21] and were still imperial property in the middle of the second century when Galen collected specimens there.[22] These properties perhaps fell to Augustus as spoils by analogy with *manubiae* ("spoils of war"). For, although the view has been expressed that *manubiae* were not the property of the *imperator*, but of the state, and that his rights were (in effect) restricted to the choice of some public purpose to which to devote them,[23] the evidence seems to me to prove the opposite, that the imperator did take *manubiae* as his property — and the role of *manubiae* as one source of Augustus' expenses (*impensae*) as recorded in the *Res Gestae* is well known.[24] If much of the spoils of Egypt had to go to the soldiers or political allies[25] or be spent in Rome, some could be retained by Octavian himself and pass to his successors.[26] Again, the troops

17. Pliny, *NH* 18, 114.

18. Pliny, *NH* 12, 113, 123.

19. Jos., *BJ* 1, 316, not mentioned in *AJ* 15, 95. See H. Buchheim, *Die Orientpolitik des Triumvirn M. Antonius* (Heidelberg, 1960), 68–69.

20. It is possible, though it is not stated, that the balsam plantations were among the territories returned by Octavian to Herod in 30 B.C., Jos., *BJ* 1, 396 = *AJ* 15, 217. In that case the plantations will have come to the Fiscus when the property of Archelaus was confiscated in A.D. 6 (see n. 113).

21. Jos., *AJ* 16, 128. Cyprus was now (12 B.C.) a public province.

22. Galen (ed. Kühn), 14, 7.

23. F. Bona, "Sul concetto di 'Manubiae' e sulla responsibilità del magistrato in ordine alla preda," *Stud. et Doc. Hist. et Iur.* 26 (1960): 105.

24. See U. Wilcken, "Zu den Impensae der Res Gestae divi Augusti," *S-B Deutsche Ak. Wiss.* 27 (1931): 772.

25. Dio 51, 17, 7–8.

26. There are, of course, difficulties here in that real property did not normally form a part of booty, or *manubiae*. The properties concerned are ones of which Antonius was able to dispose freely, and it was perhaps in the practice of the Triumviral period that the origins of Augustus' rights to the properties lay.

of Petilius Cerealis could support their demand for permission to sack the Colonia Trevirorum by offering to let all the booty go to the Fiscus.[27]

Most wars in the Empire were not profitable (hence the increasing diffi-culty of supporting the army); only Trajan, by his conquest of Dacia, made a substantial gain and was able not only to have "from the spoils" (*ex manubiis*) inscribed on buildings in the Forum Traianum,[28] but also to acquire mines in Dacia, which we find being supervised by a procurator who was one of his own freedmen.[29]

But to return to imperial properties. The well-known inscription of an imperial estate in Africa, the Saltus Burunitanus, shows the peasants com-plaining of wrongs done to them "by the contractors of the 'fiscal' lands [*a conductorib(us) agrorum fiscalium*]."[30] An equally interesting and important inscription from Saepinum,[31] one of the best examples of imperial "bureau-cracy" at work, contains three letters concerned with imperial flocks in the Abruzzi. The first, in chronological order, is from an imperial slave, Septi-mianus, to Cosmus, the *a rationibus* (the official in charge of the accounts) of Marcus Aurelius, complaining of interference with "the lord's sheep" (*oves dominicae*) by the officials of Saepinum and Bovianum and asking for the interference to be halted "lest the lord's property [*res dominica*] suffers any loss." Then Cosmus writes to the praetorian prefects requesting measures "so that by your favour the interest of the *fiscus* will be safeguarded," and finally the prefects write to the magistrates of Saepinum warning them to abstain from conduct which will result in "a great loss to the *fiscus*." A papyrus from the Hermopolite nome, dating from 135, shows a division of leased domain land (*ousiakon ktēma*) with a reference to payments to the Fiscus.[32] Over and above these documentary uses there are numerous references in legal sources to the ownership or sale of land by the Fiscus.[33]

Among imperial properties, mines occupied a specially important place. They might be gained by conquest, like those of Cyprus and Dacia, but there

27. Tac., *Hist.* 4, 72.

28. Aulus Gellius, *NA* 13, 25.

29. *CIL* III, 1312, "To M. Ulpius Hermias, freedman of Augustus, procurator of the gold mines" (*M. Ulpio Aug./lib. Hermiae proc./aurariarum*).

30. *ILS* 6870.

31. *CIL* IX 2438; *FIRA*[2] I, 61. See A. Passerini, *Le coorti pretorie* (Rome, 1939), 251–52.

32. *P. Ryl.* 157. Compare the fragmentary *BGU* 1576, a letter from an official to a pro-curator dating to 133–35 or 147–48, with mentions of (l. 10) *o kyriakos logos* (the lord's ac-count), "the revenues of the estate" (l. 16), and (l. 23) "the *fiscus.*"

33. *Dig.* 22, 1, 16, 1; 39, 4, 9, 8; 49, 45, 13–14; 49, 14, 47, 1; 49, 14, 50; 50, 6, 6, 10–11; Paulus, *Sent.* 1, 6a. 5, 5, 12, 23.

were other ways by which they might come to the emperor. A passage in
Pliny's *Natural History* implicitly illustrates some of these processes. After the
Cyprus mines, he says, the best copper came from a mine owned by Sallustius
Crispus in the Alps and the next best from one owned by Livia in Gaul. These
two soon failed and were replaced by the Mons Marianus.[34] The historical
sequence which lies behind this passage is clear. Sallustius Crispus died in
A.D. 20, and some at least of his property passed, by inheritance or legacy,
into imperial possession.[35] Livia died in 29 and Tiberius was her heir. Sextus
Marius, the richest man in Spain, was condemned in 33 and his mines were
taken by Tiberius.[36] An inscription shows a *silver* mine in Aquitania being
worked by imperial slaves in Tiberius' reign;[37] a procurator of Marius' mine
is attested in later years.[38]

The best-known imperial mine is of course the Metallum Vipascense in
Lusitania. The two inscriptions relating to it show that it was controlled by
a procurator and that payments by the lessees of the shafts, and fines for the
non-observance of the regulations, were paid to the Fiscus.[39] The system by
which the shafts were leased individually to contractors is the same as that
found in the Dacian mines.

The Fiscus in Litigation

With the continuing expansion of fiscal properties, the question of the position of the Fiscus as a party to private contracts inevitably became of major
importance. In the nature of the case the employees of the emperor could
often prevent the processes of justice or ignore them altogether; and to become involved in litigation against the Fiscus, or to be a debtor to it, was
a dangerous business. The situation is illustrated by one of the earliest literary references to the Fiscus, in Seneca's *de beneficiis*—the paragraph discusses
when it is allowable to break a promise and when it is not (he would keep
an engagement for dinner if it were cold but not if it were snowing, and so

---

34. Pliny, *NH* 34, 2–4.

35. See O. Hirschfeld, "Der Grundbesitz der römischen Kaiser," *Kleine Schriften* (Berlin,
1913), 529.

36. Tac., *Ann.* 6, 19. See text to n. 115 below.

37. *CIL* XIII, 1550 (Aquitania, Ruteni) has "To Smargadus, the overseer . . . of the *familia*
of Tiberius Caesar [employed] in the mines"; Strabo 191 mentions silver mines among the
Ruteni. See O. Davies, *Roman Mines in Europe* (Oxford, 1935), 80–81.

38. *CIL* II, 1179. Cf. *CIL* XIV, 52 (Ostia) *Dorotheus Aug. lib. proc. massae Marian(ae).*

39. *FIRA*² I, 104, 105.

forth) and ends with the sentence, "I shall go down to act as guarantor, because I have promised; but not if you will ask me to act as a guarantor for an indefinite sum of money (or) put myself under an obligation to the *fiscus*."[40] Equally relevant is a passage in an oration by Dio Chrysostom, where he is defending his record as a citizen—among the malpractices of which he was not guilty was that of delating a fellow citizen for being in possession of estates belonging to the emperor.[41]

Debts to the Fiscus are frequently mentioned in the sources. Tiberius remitted the debts of Sardis "to the *fiscus* or the *aerarium*,"[42] and if it seems improbable that a *community* could have become indebted to the imperial estate, instances can be given—the debts of Chios to the imperial procurators which were paid by Herod,[43] or the story in Philostratus of how Quirinius, the sophist, when the counsel for the Fiscus (*advocatus fisci*) in Asia, had unwillingly to take a case in which informers had denounced a small city for payment of a large sum.[44]

But even in the Republic provincial communities could become indebted to individual Romans; Cicero, for instance, reports from Cilicia a case in which the Salaminii in Cyprus were in debt to two Romans, M. Scaptius and P. Matinius. Appius Claudius Pulcher had given Scaptius cavalry to help him exact the money.[45] The earliest instance of a communal debt to the Fiscus is perhaps the case mentioned in an inscription of A.D. 1/2 from Lykosoura, in Arcadia, when one Nicasippus "paid the *fiscus* from his own pocket."[46]

Debts to the Fiscus tended to accumulate, and the *Historia Augusta* records that Hadrian remitted "huge sums of money owed by private people to the *fiscus*."[47] Dio mentions his remission of "debts to both the Fiscus and the Aera-

---

40. *de benef.* 4, 39, 3.

41. *Or.* 46, 8.

42. Tac., *Ann.* 2, 47, 3.

43. Jos., *AJ* 16, 2, 2 (26).

44. Philos., *VS* 2, 29.

45. Cic., *Att.* 5, 21, 10.

46. *Syll.*³ 800. The new date is demonstrated by A. J. Gossage, "The Date of *IG* V (2), 516 (*SIG*³ 800)," *PBSA* 49 (1954): 51. Gossage notes (p. 55, n. 2) a letter from Professor A. H. M. Jones suggesting that *phiskos* here may refer to "the emperor's financial department, including his private revenue," and mentioning as a parallel Jos., *AJ* 16, 2, 2 (26). I owe this reference to Mr. G. W. Bowersock. For imperial (private) procurators attested in Achaea in Augustus' reign, see H. G. Pflaum, *Les carrières procuratoriennes équestres sous le Haut-Empire romain* (Paris, 1960–61), 1070–71.

47. *HA, Had.* 7, 6.

rium."[48] It is not clear which of these remissions is referred to in the Roman inscription, proclaiming a remission by Hadrian, which uses the term "a debt to the *fisci*" (*debitum fiscis*).[49] It is possible that the reference is to arrears of taxation due to the provincial Fisci (and hence theoretically to the Aerarium)[50] or, perhaps, that "fisci" here is shorthand for "to the *aerarium* and the *fiscus*."

One of the processes by which debts to the Fiscus were collected seems to be hinted at in the edict of Tiberius Iulius Alexander, where a reference is made to the selling-up of the property of people "who, allegedly, entered into contracts with people who collected back payments [*anabolika*] to the *fiscus*":[51] "anabolika" here can only mean "back payments"[52]—the right to collect them was presumably sold to private persons. These processes are further illustrated by a papyrus from the reign of Commodus in which the prefect of Egypt writes to the *stratēgoi* of Thebais, Hepta Nomoi and Arsinoe, to say that goods sequestered in respect of debts to the Fiscus should be sold if the debts are not paid within six months.[53]

The process by which the Fiscus gradually claimed more than the legal rights of private persons was thus a major source of tension. Tacitus, praising the early years of Tiberius, says "and when it came to disputes with private people, they were settled in a court of law."[54] The phrase is taken up and expanded by Dio in commenting on the case of Lucilius Capito, the procurator in Asia under Tiberius: "It was not allowed at that time to those administering the Emperor's property [*autokratorika chrēmata*] to do more than collect the prescribed revenues, and in case of dispute they had to plead in the *agora* according to the laws just like private people."[55] Capito had given orders to soldiers and was punished for it. But in the same reign Herennius Capito, the procurator of Jamnia, an imperial property, was able to send troops to pursue the Jewish prince Agrippa to recover "300,000 pieces of silver owed

48. 69, 8, 1². Compare Dio's reference, 71, 32, 2 (272), to the remission of debts to the *to basilikon* and the *to dēmosion* by Marcus Aurelius.

49. *ILS* 309.

50. On provincial Fisci (the funds held by governors) and their relation to the Aerarium, see Jones (n. 6), 22–23.

51. *OGIS* 669 and the revised text by H. G. Evelyn-White and J. H. Oliver, *The Temple of Hibis in El Khārgeh Oasis*, Part II: *Greek Inscriptions* (New York, 1938), no. 4, ll. 20–21.

52. See R. Macmullen, "The Anabolicae Species," *Aegyptus* 38 (1958): 184, on pp. 192–93.

53. H. Zilliacus, *Vierzehn berliner griechische Papyri* (Societas Scientarum Fennica. Commentationes Humanarum Litterarum XI, 4, Helsingfors, 1941), no. 3, l. 13.

54. *Ann.* 4, 6.

55. 57, 23, 5.

by him to Caesar's treasury in Rome"—clearly a private debt.[56] Thus Pliny in the *Panegyric* can praise Trajan at length for ensuring that justice was done in cases involving the Fiscus.[57]

Emperors sometimes judged fiscal cases themselves, as Pliny hints in another passage: "[Y]ou did not sit in judgement to enrich the *fiscus*";[58] a report on such a case before Marcus Aurelius appears in the *Digest*.[59] But in his main passage on fiscal cases (*Pan.*, 36, 4) Pliny mentions what he calls "a tribunal . . . invented for the Principate," apparently a reference to Nerva's institution of a praetor "who will pronounce judgement between the *fiscus* and private people" (*qui inter fiscum et privatos ius diceret*).[60] Nothing more is heard of this post.

Nothing shows more clearly both the volume of litigation in which the Fiscus was engaged, and its legal status, than the appearance of the post of counsel for the Fiscus (*advocatus fisci*), instituted by Hadrian.[61] A private person could, but the state (or any part of it) could not, litigate and engage a legal adviser. The post was salaried and its occupants were not permitted to represent private persons, other than their close relations or orphans (*pupilli*), against the Fiscus.[62] A counsel for the Fiscus (*advocatus fisci*) might be concerned with a particular area of Italy or the provinces,[63] with a single piece (*tractus*) of imperial property,[64] or with a certain type of imperial revenue.[65] While they were mainly concerned with representing the Fiscus in litigation, a couple of passages in the *Digest* show that they had the right to give judgement in cases where the freedom of a man who, if a slave, would be included with property due to the Fiscus was in question.[66]

---

56. Josephus, *AJ* 18, 6, 3 (158). Agrippa had been in Rome a few years earlier, had been a friend of Tiberius' son Drusus, and had exhausted his fortune (*AJ* 18, 6, 1). Pflaum, *Carrières procuratoriennes*, no. 9, argues that Capito was acting as "collector of rents [or taxes]" (Philo, *Leg.* 199) and pursuing arrears of tribute. But Josephus' wording makes this view untenable.

57. *Pan.* 36, 3–4.

58. *Pan.* 80, 1.

59. *Dig.* 28, 4, 3.

60. *Dig.* 1, 2, 2, 32.

61. *HA, Had.* 20, 6.

62. *Dig.* 3, 1, 10; *Frag. de iure fisci* 2, 16–17.

63. E.g., *EE* V, 1203.

64. E.g., *AE* 1908, 18.

65. E.g., *CIL* IX 2565: "to the counsel for the *fiscus* in the office concerned with inheritances."

66. *Dig.* 49, 14, 3, 9 (a rescript of Hadrian); 49, 14, 7.

Apart from cases like that of Lucilius Capito, where legal processes were obviated by the simple use of force, the Fiscus gained in the course of the first two centuries a number of recognized privileges (a reflection not only of the increasing pre-eminence of the emperor but also of the importance attached to ensuring fiscal revenues). The most important privilege was that of *prōtopraxia*, which appears in Egyptian documents as the right to proceed against third parties who had acquired property from debtors to the Fiscus and in legal sources as an extended "right of seizure of property belonging to a debtor" (*ius pignoris*).[67] Similarly, the Fiscus had the right to satisfy its own claims before those of other creditors were met.[68] Of the numerous other privileges attested,[69] a few, of different types, can be given for illustration. Manumissions made with the purpose of defrauding the Fiscus were annulled.[70] The Fiscus took interest due from contracts but did not pay it;[71] the interest it received was at a standard rate (6 per cent per annum), and where it succeeded to a creditor to whom a lower rate was being paid, the rate was raised.[72] If a procurator of Caesar had promised double or triple restitution in the case of recovery by virtue of a superior title (*pro evictione*), he could none the less be held liable only for simple restitution.[73] The right of seizure of property belonging to a debtor arising from a sale of property to someone under twenty-five was automatically available to the Fiscus—but to private persons only by the princeps' concession (*beneficium principis*).[74]

While these and other privileges were established to protect the interests of the Fiscus, some regulations were made to prevent abuses and guarantee the rights of private persons. Some of these amounted to no more than an assurance (which could not be taken for granted) that normal legal rules

---

67. See *P. Strasb.* 56 (II/III A.D.), Text A, 2, l. 10 ". . . [the right of] *prōtopraxia* is preserved for the *fiscus*, the city's treasury [*poleitikos logos*], and others"; cf. *P. Stras.* 34 (Antinoopolis, A.D. 180–192), l. 25; *BGU* 1573 (Arsinoite nome, 141/2), l. 15; *PSI* XII, 1237, *recto* l. 6 (A.D. 162). Also *P. Lips.* 1, 9, l. 34, as given in Preisigke, *Wörterbuch*, s.v. φίσκος. The legal character of *prōtopraxia* and the Fiscus' rights "velut ius pignoris" or "pignoris vice" are discussed by F. Wieacker, "Protopraxie und 'ius pignoris' im klassischen Fiskalrecht," *Festschrift P. Koschaker* I (Weimar, 1939), 218.

68. Paulus, *Sent.* 5, 12, 10.

69. See the rather muddled list in Bolla (n. 1), 78–79.

70. E.g., *Dig.* 40, 9, 16, 3; 40, 1, 10; *Frag. de iure fisci* 2, 9.

71. *Dig.* 22, 1, 17, 5.

72. *Dig.* 22, 1, 17, 6; 49, 14, 6.

73. *Dig.* 49, 14, 5.

74. *Dig.* 27, 9, 2. This passage raises further legal problems which are not relevant to the present argument.

would apply to the Fiscus—though even here special conditions were often immediately attached. Thus it is stated that it was possible to claim "balancing of accounts" (*compensatio*) in relation to debts to the Fiscus, but the claim had to be made within two months;[75] or again that where the Fiscus succeeded to a creditor the legal position remained unaltered, but only with regard to past transactions, for afterwards "it [the Fiscus] will keep its own preroga-tive."[76] Delations for the benefit of the Fiscus were profitable and safe; so it had to be laid down that cases involving the status of persons dead more than five years could not be raised "either privately or in the name of the *fiscus*,"[77] or that the onus of proof in a fiscal case lay with the accuser.[78] Abuses could attend the actual execution of fiscal claims; so, for instance, Marcus Aurelius and Verus laid down that in selling-up property procurators should get a fair price "according to the present evaluation,"[79] while Severus and Caracalla sent a rescript to ensure that the "disposal by sale" (*distractio*) by a procurator of goods "in dispute" (*in controversia*) should be postponed.[80]

Thus, even in his capacity as a property owner, the princeps steadily as-sumed a more and more privileged position by comparison with ordinary citizens—and, specific privileges apart, there was pressure on magistrates to look the other way when cases between private people and imperial procura-tors arose; "and certainly when it comes to a pecuniary case involving the *fiscus*, of a kind which is the concern of a procurator, he [the proconsul] will do well to abstain."[81] More significant, however, even than privileges of this type are the extra sources of income which the princeps acquired and which went to the Fiscus. In gaining these extra sources of income the Fiscus did not, however, absorb regular revenues due to the Aerarium. It took neither the tribute from imperial provinces nor any established indirect taxes. But the Fiscus benefitted from inheritances which fell to individual emperors and also took a share of various irregular sources of income, *bona caduca* (unclaimed property), *bona damnatorum* (property of persons condemned on criminal charge), special taxes, fines, and penalties which might otherwise have gone to the Aerarium.

75. *Dig.* 16, 2, 12; 49, 14, 46, 4.
76. *Dig.* 16, 2, 12; 49, 14, 3, 7; 49, 14, 6.
77. *Dig.* 40, 15, 1 *praef.*
78. *Dig.* 49, 14, 25.
79. *Dig.* 49, 14, 3, 5.
80. *Dig.* 49, 14, 22 *praef.*
81. *Dig.* 1, 16, 9 (Ulpian, *de officio proconsulis*).

Legacies and Inheritances

Like prominent republican political figures, Augustus and his successors could expect to inherit or receive legacies from friends and political allies—and some emperors made it clear that they expected legacies from others as well.[82] The word "fiscus" appears little in this connection, for, in accordance with the law, the heir or legatee had to be a person, a particular emperor. The only instance is where Suetonius mentions Nero's regulation "that the wills of those who showed ingratitude to the Emperor should belong to the *fiscus*";[83] that (under Domitian) the same fate awaited the property of the grateful and the ungrateful is clear from Pliny's *Panegyric*: "No longer can a single heir inherit all, sometimes under the pretext that his name is there in writing, sometimes that it is not."[84] It is clear enough that numerous properties which came to an emperor by legacy or inheritance remained the property of his successors as such.[85]

Bona Caduca (Unclaimed Property)

The pressure to make testamentary dispositions in favour of the emperor affected, normally, only the upper classes in Rome. The Fiscus' reception of *bona caduca*, however, was of far wider social application and occupies most of the space in legal sources on the Fiscus. It seems clear that like *bona damnatorum*, to be discussed below, *bona caduca* or *vacantia* (unclaimed or vacant property) was divided between the Aerarium and the Fiscus—thus Pliny, again in the *Panegyric*, has "Both the *fiscus* and the *aerarium* used to be enriched not so much by the *lex Voconia* and the *lex Iulia* as from the singular and unique charge of high treason [*maiestatis crimen*]."[86] The Lex Voconia of 169 B.C. forbade those in the richest class to make women their heirs and limited the proportion of legacies in a will.[87] "Iuliae leges" is probably a shorthand way

---

82. The evidence is given in full by R. S. Rogers, "The Roman Emperors as Heirs and Legatees," *TAPhA* 77 (1947): 140, and intelligently discussed by J. Gaudemet, "'Testamenta ingrata et pietas Augusti': contribution à l'étude du sentiment impérial," *Studi Arangio-Ruiz* 3 (Naples, 1953): 115.

83. Suet., *Nero* 32, 2.

84. Pliny, *Pan.* 43, 1.

85. See, e.g., Hirschfeld (n. 35), 518–19.

86. Pliny, *Pan.* 42, 1.

87. On the difficulties surrounding the exact provisions of this law, see P-W XII, 2418–30, and B. Biondi, *Successione testamentaria e donazione*[2] (Milan, 1955), 134–35. Moreover, the

of referring to both the *lex Iulia de maritandis ordinibus* (the Julian law regulating marriage between the social orders) and the *lex Papia Poppaea* (which legal sources sometimes refer to jointly as the *lex Iulia et Papia*). The Fiscus' claim to *bona caduca* is first attested in the reign of Tiberius — "the property of the wealthy Aemilia Musa who died intestate was claimed for the *fiscus*"[88] — and thereafter was well established. In the second century Artemidorus could use as a passing example the case where a man dies, "his goods have been seized by the Fiscus," and his wife is left to carry on a legal battle for their recovery.[89] The origin of this right, however, is not easy to determine. The preface to the main papyrus copy of the Gnomon (Code of Regulations) of the Idios Logos (the Private Account), which is largely concerned with the Fiscus' claims to *bona caduca*,[90] begins by referring to the instructions "which the deified Augustus established for the administration of the Idios Logos" but does not mention him specifically in any of the later clauses. Strabo describes the Idios Logos as the official "who investigates [enquires into] the properties that are without owners and that ought to fall to Caesar."[91] It is probable that a Ptolemaic precedent was taken over directly, for, although it cannot be formally proved that the Ptolemaic Idios Logos received "properties that are without owners" (*adespota*), it is likely,[92] and there are indications that the practice was known in the Seleucid territories also.[93] But exactly how the Fiscus' rights to *bona caduca* entered Roman legal practice outside Egypt[94] is not at all clear. Tacitus says that the *lex Papia Poppaea* was brought in "to enrich the *aerarium*" and describes its effects with the words "so that . . .

---

reference to the *lex Voconia* is a puzzle in itself, since its provisions ought to have been superseded by those of the Lex Falcidia of 40 B.C.

88. Tac., *Ann.* 2, 48, 1.

89. Artemidorus, *Oneirocritica* 4, 56.

90. See the edition by S. Riccobono, *Il Gnomon dell'Idios Logos* (Palermo, 1950), text (pp. 31–32) paras. 4, 9, 10, 16, 18, 19, 20, 22, 23, 24, 27, 30, 31, 33, 45, 50, 112, and commentary (pp. 95–96), and also R. Besnier, "L'application des lois caducaires d'Auguste d'après le gnomon de l'idiologue," *RIDA* (*Mélanges de Visscher* I) 2 (1949): 93.

91. Strabo 797. This is confirmed by *P. Oxy.* 1188 (A.D. 13), e.g., ll. 4, 10, 15–16.

92. See C. Préaux, *L'économie royale des Lagides* (Brussels, 1939), 409.

93. See the "Extract from the Registry Law of Succession" on a Dura parchment, C. B. Welles, R. O. Fink, and J. F. Gilliam, *The Excavations at Dura-Europos*, Final Report V.1: *The Parchments and Papyri* (New Haven, 1959), no. 12 (pp. 76–79).

94. The operation of the principle in Egypt is illustrated by the edict of Tiberius Julius Alexander (see n. 48), ll. 38–39, on abuses concerned with delation of properties due to the Idios Logos. Note also *Archiv für Papyrusforschung* 3, 61, a judgement by the Idiologos given on 22 Nov. 136, in which *bona vacantia* are taken "to the *kyriakos logos*."

properties without owners will fall to the people as a universal parent."[95] In the reign of Trajan we find a system by which cases under the Lex Iulia et Papia were reported to the Aerarium, but the property concerned was liable to go to the Fiscus.[96] In 129 the Senate was concerning itself, in the Senatus Consultum Iuventianum, with the claims of the Fiscus to inheritances,[97] and various imperial constitutions of the second century had the same object.[98] All we can say, therefore, is that the Fiscus' reception of *bona caduca* had some Hellenistic precedents, became recognized alongside the claims of the Aerarium in the course of the first century, and was established and predominant in the second. The right of the Fiscus to all *bona caduca* was first proclaimed by Caracalla.[99]

In this connection two instances of what appear to be extensions of the principle may be noted. The Ptolemaic Idios Logos is most often attested receiving a "penalty" [*prostimon*] for the occupation and planting of desert royal land.[100] Vespasian perhaps followed this precedent in selling off unallotted portions (*subseciva*) of public land and taking the proceeds for the Fiscus.[101] Then, in the first and second centuries A.D., we find the gradual emergence of a principle whereby treasure trove tended to fall to the emperor. The complexities of this subject are great, but it is clear at least that there are no known Hellenistic precedents.[102] The earliest hint of the principle, if we leave out of account Nero's treasure hunt in Africa, which is probably not relevant, comes from Calpurnius Siculus, who describes how (in explicit contrast with

95. Tac., *Ann.* 3, 25 and 28.

96. See, e.g., *Dig.* 49, 14, 13 (from Paulus, *liber primus ad legem Iuliam et Papiam*) on two edicts by Trajan, and further second-century regulations; and also 49, 14, 15, 42, 49.

97. *Dig.* 5, 3, 20, 6–7. See Biondi (n. 87), 145.

98. Note, e.g., Gaius, *Inst.* II, 285, an *S.C.*, following on an *oratio* of Hadrian, by which *fideicommissa* (bequests) for the benefit of *peregrini* (foreigners, non-citizens) were claimed for the Fiscus, and *Dig.* 49, 14, 1, 2–3, a rescript of Antoninus Pius, referring back to a constitution by Titus.

99. Ulp., *reg.* 17, 2: "Nowadays by the constitution of the emperor Antoninius all *bona caduca*—apart from cases where the right of children and parents is involved—are claimed by the *fiscus*."

100. Préaux (n. 92), 406 and 409.

101. *Corpus agrimensorum rom.*, Teubner ed., p. 41 (Agennius Urbicus, *de controversiis agrorum*), "he obtained a significant sum of money for the *fiscus* by selling off the unallotted portions," and pp. 96–97 (Hyginus, *de generibus controversiarum*), "the deified Vespasian . . . claimed for himself all unallotted portions." Cf. also Vespasian's claim to land confiscated in Judaea after the revolt of 66–70, Jos., *BJ* 7, 216–17.

102. See G. F. Hill, "Treasure-Trove: The Law and Practice of Antiquity," *Proc. Brit. Acad.* 19 (1933): 219, where the passages I mention, except that from Juvenal, are fully discussed.

some recent period) a man digging or ploughing can do so without the *fear* of striking some buried object.[103] Then we have the story of how Atticus, the father of Herodes Atticus, found "a fabulous treasure" in a house of his in Athens; he reported the find to Nerva and had to be reassured twice before feeling safe to keep it.[104] Juvenal, in his satire on Domitian's council, enunciates the principle "whatever is rare and beautiful . . . belongs to the *fiscus* . . . it will be donated therefore lest it be lost."[105] And in the second century various explicit regulations of the Fiscus' claims were made.[106] Juvenal's words may suggest that the right arose, by a familiar process, from the custom of sending rarities or valuable curiosities as presents to the emperor.[107]

Bona Damnatorum
(Property of Persons Condemned on Criminal Charge)

With *bona damnatorum* much the same pattern of development can be traced —a possible Ptolemaic precedent and then a gradual intrusion of the Fiscus on the rights of the Aerarium, followed ultimately by formal recognition. There is some evidence that in the Ptolemaic period the property of condemned persons was taken by the king, that is by the Idios Logos.[108] The Gnomon of the Idios Logos lays down that the goods of those condemned on capital charges, or those who have gone into voluntary exile, should go to the Fiscus, with the exception of a tenth for each son and the cash dowries of their wives (plus a twelfth which Antoninus Pius allowed the condemned themselves).[109] Provisions for restoring their dowries to the wives of condemned men (or, possibly, debtors to the Fiscus) are also mentioned in the edict of Tiberius Iulius Alexander: "[D]owries, being the prop-

103. Calp. Sic., *Eclogae* 4, 117–21: "Now a digger does not fear to wield his fateful spade, and if fortune yields it, can use the gold which he finds; nor does the ploughman, as recently, fear while he turns his furrows, lest a lump of metal may sound against the plough share which strikes it."

104. Philos., *VS* 2, 1.

105. Juv., *Sat.* 4, 54–56.

106. See *HA*, *Had.* 18, 6; *Inst.* 2, 1, 39, *Dig.* 49, 14, 1, *praef.*, 3, 10–11, and Hill (n. 102), 243–44.

107. See Pliny, *NH* 7, 74–75; 10, 84; 19, 39; Sen., *Ep. Mor.* 95, 42.

108. Préaux (n. 92), 407 and 409–10. Note also that under the Seleucids the property of men convicted of treason was confiscated: E. Bikerman, *Institutions des Séleucides* (Paris, 1938), 121.

109. Para. 36. Compare Dio 47, 14, 1, on similar provisions made by the Triumvirs for the proscriptions of 43–42 B.C.

erty of others and not of the husbands who received them, the deified Augustus has ordered—as also the prefects—that they shall be paid from the *fiscus* to the women."[110] The reference to Augustus makes continuity with Ptolemaic practice probable, but, as with *bona caduca*, does little to solve the problem of how the principle came to be applied outside Egypt.

The first clear case from Rome itself comes from the reign of Tiberius, the condemnation of C. Silius in 24: "[T]he emperor's gifts were deducted and the claims of the *fiscus* were met one by one."[111] But partial precedents might have been afforded by the cases of Cornelius Gallus in 26 B.C.—the Senate voted that he should be condemned and that his property should be confiscated and given to Augustus[112]—or of Archelaus of Judaea; when the latter was condemned in A.D. 6, his property was confiscated for the benefit of the emperor.[113] The words Tacitus uses in the case of Silius, however, seem to imply that the Fiscus' claims might arise from real or alleged benefits on the part of the emperor; the same principle was perhaps applied when, as it seems, the entire property of Seianus was taken for the *fiscus*—"Seianus' property was to be withdrawn from the *aerarium* and absorbed by the *fiscus*."[114] Tacitus clearly regards this as improper, as he does in the case of Sextus Marius—"his copper- and gold-mines, although confiscated by the state, were appropriated by Tiberius."[115] None the less, he could refer without comment two chapters earlier to the fact that the goods of the condemned were taken either by the Aerarium or the Fiscus,[116] and the division between them is stated clearly by Pliny in a passage of the *Panegyric* quoted above (text to n. 86)—it was chiefly the charge of *maiestas* (treason) which enriched both Aerarium and Fiscus.

Once again the legal basis, if any, of the Fiscus' claims at this period is en-

110. L. 25. Dittenberger (*OGIS* 669, commentary) takes it that the reference is to the condemned persons (*damnati*). It is possible that *debtors* to the Fiscus are meant—so W. Schubart, *Archiv f. Papyrusforschung* 14 (1941): 37–38.

111. Tac., *Ann.* 4, 20.

112. Dio 53, 23, 7.

113. Jos., *BJ* 2, 7, 3 (111), cf. *AJ* 17, 13, 2 (344). At the death of Herod in 4 B.C. the procurator of Syria had come to Jerusalem "to take charge of Herod's estate"; see Jos., *BJ* 2, 2, 2 (16–19), 3, 1–2 (41–54), *AJ* 17, 9, 36 (221–23).

114. Tac., *Ann.* 6, 2.

115. Tac., *Ann.* 6, 19. See text to n. 36 above. It is worth noting that Dio 58, 22, 2 states that Marius was a friend of Tiberius and had *thus* become rich. This might therefore be another case in which imperial gifts were being recovered.

116. Tac., *Ann.* 6, 17, "as so many had been condemned and their estates sold that coined money was retained by the *fiscus* or the *aerarium*."

tirely unknown. Philo, however, in describing the condemnation of Flaccus, makes clear that some proportion of the property at least had to go to the Aerarium: "A clear proof of this [of Flaccus' great wealth] is that while a vast number of properties belonging to condemned persons was sold by public auction, that of Flaccus alone was reserved for the emperor, a few articles only being excepted so as not to run counter to the law enacted about persons convicted on these grounds."[117] But the claims of the Fiscus continued to grow, and, as Josephus says of some Jews condemned in Cyrene in the reign of Vespasian, a governor could expect to have the rich prosecuted without check if he confiscated their property for the emperor.[118] The Fiscus normally retained property it confiscated (in contrast to the Aerarium, which sold such properties), though an Athenian inscription refers to those who have bought the property of Hipparchus, and others, sold by the Fiscus.[119] Attempts were made to check the process; thus Trajan wrote in a rescript, "I know that my predecessors' avarice claimed the property of the exiled for the *fiscus*, but something other befits my clemency."[120] Similarly, Hadrian noted that most governors had been in the habit of selling the personal effects of executed prisoners (*pannicularia*) and turning over the proceeds to the Fiscus—but that was overly conscientious.[121] These were both of course extensions of the principle, but Hadrian (according to the *Historia Augusta*) went further in attempting to cut down the Fiscus' claims and announced that henceforward *bona damnatorum* would go solely to the Aerarium (*damnatorum bona in fiscum privatum redigi vetuit, omni summa in aerario publico recepta*).[122] His lead was not followed, and the legal sources make clear that the consequence of "confiscation of property by the state" (*publicatio bonorum*) was the reception of the goods by the Fiscus.[123]

---

117. Philo, *In Flaccum* 150.

118. Jos., *BJ* 7, 9, 2 (446).

119. The Athenian inscription is given by Abbot and Johnson, *Municipal Administration* no. 90, and re-edited by J. H. Oliver, *The Ruling Power* (*TAPhS* 43, 4, Philadelphia, 1953), 960–61. See ll. 3–5 and ll. 30–31.

120. *Dig.* 48, 22, 1.

121. *Dig.* 48, 20, 6.

122. *HA, Had.* 7, 7.

123. See, e.g., *Dig.* 48, 2, 20; 48, 20, 7–10 passim; 49, 14, 22, *praef.*; 45, 2; 45, 11; *Frag. de iure fisci* 2, 20. Compare the casual references in Plut., *Mor.* 484a—a condemned man "lost his property which was taken by Caesar's treasury [*tamieion*]"; and Euseb., *HE* 6, 2, 12, referring to the condemnation of Origen's father in 203—"and my father's property was taken by the imperial treasuries."

Fines and Penalties

From the taking of *bona damnatorum* it was only a short step to the taking of fines for lesser offenses. The Gnomon shows the Fiscus receiving penalties for breaches of status regulations,[124] and a number of scattered "penalties" (*poenae*) due to the Fiscus are attested in the *Digest* and the *Fragmenta de iure fisci*.[125] More interesting, and much more difficult to understand in legal terms, are cases where penalties become due to the Fiscus as a result of spontaneous private action. These cases divide into two types: contracts, where the parties agree in case of breach to pay a penalty (*prostimon*) to the Fiscus over and above what is paid to the injured party; and sepulchral imprecations, where a man has inscribed on his tomb a penalty (payable, usually, by anyone who puts in another body) which will be due to the Fiscus, or to a local community (or both); and in such cases a sum sometimes also allotted to the informer who brings the case. The institution of the *prostimon* in private contracts is attested in Ptolemaic Egypt; the sum went to the king, but the force of the contract was in this respect, so far as is known, conventional rather than legal.[126] The same institution is found at Dura in the Parthian period; the formula of the penalty is "to the king's treasury [*to basilikon*] the same amount."[127] Documents of the Roman period from Dura show the institution continuing; a divorce contract of A.D. 204 has "and to the *fiscus* the same

124. Paras. 43 and 44. Cf. para. 105—confiscation of half property for lending money at over 12 per cent.

125. *Dig.* 47, 12, 3, 5, a rescript of Hadrian laying down a fine payable by those "who bury corpses inside the city"; see Paulus, *Sent.* 1, 21, 2: this was punished "extra ordinem"; 49, 14, 1, *praef.*: occasions of "denunciation to the *fiscus*" (*nuntiatio ad fiscum*)—"that a house has been destroyed." The *S.C. de aedificiis non diruendis* ("decree of the Senate against the demolition of buildings for profit") of A.D. 44 and 56 (*FIRA²* I, 45) had laid down a fine payable to the Aerarium. *Frag. de iure fisci* 1, 8, gives a fine payable to the Fiscus by a man "who contrary to the edict of the deified Augustus bought disputed property from someone who had no title to it" and 1, 9 gives a fine "which is claimed now by the *fiscus*" for selling or acquiring fugitive slaves (*fugitivi*). Compare also the curious inscription from Cilicia, *IGR* III 864 = *OGIS* 579, "They decided: if someone is caught using a Cilician measure, he is to give twenty-five denarii to the *fiscus*," and a decree of Mylasa in 209/211 (*OGIS* 515 = Abbott and Johnson, no. 133) which lays down (ll. 25–27) a fine for illegal exchange—"a free man will pay to the most sacred treasury of our lords, the divine emperors . . ."

126. Préaux (n. 92), 408. See A. Berger, *Die Strafklauseln in den Papyrusurkunden* (Leipzig and Berlin, 1911), 31.

127. *Dura Final Report* V.1, nos. 19 (l. 17), 20 (l. 21). The formula is restored in nos. 21, 22, 24.

amount,"[128] and another from A.D. 254 a penalty paid "to the most sacred treasury" (*to iērotaton tameion*).[129] In Egypt, on the other hand, while the institution of the *prostimon* continues in contracts of the Roman period, it is paid "to the public treasury" (*to dēmosion*).[130] A clear example of the institution in the western provinces comes from an inscription recording a benefaction to the *collegium fabrum Narbonensium* (the social club of engineers in Narbo) in A.D. 149; the funds, if misused, were to revert "to the *fiscus* of the [our] great princeps."[131] But, while the facts are thus well attested, the legal basis of the institution remains entirely obscure.[132] In spite, however, of the dubious legal basis of such penalties we do find a case, the long inscription relating to the bequest by Vibius Salutaris to Ephesus in 104, in which the proconsul of Asia approves the decrees of the city relating to the benefaction and fixes fines, due to the Fiscus, for transgression: "I wish him [the offender] to pay forthwith a penalty to the temple of the greatest goddess Artemis 25,000 denarii and to the *fiscus* of our lord Caesar" (ll. 278–81).[133] Only two passages in the *Digest* refer to such penalties, and they contradict each other; in the one case an agreement to submit to arbitration (*compromissum*) has been made with the provision of a penalty (*poena*) payable to the Fiscus, but invalidly—"the *fiscus* acquires nothing under this judgement."[134] The other reference comes in the list of occasions of "denunciation before the *fiscus*" (*nuntiatio ad fiscum*) which forms the preface of Callistratus' *de iure fisci*—"or that a penalty is due to the *fiscus* under a private contract."[135] This is perhaps an interpolation.

Even greater difficulties attend the subject of sepulchral fines (*multae sepul-*

128. Ibid., no. 31. Upper text, ll. 19–20, lower text, ll. 47–48 "and the same amount to the *fiscus*."

129. Ibid., no. 32, l. 17.

130. Berger (n. 4), 32–33.

131. *CIL* XII 4393, ll. 15–16.

132. See the discussion by G. Wesenberg, *Verträge zugunsten Dritter: Forschungen zum römischen Recht*, Bd. I, Abh. II (Weimar, 1949), 70–71.

133. *IBM* 481, ll. 278–81 partially reprinted in B. Laum, *Stiftungen in der griechischen und römischen Antike* 2 (Berlin, 1914), no. 74, and Abbott and Johnson, no. 71. See now *I. K. Ephesos* I^a, 27, ll. 406–10. The reading of these lines can be confirmed by comparison with ll. 220–21 (= *I. K. Ephesos* I^a, 27, ll. 323–25). Further examples of endowments with penalties to the Fiscus are given by Laum, *Stiftungen*, nos. 19b (Eleusis, second century A.D.), 72 (Attaleia, second century), 124 (Iasos). See also K. M. T. Atkinson, "The 'Constitutio' of Vedius Pollio at Ephesus," *RIDA*, ser. 3, 9 (1962): 262, on p. 287 (where the legal complexities are not appreciated).

134. *Dig.* 4, 8, 42.

135. *Dig.* 49, 14, 1, *praef.*

chrales). There is nothing to show that, even though they habitually specify particular sums to be paid, they had any basis in either Hellenistic or Roman law—and it is perhaps best to regard them as a convention of religious origin.[136] Although many of these inscriptions make the penalty payable to the Fiscus, various other beneficiaries are named: gods, local communities, *collegia* (associations), or the Aerarium.[137] The explanation of the custom cannot therefore lie in the nature of the Fiscus and we have no evidence as to how, if at all, the proceeds accrued to it.

Extraordinary Taxes

Finally, among the revenues of the Fiscus, come various exactions and irregular forms of taxation. Of these the most important is probably the *aurum coronarium* (crown gold). Only one text, and that a third-century papyrus, makes a formal statement that the *aurum coronarium* went to the Fiscus;[138] but it is clear from the nature of the institution, which was from the earliest times a personal gift from subject communities to a ruler or conqueror,[139] that the proceeds must have gone to the emperor himself, as they had to republican generals.[140] With the ever increasing frequency with which *aurum coronarium* was demanded, it must have been a major source of revenue.[141] Then Caligula, when in need of cash, invented a number of taxes, including one on prostitutes;[142] one and a half centuries later, in the reign of Commodus, we find soldiers in the Crimea collecting this tax and (apparently) paying it to the Fiscus.[143] That it in fact went to the Fiscus seems to be con-

136. Wesenberg (n. 132), 75–78.

137. See, e.g., the indices of *IGR* (s.v. *multae sepulchrales*) and *FIRA*² III, 257–58.

138. A Berlin papyrus first published by G. Parthey, *Nuove Memorie d. Instituto Arch.* 2, 455, no. 21, and restored by U. Wilcken, *Griechische Ostraka* I (Leipzig and Berlin, 1899), 300, which has the expression "the *stephanos* which formerly used to go to the king's treasure [*to basilikon*] and now goes to the *fiscus*." *Aurum coronarium* may be the payment referred to in the Opramoas inscription, *IGR* III, 739, II, 59–60: "paying to the full the *eusebeia* of the people to the *fiscus*"; *eusebeia* suggests a payment which was not formally an obligation (compare the same inscription, III, 88–89, his payment of *tribute*). Similarly, *P. Giss.* 61 (Heptakomia, A.D. 119) shows a *logia* (special collection) being made for the benefit of the Fiscus not long after an emperor's accession.

139. Th. Klauser, "Aurum Coronarium," *Röm. Mitt.* 59 (1944): 129.

140. See, e.g., Cic., *in Pisonem* 90, *de leg. ag.* 2, 59; *Res Gestae* 21, 3; Pliny, *NH* 33, 54.

141. See S. L. Wallace, *Taxation in Egypt from Augustus to Diocletian* (Princeton, 1938), 281–84.

142. Suet., *Calig.* 40.

143. *CIL* III, 13750 = Latyschev, *IOSPE* I² 404. See l. 39 (41 in *CIL*).

firmed by the *Historia Augusta*, which relates that Severus Alexander diverted the proceeds of it from his private treasury to the construction of buildings in Rome.[144] Nero, faced with the revolt of Vindex, laid a tax of the equivalent of a year's rent on lodgers in Roman houses (*inquilinos privatarum aedium atque insularum pensionem annuam repraesentare fisco*),[145] while Galba confiscated the revenues of Lugdunum for the benefit of the Fiscus.[146] The most curious example of a tax (if that is what it is) which went to the Fiscus is attested in the *S.C. de sumptibus ludorum gladiatorum minuendis* (a decree of the Senate on reducing expenditures on gladiatorial games).[147] From this it appears that the Fiscus had up to then (A.D. 177–180) taken a surcharge of a third or a quarter of the price of gladiators supplied for games given by provincial magistrates. But we are no nearer understanding the situation reflected in this decree than when Mommsen discussed it.[148]

Benefactions

Because "fiscus" is the predominant *legal* term used in speaking of the imperial wealth a survey of its use tends to emphasize the rights of the imperial estate and the revenues due to it. On a few occasions, however, it is used in connection with imperial benefactions. Both Otho and Vitellius, for instance, promised to pay their soldiers' *vacationes* (payments for exemption from military duty) out of the Fiscus.[149] The immense gifts which Nero had made to his friends and favourites were recovered, as far as possible, and put in the Fiscus (whence, presumably, they had come) (*reliquias Neronianarum sectionum nondum in fiscum conversas*);[150] the gifts had included land, capital, and "equipment for crimes."[151] The following age witnessed more respect-

---

144. *HA, vita Sev. Alex.* 24, 3, "he forbade paying the tax on pimps, female and male prostitutes into the sacred treasury [*sacrum aerarium*], but re-directed it to public enterprises, on restoring the theatre, the circus, the amphitheatre, and the running track." The terminology of the *Historia Augusta* is variable, but the use of "sacred," commonly employed for things pertaining to the emperor, makes it probable that the Fiscus is being referred to.

145. Suet., *Nero* 44, 2. Cf. Dio 61, 5, 5, "he soon exhausted the treasures in the *fiscus* [*to basilikon*], and soon found himself in need of new revenues, and consequently unusual taxes were imposed."

146. Tac., *Hist.* 1, 65.

147. *FIRA*² I, 49, republished, with commentary and translation, by J. H. Oliver and R. E. A. Palmer, "Minutes of an Act of the Roman Senate," *Hesperia* 24 (1955): 320.

148. *Ges. Schr.* 8, 499–500, esp. p. 527.

149. Tac., *Hist.* 1, 46, 58.

150. Tac., *Hist.* 1, 90.

151. Tac., *Hist.* 1, 20.

able benefactions; Vespasian was the first to pay rhetors a regular salary "from the *fiscus*."[152] Nerva returned the property to men from whom Domitian had taken it, if any remained "in the *basileion*" (i.e., the *fiscus*), and made many benefactions "from his own property [the property he already possessed as a private person—see below] and from *ta basilika*."[153] The monument of Trajan's general, C. Iulius Quadratus Bassus, was paid for "by the *fiscus*,"[154] while Trajan also built an aqueduct at his own expense (i.e., "of his own *fiscus*").[155] Fronto, writing to Lucius Verus, mentions an occasion on which Antoninus Pius had paid an impoverished senator the expenses of his praetorship "from your *fiscus*."[156] Pertinax, on coming to the throne, found "the *basileion*" empty of cash and had to sell various possessions of Commodus to make the promised donations to soldiers and people.[157] Finally, it seems likely, if not certain, that Pliny is speaking of imperial purchases of corn to subsidize the *annona* (corn supply) when he says in the *Panegyric* "the *fiscus* buys whatever it seems to be buying"[158]—previous special purchases for this purpose, it is implied, had in effect been disguised extra exactions. It is attested that Augustus, Antoninus Pius, and Severus Alexander bought corn for distribution to the people[159] and that Tiberius kept the price down by cash subsidies from his own pocket.[160]

152. Suet., *Div. Vesp* 18, 1. See Hieronymus, *ad Ol.* CCXVI. 4 (A.D. 88), "Quintilian . . . received a salary from the *fiscus*." Dio (as in Zonaras) 66, 12, 1a, has "he established teachers . . . who received their salary from the *aerarium* [*to dēmosion*]." Suetonius' wording is clearly to be preferred.

153. Dio 68, 2, 1–2.

154. *AE* 1933, 268 *ad fin.*

155. See *CIL* XI, 3309 (Forum Clodi). Compare, e.g., the imperial building inscriptions: *ILS* 218, 245 *impensa sua* (his own expense), 280 *sua pecunia* (his own money), 290, 293 *sua pecunia*.

156. Cornelius Fronto (ed. Van Den Hout), 128. Compare Vell. Pat. 2, 130, 2, where "patrimonium" is used in connection with an imperial benefaction.

157. Dio 73, 5, 4 (310). Compare the occasion (Dio, ed. Boissevain, III, 280, fr. 1, and *HA, Marc. Ant.* 17, 4–5) on which Marcus Aurelius sold off palace treasures to raise cash for a war.

158. Pliny, *Pan.* 29, 5.

159. Augustus, *Res Gestae* 5, 2; 15, 1; 18; Suet., *Div. Aug.* 41, 5. On Antonius Pius, *Vita* 8, 11, "he relieved a scarcity of wine and oil and wheat with loss to his own treasury by buying these and distributing them to the people for free." Severus Alexander, *Vita* 21, 9.

160. Tac., *Ann.* 2, 87.

Conclusion

It is thus clear that most references to the Fiscus do not concern either public funds or their administration. Only three items of evidence, to my knowledge, seem to show the Fiscus as a branch of public financial administration. The first comes from Suetonius' *Augustus*, an incident in which Livia asked for a grant of citizenship for a Gaul who was *tributarius* (liable for payment of tribute); Augustus refused, but offered immunity from tribute instead— "he would more willingly suffer a loss to the *fiscus* than the prostitution of the honour of Roman citizenship."[161] It is not, perhaps, impossible that the sense of the passage is that in offering immunity Augustus would have been offering to pay the man's tribute himself, from the Fiscus, just as, when he granted the cities of Asia immunity after an earthquake in 12 B.C., he paid the equivalent of their tribute to the Aerarium.[162] But this is not the obvious meaning of the sentence. Alternatively "fiscus" here might refer to the provincial Fiscus (the *fiscus Gallicus* as in *ILS* 1514), but this seems unlikely in the context. The second occasion is the well-known reference in Pliny's *Natural History* to Annius Plocamus, "qui maris Rubri vectigal a fisco redemerat."[163] It is normally taken that Annius Plocamus had contracted for the 25 per cent customs duty at the Red Sea ports.[164] Pliny's story, however, concerns Plocamus' freedman who was sailing "circa Arabiam" (presumably round the south or east coast of Arabia) and was blown by north winds past Carmania to Ceylon. The area the story indicates is therefore the Persian Gulf, and there may be more than an accidental connection between this and the fact that it was precisely here that one of the main pearl fisheries of the ancient world lay.[165] What appears to be a list of imperial revenues, given by Statius, includes "all that is collected by the diver who searches the Eastern Sea."[166] If I suggest that what Plocamus contracted for from the Fiscus was not the Red Sea *portorium* (a public tax) but the right to exploit these pearl fisheries, I need hardly emphasize that I am doing no more than hazarding a guess.

161. Suet., *Div. Aug.* 40, 6.

162. Dio 54, 30, 3. I owe the suggestion of the interpretation offered here to Miriam Griffin.

163. Pliny, *NH* 6, 84.

164. Wallace (n. 141), 257, de Laet (n. 2), 306–7, D. Meredith, "Annius Plocamus: Two Inscriptions from the Berenice Road," *JRS* 43 (1953): 38.

165. See P-W XIV, 1687–88. Pliny, *NH* 9, 106, gives the location of the pearl fisheries as "around Arabia in the bay of the Red Sea which is in Persia."

166. Statius, *Silv.* 3, 3, 92.

The Ptolemies, and the Romans after them, held monopolies of other valuables,[167] and if there is no evidence of a royal pearl monopoly in the ancient world, there is at least an instance of one from India.[168] The third item is a papyrus, dating to A.D. 139,[169] a petition to the *epistratēgos* from a guard of a custom house at Socnopaiou Nesos, accusing two of his superiors of cheating the Fiscus (*kyriakos logos*) and asking for their books to be examined "in order to find out if the tolls in them went to the Fiscus." It seems beyond doubt that the document shows tolls being paid to the Fiscus.[170]

These three cases could of course be explained by the assumption that the regular revenues of imperial provinces went to the Fiscus. But to accept that would be to accept either that these revenues became the property of the emperor or that the term "fiscus" was systematically ambiguous. It is preferable, therefore, to admit that these passages cannot be readily fitted into the pattern suggested here; it is still possible to claim that that pattern, with which most uses of "fiscus" accord, gives a true conception of how the financial structure of the Empire developed.

Moreover, even if, as is likely, the lines of distinction between imperial and public funds drawn here come to require some modification, it must be recognized that the distinction between them did survive throughout the entire period with which we are concerned. For Dio, writing in the first half of the third century, distinguishes clearly between *to basilikon* (i.e., the Fiscus) and *to dēmosion* (i.e., the *aerarium*).[171] A passage in his account of Augustus, which is often quoted as proof that the distinction had vanished, shows in

167. See P-W XVI, 159–60, 194–95.

168. P-W XVI, 191.

169. *P. Amh.* 77 = Wilcken, *Chrestomathie*, no. 277 = *Sel. Pap.*, no. 282.

170. So Wallace (n. 141), 260–61. I thought earlier that the mention of the Fiscus might be connected with the fact that the guard's superior, Polydenus, is reported in the papyrus (ll. 20–21) to have enlisted the aid of Heraclas, "one of the swordbearers of the [imperial] estate," in order to have him taken "to the office of the procurator of the imperial estates" to be beaten. But Professor H. C. Youtie, who has very kindly discussed the papyrus with me by letter, points out that Heraclas might have been brought in simply as an armed thug and the office of the local procurator of imperial estates used as a convenient place for the beating. I am also very grateful to Professor Youtie for providing me with some other papyrus uses of φίσκος discussed in this chapter.

171. See nn. 48, 145, 153, and cf. Dio 71, 33, 2 (273), and 79, 12, 2² (463). Though see n. 152. For the survival of the distinction in the third century, see also *Dig.* 3, 6, 1, 3 = *Cod. Just.* 7, 49, 1; *Dig.* 39, 4, 9, 3 = Paulus, *Sent.* 5, 1ᵃ, 4; *CIL* VIII, 17639 = Abbott and Johnson, no. 152, ". . . owed to the people or to the *fiscus*" and cf. Cyprian, *de opere et eleemosynis* 19, "a treasure entrusted to God can neither the state snatch nor the Fiscus seize."

fact that it remained (for he writes in the present tense) and that it was the complexity of the working relations of the two funds which made it diffi-cult for a historian, reading his sources, to tell from which money had been drawn on a particular occasion.[172]

Finally, something must be said about the status and functions of imperial wealth and properties. Up to the death of Nero the property of one emperor could descend to his successor by inheritance. But in 68 there is a break in family connection, and three further breaks in 69. None the less, we find that the Julio-Claudian properties passed into the hands of those who replaced them on the throne—Galba could call in Nero's gifts, Otho and Vitellius ap-peared to find the delights of luxurious living in the imperial palaces the only consolation of supreme power,[173] and Vespasian could sell off imperial palaces in Alexandria.[174] Another break occurred in 96, but again we find that Trajan could sell properties confiscated by Domitian.[175] Thus it is clear that, as early as the first century, the existence of a vast mass of imperial properties, palaces and slaves exerted its own force on the course of events, providing as it did a setting—and a staff—for anyone who seized the throne and making the ordinary laws of inheritance irrelevant.

It was still the case, none the less, that the private property of anyone who came to the throne became absorbed in the fiscal properties and descended with them to succeeding emperors.[176] But the facts of the case meant that

172. 53, 22, 3–4, "Therefore I have no opinion to record as to whether a particular emperor on a particular occasion got the money from the public funds [*ek tōn dēmosiōn chrēmatōn*] or gave it himself. For both courses were frequently followed; and why should one enter such expenditures as loans or as gifts respectively, when both people [*dēmos*] and the emperor are constantly resorting to both the one and the other indiscriminately."

173. Otho taking over Nero's slaves, Dio 64, 8, 3–9, 1, and holding a dinner in the Pala-tium: Tac. *Hist.* 1, 80–81, Dio 64, 9, 2–3. On Vitellius' enjoyment of imperial luxuries, Dio 65, 2–4.

174. Dio 65, 8, 4.

175. Pliny, *Pan.* 50.

176. This is perhaps the explanation of the story in *HA, vita Ant. Pii* 4, 8—his wife scolded him for parsimony, and he replied, "Foolish woman, now that we have transferred to the position of emperors, we have lost even what we once had." By contrast, Pertinax, coming to the throne after the murder of Commodus, divested himself deliberately of his property and gave it to his son and daughter, whom he sent off to live with their grand-father. Dio 73, 7, 3 (311–12). See Herodian 2, 4, 9; *HA, vita Pert.* 13, 4. I suspect that we have an example of a property which became, and remained, part of the *patrimonium*, when its owner came to the throne, in the Horrea Galbae. See Platner and Ashby, *Topographical Dictionary*, 261. Another example is the Figlinae Domitianae ("Domitian's potteries")—see H. Bloch, *I Bolle laterizi e la storia edilizia romana* (Rome, 1938), 336–39.

the imperial properties came to be regarded as something more than the personal property of each emperor in turn. Thus Pertinax refused to have his name inscribed on imperial buildings, saying that they belonged to the state, not to himself.[177] Ulpian was in some doubt as to whether an *interdictum prohibitorium* (a prohibitory interdict which is intended to prevent interference with enjoyment of public places etc.) is at all applicable to fiscal properties "since fiscal properties are as it were the private property of the princeps."[178] Various other legal passages of the same period show fiscal properties attaining a status comparable to that of *loca publica* or *religiosa* (public or religious properties).[179] The historical development was not the gradual absorption by the emperor of public properties but the acquisition of a "public" character by imperial properties, a process which accurately reflected the fact that the fiscal properties played in the Empire that role which the now depleted "public land" (which Cicero had described as the *patrimonium* of the *res publica*)[180] had played in the Republic. They provided, that is, both a steady revenue for public purposes and a reserve from which, by selling some off, a large capital sum could be realized in emergencies.

The further development of this process, which followed on Severus' division of the fiscal properties and revenues between *patrimonium* and *ratio privata*, must be discussed elsewhere. This study of what "fiscus" meant in the early Empire has inevitably emphasized the legal aspects of imperial property and cannot give a full picture of the historical processes involved. The development of imperial properties, and of the emperor's financial claims, is merely one aspect of that process by which a princeps grew imperceptibly into a king (*basileus*) and his household into a court. For, whatever further revenues accrued, property remained the basis of imperial wealth, and the emergence of the Fiscus symbolized and completed the victory of aristocratic power and riches over the institutions of the *res publica*.

177. Herodian 2, 4, 7.

178. *Dig.* 43, 8, 2, 4.

179. E.g., *Dig.* 49, 14, 3, 10; 18, 1, 72, 1; cf. 30, 39, 8–10. The distinction was still maintained, however; *AE* 1945, 80, shows a man who was "procurator of the public and the fiscal buildings of the sacred City" (*proc(urator) oper(um) publ(icorum) et fiscal(ium) Urb(is) sacrae*) early in the reign of Severus. See also Herodian 2, 4, 6—Pertinax announced that uncultivated land could be freely occupied "even if it belongs to the king."

180. *de lege agraria* 1, 21, 11, 101.

CHAPTER FOUR

The Aerarium and Its Officials
under the Empire[*]

Imagine if our own Chancellor of the Exchequer were chosen by lot out of the young gentlemen who had most recently passed the Civil Service examination!

— G. G. Ramsay on Tacitus, *Annals* 13, 29

No analysis of the political character of the Empire can avoid the question of finance. The various sources of revenue of the emperor and the *res publica*, the role of the private wealth of the emperor, the nature of his control over public funds, the question of how and when various public revenues were taken by him—a satisfactory political interpretation of the early Empire must take account of all these.

This chapter attempts merely to take a second preliminary step towards such an interpretation.[1] Its aim is to set out as clearly as possible the evidence as to the nature of the Aerarium and the functions of its officials, and, above all, to avoid the anachronistic approach which our language itself so readily invites. Not all anachronistic views of the subject have had the beautiful obviousness of Ramsay's contribution: even to speak of the "world-wide financial administration"[2] of the Aerarium will prove to be misleading.

[*]First published in *JRS* 54 (1964): 33–44. I should like to thank Professor Sir R. Syme for information on the status of *Praefecti aerarii*, Dr. J. M. Kelly for discussing with me the jurisdiction of the *Praefecti*, and Dr. Miriam Griffin for reading this chapter in typescript and suggesting various corrections and improvements. The errors which remain are my own.

1. See "The Fiscus in the First Two Centuries," *JRS* 53 (1963): 29 (chapter 3 in this volume).

2. C. H. V. Sutherland, "*Aerarium* and *Fiscus* during the Early Empire," *AJPh* 66 (1945): 151ff., on p. 154.

The Building

The temple of Saturn (*aedes Saturni*) which stood at the foot of the road up to the Capitol Hill (*clivus Capitolinus*), on the edge of the Forum, was dedicated probably at the inception of the Republic, and from that time on was the main depository of the state.[3] In 78 B.C. the Tabularium, a considerably larger building, was constructed to the west of the temple of Saturn; we know of the fact, and the name, only from two inscriptions, one of which survives.[4] The name implies that, like the Aerarium, it held state archives (*tabulae*); the absence of any reference in literature makes it impossible to determine what division of functions was intended.

The temple of Saturn itself, rebuilt or repaired by Munatius Plancus in 42 B.C.,[5] and restored again in the fourth century,[6] is shown in part on a fragment of the Forma Urbis (inscribed plan of the city) made by order of Septimius Severus.[7] Neither the plan nor the existing remains make clear where exactly the money, bullion, documents, and so forth were kept. Lugli has noted some traces of a room situated within the right-hand projection of the podium, with a single door opening into the Forum, and regards that as the Aerarium itself.[8] This view must remain in doubt. Beside (or behind) the temple lay the Area Saturni (the open space next to the temple). An inscription gives a dedication by the *negotiatores* (entrepreneurs) of the Area Saturni to an urban quaestor;[9] the space was evidently supposed to be public property, for another inscription shows the two praetors of the Aerarium redeeming it "by the authority of a decree of the Senate" from private possession.[10]

---

3. See Platner and Ashby, *Topographical Dictionary*, 463–65.

4. Ibid., 506–8.

5. Suet., *Div. Aug.* 29; *CIL* VI 1316 = *ILS* 41; *CIL* X 6087 = *ILS* 886.

6. *CIL* VI 937 = *ILS* 3326.

7. See G. Carettoni, A. M. Colini, L. Cozza, and G. Gatti, *La pianta marmorea di Roma antica (Forma urbis Romae)*, X Repartizione del Commune di Roma (Rome, 1960), Tab. XXI fr. 18d, text p. 75.

8. G. Lugli, *Monumenti minori del Foro Romano* (Rome, 1947), 29–30. He uses (p. 32) the expression "*aerarium sanctum o sanctius aerarium.*" A few texts (Livy 27, 10, 11; *ad Att.* 7, 21, 2; Caesar, *BC* 1, 14, 1) seem to show that there was a physical sub-division of the Aerarium called the "aerarium sanctius." It is not clear whether this is what Lugli means.

9. *CIL* I² 810 = XIV 153 = *ILS* 892. This dates to before 28 B.C. See *PIR*² A 54.

10. *CIL* VI 1265 = *ILS* 5937.

The Officials

Throughout the Republic the Aerarium was in the charge of two quaestors (Polybius mentions that one of them was in charge of the keys).[11] Then in 45 B.C., according to Dio, Julius Caesar appointed two aediles.[12] In a major late republican inscription, the *tabula Heracleensis*, however, we find *per q(uaestorem) urb(anum), queive aerario praerit* (through the urban questor or through whoever will be in charge of the Aerarium).[13] In 29 B.C. Octavian gave the Senate the annual choice of two *praefecti* of praetorian rank for the post;[14] in 23 he changed the system again and had two of the praetors of the year selected by lot,[15] and this arrangement remained until A.D. 44. In that year Claudius, the traditionalist, gave the job to two quaestors once more, with the difference that they were appointed by himself, served for three years, and were promised "exceptional promotion" (*extra ordinem honores promisit*) in advance.[16] Finally, in A.D. 56 Nero appointed two *praefecti*, selected by himself from among ex-praetors,[17] and this (with an interval in 69 when praetors are found in charge)[18] remained the system thereafter. In the first and second centuries the post ranked with praetorian provincial commands, and a *praefectus aerarii* (prefect of the Aerarium) could expect to proceed, like Pliny (*Pan.* 92; cf. *Ep.* 9, 13, 11), directly to the consulate. The last known prefect of the Aerarium held office about the middle of the fourth century.[19]

Of the minor officials little is known except their titles. Inscriptions reveal *scribae librarii quaestorii ab aerario* (scribes [and] clerks of the quaestor's office at the Aerarium), *viatores quaestorii* (messengers of the quaestor's office), a *tabularius viatorum quaestoriorum ab aerario* (a record keeper of the quaestor's messengers) and a *publicus promotus ad tabulas quaestorias transcribendas* (a public slave promoted to the office of copying records in the quaestor's office).[20] The most important of them, the scribes, occasionally come into the light of history; Cicero says in the *Verrines* "the public records and the fates of the

11. 23, 14, 5–6.

12. 43, 48, 3.

13. *CIL* I² 593 = *ILS* 6085 = Riccobono, *FIRA²* I 13, ll. 46–47.

14. Tac., *Ann.* 13, 29; Suet., *Div. Aug.* 36; Dio 53, 2, 1. See *CIL* XIV 2604 = *ILS* 965. Cf. Mommsen, *Staatsrecht* II³, 558, n. 1.

15. Tac. and Suet. (n. 14); Dio 53, 32, 2.

16. Tac. (n. 14); Suet. *Div. Claud.* 24; Dio 60, 24, 1–3; *CIL* VI 1403 = *ILS* 966.

17. Tac., *Ann.* 13, 28–29; Dio 40, 24, 1–2. See *CIL* VI 1945 = *ILS* 1933.

18. Tac., *Hist.* 4, 9.

19. *I. L. Alg.* I, 1286: For the date, *I. L. Alg.* I, 1276. Compare *CIL* XI 4181 = *ILS* 1233.

20. *Diz. Epig.* 1, 305–7.

magistrates are committed to the trust of these people,"[21] while Plutarch describes how Cato the Younger, as quaestor, had difficulty in establishing his authority with them and getting two of them dismissed.[22] The scribes, who, like the lower officials, were organized in three panels (*decuriae*) which served in annual rotation, were of relatively high social status and might claim to be equestrians. Some went on to hold equestrian posts.[23]

Non-Financial Documents

The most important non-financial documents in the Aerarium were copies of laws (*leges*) and decrees of the Senate, which did not become valid until the copies were deposited.[24] One of the senatorial decrees given by Josephus provides some evidence, not easy to interpret, of the filing system used—"a decree of the senate, copied from the treasury [*to tameion*], from the public records of the quaestors . . . second tablet, first column."[25] Some documents were also inscribed on the wall of the temple.[26] The problem of the falsification even of important documents clearly caused considerable difficulties; during his quaestorship in 64 Cato had to resist attempts to get bogus senatorial decrees recorded, and on one occasion refused to accept one until the consuls swore to it.[27] The Lex Iunia et Licinia of 62 laid down that "it would not be allowed to deposit secretly a law in the Aerarium."[28] The deposition of a law or a decree of the Senate was a formal act, and the effect of a senatorial decree could be annulled if the process of "deposition in the Aerarium" (*delatio ad aerarium*) could be halted in time.[29] Thus after the hasty condemnation

21. *Verr.* II.3, 183.

22. Plut., *Cato Minor* 16.

23. See A. H. M. Jones, "The Roman Civil Service (Clerical and Sub-Clerical Grades)," *JRS* 39 (1949): 38 = Jones, *Studies in Roman Government and Law* (Oxford, 1960), 151. Cf. E. Fraenkel, *Horace* (Oxford, 1957), 14–15.

24. Livy 39, 4, 8; Sisenna Fr. 117 Peter; Suet., *Div. Jul.* 28; Cic., *ad. fam.* 12, 1, 1; Serv., on *Aen.* 8, 322, and on *Georg.* 2, 502. Cf. Cic., *De leg.* 3, 20/46.

25. Jos., *AJ* 14, 10, 10 (219).

26. *CIL* I² 587 = Riccobono, *FIRA²* I 10 *ad fin.*; Dio 45, 17, 3. Cf. (?) Varro, *LL* 5, 42. See Lugli (n. 8), 38.

27. Plut., *Cato Minor* 17.

28. Schol. Bob. Sest. p. 310 Or. = 140 Stangl. The view, argued by Mommsen, *Staatsrecht* II³, 546, n. 2, and normally accepted since, that the law made it obligatory to deposit copies of *proposed* legislation in the Aerarium seems to me unsound. It rests in effect only on Cic., *De leg.* 3, 4/11. For a conclusive disproof of Mommsen, see F. von Schwind, *Zur Frage der Publikation im römischen Recht* (1940), 26–27.

29. Suet., *Div. Aug.* 94, 3.

of Clutorius Priscus by the Senate in A.D. 21 it was resolved that an interval of ten days should be left before decisions of the Senate were recorded in the Aerarium.[30]

In this period, the early Empire, there is a certain conflict of evidence as to which officials looked after the public records. Dio, under the year 11 B.C., records that the quaestors were ordered to keep decrees of the Senate, because of negligence by the tribunes and aediles who had previously had the job.[31] Under A.D. 16 he mentions that the public documents had been lost or damaged in the course of time, and that three senators were appointed to put them in order.[32] Three inscriptions appear to refer to these senators. One has C. Ummidius Durmius Quadratus, quaestor of Divus Augustus and Tiberius (i.e., in A.D. 14), aedile, praetor (in 18), and (at the same time?) "keeper of the public records."[33] Then L. Coiedius Candidus, who was quaestor of the Aerarium in the first year of Claudius' new system, was also "keeper of the public records"—again possibly at the same time.[34] Finally a building inscription from Rome dating to 46 has "through" (*per*) . . . three names . . . "keepers of the public records."[35] Thus it is not clear what division of functions there was, a confusion not helped by Tacitus' description of the job transferred by Claudius in 44—"the charge of the public records."[36]

Pliny the Younger, however, listing his duties as prefect of the Aerarium, says, "I make up the records,"[37] and it is clear that documents continued to be kept at the Aerarium, as they had been before. Official oaths had been taken at the Aerarium in the Republic, and recorded there;[38] when Marcus Aurelius instituted a register of births, it was kept "with the prefects of the Aerarium of Saturn," and registration required a formal declaration (*professio*) by the father before the prefect.[39] Then there was the register of embassies currently in Rome, of which the purpose had originally been financial but, in the Empire, was so no longer. Plutarch, in the *Roman Questions*, asks why embassies to Rome go to the temple of Saturn and register with the prefects of the

30. Tac., *Ann.* 3, 51, 3; Dio 48, 20, 4.

31. Dio 54, 36, 1.

32. Dio 57, 16, 2.

33. *CIL* X 5182 = *ILS* 972. See *PIR*[1] U 600.

34. *CIL* XI 6163 = *ILS* 967. See *PIR*[2] C 1257.

35. *CIL* VI 916 = VI 31201, where the reading in Anon. Einsiedl. (the only authority for the inscription), first rejected by Mommsen and then, in *Staatsrecht* II[3], 558, n. 3, accepted, is restored, unjustifiably in my opinion.

36. Tac., *Ann.* 13, 28, 5.

37. Pliny, *Ep.* 1, 10, 9.

38. Val. Max. 2, 8, 1; Appian, *BC* 1, 137; *CIL* I[2] 582 = Bruns, *Fontes*[7], no. 8, 1, 17.

39. *HA*, *vita Marc. Ant.* 9, 7–8; *vita Gord.* 4, 8. Cf. Serv., *ad Georg.* 2, 502.

Aerarium. The answer is that formerly the Aerarium officials had sent them gifts, looked after those members who fell ill and provided a public funeral for those who died. Cicero mentions that three ambassadors from Asia tried to cheat the Aerarium—"They wanted to falsify our records; for they declared having nine slaves, when in fact they had come with no companions at all."[40] But by Plutarch's time the Aerarium officials had ceased to make any actual provision for embassies, for the number had become too great.[41]

Farming Out (*Locatio*) of Public Contracts

In the first part of the Tabula Heracleensis, which refers to the upkeep of roads in Rome, we have the provision that the farming out should be carried out by the aedile concerned through the quaestor, or other official, of the Aerarium, who should also pay out the cash.[42] Similarly, Cicero says that provincial land could not "subsignari apud aerarium," that is, be given as a pledge in the farming out of contracts.[43] Such *locationes* are presumably being referred to when Dio says that in 42 Claudius corrected irregularities on the part of the praetors of the Aerarium "who were conducting sales and leases."[44] The documents of contracts were kept in the Aerarium—Plutarch asks, "why do they use the temple of Saturn as the treasury of public monies and at the same time as the safeguard of contracts"?[45] The Lex Malacitana (the charter of the Spanish city of Malaca) lays down that the "pledging of landed property" (*obligatio praediorum*) in the farming of municipal revenues should be carried out on the model of the procedure in Rome—". . . that the people and the property will be put under legal obligation to the Roman people as if they had become sureties and guarantors, and the landed property had been submitted and registered as security before those who are in charge of the Aerarium in Rome" (. . . *uti ii e[a]ve p.R. obligati obligatave essent, si aput eos, qui Romae aerario praessent ii praedes i[i]que cognitores facti eaque praedia subdita subsignanda obligatave essent).*[46]

---

40. *Pro Flacco* 18/43.

41. Plut., *QR* 43 (*Mor.* 275 B–C). For further references, Mommsen, *Staatsrecht* II[3], 553–54, III[3], 1151–53.

42. *CIL* I[2] 593 = *ILS* 6085 = Riccobono, *FIRA*[2] I 13, ll. 46–49.

43. *Pro Flacco* 32/80.

44. Dio 60, 10, 3.

45. Plut., *Q. R.* 42 (*Mor.* 275 A).

46. *CIL* II 1964 = *ILS* 6089 = Riccobono, *FIRA* I[2] 24, col. 4, ll. 34–35. Compare the fragmentary provision of the Lex Agraria of 3 B.C., *CIL* I[2] 585 = Bruns, *Fontes*[7], no. II, l. 46.

Debts to the State

Debts to the state arose mainly from contractual obligations or from the imposition of fines.[47] In the Republic the censors on leaving office would deposit at the Aerarium a list of public debtors (*aerarii*).[48] One example of censorial action is that of Camillus and Postumius, who laid a fine on all those who had attained old age in celibacy and reported the names to the Aerarium.[49] In A.D. 58 we find the quaestors of the Aerarium entering in their books fines (*multae*) imposed by a tribune.[50] Then there were debts arising from contracts; on Octavian's abolition of debts in 29, where Suetonius has only "he burnt the records of old debts to the Aerarium, which were by far the most frequent source of blackmail,"[51] Dio has "he cancelled all obligations which had been given to the Aerarium [*to dēmosion*] previous to the battle of Actium, except those secured by buildings, and he burnt the old records of those who had been indebted to the public."[52]

Debts to the Aerarium tended to accumulate. Cato the Younger found many outstanding debts of private people to the state, and vice versa.[53] In the Empire, Vespasian, Hadrian, and Marcus Aurelius all cancelled long-standing debts to the Aerarium.[54] The situation naturally lent itself to delation, and one Paetus appears in Nero's reign "who was notorious for his acquisition of confiscated property from the Aerarium." Evidently he tried to prosecute people whose names the Aerarium officials had in fact crossed off—since the story is rounded off with the comment that "the records in which he traced back forgotten debts to the Aerarium had burnt."[55]

The question now arises of the role of the Aerarium officials in the recovery of debts, and, from that, the development of their independent jurisdiction. In the early Republic we find the quaestors seizing and selling up

---

47. Two extant republican laws, the (*CIL* I² 582 = Riccobono, *FIRA* I² 16 = Bruns, *Fontes*⁷, no. 8, l. 11.) and (*CIL* I² 583 = Riccobono, *FIRA* I² 7 = Bruns, *Fontes*⁷, no. 10, l. 57), provide for the naming of guarantors (to the quaestors of the Aerarium by a man who has suffered a fine or condemnation).

48. E.g., Livy 29, 37, 12.

49. Val. Max. 11, 9, 1. See Broughton, *MRR* I, 82.

50. Tac., *Ann.* 13, 28, 3.

51. Suet., *Div. Aug.* 32, 2.

52. 53, 2, 3.

53. Plut., *Cato Minor* 17, 2.

54. Dio 66, 10, 2a (Vespasian); 69, 8, I² (Hadrian); 71, 32, 2 (Marcus Aurelius). See "The Fiscus in the First Two Centuries," *JRS* 53 (1963): 29 (chapter 3 in this volume).

55. Tac., *Ann.* 13, 23. The interpretation of this passage is by no means secure.

bona damnatorum (property of persons condemned on criminal charges) immediately after a condemnation.[56] Cato the Younger, however, appears to have acted on his own initiative in recovering public money which had been distributed by Sulla to his followers.[57] Similarly, in A.D. 56 we find a quaestor of the Aerarium blamed "for having extended his right of compulsory sale [*ius hastae*] oppressively towards the helpless."[58] But, more than that, we find them exercising a jurisdiction of their own. The earliest reference is Dio's description of how Claudius used to sit beside magistrates as they held trial — the consuls and praetors and in particular those in charge of the finance.[59] Then we have Pliny's account of himself at work as prefect of the Aerarium: "I give jurisdiction, subscribe petitions, make up the records, and write innumerable — quite unliterary — letters." The first two phrases both imply the exercise of jurisdiction, and the implication is confirmed by the words which Euphrates, quoted in the same letter, uses to describe Pliny's labours "conducting public business, presiding at trials, judging, displaying, and administering justice."[60]

It is possible that such jurisdiction began in the period (23 B.C.–A.D. 44) when the post was held by praetors, and one reference from this period seems to show them issuing an edict. Suetonius records that Claudius before his accession, "having been forced to pay his entry fee to a priestly college, was reduced to such straitened circumstances that he was unable to meet the obligation incurred to the Aerarium; whereupon by edict of the prefects [*edictum praefectorum*] his property was advertised for sale to meet the deficiency in accordance with the law regulating confiscations [*lex praediatoria*]"[61] — the term "prefects" is used anachronistically. Cases seem to have been heard at the Aerarium itself; Nero, according to Suetonius, removed cases "from the Aerarium . . . to the Forum and the court of the *recuperatores* [assessors]."[62] That should mean that the jurisdiction itself was transferred to the *recuperatores*; but then Pliny in the *Panegyric* waxes enthusiastic over the change in the Aerarium since the death of Domitian: "What a pleasure to see peace

56. Livy 4, 15, 8; 38, 60, 8; Dion. Hal. 11, 46, 4.

57. Plut., *Cato Minor* 17, 6. See Dio 47, 6, 4.

58. Tac., *Ann.* 13, 28, 5.

59. Dio 60, 4, 4. The reference in Dio's phrase is made clear by other passages — 43, 48; 53, 2, 1; 60, 10, 3.

60. Pliny, *Ep.* 1, 10, 9–10.

61. Suet., *Div. Claud.* 9, 2. Compare Lex Malacitana (*CIL* II 1964 = *ILS* 6089 = Riccobono, *FIRA* I² 24), col. 4, ll. 50–51.

62. Suet., *Nero* 17. Cf. Suet., *Dom.* 9.

and quiet restored to the Aerarium, to see it as it was before the day of informers [*delatores*]. Now it is a real temple and sanctuary of a god."[63]

In the second century we find them concerned with the reporting (*delatio*) of *bona caduca* (unclaimed property) to the Aerarium,[64] and semi-judicial
functions might grow out of that.[65] There were also other semi-judicial functions like settlements out of court with respect to maintenance (*transactiones
alimentorum*) "before the prefect of the Aerarium."[66] But they also appear
giving criminal judgements; we have references to an informer summoned
"three times by edict" by the prefect of the Aerarium[67] and to conviction
for fraud before a prefect.[68] The *Sententiae et epistulae* of Hadrian even has a
case of a man condemned "to the quarries" by the prefect of the Aerarium
"in compliance with the Lex Aelia Sentia."[69]

This development of an independent jurisdiction is one example of a process typical of the Empire in which both the growth of the informal *cognitio*
procedure and the pressure of business on the holders of *imperium* contributed to the de facto exercise of jurisdiction by the holders of a wide range
of posts, including common soldiers.[70]

The Accounts of Promagistrates

The late Republican procedure is fairly well known. At the beginning of a
provincial command the Senate voted a sum to be paid out of the Aerarium
and taken by the governor to his province (*ornare provinciam*);[71] it was not unknown for the governor in fact to leave it behind in Rome earning interest.[72]
It is clear that what was voted from the Aerarium itself was only part of the

63. Pliny, *Pan.* 36.

64. *Dig.* 49, 14, 13 and 15. "The Fiscus in the First Two Centuries," *JRS* 53 (1963): 29
(chapter 3 in this volume).

65. See *Dig.* 49, 14, 42 *pr.*

66. *Dig.* 2, 15, 8, 19.

67. *Dig.* 49, 14, 15, 4.

68. *Dig.* 49, 14, 42, 1.

69. *Corpus Gloss. Lat.* III, p. 31, ll. 50–51.

70. See R. MacMullen, *Soldier and Civilian in the Later Roman Empire* (Harvard, 1963),
54–55.

71. Cic. *ad Att.* 3, 24, 1; Q. *f.* 2, 3, 1; *in Pis.* 5; Suet., *Div. Jul.* 18. See A. H. M. Jones, "The
Aerarium and the Fiscus," *JRS* 40 (1950): 22 = *Studies*, 101.

72. Cic. *in Pis.* 86; *de imp. Pomp* 37. Note also the fact that Cicero was able to draw money
in his brother's name from the Aerarium while the latter was in his third year as proconsul
of Asia, Q. *f.* 1, 3, 7.

funds that the governor would need during his tenure; when a subsidiary vote was made for Caesar in Gaul Cicero thought he might have got by "with the booty which he had previously won."[73] Alternatively, it was possible to authorize the promagistrate to draw money on the spot; Pompey in 67 was given authority[74]—from the provincial *fisci* (treasuries) and the *publicani*.[75] It is important to note that the evidence for these procedures shows the Aerarium playing no role beyond the handing-out of a lump sum, or an annual sum, in Rome.

The Empire provides no direct evidence for similar procedures. Some change in the system will have come when senatorial governors began to receive a fixed salary—which Dio says began with Augustus[76] and which was certainly the case in the late first and early third centuries.[77] They also received, at least in Augustus' time, a fixed allowance "for mules and tents."[78] But we do not know whether proconsuls, or *legati Augusti pro praetore*, or both, were voted sums by the Senate at the start of their governorships.

Nor do we know whether such votes were regularly made to the emperor. Jones surmises that recurrent grants were made to the emperor in respect of his "province" but admits that there is no direct evidence.[79] In fact, there are a few items of evidence. Jerome's *Chronicle* records under A.D. 67 that 10 million sesterces were decreed to Nero by the Senate as expenses.[80] Marcus Aurelius asked the Senate to vote funds for a war; Dio states explicitly that the procedure was exceptional: "Marcus also asked the Senate for money from the Aerarium [*to dēmosion*], not because such funds were not already at the emperor's disposal, but because he was wont to declare that all the funds, both these and others, belonged to the Senate and to the people."[81] Finally, a curious passage in the *Historia Augusta* states that Commodus pretended to be setting sail for Africa "so that he could get funds for the journey";[82]

---

73. *de prov. cons* 28; cf. *Pro Balbo* 61 and Plut. *Caes.* 28. It is not clear whether this means that more money would be sent out from Rome or that he would be allowed to spend more in the province.

74. Plut. *Pomp.* 25; cf. App. *Mith.* 94.

75. See Jones (n. 71), 23 = *Studies*, 103–4.

76. Dio 53, 15, 4–5.

77. Tac., *Agric.* 42, 3; Dio 78, 22, 5.

78. Suet., *Div. Aug.* 36.

79. Jones (n. 71), 24 = *Studies*, 104–5.

80. Compare Orosius 7, 7, 8.

81. Dio 71, 33, 2.

82. *Vita com.* 9, 1.

the reference, it seems, can only be to a sum voted by the Senate from the Aerarium.

With emperors and governors alike, therefore, the evidence is too slight for any conclusion as to what the regular system was. But some light is thrown on the position by references to the procedure known as *delatio ad aerarium*, that is, the registration at the Aerarium of the names of subordinate officials by their superiors, as a way of regularizing their position and ensuring their pay. The clearest evidence comes from the decree of the Senate of 11 B.C., recorded by Frontinus, which established the post of *curator aquarum* and the staff for it—"and that whatever attendants it is permitted to the water commissioners [*curatores aquarum*] by this decree of the Senate to employ, they shall report them to the Aerarium [*ad Aerarium deferrent*] in the next ten days; and as for those whose names shall be thus reported [*quique ita delati essent*], to them the praetors of the Aerarium shall grant and allocate, as annual rations, as much as the prefects in charge of corn distribution [*praefecti frumento dando*] are wont to give and allot."[83] By contrast, Cicero in Cilicia carries out the process of *delatio* retrospectively, while preparing his *rationes* (accounts) for deposit—"as for benefits, be informed, that by me military tribunes, prefects, and comrades-in-arms—so long as they were mine—have been registered [at the Aerarium]."[84] The process was evidently not automatic, and to be "delated" seems normally to have been a special favour. Cicero says of Balbus "that Caesar when he was praetor and consul registered him as *praefectus fabrum* [prefect of engineers]."[85] Atticus refused "prefectures *delatae* by many praetors and consuls" (*multorum consulum praetorumque praefecturas delatas*), or rather accepted the honour but refused both the duties and the pay.[86]

Early imperial documents confirm the honorific nature of the *delatio*: Q. Aemilius Secundus, in Augustus' reign, a *praefectus fabrum* "reported to the Aerarium by two consuls";[87] C. Julius Aquila "registered twice at the Aerarium as *praefectus fabrum* by the consul" (*[pr]aef. fabr. bis in aerarium delatus a cos.*);[88] Claudius Chionis "registered at the Aerarium as travelling companion of a proconsul of Asia" in the first century.[89] Surprisingly, we also find

---

83. Frontinus, *De aquae ductu* 100.

84. *Fam.* 5, 20, 7.

85. *Pro Balbo* 63.

86. Nepos, *Att.* 6.

87. *CIL* III 6687 = *ILS* 2683. See *PIR*² A 406.

88. *CIL* III 6983 = *ILS* 5883 = *IGR* III 83. See H. G. Pflaum, *Carrières procuratoriennes* (Paris, 1960–61), no. 21.

89. *ILS* 8860 = *OGIS* 494. Revised text and commentary, *Ins. Didyma* 272.

two imperial freedmen *accensi* (attendants) "delated": Antemus "freedman of Tiberius Caesar Augustus in charge of the accounts, attendant, registered by Augustus" (*Ti. Caesaris Aug. l(iberto) a rationi[b.], accenso delat(o) ab Aug.*),[90] and Eutactus "freedman of Augustus, procurator, attendant, registered by the divine Vespasian" (*Aug. lib. proc., accenso delat(o) a divo Vespasiano*).[91] Here too the *delatio* will have been a mark of special favour.

The majority of these instances show *delatio* by consuls or emperors in Rome. But one refers to a proconsul of Asia, and continued payments by the Aerarium for provincial officials are attested by Modestinus, writing in the first half of the third century, who refers to "military tribunes, prefects, companions [*comites*] of the legates who are registered at the Aerarium or in the *commentarii* [records] of the princeps."[92] This evidence is the more valuable because it refers to officials in imperial provinces. The responsibility of the Aerarium for paying the quaestor's scribes (*scribae*) in a public province is attested in Pliny's letters.[93]

In the Republic a provincial governor had to present his accounts (*rationes*) to the quaestors of the Aerarium on his return. There were recurrent conflicts over what exactly had to be recorded, but the actual presentation of accounts is well attested.[94] A law of Julius Caesar laid down a stricter procedure; Cicero reports from Cilicia that in accordance with it he has left copies of his accounts at two cities in the province and has sent a third to the Aerarium.[95] The only reference to this procedure from the imperial period comes from a passage of Paulus in the *Digest*: "[no action lies against him] who, on leaving his province, retains the money which was in his possession after reporting to the Aerarium."[96] There may have been a distinction between proconsuls and imperial legates in this matter, but there is no hint of it here.

It is the essential point in the understanding of what the Aerarium was (or rather was not) that the purpose of these accounts was essentially retrospective; their function was to provide a check on the individual governors. There is not the slightest evidence to suggest that the Aerarium officials ever put these accounts together or made up general accounts of the state. That was done for the first time by Augustus, and in doing so he was not reduplicating any function performed by public officials. Dio and Suetonius record

---

90. *CIL* VI 8409.
91. *CIL* VI 1962 = *ILS* 1943.
92. *Dig.* 4, 6, 32.
93. Pliny, *Ep.* 4, 12, 2–4. See below.
94. E.g., Aulus Gellius, *NA* 4, 18, 7–12; *Verr.* II.1, 36–37; 57.
95. *Fam.* 5, 20, 2; *Att.* 6, 7, 2; *In Pis.* 61.
96. *Dig.* 48, 13, 11, 6.

that "the accounts of the empire" (*rationes imperii*) were published (how frequently is not stated) by Augustus, by Tiberius until he retired to Capri, and by Gaius.[97] Some idea of what these "accounts" contained can be gained from what is said of the financial documents which Augustus handed over in 23,[98] and left in A.D. 14; the latter listed troops, revenues, and expenditures and the amounts of cash in the Aerarium, the provincial *fisci* (treasuries), and the arrears of the indirect taxes in the hands of the tax farmers.[99] It should be emphasized that Augustus' financial report had nothing in common with the accounts of a governor, for they were concerned with the public finance of the whole Empire. Some of the information used in compiling the *breviaria* may well of course have come from the accounts in the Aerarium. Plutarch reveals that Cato the Younger, after his term as quaestor, continued to send slaves to copy the financial documents there and thus kept himself well informed.[100]

Cash Payments

The essential function of the Aerarium was to be the depository of state valuables. In the early Republic legionary standards (*signa*) were stored there,[101] and in 49 Caesar found there, along with the gold and silver, a quantity of silphium;[102] Pliny the Elder lists the amounts of gold and silver, in cash and bullion, contained there at various points down to 49.[103] The primary task of the officials, symbolized by a pair of scales which stood in the temple,[104] was to make payments in and out.[105] They made such payments, not on their own initiative, but only on the authority of the Senate. This fact, stated explicitly by Polybius,[106] is well illustrated in later sources. At the beginning of the Lex Cornelia de XX Quaestoribus (the Cornelian law concerning the twenty quaestors) we have "the quaestor, who shall have the Aerarium as his province is to pay that sum to that scribe, or [those] scribes, or to his heir"

97. Suet., *Calig.* 16; Dio 59, 9, 4.

98. Suet., *Div. Aug.* 28; Dio 53, 30, 1–2.

99. Tac., *Ann.* 1, 11, 5–6; Suet., *Div. Aug.* 101; Dio 56, 33, 2. See Jones (n. 71), 23 = *Studies*, 103–4.

100. Plut., *Cato Minor* 18, 9.

101. Livy 3, 69, 8; 4, 22, 2; 7, 23, 3.

102. Pliny, *NH* 19, 40.

103. Pliny, *NH* 33, 55–56.

104. Varro, *LL* 5, 183.

105. See, e.g., Plut., *Tib. Grac.* 10, 5; *Pro Fonteio* 2/3.

106. 6, 13. See Jones (n. 71), 22 = *Studies*, 101.

(*quaestorque quei aerarium provinciam optinebit eam pequniam ei scribae scribeisque heredive eius solvito*).[107] Cicero retails the Senate's instructions for the erection of a statue to P. Servilius "that Gaius Pansa Aulus Hirtius the consuls, either or both, if they see fit, should direct the urban quaestors to make a contract for the construction and the placement on the Rostra of the said pedestal and statue and see to it that the sum agreed be allocated and paid to the contractor."[108] A slightly different formula occurs in the decree of the Senate (*senatus consultum*) relating to the Secular Games of 17 B.C. "that the consuls, either or both, in future commemoration of the event erect one column of bronze and one of marble, and also contract for the construction of the work, and direct the praetors in charge of the Aerarium that the sum agreed be paid to the contractors" (*uti cos. a(lter) a(mbo)ve ad f[uturam rei memoriam columnam] aheneam et alteram [m]armoream . . . [. . . eo loco statuant et id opus eidem] locent, praetoribusque q(ui) [a(erario)] p(raesint) imperent uti redemptoribus ea[m summam qua locaverint solvant]*).[109] The decree of the Senate for the secular games of 204 provides further evidence "towards these games and sacrifices . . . let the payments be made from the Aerarium of the Roman people."[110]

The Senate thus retained the right to vote funds from the Aerarium. Emperors too could dispose of public funds, as Dio explicitly states.[111] The three latest references to the prefects of the Aerarium at work show them making payments on the instructions of an emperor. The references are in three "letters" of Valerian given in the *Life* of Aurelian. One is addressed to the city prefect (*Praefectus Urbi*) and gives instructions for Aurelian to receive provisions as a reward for his services—"the rest will be provided by the prefects of the Aerarium"; the second tells Aelius Xiphidius, the prefect of the Aerarium, to provide Aurelian with materials and cash "to hold the circus games [*circenses*]"; the third is addressed to the Senate on the opening of the Sibylline books—"whatever costs there might be, I have ordered to be paid by the prefect of the Aerarium in a letter sent to him."[112] The genuineness of the letters may legitimately be doubted; but the evidence they provide is re-

---

107. CIL I[2] 587 = Bruns, *Fontes*[7], no. 12 = Riccobono, *FIRA* I[2] 10, ll. 2–4.

108. Cic., *Phil.* 9, 7/16.

109. *CIL* VI 32323 = Riccobono, *FIRA* I[2] 40 = Ehrenberg and Jones, *Documents* 30B, ll. 61–63. For the *s. c.* of 11 B.C. (establishing the *curatores aquarum*), see text to n. 82.

110. *CIL* VI 32326 l. 29 (cf. VI 32324 l. 5).

111. 53, 22, 4. See *JRS* 53 (1963): 41 (chapter 3 in this volume). Marcus Aurelius' request to the Senate to vote funds (see text to n. 81) suggests that, in purist theory though not in practice, the sole right of the Senate was still recognized.

112. SHA, *vita Aurel.* 9, 7; 12, 1; 20, 8.

liable, for it shows the officials of the Aerarium doing what they had always done, making payments on the authority of others.

Financial Decisions

It will already be abundantly clear that the Aerarium could not have been the source of policy decisions about finance. It will, however, be worth listing the few occasions on which the Aerarium officials appear on the political stage. In the *Ad Herennium* we find the urban quaestor telling the Senate "the Aerarium cannot afford such a largess" (the Lex Frumentaria, which fixed the price of corn, of 100 B.C.).[113] Under Tiberius a senator rose in the Senate to claim compensation for the undermining of his house by the construction of a public road; the praetors of the Aerarium resisted the claim, so Tiberius paid himself.[114] In A.D. 70 the praetors of the Aerarium, "complaining about the poverty of the public treasury [i.e., the Aerarium], demanded to put a limit to expenditure."[115] Finally, there is a rather different type of case, recorded in Pliny's letters. The scribe of a provincial quaestor died before the payment of his salary. On his return the quaestor consulted the emperor as to what should be done with the money, and he sent the matter to the Senate. It was dealt with as a case between the prefects of the Aerarium and the heirs, each side employing a counsel (*advocatus*).[116] Nothing could illustrate more clearly the comparatively humble role of the Aerarium officials.

Their unimportance—in this sense—is confirmed by the fact that attempts at financial policy making in the early Empire (in so far as there were any) were not made by or through them. In A.D. 6 we find Augustus appointing three consulars chosen by lot to cut public expenditure.[117] In 42 Claudius appointed three praetorians to recover money owed to the state.[118] In 56 Nero put 40 million HS into the Aerarium "to maintain public credit,"[119] and six years later he placed three consulars in charge of the public revenues, abusing earlier emperors for spending ahead of income and claiming that he him-

113. *Ad Herenn.* 1, 12, 21. See Broughton, *MRR* I, 575–76.

114. Tac., *Ann.* 1, 75, 3–4.

115. Tac., *Hist.* 4, 9.

116. Pliny, *Ep.* 4, 12, 2–4.

117. Dio 55, 25, 6.

118. Dio 60, 10, 4. Compare the recovery of public money by C. Sentius Sturninus as consul of 19 B.C., Vell. Pat. 2, 92.

119. Tac., *Ann.* 13, 31, 2. The nearest parallel to this phrase seems to be Livy 7, 27, 4 and 23, 48, 9.

self had been subsidizing the Aerarium to the extent of 60 million HS per year.[120] In 70 a commission of senators was selected by lot to restore the public records and place a limit on expenditure.[121] Under Nerva in 97 the Senate selected five senators "to reduce public expense";[122] it may have been on their recommendation that Nerva cut expenditure by abolishing some sacrifices, horse races, and other spectacles.[123]

Conclusion

This chapter is designed only to outline the functions performed by and at the Aerarium itself. The evidence shows that the Aerarium was a depository for cash and documents, some of which related to finance, and that the chief functions of its officials were to accept the cash and documents when lodged there, to preserve them, and to make payments when required to do so. They paid out in Rome, and the transport of the cash to where it was supposed to be used was a matter for the recipient.[124] They accepted accounts from provincial governors on their return, but kept no general accounts of the state's finances, and were in no way responsible for financial policy. So far as can be seen, the advent of the Empire made no difference to their duties except to add some judicial functions.

A number of questions remain. Some are concrete—what cash actually came into the Aerarium, from what sources of revenue and from what geographical areas? Others are more matters of terminology (though still important for the interpretation of the Empire as a political institution). How long did the various revenues of the *res publica* continue to be called "public"? How are we to see the contrast between Aerarium and Fiscus? It may be hoped that such questions may now be approached from a more secure standpoint.

120. Tac., *Ann.* 15, 18, 4.

121. Tac., *Hist.* 4, 40; see 4, 9.

122. Pliny, *Ep.* 2, 1, 9; *Pan.* 62, 2.

123. Dio 68, 2, 3.

124. Note Nic. Dam., *FGrH* 90 F. 130, xviii: in 44 Octavian sent for the money which Caesar had sent to Asia for the Parthian war, and when it arrived, along with the tribute of Asia, abstracted what fell as inheritance to himself and put the public money in the Aerarium.

CHAPTER FIVE

Cash Distributions in Rome
and Imperial Minting*

In the spring of 1989 I had the pleasure of making a journey through those areas of southern Turkey which were regarded in antiquity as belonging to Syria.[1] My purpose was to acquire at least a general conception of the geography of the northern part of ancient Syria; for the whole region which stretches from the Mediterranean to the desert and the Tigris, and from the Taurus to Egypt was due to form the subject of my book on the Roman Near East.[2]

Starting from Ankara, we crossed the central plateau of Anatolia and took the modern road which by-passes the Cilician Gates. At that point, if one leaves the modern road where it debouches from the mountains onto the Cilician plain, and climbs up one of the limestone hills which form the lower reaches of the Taurus, one finds a stretch of Roman road, perfectly preserved over a distance of some two kilometres; as was normal, the route chosen followed the crest of the hill rather than the valley.[3] I do not know of any

---

*First published in French, as "Les congiaires à Rome et la monnaie," in A. Giovannini, ed., *Nourrir la plèbe: actes du colloque tenu à Genève les 28 et 29.IX.1989 en hommage à Denis van Berchem* (1991), 143–59. I would like to thank C. J. Howgego and C. E. King very warmly for information and critical observations which have greatly contributed to improving this chapter.

1. I am extremely grateful to my companion on that journey, Dr. C. S. R. Lightfoot, then assistant director of the British Institute at Ankara, whose knowledge of the area, and boundless energy and enthusiasm, made it possible both to cover the whole region in a few days and to visit various remote and inaccessible sites.

2. *The Roman Near East, 31 BC–AD 337* (1993).

3. For this stretch of road, see W. M. Ramsay, *Cities of St. Paul* (1907), with the map on p. 106, and pl. 2. See also M. Hellenkemper and H. Hild, *Neue Forschungen in Kilikien* (1986), 96–97 and pls. 139–40. Moreover, Dr. David French was kind enough to inform me by

scene which expresses more powerfully the nature of the Roman Empire. For in reality it is not a matter of *a* Roman road but of *the* Roman road: that is to say, that major route which ran from northern Italy and the Danube, then through the Balkans to Byzantium, and across Anatolia to Syria and the Euphrates frontier.[4]

From this section of the road one could see the snow-capped peaks of the Taurus to the north, and to the south the Cilician plain and the Mediterranean, and could imagine oneself to be at the very heart of the Empire. For this narrow road, a mere three metres or so in width, which—in its present form at least—would not have allowed more than two soldiers to march abreast, was in reality the link which maintained the unity of the Empire as an integrated system. But to think of the Roman Empire as a system of communications extended in space is necessarily to think of that important work on the provisioning of the army in kind—the *annona militaris*—published by Denis von Berchem in 1937, which has stimulated so much reflection by integrating our conceptions of the road system, of the movements of troops, of the delivery of supplies for them, and of taxation.[5]

But, on the following day, I had yet another occasion to contemplate the contribution made by Denis von Berchem to our conception of the Roman Empire as an organisation, or as a spatial system. For, after crossing the Amanus, we arrived in the plain of Antioch, and made our way to the coast. All that I had previously come to understand of the nature of this small region was owed to the magisterial article on the port of Seleucia in Pieria published by van Berchem in 1985.[6] Like pilgrims, so to speak, we traversed the enormous cutting and tunnel there, carried out on the orders of Vespasian and Titus to divert from the port a stream coming down from Mount Coryphaeus (the south-west point of the Amanus). Furthermore, by climbing up to the acropolis of the ancient city, we gained a magnificent view of the port, now filled with earth (and used for growing tomatoes), but perfectly visible from above.

As is indicated by the title of his article, "The Port of Seleucia in Pieria and

---

letter that the stretch of road in question, although certainly a section of the great trans-Anatolian route, should in its present state be regarded as a reconstruction dating to the late Empire.

4. On the Anatolian section of this route, see D. French, *Roman Roads and Milestones of Asia Minor* I: *The Pilgrim's Road* (British Institute of Archaeology at Ankara, Monograph 3; BAR Int. Ser., 105, 1981).

5. D. van Berchem, *L'annone militaire dans l'Empire romain au 3ᵉ siècle* (1937).

6. D. van Berchem, "Le port de Séleucie de Piérie et l'infrastructure logistique des guerres parthiques," *Bonner Jahrbücher* 185 (1985): 47–87.

the Logistical Infrastructure of the Parthian Wars," van Berchem's interest in the port was not solely that of an archaeologist, but was directed, once again, to the better understanding of the organic unity of the Empire. He took the occasion to associate with his study of the port a revision of the Latin inscription from near Antioch, which records the work of canalisation of the Orontes, also carried out under Vespasian.[7] As a result, it became possible to bring ships up the river as far as Antioch, and possibly further, to the lake itself.[8] It was striking to observe that today there is absolutely no traffic on the river between Antalya and the sea; and it takes some effort to envisage the modern town as a secondary "capital" of the Empire and as the strategic centre of the Roman Near East.

The reader might begin to ask what precisely is the link between the roads and ports of the Roman Near East and the cash distributions, or *congiaria*, carried out by the emperor in Rome. One such link of course is provided by another of the seminal works of van Berchem, on the distributions of corn and cash to the Roman plebs.[9] But this link does not merely consist in the successive works of a contemporary historian. There is a more profound underlying conception, which consists in the will to envisage in an absolutely concrete way the actual functioning of the imperial system. As an expression of that, van Berchem tended always to leave aside abstractions and theories of government, to offer us instead a "real" Roman Empire, of peasants and harvests, roads, ports, and soldiers, quartered in camps or marching along the roads of the Empire. To maintain these soldiers, the state had to find the means to provide them either with regular pay in cash, or with supplies of food in kind, or both. In either case the state was obliged to transport across the vast expanses of the Empire enormous quantities of cash or provisions.[10]

Let us leave aside the question of the provisioning of the army in kind— of the *annona militaris*, if one wishes to use the term. Equally, when we arrive finally at the city of Rome, let us leave aside the question of how it was provisioned, whether by commercial means or by the free distributions of corn established by the legislation of Clodius in 58 B.C., and maintained throughout the imperial period. Let us concentrate instead on coin, that imperial coin of which two of the most important functions, but not the only

7. *Mus. Helv.* 40 (1983): 185–96, revised in *Bonner Jahrbücher* (n. 6), 85–87, whence *AE* 1983, no. 927.

8. Pausanias, *Description of Greece* 8, 29, 3, refers to the work of canalisation and its purpose, without actually naming the emperor who gave orders for it.

9. *Les distributions de blé et d'argent à la plèbe romaine* (1939).

10. I will allow myself to mention also, while thinking of space and movement, D. van Berchem, *Les routes et l'histoire. Études sur les Helvètes et leurs voisins dans l'Empire romain* (1982).

ones, were on the one hand that of being brought to the military camps for distribution to the soldiers as *stipendium* (pay) or *donativum* (largesse), and on the other that of being distributed in *congiaria* to the Roman plebs. In my view, this latter function remains more mysterious than people have believed.

It has to be admitted that when I begin to read the major numismatic collections, and even the introductions to Roman coinage designed for students, such as the excellent one published by Andrew Burnett,[11] I find myself still quite confused. I find myself in a world which I understand only very partially, and in which, as it seems, no one directs their energies to clarifying the particular questions which interest me. The "berchemian" will to envisage concretely the various aspects of the Roman monetary system seems to be largely absent.

Let me give one example. In order to mint its coins, the state, obviously enough, had to procure vast quantities of gold, silver, copper, or other base metals. How? The answer is not as clear as one might suppose. Was it perhaps by the direct exploitation of imperial mines? Perhaps, in certain cases.

We could think of the copper mines at Phaeno (which in the fourth century lay within the borders of Palaestina, and are now within those of Jordan). They were exploited by the state in the early fourth century and were used for the detention of Christian martyrs who were put to forced labour.[12] But did the state utilise the copper for its own minting? The answer is not certain. In the second century at any rate, we know that the imperial mines in Lusitania had been exploited by leasing them out to contractors against a payment in cash; even as regards the 50 per cent of the ore which the state claimed, it seems that the state in practice took its share in cash.[13] And if we go further back, to the beginnings of the imperial system, there is no reason to think that, under Augustus, for example, a category of imperial mines existed. From where, and through what means, did Augustus, or the Roman state of his time, obtain the silver which was required for minting denarii? I do not know. And, so far as I know, the question has not been asked.

11. A. Burnett, *Coinage in the Roman World* (1987). Note also now C. J. Howgego, *Ancient History from Coins* (1995).

12. On the exploitation of these mines, and on the condemned Christians who worked there, see F. Millar, "Condemnation to Hard Labour in the Roman Empire, from the Julio-Claudians to Constantine," *Papers of the British School at Rome* 52 (1984): 124–47, esp. 140–41 (chapter 7 in this volume).

13. See esp. C. Domergue, *La mine antique d'Aljustrel (Portugal) et les tables de bronze de Vipasca* (extrait de *Conimbriga* 22, 1983).

But let us admit that with the passage of time the emperors were progressively more in a position to exploit "imperial" mines directly and to acquire stocks of metal from them. How were the ores transported from the mines to be refined and then minted? Was it by means of wagons moving along the roads? In that case, who protected such wagons against robbers? Or was it, if geography permitted, by boat?

As regards the western part of the Empire in the period from the first to the third century, there is at least one question which can be answered. The goal of any such process of transport must have been Rome itself. For it seems certain that after the reign of Nero the sole mint (or mints) which produced coins in gold and silver for the Roman West was (or were) situated in Rome.[14]

Therefore, the monetary system of the Empire depended absolutely on the arrival in Rome of the necessary stocks of metal. But it does not follow from that that what was concerned was always newly mined ore, or metal newly refined from ore. There was another possibility, the re-minting of already existing coins which had arrived in Rome in the form of taxes. But that possibility raises an even more difficult question. Is it true that a large part of the taxation revenue of the Empire actually was transported to Rome in the form of coin? Let us recall the "model" of the finances of the Empire offered by Keith Hopkins.[15] The model is as follows. The 50 million inhabitants of the Empire paid some 10 per cent of the "gross national product" in taxes. These taxes were transported from the richer provinces to the poorer ones where (on the whole) the army was stationed, thus producing a sort of integrated inter-regional market, or system of circulation.

Hopkins has nothing to say about the means by which so enormous a quantity of coins could have been transported. If we follow his calculations, we are talking of an annual revenue of some 824 million sestertii, or 206 million denarii. If we think of denarii, the total weight of silver would have been of the order of 775,000 kilograms.[16] To transport such a quantity all

14. See, e.g., J. P. C. Kent, "The Monetary System," in J. Wacher, ed., *The Roman World* II (1987), 568–85. It must be admitted that we understand very little about the actual working of the mint at Rome. See R. A. G. Carson, "System and Product in the Roman Mint," in R. A. G. Carson and C. H. V. Sutherland, eds., *Essays in Roman Coinage Presented to Harold Mattingly* (1956), 227–39; M. Peachin, "The Procurator Monetae," *Numis. Chron.* 146 (1986): 94–106.

15. K. Hopkins, "Taxes and Trade in the Roman Empire (200 BC–AD 400)," *JRS* 70 (1980): 101–25.

16. According to Kent (n. 14), 570, the denarius weighed on average 3.76 grams.

at one moment, it would have been necessary, following the calculations of A. H. M. Jones, to assemble 1,610 wagons, each drawn by 4 oxen, thus 6,440 animals in all.[17]

Naturally, these calculations are purely theoretical. In reality what was involved was thousands of separate journeys by land or voyages by sea, of which many will obviously have amounted to no more than local or regional movements. But it is essential to insist on the fact that these journeys or voyages, serving the function of distributing their pay to the soldiers, were absolutely essential to the functioning of the Empire. We can, for instance, gain an impression of such a voyage by reading Arrian's *Periplus*. For Arrian records how, as *legatus* (imperial governor) of Cappadocia, he sailed eastwards from Trapezus along the coast of the Black Sea, to visit and inspect the auxiliary forts. At two points in his narrative he describes how he distributed pay to the soldiers.[18] On the first of these occasions five cohorts were involved, thus amounting in principle to some 2,500 men. Given the difficulty of calculating the pay levels of the higher ranks, any estimate of the sum involved must be hypothetical. But, in order to try to envisage concretely what was involved, let us suppose that at this point Arrian had to pay out 100,000 denarii, or 375 kilograms of silver. Such a sum could have been carried in one heavy wagon; on this occasion, of course, it was carried on ship.

To catch a glimpse of the transportation by land of military pay, we need only have recourse to the last letter contained in the second of the two very important papyri from Panopolis, dating to A.D. 300. In this letter the procurator of the Lower Thebaid gives instructions for the provision of a sum of military pay as follows: "to Valerianus, the commander [*praepositus*] of the most noble spearmen [*lancearii*] of *legio III Diocletiana* stationed with you, 50 lbs. of silver and 4 purses [*folles*] of money, which makes 33 talents and 500 denarii, together with a team of four mules and a carriage and a driver."[19]

---

17. See A. H. M. Jones, *The Later Roman Empire* (1964), 830–31. The heaviest wagon (*angaria*) used on the *cursus publicus* (the state transport system) of the late Empire was supposed to carry a maximum load of 1,500 Roman pounds, each of 321 grams, hence a total of 481.5 kilograms. This figure will be used here on the assumption that there was no systematic change in the maximum size of the wagon between the early Empire and the late.

18. Arrian, *Periplus Mari Euxini* 6; 10.

19. T. C. Skeat, *Papyri from Panopolis in the Chester Beatty Library, Dublin* (1964), 105–7. On the level of military pay and *donativa* in this period, see R. Duncan-Jones, "Pay and Numbers in Diocletian's Army," *Chiron* 8 (1978): 541–60, revised in *Structure and Scale in the Roman Economy* (1990), 105–17; J. Jahn, "Zur Entwicklung römischer Soldzahlungen von Augustus bis auf Diocletian," *Studien zu Fundmünzen der Antike* 2 (1984): 53–74.

I cannot calculate the total weight of the pay due to be transported in this carriage (*ochema*); it is more important to make the effort to imagine the thousands of local journeys of this type, repeated across the vast expanse of the Empire.

However, I have deliberately left aside a question of central importance for our purposes: what proportion of journeys of this type had as their destination the city of Rome? In my opinion we would be entitled to exclude the possibility that the totality of the taxation revenues in cash from all the provinces was first transported to Rome, then to be re-directed to other provinces. It is at least very probable that a large proportion of the taxation revenues circulated directly from one province to another, without going to Rome. It should be stressed, however, that to the best of my knowledge our documentation on this question is precisely nil.

However, even if only a modest proportion of the taxation revenues from the provinces flowed each year to Rome in the form of coin, we must at any rate suppose that the indirect (not direct) taxes levied in Rome and Italy were not sufficient for the needs of the capital. By "indirect taxes" I mean the *vicesimae hereditatium* and *libertatis* (the 5 per cent taxes on inheritances and manumissions), the *centesima rerum venalium* (the 1 per cent tax auction tax), and the *portoria* (tolls).[20] At any rate, whether from Rome and Italy or from the provinces, quite significant sums were required each year in Rome merely to pay the soldiers stationed there, let alone for other purposes. For instance, in the reign of Septimius Severus, to which I will return later in connection with *congiaria*, the total annual pay of the units stationed in Rome was perhaps something of the order of 12 million denarii.[21] If these sums were still paid in three *stipendia* (instalments), some 4 million denarii will have been required each time, and for the transport of this sum thirty wagons will have been required, each drawn by four oxen. In any case, if these calculations are

20. For the very low level of administrative or fiscal activity in Italy on the part of the Roman state during the earlier Empire, see F. Millar, "Italy in the Roman Empire, Augustus to Constantine," *Phoenix* 40 (1986): 295–318 (chapter 17 in this volume).

21. For the total number of soldiers in the various units stationed in Rome under Septimius Severus, see E. Birley, "Septimius Severus and the Roman Army," *Epigraphische Studien* 8 (1969): 63–82, reprinted in *The Roman Army: Papers, 1929–1986* (1988), 21–40. According to these calculations the total number of soldiers in the praetorian cohorts, the urban cohorts, and the *vigiles* (fire brigades) was some 23,000. As is well known, the pay levels of these various units (and even more, evidently, that of the various grades between *miles gregarius* [common soldier] and centurion in these units) is very difficult to determine. As a rough basis I have estimated their average annual pay at 500 denarii, or 2,000 sestertii.

not entirely misleading, some 6 per cent of the revenues of the Empire will have been required each year for the payment of military units stationed in Rome. It thus becomes very probable that the revenues of Italy, where until Diocletian no direct taxes were raised, will not have sufficed for the needs of the state in Rome, and consequently that there must have been a constant inflow of provincial revenues to Rome.

If this is correct, is it not curious that this enormous traffic, in ore, in ingots of refined metal, or in coin, has left so little trace in our evidence? No stories of ships which sank, taking with them a whole cargo of provincial revenue in cash? No robbers or bandits who gained fame by intercepting a column of wagons loaded with coins en route to a port, or being transported towards Rome? No case of a soldier with the task of escorting such a waggon, who instead helped himself to a sack of coin and disappeared? So far as I know, we can find no anecdotes of this sort. However, if our literary sources fail us, it is always possible that some of the known hoards, on land or sea, derived in reality from imperial consignments of coin.[22]

I have just stated that it is at least very probable that a significant volume of provincial revenue was transported to Rome in cash for the payment of the troops there. But we must remember also the fact to which reference was made earlier, namely that it must also have been necessary to transport to Rome (in whatever form) large quantities of gold, silver, and base metals to be minted—or re-minted—at the mint in Rome. The two categories may of course have overlapped, and both may have performed similar functions (e.g., the units in Rome could have been paid either in coins brought as taxation revenue or in newly minted coins).

At any rate, even if we think only of minting (or re-minting), the quantities concerned were considerable. According to Andrew Burnett, for example, in the second century some 1 million aurei (gold coins) per year may have been minted in Rome.[23] For that purpose some 7,850 kilograms of gold would have been required,[24] and if it had been necessary to transport them at a single moment some sixteen heavy wagons would have been needed.

---

22. I mention only a few examples, for which I am entirely indebted to information from C. J. Howgego and C. E. King; P. Salama, "Les trésors maxentiens de Tripolitaine," *Libya Antiqua* 3–4 (1966–67): 21–27; R. A. G. Carson, "A Treasure of Aurei and Multiples from the Mediterranean," in P. Bastien, F. Dumas, H. Huvelin, and C. Morrison, eds., *Mélanges de Numismatique, d'Archéologie et d'Histoire offerts à Jean Lafaurie* (1980), 59–73.

23. Burnett (n. 11), 50. It should be made clear that Andrew Burnett himself presents this figure only as a hypothesis. But it will be retained here as a means of producing a framework for comparison, and for posing questions.

24. Kent (n. 14), 570, states that the average weight of an aureus was 7.85 grams.

But, if this figure of 1 million aurei per year has any validity, it is also very revealing as regards *congiaria*, to which we will return later.

It is at any rate certain that the mint of Rome produced considerable quantities of coin in gold, silver, and base metals. But the question of *what* was minted remains entirely obscure. In order to strike new coins, did they remint existing coins, delivered to Rome as taxation? Or was it normal to use ingots derived more or less directly from mining? Or stocks of metal previously stored up in Rome? Or perhaps even ornaments, gold or silver statues, and decorative objects of that sort?[25] All this possibilities are discussed in a paper by C. J. Howgego,[26] who contests, not without justification, various conclusions arrived at in a now classic paper by Michael Crawford.[27] Howgego's principal purpose is to dispute Crawford's theory that ancient states struck coins solely in order to be able to make their own necessary payments. In itself, this theory is certainly too inflexible. But, beyond that, it rests on a presupposition which is by no means beyond question: that is to say that, in order to make payments, an ancient state needed normally to strike *new* coins. But, for example, the idea that every payment made to each of the 300,000 to 400,000 soldiers in the Roman army[28] will normally have been carried out in new coin is surely absurd, presupposing as it does an inconceivably vast scale of minting. On this basis, the imperial mints would have had to mint, or re-mint, perhaps some 105 million denarii each year in the second century.[29] But it is generally known that in the imperial period the coins in circulation included some minted even as much as a century earlier. There is, in other words, no need to suppose that, when soldiers were paid, they received only newly minted coins.

One could however pose the question of *donativa* (largesses) in this context. It is surely possible that a *donativum*, being in principle a personal gift from the emperor to the individual soldier, was regularly paid in newly

25. For some examples of the melting down and minting of treasures or stocks of ornaments, see F. Millar, *The Emperor in the Roman World* (1977; 2nd ed., 1992), 144–47.

26. C. J. Howgego, "Why Did Ancient States Strike Coins?," *Numis. Chron.* 150 (1990): 1–25.

27. M. Crawford, "Money and Exchange in the Roman World," *JRS* 60 (1970): 40–48; revised version in Italian in M. Crawford, *La moneta in Grecia e a Roma* (1982), chap. 5.

28. As is well known, the question of the total size of the Roman army in the Empire remains open to discussion. See, e.g., A. R. Birley, "The Economic Effects of Roman Frontier Policy," in A. King and M. Henig, eds., *The Roman West in the Third Century* (BAR Int. Ser. 109, 1981), 39–53; R. MacMullen, "The Roman Emperor's Army Costs," *Latomus* 43 (1984): 571–80.

29. So MacMullen (n. 28), 580.

minted coins. This is precisely the question which forms the subject of an important work by P. Bastien, dealing with *donativa* in the late Empire, their relation to minting, and the utilisation for these occasions of specific types of coin.[30] Bastien asks the precise question: were there coins which were struck specifically for *donativa*? His reply is that there were, at least for the more important occasions.

I am not in a position to review with any confidence the production of coins in the fourth century. So, as regards this question, I would only wish to say that to me the Panopolis papyrus of A.D. 300, referred to earlier,[31] suggests a significantly different procedure: that is to say that the two formally distinct types of payment to soldiers—*stipendium* and *donativa*—were both carried out by the use of a mixture of coin, none of which seems to give the impression of being a special new issue. In the last letter in the papyrus, referred to above (text to n. 19), the writer speaks also of a quantity calculated in pounds of silver.

As regards the soldiers who belonged to legions or auxiliary units stationed in the provinces, I see no reason to believe that there was a system for the payment of either *stipendium* or *donativa* which necessitated the striking of new coins. In the case of legions or auxiliary units in the western provinces, such a system would have required the transport to the mint of Rome of enormous quantities of coins or ingots, a constant process of minting, or re-minting, at Rome, and then the transport of the coins back to the provinces. Everything is possible. But I can find no trace of such a system in our evidence.

But none the less we need to be cautious. I have so far left aside another type of payment made by the Roman state for the benefit of soldiers. I mean the *praemia* (discharge benefits) paid to legionary veterans at the moment of their discharge from service (or at any rate to those who survived to the required age of about forty-five). As is well known, we are concerned with relatively substantial sums compared to the annual *stipendium*. During the first two centuries of the Empire the *praemium* granted to a veteran seems to have been some 12,000 sesterces, or 3,000 denarii, which was equivalent to the pay for about twelve years of service in the first century and (if the *praemium* remained the same) about ten after Domitian.[32] So far as I know, no one has attempted to calculate how many soldiers will have survived until the age

---

30. P. Bastien, *Monnaie et donativa au Bas-Empire* (*Numismatique romaine* 17, 1988), 37.

31. Text to n. 19.

32. See the classic article of P. A. Brunt, "Pay and Superannuation in the Roman Army," *PBSR* 18 (1950): 50–71; and also Jahn (n. 19).

of discharge (after twenty-five years) and will thus have received their *praemia*. So the total expenditure each year is quite uncertain. But in any case, in this instance too we find ourselves confronted with the same problem, that of geography and transport. Obviously, the vast majority of the soldiers in the Roman army were stationed in the provinces, and generally in areas on, or at any rate near, the actual frontiers. I would presume that it was therefore in the camp itself that the soldier received his discharge and his *praemium*— in the time of Augustus at least, 3,000 denarii or 120 aurei. It will be worth noting that 120 aurei will have weighed about 1 kilogram, but 3,000 denarii rather more than 11 kilograms.

Or is it possible to imagine, on the contrary, that in order to receive his *praemium* every discharged legionary had to present himself in Rome? Surely not. But, before giving a confident answer, we have to take into account some relevant analogies. Firstly, the auxiliary units were also stationed in the provinces. But it was at Rome, on the Capitol, that the bronze tablets recording the privileges given to auxiliaries of any one province, when discharged en masse, were put up.[33] The documents which we have which relate to this process are secondary ones, namely the portable *diplomata* (certificates), each in the name of one auxiliary soldier, discharged, along with many others, on such an occasion. Were these individual, passport-sized, bronze *diplomata* despatched automatically to each soldier in his camp? Surely not. The evidence quite clearly suggests that any auxiliary veteran who wanted an individual *diploma* had to get a copy of the text which was inscribed on the Capitol and have it attested by witnesses. Therefore, either someone had to go to Rome to get the copy made, or the veteran had access to a copy held somewhere else, presumably in his province. But the latter possibility is a pure hypothesis. What the individual *diploma* referred to as its source was the bronze tablet put up on the Capitol. The communications, and the geographical relationships, involved remain mysterious.

So far as we know, discharged auxiliaries did not receive a *praemium*. But it is precisely one of the individualised *diplomata* recording the rights which auxiliaries received on discharge which must make us hesitate before expressing any certainty as to how and where the *praemia* in cash to which the discharged legionaries (by contrast) were entitled were delivered to them. For it is an auxiliary *diploma* of A.D. 65 which records that the *aerarium militare*

33. For valuable discussions of *diplomata* and the privileges granted to discharged auxiliaries, see W. Eck and H. Wolff, eds., *Heer und Integrationspolitik: Die römische Militärdiplome als historische Quelle* (1986). See also M. M. Roxan, "The Distribution of Roman Military Diplomas," *Epigr. Stud.* 12 (1981): 265–308.

(military treasury), out of which legionary *praemia* were paid, was an actual building, or structure, situated on the Capitol:[34] "Copied down and checked from the bronze tablet which has been put up in Rome in front of the *aerarium militare*, on the statue base of the Claudii Marcelli."

Even if the valuable discussion of this text by Mireille Corbier does not succeed in pointing to an exact localisation for the *aerarium militare*,[35] its importance is none the less clear. As regards the older "treasury," the Aerarium Saturni, situated (in some way which is not clear), in the ancient temple of Saturn, it is certain that it retained until the imperial period its archaic function as a storehouse of valuables and as an archive of official documents. But although we have some evidence on this point, for instance a letter of Pliny the Younger,[36] it remains difficult to conceptualise the functioning of the Aerarium Saturni as a government "office," or to understand the role of the prefects of the Aerarium Saturni. So far as I know, since my article of 1964,[37] the study of the two treasuries has been pursued systematically only by Mireille Corbier, and even then primarily as regards the prosopography of the relevant officials.[38] The continued existence, at the centre of a vast empire, of an institution whose fundamental character was strikingly archaic serves to raise once again the question of the role of the city of Rome within the imperial financial system. Was it the case, or not, that vast numbers of coins were regularly transported to Rome, and then re-exported to the provinces? The question applies to the ancient Aerarium Saturni. But, now that we know that the *aerarium militare* was also some sort of physical structure situated on the Capitol, we have to ask ourselves whether we should conceive of it too as a sort of government "office," concerned with paper transactions; or was it too a physical "treasury" or storehouse, to which coin was brought from the provinces and then re-exported, to be paid out as *praemia* to discharged legionaries? What does seem inconceivable is that each discharged legionary would have had to come to Rome from the province where he had been stationed in order to receive his *praemium*.

At any rate, for all the complex questions relating to the stockpiling at

34. Published by S. Dušanic, "A Military Diploma of AD 65," *Germania* 56 (1978): 461–65; *AE* 1978, no. 658; M. M. Roxan, *Roman Military Diplomas, 1978–1984* (1985), no. 79.

35. M. Corbier, "L'aerarium militaire sur le Capitole," *Cahiers du groupe de recherches sur armée romaine et les provinces* 3 (1984): 147–60.

36. Pliny, *Epp.* 1, 10.

37. F. Millar, "The Aerarium and Its Officials under the Empire," *JRS* 54 (1964): 33–40 (chapter 4 in this volume).

38. M. Corbier, *L'aerarium Saturni et l'aerarium militare: administration et prosopographie sénatoriale* (1974).

Rome of enormous quantities of ore, we need to refer once again to an important paper by Mireille Corbier, who makes the essential comparison between treasures and storehouses (*horrea*);[39] that is to say that she has seen that coins too were a type of product, which needed to be manufactured, transported, and stored.

However, even if we leave aside the difficult question of the *praemia* of the legionaries, it is obvious that it must have been necessary to maintain stocks of coin in Rome, sufficient to provide not only for the annual pay of the praetorians while in service, but for the *praemia* which they received on discharge. Given the relatively small numbers of praetorian soldiers, probably some 5,000, and then 10,000 in the reign of Septimius Severus,[40] the sums necessary for paying their *praemia* will have been correspondingly modest. But we have to remember that the *praemium* received by a praetorian was higher, and that it was paid after a shorter period, sixteen years. In relation to the numbers serving, therefore, payments will have been more frequent, and the chances of the individual surviving to the relevant age will have been higher.

As regards the praetorians, there was another reason why it will always have been necessary to have available very large stocks of coin in Rome, namely *donativa*, which could on occasion be as high as 5,000 denarii per praetorian soldier. For example, after the murder of Geta in 211, Caracalla made a payment of 2,500 denarii to each praetorian,[41] hence a total of at least 25 million denarii, or, if the payment were made in gold, about 1 million aurei. If we accept the suggestion made by Andrew Burnett (text to n. 23 above), that was the equivalent of the typical annual production of aurei for the whole Empire.

These extended preliminaries have been necessary, I suggest, in order to locate the imperial distributions of cash to the plebs of Rome (*congiaria*) in the wider context of the financial and monetary system of the Empire. As I indicated earlier (text to n. 21 above), I would like to focus attention on the reign of Septimius Severus, above all because it is in relation to the celebration of the tenth anniversary of his rule in A.D. 202 that Cassius Dio offers us the most detailed description of such a distribution:[42] "On the tenth anniversary of his reign Severus offered to all those who were in receipt of the [regu-

---

39. M. Corbier, "Trésors et greniers dans la Rome impériale (Ier–IIIe siècles)," in *Le système palatial en Orient, en Grèce et à Rome* (*Actes du Colloque de Strasbourg*, 1985) (1987), 411–43.

40. See n. 21 above.

41. Herodian 4, 4, 7; for other figures see J. B. Campbell, *The Emperor and the Roman Army* (1984), 170–71.

42. Cassius Dio 77, 1, 1 (ed. Boissevain, III, 357).

lar] distributions of corn, and also to the praetorian soldiers, chrysoi [aurei]
equal in number to the years of his rule . . . on this munificence [*dorea*] 50
million drachmai were expended." It is clear from this that the sum due was
calculated in aurei, each person receiving ten, while the list of those entitled
was drawn directly from the list of those in receipt of the regular monthly
distributions of corn. Leaving aside the praetorians, Dio's figures imply that
the list contained 200,000 persons. His description does not of course tell us
in which type of coin payment was made: 10 aurei each, or 250 denarii, or
1,000 sestertii?

At any rate, while Dio explains the rationale for the level of distribution
in terms of aurei (one per head for each year of the reign), he expresses the
total in drachmai = denarii. The total given, 50 million, is very significant,
if we put it into relation with the estimate by Keith Hopkins of the total
annual revenue of the Empire, perhaps some 250 million denarii, or 1 billion
sestertii, *per annum* in this period.[43] Hence the distribution made to the plebs
of Rome in A.D. 202 may have been the equivalent of a fifth of the public
revenues for a year. It is certainly essential to use the term "equivalent," for in
principle such a *liberalitas* was not drawn from public funds, but had the character of a personal gift from the emperor.[44] There is a clear contrast with the
frumentum publicum (public corn), originally established by the legislation of
Clodius in 58 B.C. — a contrast which remains, even though it was precisely
the recipients of the monthly public corn ration who were designated as the
objects of the Emperor's ad hoc demonstration of liberality in cash.

Here too, as regards the distribution of coin, we have to try to envisage the
physical processes involved. Was the *liberalitas* paid in silver denarii? In that
case we would have to remember that 50 million denarii would have weighed
188,000 kilograms. To transport such a mass of coin at one moment, if that
had been necessary, would have required 390 heavy wagons, each drawn by
4 oxen, hence 1,560 oxen in all.

Suppose by contrast that the payment were literally made in aurei: 2 million aurei (twice the entire annual production at the level suggested by
Andrew Burnett), each weighing some 7.20 grams, would have weighed
about 14,400 kilograms. Therefore, some 30 heavy wagons and 120 oxen
would have been required to transport it. It does therefore seem quite likely
that the actual payment corresponded in form to the symbolic basis of the
occasion: one aureus per year for each of the ten years of the reign, paid to

43. Hopkins (n. 15), 117, 119.

44. For the ideology of imperial largesse, see esp. P. Veyne, *Le pain et le cirque: sociologie
historique d'un pluralisme politique* (1976), 534–730, translated, and somewhat abbreviated, as
Bread and Circuses: Historical Sociology and Political Pluralism (1990), 292–482.

each of the 200,000 recipients of the *frumentum publicum*. For otherwise the payment, if made in the form of 250 denarii per head, would have involved a weight of just under a kilogram for each person.

But even in the former case, the use of aurei, we need to try to envisage just what will have been involved in preparing a stock of 2 million aurei for distribution. First, if newly minted coins were to be used, it may have been necessary to triple the size of the normal output of aurei: for a *congiarium* was a special occasion, over and above the normal uses to which aurei were put, whatever these were. Alternatively, if the distribution were to depend on the stock of aurei currently in circulation, it would have been necessary to take steps to collect a sufficient quantity, perhaps starting several years in advance, to transport them to Rome, and to stockpile them. Severus was absent from Rome from 197 to mid-202,[45] so this process, if it were needed, may have taken place largely in his absence, with reserves building up as against his return, and the planned *liberalitas*. Alternatively, there may have been vast stocks of coin already to hand in Rome. But where? Possibly in the temple of Saturn—but, as indicated above, the *liberalitas* was supposed to be a private gift from the emperor. Alternatively, it is possible that the coins were stored in the *apothekai* (magazines) for Egyptian and Arabian products which, according to Cassius Dio, were situated between the temple of Peace and the Palatine.[46] Unfortunately this is one of the areas of the centre of Rome whose character and function in the imperial period remains particularly mysterious.[47] Or, as Denis van Berchem once suggested, were the stocks of coin kept somewhere in the Forum of Trajan?[48] Quite strong support for this hypothesis is offered by the reference in the *Fragmenta Vaticana* to "the imperial treasurers who have their positions in the Forum of Trajan";[49] it is surely relevant that, according to a scholion on Juvenal (10, 24), senators had *arcae* (chests) there for the safe-keeping of silver and coin. Moreover, the *Historia Augusta* records that Commodus, when he gave a *congiarium* as a boy, presided at the distribution while taking his seat in the "basilica of Trajan," which certainly means the basilica of Trajan's Forum.[50] It would then be possible to

45. See H. Halfmann, *Itinera Principum* (1986), 217–18.

46. Cassius Dio 72, 24, 1. For the stores of valuables and edible products in the possession of the emperor, see Millar (n. 25), 144–53.

47. See now E. M. Steinby, ed., *Lexicon Topographicum Urbis Romae* III (1996), s.v. "Horrea piperateria" and "Horrea Vespasiana."

48. Van Berchem (n. 10), 165.

49. Ulpian, *Frag. Vat.* 134: *Arcari Caesariani, qui in foro Traiani habent stationes.*

50. *HA, V. Commodi* 2, 1: *adhuc in praetexta puerili congiarium dedit atque ipse in basilica Traiani praesedit.*

imagine that the coins required had been stockpiled, for a shorter or longer period, somewhere in the Forum complex, perhaps not far from the *tribunal* on which, as we know from representations on coins, the emperor would take his seat. But, even as regards very short-distance movements such as these, it should still be stressed that bringing out some 14,000 kilograms of gold coins must have meant some 350 to 400 sack-loads to be carried by porters (*saccarii*) on their backs.

However, that may be enough of these necessarily speculative calculations. It may be more appropriate to conclude by recalling that, in his book on the distributions of corn and money to the Roman plebs, published more than sixty years ago, Denis van Berchem expressed a hope which we would have to admit has not yet been fulfilled: that a history of the imperial finances might soon be published which would provide a new conception of this still obscure aspect of Roman institutions.[51] Such a study is still awaited, and the Empire continues to keep its secrets.

51. Van Berchem (n. 10), 127.

CHAPTER SIX

Epictetus and the Imperial Court*

What we know of Roman political life under the early Empire we owe mostly to senatorial writers, and to an equestrian, Suetonius; a single imperial freedman, Phlegon of Tralles, has left some scraps of information about the court in his own time and before.[1] It is therefore worth paying some attention when we have a lengthy text which reproduces the observations on human life and fortune of a man who was himself the slave of an imperial freedman. Epictetus has been little used as a historical source; it is the aim of this chapter to bring out both the extent and the value of his references to Roman society and politics in his own time.

Before we can assess the value of these references, we must examine both the experience on which they are based and the authenticity of the text in which they occur. Epictetus originated from Hierapolis in Phrygia; according to an inscription he was born a slave.[2] Either by birth or sale, he belonged to Epaphroditus, the freedman and *a libellis* (the official in charge of petitions) of Nero, who after Nero's death survived unharmed until relegated, and then (in 95) executed, by Domitian.[3] Whether Epaphroditus remained *a libellis* under the Flavians is not clear, though the likelihood is that he did not. This

---

*First published in *JRS* 55 (1965): 141–48. An earlier version of this chapter was read to the Oxford Branch of the Classical Association on 12 November 1964. I should like to thank those present for the helpful discussion which followed, and also Professor Sir Ronald Syme for his advice and assistance, especially on points of prosopography. My quotations of passages in English owe much to the Loeb Epictetus by W. A. Oldfather (1925, 1928).

1. Jacoby, *FGrH* 257, F 36, XIV; F, IV.

2. For the full testimony, see the Teubner ed. H. Schenkl (1894), XIV–XXIII, and *PIR²* E 74.

3. *PIR²* E 69. Dio 67, 14, 4–5, dates the execution to 95.

view would be supported if we could be sure that it was the same Epaphroditus who encouraged Josephus in the writing of his *Antiquities*, completed
in 93–94. For Josephus describes this man as "taking special pleasure in the
experiences of history, conversant as he himself has been with large affairs
and varying turns of fortune."[4]

It is unfortunately not clear whether Epictetus was in Rome as early as
the reign of Nero. He does however refer in his Dissertations to a number
of incidents in that reign—the reply of Demetrius the Cynic when threatened with death by Nero,[5] a discussion between Paconius Agrippinus and
Florus (L. Mestrius Florus, the patron of Plutarch?)[6] as to whether the latter
should take part in a theatrical performance put on by Nero,[7] the scene at
the execution of Plautius Lateranus in 65,[8] a conversation between Thrasea
Paetus and Musonius Rufus on the dangers of death and exile,[9] or the calm
reaction of Paconius Agrippinus to the news of his exile in 66.[10] There are
also some stories (discussed below) about his master, Epaphroditus, one of
which is explicitly dated to before the execution of Lateranus. Such stories
might indicate that Epictetus was already in Rome; but, especially as most
of them belong in the Stoic martyr tradition, they cannot prove it.

All that we can be sure of is that he was in Rome in the Flavian period,
when he was a friend and disciple of Musonius Rufus.[11] He tells an anecdote
of Musonius' reaction to the news of Galba's death[12] and records a conversation between himself and Musonius in which they referred to the burning
of the Capitol in 69 (or possibly the burning in 80),[13] and another where they
talked about the cruelty of Epaphroditus.[14] Then there are a couple of refer-

---

4. Jos. *AJ* 1, 8. The question of the identification cannot be formally decided. Th. Frank-
fort, "La date de l'autobiographie de Flavius Josèphe et des oeuvres de Justus de Tibériade,"
Rev. Beige de Phil. et d'Hist. 39 (1961): 52, esp. 56–57, shows that there are no firm chronological grounds for dismissing the identification.

5. 1, 25, 22. This could have been on any one of a number of occasions between 60 and
66. See *PIR²* D 39.

6. *PIR¹* M 380; P-W, s.v. "Mestrius" (3).

7. 1, 2, 12–18.

8. 1, 1, 19. Cf. Tac., *Ann.* 15, 60, 1–2.

9. 1, 1, 26–27.

10. 1, 1, 28–32 = fr. 21 Schenkl. Compare Tac., *Ann.* 16, 33, 3 and see *PIR¹* P 16.

11. See Cora E. Lutz, "Musonius Rufus, 'The Roman Socrates,'" *Yale Class. Stud.* 10
(1947): 3, esp. 8–9.

12. 3, 15, 14.

13. 1, 7, 32. Cic., *de amicitia* 37 and Plut., *Tib. Grac.* 20, 4, quoted by Souilhé ad loc., do
not suffice to prove that "burning the Capitol" was a proverbial expression.

14. 1, 9, 29–30. This could of course date to before the banishment of Musonius in 65.

ences to another pupil of Musonius, Euphrates the philosopher and rhetorician, though neither of them clearly indicates personal acquaintance.[15] He also quotes verbatim a dialogue (not mentioned in any other source) between Helvidius Priscus and Vespasian, who had ordered him not to attend the Senate:

> "It is in your power not to allow me to be member of the Senate, but so long as I am one I must attend its meetings." "Very well then," he [Vespasian] said, "when you attend, hold your peace." "Do not ask me for my opinion and I will hold my peace." "But I must ask for your opinion." "And I too must answer what seems right." "But if you speak, I shall kill you."[16]

The reference to Vespasian asking opinions (*sententiae*) shows that the dialogue, if authentic, took place during one of Vespasian's consulates (probably 71 or 72, since Helvidius seems to have been executed fairly early in the reign). Then Epictetus mentions the banishment under Domitian of Gratilla (Verulana Gratilla, possibly the wife of Arulenus Rusticus) and the courage of another woman who persisted in sending a boatload of supplies to her.[17]

This period of Epictetus' life ended when Domitian expelled the philosophers from Rome, probably in 92–93.[18] Epictetus retired to Nicopolis in Epirus, where he remained. It should be noted that there is no evidence as to whether Epictetus had previously been manumitted by Epaphroditus, or as to what his status was at this time or later.

It was at Nicopolis that he had as his pupil, among many others, Arrian; and it is to the four books which remain of Arrian's transcript of Epictetus' homilies and dialogues that we owe the vast majority of what we know about him.[19] In the letter to Lucius Gellius (perhaps L. Gellius Menander, a prominent Corinthian of the Hadrianic period),[20] which forms the preface to the existing text, Arrian claims that he wrote down Epictetus' words exactly as they were spoken and deliberately avoided any process of literary composition.[21] Internal evidence supports this claim. For instance, the

15. 3, 15, 8; 4, 8, 17–20.

16. 1, 2, 19–21. Note 4, 1, 123, a reference to the condemnation of Helvidius. *PIR*² H 59 notes neither passage.

17. 2, 7, 8.

18. For a discussion of the date, see A. N. Sherwin-White, *JRS* 47 (1957): 126–27.

19. For a discussion of the tradition about Epictetus' works, see vol. I of the Budé text by J. Souilhé (Paris, 1943), XII–XIII.

20. See *PIR*² G 132 and *Corinth* VIII.2, no. 93.

21. *Praef.* "I have not composed these *Words of Epictetus* as one might be said to 'com-

Dissertations use the *koine* whereas elsewhere Arrian writes in Attic,[22] and the homilies in the first book at least come in chronological order.[23] Epictetus' teaching, which seems to have centred round the reading out of passages from Stoic writers, sometimes took the form of homilies on general topics, sometimes of homilies to, or dialogues with, one of his regular pupils or a visitor from Rome or elsewhere, and sometimes of imaginary dialogues in which Epictetus himself took both parts.[24]

The date of the Dissertations (given that we do not know how long Arrian stayed) can be established within a year or two. Firstly, we know the reign from a comparison Epictetus makes between the coinage of Nero and of Trajan.[25] Then, giving examples of major wars, Epictetus ends "and now the Romans against the Getae"[26] — that should mean at least that he was speaking before the outbreak of the Parthian war in 113. Moreover a number of passages (discussed below) indicate that the time was one at which the emperor was in Rome (so 99–101, 102–4, or late 106–early 113). But the vital passage is the long dialogue between Epictetus, and a Roman visitor called Maximus, described as "commissioner" (*diorthōtes*) and "judge" (*kritēs*) of the Hellenes. There is no concrete argument against identifying this man with the Maximus to whom Pliny writes in *Ep.* 8, 24, about his appointment "to set in order the conditions of the free cities" (*ad ordinandum statum liberarum civitatum*) in Greece.[27] Book VIII of the letters belongs in about 108,[28] and this letter should be fairly close in date to the dialogue, which implies clearly that Maximus is on the way to take up his post. Moreover, Arrian was suffect consul about 130;[29] if this was at the standard age of forty-two or so,[30] Arrian

---

pose' books of this kind, nor have I of my own act published them to the world; indeed, I acknowledge that I have not 'composed' them at all. But whatever I heard him say I used to write down, word for word, as best I could, endeavouring to preserve it as a memorial for my own future use, of his way of thinking and the frankness of his speech."

22. See K. Hartmann, "Arrian und Epiktet," *Neue Jahrbücher* 15 (1905): 248, on 275.

23. See 1, 18, 15 and 29, 21 and Hartmann (n. 22), 259. Cf. n. 69 and the text to it.

24. See I. Bruns, *De Scholae Epicteti* (1897) and, for the form of the Discourses, see Th. Colardeau, *Étude zur Épictète* (1903), 283–84.

25. 4, 5, 17–18. See T. O. Mabbott, "Epictetus and Nero's Coinage," *Class. Phil.* 36 (1941): 398.

26. 2, 22, 22.

27. 3, 7. Compare M. N. Tod, "The *Corrector* Maximus," *Anatolian Studies Presented to W. M. Buckler* (1939), 333, esp. 336–37.

28. See R. Syme, *Tacitus* (1958), 661.

29. *PIR*² F 219.

30. Suggested by Syme (n. 28), *App.* 18, and fully documented by J. Morris, "Leges Annales under the Principate," *Listy Filologické* 87 (1964): 316.

will have been about twenty, just the age one would expect, when he sat at the feet of Epictetus.

This then is the setting in which Epictetus was speaking, Nicopolis about the year 108. Even Stoics are human, and one cannot but note how often Epictetus' mind turned to Rome and Roman life, which he had left some fifteen years before. He mentions details of topography, the Aqua Marcia[31] or the altar of Febris on the Palatine,[32] scenes from the circus or the theatre — as when a man covered his head while the horse he backed was running and had to be revived with sponges when it won[33] — or from the Saturnalia.[34] Then he refers to the freeing of a slave before the praetor (and payment of the *uicesima libertatis*, that is, the 5 per cent tax paid on setting a slave free),[35] to meeting a consul in the street[36] or to a man's rejoicing on being elected tribune:

> "He has been honoured with a tribunate," someone says. All who meet him offer their congratulations; one man kisses him on the eyes, another on the neck, his slaves kiss his hands. He goes home; he finds lamps being lighted. He climbs up the capitol and offers sacrifice.[37]

The scene he portrays of a host boring his guests with accounts of his heroic deeds on campaign in Moesia[38] might reflect life in Rome — but equally well anywhere in the Empire. But he also mentions explicitly how Roman ladies of easy virtue kept copies of Plato's *Republic* because he advocated the sharing of wives,[39] or relates an incident when he was in company with the Roman philosopher Italicus.[40] He also describes how a bold philosopher could approach a man of consular rank and question him about the care of his soul until the man would be provoked to strike him — "this was the pursuit I too was very fond of once upon a time, before I fell to my present state."[41]

At one point, talking about advertising for patients by doctors in Rome, he

---

31. 2, 16, 30–31.

32. 1, 19, 6. See K. Latte, *Römische Religionsgeschichte* (1960), 52.

33. 1, 11, 27. See also 1, 29, 37 — gladiators owned by Caesar begging to fight.

34. 1, 25, 8; 29, 31; 4, 1, 58.

35. 2, 1, 26–27. On the *vicesima libertatis*, see also 4, 1, 33.

36. 3, 3, 15 and 17.

37. 1, 19, 24.

38. 1, 25, 15.

39. Fr. 15 Schenkl.

40. 3, 8, 7. It is not quite impossible (but not particularly probable) that this was the poet, Silius Italicus. See Schanz-Hosius II[4] (1935), 526–27.

41. 2, 12, 17–25.

complains in the manner of exiles that things have changed since his time;[42] his testimony is perhaps equally out of date in a passage—which should reflect conditions under Domitian—where he describes how soldiers act as spies in Rome: wearing civilian dress, they encourage people to speak ill of the emperor and then arrest them.[43] The same should be true when he speaks of the possibility of being forced to kiss the feet of Caesar.[44] On the other hand, we find him mentioning adoption by the emperor—"yet, if Caesar adopts you, no one will be able to endure your conceit."[45] The reference, and the tone of it, is striking enough when made in the reign of Trajan. But, more specifically than that, in 108 Hadrian was suffect consul, and during his consulship (according to the *Historia Augusta*) was told by Licinius Sura that Trajan was going to adopt him.[46] Do Epictetus' words reflect contemporary rumour and speculation on the issue?

Since Rome and Roman political life loomed so large in the mind of Epictetus, it is not surprising that when he came to discourse to his pupils on what men imagined to be good fortune or bad, freedom or slavery, he should frequently use as examples cases involving the favour or disfavour of the emperor. Some of these are real incidents, some imaginary or typical cases. We also find him on occasion, as with Maximus, in conversation with real individuals passing through, or living in, Nicopolis, and discussing with them their attitude to the emperor and to the punishments or rewards which he had to offer. In setting this evidence out it will be easiest to start with those items which involve imperial slaves and freedmen, and move on to friends of Caesar (*amici Caesaris*), senators and equestrians, and finally provincials. It is of course necessary to remember the advantages and disadvantages of Epictetus' viewpoint as the slave of an imperial freedman, and the fact that his own experience of Rome was some fifteen years out of date.[47]

First we have two stories about Epaphroditus as *a libellis*. The first relates how Epaphroditus approached Plautius Lateranus to enquire about some concern of his, and got the reply, "If I want anything I will speak to your

42. 3, 23, 27: "I have told you, brother, how I climbed up to the crest of the hill; well now, I begin to be besieged again."

43. 4, 13, 5.

44. 4, 1, 17. See Pliny, *Pan.* 24, 2 comparing Domitian and Trajan on this point.

45. 1, 3, 2.

46. *HA, Had.* 3, 10. See *FIRA*² A 184. But cf. Syme (n. 28), 232–34.

47. For a good analysis of the extent to which Epictetus' teaching reflects his experience of Rome under Domitian, see C. G. Starr, "Epictetus and the Tyrant," *Class. Phil.* 44 (1949): 20, which I ought to have known before writing this article, but did not.

master."[48] The story is only brought in as an example of exceptional courage—and thus illustrates perfectly the power of freedmen in Nero's reign.
The second story shows a man clinging in tears to the knees of Epaphroditus and exclaiming that he has only a million and a half sesterces left to his
name.[49] To Epictetus this illustrates the absurd lack of proportion induced by
the luxuriousness of Roman life, as compared with the modest manners of
Nicopolis. Perhaps, however, the man was a senator who needed Epaphroditus' help in appealing for a subvention from Nero to maintain the necessary
census of 1 million or 1.2 million sesterces.[50]

The third story about Epaphroditus seems to come from the period when
he was no longer *a libellis*. "Epaphroditus owned a certain cobbler whom
he sold off as being no good at his job. Then by some chance the man was
bought by one of the members of Caesar's household [*Caesariani*] and became the emperor's cobbler. You should have seen how Epaphroditus paid
court to him—'What is the good Felicio doing, I pray you?' And then if
anyone asked us, 'What is Epaphroditus doing?' he was told, 'He is in consultation with Felicio.'"[51] The point that the accident of proximity to the
emperor might lend a fortuitous importance to the occupants of the most
humble posts had been made even more forcibly in the preceding passage.
"If only it were only the tyrants and not their *cubicularii* [chamberlains] also
[who have to be courted]. How is it that a man can suddenly gain a reputation for sagacity when Caesar puts him in charge of the imperial lavatory?
How is it that we at once start saying 'Felicio spoke so wisely to me'? If only
the man might be deposed from the lavatory, and seem a fool once more."[52]
This is given as a typical instance, not as a historical anecdote. There seems
to be no other evidence for the post in question (which it is implied would
be held by one of the chamberlains).

Then the friends of Caesar—the type of worldly success on which Epictetus pours most scorn. For instance, he represents a man contemplating how
he can best ensure his safety (using the image of a traveller fearing attack by
robbers). "What shall I do? I shall become a friend of Caesar. While I am
his companion no one will injure me. But before I can become that, how

48. 1, 1, 20. For the justifiable emendation of the text to make Lateranus the author of
this remark, see the Budé edition.

49. 1, 26, 11–12.

50. Dio 54, 26, 3 gives 1 million, Suet., *Div. Aug.* 41, 1.2 million. For subventions by
Nero, Suet., *Nero* 10; Tac., *Ann.* 13, 34, 2–3, cf. 15, 53, 2.

51. 1, 19, 19–21. An imperial *sutor* (cobbler) is attested on *ILS* 1787 (A.D. 13).

52. 1, 19, 17–18. On the power of members of the imperial *familia*, note also 4, 13, 22.

much must I suffer and endure, how often must I be robbed by how many! And if I do become his friend, he too is mortal."[53] Similarly he represents a man, the holder of two consulships, protesting that he at least is free— "I am of free birth, a senator, a friend of Caesar, I have been consul and I own many slaves"—but even he can be compelled by Caesar.[54] Then there is a discussion about what true misfortune is—not to be an friend of Caesar? But Caesar's friend knows neither security nor freedom. He cannot sleep for people coming one after another to say that Caesar is awake, Caesar is coming out; he has failed, that is, to be present in the early morning to be admitted with the other friends.[55] If he is not invited to dine by Caesar, he is slighted; if he is, he dines like a slave at his master's table. What is he afraid of—a whipping? Nothing so ignoble. He is afraid of losing his head.[56]

Comparable with this is what Epictetus says to a prominent Roman called Naso who has come with his son to visit him[57]—"What could anyone imagine you to want. You are rich, you have children, a wife, and many slaves; *Caesar knows you,* you have many friends in Rome, you can perform your duties and return kindness with kindness and injury with injury"—but he lacks the really important things.[58]

Then there were ordinary senators and equestrians, who depended on the emperor for promotion and benefits, or feared his punishment or displeasure. Caesar is men's master—for men fear not Caesar, but death, exile, confiscation, imprisonment, disenfranchisement; they do not love Caesar—unless (he adds in parenthesis) he is a man of great merit—but they love wealth, a tribunate, a praetorship, a consulate.[59] The desire for office is an easy target: "For the sake of these mighty and dignified offices and honours you kiss the hands of another man's slaves—and are thus the slaves of men who are not free themselves."[60] Then we get a more general picture of ambition (*ambitus*) and its rewards: "If you wish to be consul you must give up your sleep, run

53. 4, 1, 95.

54. 4, 1, 6–13.

55. Cf. Suet., *Div. Vesp.* 21; Pliny, *Ep.* 3; 5, 9.

56. 4, 1, 45–48.

57. Almost certainly not the young Iulius Naso, whose candidature for *honores* (public office) had been supported a couple of years earlier by Pliny, *Ep.* 6, 6. But he might be the proconsul of Africa about 107, C. Cornelius Rarus Sextius Na[so?], possibly the same as a suffect consul of 93. See Syme (n. 28), 638, 805. Epictetus' words would suit a man of that status.

58. 2, 14, 18.

59. 4, 1, 60.

60. 4, 1, 148.

around, kiss men's hands, rot away at other men's doors . . . send presents to many and daily *xenia* [guest-gifts] to some. And what is the result? Twelve bundles of rods, sitting three or four times on the tribunal, giving games in the Circus, and distributing meals in little baskets"—*sportulae*, that is.[61] Epictetus' picture forms an admirable complement to what we know from Pliny, especially *Ep*. VI, 19, about senatorial canvassing.

Elsewhere Epictetus expatiates on the worthlessness of what the emperor has to give, or to refuse. Let the chamberlains bar you access to the emperor; if you do not care about entering, you are not really excluded. A man is given a province or a procuratorship—can he be given the wisdom to exercise it? We then get a comparison of the distribution of provinces, praetorships, and consulships with the custom of scattering figs and nuts for children to fight over.[62]

These are mere abstract examples. More interesting is Epictetus' dialogue with, or homily to, Maximus the commissioner (*corrector*).[63] First Epictetus demonstrates that Maximus does not really follow his pretended Epicurean principles. If he really consults only his pleasure, he can rob the Greeks as he wishes; he has powerful friends in Rome, and the Greeks are too feeble to accuse him anyway.[64] Then there is a fragment of dialogue. "What need have you of philosophical doctrines?" "But I am judge over the Greeks." "Do you know how to judge? What caused you to know that?" "Caesar wrote *codicilli* (a letter of appointment) for me." "But how did you come to be a judge? Whose hand did you kiss—Symphorus' or Numenius'? [evidently imperial freedmen, whether real or notional is not clear].[65] Before whose bedroom door did you sleep? To whom did you send presents? After all, do you not see that the office of judge is worth no more than Numenius is?"[66] One may contrast Pliny's reference to the same office: "You bring with you the excellent reputation you won during your quaestorship . . . you bring the emperor's recommendation [*testimonium*] and experience as tribune, praetor, and as holder of your present mission [*legatio*], granted as a prize."[67]

61. 4, 10, 20–21. On senatorial ambition, cf. 1, 25, 26–27; 4, 1, 55 and 173.

62. 4, 7, 19–24. There are references to the terrors of audience with Caesar in 1, 30, 7 and 4, 7, 1.

63. 3, 7. The view of Hartmann (n. 22), 261, that the dialogue is a fiction narrated by Epictetus and relating to an incident some years back, involves believing that Arrian's introduction to it is straightforwardly false. There is no basis for such a belief.

64. 3, 7, 13.

65. Though *ILS* 1684 reveals a freedman of Trajan, M. Ulpius Symphorus.

66. 3, 7, 29–31.

67. *Ep*. 8, 24, 8.

With that we can come to a story related by Epictetus, one of the best and
most revealing anecdotes in the work. It concerns a man older than himself,
Epictetus says, who had earlier passed through Nicopolis on his way back
from exile (the occasion was very probably the return of exiles in 96 after the
abolition of the *acta* [official acts] of Domitian). Speaking to Epictetus he had
inveighed against his former life and expressed his resolve to pass the rest of
his time in peace and quiet. "As soon as you catch a whiff of Rome," Epictetus had said, "you will forget all this. And if admission [*parodos*] to the court
is granted, in you will rush, rejoicing and thanking God." The man denied
it. But before he even reached Rome, messages (*pinakides*) from the emperor
reached him. He forgot his resolution, and gained post after post. He is now,
says Epictetus, *praefectus annonae* (the prefect in charge of the supply of corn
and other food) in Rome.[68]

It is unfortunately difficult to identify the prefect in office about 108. Sulpicius Similis, later praetorian prefect at the end of Trajan's reign and under
Hadrian, would be suitable, in that he rose from being a mere centurion at
some point in Trajan's reign[69] to the prefecture of the Annona and then, between March and August 107, to that of Egypt.[70] The identification is not
quite impossible, though Sulpicius' period at the Annona would be a little
too early for comfort—or might the first book, which contains this story,
belong in 107, and the third, which has the dialogue with Maximus, in say
the winter[71] of 107–8? The difficulty would remain that the man in Epictetus seems to be of higher rank than centurion. Otherwise we know only of
Rutilius Lupus who is attested in this post on an inscription datable to between 103 and 111,[72] before moving to Egypt in 113. But if an identification
is difficult, there is a slight compensation in that the following passage portrays the prefect receiving a petition to allow the export of some grain, "I
beseech you to allow me to export a small quantity of corn"[73]—which adds
a little to the rather scanty evidence on his functions.

It was one of the striking peculiarities of the Empire as a political system
that the personal judgements and actions of the emperor affected not only

68. 1, 10, 2–6.

69. Dio 69, 19, 1.

70. P-W, s.v. "Sulpicius" (104). See A. Stein, *Die Praefekten von Ägypten* (1950), 53–55.

71. Note in 3, 7, 3 (Maximus) "during the winter," and 3, 9, 3 (the man from Cnossus—
see below) "after the winter."

72. *AE* 1940, 38. See Stein (n. 70), 55–58.

73. 1, 10, 10. The previous sentence perhaps also refers to the prefects of the Annona—
"For what else do they do but all day long cast up accounts, dispute, consult about a bit of
grain, a bit of land . . ."

the members of the governing class in Rome but a wide range of individuals in the provinces (especially in the Greek East, where contacts with Rome and the court were so much closer). Of this too we get evidence in Epictetus.[74] There is for instance a dialogue—probably, but not certainly, one of those invented as an example by Epictetus, since there is no setting or introduction—between Epictetus and a man on his way to Rome to stand trial before Caesar on a capital charge. Epictetus replies with some rather inadequate comfort: he too risks his life from earthquakes at Nicopolis, the man is equally in danger of his life crossing the Adriatic, banishment is merely not living in Rome, and if he does not wish to go to Gyarus, suicide is possible.[75]

Then we have another dialogue—this time clearly historical—between Epictetus and another man on his way to Rome to appear before the emperor.[76] The man's aim was to get himself elected *prostatēs* of the Cnossians, that is, patron of the Roman colony of Cnossus—Colonia Iulia Nobilis Cnossus—founded by Octavian probably in 36. It happens that we know that such an office really existed, for a Latin inscription from Cnossus shows a man who was a *duovir* there, *flamen* (priest) of Vespasian and also patron of the colony (*patro[nus Coloniae]*).[77] It emerges from his conversation with Epictetus that the would-be patron was the perfect type of a local magnate under the Empire. He was a rich man, who possessed land and cattle, and gold and silver plate. In his youth he had studied rhetoric, had pleaded cases himself, and had then entered political life and held various offices. Now he wanted this further honour and was sailing to Rome—changing ships at Nicopolis—at his own expense, in winter, to fight the case. Evidently there was some opposition; the circumstances were perhaps not unlike, for instance, the business recorded on a Lycian inscription from the reign of Antoninus Pius: a Lyciarch, Jason, son of Nicostratus, was voted honours by the *koinon* (common council of a league of cities), then accused of something unspecified by one Moles. An ambassador was sent to the emperor to testify to the virtues of Jason; and the emperor wrote back to the *koinon* evidently approving the honours.[78]

That the emperor himself was concerned in the Cnossus case only emerges towards the end of the dialogue, when Epictetus compares the man's anxi-

74. Note, for instance, 2, 13, 11 which lists among unworthy causes of anxiety "about what Caesar will think."

75. 2, 6, 20–23. On trial and condemnation by Caesar, see also 2, 19, 17–18 and 3, 8, 2. Banishment to Gyarus is a recurrent theme: 1, 25, 19–20; 3, 24, 100; 4, 4, 34.

76. 3, 9.

77. *AE* 1908, 215 = *Inscr. Cret.* I, VIII, 54.

78. *IGR* III, 704, Col. III.

eties with his own real freedom—"patron or not patron, what do I care? But you care. I am richer than you are; I am not going to worry about what Caesar is going to think of me."[79]

Even outside the considerable range of trifling local matters which a Roman emperor found himself dealing with personally, his existence overshadowed and influenced the forms of local life. Thus it is not irrelevant to mention some illustrations Epictetus gives of life and politics in Nicopolis. All men are slaves in reality, he says—and quotes the customary acclamation of the Nicopolites, "Yea, by the fortune [*tychē*] of Caesar we are free men."[80] The paradox needs no comment. Then we get a vivid picture of the procurator of Epirus appearing in the theatre at Nicopolis, showing undignified fervour in applauding—supported by a claque of slaves—a comic actor, and being abused by the mob for it. He complains to Epictetus, who replies that if the people see their governor, the "friend" and procurator of Caesar, showing his feelings by shouting and jumping up and down in the theatre, they will do likewise.[81] The scene, and Epictetus' view of it, offers a complement to, and contrast with, that in Saint John, when the crowd shouts at Pilate, "If you release him, you are no friend of Caesar."[82]

As for the procurator of Epirus, the only known holder of the post from this period is Cn. Cornelius Pulcher, who was there sometime between 103 and 114.[83] He is an interesting figure, the descendant of a distinguished family at Epidaurus, military tribune of the *legio IV Scythica* in Syria,[84] duovir at Corinth, *agōnothetēs* (president) of three series of games at Corinth, the *Traianeia*, *Isthmia*, and *Caesaraea*, and of the *Sebasteia* and *Asclepeia* at Epidaurus, *archiereus* (high priest) of Greece, and Helladarch for life of the *koinon* of the Achaeans (all before he was procurator of Epirus); later he was *iuridicus* (judicial commissioner) in Egypt and priest of Hadrianos Panhellenios. An identification with the procurator of about 108 is mere speculation. But if the procurator whom Epictetus rebuked had in fact been a prominent *agonothetēs* in Greece over the previous few years, one of the things Epictetus says to him gains an added point and relevance: "Stage as many contests as you will in your own house, and proclaim him victor in the Nemean, Pythian, Isthmian, and Olympic games."[85]

79. 3, 9, 18.
80. 4, 1, 14.
81. 3, 4.
82. Jn. 19, 72.
83. *PIR*² C 1424. See H. G. Pflaum, *Carrières procuratoriennes* (1960–61), no. 81.
84. Perhaps as a sinecure: see *JRS* 53 (1963): 196–97.
85. 3, 4, 11.

If that hint of identification is not misleading, Epictetus was not the only pundit to give this man the benefit of his advice. For it was to Cornelius Pulcher that Plutarch addressed his treatise *On Gaining Profit from One's Enemies*, which begins with a reference to Pulcher's mild and beneficial political activities — and to the fact that he was an assiduous reader of Plutarch's *Political Precepts*.[86]

Finally, there is a brief dialogue, which Epictetus reports, between himself and a man who held the priesthood of Augustus at Nicopolis. Epictetus had said, "Drop the business; you will spend a lot of money for nothing." "But they will write my name on contracts." "And will you be present to say to those who read them out — 'that is my name they have written?' And even if you can be present every time now, what about when you are dead?" "My name will live after me." "Write it on a stone and it will live after you. Who will remember you outside Nicopolis?" "But I shall wear a crown of gold." "If you want a crown at all, take one of roses and wear it; you will look more elegant in that."[87] Like the post of *sevir augustalis* so much valued by Trimalchio,[88] the man's priesthood in the passage illustrates perfectly the political functions of emperor worship, in providing for the wealthy classes honorific positions which both gave them prestige and identified them with the regime.

Such is some, by no means all, of the testimony Epictetus can provide for the social and political life of his time. A number of problems have to be faced if the testimony is to be used as historical evidence. Firstly, can we trust Arrian's statement that the text of the Dissertations consists of the words of Epictetus as recorded verbatim by him? Given the possible limits of accuracy in such a procedure, I can see nothing in the Dissertations to prove the claim incredible. Secondly, can we trust Epictetus' statements about incidents and historical events occurring up to some forty-five years before the moment of speaking? None of his statements is directly refutable from any other source, and some are confirmed,[89] and where he adds facts not otherwise known, these fit with what we know from other evidence.

It is a quite different problem to decide how far it would be valid to take over Epictetus' attitudes to, and valuation of, the institutions and customs he mentions. The slave of Epaphroditus exiled under Domitian would not be likely to view the values and aspirations of Roman society with much

86. *Mor.* 86 B–D.

87. 1, 19, 26–29.

88. Petronius, *Sat.* 30, 71.

89. One might note especially his statement in 3, 3, 3 that it is forbidden to reject imperial coins, which is confirmed by Paulus, *Sent.* 5, 25, 1.

enthusiasm; and the philosopher on show for culturally minded travellers at Nicopolis had a certain role to play as a critic of the world and its occupations. None the less, actions and events in a bygone society must be seen, in the first instance, in terms of the attitudes to them—all the attested attitudes—expressed by contemporaries. For that reason Epictetus' viewpoint, unique in our sources, makes his testimony all the more valuable—and specifically as a complement to the very different viewpoint of Pliny the Younger.

Moreover, the considerable quantity of factual information Epictetus provides covers a wide range of topics, from the workings of the court to the life of the Greek cities. He should thus take his place as a historical source alongside his two direct contemporaries, Plutarch and Dio of Prusa.

Postscript

This chapter had its origin in the collection of material for a book on the imperial court from Augustus to Constantine, not in the study of Epictetus or of Arrian (neither has received any full modern study, which both richly deserve). To pick out such material, as has been done here, must inevitably give a partial and distorted picture of Epictetus' teaching, which is primarily concerned with conduct in ordinary life, and uses examples from many spheres other than politics. None the less, the political aspect of his teaching could be regarded as subversive, as is made explicit when an (imaginary?) interlocutor asks "Do you philosophers, then, teach us to despise our kings?"[90] It may have been partly for this reason that Arrian, as he explains in his introductory letter, did not spontaneously publish his transcripts, and was only provoked into doing so by the circulation, against his will, of unauthorized copies. Also we do not know whether he published them during the period (up to about 140) of his career as a Roman senator, or during the following period when he lived, wrote, and held local magistracies in Athens.[91] All that we know is that the work was in circulation by the early 150s when Aulus Gellius, as a student, heard a passage from it read out in the villa of Herodes Atticus near Athens.[92]

By this time it was possible to look back on the earlier emperors, especially the Julio-Claudians, as an unfortunate aberration. Marcus Aurelius could talk

90. 1, 29, 9.

91. See *PIR*² F 219.

92. Aulus Gellius, *NA* 1, 2, 6–13. The date can be roughly calculated from the fact that Gellius, now "apud magistros" (1, 2, 1), had been an *adulescens* attending *grammatici* (grammarians) in Rome in the urban prefecture of Erucius Clarus (7, 6, 12; 13, 18, 2–3), who died in office in 146 (*PIR*² E 96).

about tyrants and advise himself not to "Caesarise";[93] Fronto could pour contempt on the acts and the intellectual abilities of the Julio-Claudians in a letter to Lucius Verus.[94] Some of Epictetus' attitudes might thus have been acceptable, as referring to a bygone age. But the Dissertations are still unique; no other work read and valued in Roman society dealt so harshly with the values of status and ambition on which that society was based.

93. *Meditations* 6, 30.
94. *Ad Verum* 2 (Naber 123; Van Den Hout 117).

CHAPTER SEVEN

Condemnation to Hard Labour in the Roman Empire, from the Julio-Claudians to Constantine*

Introduction

In A.D. 258 a group of Numidian bishops, condemned to the mines of their province, wrote as follows to Cyprian, bishop of Carthage, at that moment in exile:[1]

> Therefore they who were condemned with us give you before God the greatest thanks, beloved Cyprian, that in your letter you have refreshed their suffering breasts; have healed their limbs wounded with rods [*fustes*]; have loosened their feet bound with fetters; have smoothed the hair of their half-shorn head; have illuminated the darkness of the dungeon; have brought down the mountains of the mine to a smooth surface; have even placed fragrant flowers to their nostrils and have shut out the foul odour of the smoke.

Even our scattered and inadequate evidence is enough to make it clear that from the second century onwards condemnation to hard labour in mines or

*First published in *PBSR* 52 (1984): 123–47. Versions of this chapter were given as lectures at the Institut de Droit Romain in Paris, in February 1980, and at a conference on "Il regime romano e le strutture economiche e sociali dell'impero romano," held at the British School in Rome in March 1983. I am grateful for comments and information to various members of the audiences, especially Andrea Caradini and John Bodel; to Philip Stadter for references on the tattooing of slaves and convicts; and to Roger Hood, Reader in Criminology at Oxford, for some illuminating questions and points.

1. Cyprian, *Ep.* 77, 3 (trans. Wallis, 1868, with corrections); cf. also Cyprian's previous letter to them, 76, 2.

quarries was a familiar fate for Christians.[2] Tertullian, who might well count not only as the finest writer of rhetorical Latin from the imperial period,[3] but as the most acute and observant satirist of imperial society and government, had already deployed the theme of the savage punishments now in use to satirise pagan worship and its objects—pieces of stone or metal extracted from the ground and fashioned by human hands (*Apol.* 12, 3–5):

> You place Christians on crosses and stakes. What statue is not first shaped by clay moulded on a cross or stake? It is on a gibbet that the bodies of your gods are first dedicated. You tear with hooks at the sides of Christians. But all the parts of your gods are even more vigorously worked with axes, planes, and rasps. We place our heads on the block; your gods are without heads until lead and glue and wedges are applied. We are driven to face the beasts—those indeed which you place beside Liber, Cybele, and Caelestis. We are burned with fire; so too are they, as they leave the crude ore. We are condemned to the *metalla* [mines or quarries]; these are the origins of your gods. We are relegated to islands; by custom your gods are born and die on some island.

Later Tertullian returns to the theme of the mines (*Apol.* 29, 2–3):

> For [if the gods had the powers attributed to them] they would first defend their own statues and images and temples, which in fact, I rather think, the soldiers of the Caesars stand on watch to protect. Moreover, as I believe, the very materials of which they are made come from the *metalla* of the Caesars, and all the temples depend on Caesar's nod.

These passages presuppose and reflect a number of profound developments in the nature of the state and its relation to its subjects which took place in the imperial period. Firstly comes the regular application to free people, or at least to those of low social status, of savage means of physical punishment designed to produce a painful and lingering death. Some, perhaps all, of these punishments were regularly carried out in public, as an aspect of shows for popular amusement. Secondly, there is the appearance of forms of exile which involved not merely exclusion from an area, as in the Republic, but direction to a particular place. This was true in some cases of the milder form of

2. See J. G. Davies, "Condemnation to the Mines: A Neglected Chapter in the History of the Persecutions," *University of Birmingham Historical Journal* 6 (1957–58): 20.

3. See T. D. Barnes, *Tertullian: A Historical and Literary Study* (1971), esp. chap. 14: "The Christian Sophist"; R. D. Sider, *Ancient Rhetoric and the Art of Tertullian* (1971).

exile, *relegatio*, and invariably of the more severe form, *deportatio*. In the developed system *deportatio* was the harshest penalty applicable to upper-class persons, except for particularly offensive or dangerous crimes, such as parricide, treason, and later arson. With these exceptions, there did not develop any clear relationship between type of crime and form of penalty. Social status, not the specific crime, became the determining factor. In these two forms of exile, defined in the course of the first century A.D., there thus evolved, for convicts of high status, something resembling a custodial penalty, a feature unknown to the Republic. Thirdly, we find quite different forms of custodial penalty, which applied (in principle) only to slaves and lower-class persons; it is these, which involved hard labour, which form the subject of this chapter.

This last development gives rise to major questions which involve the nature of state and society. Does the use of convicts for hard labour imply the pursuit of strictly economic objectives by the emperors, or some emperors? Does it, as has been suggested, reflect the relative decrease in the inflow of slaves after the cessation of major wars of conquest? On this view the use of convicts, who were reduced, as we shall see, to slave status, will have been an attempt to find a partial substitute for slave labour.[4] The question is given added significance by the claim made by G. E. M. de Ste. Croix in *The Class Struggle in the Ancient Greek World* (1982) that it was precisely the enforced partial shift from the exploitation of slaves to the exploitation of the free poor which produced the more savage penalties applied in the imperial period to lower-class convicts.

There are also other problems, which equally relate to the nature of the imperial state. What forms of establishment for the temporary, long-term, or permanent retention of prisoners or convicts existed? In returning, a little later in the *Apology* (44, 3), to criminals and their treatment, Tertullian mentions the institution of the prison (*carcer*) as well as the mines: "It is with your people [pagans] that the prison is packed, with yours that the *metalla* groan, with yours that the beasts are fattened, with yours that those giving shows can maintain their gangs of convicts [*noxiorum greges*]." As we shall see, while the *carcer* was employed for the retention of prisoners awaiting trial or punishment, any tendency for it to be used as a place of sentence was always resisted. At no stage was the concept of a prison sentence, for a term or for life, ever adopted. But if that is clear, more important questions arise concerning the status and management of the *carceres* which existed in the

4. E.g., U. Täckholm, *Studien über den Bergbau der römischen Kaiserzeit* (1937), 132; S. Mrozek, "Les esclaves dans les mines d'or romaines en Dacie," *Archeologia* 15 (1964): 119, in Polish with Russian and French résumés, pp. 126–28.

provinces. Are we to imagine a chain of institutions set up by the Roman state as such, and staffed by its employees—and, if so, by civilian employees or by soldiers? It will be suggested that while there is some evidence for such a development, the basic pattern was quite different, namely the dependence of Roman officials on the prisons which were owned and run by provincial cities. The same, it will be suggested, is true of one category of hard-labour penalty whose character has often been misunderstood, that is to say, *opus publicum* (public labour).

Whether or not these suggestions will prove acceptable, it can at least be claimed both that no system of punishment can be understood except in the framework of the relevant state and society, and that we can afford to make no presumptions about the types of establishment in which punishment might be inflicted. In the Roman Empire city prisons might be the only ones available for locking up prisoners before trial or execution; and "public" works in cities certainly provided one form of long-term sentence. Furthermore, convicts sentenced to death by Roman governors were available for use by city magistrates putting on gladiatorial or wild beast shows. Here too, therefore, the city was in a position to provide the machinery which the state as such lacked.

What other contexts were possible for hard-labour sentences? It is certain that *slaves* could be punished by being sent to work in private mills or bakeries. Is it therefore possible that free convicts were treated similarly? If so, the question arises as to what range of economic functions might gain a labour supply by this means. The more extensive the range of such functions, and the scale of convict labour, the more relevant this pattern would be to the apparent diminution in the supply of slaves.

It is certainly implied by Tertullian that it was common, and perhaps even typical, for mines or quarries to be in imperial possession, and to be worked, at least in part, by convicts. Various questions therefore arise. Was it a precondition of the growth of convict labour that there should have been imperially owned establishments in which the convicts could work? Was convict labour employed in any and all types of imperial property (e.g., agricultural properties or manufacturing establishments), or only in mines and quarries? If the latter, were the reasons for such a deployment of the labour which was thus available in any sense economic, or of a quite different character? If economic, is this perhaps to be taken in the restricted sense, which Tertullian might be taken to imply in *Apol.* 12 and 29, of ensuring the direct supply of valuable metals and marble for public works or cult statues?

However, even if imperial mines or quarries were the normal places of work for convict labour, there remains the question of the organisation and supervision of that labour. On the one hand it is quite certain that it was common (at least) for imperial properties of all types to be leased out to private tenants or contractors. That being so, it is in principle possible that convicts were put to work for such contractors and were therefore, in the first instance, subject to private exploitation. Whether such a system operated or not, it is on the other hand also certain that soldiers were employed in guarding some mines and quarries. It is an important feature of the imperial system that the army constituted the only source of manpower, in the employment of the state, which could be deployed for police functions or for low-level administrative ones. In his references to prisons and to soldiers guarding temples, as well as his allusion elsewhere (*Apol.* 2, 8) to the role of the military post (*militaris statio*) in repressing brigandage, Tertullian touches also on the equally large and difficult question of the maintenance of public order in the provinces. The evidence may well suggest, though certainly cannot prove, a steady extension of the police functions of the Roman army during the imperial period, with a consequent dilution of the military manpower grouped in units and available for strategic and tactical use against external enemies.[5] The potential relevance of that to the history of the third and fourth centuries need hardly be stressed.

In this area, as in other aspects of the interconnected web of themes outlined above, our evidence hardly allows us to write an actual history showing how institutions evolved. If nothing else, the concentration of our legal evidence in the late second and early third centuries produces a distortion which can never fully be overcome. None the less, these legal sources themselves do at least permit an insight into attitudes and presumptions which illuminate not only economic, administrative, and penal history, but conceptions of social class and of the treatment of the human body. Since it is precisely the latter which is of crucial importance, it is necessary to begin with liability to flogging and cruel punishments before moving on to imprisonment and hard labour.

Beating and Cruel Forms of Execution

The rapid extension of the range of criminal punishments in use, which characterises the imperial period, has been discussed many times; so has the reser-

---

5. There is no general up-to-date discussion of this important question. Note, e.g., O. Hirschfeld, "Die Sicherheitspolizei im römischen Kaiserreich," *Kleine Schriften* (1913), 576; G. Lopuszanski, "La police romaine et les Chrétiens," *Ant. Class.* 20 (1951): 1; R. Mac-Mullen, *Soldier and Civilian in the Later Roman Empire* (1963), 55–56.

vation of the more cruel and humiliating penalties for lower-class convicts, which was already an established principle at least by Hadrian's reign.[6] To place hard labour penalties in their correct context, it is only necessary therefore to recall the main features of the nexus of presumptions which associated lower social class with liability to beatings, to cruel forms of execution, and to hard labour in various forms.

As is well known, the social dividing line which determined liability to, or exemption from, these punishments lay just below the status of *decurio* (town councillor) or veteran. However variable and tangential the numerous allusions to this principle from the second century and onwards may be, we can be confident that a general principle of this character was generally accepted. The presumption of the incompatibility between decurial status, implying qualification for local offices, and exposure to flogging is neatly illustrated in Callistratus' discussion of whether it was acceptable for traders, liable to flogging by the local magistrates, to attain the decurionate or city *honores* (magistracies); it was in fact allowable, he says, but *inhonestum* (degrading), and only acceptable if made absolutely necessary by a lack of *honesti uiri* (men of standing) with adequate wealth (*Dig.* 50, 2, 12). Exemption could itself be described as an *honor*: according to Arrius Menander veterans and their sons have the same *honor* as *decuriones*, namely exemption from condemnation to metallum, to *opus publicum* (see below), to the beasts, or to being beaten with rods (*fustes*) (*Dig.* 49, 18, 3). The sons of *decuriones* were similarly protected, and Ulpian concludes that this exemption from beating and condemnation to *metallum* applied even to a son born to a father who had then been a *plebeius* (a person of below town councillor rank), but who subsequently gained the *honor decurionis* (status of a decurion). An equally complex case law applied if a father lost his decurial rank by being removed from the *ordo* (membership of the town council) or relegated (*Dig.* 50, 2, 2). Given the close connection between social rank and immunity from degrading and painful intrusions on the body, the question naturally arose as to whether if a beating had been administered, even improperly, rank was lost with it. So, for instance, Gordian III replied in 238 to a man named Iovinus: "Your uncle need fear no disgrace to his standing [*existimationis infamiam*] on the grounds of his having been beaten with rods, if this had not been preceded by a sentence imposing the stain of *ignominia* [disgrace]" (*App. Leg. Rom. Wis.* 1, 1).

6. E.g., Th. Mommsen, *Römisches Strafrecht* (1899), 897–98; U. Brasiello, *La repressione penale in diritto romano* (1937), 189–90; P. D. A. Garnsey, *Social Status and Legal Privilege in the Roman Empire* (1970); Garnsey, "Why Penal Laws Become Harsher: The Roman Case," *Natural Law Forum* 13 (1968): 141. Note also P. A. Brunt, "Evidence Given under Torture in the Principate," *ZSS* 117 (1980): 256.

The association of condemnation to hard labour with violent intrusion on the body extended to tattooing, normally performed on the face, but after Constantine's proclamation of 315/16 on other parts of the body (*CTh* 9, 40, 2 = *CJ* 9, 47, 17):

> If anyone has been condemned to a gladiatorial school or a *metallum* in accordance with the seriousness of the crimes in which he has been de- tected, let there on no account be marking on his face, since the penalty of his condemnation can be fulfilled merely by marking on the hands and calves, so that the face, which is formed in imitation of the divine beauty, may in no way be disfigured.

To use marking (almost certainly tattooing—*scribtio*—rather than branding) as the sign or accompaniment of criminal penalties was, of course, to apply to freemen treatment originally reserved for slaves. We may note the incident in Petronius, *Sat.* 103–4, in which Encolpius and Gitus, to disguise them- selves as fugitive slaves, have their heads shaved (or half-shaved?—105, 2) and their faces marked with ink.[7] This parallelism, as is generally accepted, runs through the evolution of harsher penalties under the Empire and is one of its primary features. Indeed, Macer so far assumed the parallel as to invert it, writing that slaves were punished in the same manner as *humiliores* (lower- class persons)—except that, for the same offence, a free man would be beaten with rods (*fustes*) and a slave with whips (*flagella*) and returned to his master (*Dig.* 48, 19, 10, *pr.*; see further below). This distinction none the less left the free man of low status much closer to the slave than to an upper-class free man. Both the (marginal) distinction in the type of beating and the much more fundamental distinction over liability or otherwise to hard labour are visible for instance in the reply of Antoninus Pius to a provincial governor about the despoiling of a shipwreck (*Dig.* 47, 9, 4, 1):

> If it appears that booty of a more significant sort has been sought by force, you will relegate free men for three years, or, if they are of hum- bler rank [*sordidiores*], you will have them beaten with *fustes* and put to *opus publicum* for the same period; as for slaves, you will have them beaten with whips and condemn them to *metallum*.

7. I had earlier assumed that Constantine was speaking of *branding* (on the face or else- where). But the characteristic expressions used—*scribtio, frontes litterati* etc.—clearly suggest tattooing, as does a fair volume of comparative evidence; see J. W. B. Barns and H. Lloyd- Jones, "Un nuovo frammento papiraceo dell'elegeia ellenistica," *St. It. Fil. Class.* 35 (1963): 205. I am also grateful to Professor C. P. Jones for letting me see his then unpublished paper, "Stigma: Tattooing and Branding in Graeco-Roman Antiquity," *JRS* 77 (1987): 139.

There was, however, something more than a parallelism in the treatment of free men of low status and slaves, for those condemned to the various forms of hard labour included not merely free men suffering a penalty which gave them the effective status of slaves, but actual slaves enduring a further punishment for disobedience or crime. Thus, in the passage quoted above, Macer continues (48, 19, 10 *pr.*):

> And for those offences for which a free man is beaten with rods and put to *opus publicum*, a slave is ordered to be beaten with whips and returned to his master under the penalty of being in shackles [*vincula*] for the same period. If, when it is ordered that he should be returned to his master under penalty of *vincula*, he is not accepted, it is ordered that he should be sold and, if no buyer is found, that he should he given over to *opus publicum*, and moreover in perpetuity.

Thus by different routes both free men of low status and slaves might finish up condemned to *opus publicum*, whose nature will be discussed later, as they might also to *metallum*. Slaves might also be returned to their master on the strict condition of being kept in shackles. That penalty too came on occasion to be extended to free men and was quite distinct from temporary retention in prison—*carcer* or *custodia* (discussed in the next section). The master had of course always had the power to shackle his slave if he so wished, or to put him to work in particularly laborious or degrading conditions, or both. Such steps are perhaps to be understood as the background to the famous description in Apuleius' *Metamorphoses* of men working in a mill:[8]

> Their skins were seamed all over with the marks of old floggings, as you could easily see through the holes in their ragged shirts that shaded rather than covered their scarred backs; but some wore only loin-cloths. They had letters branded [or rather tattooed—*frontes litterati*—see above] on their foreheads, and half-shaved heads and irons on their legs. Their complexions were frightfully yellow, their eyelids caked with the smoke of the baking ovens, their eyes so bleary and inflamed that they could hardly see out of them and they were powdered like athletes in the arena, but with dirty flour, not dust.

The men must be intended to be understood by the reader as being of slave status. But the half-shaven heads and the shackles recall the Christian convicts of the 250s in the *metalla* of Numidia, and the tattooed foreheads the

---

8. *Met.* 9, 12, trans. Graves. See F. Millar, "The World of the *Golden Ass*," *JRS* 71 (1981): 63, on p. 65 (chapter 15 in this volume).

custom which Constantine abolished (or rather altered), while the marks of beatings on the back indicate convicts and slaves equally. Are these men slaves enduring punishment by their own master, or slaves sent by their master to a mill owned by someone else, or consigned there by public authority (see below)? Or might public authority have already come to deploy convicts of free status as a labour force for such private establishments? The question may be postponed for a moment while we look at the (relatively unimportant) use of prison and shackles in the detention of free men. But this passage, apart from its value as one of the most vivid presentations from antiquity of what the extraction of value from the poor really meant, is highly significant precisely because we *cannot* be quite sure whether the victims are slaves, or slaves sent for punishment, or convicts.

Carcer or *Custodia,* and *Vincula*

In 59 B.C. Cicero wrote to his brother Quintus, then proconsul of Asia, mentioning among other things an escaped slave who had been apprehended in Ephesus: "a certain Plato of Sardes . . . arrested the man and handed him over to *custodia* in Ephesus, but whether to public custody or to a *pistrinum*, I have not been able to determine adequately from his letter."[9] The letter illustrates perfectly the use of a mill or bakery as a place of detention and punishment for slaves (see below). The alternative was *publica custodia*, the public prison of the city. The evidence on city prisons in the areas under Roman rule has never been fully collected;[10] but Vitruvius, for instance, regards a treasury (*aerarium*), *carcer*, and *curia* (council house) as the standard public buildings which ought to be placed next to the forum of a *municipium* (5, 2, 1). Anecdotal evidence reveals for example the prison (*phylakē*) in the *colonia* of Philippi where Paul and Silas passed a somewhat disturbed night after being beaten on the orders of the *duoviri* (*Acts* 16, 22–40). Similarly the martyr acts illustrate the presence of city prisons at Lugdunum and Smyrna; the prisons are under the control of the city magistrates and, as at Philippi, staffed by city employees. They function as places where Christians are locked up to await trial before the governor.[11] In Apuleius' *Metamorphoses* we find city magistrates, acting independently, having a slave who is suspected of a crime

9. *Ad Qf.* 1, 2, 14 (Shackleton-Bailey 2).

10. See *RE* and Daremberg and Saglio, s.v. "Carcer"; *RAC*, s.v. "Gefangenschaft." [See now J.-U. Krause, *Gefängnisse im Römischen Reich*, Habes 23 (1966)].

11. H. Musurillo, *Acts of the Christian Martyrs*, no. 5 (= Eusebius, *HE* 5, 1, 8; 27) (Lyon); no. 10, 10–17 (Smyrna).

placed in the *publica custodia* (public prison) before enduring trial by torture the next day (7, 2, 2). Prisons, however, represent a prime instance of the interdependence of city institutions and of provincial government. Also in the *Metamorphoses*, a woman condemned in Corinth by the governor, who is resident there, is kept in the *publicus carcer* until a soldier comes to collect her for execution in a public show (10, 28; 34). By contrast with the martyr acts set in Lugdunum and Smyrna, the governor here makes spontaneous use of the city prison; similarly, martyr acts set in the third century show soldiers carrying out arrests and placing the victims in a prison (*carcer*) before trial.[12] In Carthage, indeed, where (quite exceptionally) an urban cohort was stationed, the *Acts* of Perpetua and Felicitas reveal that in the early third century there were two prisons, a city one, where the martyrs are first placed (3, 5–9; 6, 7), and a camp prison (*carcer castrensis*), under an *optio, praepositus carceris* (an *optio* in charge of the prison), to which they were transferred with a view to being put before the beasts in a camp show, *castrense munus* (7, 9–9, 1). But even the city prison was subject to abuses by soldiers (3, 6).

It is not impossible that with the passage of time soldiers came to be used not only to collect condemned persons from prison, or to arrest suspects and bring them to city prisons, but to run the city prisons themselves. It is indeed exactly this possibility which Trajan firmly resisted, when Pliny wrote from Bithynia to ask approval for the step (which he had indeed provisionally taken) of adding some soldiers to the "public slaves of the *civitates* [cities]" who had up to then managed the *custodiae*. Trajan was eager both that military discipline should not be corrupted and that too many men should not be withdrawn from their units (Pliny, *Ep.* 10, 19–20). It may well be that both of these developments did come about later. But since there were strictly military *custodiae* as well as (in principle) city ones, the chances of our being able to trace developments in this area seem as yet slight. A new inscription from Bostra, for instance, is a dedication set up by the "*officiales* of the prisoners" under Gordian III to the *praepositus* of the *custodiae* (cells), a centurion of the *legio III Cyrenaica*.[13] A military prison proper, or a city prison run by soldiers? By contrast, legal sources of the second and early third centuries appear to regard *carcer* as an *alternative* to handing over to the soldiers, as a way of detaining defendants (*Dig.* 48, 3); but certainly the frequent references in the same chapter to the *custodia* exercised by soldiers do not seem to refer only or specifically to defendants from within the army.

12. Ibid., nos. 12, 14.

13. M. Sartre, "Nouvelles inscriptions grecques et latines de Bosra," *Ann. Arch. Arab. Syr.* 22 (1972): 167, on p. 175, no. 8; see *BE* 1973, no. 501.

There may well be a significant evolution here, but the ambiguity of the scattered evidence makes it impossible to prove. What is clear, however, is that the *principle* was maintained that prisons were not intended for long-term sentences but only as places of short-term detention for defendants, or persons awaiting execution. It is, however, obvious, from the very passage which provides the clearest expression of this principle, that it was not always observed in practice: "Governors are in the habit of condemning men to be detained in prison or kept in *vincula* [shackles]; but it is not right for them to do so. For penalties of this type are forbidden. Prison ought to be regarded as being for the detention of men, not for their punishment" (*Dig.* 48, 19, 8, 9, Ulpian). Even such temporary detention normally involved the defendant or convict being chained, and hence was regarded as inflicting *infamia* (disgrace). Severus and Caracalla had to reassure a man that if he had been thrown into prison *per iniuriam* (unjustifiably), without a sentence carrying *infamia* having been passed, he need not fear that his *existimatio* (reputation) had been damaged (*App. Leg. Rom. Wis.* 1, 2). The severity of the conditions can be judged from Constantine's well-known instructions on the production of prisoners awaiting trial:[14]

> Meanwhile the man who has been produced in court shall not be put in manacles made of iron that cleave to the bones, but in looser chains, so that there may be no torture and yet the custody may remain secure. When incarcerated he must not suffer the darkness of an inner prison, but he must be kept in good health by the enjoyment of light, and when night doubles the necessity for his guard, he shall be taken back into the vestibules of the prisons and into healthful places. When day returns, at early sunrise, he shall forthwith be led out into the common light of day that he may not perish from the torments of prison, a fate which is considered pitiable for the innocent but not severe enough for the guilty.

Constantine's words imply both that a more positive punishment than mere imprisonment was thought appropriate for convicts, and (once again) that there was no accepted concept of a prolonged prison sentence with any purpose, whether retributive, economic, or reformative. None the less, when Galerius' edict of toleration was issued in 311, Donatus, the addressee of Lactantius' *De Mortibus Persecutorum*, had been in a *carcer* for six years (35, 1–2; cf. Eus., *HE* 9, 1, 7).

14. *CTh* 9, 3, 1, trans. C. Pharr; some variants in *CJ* 9, 4, 1.

Theory and practice might also diverge in the matter of the penalty of *vincula*. Given that, as mentioned above, persons in prison were also normally shackled (unless bribes were used to avoid this, *Dig.* 48, 3, 8), many references to *vincula*, or *vincula publica*, are simply to imprisonment. But it is clear that *vincula* could in practice function as an alternative to prison; this is clearly implied, for instance by Ulpian, cited above (*Dig.* 48, 19, 8, 9). Being an alternative to prison, it was in principle a temporary measure of detention, applied to free defendants (*Dig.* 48, 3, 3). As a *penalty*, being kept in *vincula*, for either a specified period or in perpetuity, was appropriate only for slaves (text to n. 8 above). It appears for instance in the Lex Metalli Vipascensis: a slave guilty of stealing from the mine is to be sold outside the bounds of the mining area, and on condition that he should be in *perpetua vincula* (in chains for life) — that is, while in private possession (*FIRA*² I, no. 104, ll. 25–30). None the less, here too the treatment of slaves might influence that of free convicts. The imperial *mandata* (instructions) forbade any (free) person from being kept in *perpetua vincula* (*Dig.* 48, 19, 35). Caracalla, however, wrote in 214: "What you allege is incredible, namely that a free man has been condemned to be kept in chains in perpetuity; for this procedure can scarcely be followed even as regards (a person of) servile status" (*CJ* 9, 47, 6). We cannot tell whether it was common in practice for this regular slave penalty to be applied to free men. But even temporary application of *vincula*, like being thrown into prison (above), will have been regarded as damaging to status. This is perfectly clear from Ulpian's inclusion of persons in chains among the categories who could claim restitution because they were not in a position to appear in a case. His words also illustrate once again the variety of agencies who might keep a man under arrest: "Those are in the same category who are being kept under arrest by soldiers and *statores* [military grooms] or by municipal servants, if it is proved that they could not have appeared for their case. For we have defined those as being *in vinculis* who are bound in such a way that they cannot appear in public without indignity [*sine dedecore*]" (*Dig.* 4, 6, 10).

The Nature of *Opus Publicum*

Imprisonment therefore was not (in principle) a recognised long-term penalty, whatever might happen to individuals, sometimes even before resolution of their case, like Paul, who was kept for two years in the "*praetorium* [governor's residence] of Herod" in Caesarea (*Acts* 23, 35; 24, 27), or the people about whom the *koinon* (common council of a league of cities) of

Bithynia complained to Severus Alexander, who were prevented from pursuing appeals by military guards under the orders of procurators or governors.[15] *Opus publicum*, however, clearly was a regular custodial penalty, frequently referred to in legal sources. Its nature and context—that is to say, the administrative and social context in which the labour of the convicts was to be performed—has not always been clearly understood. We could imagine that the reference is to public works in Rome, or works such as temples or walls, provided for a city by the emperor and paid for by him, or works carried out under the orders of a governor, for which labour and expertise might be provided, at least in part, by the army.[16] We might well expect, alternatively, that convict labour would have been used for the repair of dykes in Egypt, or for the building and repair of roads (*munitiones viarum*) throughout the Empire. In fact, however, as is well known, labour for the dykes was provided by the corvée system, and we have only two isolated items of evidence (see below) for condemnation to *munitiones viarum*. Similarly, construction and repair of the public works, temples, and aqueducts of Rome itself was carried out either by direct labour, the imperial and public *familiae* (gangs of slaves) for the aqueducts, or by contract. Though private contractors *might* have had the use of slave convict labour, there is nothing to suggest that those in Rome did.[17] For the use of convict labour in major "imperial" works outside Rome there appear to be at the most two items of evidence, both associated with projects begun, but not completed, by Nero. Josephus describes Vespasian in 67 as sending 6,000 Jewish captives (who were not, strictly speaking, convicts) to Nero at the Isthmus, *presumably* for labour there (*BJ* 3, 540); and Suetonius (*Nero* 31) reports that for his canal projects between Misenum and Ostia, Nero "ordered that whoever was in *custodia* [awaiting trial or execution?] anywhere should be deported to Italy, and that those convicted of a crime should not be condemned except *ad opus*." There is no evidence as to whether this order was ever carried out.

There is, therefore, little or nothing to support the idea, entirely plausible in itself, that those subjected to the regular penalty of *opus publicum* were systematically employed on the "public work" of the Roman state. Lack of such evidence cannot of course disprove such a possibility. But it does make it reasonable to enquire whether there was not some different context to

15. *Dig.* 49, 1, 25 = *P. Oxy.* 2104. See F. Millar, *The Emperor in the Roman World* (1977), 392–93 (henceforth *ERW*).

16. See, for instance, R. MacMullen, "Roman Imperial Building in the Provinces," *HSCPh* 64 (1959): 207.

17. See P. A. Brunt, "Free Labour and Public Works at Rome," *JRS* 70 (1980): 81.

which the term *opus publicum* might have applied. Two general considerations suggest that the reference is to the "public work" of the provincial (or Italian) cities. Firstly, there is the well-known semantic shift by which in the general vocabulary of the imperial period "publicus" tends to be applied to things associated with the cities, rather than with the "res publica" of Rome. Ulpian indeed protested, in vain: "Things belonging to a *civitas* are improperly called 'public,' for only those things are 'public' which belong to the *populus Romanus*" (*Dig.* 50, 16, 15). But it was already well established that even the term *res publica* itself commonly meant simply "a city," of any status.[18] Secondly, to support the possibility that "public work" could mean hard labour in the service of a city, even though the condemnation had been pronounced by a provincial governor, there is the fact that such condemnations by governors frequently led to convicts appearing in the arena, either as gladiators or as passive victims for the beasts, in shows put on by city magistrates or high priests of provincial councils. Condemned criminals could, of course, be used in the shows put on by magistrates or by the emperor in Rome itself. This seems to be first attested in 65 B.C., and continued under the Empire.[19] Criminals might also be sent to Rome from the provinces to die in the arena. Strabo saw a famous bandit who had been sent from Sicily to be killed by beasts in a show in Rome (*Geog.* 273); and, for instance, Bishop Ignatius of Antioch, on his way under guard to Rome in the reign of Trajan, was happily anticipating being "ground by the teeth of beasts" (*Ep. Rom.* 4, 1–2). In the early third century Herennius Modestinus wrote: "A governor ought not to release *damnati ad bestias* [persons condemned to be thrown to the beasts] as a favour to the people. But if they are of such strength or skill that they can worthily be exhibited to the Roman *populus*, he ought to consult the emperor" (*Dig.* 48, 19, 31).

In these cases therefore the Roman state not only, in the person of the governor, passed sentence but also provided the organisation and context for execution. However, the implication which might be drawn from Modestinus' words, that governors themselves might also give shows in the provinces, at which criminals condemned by them might meet their deaths, is misleading. Governors might well be *present* at such shows, but all our evidence indicates that the persons giving them would normally be city magis-

18. See A. Mócsy, "Ubique res publica," *Acta Antiqua Academiae Scientiarum Hungaricae* 10 (1962): 367.

19. For Caesar's aedilician games in 65 B.C., see Pliny, *NH* 33, 53 (*noxii*—or slaves being punished?). See G. Ville, *La gladiature en Occident des origines à la mort de Domitien* (1981), 232–33. Cf. L. Robert, *Les gladiateurs dans l'Orient grec* (1940), 320–21.

trates or provincial high priests. Thus in the *Acts* of Polycarp (12) the proconsul tries the bishop in the stadium at Smyrna, but it would have been the Asiarch, Philippus, who produced beasts, if the permitted days for *venationes* (animal hunts) had not already been past. Similarly, in the *Golden Ass*, a woman condemned in Corinth by the proconsul of Achaea (see above) is due to die in a show put on by a *duovir quinquennalis* (colonial censor) of the city.[20] As happens in this case, and whether the governor was present or not, local office-holders could acquire condemned persons for use in the shows they put on, possibly buying them from the imperial *fiscus* (treasury).[21]

It is not necessary to enter into the complex details of the different handling of those condemned "to the beasts" or *in ludum* (to be trained as gladiators). The essential point is simply that just as the Roman state, except in the army camps, possessed no prisons for short-term detention, it also had no social or ceremonial framework of its own, outside the city of Rome, for executions which were felt to require some means more impressive than the sword or the cross. This function, too, therefore devolved on the institutions of the cities or provincial councils.

This fact, therefore, may also support the possibility that "public work" took place in the same context. But Pliny's correspondence with Trajan provides a more direct connection (10, 31–32). Pliny reports that in many *civitates*, especially Nicomedia and Nicaea, persons who had been condemned *in opus*, or *in ludum* or to similar sorts of penalty, were acting as public slaves (of these cities) and were even receiving pay. Pliny thought it too severe to return them to their *poenae* (penalties), and not quite decent (*satis honestum*) to retain them in public service (*in publiciis officiis*)—even ones filled by slaves. It was also not clear how they had evaded the due penalties, though some were alleged to have petitioned proconsuls or their *legati*. Trajan replied that those condemned within the past ten years, and not released on proper authority, should be returned to their *poenae*. Those who were older and had been condemned more than ten years earlier should be distributed "to those *ministeria* [functions] which are not far from a *poena*. For men of that sort are accustomed to be put to [work in] a bath-house, the cleaning out of drains, and also the building of roads and [?] streets [*vicorum*]."

It is clear from this that all the various categories of condemned had remained within the context of the cities, and that some had been condemned specifically *in opus*. It was presumably this apparently established category

20. Apuleius, *Met.* 10, 18; Millar (n. 8), 68–69.
21. So *ERW*, 194–95.

to whom Trajan referred at the end of his letter, as persons who normally carried out work, of a punitive kind, on the utilities of the cities.

If this was what the lawyers meant by *opus publicum*, it is immediately evident how and why it differed so profoundly from any form of condemnation to the mines. Firstly, the question of transporting the condemned to distant regions did not arise; they were put to work in their own city. Secondly, although it was a humiliating and degrading penalty, it was less so than *metallum* or *opus metalli* (from which it was totally distinct; see below). Thirdly, it was common to impose it for limited periods. Fourthly, the occasion did not arise for discussing, as with those condemned to the mines, whether they were "slaves of the *fiscus*" or "slaves of the *poena* [penalty]." For, although they too were condemned by provincial governors, they were not at work in "the mines of Caesar," but in cities.

This penalty seems regularly to have been preceded by flogging with rods (*fustes*) (for free men, see above), and involved heavy and humiliating labour. The *Oneirocritica* of Artemidorus (1, 21) also makes clear that convicts of this category had half of their heads shaved, evidently to aid identification in case of escape: "[W]henever someone [dreams that he] has his head half-bald and is of a bad conscience, he will be condemned to the penalty of public work [*ergon dēmosion*]. For in this instance too this is the mark of the condemned." As in the case of all other physically degrading penalties, exemption was granted to decurions (*CJ* 9, 47, 3), and to veterans and their sons (47, 5). On the other hand there is no specific indication that those engaged on *opus publicum* had to wear chains.[22] And above all the penalty might be imposed for relatively short periods, such as one year (*Coll.* 11, 3, 1 = *Pauli Sent.* 5, 18, 1) or two to three years (preceded by beating with *fustes*), as Hadrian laid down for those lower-class persons who assisted in the moving of boundary stones.[23] The maximum period mentioned for fixed-term condemnation to *opus publicum* is ten years; but condemnation in perpetuity was also possible. So, according to Paulus, nocturnal house-breakers were to be beaten with *fustes* and sent to *metallum*; diurnal ones, after beating with rods (*fustium castigatio*), went to *opus publicum*, either temporary or permanent (*Dig.* 47, 18, 2). Flight during the sentence might lead to doubling of the sentence, or its perpetuation, or transfer to *opus metalli* (*Dig.* 48, 19, 8, 7). Though Pliny (above) seems not to have enquired as to whether any of those condemned *in opus* had been serving fixed terms, it seems in general that those enduring *opus*

22. Brasiello (n. 6), 360–61, is wrong to associate this penalty with *vincula publica*.
23. So *Coll.* 13, 3, 2; *biennio* in *Dig.* 47, 21, 2.

publicum could expect eventual release. So Diocletian and Maximian replied to one Vitalis (*CJ* 9, 47, 14): "If the day fixed in advance by a sentence laying down a fixed-term penalty of *opus publicum* has not yet passed, it is right for it to be awaited, since it is in the public interest that a penalty should not lightly be remitted, lest anyone rush recklessly into wrongdoing" (a relatively rare reference to the deterrent purpose of penalties).

Opus publicum is formally attested from Pliny's correspondence with Trajan until the first half of the fourth century, when Firmicus Maternus refers to it (*Math.* 7, 24, 2); and it was among the penalties suffered by Christians in the East under Licinius.[24] A single later imperial letter, of uncertain date (383 or 391) and insecure text, seems to refer to *opus publicum*, and at any rate makes the link between social status, beating, and physical labour: those who harbour deserters "will encounter the law in proportion to their rank and person. If indeed he is liable to be subject to physical punishment . . . , he will be beaten with *fustes* or [and?] directed to *metallum* [or?] to *opus publicum*" (*CTh* 7, 18, 8).

The place of *opus publicum* in the scale of habitual punishments is thus fairly clear: in the *Sententiae Pauli* (5, 17, 2) it is classed, along with *vincula* (see above), among the *minimae poenae* (the lightest punishments). Antoninus Pius described the *condicio* (situation) of a person condemned to *opus publicum* as being comparable with that of a *deportatus* (*CJ* 9, 47, 1). If so, that meant confiscation of property and loss of all rights of testament and inheritance. In other respects the parallel is surely misleading; for *deportatio*, which involved no physical injury or restraint, was the most severe penalty to which (for most crimes) the upper classes could be condemned, while *opus publicum* was reserved for the lower classes.

If we can locate it (more or less) as a legal penalty, the same is barely true of its economic and social aspects. Given the values attached in the imperial period to city life and its physical manifestations, it must have some significance that one of the few attested forms of long-term penalty involved physical labour in the service of urban utilities. To the list of functions mentioned by Pliny nothing can be added except (probably) that of working a treadmill (*antlia*): Artemidorus in the *Oneirocritica* (1, 48) reports one dream which involved walking without advancing and one of water flowing from a man's feet, both of which turned out to have foretold condemnation to the treadmill. As with most of Artemidorus' cases, it would be reasonable to assume that these incidents reflect the town life of the Greek East in the second century.

24. Eusebius, *VC* 2, 20, 3; Sozomenus, *HE* 1, 7, 3.

No such context can be supplied for Suetonius' two isolated reports, that Tiberius condemned an equestrian *in antliam* (*Tib.* 51), and that Gaius had many men of honourable rank (senators and equestrians) tattooed (*deformatos . . . stigmatum notis*) and sent to the *metalla* (see below) and road building (*munitiones viarum*) or *ad bestias* (*Cal.* 27). The implication might well be that condemnation to hard labour was already customary in that early period for persons of lower rank. But there is nothing whatever to suggest the social context in which the labour was performed. The allusions in Pliny (*Ep.* 10, 31–32) and Suetonius appear in any case to provide our only evidence that roads might be built by convict labour.[25] To complete our confusion, road building is here linked directly with *metalla* (evidently meaning quarries rather than mines). But in the period for which we have some evidence, *metallum* was a quite distinct penalty from *opus publicum*, far more severe — and perhaps of greater economic significance.

Condemnation to the Mines or Quarries: *Metallum, Opus Metalli,* and *Ministerium Metallicorum*

Christian evidence alone would be enough to indicate the significance of *metallum* in the minds of those subjects of the Roman Empire who faced the possibility of condemnation. But neither an institutional nor an economic nor a geographically orientated history of the exploitation of convict labour in the mines and quarries can be written. All that can be done is to pick out some suggestive features of our evidence, which is overwhelmingly legal in character and concerned with the consequences for the property and personal status of the condemned.

There is nothing to suggest that the condemnation of free men to *metallum* was a feature of republican jurisdiction. But Strabo records that the contractors (Roman *publicani*?) who formerly operated the red-sulphide mine at Pimolisene in Pontus had used slaves who had been sold off for evil-doing, and who met a quick death there (*Geog.* 562). This cannot be brought into any relation with the later evidence; but it may remind us, firstly, that the patterns of exploitation of natural resources within the Empire did not always owe anything to Rome; secondly, that, as with other hard-labour penalties, condemnation to *metallum* applied to slaves as well as low-status free men; and, thirdly, that use of convicts did not necessarily imply direct exploitation by employees of the state. Equally, the famous description, which Diodorus (3, 12–14) took from Agatharchides, of convicts working the gold mines

25. See T. Pekáry, *Untersuchungen zu den römischen Reichsstrassen* (1968), 120.

of southern Egypt in the later second century B.C., also cannot be brought into any relation with Roman use of convict labour in Egyptian mines (see below). But we need not dismiss altogether the possibility that imperial practice was derived from Hellenistic precedents. The "works in Egypt" to which Titus in 70 sent Jewish prisoners were perhaps mines (Josephus, *BJ* 6, 418).

However, it is typical of the poverty of our sources for the structure of the Empire in the first century A.D. that we hear nothing of the institution of condemnation to the *metalla*, apart from Suetonius (above), until we come to two brief allusions in Pliny's *Letters*. In the trial of Marius Priscus, the former proconsul of Africa, it was alleged that a Roman equestrian had been "beaten with *fustes*, condemned to *metallum*, strangled in a *carcer*" (*Ep.* 2, 11, 8). There is a clear emphasis on the breach of rules about social status, and a clear implication that the penalty of *metallum* was not itself unknown. Then, in a dispute which Pliny heard in Bithynia, there was recited before him the verdict of the proconsul Velius Paulus, by which a philosopher, Flavius Archippus, had been *damnatus in metallum* on being convicted of forgery (10, 58, 3). The allusion carries the same implication about the normality of the penalty; in this case, though we would naturally suppose Archippus to have been of relatively high social status, nothing suggests that his condemnation was seen as unusual. The more significant combined implication of these two items of evidence is that this penalty was in established use in both a Greek- and a Latin-speaking province.

From the next two centuries, when legal evidence provides at least some conception of what *metallum* meant, only certain basic social and economic features need be considered here.

1. Both slaves and free men could be condemned to *metallum* (formally stated by Gordian in *CJ* 9, 47, 11).

2. As we would expect, persons of higher social status were exempt. This principle is not indeed explicitly stated in Hadrian's well-known reply to the provincial council of Baetica about cattle rustling, which laid down *metallum* for persistent offenders.[26] However, rulings of Hadrian on the escape of convicts already presuppose the two different scales of penalties applied to upper- and lower-class persons, as attested subsequently; in the category of custodial penalties (*in custodiis*) *metallum* was the most severe, and escape from it could only be punished by death.[27] The social distinction happens first to be explicitly attested for *metallum* in Antoninus Pius' edict that those who stole from *metalla Caesariana* (imperial mines or quarries) should be punished

---

26. Most fully in *Coll.* 11, 7, 1–2; extract in *Dig.* 47, 14, 1 *pr.*
27. *Dig.* 48, 19, 28, 13–14. See Garnsey, *Social Status* (n. 6), 103–4.

with exile or *metallum* "in accordance with the rank of the person" (*Dig.* 48, 13, 8, 1). Thereafter, for instance, Ulpian states that decurions (and their families) cannot be condemned to *metallum* or *opus metalli* (see below), nor to the *furca* (gallows) or being burnt alive (48, 19, 9, 11–15). Mistakes did occur, of course. Thus Severus Alexander replied to a man named Demetrianus: "If it is proved that your mother was the daughter of a decurion, it will be evident that she should not have been condemned to *ministerium metallicorum* [see below] nor to *opus metalli*" (*CJ* 9, 47, 9). The reasons which are given for this distinction again relate directly to the connection between social and physical dignity, or indignity. Thus Callistratus writes: "All whom it is forbidden to beat with *fustes* ought to enjoy the same respect for rank [*honoris reveretiam*] as *decuriones*. For it is inconsistent to say that those for whom imperial constitutions have forbidden subjection to beating can be condemned to *metallum*" (48, 19, 28, 5).

3. The consequences for a person's legal status, if he or she were condemned to *metallum*, were profound. Any criminal condemnation reduced a person's *existimatio* (reputation), by, for instance, disqualifying them from public office. *Metallum* extinguished their *existimatio* altogether and (unlike *opus publicum*) removed their formal possession of the status of a free person (*Dig.* 50, 13, 5, 2–3). It was primarily in connection with this penalty that there appeared the concept of a *servus poenae*, "slave of the penalty" (see below). *Metallum* carried with it the confiscation of a person's property and the loss of all rights of inheritance or testament. The sentence was for life, unless release came by an individual or general imperial *indulgentia;*[28] though Antoninus Pius ruled that a provincial governor could release those found to be incapable of work through age or ill-health, provided that they had served at least ten years and had some living relatives (48, 19, 22).

As with many aspects of Roman criminal law, the rules about gradations and distinctions relating to convict labour in *metalla* were not entirely consistent. Hadrian replied, evidently in answer to a letter from a governor, or a private petition: "No one ought to be condemned to *opus metalli* for a fixed term [*ad tempus*]. Whoever has been condemned *ad tempus* ought not, even if he is carrying out *metallicum opus*, to be regarded as having been condemned *in metallum*; for his *libertas* [status as a free man] is retained, which those who are condemned to *opus perpetuum* lose" (48, 19, 28, 6). It is thus not clear what was the status of the slave whom a papyrus of 209 shows being released after a five-year sentence to the alabaster-mine in Egypt (*SB* 4639). A little later Herennius Modestinus implies that a fixed-term sentence was normal and

28. See, e.g., *Pauli Sent.* 4, 8, 22 (24); *CJ* 9, 49, 4; 51, 2; 4.

states that an indefinite sentence should be construed as one of ten years (47, 19, 23), while Constantine lays down a two-year condemnation *in metallum* for persons of "a rustic or impoverished condition of life" who wrongly challenged a verdict (*CTh* 1, 5, 3).

4. Three different varieties of convict labour in *metalla* are mentioned: *metallum*, *opus metalli*, and *ministerium metallicorum*. According to Ulpian the difference between the first two lay solely in the weight of the chains which the convicts wore, *metallum* implying heavier chains; those who escaped from *opus publicum* and were recaptured might be sent to *opus metalli*; escapees from the latter went to *metallum* (48, 19, 8, 6–7). There is no indication here or elsewhere as to what (if any) difference of function there was between these two categories. Ulpian's evidence, however, confirms the Christian testimony (above) that all the convicts were shackled; they were also, as Callistratus put it, "coerced with servile lashes" (49, 14, 12). Ulpian seems to imply, as regards *ministerium metallicorum*, that it was a function reserved for female convicts: "[I]t is customary for women to be condemned to *ministerium metallicorum* either *in perpetuum* or *ad tempus*. . . . If they have been condemned *in perpetuum* they are regarded as *servae poenae*; but if *ad tempus* they retain their civil rights" (48, 19, 8, 8). Since *metallici* means the persons condemned to *metallum*, it is easy to suppose that the women performed menial functions for them in the *metalla*. As we saw above, a man complained to Severus Alexander about the improper condemnation of his mother to *ministerium metallicorum* or *opus metalli*. But Hermogenianus, at the end of the third century, speaks of men being condemned to *ministerium metallicorum*, and becoming *servi poenae* (48, 19, 36).

5. Unlike *opus publicum*, which could be served in a person's native town, condemnation to *metallum* necessarily involved transportation over greater or lesser distances. The condemned acquired the status of *metallici* (and will thus have been chained) as soon as sentence was passed, "although they have not yet been brought to the place where they are due to labour" (48, 19, 10, 1). Similarly Ulpian writes, "Some provinces have them [*metalla*] and some do not. But those which do not send [convicts] to those which have" (48, 19, 8, 4). That it was presumed to be worth the effort of directing soldiers to act as escorts, sometimes over substantial distances, is an indication that this form of labour was felt to be particularly appropriate as a punishment for serious offences. There is nothing as yet to show whether this was because of the punitive nature of the labour involved, or because of the particular value of the products.

6. It will be economical to consider together the evidence, fragmentary and accidental as it is, for the types of *metalla* where convicts are known

to have worked, for their geographical locations and for the administrative framework in operation. As regards types, *metallum* is of course ambiguous as between "mine" and "quarry." Ulpian, however, states that salt-works (*salinae*) could function as an equivalent place of sentence, as could lime or sulphur quarries (48, 19, 8, 8–10). Pomponius mentions a woman condemned *in opus salinarum* and then captured in a raid by "bandits of a foreign tribe" (49, 15, 6).

As regards geographical location, we saw that Christians were serving in *metalla* in Numidia in 258; Cyprian's previous letter to them, addressed to three groups, who reply separately (*Ep.* 77–79), would imply, if taken literally, that these were gold or silver mines (*Ep.* 76, 2, 2). If so they are not identifiable. However, the geographical location of one of the three groups of confessors in the *metalla*, to whom Cyprian had written, can be determined, at least approximately. They were the bishops, presbyters, and others dwelling *apud metallum Siguense* (*Ep.* 79). Sigus lies in central Numidia, and within a radius of some forty kilometres there are onyx quarries, and mines for lead, zinc, antimony, and copper; only the latter is thought to have been exploited in the Roman period.[29] Nor can we firmly identify the alabaster mine in Egypt from which a slave was released in 209 (see above), though two possible sites are known (*ESAR* II, 240). However, Aelius Aristides (*Or.* 36 Keil, 67) describes a porphyry quarry in Egypt and says that, like other *lithotomiai*, it was worked by convicts. We can reasonably take this to be the same porphyry quarry in the Thebaid in which Christian confessors were serving in 308, before ninety-seven of them were transferred to Palestine.[30] The site, Mons Porphyrites (Gebel Dokhān), in the eastern desert of Egypt near Myos Hormos, was guarded by soldiers, as inscriptions, ostraca, and papyri attest.[31]

This quarry was therefore probably imperial property, and the same is more certainly true of the mines in Cyprus to which Christian confessors were sent in 309/10 (Eusebius, *MP* 13, 2). It is reasonable to suppose that these were the same mines of which Augustus had given Herod a share in 12 B.C. and which Galen visited in the middle of the second century. At that time the mine workings were under the direct control of an imperial procurator, and at least some of the workers were fettered.[32] A similar pattern may have obtained in Sardinia, illuminated by Hippolytus' account of the chequered

29. See U. Saumagne, *Saint Cyprien, évêque de Carthage* (1975), 152 and n. 3.

30. Eusebius, *MP* 8, 1; cf. 9, 1.

31. See K. Fitzler, *Steinbrüche und Bergwerke im ptolemäischen und römischen Ägypten* (1910), 94–95; J. Lesquier, *L'armée romaine d'Égypte* (1918), 439–44; *RE*, s.v. "Porphyrites"; D. Meredith, "The Roman Remains in the Eastern Desert of Egypt," *JEA* 38 (1952): 94. Cf. A. Bernand, *Pan du Désert* (1977), 44–45.

32. *ERW*, 184–85.

early history of the bishop Callistus (*Haer.* 9, 11–12). As the slave of a private person, he was convicted of violence by the prefect of Rome in the 180s, and sentenced to be flogged and sent to the *metalla* of Sardinia; when a letter giving instructions to the procurator of Sardinia to release Christians in the mines arrived (in 189–92), Callistus managed to get himself included. This story, however, reveals nothing about the local administration, policing, or exploitation of the mines. Rather more can be discerned, from the first decade of the fourth century, about the copper mines at Phaeno in Palestine. When Diocletian and Maximian replied to a letter from Iulianus, proconsul of Africa, reporting in 302 on the spread of Manicheeism, they laid down that in this instance the rules of status were to be disregarded: even persons who were *honorati* (holders of imperial office) or possessed of *dignitas* should have their property confiscated and be sent to the *metalla* of Phaeno or Proconnesus.[33] The *metalla* of the island of Proconnesus (Marmara) were marble quarries, while those at Phaeno were copper mines, or rather copper workings or sites in a mining area lying east of the Wadi Arabah, between the south end of the Dead Sea and Petra.[34] The Phaeno mines play a considerable part in Eusebius' account of the next decade in Palestine. It was to there that one group of confessors was sent in 307, after having their legs disabled with branding irons, and another after being emasculated (*MP* 7, 3–4). Then a group of ninety-seven sent from Egypt suffered the severing of the left tendon and the gouging out of the right eye before being sent to these mines (8, 1); the same occurred with a further group in Egypt, later dispersed to mines in Palestine and Cilicia (8, 13). None the less, by 309/10 the convicts were enjoying a degree of liberty, to the point where they were able to construct buildings to serve as churches; and some who were unable to work because of mutilation or old age had been released from labour and were living separately but in the same area (13, 1–4). The conditions were thus marked by a considerable degree of freedom on the one side, so that Epiphanius could later record that the followers of Meletius and those of Peter of Alexandria had kept themselves separate in the mines (*Panar.* 68, 2, 8); and on the other by systematic mutilation which must largely have negated any economic function which the convicts could perform. Eusebius elsewhere (*HE* 8, 12, 10) describes these Christians as being "after this [the two forms

33. *Coll.* 15, 3, 7. For the date, see T. D. Barnes, *The New Empire of Diocletian and Constantine* (1982), 55.

34. For the copper workings at Feinan, see F. M. Abel, *Géographie de la Palestine* II (1983), 41–42; H. D. Kind, "Antike Kupfergewinnung zwischen Rotem und Totem Meer," *ZDPV* 81 (1965): 56, esp. 57–64.

of mutilation] condemned to the copper mines of the province not so much for service as for the sake of ill-treatment and hardship." This combination does, however, seem to have been unique to the Christian persecutions of these few years. A few years later Constantine was to decree amputation of a foot as an *alternative* to *metallum* for slaves caught escaping *ad barbaricum* (*CJ* 6, 1, 3).

No evidence survives to illuminate the fate of the Manichees sent from Africa to Proconnesus, though the *Passio IV Coronatorum* represents Proconnesian marble being used for building projects in Rome in the Tetrarchic period. But this same narrative, of uncertain authenticity, does also record Christian confessors, in chains and subject to many lashes, working in quarries in Pannonia.[35]

That seems to complete the erratic and unsatisfactory evidence for the location of mines or quarries where convict labour is specifically attested. By contrast, the two major documents relating to the mining district of Vipasca in Lusitania (*FIRA*[2] I, nos. 104–5) contain no hint of the presence of convict labour; nor does the evidence for the imperial gold mines in Dacia, where it is certain that at least some of the work force was employed under contract,[36] or that from the famous imperial quarries at Synnada/Dokimaion in Phrygia.[37]

7. Though it would be useful to carry out a careful re-examination of mining and quarrying under the Empire, without presuppositions as to what "imperial" properties were or what economic or financial functions they performed, for the moment only a very few tentative generalisations are possible. Imperial officials concerned with mines are attested in various provinces.[38] But, though Tertullian clearly implies (text to n. 3 above) that the material for cult statues typically came from *metalla Caesarum*, it is certain that the ownership of mines and quarries was never formally or completely monopolised by the emperor.[39] The lawyers therefore record specific penalties for the theft of gold or silver from *metalla Caesariana*, or of anything from

---

35. *Passio Sanctorum IV Coronatorum*, ed. W. Wattenbach, in M. Büdinger, *Untersuchungen zur römischen Kaisergeschichte* III (1870), 321. See Täckholm (n. 4), 136–37; *RE* Supp. IX, 674, s.v. "Pannonia" (A. Mócsy); A. Mócsy, *Pannonia and Upper Moesia* (1974), 326.

36. See the full study by H.-C. Noeske, "Studien zur Verwaltung und Bevölkerung der dakischen Goldbergwerke in römischer Zeit," *Bonn. Jahrb.* 177 (1977): 271.

37. See L. Robert, *Journal des Savants* (1962): 13–14, with refs., and cf. M. Waelkens, *Dokimeion: die Werkstatt der repräsentativen kleinasiatischen Sarkophage* (1982), esp. 124–25.

38. See, e.g., Pflaum, *Carrières* III, 1053, 1061, 1063, 1065.

39. See Jones, *LRE*, 837–39.

a *metallum principis* or the *sacra moneta* (imperial mint).[40] There were certainly both private and imperial mines; it is equally certain that free labour, and normal slave labour, could be employed in both. When Tertullian elsewhere (*De Cult. Fem.* 1, 5, 1) characterises gold and silver as the product of convict labour (*poenale opus*), he is once again generalising for rhetorical purposes.

It could not even be strictly proved that all those condemned *ad metallum* worked in imperial *metalla*. It is natural, and perhaps correct, to assume that they did; and this would explain why it had to be carefully reiterated by the lawyers that such persons became not "slaves of Caesar" or "slaves of the *fiscus*" but "slaves of the penalty [*poena*]"; but in fact the same principle was held to apply to those condemned to the sword, or *ad bestias*.[41] Furthermore the other evidence for the use of imperial properties as places of detention or exile all relates to individual upper-class victims,[42] and affords little basis for the idea that such properties might have been used on an extensive scale for this purpose. The only significant hint of such a general use comes in Valerian's order of 258 that *Caesariani* (imperial slaves) who persisted in Christianity should be bound and sent off to *Caesarianae possessiones* (Cyprian, *Ep.* 81, 1, 2). There is, however, no positive indication that they were to be put to work there. Most imperial possessions, like most property in the ancient world, will have consisted of land. It is perhaps the most significant feature of the use of convict labour under the Empire that it seems never to have been employed on the most important work of all, that on the land (see below).

However, in spite of these reservations, there are clear cases of convict labour being employed in imperial mines and quarries under the control of imperial officials, and conversely no definite evidence for its being made available for private exploitation. It is therefore reasonable to assume that the convicts did work solely in *metalla Caesariana*. If that is so, then the possibility of such a form of forced labour was a function of the gradual spread of imperial ownership of properties of all types. The opportunity thus existed to combine the notion of applying physically degrading penalties to free persons with the existence of properties of various economic types. There might (in principle) therefore have been a significant general deployment of convict labour by way of direct exploitation of these properties. But in fact our inadequate evidence suggests that imperial landed properties were more often leased out for a cash rent than exploited directly through a slave

40. *Dig.* 48, 13, 8, 1; 19, 38 *pr.* = *Pauli Sent.* V, 21a, 1.
41. See, e.g., *Dig.* 28, 3, 6, 6; 29, 2, 25, 2–3; 34, 8, 3 *pr.*; 48, 19, 12; 17 *pr.*
42. *ERW*, 182.

labour force;[43] convict labour is attested only in imperial mines and quarries. The economic objectives which could thus have been sought were therefore of a comparatively limited character; the products, in the form of stone or metal, could have been put on the market, used for minting or (perhaps) for the army, or employed directly in imperial building projects; high-quality marble from imperial quarries might also—as seems clear in some attested cases—have been granted as a gift to cities for their buildings.[44] It *may* not be an accident that our clearest evidence relates once again to cities and their public works.

It remains to see if there were any other economic functions which might have been performed by convict labour. Since the treatment of long-term convicts closely resembled that of slaves—and the victims indeed included existing slaves—it will be natural to look first at forms of labour which were by convention used as a punishment for slaves.

Pistrinum

We saw earlier (text to n. 8 above) Apuleius' graphic description of men, tattooed and in shackles, working in a mill or bakery; were they slaves, slaves sent for punishment, or possibly convicted free men? What needs no demonstration is that being sent to labour in a *pistrinum* had long been a punishment which hung over slaves (e.g., Plautus, *Pseud.* 494–95).[45] Similarly, as we also saw (text to n. 9 above), a fugitive slave apprehended in Ephesus might have been detained either in a *custodia publica* or in a *pistrinum*. The implication is therefore that a *pistrinum* was a place where persons were restrained either by fetters or by being locked in, or both, and from which escape would be difficult. This could be the case even for someone who hired out his services to *pistores* (millers or bakers), like Callidromus (already an escaped slave) who was detailed by two *pistores* in Nicomedia, to whom he had hired his *operae* (services), and fled to a statue of Trajan (Pliny, *Ep.* 10, 74). It is therefore no surprise to find that Callistus, even before his condemnation to *metallum* in Sardinia (see above), had been punished by being sent to a *pistrinum* by his master in Rome, some time in the 180s.

43. *ERW*, 185–86; compare D. J. Crawford, "Imperial Estates," M. I. Finley, ed., *Studies in Roman Property* (1976), 35.

44. *ERW*, 184.

45. See also Plautus, *Asinaria* 708–9, and L. A. Moritz, *Grain-Mills and Flour in Classical Antiquity* (1958), 67–68.

Since the use of convict labour evolved in close conjunction with slave labour in other contexts under the Empire, we might well expect that *pistrina*, equipped for detention, penal in character and readily to hand everywhere, would have served the same purpose. Until the fourth century, however, the evidence is almost non-existent. Pliny reports that grain produced in part of Campania was ground in a wooden mortar, the power for the pestle being supplied by convicts in chains ("vinctorum poenali opera," *NH* 18, 112). But here, as elsewhere, there is no certain way of distinguishing (formerly) free convicts from slaves enduring extra punishment. When we reach the fourth century, there is some clear evidence for the condemnation of free persons to *pistrina*, but it all concerns the city of Rome itself. In 319 Constantine wrote to the *praeses* (governor) of Sardinia (*CTh* 9, 40, 3): "Let those who in the future appear to deserve punishment for non-serious offences be consigned to the *pistrina* of Rome. When your Sincerity begins to carry this out, all will be aware that those who, as indicated above, deserve to undergo a sentence of this sort for non-serious offences, are to be consigned to *ergastula* [work houses] or *pistrina* and sent to the City of Rome, that is the Praefectus Annonae, under suitable escort." Thereafter, more consistent evidence does not appear in legal sources until the second half of the fourth century.[46] None the less, Constantine's letter clearly attests this new category of custodial penalty for minor offenders. Once again, the purpose served is one which responds to one of the limited economic objectives of the imperial system, namely the supply of bread for the population of Rome, an innovation (as against the supply of corn) introduced in the third century.[47]

Gynaecea and Other Manufacturing Establishments

However modest the economic objectives of the imperial state may have been, they clearly underwent some expansion in the late third and fourth centuries. It is only then that we begin to have evidence of manufacturing establishments run by the state and concerned with the production and dyeing of textiles. The earliest reference to such an establishment seems to be in Eusebius' account of the presbyter Dorotheus at Antioch who, because he was a eunuch, was honoured by the emperor towards the end of the third century with the charge (*epitropē*) of the dye works at Tyre (*HE* 7, 32, 3). This

46. See, e.g., *CTh* 9, 40, 5–7; 9; 14, 3, 12; 17, 6. See J.-P. Waltzing, *Corporations professionelles* II (1896), 333–34.

47. See D. van Berchem, *Les distributions de blé et d'argent à la plèbe romaine* (1939), 104–5; G. Rickman, *The Corn Supply of Ancient Rome* (1980), 206–7.

accidental allusion reveals a development of some significance and of wholly unknown (and undatable) origin. By the end of the fourth century imperial *baphia* (dye works), *gynaecea* (woollen mills), and to a much lesser extent *linyphia* (linen mills) were scattered across the Empire, providing clothing exclusively (so far as is known) for the army and the court.[48] So far as can be discerned, the bulk of their workers were in principle free but bound to their occupation.[49] None the less we do have evidence from the first half of the fourth century for the condemnation of free people to these establishments. Under Galerius, after 305, Lactantius reports that ladies of free and even noble birth were thrown *in gynaeceum* (*De Mort. Pers.* 21, 4). Constantine, after his victory in 324, records that under Licinius Christians had been condemned to be thrown into *gynaecea* or *linyphia* "to endure unwonted and wretched toil" or (and?) to be considered "slaves of the *fiscus*" (Eusebius, *Vit. Const.* 2, 34). Finally, Constantine again, at the end of a letter to a praetorian prefect read out in Carthage in August 336, says "As for the son of Licinianus, who has been captured in flight, let him be bound with shackles and consigned to the service of the *gynaeceum* in Carthage" (*CTh* 4, 3, 6; this sentence omitted from *CJ* V, 27, 1). The man concerned was an illegitimate son of Licinius, evidently by a slave or freedwoman, whom Constantine had earlier that year ordered to have his property confiscated and to be beaten, shackled, and reduced to his original status (*CTh* 4, 6, 2).

These items of evidence, however inadequate, are enough to show that convicts represented at least one source of labour for the imperial clothing factories which had been created by the early fourth century. It may well be right to see the establishments themselves as in some way attempts to compensate for the decline of slave labour.[50] But once again the objectives of this new system, whose scale in this early period is wholly unknown, were strictly limited in character.

---

48. See Jones, *LRE*, 836–37, and "The Cloth Industry under the Roman Empire," in P. A. Brunt, ed., *The Roman Economy* (1974), 350.

49. See N. Charbonnel, "La condition des ouvriers dans les atéliers impériaux aux IVᵉ et Vᵉ siècles," in F. Burdeau et al., *Aspects de l'Empire Romain* (1964), 61, esp. 77–78. Note also, for the *fabrica* at Sardis, C. Foss, *Byzantine and Turkish Sardis* (1976), 7–8, 14–15, and "The Fabricenses Ducenarii of Sardis," *ZPE* 35 (1979): 279 (*SEG* XXIX, 1206). For the imperial dye works at Tyre, note too the sarcophagus "of Thioktistus, dyer of the most sacred imperial purple"; see J.-P. Rey-Coquais, *Inscriptions de la Nécropole* (1977), no. 28.

50. See Charbonnel (n. 49), 70–71.

Conclusions

Looked at from the point of view of penal principles and practice, the development under the Empire of custodial penalties involving the subjection of free people to beating, fettering, and hard labour represents a radical innovation both in the coercive capacities of the state and in the attitude to individuals. In spite of the immense bulk of the surviving juristic literature from this period, it would, however, hardly be possible to characterise this change as an evolution in legal *theory*, for no trace of any systematic justification or discussion of its various aspects can be discerned. There could thus hardly be a greater contrast with the intense debates and thoroughgoing applications of new penal theories in the eighteenth and nineteenth centuries, analysed in Michel Foucault's *Surveiller et punir: naissance de la prison* (1975). None the less, the juristic writing on this subject, as on many others, is heavily charged with values and presuppositions which make it an essential part of the social and ideological history of the Empire. So also is the Christian literature of reaction to savage punishments, and above all the writing of Tertullian.

In this contemporary literature the notion that convict labour might function as a substitute for a declining supply of slave labour plays absolutely no part. That will hardly occasion surprise and, of course, constitutes no proof that it did not have such a function. What is much more significant is the apparent absence of convict labour from agriculture. Yet it does not need to be stated that the use of slaves in shackles was known, or that it was common for slave owners to keep slaves locked in *ergastula* (cf. Columella 1, 6, 3), into which unwary travellers, both free and slave, might disappear by way of kidnapping (Suetonius, *Aug.* 32). However, although we might reasonably expect to find convict labour being used in agriculture, most of the possible evidence for this seems in fact to allude to slave labour. For instance, Columella's references to using as a vinedresser a *noxius* (criminal) bought *de lapide* (at the slave market) (3, 3, 8) seems clearly to refer to a slave sold as a punishment; similarly his allusion to the labour in vineyards of *alligati* (persons in bond) who were *noxii* seems to indicate people who were part of the *familia* (1, 9, 4–5). It is rather less certain whether Pliny the Elder, speaking of the current form of agricultural labour (18, 21), is necessarily referring to slaves: the tasks, he says, formerly performed with their own hands by senators and generals were now fulfilled by men with their feet in chains, condemned and tattooed on the face ("vincti pedes, damnatae manus inscriptique vultus"), who came from the *ergastula*.[51] If, as it seems, this too is a reference to slaves

---

51. For a full discussion, see R. Étienne, "Recherches sur l'ergastule," *Actes du Colloque 1972 sur l'esclavage* (1974), 249.

enduring a penal form of labour, inflicted as a punishment (cf. also *Σ* Juv. 6, 151), then there is a striking resemblance to the conditions to which the free poor were soon to be condemned. But we still have no proof of the employment of formerly free convicts in agriculture, even on the ever growing imperial estates. If the question of the shortage of slaves had indeed been of fundamental importance, then the means existed within agriculture, by far the largest section of the economy, for deploying convict labour under strict surveillance.

In fact, it may be suggested, we are not dealing with a phenomenon of that level of economic importance. Though there is absolutely no way of computing the numerical scale of convict labour, it is clear that by the second century it was a familiar and accepted fact (note the casual reference to condemnation to *metallum* in Artemidorus 1, 59). But it was deployed, as it seems, simply where degrading or intensely laborious work was available, in "public" (i.e., city) work and in the mines and quarries of Caesar. Convict labour, which was in any case in part the labour of convicted slaves, thus contributed to the utilities of the cities, to the quarrying of stones for building, and to the production of precious metals and rare minerals; perhaps also (though this is not specifically attested) to that of common metals such as iron or tin; it would also be interesting to know how widely it was employed in salt-works. It was only in the later third and fourth centuries that the state consigned convict labour to the *pistrina* of Rome, or came to possess factories where convict labour assisted (at least) in the production of clothing for the army and the court. The narrow contours of the deployment of convict labour thus represent a quite significant expression of the limits of "economic" thinking in imperial society.

What is far more clearly defined and far more significant is the reservation of these penalties to lower-class persons. The term "lower-class" here necessarily refers to the vast majority of the inhabitants of the Empire (those below the status of town councillor or veteran). We are not therefore dealing with penalties reserved for a "criminal class" or specific groups who were conceived of as subversive or dangerous. Such "bad men" (*mali homines*) — temple robbers, bandits, kidnappers, thieves — are indeed referred to by Ulpian as requiring a governor's special attention (*Dig.* 1, 18, 13 *pr.*); but the severe penalties which appeared in the Empire threatened a far wider group and reflect social rather than specifically criminological ideas. The significant fact is the close association made between social class and either exemption from or exposure to beating, shackling, being confined in prison, painful and prolonged forms of death, and employment on forms of labour which were either degrading or physically destructive, or both. In this context labour was seen, and used, as a form of violence to the body which was closely comparable to flogging, the cross, or exposure to the beasts. Tertullian was thus wholly justified in placing so much rhetorical emphasis on the various forms of laceration applied to the bodies of condemned Christians. Condemnation to custodial penalties involving hard labour exposed the victims to similar if more prolonged forms of violence to the body and was preceded as a matter of course by whipping. The economic functions of such custodial penalties were not without significance, not least in their very distinct directions and limits; but they should none the less be seen as secondary. It was only an extension of a general principle when the early fourth-century Christians went to the mines with one eye gouged out and a tendon severed: "not so much for service as for the sake of ill-treatment and hardship."

CHAPTER EIGHT

The Equestrian Career
under the Empire*

Prosopographical methods, which have revolutionized the study of republican politics, have produced for the imperial age results less spectacular in themselves but no less fundamental for our understanding of the historical processes involved. The history of the Roman governing class in this period becomes one not of violent change but of slow development and evolution, and the immense and ever increasing mass of documentary evidence enables us to observe these processes in the persons and careers of hundreds of men quite unknown to the literary sources. This is true above all of senators, for the senatorial cursus, developed in the Republic, further regularized and expanded in the Empire, affords a framework within which careers can be precisely analysed and compared. We can tell whether a man's early posts showed promise of future advancement, or whether he rose fast or slowly or received some check in midcareer, and may be able to relate a distortion of the normal pattern in the course of his advancement to historical events of his life-time. In other words, from the bare record of posts held it is often possible to form, within certain limits, a true and meaningful conception of a man's public life.

Some hundreds of inscriptions reveal, in very similar ways, the careers of people who belonged to the equestrian order (*equites*) in the first three centuries of the Empire. But, while an enormous amount can be learnt from them, the careers they reveal do not display an obvious structure—comparable with the essential core of senatorial posts and magistracies held in Rome, the vigintivirate, quaestorship, tribunate, praetorship, and consul-

*First published as a review of H.-G. Pflaum, *Les carrières procuratoriennes équestres sous le Haut-Empire romain* I–III (Paris, 1960–61) in *JRS* 53 (1963): 194–200. Some detailed points of discussion are omitted here.

ate—which could enable the assured comparison of one career with another. But, where there is enough evidence, patterns which are not explicit and obvious may still be sought. O. Hirschfeld, *Die Kaiserlichen Verwaltungsbeamten bis auf Diocletian*[2] (Berlin, 1905), 410–11, discussed theprocuratorial career with typical elegance and caution, but found that no firm results could be achieved. Pflaum's true predecessor was A. Von Domaszewski, *Die Rangordnung des Römischen Heeres* (Bonn, 1908; rev. ed. B. Dobson, 1967). On pp. 141–42 he produced a brief *schema* of grades of procuratorial posts, based on the military ranks from which promotion to each grade followed. The results, though compressed and achieved without much regard to chronological development, are far from unconvincing.

The full treatment of the subject has been left to Pflaum, who has devoted to it an immense learning and a large part of his life. The results were shown first in his *Procurateurs équestres sous le Haut-Empire romain* (1950); the three admirably produced volumes under review form the promised "thèse complémentaire" of that book and are the culmination of his work. The first two volumes deal in separate entries with some 350 individual careers (i.e., on Pflaum's definition, a case where at least two equestrian posts are attested for a man, other than the four major prefectures); in each entry the documentary and literary evidence is set out in full and is followed by a detailed discussion. The third volume gives *addenda* and then something of enormous value in itself, the lists (*fasti*) of all the various equestrian procuratorial posts in Rome, Italy, and the provinces, and finally immensely detailed indices covering persons, places, posts, and sources of evidence, and relating both to this work and the *Procurateurs*. The "tableaux d'avancement" give a tabular analysis of all the careers discussed divided by type and period. It can thus be seen that, if it were nothing else, this would be a reference work on a considerable scale and of lasting value.

It is, however, essentially not a work of reference alone, but an instrument in the demonstration of Pflaum's theses about the equestrian career (*cursus*). This dual function of the work must be reflected in any full review of it. In this chapter, therefore, I will consider Pflaum's views and the value of his contribution as a whole—which will involve some reference to the *Procurateurs*, with which this work is so intimately linked. A detailed review of the individual entries will not be included.

Pflaum's primary thesis is that the appellations *trecenarius, ducenarius, centenarius*, and *sexagenarius* (indicating an annual salary of 300,000, 200,000, 100,000 and 60,000 sesterces respectively), which are attached sometimes to the titles of equestrian posts and sometimes to the names of their holders, relate to established grades which gave the essential structure of the equestrian *career* throughout the period concerned. Two major difficulties have to be dealt with before such a view could seem probable. Firstly, as Pflaum is of course well aware, these terms do not appear on documents until the reign of Commodus. The two pages (*Procurateurs*, pp. 29–30) in which Pflaum argues his case for extending these grades back to the reign of Augustus are hardly adequate for something so fundamental to his work. Secondly, Pflaum recognized himself that there is no attested equivalent in the case of equestrians for the laws regulating minimum ages and intervals between tenure of magistracies which dictated the structure of senatorial careers (*Procurateurs*, p. 210). But what then do we make of propositions such as that the organisation of the hierarchy of posts under Tiberius still allowed certain liberties with the pattern of promotion ("L'organisation de la hiérarchie sous Tibère permettait encore à l'empereur de telles libertés avec le tableau d'avancement," *Carrières*, p. 4)—or of the many other occasions on which Pflaum speaks of the rules (*regles*) which governed equestrian promotions?

Taking these two points together, one can admit that Pflaum has shown, firstly, that posts which were in existence throughout the whole period tended to remain in the same relation of importance to each other and, secondly, that in the period from the end of the first to the middle of the third century there was a regular pattern of promotion, or rather a series of linked regular patterns. But the distinction between a system which, in the process of development and expansion, retained certain regularities and one in which there were from the beginning explicit grades and rules of promotion is fundamental. Pflaum has nowhere given a clear and full statement of his reasons for preferring the second of these views.

On general grounds, should we be ready to accept the conception of an organized "career" as fundamental to the nature of equestrian office-holding from the beginning? It may be worth detailing here some considerations relevant to the soundness of Pflaum's conclusions and their wider importance.

1. Pflaum almost totally ignores freedmen procurators. Even, for instance, in his article s.v. "procurator" in Pauly-Wissowa XXIII (which, lamentably, is merely a condensed and revised version of his *Procurateurs*) he devotes only a paragraph to them (cols. 1277–78). There he lays down that there was a distinction of principle between equestrian and freedmen procurators, because the latter hardly ever have the title *procurator Augusti*. But this is an absurdity, for a man who calls himself, for instance, *Acastus Aug(usti) lib(ertus) procurator provinciae Mauretaniae* (Acastus, Augustus' freedman, procurator of the province of Mauretania, *ILS* 1483) need not, and for stylistic reasons will not, repeat the *Aug(usti)* after *procurator*. This curious slip apart, Pflaum does,

however, seem to believe (as he indicates in *Procurateurs*, p. 34, and *Carrières*, p. 114) that freedmen procurators were systematically the *assistants* of equestrian procurators, even where the posts held are apparently identical. He might have been able to prove this in his promised *Mémoire sur les sousprocurateurs*, but alas this never saw the light of day. I find it difficult to accept. It is true that (as in Tac. *Ann.* 13, 1, Pliny *Ep.* 10, 84 or *CIL* VIII 25902) where an equestrian and a freedman procurator are mentioned together, the equestrian is mentioned first; but there is nothing in such cases to show that their functions were not identical. Pflaum admits of course that, for instance, the post of *praefectus classis* (prefect of the fleet) could at first be held by freedmen. But in discussing the career of Pompeius Macer (*Carrières*, No. 2), he has to assume, gratuitously, that his post in connection with Augustus' libraries must have been some higher function than that performed by the freedman Hyginus. Again, he does not mention the freedman, Halotus (*PIR*² H 11), on whom Galba "bestowed an important procuratorship" (an expression used by Pliny *Ep.* 7, 31, 3–4 to refer, implicitly, to the procuratorships of the *vicesima hereditatium* [the collection of the 5 per cent tax on inheritances] and the Alpes Graiae; see No. 54).

This concentration on equestrians leads to factual errors, as where (*Carrières*, p. 209) he says that the earliest evidence for districts for the collection of the *vicesima hereditatium* dates to the reign of Hadrian—ignoring *CIL* VI 8443, *Ti(berius) Claud(ius) Aug(usti) lib(ertus) Saturninus proc(urator) XX here(ditatium) prov(inciae) Achaeae*. It also means that his otherwise invaluable lists of holders of the individual posts are incomplete. They do not give a list of all the holders of these posts. But a more serious consideration is that the fact that some of the civilian posts open to equestrians could also be held by freedmen must be relevant to a proper view of them. They were not in fact such that they could only be reached via a "career."

Equestrian and freedman office-holding ought to be considered together, and compared. Curiously, Pflaum in the *Procurateurs*, pp. 198–99, lays considerable emphasis on the letter of Fronto in which he supports the petition of an imperial freedman, Aridelus, for a procuratorship "in the right form, at the right place and time" (*petit nunc procurationem ex forma suo loco et iuõ tempore*), but gives no further consideration to office-holding by freedmen.

2. By the mere process of including only men who held two or more equestrian posts Pflaum has excluded from his view men who held only a single post. But it cannot be assumed that in every case where only one post is known, further evidence would show a full "career." Equestrian posts might, it is in fact clear, be an adjunct to a man's personal standing. A Greek sophist might become *advocatus fisci* (a legal representative of the imperial emperor's

treasury) in a province (like Quirinius in Asia, Philos. *VS* II, 29, omitted by Pflaum, *Carrières*, p. 1073) or in Rome (Heliodorus, *VS* II, 32), a *procurator* (Dionysius, *JOAI* XL, 1953, 6–7) or *ab epistulis graecis* (the official in charge of the emperor's Greek correspondence) (Hadrianos, *VS* II, 10), just as Trajan's doctor, Statilius Criton, became a *procurator* (if a restoration in Robert, *La Carie* II, p. 167, no. 49 is correct). Plutarch was made *epitropos* (i.e., *procurator*) of Achaea in his old age (Euseb. *Chron.* ad 119 — I can see no reason to dismiss this) and a third-century Palmyrene, Iulius Aurelius Septimius Vorodes, was *procurator Augusti* and also *procurator centenarius* of Zenobia (*Bull. Ét. Or. Inst. Fr. Damas* IX, 1942–43, 60–61). Pflaum tends to see "careers" where perhaps there were none. He says, for instance, of P. Aelius Zeuxidemus Aristus Zeno (*Carrières*, No. 205), who was high priest (*archiereus*) of Asia and *advocatus fisci* in Phrygia and then in Asia, that he was probably too old when first appointed to go through the normal stages of the career. That is surely to misconceive the man's position — compare the Ulpii Lycini, grandfather and grandson (*MAMA* VI, 373, conflated by Pflaum, *Carrières*, p. 1074), who were both *advocatus fisci* in Phrygia. These examples suggest again that the "career" was not essential to equestrian office-holding.

3. Even with military posts the "career" is not perhaps as prevalent as Pflaum supposes. The possibility of holding a prefecture or tribunate as a sinecure is explicitly attested in the late Republic (Nepos *Att.* 6, 4; see also Cic. *ad fam.* 7, 8, 1, and *ad Att.* 5, 21, 10), and Suet. *Div. Claud.* 25 records the institution of a "a type of fictitious military post" by Claudius (see Hirschfeld, *Verwaltungsbeamten*, p. 422). Moreover it has long been recognized — though the fact is not, I think, explicitly acknowledged by Pflaum — that the office of *praefectus fabrum* (prefect of engineers) in the Empire was normally a sinecure. One might well suspect that the single military tribunate (with no legion mentioned) held by C. Julius Spartiaticus (*Carrières*, No. 24 *bis*) was nominal. In that case he perhaps never left Sparta, and his procuratorship could be considered, like some posts mentioned above, an adjunct of his local position — note that C. Iulius Laco, probably his brother (*JRS* 51 [1961]: 118), was also a *procurator*. Then C. Stertinius Xenophon (*Carrières*, No. 16) moved into the imperial service, as *archiatros* (chief doctor), from a profitable practice in Rome. Surely the tribunate and *praefectura fabrum* which he held were nominal posts given him as Claudius' *comes* (companion) on the British expedition? Similarly with the jurist Caecilius Crescens Volusianus (*Carrières*, 142) who was *praefectus fabrum* and then *advocatus fisci Romae* (i.e., *advocatus fisci* in Rome). It is worth noting the case of one P. Messius Augustinus Maecianus (son of *Carrières*, No. 231), "a youth of senatorial rank who had filled three posts of equestrian status." The posts held by a youth (*puer*) will surely have

been nominal. One might wonder how many such cases lurk in the inscriptions of "careers" (perhaps, for instance, the tribunate and the command of an auxiliary cohort, *praefectura cohortis*, of Titinius Capito, *Carrières*, No. 60?).

4. Sherwin-White established years ago (*PBSR* 15 [1939]) that careers stretching across the different types of equestrian posts only began with the reign of Claudius. But even after that there was never a common core of posts held by all equestrians or a common point of entry to equestrian posts. A man might hold his posts in Rome, or never come to Rome at all. Nor did any formal age limits for the holding of posts shape the equestrian "career."

5. Pflaum himself lays down (*Procurateurs*, pp. 165–66) that the actual level of pay for procuratorial posts could not have exhausted the possible profits to be gained from them. All holders of such posts already possessed the equestrian census of 400,000 sesterces, and many had already occupied magistracies in cities. The main profits of equestrian office may well have come from incidental benefits, gifts, or simply bribes. The pay itself was clearly not a *negligible* factor (Fronto, in recommending Appian, is careful to say that he is not moved "by ambition or greed for the procurator's salary," but we have no a priori reason for assuming that the level of pay was from the beginning the index by which procurators were graded).

Given such considerations, Pflaum ought to have established the basis of his theory by an examination of all the documentary and literary uses of *ducenarius* and the other terms. In doing this, he might perhaps have asked himself explicitly why it was precisely in the reign of Commodus that these terms came into common semi-official use. The answer in fact seems clear from his own survey in *Procurateurs*, pp. 29–30, of the gradual multiplication of equestrian posts. Ducenariate posts (to use Pflaum's classification) predominate in the first century and in the Hadrianic period are still as numerous as centenariate or sexagenariate posts. Only in the reign of Commodus, when the total of attested posts reaches 136, do we find a typical "pyramid" hierarchy (51 "sexagenariate" posts, 48 "centenariate," and 36 "ducenariate"). The process was perhaps roughly as follows. Equestrian officials, as is beyond dispute, received a yearly salary from the inception of the Principate. Up to the mid-second century the more important posts were an identifiable group with a common level of pay. Their holders might thus (occasionally) be referred to as *ducenarii*. In this period there are no documentary uses of the term, and only two literary: Suet., *Div. Claud.* 24: "[H]e conferred consular marks of honour also on procurators holding a ducenariate post" (a procurator of Pontus and Bithynia, Iunius Cilio, and of Gaul, Graecinius Laco), and Apuleius, *Met.* 7, 6: "a procurator of the princeps who filled a ducenariate post" (the date of the *Metamorphoses* is of course uncertain). In the reign of Marcus Aurelius we get the first documentary use, in an inscription from Bulla Regia, not available to Pflaum, but reported in *Fasti Archeologici* 13 (1958): 4404 (with a photograph, pl. XXVI, fig. 78), and *Studi Romani* 7 (1960): 331, and printed as *AE* 1962, 183. It details the career of one Q. Domitius Marsianus up to the post of procurator of the emperor's private property (*patrimonium*) in the province of Narbonensis and gives an example of the letters of appointment (*codicilli*) of Marcus Aurelius making him a *ducenarius*. In the reign of Commodus the number of less important posts had swollen sufficiently to make it worth while to use *ducenarius* quite commonly as a semi-official term on documents, and to use *centenarius* and *sexagenarius* (not found in literary sources with this meaning) to distinguish the lower levels. *Trecenarius* also appears, but only twice in the period covered by Pflaum. For almost a century these terms are in common use to designate grades of post; their significance is attested explicitly by Dio 53, 15, 5: "As for the procurators, the very title of their rank is derived from the level of the pay given to them," which is supported by 52, 25, 2, from the Maecenas speech; both passages relate to Dio's own time. But even in this period these terms still appear in only one in four of the careers discussed by Pflaum. Nine posts are explicitly attested, eight of them only once, as sexagenariate, ten (eight or nine of them once only) as centenariate, and seventeen (seven once only) as ducenariate. In the face of the total of 182 posts which on Pflaum's reckoning (*Procurateurs*, p. 105) are attested for this period, these figures (which are purely for guidance and do not take account of many difficulties) are not very impressive. Moreover, there are considerable variations in terminology—*procurator ducenarius* (a procurator holding a ducenariate post), *promotus ad ducenariam* (advanced to a ducenariate [procuratorship]), *ducenarius praefectus vehiculorum* (ducenariate prefect of the state wagons), *adsumptus in consilium ad HS LX* (admitted to the council with a salary of 60,000 sesterces)—which should indicate that the terms did not have an established function. In the second half of the third century *ducenarius* at least came to be an honorific term not related to specific posts.

The documentary uses of *sexagenarius* and *centenarius* give little opportunity of checking for coherence. The uses of *ducenarius* do, however, show that there were some posts, especially those in Egypt, where the level of pay was stable. Pontus and Bithynia also is a post which remained ducenariate from the mid-first to the early third century (*Carrières*, No. 325). But it is also clear that there were posts, like those of *praefectus vehiculorum*, *a studiis* (a "secretarial" post whose precise role is uncertain), the imperial domain at Hadrumetum, or member of the emperor's council (*consiliarius*), which could be held at two levels of pay. Others fluctuated in importance. The procuratorship of Thrace in this period will not fit easily into Pflaum's scheme; *Carrières*, No. 244 (A.D. 200–1) is a *sexagenarius*, but *Carrières*, No. 268 (T. Aurelius Calpurnianus) comes to the post from Moesia Inferior, which ought to be centuriate. Pflaum has to say that this was after the "intensive urbanization" (i.e., the Pizos inscription) carried out by Severus and Caracalla — but Calpurnianus' procuratorship cannot be closely dated (*PIR*² A 1471). Under *Carrières*, No. 312 the post has become centuriate again.

When we come to look at the patterns of promotion over the whole period it is clear that while the relative importance of posts remained remarkably constant, the concept of established grades is simply not relevant before the last part of the first century, since the required lesser posts are not there in sufficient numbers. From then on there are certainly established patterns of promotion, but there is nothing to show that any prescriptive rules governed them. The greatest regularity is shown in the careers of former equestrian officers and of *ex-primipili bis* (centurions who held the senior centurionate of a legion for a second time). The importance of the "praetorian" careers of the latter (see especially M. Bassaeus Rufus, *Carrières*, No. 162) is clearly demonstrated (that is, careers taking them through tribunates in the praetorian cohorts). But at all times men might enter at different points in the scale or might miss a grade, with no trace of expressions comparable with those like *adlectus* or *promotus inter praetorios* (elected or promoted into the rank of ex-praetors) which indicate the exceptional advancement of a senator (nor were there *insignia* of the different grades). Posts might gain or lose in importance — the procuratorship of the *quadragesima Galliarum* (the 2.5 per cent customs duty in Gaul and Germany), the *quattuor publica Africae* (the four indirect taxes raised in Africa), and the *argentariae Pannonicae et Delmaticae* (the silver-mines of Pannonia and Dalmatia), for instance, seem to have gained, while the *praefectura alae* (prefecture of a cavalry unit) lost; from Hadrian's reign on ex–*praefecti alae* sometimes move to relatively minor posts such as those of *censitor* (the official in charge of the census in a province) or of *epistrategus* in Egypt.

Pflaum has demonstrated both that the structure of equestrian promotions remained extremely stable and that intelligible patterns can be traced within the structure. He has not shown that any explicit rules were ever formulated for it.

What should be the final judgement on Pflaum's work? His principal thesis cannot, so far as I can see, be formally disproved; it may be the case that equestrian careers, from the inception of the principate, were structured on a series of established grades based on the level of pay. But it cannot be proved either, and the theory as such seems an unnecessary encumbrance on an otherwise readily intelligible pattern in which a number of disparate posts entrusted to equestrians gradually coalesced into something like an organized civil service. On this view, the rankings in terms of pay, explicitly attested by Dio but still appearing only in a minority of documents in the period 170–270, would be regarded as a consequence of the development and extension of equestrian office-holding, rather than as a factor determining the nature of that development.

But whatever objections there may be to the categories into which Pflaum attempts to fit his material, the patterns of promotion and office-holding which he demonstrates are undeniable and make this work a landmark in our understanding of an important aspect of the imperial administration. Against this network of interrelated patterns individual careers can be interpreted with confidence in a way never before possible. In this immense collection of material, admirably set out and analysed with devotion and insight, Pflaum has produced a major contribution to the study of the Empire, and one which can stand comparison with the works of Hirschfeld and Stein.

CHAPTER NINE

Emperors, Frontiers, and Foreign Relations, 31 B.C. to A.D. 378[*]

Introduction

"Severus . . . was in the habit of saying that he had gained a large additional territory and made it a bulwark for Syria. But the facts themselves show that it is a source of continual wars for us, and of great expenses. For it provides very little revenue and involves very great expenditure; and having extended our frontiers to the neighbours of the Medes and Parthians, we are constantly so to speak at war in their defence." So writes Cassius Dio about the extension of the eastern frontier in the 190s and the creation of the provinces of Mesopotamia and Osrhoene.[1] The significance of the passage however, extends beyond the question of the eastern frontier itself at that moment. Written by an ex-consul, and former adviser of Severus, it reveals two types of justification for conquest uttered by the Emperor himself—one straightforwardly imperialistic, the other strategic; and a critique of this from two points of view, the balance of income and expenditure, and the wider strategic commitments incurred. Whether Dio had formulated such views already in Severus' reign we cannot know; this section of his History will have been written at the earliest towards 220, and probably later.[2] If he had, we have no reason to think that he expressed them to Severus. If he did, it can only have been after the event, for his own narrative at this point makes clear that

---

[*]First published in *Britannia* 13 (1982): 1–23. Earlier versions of this chapter were given at the universities of Berlin, Bielefeld, Bochum, and Cologne in July 1979 and at Miss J. M. Reynolds's and Mr. M. H. Crawford's seminar in Cambridge in October 1979. I am grateful for comments and suggestions to Sir Ronald Syme, Professor A. L. F. Rivet, and Professor J. J. Wilkes.

    1. Dio 75, 3, 2–3 (Boissevain III, 340).

    2. For an early chronology—probably too early—of the composition of the *Roman History*, see F. Millar, *A Study of Cassius Dio* (1964), chap. 2 and pp. 193–94.

the new province of Mesopotamia was entrusted to an equestrian, and an "honour" (the status of *colonia*) given to Nisibis, either after the campaign of 195, or (less probably) after that of 198, in neither of which Dio himself took part.[3] None the less, the fact that the passage retails both the authentic views of an emperor and a critique of them by an ex-consul may encourage us to ask some general questions: how, by whom, and within what conceptual frameworks were the foreign and frontier "policies" of the Empire formulated?

We need not doubt the importance of such problems. On the one hand the results of these policies had fundamental effects on the political, social, and cultural contexts within which millions of people lived, from the lamplighters of Oxyrhynchus taking their oath by "Caesar" in 30/29 B.C.;[4] to the people of Dura who found Roman troops established in their city in the late second century and then saw it destroyed by the Persians in the 250s; or (in Ammianus' marvellous description) the inhabitants of Nisibis evacuating the city in 363 under the terms of Jovian's treaty with Shapur II.[5] On the other hand the problems involve the extent of the geographical and ethnographical knowledge available to the emperors and their advisers; the nature of the conceptual framework which they could apply to this knowledge; and their conception of the Empire itself—either (to put it at its simplest) as an offensive system designed for further conquests, or as an essentially static defensive system. Then there are more specific and concrete but equally fundamental questions. Was (for instance) a map of the German or Tripolitanian frontier, or of northern Britain, available in Rome, or wherever the emperor was? In either case how, with what delays, and in what form did short-term information reach the emperor or whoever made decisions on frontier questions? Who indeed was involved in such decisions, and what difference did it make whether at the relevant moment the emperor was in Rome, in a province, or on campaign elsewhere?

These questions are, of course, prompted by E. N. Luttwak's excellent *Grand Strategy*,[6] whose approach is to analyse the actual dispositions of troops

---

3. Dio (n. 1); Nisibis as a *colonia*: Dio 36, 6, 2. For the background, see M. G. Angeli Bertinelli, "I Romani oltre l'Eufrate nel II secolo d. C (le province di Assiria, di Mesopotamia e di Osroene)," *ANRW* II.9.1 (1976), 3; cf. D. L. Kennedy, "Ti. Claudius Subatianus Aquila, 'First Prefect of Mesopotamia,'" *ZPE* 36 (1979): 255. The exact date of the creation of the two provinces cannot be determined.

4. *P. Oxy.* 1453 = *Sel. Pap.* II, no. 327.

5. Ammianus 25, 9.

6. E. N. Luttwak, *The Grand Strategy of the Roman Empire from the First Century* A.D. *to the Third* (1976).

and frontier installations at successive periods, and to deduce from them the nature and intentions of the current imperial strategy. It remains possible, however, to doubt whether all the successive phases actually answer to Lutt-wak's analyses, and to wonder whether indeed there was a "grand strategy" rather than a series of positions arrived at by ad hoc decisions.[7] It is there-fore all the more important to ask whether we can know how the emper-ors or others could or did acquire information, form views, and formulate decisions in these areas. It may be, of course, that we cannot. As Dio him-self observed in a famous passage, under the Empire decisions were taken in secret, and what was given out was often untrue, or at least unverifiable.[8] But imperial *civil* decisions did at least produce a vast series of written pro-nouncements, letters, and verdicts, preserved in literary and legal sources and on papyri and inscriptions, which are not merely products of the imperial entourage, but which cannot be falsified (unless proved to be inauthentic) because they are performative utterances which embody rather than report imperial actions. By contrast, whereas we know that there was correspon-dence between emperors and the governors of imperial provinces on matters of frontier policy, no texts of such letters survive. There were also letters be-tween emperors and foreign kings, but our only texts of these are offered by literary sources of the fourth century (the letter of Constantine to Shapur II, and Shapur's exchange of letters with Constantius in 358), and are of un-certain authenticity.[9] Comparable problems arise with imperial pronounce-ments which are certainly authentic, the *Res Gestae* of Augustus or Julian's *Letter to the Athenians*,[10] but which contain retrospective reports, justifications or celebrations of military or diplomatic policy. Like the victory titles of emperors, or their coins, columns, or arches, these pronouncements will tell us what was claimed, while leaving us without even the certainty that the claim was not justified. The difficulty in knowing simply "what happened" is illustrated dramatically, for instance, by the total contradiction between Graeco-Roman narrative sources on the death of Gordian III and the end-ing of the Persian campaigns under Philip, and our only external document

7. So J. C. Mann, "Power, Force and the Frontiers of the Empire," *JRS* 69 (1979): 175. Note also Mann, "The Frontiers of the Principate," *ANRW* II.1 (1974), 508.

8. Dio 53, 19.

9. Constantine: Eusebius, *VC* 4, 9–13. Eusebius (4, 8) attests the preservation of a copy of the Latin original in Constantine's own hand, which he reproduces in Greek. See H. Dörries, *Das Selbstzeugnis Kaiser Konstantins* (1954), 48–49, 125–27. Shapur and Constantius: Ammianus 17, 5.

10. Julian 268A–287D.

on imperial campaigns, the so-called *Res Gestae* of Shapur I from Naqsh-i-Rustam.[11] None the less, even the most blatant of propaganda will tell us what someone wished to be believed and will by implication reveal something of the values, objectives, and presuppositions both of its author and of its intended audience. As the passage of Dio shows, it does not follow that contemporary observers assented to the claims made in propaganda. But the overall pattern of propaganda must still tell us something of the conceptual framework within which policy was formulated.

The same applies to what must, for lack of anything better, remain our main source of evidence, the historical narratives, letters, and biographies of the period. Some of these at least — for instance, the works of the two Plinies, Tacitus, Suetonius, Dio, and Ammianus — come from precisely the class of men who were called to the emperor's *consilium*, acted as his secretaries, or served on his staff. Have we any reason to suppose that even those emperors (remarkably few) who were brought up and trained as such could have acquired a conception of frontier or foreign policy which was significantly different from theirs? Even if that could be shown, many of the emperors who played the most important parts in military history — for instance, Vespasian, Trajan, Septimius Severus, Aurelian, Diocletian, and Valentinian — came to the throne in middle life, from the Senate or from equestrian posts. Chance or circumstance could have brought Tacitus, Dio, or Ammianus to the throne just as well as Trajan, Severus, or Valentinian. We would be quite wrong to *assume* that imperial policy was informed by reasoning which was superior or different in kind from that of those who recorded it in historical narratives.

A superiority of immediate concrete information — in the form of messages from the frontiers — on the emperor's part might well be supposed. But even here his dependence on his social and cultural environment is manifest, for new information could come to him from three main sources: missions sent by him across the frontiers to explore and report back; reports from governors (men, once again, like Tacitus, Agricola, Pliny the Younger, or Dio); or the arrival of foreign envoys. In all these cases his perceptions of the situation must have been profoundly affected by the conceptions and interests of those presenting the information.

11. See A. Maricq, "Res Gestae Divi Saporis," *Syria* 35 (1958): 295. This episode is described in ll. 6–9; Shapur claims that he killed Gordian in battle and that Philip then made peace on payment of a large sum. Zosimus 1, 18–19, reports that Gordian won a victory and was then killed by the troops, instigated by Philip; cf. Eutropius 9, 2, 2–3; Aurelius Victor, *Caes.* 27, 8.

What follows is offered as no more than a few tentative steps towards analysing the conditions under which the external policy of the Empire was formulated and put into effect in the four centuries between Actium and Hadrianople. The need for such an approach is widely recognised,[12] and the theme is of considerable relevance to our understanding of the nature of the Empire. The discussion will be based on literary and documentary evidence, will have to be highly selective, and will do no justice to the complexities of particular campaigns or the archaeology of individual frontiers. But it may serve to raise some questions, and to emphasize the limits imposed on policy and its execution by Graeco-Roman culture, the structure of government, time, distance, and the conventions of diplomacy. No apology is made for the use of arguments from silence. We must *as a first step* listen to what our sources explicitly tell us and refrain from making assumptions as to what they do not tell us. If we then wish to claim (for instance) that the emperors systematically gathered and stored information from traders and others, at least we shall know that this is a hypothesis.

The Agents of Decision

No one will argue that the popular assemblies in Rome still played any part in the declaration of war or the making of treaties. Nor is there any reason to think that the Senate acted as a genuine vehicle of decision in military or foreign policy matters, in the sense of being a forum of debate where contrary opinions were expressed and votes taken. That said, however, the evidence shows that up to the mid-second century it could and often did play at least a formal role in matters affecting wars, "client" kings, and foreign relations. It seems indeed to have lost this role at roughly the same time as it ceased to receive embassies from provincial communities, a process which of course always retained the formal character of diplomatic traffic.[13]

In the early Empire the Senate might be the scene of the trials of "client"

---

12. For discussions of these and comparable problems, see for instance B. H. Warmington, "Frontier Studies and the History of the Roman Empire—Some Desiderata," *Actes du IXe Congrès international d'études sur les frontières romaines, 1972* (1974), 291; A. R. Birley, "Roman Frontiers and Roman Frontier Policy: Some Reflections on Roman Imperialism," *Transactions of the Architectural and Archaeological Society of Durham and Northumberland* 3 (1974), 13; G. D. B. Jones, "Concept and Development in Roman Frontiers," *Bulletin of the John Rylands Library* 61 (1978): 115. See also Mann (n. 7), the essays in D. H. Miller and J. D. Steffen, eds., *The Frontier: Comparative Studies* (1978), and G. W. Bowersock, "The Emperor's Burden," *Class. Philol.* 73 (1978): 346.

13. F. Millar, *The Emperor in the Roman World* (1977; 2nd ed., 1992), 343 (henceforth *ERW*).

kings,[14] though it was a sign of the future that, when in 23 B.C. Augustus brought Tiridates in person to appear against an embassy from Phraates in the Senate, the latter referred the matter back to him.[15] Under Tiberius the Senate was supposed to receive reports from imperial governors and was consulted on the recruitment and discharge of soldiers, the disposition of the legions and the non-citizens auxiliaries, and on replies to kings.[16] If we may believe Strabo's contemporary account, the decision to make Cappadocia a province in A.D. 17 was taken jointly by Emperor and Senate.[17] In 19 Tiberius addressed the Senate after granting refuge to Maroboduus, arguing that the king had been a greater threat than Pyrrhus or Antiochus III.[18] Gaius had the Senate vote on the grant of various client kingdoms in 38,[19] and under Claudius it voted that treaties made by the Emperor or his *legati* should be valid as if passed by Senate and People.[20] In 49 Parthian ambassadors appeared in the Senate and were answered by a speech from Claudius;[21] Trajan in 102 sent ambassadors from Decebalus to speak in the Senate and have the peace treaty confirmed, and when the king was reported to have broken it the Senate declared him an enemy.[22] Under Hadrian embassies from Vologaeses of Parthia and the Iazyges appeared in the Senate,[23] while Marcus Aurelius formally asked the Senate to vote funds for the war of 178—but, as Dio makes clear, solely as a deliberate gesture to constitutional theory.[24] When Dio suggests in the "speech of Maecenas" that embassies from hostile and allied kings or nations should be brought before the Senate, this clearly no longer corresponded to the reality of the early third century: "[F]or, other questions apart, it is appropriate and impressive if the Senate seems to have full powers."[25] However, even in this period, as they had done from the beginning, the emperors would write reports to the Senate on their military

14. E.g., Antiochus of Commagene, Dio 52, 43; Archelaus of Cappadocia, Dio 57, 17, 3–6; Rhescuporis of Thrace, Tacitus, *Ann.* 2, 67.

15. Dio 53, 33, 1–2.

16. Suetonius, *Tib.* 30; 32.

17. *Geog.* 12, 1, 4 (534).

18. Tacitus, *Ann.* 2, 63.

19. Dio 59, 12, 2.

20. Dio 60, 23, 6. See P. A. Brunt, "Lex de Imperio Vespasiani," *JRS* 67 (1977): 95, on p. 103.

21. Tacitus, *Ann.* 12, 10–11.

22. Dio 68, 9, 7–10, 1; 10, 3–4.

23. Dio 69, 15, 2.

24. Dio 72, 33, 2.

25. Dio 52, 31, 1.

and diplomatic dealings.[26] In the 160s, when for the first time there were two Augusti, Lucius Verus' letter of report from Parthia was read in the Senate and accompanied by a speech from Marcus Aurelius.[27]

These procedures cannot be regarded as having been vehicles of debate or decision, but like the related process of voting military honours for emperors and others,[28] they were by no means irrelevant to the issues discussed here. Even these formal votes, and the orations which accompanied them, will have served to formulate the prevailing notions of what constituted success in military and diplomatic policy, and hence to form those presuppositions which would lie behind future objectives.

The question of such a slowly evolving consensus is all the more vital because, as is beyond question, external policy was in fact created throughout the period within the framework provided by the emperor, his senatorial and equestrian friends, and his "secretarial" staff. It hardly needs stating once again that our evidence provides no hint of any ministries, headquarters, or general staffs established in Rome, or in the Tetrarchic or fourth-century "capitals," and functioning independently of the emperor. It was only in the late fourth century, and in the West, that *magistri militum* (masters of soldiers) attained a real military independence of the emperors.[29]

If we look first at the bureaucratic or "secretarial" entourage, as opposed to friends (*amici*) or officers, all our evidence combines to suggest its essentially civilian character. It is not only that there is, for instance, very little trace of *commentarii* (imperial records) or other records relating to military or diplomatic matters, to match those concerned with imperial legal decisions, the foundation of colonies, or the granting of the citizenship or other *beneficia* (favours).[30] It is rather that the "secretarial" entourage of the emperors visibly developed to serve civilian purposes: the hearing of embassies and legal cases, replying to *libelli* (petitions), writing letters in Latin and Greek. There was later an *a memoria*, or later still *magister memoriae*, of uncertain function—but never, surprisingly enough, any official concerned with

26. See, e.g., Dio 54, 9, 1 (Augustus to the Senate on foreign policy issues, 20 B.C.); Suetonius, *Calig.* 44; Dio 68, 29, 1–3 (Trajan from Parthia); 77, 12, 3 (Caracalla); 73, 27, 3 (Macrinus, 218).

27. Fronto, *Ad Verum Imp.* 2, 1, 3–4.

28. To take only two examples, note the *triumphalia ornamenta* voted by the Senate to Agricola (Tacitus, *Agric.* 40), and the three statues voted to M. Bassaeus Rufus on the motion of Marcus Aurelius and Commodus, *ILS* 1326.

29. See, e.g., Jones, *LRE*, 174–78.

30. See *ERW*, 259–72. Augustus' *breviarium*, or summary report (Suetonius, *Aug.* 101), did contain details of how many soldiers were under arms.

edicts.[31] The standard assumptions about the functions of the imperial entourage are clearly expressed by Dio in the "speech of Maecenas": "Moreover, as regards legal cases, letters, and decrees of the cities, petitions of individuals, and whatever else concerns the administration of the Empire, you should have helpers and assistants from among the equestrians."[32] There is no trace here—or elsewhere—of imperial "secretaries" specifically concerned with military matters or foreign affairs. The pattern persists through the period, and beyond. The *Notitia Dignitatum* (List of Offices) lists the four established *magistri* (ministers): of the *memoria*, the *epistolae* (correspondence), the *libelli* (petitions), and the *epistolae graecae* (the Greek correspondence).[33]

Any "secretarial" functions in relation to military matters or foreign affairs must then have been performed by these primarily civilian officials. Since, as we shall see, the emperors conducted an extensive exchange of letters and embassies with foreign rulers, it is natural to think first of the *ab epistulis/magister epistolarum* (i.e., the officials in charge of the imperial correspondence), and the (much less often attested) *a legationibus* (in charge of embassies). But, in fact, the little evidence which we have for their role concerns not the reception of embassies or the preparation of letters at court, but the despatch of occasional "secretarial" officials on foreign missions. For instance, it was evidently while he was on such a mission in about 173 that Marcus Aurelius' *ab epistulis Latinis* (in charge of the Latin correspondence), Taruttienus Paternus, was held and ill-treated by the Cotini, who had promised military collaboration against the Marcomanni.[34] Then, at the end of the third century, we find Sicorius Probus, the *magister memoriae*, being sent from Nisibis by Diocletian and Galerius as ambassador to Narses, and making a speech before him with proposals for the regulation of the Tigris frontier.[35] The detailed accounts in Ammianus of the reception by the emperor of embassies and letters from foreign rulers, and the despatch of others, show important roles as ambassadors being entrusted to court officials (*praefecti praetorio, comites, tribuni et notarii*), or high-ranking officers (*magistri militum* or *duces*),[36] and in one case to a philosopher, Eustathius. As both Ammianus and Libanius make clear, he was selected personally for his oratorical powers,

31. *ERW*, 252–59.

32. Dio 52, 33, 5.

33. *Not. Dig., Or.* 19; *Occ.* 17 (minus the *epistolae graecae*).

34. Dio 71, 12, 3. The *Tabula Banasitana* attests this form of his name, see *JRS* 63 (1973): 86.

35. Petrus Patricius, fr. 14 (*FHG* IV, p. 189).

36. Ammianus 17, 5 and 14; 18, 2, 2 (*tribunus*); 19, 11, 5 (two *tribuni* with interpreters); 25, 7, 7 (praetorian prefect and, probably, *comes rei militaris*); 27, 5, 1 (*magister equitum*); 5 (*magistri*)?; 31, 7, 1 (*magister equitum*).

and Eunapius gives a highly coloured account of his success with Shapur II.[37] These narratives never show any specific role being performed by the "secretarial" *magistri*, though we do find some Alamannic ambassadors in 364 or 365 being rudely treated by Ursacius, the *magister officiorum* (the master of the offices).[38] The reason why court officials play so small a part in the accounts of the reception of embassies is quite simply that the emperors conducted all such negotiations in person through public verbal exchanges which naturally lent themselves to narrative presentation.[39] This highly personal and dramatic element was an essential feature of imperial foreign relations, and it was appropriate that Eunapius, in describing negotiations between Julian and the king of the Chamavi, made an explicit comparison with a scene on the stage.[40]

If the emperor possessed any secretarial staff specifically for the conduct of frontier policy or diplomacy, all trace of it has disappeared. As regards advisers whom he could consult, it was normal from the beginning for one praetorian prefect or both to be in attendance on the emperor,[41] as will have been the tribunes of any praetorian cohorts which were accompanying him. When an emperor was on campaign he could naturally consult the consular or praetorian *legati* of any legions which were in his vicinity, or the equestrian commanders of auxiliary units. Beyond that, in the first three centuries, if he was in Rome, he would consult whichever friends of senatorial or equestrian rank he chose to summon to him; if he was travelling in Italy or the provinces or was on campaign, the choice was inevitably restricted to those whom he had already selected to take with him as his *comites* (travelling companions). Thus, as regards Rome, Tacitus shows that Nero in 63, after receiving some Parthian ambassadors bringing a letter from Vologaeses, and interrogating the centurion who had accompanied them, consulted "among the *principes civitatis*" (the foremost people in the state) as to whether there should be peace or war.[42] The same procedure is implied in Juvenal's *Fourth Satire*, 144–49, with Domitian's *amici* hurrying to the Arx Albana "as if he were about to speak about the Chatti or the wild Sygambri, and as if from distant parts of the earth an urgent letter had come on headlong wing."

37. Ammianus 17, 5, 15: *Ut opifex suadendi* (as a master of persuasion); Libanius, *Ep.* 331; Eunapius, *Vit. Soph.* 365 (also noting that high military or civilian officials were normally sent on embassies).

38. Ammianus 26, 5, 7.

39. See further text to nn. 100–101.

40. Eunapius, *Fr.* 12 (*FHG* IV, pp. 17–19).

41. *ERW*, 127.

42. *Ann.* 15, 24–25.

Outside Rome, we see for instance Otho's advisers debating the prospects of the civil war of 69: five persons give their opinions, including his brother and his praetorian prefect, and the prime role is played by Suetonius Paulinus, on the basis of his established reputation as a military man.[43] The advisers whom Marcus Aurelius would consult on both military and civil matters[44] were with him and Commodus when he died (at Sirmium or Vindobona) in 180. Both Dio and Herodian report that it was against their advice that the young Commodus made peace, abandoned the Marcomannic war, and returned to Rome.[45] This is a cardinal instance of the essential weakness of the position of the *amici* or *comites*. It lay solely with the emperor whether to have them with him, to consult them on any particular issue, or to take their advice. They had no power base, were nobody's delegates or representatives, and could not compel him even if they were unanimous.

The other essential feature of the institution of the *consilium* in the early Empire was the absence of any distinction of function (juridical, administrative, political, or military) between its members. In this respect the structural developments of the third and fourth centuries brought some changes, not easily defined. In the century from 250 to 350 the few brief accounts we have of discussions between the emperor and advisers tend to single out persons holding specific military ranks, *praefecti*, *tribuni*, or *duces*;[46] we have no evidence to indicate whether the *magistri militum* created by Constantine began at once to act as military advisers to the emperor. When Ammianus' narrative is available, for the years from 353 onwards, we have various descriptions of councils of war: before Ctesiphon in 363; when Valentinian was hesitating in 364 between repelling the Alamannic invasion of Gaul and confronting the still vaguely reported coup of Procopius in the East; and later when he was dissuaded by his advisers from marching from Rhine to Danube against the Quadi until he had made peace with the Alamanni and had waited for the spring of 375.[47] But unfortunately only the account of the council of war held by Valens before Hadrianople in 378 gives any indication of the ranks or offices of the persons consulted: the persons of "various ranks" (*potestates variae*) included Sebastianus, the *magister peditum* (the master of the infantry) who was in favour of immediate action, and Victor, the *magister equitum* (the

43. Tacitus, *Hist.* 2, 31–33.

44. *HA, v. M. Ant.* 22. 3.

45. Dio 73, 1, 2; Herodian I, 6. For the treaty negotiations, see text to n. 101.

46. *ERW*, 125–22.

47. Ammianus 24, 7, 1; 26, 5, 8–13; 30, 3; (see further below). Note also Eunapius, *Fr.* 42 (*FGH* IV, pp. 31–33) on the discussion of the Goths' request to be allowed across the Danube.

master of the cavalry), who vainly advised awaiting Gratian and his forces.[48] The specific accounts of strategic or tactical debates within the imperial entourage are thus both rather deficient in indications of the composition of the entourage (Ammianus notes a few paragraphs later that the praetorian prefect and the *consistoriani* [members of the *consistorium*, which replaced the earlier *consilium*] were at Hadrianople)[49] and not very clear as to who was actually consulted. A much clearer impression of the military character of the entourage in the fourth century is given by Ammianus' accounts of those moments, in 363 and 364, when the death of an emperor left it with the task of selecting his successor and proclaiming him first to the army on the spot and then to the Empire.[50] Here too, as in the events leading to Hadrianople, when Gratian's only means of attempting to intervene was a letter carried from Sirmium by the *comes domesticorum* (commander of the household troops), Richomer,[51] we see the fundamental limitations placed by time, space, and delays of communication on the ways in which the Empire could function as a system.

Communication and Responsibility

It is thus clear enough, firstly, that immediate tactical, strategic, and diplomatic decisions by the emperor could only be taken on the spot wherever he and his entourage were; and, secondly, that, whatever advice he received, these decisions were taken by the emperor in person. That still leaves open the question of responsibility and decision making in relation to military or diplomatic operations conducted in the absence of the emperor. To illustrate the nature of the problem we may take two well-known instances from the first century. The first is the record of his governorship of Moesia in about 60–67 from the inscription of Tiberius Plautius Silvanus Aelianus on his family tomb at Tibur, listing the following activities:[52]

1. More than 100,000 "Transdanubians" brought across with their wives and children and chiefs or kings (and settled) "so that they paid tribute."
2. A Sarmatian threat repressed, though part of his army had been withdrawn for operations in Armenia.

48. Ammianus 31, 12, 5–7. For Sebastianus' rank, *PLRE* I, Sebassianus 2.
49. 31, 12, 10.
50. 25, 5 (Jovian), see 8, 8–11 (communications to the West); 26, 1–2 (Valentinian).
51. 31, 12, 4.
52. *ILS* 986.

3. Previously unknown or hostile kings brought to the bank of the Danube to do reverence to the Roman standards.

4. The return to the kings of the Bastarnae and Rhoxolani of their sons, and (probably) to the king of the Dacians of his brother(s), whom he had captured or taken from their enemies.

5. The acceptance from some of these kings of hostages, by which the peace of the province was confirmed and extended.

6. The deterrence (by military or diplomatic means?) of the king of the Scythians from the siege of Chersonesus, "which lies beyond the Borysthenes."

7. The despatch of corn to Rome.

The record shows features which characterized Roman frontier operations, in this area above all, throughout the period: the combined employment of force and diplomacy; the steady absorption of barbarians, whether as settlers or soldiers or both;[53] and the assumption implicit in the language of the inscription that the Danube and its banks constituted the frontier of the Empire. The inscription reflects and expresses a common stock of conceptions about frontier objectives, not all of which will have needed to be expressed in formal instructions from the emperor. We know, of course, that governors of all types received *mandata* (instructions) from the emperor, covering administrative, legal, and military matters, at least in the sense of the disposition and discipline of troops. The evidence implies, however, that by the end of the second century the *mandata* had ossified into a code which was not specific to particular provinces or circumstances.[54] There seems, however, to be no evidence as to whether the *mandata* included instructions of a strategic or diplomatic nature, whether related to the particular time and place or of a general character.[55] If such instructions were not provided, then we must either accept that there actually was no "imperial" policy for Moesia in this period, or suppose either that Nero wrote subsequently to Aelianus on specific points or that Aelianus will have consulted him before taking major steps. At least one such letter of instruction must have reached Aelianus, on

53. I am very grateful to Dr. G. E. M. de Ste. Croix for letting me see in advance app. III. of *The Class Struggle in the Ancient Greek World* (1981), which contains the most complete collection of the evidence on barbarian settlement.

54. *ERW*, 314–17, corrected as regards proconsuls by G. P. Burton, "The Issuing of Mandata to Proconsuls and a New Inscription from Cos," *ZPE* 21 (1976): 63.

55. Tacitus, *Ann.* 2, 77, implies that the *mandata* given to the *legatus* of Syria concerned his military role, but says nothing of their contents.

the detachment of some of his troops (the legion V Macedonica) for the Armenian campaign. From parallel cases it is clear that there could have been other letters of instruction, though the inscription, put up under Vespasian, would not emphasize either that or consultation of Nero. For instance, Josephus records that Tiberius wrote to L. Vitellius as governor of Syria, probably in 35, to give him detailed instructions on the resumption of diplomatic relations with Artabanus of Parthia.[56] Subsequently, Herod Antipas wrote from Galilee to make accusations against Aretas of Nabataea, and Tiberius wrote to Vitellius instructing him to take his army against Aretas. When Vitellius had reached Jerusalem, news came of the death of Tiberius, and he returned to Syria, "no longer being empowered as before since control of affairs had passed to Gaius."[57]

Precisely the same questions arise with the second instance, the governorship of Agricola in Britain in 78–84. Nothing is said by Tacitus about *mandata* from Vespasian, or about subsequent instructions from him, Titus, or Domitian, or about consultation of them by Agricola. But the statement that he did not enshrine the report of his containment of the Ordovices in a laurelled letter (18) surely implies at least that end-of-campaign reports were normal. Such reports are not mentioned again, however, until after the victory at Mons Graupius, when they were followed by the vote of *triumphalia ornamenta* (triumphal distinctions) and of a statue by the Senate—and a letter of recall from Domitian (39–40). But if there is any truth in Dio's confused report that Titus had gained an imperatorial acclamation as a result of Agricola's successes in Britain, there must have been reports to him too.[58] Tacitus' account however provides no positive reason to believe that the consolidation of northern Wales, the advance into southern Scotland and up the east coast, the battle of Mons Graupius or, on the diplomatic side, the reception of a fugitive chief from Ireland (24) or the demand for hostages from tribes in Scotland (38) followed any specific imperial plan or instructions. It is a reasonable speculation, but only a speculation, that *Agricola* 23 might reflect a decision by Titus that Agricola should halt on the Forth-Clyde line, then reversed by Domitian.[59] The recall of Agricola, combined with the very clear archaeological evidence for the establishment of the legionary fortress

---

56. Josephus, *Ant.* 18, 4, 4 (96). For the date, see Tacitus, *Ann.* 6, 31–37, and Dio 58, 26.

57. Josephus, *Ant.* 18, 5, 1 (115); 5, 3 (120–24).

58. Dio 66, 20, under A.D. 79, and mentioning the fifteenth acclamation, correctly dated to that year, together with the circumnavigation of Britain, which happened in Agricola's sixth year (83).

59. For this view, S. S. Frere, *Britannia*² (1978), 126–28.

at Inchtuthil, perhaps in 84, and its systematic dismantlement in about 87, along with the withdrawal of the *legio II Adiutrix* perhaps in the same year, and its transference to Moesia,[60] might suggest that imperial "policy" could often consist of allowing imperial governors to follow their own presumptions until external factors, a major crisis or their own excessive activity, compelled intervention. Alternatively, intervention might follow more quickly, as we see in the case of Corbulo as *legatus* of the lower Rhine army in 47. The Chauci stirred, and Corbulo moved against them, apparently reporting his action to Rome. While he was building a camp in enemy territory, a letter arrived from Claudius ordering an end to operations and a withdrawal back across the Rhine.[61] If the governor did not write to the Emperor, the equestrian procurator might, as we see in the well-known case of Classicianus' report to Nero from Britain, and the mission of Polyclitus (*Ann.* 14, 38–39).

Alternatively, a governor might write to the emperor to request his instructions before taking action. So, for instance, Domitius Marsianus, the *legatus* of Syria, wrote to Claudius to report that Agrippa I was strengthening the walls of Jerusalem, and evoked a letter from the Emperor to the king telling him to stop.[62] Similarly, Caesennius Paetus, as a *legatus* of Syria in about 72, reported to Vespasian that Antiochus of Commagene was conspiring with Vologaeses of Parthia and received instructions to invade the kingdom and bring royal rule to an end.[63]

It is easy to take such correspondence for granted, as we do the communications between Pliny in Bithynia and Trajan in Rome. But it is essential to emphasize its limitations as a decision-making procedure. First, there were the delays in time. There is no evidence that the Empire possessed any signalling procedure capable of transmitting complex messages (or indeed any long-distance signalling procedure at all). If, in fact, Augustus ever established relays of runners for carrying messages (which would have been prohibitively expensive in manpower if widely used), this procedure was quickly replaced by a system whereby messengers travelled the entire distance, and could be questioned for further information on arrival.[64] The system relied on the use of *diplomata* (permits) to requisition horses or *vehicula* (carriages), and later on the relays of horses available at the posting stations (*mansiones*). Since everything depended on the urgency of the situation and

60. See Frere (n. 59), 136–38.
61. Tacitus, *Ann.* 11, 19–20; Dio 61, 30, 4–5 (4).
62. Josephus, *Ant.* 19, 7, 2 (326–27).
63. Josephus, *BJ* 7, 7, 1–3 (219–43).
64. Suetonius, *Aug.* 49.

the physical resilience of the messengers (not to speak of the efficiency and co-operativeness of the persons supplying horses or vehicles), all that is really certain is that reports of exceptionally fast journeys over a few days by highly motivated individuals can be no guide to normal speeds; and that the speeds actually achieved must have dropped in proportion to the length of the journeys undertaken. For the relatively urgent messages with which we are concerned, the truth should lie somewhere between the 50 Roman miles per day estimated by Ramsay as typical[65] and Procopius' assumption, relating to the developed system of the late Empire, that a messenger could cover ten times the normal daily distance for a traveller in a day, that is, about 200 miles.[66] On that basis messengers going by land from Antioch to Rome, about 3,000 miles, are not likely to have taken less than a month, with a similar period for the return journey. Much faster journeys were possible by sea, of course—for instance, nine days from Puteoli to Alexandria.[67] But even where sea communications were relevant, as between Rome and Syria, they were acutely unreliable: the messengers bringing a threatening letter from Gaius to Petronius, a *legatus* of Syria, were storm-bound for three months, and arrived twenty-seven days after later messengers carrying the news of Gaius' death.[68] Moreover sea travel by official passengers or groups (like the escort which took a whole winter to bring Paul and other prisoners from Judaea to Rome) depended on the availability of trading ships. Even emperors occasionally travelled on merchant ships, and there is no clear evidence of the regular use of the imperial navy for transporting messengers.[69] In this connection we may note the evidence of *Dig.* 45, 1, 122, 1, of a nautical loan contract which allowed 200 days for a round trip from Berytus to Brundisium and back.

Thus, with the partial exception of the Rome-Alexandria voyage, the Mediterranean did not provide a medium of speedy and reliable internal communications for the Empire; the official voyages envisaged in the *Imperatoris Augusti Itinerarium Maritimum*[70] were coastal or went from island to

---

65. For discussions of the imperial communication system, see W. Riepl, *Das Nachrichtenwesen des Altertums mit besonderer Rücksicht auf die Römer* (1913), 123–240; W. M. Ramsay, "The Speed of the Roman Imperial Post," *JRS* 15 (1925): 60; M. Amit, "Les moyens de communication et la défense de l'Empire romain," *Parola del Passato* 20 (1965): 207.

66. Procopius, *Hist. Arc.* 30, cited by Riepl (n. 65), 186.

67. Pliny, *NH* 19, 3.

68. Josephus, *BJ* 2, 10, 5 (203); *Ant.* 18, 8, 9 (305).

69. C. G. Starr, *The Roman Imperial Navy* (1941), 177–78. See now W. Eck, "Tacitus, *Ann.* 4, 27, 1 und der *cursus publicus* auf der Adria," *SCI* 13 (1994): 60.

70. [See O. Cuntz, *Itineraria Romana* I (1929).]

island. So the communications with which we are concerned depended on the use of animal power on land, and all the more so after it became clear that the three key frontiers were those of the Euphrates, Danube, and Rhine. The mere fact of delay, in any case common to the Empire and its neighbours, and inbuilt into the economic and social fabric of the ancient world, did not of course prohibit consultation on military matters, any more than it prevented the constant resort of provincial embassies to the emperor, or correspondence on other matters between emperors and officials, in which intervals of several months between the composition of an imperial letter or edict and its receipt or promulgation were common.[71] Indeed it is clear that in diplomatic traffic at least it was possible to tolerate delays far greater than those strictly imposed by the conditions of travel: in 356 Constantius and Julian wrote to the praetorian prefect to say that no Roman emissary on his way to Axum or the Homeritae should remain in Alexandria for more than a year or draw rations there after that time.[72] Nor would the slowness of travel, especially by large bodies of men, affect those operations where the initiative lay in Roman hands. Thus for the invasion of Britain in 43 it was possible to concentrate not only three legions from the Rhine but one from Pannonia, which must have involved a march of two to three months to the Channel.[73] But the effect of distance and delay must either have been to allow considerable latitude to local commanders at least in the medium term, or alternatively to paralyse significant initiatives or responses while the lengthy process of consultation was carried out. This fact could on occasion be put to good effect, as in the anecdote recorded by Petrus Patricius of a governor of Moesia Inferior under Gordian III telling a delegation of Carpi that he would consult the emperor about their demands for a subvention, and that they should return after four months to hear the answer.[74]

The Concentration of Strategic Decision Making

In a different political system the effect of these irremovable limitations on communication might have been a diffusion of political and military power

71. *ERW* 39, 254.

72. *CTh* 12, 12, 2. Note that Flavius Abinnaeus spent three years escorting back *refugae* or *legati* of the Blemyes (*P. Abinn.* 1).

73. The camp of the *legio IX Hispana* in Pannonia is not known. The march must have meant going either through Noricum and Raetia or through northern Italy and across the Alps.

74. Petrus Patricius, fr. 8 (*FGH* IV, pp. 186–87). For the governor, Iulius (?) Menophilus, see Barbieri, *Albo senatorio*, no. 1071.

and hence of strategic and diplomatic initiative and responsibility. But in fact, as is clear, the opposite development occurred, and the emperors tended to concentrate the direction of military affairs more and more definitely in their own hands. In the 370s, for instance, we find the *duces* on the Danube telling the Goths that they cannot let them cross the Danube without the Emperor's permission.[75] Valens himself, on receiving the news of the threat to Thrace, sent emissaries to settle the Armenian question and hastened back from the Persian front to meet his death at Hadrianople.[76]

From the very beginning, from Augustus' wars in Spain in 27–4 B.C. onwards, the notion that direct military command was an essential imperial function was present and was of great importance. But in the first century it was still possible, as the operations of Corbulo in Armenia show, for major campaigning to be conducted in the absence of the emperor. Subsequently that ceased to be so, in either offensive or defensive warfare, and the consequences were of the greatest importance for the evolving structure of imperial rule. Why this evolution took place is not a question which allows any simple answer. But some factors are clear. The first is that the fact that the Empire was a monarchy was immediately noticed and acted upon by foreign kings and rulers, some of them at immense distances. There thus begun at once that traffic in embassies, fugitive princes, hostages, letters, gifts, and (from the emperor) the bestowal of crowns, which was one of the embodiments of the emperor's supremacy and was to be one of the most important functions of the Byzantine emperors.[77] It is necessary to stress that this very personal and monarchical element is strongly emphasized in the actual sentence structures of the relevant part of Augustus' *Res Gestae*: "*To me* from India . . . asking for our friendship . . . *to me* as suppliants these fled . . . *to me* the King of the Parthians . . . *from me* . . . the peoples of the Parthians and of the Medes" (*Ad me ex India . . . nostram amicitiam appetiverunt . . . . ad me supplices confugerunt . . . ad me rex Parthorum . . . a me gentes Parthorum et Medorum*) (31–33). Several passages in Strabo's *Geography* offer confirmation of Augustus' claims, for instance that on the British chiefs who had gained the friendship of the emperor by embassies and diplomacy and had made offerings on the Capitol;[78] or the embassy from a king in India which (as Strabo describes) Nicolaus of Damascus encountered in Antioch on its way to Augustus. The three

75. Eunapius, *Fr.* 42 (*FGH* IV, p. 31); cf. Zosimus IV, 20, 6.

76. Ammianus 31, 7, 1; 11, 1–2; 12, 1–4; Zosimus IV, 21.

77. See J. Gagé, "L'empereur romain et les rois: politique et protocole," *Rev. Hist.* 221 (1959): 22.

78. *Geog.* 4, 5, 3 (200).

ambassadors who had survived the journey were carrying a letter in Greek
in which Poros described himself as king over 600 other kings and offered
any collaboration which Augustus required: with the letter came gifts, borne
by eight slaves, naked except for scented loincloths, namely, a freak, some
large snakes, a serpent ten cubits in length, a turtle three cubits long, and a
partridge larger than a vulture.[79] This embassy in fact reached Augustus in
Samos in the winter of 20/19 B.C.;[80] and it had been there also, in the previous
winter, that an Ethiopian embassy had appeared before him. The circumstances, again described by Strabo, are of considerable significance. When
in 24–22 B.C. Ethiopian forces attacked the fort of Primis (Qaṣr Ibrîm), the
prefect of Egypt, Petronius, reinforced it in time, and when an Ethiopian
embassy arrived told them to go to Augustus:[81]

> When they said that they did not know who Caesar was or how they
> were to reach him, he provided them with an escort. They travelled to
> Samos where Caesar was, as he intended to go on to Syria and to send
> Tiberius into Armenia. They gained everything for which they asked,
> and he released them also from the tributes which he had imposed.

The diplomatic and military role in the East delegated by Augustus to Tiberius in person was in fact highly significant for the future. None the less, it is
conceivable that if the Empire could have achieved overall the secure dominance momentarily demonstrated on both the eastern and Nubian fronts in
the late 20s B.C., its frontier and diplomatic policy might indeed have been
directed from Rome or wherever in the Mediterranean the emperor happened to be. Such a state of affairs was almost secured in the middle of the
second century, when Appian gives his eye-witness report of the conduct of
diplomacy by Antoninus Pius:[82]

> The emperors, in addition to the original provinces, have added some
> further areas to their rule and have suppressed some which broke away.
> In general, possessing by good government the most important parts
> of land and sea, they prefer to preserve their empire rather than ex-
> tend it indefinitely to poor and profitless barbarian peoples. I have seen
> embassies from some of these in Rome offering themselves as subjects,
> and the Emperor refusing them, on the grounds that they would be
> of no use to him. For other peoples, limitless in number, the emperors

79. *Geog.* 15, 1, 73 (719) = Jacoby, *FGrH* 90, F. 100.
80. Dio 54, 9, 8–10.
81. *Geog.* 17, 1, 54 (820–21); cf. *JRS* 69 (1979): 127.
82. Appian, *Praef.* 7/25–28.

appoint the kings, not requiring them for the Empire. On some of the provinces they spend more than they receive, thinking it shameful to give them up even though they are loss-making. They surround the empire with a circle of great camps and guard so great an area of land and sea like an estate.

It was of Antoninus Pius also that Fronto, in the course of a speech of congratulation on the completion of a war in Britain "declared that although he had committed the conduct of the campaign to others, while sitting at home himself in the Palace in Rome, yet like the helmsman at the tiller of a ship of war, the glory of the whole navigation and voyage belonged to him."[83] Although the theme of Pius' control by correspondence from the centre reappears both in Aristides' *Roman Oration* (31–33) and in the *Historia Augusta*,[84] the element of special pleading on Fronto's part is evident. Even in the first century it had been only those emperors, such as Tiberius or Vespasian, who enjoyed an already established military reputation, who could afford to lead no war of conquest. It does not need demonstration that Claudius' invasion of Britain, lavishly celebrated in Rome and throughout the Empire, arose at least in part from the opposite case; and the fact that Pliny in his *Panegyric* can refer to no significant military achievements of Trajan before his accession surely has some relevance to the Dacian and Parthian wars which he led. Then, after the lull of Hadrian's and Antoninus Pius' reigns, we find that it is assumed that all major wars, whether defensive or offensive, are implicitly held to require the presence of the—or an—emperor. Though the gradually growing predominance of defensive warfare is undeniable, the ideal of conquest was not wholly abandoned. We need not disbelieve the *Historia Augusta*'s claim that Marcus eventually intended to create two new provinces, Marcomannia and Sarmatia, beyond the Danube;[85] according to Herodian Severus spontaneously chose to undertake the British expedition of 208–11, as a training for Caracalla and Geta;[86] and above all the extension of provincial territory to the Tigris, and at times beyond, meant—as Dio saw— a wholly new strategic commitment whose consequences for the Empire were incalculable. Whether or not the overthrow of the Parthian Empire

83. *Pan. Lat.* VIII (Galletier IV), 14, 2, Loeb trans. from *Correspondence of M. Cornelius Fronto* II, 251 (see C. E. V. Nixon and B. S. Rogers, *In Praise of Later Roman Emperors* [1994]: 132–33).

84. *HA, v. Ant. Pii* 7, 11–12.

85. *HA, v. M. Ant.* 24, 5; cf. 27, 10. See A. Birley, *Marcus Aurelius* (1966), 205–6, and Birley (n. 12), 20–21; cf. A. Mócsy, *Pannonia and Upper Moesia* (1974), 183–86, 193.

86. Herodian 3, 14, 1–2.

by the new Persian dynasty of the Sassanids was one of those consequences, Herodian's account (6, 2–3) of Roman reactions in the 220s and 230s shows very clearly how rigid were the assumptions which now prevailed as to the need for the imperial presence on all major campaigns. Letters came from the governors of Syria and Mesopotamia to say that Artaxerxes (Ardashir) was threatening the whole eastern empire. Severus Alexander consulted with his *amici* and sent an embassy with a letter warning Artaxerxes off; when this was ineffective, and the governors of the eastern provinces "were calling for him," Alexander marched via the Danubian provinces to Antioch. After further diplomatic exchanges, he mounted a triple invasion of Armenia and Mesopotamia. He was back in Antioch, probably over the winter of 232/3, when messengers brought news of German invasions across the Rhine and Danube, which demanded the presence of Alexander and the troops which he had taken east with him. The force of these reports was intensified by the reactions of those soldiers who had been transferred from the Danubian provinces. Herodian continues:[87]

> Alexander and the advisers who accompanied him were by this time even concerned about Italy, rating the German menace as very different from the Persians. The inhabitants of the eastern territories, separated as they are by a wide stretch of land and sea, hardly hear about Italy. But the Illyrian provinces are a narrow stretch of land that do not occupy much of Roman territory. This makes the Germans practically adjacent neighbours of the Italians. Reluctantly and sadly (through sheer necessity) Alexander issued the proclamation of an expedition.

However vague and confused Herodian may be, it is a fact that in this situation Alexander felt himself compelled to undertake a march of more than 2,000 miles, which cannot have taken less than about five months. By 234 he was on the Rhine frontier, where he was murdered at Moguntiacum in 235. He had ruled as sole emperor; but one direct consequence of the assumption that emperors would conduct major campaigns in person was the multiplication of emperors. This is already clear, for instance, in 260: when Valerian was captured by Shapur I in Mesopotamia, his son Gallienus, as joint *Augustus*, was conducting campaigns in northern Italy, and his grandson Saloninus, with the title of "Caesar," was commanding the Rhine frontier from Cologne. Precisely such necessities led to the formation of the Tetrarchy and then to the successive semi-dynastic combinations of emperors which characterized the fourth century. According to Zosimus, for instance, it was the

87. 6, 7, 4–5.

existence of simultaneous threats to the Empire on several fronts which induced Constantius to appoint his cousin Julian as *Caesar* in 355 and send him
to Gaul.[88]

It had already been established long before that an emperor, once in command on a particular front, took direct tactical and strategic command of it,
fighting battles and determining the geographical and physical character of
frontier installations. For instance, we owe our only precise literary reference
to the pushing forward of the German frontier in 83 to Frontinus:[89]

> Imperator Caesar Domitianus Augustus—when the Germans, in ac-
> cordance with their usual custom, kept emerging from woodland pas-
> tures and unsuspected hiding places to attack our men and then finding
> a safe refuge in the depths of the forest—by (constructing) *limites* along
> a stretch of one hundred twenty miles, not only changed the nature
> of the war, but brought his enemies beneath his sway, by uncovering
> their hiding places.

The question of whether he means to say that Domitian drove roads directly
into enemy territory[90] or constructed *limites* (roads) laterally over a distance
of 120 miles[91] is not as significant for present purposes as the fact that Frontinus represents this as a strategic choice made by the Emperor in person. He
similarly attributes to Domitian choices of other sorts: the ruse by which he
set out from Rome on the pretence of conducting a census in Gaul; a tactical
device used in battle against the Chatti; and the payment of compensation for
land on which *castella* (forts) were built during the war.[92] Again, to give only
isolated examples, the *Historia Augusta* attributes to the moment of Hadrian's
visit to Britain in 121/2 his building of the Wall "to separate the barbarians
and the Romans."[93] Dio describes Caracalla seeing to the siting of forts and
settlements on his German campaign of 213,[94] while Ammianus mentions the
fortification of Circesium by Diocletian and details the major programme
of military construction along the Rhine undertaken by Valentinian in 369
onwards.[95] J. J. Wilkes has drawn attention to the fact that inscriptions in-

88. Zosimus 3, 1.

89. *Strat.* 1, 3, 10.

90. So R. Syme, *CAH* XI (1936), 162–63.

91. So H. Schoenberger, *JRS* 59 (1969): 159.

92. *Strat.* 1, 1, 8; 2, 3, 23; 2, 11, 7.

93. *V. Had.* 11, 2.

94. 77, 13, 4 (388–89).

95. Circesium: Ammianus 22, 5, 2. Rhine: 28, 2, 1–6, cf. 30, 7, 6. See H. Schoenberger, *JRS* 69 (1969): 182–86.

creasingly advertise the responsibility of emperors for the construction of defensive works along or near the frontiers: "[F]ollowing the subjugation and control of the Franks through the excellence of Constantine, the *castrum* (fort) of the *Divitenses* was constructed in their territory in the presence of the Emperor himself."[96]

Direct tactical command necessarily brought with it the direct management of diplomatic contacts, which would otherwise have been handled, at least in the first instance, by provincial governors, or later *duces*, *comites*, or *magistri*. Contacts with the Parthian and, later, Persian kings were always conducted by emissaries, who would speak before the emperor or king in person; Augustus' grandson Gaius might meet the king of the Parthians on the Euphrates,[97] but the only occasion on which emperor and king came face to face was the capture of Valerian. With lesser peoples the emperor might actually confront their kings in person, as Trajan did with a succession of kings and dynasts on his Parthian campaigns.[98] So too Ammianus offers a remarkable description of Valentinian negotiating from a boat on the Rhine with Macrianus, the king of the Alamanni, who was standing on the bank.[99]

Thus when Commodus rejected the advice of his *comites* to continue the Marcomannic war in 180 the mechanism of decision was that he received an embassy from the Marcomanni and Quadi and made peace with them on the following terms: the return of prisoners and deserters; the provision of a fixed quantity of corn each year; the supplying of weapons and of 13,000 soldiers from the Quadi and less from the Marcomanni; the restriction of their assemblies to once a month, in the presence of a Roman centurion; and no attacks on the Iazyges, Buri, or Vandals. In return he withdrew the forts placed in their territory. Comparable terms were granted to an embassy from the Buri on the borders of Dacia, with the additional provision that they should leave an uninhabited zone forty stades wide along the frontier.[100]

The close combination of military and diplomatic functions, and the personal management of both by the emperor, appear even more clearly in Dexippus' notable description of Aurelian's negotiations with the Juthungi in Pannonia in 270 or 271. He had defeated them and driven them back to the Danube and now proposed to receive an embassy. To instil the due measure of fear (which seemed to be lacking), he received them dressed in his

96. *CIL* XIII, 8502 = *ILS* 8937; see J. J. Wilkes, "British Anonymity in the Roman Empire," in D. E. Johnston, ed., *The Saxon Shore* (1977), 76.

97. Velleius 2, 101.

98. Dio 68, 18–19; 21 (Abgar of Osrhoene, cf. Arrian, *Parth.*, fr. 46*).

99. 30, 3, 4–5.

100. Dio 72, 1–3 (282–84).

purple cloak, seated on a tribunal, with his officers on horseback about him
and the army on parade. When given permission to speak, the ambassadors
addressed him through an interpreter and represented themselves as willing
to make peace from a position of strength. The Emperor made a speech in
reply, contemptuously rejecting their demands.[101]

Information and Conceptual Frameworks

Within the few years before his death in 275 Aurelian had marched east and
in two campaigns destroyed the brief "empire" of Palmyra, and then west
and brought to an end the Imperium Galliarum. The Empire was thus substantially restored, but without the territories beyond the upper Rhine, and
without Dacia, definitely abandoned perhaps in 271. Aurelian thus represents
one of the extreme examples of the direct control of military operations by
emperors and of the sheer extent of the marches undertaken by those of the
third and fourth centuries—and the last example of one who carried this
burden without at least one co-emperor. But his strategic choices may also,
as we shall see below, reflect one set of presuppositions on the part of educated inhabitants of the Empire as to the shape and strategic character of the
Roman world.

These general presuppositions—not necessarily unanimous, as Dio's criticism of Severus shows—are of crucial importance precisely because of what
seems on our evidence to have been the relative lack of short- or medium-
term information on peoples and geographical features beyond the Empire.
Three interlinked factors are involved here: the means by which information could be obtained; the forms in which it could be presented; and the
conceptual frameworks within which it could be used to produce decisions
about frontier policy. It will be obvious that these are immense topics, as to
which only a few suggestions and items of evidence can be presented here.

First, then, there seem to be relatively few cases, all in the early empire,
and all concerned with prospective Roman expeditions, where long-distance
missions were sent to explore enemy territory for military purposes. Augustus despatched Dionysius of Charax to the East "to write an account of everything" (*ad commentanda omnia*) in advance of Gaius Caesar's expedition.[102]
More detail is reported of the party of praetorians under a tribune which
was sent by Nero to Ethiopia with a view to an expedition there. Their re-

101. Jacoby, *FGrH* 100, F. 6; see F. Millar, "P. Herennius Dexippus," *JRS* 59 (1969): 12,
on p. 25 (= chapter 13 in this volume).

102. Pliny, *NH* 6, 141.

port described the flora and fauna of the region, the political structure of the kingdom, and the size of the army. More specifically, they gave the total distance between Syene and Meroe and the length of the stages from town to town.[103]

This last was of course a crucial question, whether it related to bodies of troops marching by land or to fleets moving along a coastline. Information on these points is a conspicuous feature of the *Periplus of the Euxine* (*The Voyage round the Black Sea*) sent to Hadrian by Arrian while he was governor of Cappadocia in 131/2.[104] Only the first part (chaps. 1–11) describes an actual voyage by Arrian as governor, from Trapezus to Sebastopolis, the last auxiliary post on the east coast of the Euxine. He then adds a detailed guide to the coasting voyage from Byzantium to Trapezus, thus outside his province (12–16). At this point (17) Arrian writes: "Since I have heard of the death of Cotys, king of the Cimmerian Bosporus, I have taken the trouble to describe to you the voyage as far as the Bosporus, so that if you are considering matters relating to the Bosporus you may be in a position to do so without being ignorant of the voyage there." The work is therefore completed (18–25) with a full description of the voyage round the north and west coasts from Sebastopolis to Byzantium, with indications of distances and the capacity of the harbours.

This is not, of course, an example of an exploratory expedition. But the information is offered for the same purpose as that gained by the first-century expeditions, as a guide to movement in an area where intervention might be required. The particular feature of the core of information provided — the names of stopping places and the distances between them — was that it could either be presented in literary form or be tabulated in the form of lists following particular routes or represented schematically on a map which did not have to be in proper topographical scale or proportion. So, for instance, a large number of the major sea and land routes could be tabulated verbally in the *Itinerarium Antonini*. One section (123, 8–147. I) lists the stages of the key route from Rome to Antioch via the Balkans and Asia Minor, endlessly traversed by emperors, and another (217, 5–231, 3) gives what may have been Caracalla's route along the Danube in 214. The listing of the legions in their

103. Pliny, *NH* 6, 181–86; 12, 18–19; Seneca, *NQ* 6, 8, 3–5. See J. Desanges, *Recherches sur l'activité des Méditerranéens aux confins de l'Afrique* (1978), 323–25.

104. See the edition by G. Marenghi, *Arriano, Periplo del Ponto Eusino* (1958). Note also H. F. Pelham, "Arrian as Legate of Cappadocia," in *Essays* (1911), 212, and P. A. Stadter, *Arrian of Nicomedia* (1980), 32–41. An English translation and discussion of this extremely important text for frontier studies would be of great value.

long-established camps on the Danube may suggest a military purpose, as does the connection, proposed by D. van Berchem, with the *Historia Augusta*'s report of Severus Alexander's procedure for announcing in advance his route from Rome "to the barbarian frontiers" (*ad fines barbaricos*).[105]

Such tabulations, essential for any movements within the Empire, whether of troops, the imperial entourage, or both, could also be extended outside the Empire if the relevant information was available. We can see an example in the *Parthian Stations* of Isidorus of Charax, which describes the major routes through the Parthian Empire as far as Arachosia.[106] In the second century the *Geographia* of Ptolemy, extending as far as India, grouped place-names by areas and located them by latitude and longitude. The absence of any sequential listing by routes must indicate that it could not have been intended for practical purposes, military or otherwise. Nor is it certain whether actual maps accompanied the text.[107] For a schematic map incorporating practical information we must of course look to the *Tabula Peutingeriana*, generally accepted as going back to a map of the late Roman period (and emphasizing Rome, Constantinople, and Antioch), which may hypothetically derive in part from earlier models, even from the map of Agrippa.[108] The original was designed functionally in two senses: to be used in roll form, and to indicate land routes (but not sea routes) schematically over the area from the Atlantic to Central Asia, marking distances, basic geographical features, towns, and types of accommodation. There is nothing strictly to prove the official character of the original, and nothing even to suggest a military function. But a fragment of a comparable map—offering a schematic representation of a route round the Euxine—was found on the cover of a soldier's shield from Dura-Europos. This too gives essentially a sequence of places and distances;

105. *HA, v. Sev. Alex.* 45, 2. See D. van Berchem, "L'annone militaire dans l'Empire romain du IIIe siècle," *Mém. Soc. Nat. Ant. Fr.*, 8e ser., 10 (1937): 117–201; cf. *ERW*, 31–33. For all questions relating to *itineraria* and maps, note the invaluable discussions in A. L. F. Rivet and Colin Smith, *The Place-Names of Roman Britain* (1979); for the *Itin. Ant.*, pp. 150–54.

106. For the text, see *Geog. Gr. Min.*, 1, 244–55. See A. S. Nodelman, "A Preliminary History of Characene," *Berytus* 13 (1960): 83, on pp. 107–8, arguing against a possible identification with Dionysius of Charax, and suggesting a date in the later first century.

107. See *RE* Supp. X (1965), cols. 680–833, s.v. "Klaudios Ptolemaios"; Rivet and Smith (n. 105), 103–31.

108. See the invaluable facsimile edition, with accompanying volume of discussion and commentary, by E. Weber, *Tabula Peutingeriana: Codex Vindobonensis 324. Vollständige Faksimile-Ausgabe im Originalformat* I–II (1976). For the functional character of the map, see esp. A. Levi and M. Levi, *Itineraria Picta: contributo allo studio della Tabula Peutingeriana* (1967).

if conceived of as giving a visual impression of the actual topographical re-lationships of the places, it would be wholly misleading.[109]

We need not doubt that itineraries, whether in the form of sequential lists of places or of schematic maps, could be used for military movements within the Empire and (where towns, roads, and information about them existed) outside it. Vegetius indeed advises that itineraries should be issued for all troop movements showing distances, types of roads, short-cuts, stop-ping places, mountains, and rivers. But, writing in an era of defensive warfare (probably under Theodosius I), he assumes that such movements will have taken place through existing Roman provinces — "so much so that the more careful generals are claimed to have had the *itineraria* of provinces where they needed to operate not merely listed but also pictured."[110]

Visual representation thus seems to have been secondary to schematic, or even purely verbal, tabulation of towns and stages. We cannot, unfortunately, form any clear conception of the map (?) — *geōgraphia* — in the form of a tab-let (*pinakion*) and containing *diagrammata* (plans?), for which Julian wrote to thank Alypius, who may then have been *vicarius* of the provinces of Brit-ain.[111] That suggests the possibility that office-holders could use visual means to inform emperors — though the vicariate was a civil, not a military, office, and we do not know what region the map represented. But it still leaves a more fundamental question: if the Roman maps of which we can form any clear conception did not provide a realistic projection of land-masses (or still less of seas or the mutual relations of islands in seas), was it in principle possible for an emperor, or anyone else, to conceive of the overall military situation in global strategic terms, or to consider for instance whether a fron-tier on the Elbe might have provided shorter lines of communication than one on the Rhine?[112] All that can be said is that our explicit evidence does not seem to provide any clear instances of the use of maps in strategic or

109. F. Cumont, "Fragment de bouclier portant une liste d'étapes," *Syria* 6 (1925): 1; *Fouilles de Dura-Europos* (1926), 323–24.

110. Vegetius, *Epit. rei mil.* 3, 6. See T. D. Barnes, "The Date of Vegetius," *Phoenix* 33 (1979): 254. The remarkable description of the arrangements for the march of an army unit in Ambrose, *In Psalmum CXVIII*, Sermo 5, 2 (Migne, *PL* 15, 1250–51), also refers to move-ments through provincial territory. I owe this reference to G. M. Koeppel, "A Military *Itinerarium* on the Column of Trajan: Scene L," *Röm. Mitt.* 87 (1980): 302, on p. 305, n. 24.

111. Julian, *Ep.* 30 Hertlein; 10 Bidez-Cumont; 7. See Rivet and Smith (n. 105), 71.

112. This is, as need hardly be said, the theory put forward in the classic chapter of R. Syme, "The Northern Frontiers under Augustus," *CAH* X, 340–81, esp. 353–54. For a different view, P. A. Brunt, *JRS* 53 (1963): 172–73.

tactical planning as opposed to subsequent representations of the terrain of campaigns.[113]

The clearest example of the latter is provided by the *situs depicti* (maps?) which Corbulo sent back from the Caucasus, and which according to Pliny the Elder misdescribed the Caucasian Gates (the Pass of Dariel) as the "Caspian Gates."[114] Pliny's *Natural History* indeed lists a number of occasions on which increased geographical knowledge had resulted from rather than preceded military operations. Thus Aelius Gallus' Arabian expedition—precisely a case where routes and distances had *not* been explored in advance—produced a report on the population and economy of Arabia Felix (6, 160–61); the Baltic was first explored by a Roman fleet under Augustus (2, 167); Suetonius Paulinus reported on the Atlas region and beyond after his operations in 41/2 (5, 11–15); and Corbulo and Licinius Mucianus managed to produce divergent views on the source of the Euphrates (5, 83).

Of course we have a number of geographical and ethnographical descriptions of large areas beyond the Empire, for instance, Strabo on Germany,[115] Pliny the Elder on the Parthian Empire,[116] Ammianus on the Persian Empire[117] or, perhaps the most significant of all, Tacitus' *Germania*. Its importance for us lies in the combination of its relevance to military relations between the Empire and the German tribes ("so long is the conquest of Germania taking," 37, 2) with its dependence on earlier literary sources, only occasionally supplemented by contemporary episodes (8: Veleda; 29: the *agri decumates*; 33: massacre of Bructeri; 37: recent campaigns). Indeed all the writers mentioned depended on literary sources of varying dates: Pliny finds it necessary to explain that what he says on central Asia will differ from what has been said by earlier writers, since he has gained information "from the recent operations conducted by Domitius Corbulo and from kings sent thence as suppliants or royal children as hostages."[118]

In default of any formal archives relating to external policy, for which we have no specific evidence at all, or of an active pursuit of intelligence,

---

113. This conclusion seems to me to emerge from the survey by R. K. Sherk, "Roman Geographical Exploration and Military Maps," *ANRW* II.1 (1974), 534. Note also the suggestion by Rivet and Smith (n. 105), 196–97, that for North Britain the Ravenna Cosmographer was using a map with ethnic and place names revised as a result of Severus' campaigns of 208–11.

114. Pliny, *NH* 6, 40.

115. *Geog.* 7, 1, 2–3, 1 (290–95).

116. *NH* 6, 112–41.

117. 23, 6.

118. *NH* 6, 23.

which seems to have been operated only (at best) when a Roman expedition was in prospect, any supplementation of the common stock of notions about the world beyond the frontiers would thus tend to come either in the wake of military operations or as a product of the ceaseless diplomatic traffic of suppliants, hostages, and embassies. Thus under Claudius an embassy came from a king in Ceylon and delivered information about the location, geography, and topography of the island.[119] Round the fringes of the Empire itself such diplomatic traffic was intense, and its scale and importance cannot be explored here. Apart from examples already given,[120] one of the papyri from Dura-Europos (*P. Dura* 60B) happens to reveal a Parthian envoy on his way to (or from) Severus and Caracalla in about 208. Similarly Pliny sent on to Trajan in Rome a letter carrier (*tabellarius*) from king Sauromates of the Bosporus, giving him a *diploma* (a permit to requisition transport) on the grounds that the king had written to say that the information which the man carried was urgent. An embassy from the Bosporus, en route simultaneously, was pursuing a more leisurely course.[121] It is important to stress that the requests, accusations, self-justifications, or reports which flowed into the emperor through such diplomatic traffic all emanated from interested parties attempting to gain the help or protection of the emperor. The more quickly the emperor felt obliged to act, the more limited would be the choices open to him. In the early Empire a full examination of rights and wrongs might involve the conflicting parties, or their emissaries, travelling to appear before the emperor in Rome. So for instance the complex issues and mutual accusations as between Herod of Judaea and Aretas of Nabataea, in which either or both kings might have been deposed, were finally resolved in a hearing before Augustus in about 8–7 B.C. at which Nicolaus of Damascus spoke.[122] By the fourth century the more characteristic pattern was the direct control of military and diplomatic affairs by the emperor in the field, which has already been discussed.

Thus the burden of proof must rest on those who would claim that emperors both could and did draw on systematic sources of up-to-date information from beyond the frontiers. Caracalla could write to the Senate in about 215 to say that strife between the two claimants to the Parthian throne was of great advantage to the Roman state;[123] but neither he nor his successors, Elagabal and Severus Alexander, had any means of anticipating that the

119. *NH* 6, 84–88.
120. See the second and the immediately preceding sections above.
121. Pliny, *Ep.* 10, 63–64, 67.
122. Josephus, *Ant.* 16, 10, 8–9 (335–55).
123. Dio 77, 12, 2a–3 (387).

Parthian Empire was about to collapse and that a new Persian dynasty would arise which would fundamentally alter the level of conflict on the eastern frontier. Similarly, Julian brushed aside the suggestion made in 362 by his advisers, that he should attack the Goths, saying that he sought "better enemies" (the Persians). It was perhaps at the same moment that he contemptuously told an embassy of Goths to look to arms if they wished to alter the terms of their treaty.[124] If he in fact anticipated a serious movement on their part, as Eunapius alleges,[125] he did not act on it, preferring the supposed greater glory of a Persian war. There was no mechanism for securing advance warning of the movements of the Huns in the following years or of their impact on the Goths, until the latter and other peoples living north of the Danube sent embassies in the mid-370s asking to be allowed to cross the river and settle in Roman territory.[126] The vivid excursus on the Huns with which Ammianus introduces this major event is the first significant account of them in Graeco-Roman literature[127] and was of course written at least a decade after the disaster of Hadrianople.

Thus what A. Alföldi once called "the moral barrier on Rhine and Danube"[128] seems to have been an information barrier also. But it was so partly because of one element in the conceptual framework within which the educated inhabitants of the Empire saw their world. There is ample evidence to suggest that after the great expansion of the Augustan period people regarded the Empire as a coherent geographical and strategic entity bounded by the three great rivers: Rhine, Danube, and Euphrates.[129] A conflict thus arose between that conception and the long tradition and ideology of continuing conquest.[130] When in Fronto's words "the *imperium* of the Roman People was extended by the emperor Trajan beyond the hostile rivers,"[131] Florus could rejoice that the Empire had found its youth again, and Tacitus

124. Ammianus 22, 7, 8; Libanius, *Or.* 12, 78.

125. Eunapius, *Fr.* 22. 1 (*FHG* IV, p. 23).

126. Ammianus 31, 1–4; Eunapius, *Fr.* 42 (*FHG* IV, pp. 31–33).

127. 31, 2: cf. Eunapius, *Fr.* 45 (*FHG* IV, p. 30); Zosimus 4, 20.

128. *The Congress of Roman Frontier Studies, 1949,* ed. E. Birley (1952), 1.

129. See, e.g., Josephus, *BJ* 2, 16, 4 (363; 377); Statius, *Silv.* 5, 1, 89–90; Tacitus, *Ann.* 1, 9, 4, 5. For the function of the Euphrates as a symbolic frontier, see, e.g., Strabo 16, 1, 28 (748); Velleius 2, 101; Suetonius, *Cal.* 14; Josephus, *BJ* 7, 5, 2 (105); *Ant.* 18, 4, 5, (101–2); Dio 59, 27, 3. For the Danube, see text to nn. 52–55 above.

130. For a good collection of the evidence, see P. A. Brunt, "Laus Imperii," in P. D. A. Garnsey and C. R. Whittaker, eds., *Imperialism in the Ancient World* (1978), 159, reprinted in *Roman Imperial Themes* (1990), 288.

131. Fronto, *Princ. Hist.* 4.

could complain of the inertia of earlier emperors in terms which strikingly recall the content of the poem on the Dacian war which Pliny's friend Caninius Rebilus composed in Comum.[132] Yet the three new provinces beyond the Euphrates could be given up by Hadrian with only relatively mild hostile comment from our sources: according to the *Historia Augusta* he justified this step by quoting the Elder Cato on the difficulty of holding Macedonia as a province.[133] It could even be reported that he had also thought of giving up Dacia beyond the Danube and been restrained by his *amici*, who urged him not to betray the Roman citizens who had immigrated to it.[134]

When Appian began writing his *Roman History* under Antoninus Pius, he still thought of the boundaries as Euphrates, Danube and Rhine, with the Upper German territories beyond the Rhine and Dacia as mere additions: "[B]ut going beyond these rivers in places they rule some of the Celts over the Rhine, and the Getae over the Danube, whom they call Dacians."[135] The concept of the Empire as a stable defensive system based on an outer ring of fixed camps is clearly present in Aristides' *Roman Oration* (80–84) and persists in Herodian, writing a century later, when it was rapidly ceasing to be appropriate: "Augustus . . . fortified the Empire by hedging it around with major obstacles, rivers and trenches and mountains and deserted areas which were difficult to traverse."[136]

This concept became out of date in two ways. Dacia had been taken by Trajan, and involvement beyond the Euphrates was resumed, with uncertain results, under Marcus and Verus, and reached a decisive stage under Severus. The subsequent fates of these two areas form an instructive contrast. Dacia was finally abandoned in the early 270s, but our sources barely notice the fact.[137] Moreover, writers of the later third and fourth centuries again tend to treat the Danube as the established frontier of the Empire, with no hint that there had once been a substantial provincial area beyond it.[138] Not only

132. Florus, *Epit. praef.*; Tacitus, *Ann.* 4, 32; cf. Pliny, *Ep.* 8, 4.

133. Fronto, *Princ. Hist.* 10; Eutropius 7, 6, 2; Festus, *Brev.* 14, 20; *v. Had.* 5, 3.

134. Eutropius 7, 6, 2. Fronto (*Princ. Hist.* 10) claims that Hadrian actually gave up Dacia.

135. Appian, *Praef.* 4/14–15. Cf. Pausanias 1, 9, 5, for very similar conceptions.

136. Herodian 2, 11, 5.

137. The few lines of Eutropius 9, 55, 1 represent the fullest account of the abandonment, and the creation of Dacia Ripensis south of the river. Repeated in *HA, v. Aurel.* 39, 7. Cf. Festus, *Brev.* 8. See H. Vetters, *Dacia Ripensis* (1950).

138. Cf. text to n. 75 (crossing by Goths); *Pan. Lat.* X (Galletier II), 2, 6; XI (Galletier III), 6, 6. Note *Pan. Lat.* VIII (Galletier IV), 3, 3: *Dacia restituta*, referring to Dacia Ripensis. When Anon. Vales. 1, 135/13 gives the origin of Licinius as "ex nova Dacia," this is an implicit allusion to the old province.

that, but historians of the fourth century and after—including Eutropius, who had actually recorded the abandonment of Dacia—describe the treaty by which Jovian gave up Nisibis, Singara, and five districts across the Tigris as a disgrace which had never occurred before in the history of Rome.[139] The pre-eminence of eastern wars was deeply rooted in Graeco-Roman culture and was concretely embodied in the strategic priorities chosen by emperors. There, but not elsewhere, the view of Septimius Severus had long triumphed over that of Dio.

Conclusion

This sketch of some issues relating to the way frontier and foreign policy was conducted by the imperial monarchy cannot by its nature even suggest firm conclusions. Given the haphazard nature of our literary evidence, arguments from silence must always be fragile. They may, none the less, serve the purpose of preventing the interpretation of archaeological evidence in the light of naive assumptions as to information, communication, and responsibility. Even where archaeological evidence of the alignment of frontiers, the siting of camps, or the building of roads seems clearly to demonstrate the operation of coherent plans based on good geographical knowledge, we must still ask whose knowledge, and whose plans. What this chapter can do, therefore, is to focus attention on some issues and to put forward some tentative propositions which, if they prove on further examination to be valid, will have some relevance to how we understand the Empire as a system, and the choices made within it in relation to other peoples.

1. These choices have to be seen in the light of the culture (in both the broad and the more specific sense) of the Graeco-Roman world, whether this be in the use of historical precedents and models, in the types of training for warfare which the upper class received, or in contrasting attitudes to the northern barbarians and to Parthia or Persia. For what it is worth, it may be noted that the explicitly military literature of the Empire is either concerned to deploy precedents from existing narrative histories, or is tactical rather than strategic in character, or both.[140] The surviving literature from

139. Eutropius 9, 17, 1–2; Festus, *Brev.* 29; Ammianus 25, 7; Zosimus 3, 31–32.

140. E.g., Onasander, *Strategemeta*; Frontinus, *Strategemata*; for Arrian, *Techne Taktike*, see F. Kiechle, "Die 'Taktik' des Flavius Arrianus," *45. Ber. Röm-Germ. Kom. 1964* (1965), 87; for Arrian, *Ektaxis*, see A. B. Bosworth, "Arrian and the Alani," *HSCPh* 81 (1977): 217, esp. 232–55, and cf. P. A. Stadter, *Arrian of Nicomedia* (1980), 41–49; Polyaenus, *Strategemata* (addressed to Marcus Aurelius and Verus). The anonymous *de rebus bellicis* (see the new text and dis-

the first four centuries of the Empire provides nothing remotely comparable with the strategic-diplomatic manual which Constantine Porphyrogenitus wrote for his son in about 950.[141]

2. The types of decision which could be made must have been limited by the character of the information available, both on a longer- and short-term basis. It is perhaps significant that one subject on which our literary sources, at least those of the early Empire, provide relatively clear and concrete information is the number and positioning of the legions (and, to a much lesser extent, the auxiliaries). The transfer of legions from province to province and the raising of new ones were clearly essential elements in the types of strategic decision making open to emperors.[142]

3. The character of the bulk of the short-term information reaching the emperor must have depended on the interests and objectives of persons (mainly individual rulers, or would-be rulers) beyond the Empire, or on the presumptions of governors or military commanders on the frontiers.

4. How the Empire *could* respond to any perceived necessity on the frontiers will have been determined first by the degree of initiative allowed to commanders in the area, and the extent to which they operated within the explicit terms or unspoken general assumptions of any imperial "grand strategy."

5. In so far as decisions were held to be required at the centre, that is, by the emperor, it is essential to remember the crude fact that the emperor could be aware of nothing beyond the reach of his own eyes except what someone wished or felt obliged to tell him. With all communications made to him we have to recall constantly the controlling factors of space and time, that is, the delays of up to some two months before a messenger could reach him, and up to a further two months for the return journey to the area concerned; and

---

cussions, edited by M. W. C. Hassall and R. I. Ireland, BAR Int. Ser. 63, 1979) is of course more original, being concerned with practical measures for the defence of a static frontier.

141. Constantinus Porphyrogenitus, *de Administrando*, ed., trans., and com. G. Moravcsik and R. J. H. Jenkins, I–II (1949–62). For its importance as a source of ethnographical information on the area north of the Black Sea, see D. Obolensky, *The Byzantine Commonwealth: Eastern Europe, 500–1453* (1971), esp. 24–25.

142. See Josephus, *BJ* II, 16, 4 (345–401), the speech of Agrippa II; Suetonius, *Vesp.* 8; Tacitus, *Ann.* 4, 5; *Hist.* 1, 8–11; 2, 81. Note esp. Dio 55, 23–24, on the positioning of those legions which had existed under Augustus and were still in service, and those raised by successive later emperors. It will be recalled that according to Suetonius, *Tib.* 30, Tiberius used to consult the Senate "de legendo vel exauctorando milite ac legionum et auxiliorum discriptione" (see translation in text to n. 16).

the much longer delays certainly involved in the journeys of ambassadors from beyond the Empire.

6. Even more important, it is essential to envisage the military-diplomatic relations of the Empire not so much in geographical or even ethnographical terms but as networks of relationships partly created by symbolic acts (the sending of hostages, exchanges of gifts, the grant of crowns) and by verbal exchanges, conducted on the Roman side by governors and local command-ers, but above all by the emperor in person. It may be worth noting that Gaius gives as the prime example of an obligation valid for a *peregrinus* (non-citizen) the occasion when our emperor (*imperator noster*) formally asks the *princeps* of some foreign people, "do you solemnly promise that there will be peace"? (*pacem futuram spondes?*)[143]

7. In accordance with the long-established traditions of Roman public life the position of emperor was from the beginning both civil and military. It is also clear that those emperors of the first century and a half who had no established military reputation actively sought major campaigns while they were on the throne. Yet a qualitative change seems to occur in the middle of the second century, in terms of which, from then until the end of the fourth, it is assumed that all major campaigns, defensive or offensive, require direct command by the (or an) emperor in person.

8. This assumption led directly to the need for a multiplication of emper-ors, and thus to the Tetrarchy, the complex co-emperorships of *Augusti* and *Caesares* in the fourth century, and ultimately to the division of the Empire in the fifth.

9. It cannot be specifically proved—and therefore should not be assumed—that an emperor, whether receiving embassies in Rome or replying to mes-sages from provincial governors, or (progressively) taking command in the field himself and confronting barbarian chiefs or delegations or Persian emis-saries while on campaign, had access to privileged archives of information in strategic matters, or that he had any advice on which to draw except that pro-vided by the *amici*, *comites*, or *consistoriani* whom he consulted, but by whom he could not be bound.

10. For these reasons the emperor's strategic choices and orders and the replies which he made in formal verbal exchanges with foreign embassies could only be determined by the general values of Graeco-Roman culture, of which he himself was a product. When that culture changed, as with the victory of Christianity, so did some of the values which informed foreign relations; Constantine's letter to Shapur II is perhaps the first symbol of that.

143. Gaius, *Inst.* 3, 94.

11. Of all the fundamental choices made, the most significant was the occupation of Mesopotamia and the readiness to fight repeated wars for it. Trajan's brief conquest marked not an end but a beginning, and it was here that the ethos of imperialism had its most lasting effects. Plotinus may have been quite misguided (or is it we?) in thinking that if he joined Gordian III's Persian expedition he might make contact with the philosophers not only of Persia but of India.[144] But most emperors also implicitly agreed with Julian that the Persians were the "better enemies."

To illustrate the concrete conditions of imperial rule to which these developments led—and to exhibit the counter-example of an Emperor who did *not* prefer the eastern front—it may be useful in conclusion to sketch the movements and military preoccupations of Valentinian I as portrayed in Ammianus' narrative. He came to the throne in 364 by the choice of the imperial entourage on the march through Bithynia and, once he had reached Constantinople, appointed his brother Valens as joint *Augustus*. The brothers marched west, and at Naissus divided their accompanying *comites* and *magistri*, and then, after moving on to Sirmium, separated, Valentinian going to Milan and Valens back to Constantinople. In Gaul later in the year Valentinian hesitated between staying to confront an Alamannic invasion and returning to protect Pannonia against the pretender Procopius; he finally followed the view of the majority of his advisers and the pleas of embassies from the Gallic cities and stayed in Gaul (26, 9–13). There he remained for nearly a decade, repeatedly engaged in campaigns on the Rhine, mainly against the Alamanni, writing to the kings of the Burgundii to evoke their aid (28, 5, 10) and making the last crossing of the Rhine by a Roman emperor (29, 4, 1–6). He was building a fort near Basel in 374 when a letter arrived from Petronius Probus, praetorian prefect of Illyricum, reporting raids by the Quadi and Sarmatians on Pannonia. The *notarius* (secretary) Paternianus was sent to investigate and sent back reports to confirm. Valentinian was eager to set out at once on the considerable march to Pannonia (Ammianus elsewhere shows Constantius II at Sirmium as being forty stages' march from Argentorate).[145] But his advisers persuaded him to wait for the spring, when supplies would be available, and to make peace with the Alamanni first. As we saw before (text to nn. 98–99 above), he did so by negotiating from a boat in the Rhine with King Macrianus standing on the bank, and then returned to Trier. In the spring of 375 he marched from Trier to Carnuntum, and then after three

144. Porphyry, *v. Plot.* 3.
145. 16, 12, 70.

months moved to Aquincum, finally settling for the winter at Brigetio (30, 5). There ambassadors from the Quadi appeared and were granted a treaty. But when admitted into the *consistorium*, they were too ready to excuse their previous conduct. The Emperor was enraged, suffered a fit of apoplexy, and died shortly after (30, 6).

The story exemplifies perfectly the constraining factors of time, distance, and information within which an emperor, like anyone else, had to operate. Its ending also illustrates the irreducibly personal character of the combined management of war and diplomacy. We are still a long way from explaining why these responsibilities pressed over more heavily on the emperor in person. But granted the fact of that development over the previous four centuries—the opposite of what we might have presumed in an immense, relatively stable and highly civilized Empire—Valentinian's apoplexy at least is wholly intelligible.

CHAPTER TEN

Government and Diplomacy in the Roman Empire during the First Three Centuries[*]

The diplomacy of the Roman Empire in the period of its greatest extent and stability, let us say until towards the middle of the third century A.D., has received very little attention. A recent collection of studies on ancient diplomacy ignores it altogether.[1] It is true that in this period the Empire faced no major external threat, and remarkably few significant internal revolts. The great Jewish revolt of A.D. 66, culminating in the siege of Jerusalem in 70, which absorbed almost one-seventh of the entire Roman army, offers a clear indication of how much the Empire owed to the absence of national identities within its borders.[2] The period of stability ended precisely with the overthrow in the 220s of the relatively weak Parthian Empire, centred on Babylonia, and the rise of what was to become a serious external threat, the new Persian dynasty, the Sassanians or Sassanids. Observers in the Roman Empire were immediately conscious of how much had changed. Near the end of his great *Roman History* in eighty books, which began with the arrival of Aeneas in Italy and concluded with his own second consulship in 229, Cassius Dio writes (80, 3, 1–4):

> But the situation in Mesopotamia became still more alarming and in-
> spired a more genuine fear in all, not merely the people in Rome, but
> the rest of mankind as well. For Artaxerxes, a Persian, after conquering

*First published in *International History Review* 10 (1988): 345–77.

1. E. Olshausen and H. Biller, eds., *Antike Diplomatie* (Darmstadt, 1979).

2. For revolts, or their absence, and national identities and their general absence, see, e.g., S. L. Dyson, "Native Revolt Patterns in the Roman Empire," in *ANRW* II.3 (1975), 138–75; M. Goodman, *The Upper Class of Judaea: The Origins of the Jewish Revolt of A.D. 66* (Cambridge, 1987); F. Millar, "Empire, Community and Culture in the Roman Near East: Greeks, Syrians, Jews and Arabs," *Journal of Jewish Studies* 38 (1987): 143–64.

the Parthians in three battles and killing their king, Artahanus, made a campaign against Hatra, in the endeavour to capture it as a base for attacking the Romans. . . . He accordingly became a source of fear to us; for he was encamped with a large army so as to threaten not only Mesopotamia but also Syria, and he boasted that he would win back everything that the ancient Persians had once held, as far as the Grecian Sea, claiming that all this was his rightful inheritance from his forefathers.

The Persians never did reach the Aegean, though four centuries later their invasion and brief conquest of Syria and Palestine, and Heraclius' great counter-invasion, were to form the background to the sudden and wholly unexpected conquests of Islam. Long before that, however, the imperialist self-image of the new dynasty had produced, in the form of the great inscription of Shapur I at Naqsh-e-Rustam in Iran, the first documentary representation which we have of the external relations of the Roman Empire as seen from outside:

> When at first we had become established in the empire, Gordian Caesar raised in all of the Roman Empire a force from the Goth and German realms and marched on Babylonia [Assyria] (Asuristan) against the Empire of Iran and against us. On the border of Babylonia at Misikhe, a great "frontal" battle occurred. Gordian Caesar was killed and the Roman force was destroyed. And the Romans made Philip Caesar. Then Philip Caesar came to us for terms, and to ransom their lives, gave us 500,000 *denarii*, and became tributary to us. And for this reason we have renamed Misikhe Peroz-Shapur.
>
> And Caesar lied again and did wrong to Armenia. Then we attacked the Roman Empire and annihilated at Barbalissos a Roman force of 60,000 and Syria and the environs of Syria we burned, ruined and pillaged all. In this one campaign we conquered of the Roman Empire fortresses and towns: the town of Sura, Barbalissos . . . a total of 37 towns with surroundings.
>
> In the third campaign, when we attacked Carrhae and Urhai [Edessa] and were besieging Carrhae and Edessa Valerian Caesar marched against us. He had with him a force of 70,000 from Germany, Raetia, Noricum. . . . And beyond Carrhae and Edessa we had a great battle with Valerian Caesar. We made prisoner ourselves with our own hands Valerian Caesar and others, chiefs of that army, the praetorian prefect, senators; we made all prisoners and deported them to Persis.
>
> And Syria, Cilicia and Cappadocia we burned, ruined and pillaged. In that campaign we conquered of the Roman Empire the town of

Samosata, Alexandria on the Issus . . . all these cities with their sur-
roundings.[3]

This passage begins with Shapur's accession in 240–41, and culminates with
the capture of Valerian in 260, the first and only occasion on which a Roman
emperor was captured alive. As such, it represents very accurately the drastic
nature of the third-century crisis of the Empire. While the crisis was overcome, and the Empire in A.D. 400 still ruled a larger area than it had in A.D. 40,
its strategic centre of gravity had shifted irreversibly eastwards, with consequences too obvious to need spelling out here.

Essentially, therefore, Cassius Dio's report, and Shapur's triumphant proclamation, put up in three languages far away in Iran, reflect a fundamentally
new phase in the history of the Empire. In this phase an emperor may be
captured in person in the field, be killed in battle (as Shapur alleges of Gordian III, in fact, perhaps killed by his own men), have to treat for terms, or
pay his enemy money to obtain peace. Gordian III is also described as bringing against Persia forces which include contingents of Goths and Germans.
If that claim is based on fact, it represents one of our earliest items of evidence of Gothic forces serving under Roman command and suggests their
arrival on the shores of the Black Sea some time in the later second century;
other documentary evidence shows that units of Goths had been enrolled in
the Roman army by the early third century.[4] Goths, too, were to have an important role in the later history of the Empire. The first Roman emperor certainly to die in battle was Decius, killed by the Goths in 251; the second was
Valens, when his forces were crushed by the Goths at Hadrianople (Edirne
in European Turkey), deep in the Roman provinces, in 378.

As we shall see, and as the enrolment of Goths considerably earlier than
previously attested itself illustrates, many features of the Roman state during the crisis of the Empire have their origin in the earlier period of general stability and security. None the less, there are features which make the
period before the rise of Sassanid Persia distinctive, and which raise particular problems as to the nature and conduct of Roman diplomacy as it then
was. Although the subject has attracted relatively little attention, it was not
unimportant. For, even given a remarkable degree of external security and
the absence of major external threats, the frontiers of the Empire, stretching
over several thousand miles, inevitably brought it into contact with a large
variety of peoples, speaking different languages and at very different stages

3. The inscription, in Parthian, Middle Persian, and Greek, is quoted from the translation by R. N. Frye, *The History of Ancient Iran* (Munich, 1984), 371–73.

4. See M. Speidel, "The Roman Army in Arabia," *Roman Army Studies* 1 (1984): 254–58.

of development. Whether we think of purely local contact, aimed at solving disputes or controlling the movements of traders and pastoralists, or of important negotiations conducted centrally, some means for the adjustment of relations clearly had to exist, and did.

Still, it is easy to see why the subject has not occupied a central place in our conception of the early Empire as a political system—the bibliography of this topic is by no means extensive[5]—for it is marked by striking anomalies and contradictions. First, whose Empire was it? What body or person was the sovereign? In fact, as we shall see, the public official discourse of the early imperial period was unambiguous in representing the Empire as that of the *populus Romanus*, the Roman People as a collectivity.[6] But whatever functions the assemblies of the Roman people still fulfilled, the conduct of foreign relations was not one of them. Indeed, even in the Republic, it had been one of the features distinguishing the city-state of Rome from a typical Greek democracy, that ambassadors from foreign powers never came before the assemblies of the people. The people had once voted on declarations of war and the making of peace treaties, but that function too disappeared in the later Republic.[7]

Embassies from foreign powers had in fact always appeared before the Senate: as Polybius rightly noted in the course of his well-known analysis of the Roman constitution, the reception of embassies was one of the Senate's most important functions, and also one which tended to give foreigners the (false) impression (shared however by many moderns) that the Senate could be regarded unambiguously as the "government" of Rome (Polybius 6, 13, 7–8). This central role of the Senate was remembered, and still claimed,

5. The major background survey of the evidence is C. Phillipson, *The International Law and Custom of Ancient Greece and Rome* I–II (London, 1911); for the Roman Empire the most important discussions are J. Gagé, "L'Empereur romain et les rois," *Revue Historique* 221 (1959): 221–60; and M. Lemosse, *Le régime des relations internationales dans le Haut-Empire romain* (Paris, 1967). The present chapter also draws on some aspects of F. Millar, "Emperors, Frontiers and Foreign Relations, 31 B.C. to A.D. 378," *Britannia* 13 (1982): 1–23 (chapter 9 in this volume).

6. For this theme, see F. Millar, "Imperial Ideology in the Tabula Siarensis," in J. González, ed., *Estudios sobre la Tabula Siarensis* (Madrid, 1988). Add a typical example not used there: Pliny, *Nat. Hist.* 3, 136, quotes the inscription from the triumphal monument set up to commemorate Augustus' subjection of a long list of Alpine peoples: "[B]ecause under his command and auspices all the Alpine *gentes* [peoples] . . . have been brought under the *imperium* of the *populus Romanus*."

7. See J. W. Rich, *Declaring War in the Roman Republic in the Period of Transmarine Expansion* (Brussels, 1976).

throughout the period of the Empire with which we are concerned. Our clearest indication of the importance attached to it is in the fictitious speech which Cassius Dio, in his *Roman History*, puts into the mouth of Maecenas, supposedly addressing Augustus (53, 31, 1):

> Moreover, as regards other matters, you would seem to me to be arranging things for the best, if as regards embassies both from enemies and from allies, whether kings or peoples, you were to bring them first before the Senate. For, other considerations apart, it is both appropriate and impressive for the Senate to give the appearance of being sovereign in all things, and that there should be a plurality of people to appear as adversaries in the case of those of them [foreign envoys] who are contumacious.

Though the narrative setting of the speech is the reign of Augustus, its contents were undoubtedly intended to refer to Dio's own time. The words were perhaps written about A.D. 230; in which case, they carry a particularly appropriate message. For, on our evidence (see further below), precisely during the course of the second century had embassies from both outside and inside the Empire ceased to appear before the Senate, and come instead to be directed solely to the emperor in person.[8]

The relationship between the emperor and the Senate thus points towards two further elements of ambiguity in the character of the Empire as a sovereign state. In spite of the formal emphasis on the sovereignty of the Roman people, a wide range of evidence illustrates the fact that from the beginning of the reign of Augustus, diplomatic traffic from outside the Empire tended markedly to direct itself to the emperor in person, wherever he happened to be, as to the effective head of government. Yet for at least a century and a half after the battle of Actium in 31 B.C., which ensured the sole rule of the future Augustus, embassies and allied kings from outside the Empire might also appear to speak before the Senate in Rome. The legacy of the origins of the monarchy from within a republic was thus to be remarkably durable. Nothing shows more clearly than the words which Dio puts into the mouth of Maecenas that this role of the Senate was no ornament but a valued function which was to be recalled decades after it had apparently lapsed into disuse.

However, valued as it clearly was, the diplomatic and foreign-relations role of the Senate had been overshadowed from the reign of Augustus by that of the emperor. This aspect of his function plays an important part in the *Res Gestae*, the record of his achievements, which Augustus composed

8. See R. J. A. Talbert, *The Senate of Imperial Rome* (Princeton, 1984), esp. 425–30.

himself, and left behind on his death, to be inscribed on two bronze tablets which flanked the entrance to his massive Mausoleum on the Campus
Martius in Rome (chap. 35):

> To me there were often sent embassies from kings in India, never pre-
> viously witnessed before any *dux* [general] of the Romans. The Bastar-
> nae and the Scythians sought our *amicitia* [friendship] by embassies, as
> did kings of the Sarmatae living on this side and the other side of the
> river Tanais [the Don], and the king of the Albani, the Hiberi, and the
> Medes. To me there fled suppliant kings of the Parthians . . . [and other
> peoples]. To me the king of the Parthians, Phraates, son of Orodes, sent
> all his sons and grandsons to Italy as hostages, not after defeat in war
> but seeking our *amicitia* by the use of his children as pledges. Several
> other *gentes* tried the faith [*fides*] of the *populus Romanus* while I was
> *princeps*, who had never previously had any exchange of embassies and
> *amicitia* with the *populus Romanus*.

Contemporary evidence confirms that such embassies did reach Augustus,
from both West and East.

The geographer Strabo describes how British kings had gained the friendship of Augustus by sending embassies, and paying court, and had made offerings on the Capitol in Rome (*Geography* 4, 5, 3, 200). The latter point again
illustrates the ambiguity of sovereignty in the early Empire, for by a long-
established tradition of the Republic, which persisted into the Empire, foreign peoples and rulers symbolised their acceptance of Roman hegemony by
offering sacrifices or making permanent dedications on the Capitol, therefore in or near the ancient temple of Jupiter Optimus Maximus; it was there
too that copies of treaties had long been deposited.[9] That same ambiguity appears in the inscription from Apamea in Syria recording a local dynast from
this region in the time of Augustus, called Dexandros, "[who] by the decree
of the deified Augustus, because of his friendship and loyalty to the Roman
People, was inscribed as friend and ally on bronze tablets on the Capitol."[10]
But this inscription introduces yet another form of ambiguity to which we
shall return.

As regards embassies from far beyond the Empire, to the East, our best
evidence comes again from Strabo, who quotes the account of an Indian embassy on its way to meet Augustus given by another contemporary, Nicolaus
of Damascus (Strabo, *Geography* 15, 1, 73, 719):

9. R. Mellor, "The Dedications on the Capitoline Hill," *Chiron* 8 (1978): 319–30.
10. *Année Épigraphique* 1976, no. 678.

He says that at Antioch, near Daphnê, he chanced to meet the Indian ambassadors who had been despatched to Caesar Augustus; that the letter plainly indicated more than three ambassadors, but that only three had survived (whom he says he saw), but the rest, mostly by reason of the long journeys, had died; and that the letter was written in Greek on a skin; and that it plainly showed that Porus was the writer, and that, although he was ruler of six hundred kings, still he was anxious to be a friend to Caesar, and was ready, not only to allow him a passage through his country, wherever he wished to go, but also to cooperate with him in anything that was honourable. Nicolaus says that this was the content of the letter to Caesar, and that the gifts carried to Caesar were presented by eight naked servants, who were clad only in loin-cloths besprinkled with sweet-smelling odours; and that the gifts consisted of the Hermes, a man who was born without arms, whom I myself have seen, and large vipers, and a serpent ten cubits in length, and a river tortoise three cubits in length, and a partridge larger than a vulture.

We happen to know from Cassius Dio's *Roman History* that this embassy, or what was left of it, appeared before Augustus when he was spending the winter of 20–19 B.C. on Samos (54, 9, 8–10). Augustus had also spent the previous winter on Samos, and there an Ethiopian embassy had reached him, sent on by the prefect of Egypt. Strabo again gives a very illuminating account of the reaction of this Ethiopian embassy, originally sent by Queen Candace, when the prefect told the embassy that they must go on from him to the Emperor (*Geography*, 17, 1, 54, 820–21):

Meantime Candace marched against the garrison with many thousands of men, but Petronius set out to its assistance and arrived at the fortress first; and when he had made the place thoroughly secure by sundry devices, ambassadors came, but he bade them go to Caesar; and when they asserted that they did not know who Caesar was or where they should have to go to find him, he gave them escorts; and they went to Samos, since Caesar was there and intended to proceed to Syria from there, after despatching Tiberius to Armenia. And when the ambassadors had obtained everything they pled for, he even remitted the tributes which he had imposed.

The ambassadors' reaction introduces, very early in the history of the Empire, a question to become of ever increasing relevance, especially from the middle of the second century onwards. If it were necessary to appear before

the emperor, as it often was, where was he to be found? The remarkable mo-
bility of emperors, whose journeys are the subject of a valuable recent study,[11]
is a crucial and underestimated aspect of the Empire as a political system.

But, wherever the emperor happened to be, the leaders of most groups
from beyond the borders of the Empire understood from the beginning that
it was to him in person that they should go on diplomatic business. At this
point we encounter further ambiguities. It is by no means clear that any concept of the borders of the Empire prevailed, or that there would have been
any agreement about which regions or peoples lay within the Empire, and
which outside it. Fixed and visible frontier installations (walls, pallisades,
lines of forts) were created in some areas in the course of the imperial period,
for instance in the form of Hadrian's Wall, or the defences of southern Germany. But it is not certain even that these were regarded as marking legal
borders between Roman and non-Roman territory. They were in any case an
exception. In many areas there will have been no definable moment when
the traveller will have known that he was entering or leaving the Roman
Empire. Moreover, the Empire, especially as it was under Augustus, incorporated a large number of regions ruled by allied kings (the so-called client
kings), for instance, in the Alps, Thrace, Eastern Anatolia, the Syrian region,
Arabia, and Mauretania.[12] There is no unambiguous way of saying whether
such regions formed part of the Roman Empire or not. In some sense they
clearly did. Strabo, bringing his *Geography* to a close with a description of
the division of the provinces between the Roman people and the Emperor
(i.e., those provinces whose governors he appointed), ends by saying categorically "kings and dynasts and tetrarchies belong to his part, and always
have done so" (18, 3, 25, 840). But if the criterion of belonging to the Empire were taken as the payment of tribute, then these "client" kingdoms did
not belong to it. As a subject of the tetrarch Herodes Antipas, and living in
Galilee, Jesus paid no tribute to Rome. The issue of whether or not tribute
should be paid by Jews arose, as the Synoptic Gospels agree (Mark 12:13–17;
Matt. 22:17–22; Luke 20:21–26), when Jesus visited Jerusalem, now under
direct Roman rule. But it would be an over-simplification to say that Jesus
was not a subject of the Empire.

None the less, the step-by-step absorption of the "client" kingdoms was a
significant, if protracted, process. Not until A.D. 46 could anyone have walked

11. H. Halfmann, *Itinera Principum: Geschichte und Typologie der Kaiserreisen im römischen
Reich* (Stuttgart, 1986).

12. On these kings, see D. C. Braund, *Rome and the Friendly King: The Character of Client
Kingship* (London, 1984).

round the shores of the Mediterranean while remaining all the time either in Italy or provinces paying tribute to Rome. And not until the second century did the Empire acquire a strategic shape and character such that its defence need not depend to any significant degree on "client" kingdoms.[13]

If our concern is with the nature of the Empire as a diplomatic system, however, the mere fact of the extension of provincialisation will not remove — indeed, rather accentuates — the ambiguities with which we are faced. For quite apart from those unsubdued tribal peoples who remained within the bounds of the Empire, many provinces, especially in the Greek East, contained "free" cities which governors were not supposed to visit, and which lay outside their jurisdiction. One of these, Aphrodisias in Caria, took the precaution early in the third century of inscribing on the wall of its theatre a long series of imperial letters confirming its privileged status. The publication of this archive in 1982 provided a rich store of illustration of the diplomatic practices governing exchanges between such a city and the emperor.[14] In particular, when a new emperor came to the throne, the city council would pass a decree expressing the city's joy at his accession, and ambassadors would be sent who would hand over the decree, accompanying it with a brief speech, heard by the emperor in person. He then addressed to the city a letter in Greek, which was brought back to their homeland by the ambassadors. The custom continued at least until the middle of the third century. The latest document added to the archive wall at Aphrodisias is a reply from the Emperor Decius and his son Herennius, dated to A.D. 250 (no. 25, trans. Reynolds):

> Imperator Caesar C. Messius Q. Traianus Decius, Pius, Felix, Augustus, holding tribunician power for the third time, consul for the second time, designated for the third, father of his country, proconsul, and Q. Herennius Etruscus Messius Decius, Pontifex Maximus, holding the tribunician power for the first time, consul designate, to the Magistrates, Council and People of the Aphrodisians, greetings. It was to be expected, both because of the goddess for whom your city is named and because of your relationship with the Romans and loyalty to them, that you rejoiced at the establishment of our kingship and made the proper sacrifice and prayers. We preserve your existing freedom and all the other rights which you have received from the emperors who

---

13. For this theme, note the very stimulating analysis by E. N. Luttwak, *The Grand Strategy of the Roman Empire from the First Century A.D. to the Third* (Baltimore and London, 1976).

14. J. Reynolds, *Aphrodisias and Rome* (London, 1982).

preceded us, being willing also to give fulfilment to your hopes for the future. Aurelius Theodorus and Aurelius Onesimus carried out the duties of ambassadors. Farewell.

It would, however, be a mistake to conclude that the elaborate diplomatic protocol which characterizes this letter is a function specifically of Aphrodisias' status as a free city, or, as other documents in the archive put it, "removed from the *formula* [*typos*] of the province." For what is distinctive about the archive is not that, but lies in the clear indication it gives of the particular privileges such a "free and immune" city enjoyed: for instance, non-payment of Roman taxes, exemption from visits by the proconsul of Asia, and even exemption from claims on the services of its citizens made by other cities in the province or by the provincial council. Precisely because these privileges were exceptional, repeated "diplomatic" activity was required to ensure their protection and preservation.

Such activity, directed to the emperor, did not in itself mark Aphrodisias as a "free" city, nor ought it to lead us to characterize Aphrodisias as a place which belonged notionally, though of course not geographically, beyond the borders of the Empire. The truth is exactly the opposite, that most of the evidence for exchanges which have the *form* of diplomatic dealings between the emperor and a foreign sovereign power in fact comes from his dealings with cities and communities unambiguously subject to the Roman Empire, which paid tribute to it, and which were in every sense within its borders.[15]

Our extensive knowledge of the form and nature of these exchanges is largely, but not wholly, a function of a feature of Graeco-Roman culture which Ramsey MacMullen aptly nicknamed "the epigraphic habit":[16] that is to say, the custom illustrated above of inscribing in public, on stone or bronze, documents which were felt for various reasons (glory, status, preservation of privileges) to be worth publicizing in permanent form. The mass of our evidence for "diplomatic" exchanges with the emperor comes from cities like Aphrodisias, in the Greek-speaking part of the Empire. It is impossible to tell for certain whether the much smaller number of such documents from the Latin-speaking West is a product of the lesser involvement of communities from this region in such diplomatic traffic, or their less-developed attachment to the epigraphic habit, or (as is quite likely) both.

We may be certain, at any rate, firstly, that long before the establishment of monarchic rule by Augustus, embassies from provincial and allied com-

15. For this topic, see *ERW*, esp. chap. VII.

16. R. MacMullen, "The Epigraphic Habit in the Roman Empire," *American Journal of Philology* 103 (1982): 233–46.

munities had addressed themselves not only to the Senate in Rome but to individual Roman commanders in the field; and, secondly, that immediately after the battle of Actium in 31 B.C., such communities were aware that the source of authority had been decisively concentrated in one man and acted accordingly. We may take as a clear example the reply which Octavian, the future Augustus, wrote from Ephesus to the small Syrian city of Rhosus, some time between the battle on 31 September and the end of the year. It was addressed in formal style to "the magistrates, council, and people of the sacred, inviolate, and autonomous city of the Rhosians," and began with the standard greeting:

> If you are well, it is well; I too, with my army, am well. The ambassadors sent by you . . . having come to me at Ephesus, addressed me on the matters on which they had instructions. On receiving them I found them to be patriotic and good men, and accepted the honours and the gold crown. When I come to those parts I will do my best to be of service to you and to preserve the privileges of the city.

Once again we owe our knowledge of this exchange entirely to the fact that the city decided to have this and other related documents inscribed publicly.[17] It would be possible to cite comparable examples from the following centuries but is surely unnecessary. Such exchanges can be shown to have been initiated by all types of cities or self-governing communities. The composition of decrees, the sending of embassies, the reception of these embassies at a formal session by the emperor, the delivery of the written decrees to the accompaniment of a brief oration, and the bringing back of a reply: such formal exchanges were common both to places which stood in some legalistic sense "outside" the imperial system, and to ones which might be presumed to have been far inside it, to have been in a real sense part of the Roman *res publica* itself—by that I mean regular *coloniae* (colonies), formally established by the *populus Romanus* "of which those colonies can be regarded as being miniature effigies and as it were representations," as Aulus Gellius put it in the second century (*Noctes Atticae* 16, 13). But such colonies, whether situated in Italy, all of whose inhabitants were Roman citizens, or in the provinces, in which case the status of colonies itself automatically conferred the Roman citizenship, none the less addressed themselves to the emperor, and were addressed by him, in precisely the "diplomatic" manner, more suggestive of equal sovereign states, described above. The same is also true of

17. R. K. Sherk, *Roman Documents from the Greek East (Senatus Consulta and Epistulae to the Age of Augustus)* (Baltimore, 1969), no. 58, III.

tribute-paying communities, enjoying no specific Roman status, situated in the Latin-speaking western provinces. So, for instance, we find Vespasian in the 70s replying to an embassy from a totally obscure community in northern Corsica. Once again our knowledge of the exchange is owed entirely to the inscription which the community later put up:

> Imperator Caesar Vespasianus Augustus to the magistrates and senators of the Vanacini, greeting.
>
> I am pleased to learn that Otacilius Sagitta, my friend and procurator, exercised his authority over you in such a way as to earn your commendation. On the controversy which you are engaged in with the Mariani . . . The business was conducted by the ambassadors Lasemus son of Leucanus, priest of Augustus, and Eunus son of Tomasus, priest of Augustus.[18]

In this case the real subordination of the community to imperial control is made perfectly explicit, while the conventional diplomatic form is maintained.

We are not, however, entirely dependent for our knowledge of the nature of these exchanges on the determination of provincial towns to immortalize in public form the answers they received from emperors. While diplomatic (or other) archives, in the sense familiar from more recent periods of history, are unknown, a scattering of comparable texts exists preserved on perishable materials, notably private copies found on papyri from Roman Egypt. One striking example, almost (in a weak sense) deserving the term "archive," is provided by a group of papyri showing exactly comparable embassies, with replies in letter form, being directed to emperors from Claudius in the mid-first century to Severus Alexander in the early third, by the world-wide association (literally "oecumenical synod") of Greek actors, that is, professionals who performed at the major festivals.[19]

The reception of such embassies was a regular public occasion for the emperors, and hence for that reason a fruitful source of anecdotes illustrating their notoriously wide range of personal peculiarities. It is significant that while jurisdiction, another role performed by emperors in person, was often delegated, especially from the early third century on, the hearing of embassies almost never was. The sole exception is provided by Augustus, in advanced old age.[20]

18. *Corpus Inscriptionum Latinarum* X, no. 8038.

19. *ERW*, 460–61.

20. Cassius Dio, *Roman History* 54, 33, 5; 56, 25, 7.

It would be to diverge too far from the purpose of this chapter to ask how far the maintenance (on the part of provincial governors as well as of the emperor himself) of a sort of universal fiction of local sovereignty and entitlement on the part of provincial cities to conduct diplomatic-style relations in the manner of an independent state contributed to the stability of the Empire, and the acceptance of it, or at least absence of consistent opposition to it, among the ruling classes of the provinces. The diplomatic system of the Empire, as sketched above, did, however, implicitly remember and recognise the fact that the vast majority of the locally self-governing cities and communities of the provinces had once been genuinely independent, and had come within the orbit of Roman provincial government and of the payment of tribute to Rome, in a complex variety of ways, from alliance to outright conquest.

In the Roman Empire, therefore, even in Italy itself (most of whose cities were also not creations of Rome and had once been independent), diplomatic forms more suggestive at first sight of foreign relations were carefully preserved. Moreover, it is highly significant that the structure of the imperial court, or entourage, was clearly marked by the need to be able to make the necessary replies in appropriate form. In the speech which Cassius Dio in his *Roman History* puts into the mouth of Maecenas, addressing Augustus, he interestingly suggests restricting embassies from provincial cities to matters requiring a decision (*diagnōsis*) from the emperor, that is, to disputes between at least two cities; other requests should be sent on by the local provincial governor (52, 30, 9). So ingrained was the conception that disputes between city embassies ought to be heard by the emperor, that even Dio, whose attitudes were strongly hierarchical, could not envisage the ending of this imperial role. More pertinent here, however, at a later point in the speech Maecenas is even made to envisage all the chief functionaries at the emperor's side, other than the praetorian prefects, and officials concerned with finance, being employed to answer, in various forms, the addresses and petitions made by both cities and individuals (52, 33, 5): "Moreover, as regards judicial hearings and letters, the decrees of the cities, and the petitions of individuals, and whatever else is relevant to the government of the Empire, take aides and assistants from the equestrian order."

A wider and much-disputed issue is being touched on here, namely the extent to which the imperial system was primarily passive, directed to a significant degree to answering requests or solving disputes emanating from below. It may suffice to say here that the (admittedly unsatisfactory) evidence does indeed reveal imperial secretaries with functions of the sort suggested by Dio through "Maecenas": men with titles such as *a cognitionibus* (to do with judicial cases), *ab epistulis* (to do with letters), and *a libellis* (to do with petitions). But, in a way which remains very puzzling, the evidence reveals no imperial "secretaries" whose titles suggest responsibility for the positive or general forms of instruction which emperors did indeed issue: the *mandata*, or codes of instruction given to provincial governors and other officials; or imperial *edicta*, general pronouncements which were not (in principle) addressed to any one community or individual. It remains quite unclear which "secretaries," if any, were concerned in the composition of the sometimes extensive, detailed, and declamatory imperial *edicta*.

The fact that our evidence does not even record the titles of any officials concerned with these two important types of imperial pronouncement merely accentuates a more general and profound problem, firstly, as to the working of the imperial court as a whole as a bureaucratic or governmental system and, secondly, as to the specific role of the emperor in deciding the content of imperial replies, or even, perhaps, in the actual composition of the relevant texts. The problem is not decided by the mere fact that our sources invariably talk *as if* all forms of imperial pronouncement came from the emperor himself. None the less, two considerations serve to establish a framework for the question. Firstly, there is nothing in our entire evidence to suggest that any form of imperial pronouncement could be issued in his name, or as from him, by any imperial agency functioning from a place from which the emperor himself was absent—for instance from Rome, if the Emperor were currently at an imperial villa elsewhere in Italy, or in the provinces, or on campaign. All imperial pronouncements emanated at least from the immediate vicinity, or entourage, of the emperor.

Secondly, it would be reasonable, and in accordance with the basic character both of Roman political life and of Roman law, to see verbal, or oral, pronouncements as primary, and their written manifestations as secondary. Roman law depended fundamentally on verbal statements made by parties to legal transactions, rather than on written documents: it is striking that the legal writer Gaius, of the middle of the second century A.D., imagines the emperor requiring the *princeps* of a foreign *populus* to make a verbal promise to keep the peace—"pacem futuram spondes?" (*Inst.* 3, 94). Equally, for instance, an *edictum* had originally been literally that, a pronouncement "spoken out" to the people by a magistrate, normally from the Rostra, the speaker's platform in the Forum in Rome.

It is important to stress that the role of issuing verbal pronouncements or decisions remained an essential element in the functions of the emperor. He delivered *orationes* (speeches) to the Senate (though these could be read in his absence by his quaestor, the *quaestor Caesaris*); he also made *orationes* on occasion to the people, and *orationes* or *allocutiones* to the soldiers in Rome or the army in the field. Both coins and the representations of the imperial military role on the Column of Trajan and the Column of Marcus Aurelius give particular prominence to this latter role. The emperor also, as mentioned above, gave jurisdiction; as with any other person giving jurisdiction, the verdict (*decretum* or *sententia*) had to be read out by him, often from a written text so as to ensure complete accuracy. Finally, as noted earlier, the emperor heard embassies from provincial communities in person and had to make at least a provisional response verbally at the time, even though the definitive reply was invariably embodied subsequently in a letter.

It was precisely such letters, as we have seen, which formed the type of imperial pronouncement most frequently enshrined by these provincial communities in permanent inscriptions; hence they are among the documents whose formal character is best known to us. That still leaves open, however, the question of by whom they were in reality composed. Somewhat similar problems arise with imperial answers to *libelli*, or written petitions from individuals. These were, originally at least, handed to the emperor in person; and the replies, referred to in the second century as *subscriptiones*, were in principle literally "written under" the petitions themselves, and given back. There is no need here to go into the complex question of the evolution of the *libellus* system, except to say that it does bear in an important way on major questions in Roman law, for imperial replies to *libelli* from private persons make up almost the whole of the *Codex Justinianus* and are extensively quoted in the *Digest*, in other legal sources from Gaius onwards, and on inscriptions and papyri. They appear in large numbers in the *Codex* and *Digest* precisely because they are being quoted as sources of law. Current arguments have not yet established whether we should see this branch of law-making as a function of the emperors themselves, or allow it to be reclaimed for the jurists, including major ones such as Papinian, who successively occupied the secretarial post at the emperor's side called *a libellis* (to do with *libelli*), or later *magister libellorum*. It might well be necessary here, too, to distinguish clearly between responsibility for the essential content of such a reply (which might often be of a yes-no form) and the composition of a text expressing the answer in appropriate legal language, with explanation and justification where required.[21]

21. For the complex issues relating to *libelli* presented to the emperor, and to the composition of the replies, see T. Honoré, *Emperors and Lawyers* (London, 1981); F. Millar, "A New Approach to the Roman Jurists," *JRS* 76 (1986): 272–80 (chapter 19 in this volume), and "L'Empereur romain comme décideur," in C. Nicolet, ed., *Du pouvoir dans l'antiquité: mots et réalités* (Paris, 1990), 207–20.

By the second century, it was possible for such *libelli* to be forwarded to the emperor by provincial governors, accompanied by a covering letter, both carried by messengers. Such an exchange, which took place in the reign of Marcus Aurelius, provides one of the very few glimpses we ever get of the archives of the emperors and how they were managed. Once again, however, the glimpse is indirect. The source is again an inscription, a bronze tablet discovered at Banasa (Morocco), and evidently put up by the beneficiaries of the imperial grants in question. The two imperial letters quoted are in response to letters from two successive governors of the Roman province of Mauretania Tingitana, each forwarding a *libellus* asking for the Roman citizenship for a chief of a tribal people in that region, the Zegrenses, or for members of his family:

[c. A.D. 168] Copy of a letter of our Emperors Antoninus and Verus, Augusti, to Coiiedius Maximus: we have read the *libellus* [petition] of Julianus the Zegrensian attached to your letter, and although the Roman citizenship is not normally granted by imperial *indulgentia* to those tribesmen unless earned by the highest deserts, yet since you affirm that he is among the most prominent among those peoples of his and most loyal in his prompt obedience in our interests (and we do not think that many households from among the Zegrenses will be able to claim the same of their services) and since [?] we wish as many as possible to be aroused by the honour conferred by us on that house to emulate Julianus, we do not hesitate to give the Roman citizenship, without prejudice to the law of the tribe, to him, his wife Ziddina, and their children Julianus, Maximus, Maximinus, Diogenianus.

[A.D. 177] Copy of a letter of the Emperors Antoninus and Commodus, Augusti, to Vallius Maximianus: we have read the *libellus* of the chief of the tribes of the Zegrenses and have noted the favour with which he is regarded by your predecessor Epidius Quadratus, and also moved by the latter's testimonies, and the services and evidence of his conduct which he himself puts forward, have given to his wife and children the Roman citizenship, without prejudice to the law of the tribe. In order that this may be recorded in our *commentarii* [records] find out what the age of each is and write to us.

Copied down and checked from the record [*commentarius*] of those given the Roman citizenship by the Divine Augustus [names of preceding emperors] . . . which the freedman Asclepiodotus produced, as it is written below:

In the consulship of Imperator Caesar L. Aurelius Commodus Aug. and M. Plautius Quintilius, on the day before the nones of July, at Rome [6 July 177]

Faggura, wife of Julianus, princeps of the tribe of the Zegrensians, age 22, Juliana, age 8, Maxima, age 4, Julianus, age 3, Diogenia, age 2, children of Julianus mentioned above:

At the request per libellum of Aurelius Julianus, princeps of the Zegrensians supported by Vallius Maximianus by letter [*suffragante . . . per epistulam*], to these we have given the Roman citizenship, without prejudice to the law of the tribe, and without diminution of the *tributa* and *vectigalia* of the *populus* and the *fiscus*.

Carried out on the same day in the same place under the same consuls. Asclepiodotus, freedman: I have checked it:

Witnesses:

M. Gavius Squilla Gallicanus	[consul, 150]
M. Acilius Glabrio	[consul, 152]
T. Sextius Lateranus	[consul, 154]
C. Septimius Severus	[consul, 160]
P. Juilius Scapula Tertullus	[consul, 160–6]
T. Varius Clemens	[ex–*ab epistulis*]
M. Bassaeus Rufus	[ex–praetorian prefect]
P. Taruttienus Paternus	[praetorian prefect by 179]
Sex [Tigidius Peren]nis	[probably praetorian prefect]
Q. Cervidius Scaevola	[lawyer, prefect of *Vigiles* (fire brigade), 175]
Q. Larcius Euripianus	
T. Flavius Piso	[prefect of the corn supply, 179][22]

What is relevant in this context is, firstly, the unexpected revelation of a continuous system of recording the names of persons granted the Roman citizenship, going all the way back to the first emperor, Augustus, who had died more than a century and a half earlier. It must remind us that we *may* seriously underestimate the sophistication of an imperial archival system to which we have no direct access; and it must at least raise the question of whether any comparable archival system recorded diplomatic and foreign relations be-

---

22. M. Euzennat, J. Marion, and J. Gascou, *Inscriptions antiques du Maroc* II: *Inscriptions latines* (Paris, 1982), no. 94.

yond the imperial frontier. Secondly, once again, it may remind us that "the imperial frontier" itself is not an unambiguous concept. Roman dealings with the unsubdued tribal peoples of western Mauretania had themselves in part the character of foreign, or diplomatic, relations. In this instance, Roman citizenship is being sought by someone who clearly lay at best on the margins of the urban, literate world of Graeco-Roman culture. The document also touches on another ambiguity characteristic of what we might otherwise want to call Roman "foreign" policy. Like the Herodian kings who ruled one area or another in the Palestine region in the first century, or the kings of the Bosporan kingdom (the eastern Crimea and western Tuman peninsula across the straits) throughout the whole period with which we are concerned, this family of Moroccan tribal chiefs was henceforth to hold Roman citizenship. The citizenship was another respect in which the nature of a strict "frontier" between Roman and non-Roman does not apply. Finally, it is striking that even at this late stage there is a reflection of the ambiguous sovereignty prevailing in the Roman state itself. The taxes and duties which the beneficiaries will still have to pay are due both to the imperial *fiscus* (treasury) and to the *populus*.

If we come back to the governmental and bureaucratic practice of the imperial court, Cassius Dio, it will be recalled, had specified letters as one area where the emperor would certainly need an aide of equestrian rank (52, 33, 5, cited above). It is noticeable, however, that here, in clear contrast with the passage where he speaks of the reception of foreign embassies by the Senate (53, 31, 1, cited above), he is thinking of the internal working of the Empire. Some of this imperial correspondence was addressed, invariably in Latin, to officials, in particular provincial governors; Pliny the Younger's correspondence with Trajan from the province of Pontus and Bithynia is only the best-known example of a standard form of exchange, which represents a central element in how the Empire was governed. Two specimens are, of course, incorporated into the document from Banasa just quoted. Equally, imperial letters to cities in the Latin-speaking part of the Empire, of which only a rather modest number is preserved, were also naturally written in Latin.

But very different considerations applied to cities and provincial councils in the Greek-speaking half of the Empire. Here, all the letters from emperors and from governors, which inscriptions put up by these cities reveal, are written in Greek. The suspicion that the original letters might have been translated from Latin in the city concerned, in order to make them more readily intelligible to passers-by who stopped—as they might when entering the theatre of Aphrodisias—to read the inscribed documents, is natural, but in fact not justified. For those inscribed archives, or perhaps pseudo-archives, which also incorporate letters between officials, which were originally written in Latin, leave the texts in Latin and do not translate them.[23]

It thus seems highly probable that the Greek cities of the eastern part of the Empire were paid the compliment, in yet another and very precise respect, of having letters addressed to them which had been written in Greek, or translated into Greek, at the imperial court itself. In this sense too, therefore, they were treated as foreign powers, to whom a diplomatic form of address was appropriate. The probability that this was so becomes a certainty when we consider the relatively well-known history of the office of *ab epistulis* (to do with letters).[24] This office existed in some form from the beginning of the Empire and comes more clearly into view in the middle of the first century A.D., when it was primarily occupied by freed slaves from the imperial household. Precisely this aspect served to give it and comparable offices some prominence in historical and biographical sources such as Tacitus and Suetonius; for it was generally felt, looking back some decades later, that in the middle of the Julio-Claudian period, and in particular in the reign of Claudius (A.D. 41–54), imperial freedmen serving in close proximity to the emperor had exercised an excessive, damaging, and corrupting influence. In the course of the following period, positions such as *ab epistulis, a libellis,* and *a rationibus* (to do with accounts) began to pass instead into the hands of men of free birth belonging to the rank immediately below the Senate, the equestrian order—a process complete by the reign of Hadrian (A.D. 117–38), when one of the *ab epistulis* was the biographer Suetonius. At the same time, however, we find the emergence of a separate post defined as *ab epistulis Graecis* (to do with letters in Greek). Such a post, or one defined in closely comparable terms, had been attested on some occasions in the middle of the first century. Indeed it is striking that these posts are the earliest "secretarial" posts alongside the emperor to appear on public inscriptions as being held by men who are not freed slaves but Roman citizens of equestrian rank. Both the known examples from this period are in fact Roman citizens of Greek origin. Tiberius Claudius Balbillus appears in a Latin inscription from Ephesos as *ad legationes* (to do with embassies) *et res[ponsa Graeca?* (and replies in Greek?)]—it is typical that the text should be broken at the crucial point. This problem at least does not appear in the Greek inscription from Cos,

23. For a prime case, see the exchanges relating to the temple of Zeus at Aezani in the province of Asia: U. Laffi, "I terreni del tempio di Zeus ad Aizanoi," *Athenaeum* 49 (1971): 3–53.

24. For this office, or evolving separate offices, see *ERW*, esp. chap. III, pts. 5–6, and V, pt. 2.

his native city, honouring Claudius' doctor, C. Stertinius Xenophon, who is also described as holding the post of *epi tōn Ellēnikōn apokrimatōn* (to do with pronouncements, or replies, in Greek). How exactly we should translate *apokrima* is not clear, but hardly matters in this context, as the sphere of activity is clear enough. It is equally so in the entry in a Byzantine lexicon which describes another Greek, of the second half of the first century, Dionysius of Alexandria, as "in charge of the *epistolai* and *presbeiai* [embassies] and *apokrimata*." From the reign of Hadrian onwards, the role is well attested, and in particular it is known to have been held by a number of the fashionable and famous Greek orators celebrated in the *Lives of the Sophists* of Philostratus, written in the first half of the third century. That fact alone would tend to suggest that their role related to the formulation of imperial letters in correct Greek style. And, in fact, this function is made quite explicit in what Philostratus says of one of these men, Aspasius, who held office in the early third century. The other Philostratus mentioned was the writer's nephew (*Vit. Soph.* 2, 33):

> The epistle composed by Philostratus called *How to Write Letters* is aimed at Aspasius, who on being appointed imperial secretary wrote certain letters in a style more controversial than is suitable; and others he wrote in obscure language, though neither of these qualities is becoming to an emperor. For an emperor when he writes a letter ought not to use rhetorical syllogisms or trains of reasoning, but ought to express only his own will; nor again should he be obscure, since he is the voice of the law, and lucidity is the interpreter of the law.

In the course of the second century, the division of functions naturally led to the other secretary concerned with letters being described as *ab epistulis Latinis*. It would not be unreasonable to suppose that their respective functions were already not very different from those later described in the *Notitia Dignitatum* (List of Offices) of around A.D. 400:

> *Magister epistolarum*: deals with embassies from cities, *consultationes* [enquiries by letter from officials] and *preces* [petitions].

> *Magister epistolarum graecarum*: those letters which are customarily issued [*emitti*] in Greek he either dictates himself or if dictated in Latin translates into Greek.

Thus, in evidence from various periods, while a clear functional connection is made between incoming embassies and the letters which needed to be written in reply to them, the latter role tends to be the more prominent, and to determine the titulature of the officials concerned. Far more important for our purposes, however, is the contrast between the very clear effect on the structure and functioning of the imperial entourage of the respect paid to the Greek cities of the Empire on the one hand, and the total absence on the other of any precise apparatus to handle diplomatic relations beyond the frontier.

As regards a large proportion of the areas with which the Empire was in some permanent or repeatedly renewed relationship, we could simply suppose that the same apparatus designed for "internal" exchanges of a diplomatic type could be applied without difficulty—indeed, in the case of "client" kings without any clear distinction—to relations which might be regarded as "external." It can, for instance, be assumed without question that Greek was the diplomatic language of all letters to and from kings on the eastern perimeter of the Empire, from the Bosporan kingdom on the north coast of the Black Sea to Armenia, Commagene (finally absorbed in about A.D. 72), Osrhoene on the other side of the Euphrates, absorbed in A.D. 213–14, Nabatea (Arabia), absorbed in A.D. 106, and even Parthia itself, as well as its Persian successor empire of the 220s onwards. We have in the case of the Parthian Empire a precise parallel in the respect shown to the "Greekness" of the Greek cities within its borders. For the only documentary example which we have of a letter written by a Parthian king is one written in A.D. 21 by Artabanus III to the city of Seleucia on the Eulaeus, the ancient Susa in present-day Iran.[25] As with the numerous letters of Roman emperors to Greek cities, of which some examples are mentioned above, we owe our knowledge of this letter to the fact that the city concerned had it publicly inscribed. It follows, however, and could not be doubted on more general grounds, that the Parthians will always have had the capacity to conduct diplomatic relations with the Roman Empire, or specifically with the emperor, in Greek. This will have remained true even in the later period, when it is generally thought that, in broader cultural terms, the long-lasting influence of the Greek culture imported into the Middle East by Alexander had begun perceptibly to decline. So, for instance, there is the evidence of a wonderful new discovery, a bronze statue of the Greek hero Herakles, captured by the Parthian king Vologaeses in A.D. 150 in the course of his conquest of the little kingdom of Mesene, at the head of the Persian Gulf, and dedicated by him in the temple

25. C. B. Welles, *Royal Correspondence in the Hellenistic Period* (New Haven and London, 1934), no. 75.

of Apollo situated in another Greek city, Seleucia on the Tigris. The fact is recorded on a bilingual inscription, in Greek and Parthian (the latter written in Aramaic letters) on the statue itself.[26]

We can thus assume without difficulty that when the emperor Macrinus, who seized power after the murder of Caracalla in Mesopotamia in 217, sent "friendly messages, and returned captives" to the Parthian king Artabanus, the letter and any accompanying exchanges were in Greek (Cassius Dio 79, 29, 2). Greek was to remain one of the royal languages of the new Persian Empire, as is illustrated most clearly by the great inscription of Shapur I from Naqsh-e-Rustam (text to n. 3 above), set up in three languages, Greek, Middle Persian, and Parthian.

The same predominance of Greek as an international language can be assumed for all the kingdoms, of varying size and stability, which were to be found in the broad zone between the Red Sea and the Black Sea. An inscription from the city of Priene in Asia Minor happens to allude quite casually to the fact that as early as 129 B.C. an ambassador had gone "to Petra of Arabia," the Nabatean capital, for what purpose is not known.[27] We can be certain that the ambassador from this Greek city did not devote himself to studying the Nabatean language (a dialect of Aramaic) before he set off. The Nabateans' official use of Greek is shown not only on their coinage of the Hellenistic period but also, for instance, in dedications which one of their kings, Rabbel, like other kings, placed on the Capitol in Rome. In fact, it was made for him by his ambassadors, described in Greek as *presbeutai*.[28] The same will, beyond question, apply to the dynasty of the kings of the Bosporus, since the language of the kingdom and the cities within it was entirely Greek. In the correspondence between Pliny the Younger, as governor of Pontus and Bithynia, and Trajan, we happen to catch a glimpse of a letter being transmitted by Sauromates I (A.D. 93/4–123/4) to Trajan. Indeed, we find a complex set of exchanges proceeding simultaneously. A messenger (*tabellarius*) from the king arrives in Bithynia carrying a letter to Trajan, and also one to Pliny himself, urging him to send the messenger onwards with all speed, as the letter to the Emperor contains things he urgently needs to know. At the same time an embassy from the Bosporus, or more precisely from the king, is pur-

---

26. Published in *The Land between Two Rivers: Twenty Years of Italian Archaeology in the Middle East* (Turin, 1985), 423–25, no. 231.

27. See G. W. Bowersock, *Roman Arabia* (Cambridge, Mass., 1983), 22.

28. A. Degrassi, "Le dediche di popoli e re asiatici al popolo romano e a Giove Capitolino," *Bulletino della commissione archeologica communale di Roma* 74 (1952): 19–47, on p. 34, no. 20 = *Scritti vari di Antichità* I (Rome, 1962), 415–44.

suing a more leisurely journey through Bithynia on its way to Rome (Pliny, *Letters* 10, 63; 64; 67).

The embassy was probably intending to present itself before Trajan, but it could still have been brought by him before the Senate. For the latest definite evidence which we have for such an appearance relates to the following reign, that of Hadrian (A.D. 117–38). The kings of the Bosporus were the most stable and long-lasting of all the "client" dynasties of Rome, and the only one which minted (or was allowed by Rome to mint?) gold coins. The coins invariably portrayed both King and Emperor. But the titulature of the kings implicitly expressed a dual loyalty, which reflected the dual sovereignty inherent in the Empire itself: *philokaisar* and *philorōmaios*. What that meant is spelled out in a Latin inscription in honour of Sauromates I, put up in Panticapaeum in the Crimea by the *colonia* of Sinope on the opposite coast of the Black Sea: "King Ti[berius] Iul[ius] Sauromates, an outstanding friend of the Emperor and of the *populus R[omanus]*."[29]

If this dual sovereignty was more important, and was reflected in our sources for a longer period than has been realized, it is still the case that actual communications with foreign powers, and even "client" kings, were always conducted by the emperor. If he chose also to bring foreign rulers, and embassies from them, before the Senate, that was at all times a gesture which did not affect the realities of decision making. It is worth noting the elaborate form which this gesture took on the latest occasion of its use, so far as our narrative sources indicate, that is, in the reign of Hadrian. This is how Cassius Dio, writing a century later, records the relevant episode (69, 15, 2):

> When ambassadors were sent by Vologaeses [king of Parthia] bringing charges against Pharasmanes [king of Iberia in the Caucasus] and by the Iazyges, who wished to have peace confirmed, he introduced them into them into the Senate; and being commissioned to prepare the answers, he composed them himself and read them to them.

By "them" Dio seems to mean not the Senate collectively (which he refers to in the singular) but the ambassadors. Whether or not Dio is right in his clear implication that Hadrian wrote the letters himself, what he says raises acute problems about the nature of Roman diplomacy in this period, some of which have already been adumbrated.

Firstly, the practice of bringing foreign embassies before the Senate may have continued longer than has been previously supposed, and indeed into the lifetime of Cassius Dio. For a very fragmentary Latin papyrus, recently

29. I. Struve, *Corpus Inscriptionum Regni Bosporani* (Moscow, 1965), no. 46.

discussed for the first time as a historical source, is certainly an extract from the *acta* (proceedings) of the Senate, dates to the reign of Commodus (A.D. 180–92), and seems to show exchanges with an embassy (*[l]egatio*) which may be one from the central European tribe known as the Buri; at any rate, in a typically frustrating way, the word Bu[ri?] can be read in the papyrus. It was already known from Cassius Dio (72, 3, 1–2) that Commodus had "granted peace" to this Germanic people early in his reign.[30]

Secondly, there are questions of procedure. In its dealings with foreign peoples, the Senate had always used, for the reception of embassies, a minimally adjusted version of its standard proceedings. It functioned essentially by the presentation of the relevant subject matter by the presiding magistrate, usually a consul or praetor, the giving of opinions by the more senior senators in order of precedence, and where necessary a vote by division. Embassies, whether appearing singly or in competition or dispute with each other, were simply heard after being introduced by the presiding magistrate, and the rest of the procedure continued as normal. As with the emperor, one could say that diplomacy was simply "embedded" in a more general framework of government, in which verbal exchanges and pronouncements played a predominant part. Like the emperor, the Senate had at its disposal no specific agency for the bureaucratic or professional management of foreign relations, or for the preparation of missives to foreign powers. It was, however, normal for inscribed texts of treaties to be put up on the Capitol (texts to nn. 9–10 above).

In the Republic, the Senate had also performed the diplomatic function of sending embassies from within its own ranks to negotiate with foreign powers. Once again, the function was embedded in the more general exercise of a public political role, and no core of specialist diplomats existed. In the Empire, however, no trace of this function can be found at all. By an odd paradox, the only embassies which the Senate now sent were ones with the function of addressing the emperor himself or members of his family.

The active conduct of foreign relations therefore rested entirely with the emperor, his advisers, and his entourage. But various problems suggested by Dio's account of Hadrian's dealings with the embassies from Vologaeses and the Iazyges still present themselves. We can be sure, as mentioned above, that letters from and to Vologaeses will have been in Greek, just as the Parthian ambassadors may well have spoken in the Senate in Greek. Whoever was "in charge of Greek letters" and perhaps simultaneously responsible for receiving

---

30. R. J. A. Talbert, "Commodus as Diplomat in an Extract from the Acta Senatus," *ZPE* 71 (1988): 137–47.

embassies could have dealt with Parthia exactly as he dealt with a Greek city within the Empire.

But if the rules and the language of diplomatic contact presented no problems as between a Roman emperor and a Greek-speaking, or Greek-using, kingdom, what of the Iazyges, a people of Iranian origin inhabiting the territory between Roman Dacia and the lower course of the Danube before it reaches the Black Sea? It is striking how our sources repeatedly describe verbal contacts with the barbarian peoples of Europe, as of Africa, while only rarely making the slightest allusion to the mechanics of how these exchanges were conducted.

The first thing that has to be made clear is that there is no sign of anything that could be described as permanent diplomatic representation on either side. The Romans maintained no resident ambassadors or legations either in "client" kingdoms or among any other peoples with whom they had diplomatic or military contacts. The nearest to a Roman representative that our sources offer would be the officers of military units, which are occasionally found stationed in allied kingdoms. Even this is not common; but we do find some Roman forces stationed in the kingdom of the Bosporus, mentioned above; Roman forces were supporting a Roman nominee to the throne there in A.D. 51 (Tacitus, *Annals* 12, 15); and Josephus records that there were as many as 3,000 Roman troops in this general area in A.D. 66 (*Jewish War* 2, 16, 4, 366). Others are also attested from time to time in the Caucasus. A famous Greek inscription from Harmozica (Tiflis) of A.D. 75 also shows Vespasian, Titus, and Domitian having fortifications built "for King Mithridates of the Hiberi, son of King Pharasmanes and Iamaspos [?] his son, *philokaisar* and *philorōmaios*, and for the people of the Hiberi."[31] This almost certainly means that Roman forces were present. They are more clearly attested in a Latin inscription put up by a *legatus* of the *legio XII Fulminata*, from near Baku on the Caspian Sea under Domitian (A.D. 81–96)—notable as the easternmost Latin inscription so far known (*Ann. Épig.* 1951, no. 263).

However, neither permanent military occupation by Roman forces nor any other standing Roman presence should be assumed as the norm for any of the "client" or allied states on Rome's borders. Indeed, as regards military relations, the current went the other way. It was extremely common for barbarian or semi-barbarian peoples on Rome's borders to provide auxiliary units for the Roman army. This is an important topic which cannot be pursued here, though we may note that such units included Bosporani, and

---

31. *OGIS* 379 = M. McCrum and A. G. Woodhead, *Select Documents of the Principates of the Flavian Emperors* (Cambridge, 1961), no. 237.

that Arminius, the victor of the famous defeat of the Roman *legatus*, Quinctilius Varus, in the battle of the Teutoburger Forest in A.D. 9, had not only led Cheruscan forces in Roman service, but was himself a Roman citizen, and even had the status of *eques* (Velleius Paterculus 2, 118, 2). It is more important to stress that the provision of military contingents for service with Rome is well attested as a specific provision of peace treaties concluding hostilities; one example will be given below.

If there was no permanent Roman diplomatic representation among allied peoples, the same is also true in the reverse direction. The notion of established representation at the political centres of foreign peoples, whether monarchies or not, was unknown in antiquity. The only representatives of foreign powers who might be living in Rome were of a different sort, namely hostages. A considerable volume of literary and inscriptional evidence illustrates the presence in Rome of hostages from a variety of regions beyond the Empire. They could indeed be regarded, as by Pliny the Elder, supplementing his knowledge of the Caucasus region, as sources of geographical information (*Nat. Hist.* 6, 23), or of course as Roman nominees in disputes over the occupancy of thrones in "client" kingdoms. There is only a narrow line between these and the children whom "client" kings often sent to Rome to be educated, as Herod the Great did with two of his sons. When Roman coinage claimed, as it on occasion did, that a king had been "given" (*datus*) to a people beyond the borders, it was often a hostage or royal child, already available, and suitably Romanized, who was sent out in this role.[32]

It is only, however, in a very loose sense that such hostages or members of royal families, more or less voluntarily resident in Rome, could be considered as diplomatic representatives. To make such a claim would be on the contrary to miss the essential point that all diplomatic transactions were conducted ad hoc either by the dispatch of ambassadors to the seat of power, or on occasion by face-to-face negotiations conducted in person by the emperor, or a member of his family, with a foreign king.

The latter is more fully attested in the following period, the "crisis" of the third century, and increasingly so in the fourth century, where a detailed narrative is available from Ammianus Marcellinus. But diplomacy at a distance, as conducted by Rome, is not so easy to grasp. As we have seen in sufficient detail already, the opposite process, the arrival of foreign ambassadors in Roman territory, is frequently described. For instance, the documents from the famous archaeological site of Dura-Europos on the Euphrates show a Parthian ambassador on his way to appear before Septimius Severus and

32. See Braund, *Rome and the Friendly King* (n. 12), 9ff.

Caracalla. The governor of Syria Coele gives instructions that he is to be offered upkeep in the normal manner:

> Marius Maximus to the *tribuni* and *praefecti* and *praepositi numerorum*, greeting:
> I have attached a copy of the letter which I have written to Minicius Martialis, *procurator* of our *Augusti*, so that you may take note of it. Take care that the quartermaster's offices of the units [*numeri*] through which Goces, an ambassador of the Parthians, sent to our Lords the most valiant Emperors, is in transit. Offer him upkeep according to the normal form. Report to me whatever is spent in each unit.[33]

The document shows quite clearly that, as with the Bosporan embassy on its way through Bithynia which Pliny sent on, the movement of ambassadors sent to appear before emperors far away in Rome or elsewhere was a routine matter. If, as seems likely, the document from Dura dates to A.D. 208, the ambassador may in the end have had rather a long way to go, for in that year Severus, with his two sons, Caracalla and Geta, set off to campaign in Britain, where he died at York in 211. If Goces did only encounter Severus on campaign, facilities were still likely to have been available for his reception. A writer of the second century, Hyginus, describing a model military camp in which the imperial entourage was present, mentions the *quaestorium*, which housed ambassadors of the enemy and hostages, and in which booty, if any, was stored.[34]

We shall come later to some evidence which does clearly illustrate the reception by the emperor of barbarian embassies while on campaign. But the problem still remains of what procedures were used by the emperors in communicating with foreign powers. The notion of letters from the emperor to kings is clearly attested. For instance, Suetonius happens to mention that Tiberius did not use the name "Augustus" except in letters to kings and dynasts (*Tib.* 26). The fact that he also used it in letters to cities does not entirely invalidate the notion that writing letters to kings and dynasts was a specific imperial function, in which the emperor needed to emphasize his superior status. However, such letters, like those to cities discussed above, might in many cases have been carried back by ambassadors who had appeared before the emperor. In consequence, no procedure was required

33. Recently discussed by M. L. Chaumont, "Un document méconnu concernant l'envoi d'un ambassadeur parthe vers Septime Sévère (P. Dura 60B)," *Historia* 36 (1987): 422–47.

34. Hyginus, *de munitionibus castrorum* 18, ed. and trans. M. Lenoir, *Pseudo-Hygin des fortifications du camp* (Paris, 1979).

beyond the writing of the letter itself. But suppose no foreign embassy were to hand, and it was necessary to communicate spontaneously with a foreign power, or to conduct negotiations beyond the frontier? In the case of a king whose loyalty to the Empire was beyond question, it might have been feasible for a mere messenger to carry a letter, the counterpart of the *tabellarius* of Sauromates I on his way to deliver a letter to Trajan (Pliny, *Ep.* 10, 63, 64, 67). Such a procedure seems, however, not to be concretely attested, though it may have been employed. For any delicate situation, it is much more probable that a high-status emissary will have gone. But here too the evidence is remarkably sparse. A modest Greek historian of the mid-third century, Herodian, does however record something of the sort, in typically vague terms. In describing the exchanges after the rise of the new Persian Empire in the 220s, he relates that Severus Alexander sent Artaxerxes/Ardashir an embassy (*presbeia*) with a letter warning him of the dangers of serious conflict with Rome (6, 2, 3–4). But he says nothing of the rank or function of the person, or persons, who constituted the embassy. Then, when Alexander had reached Antioch on his way to the eastern frontier, he sent another *presbeia*. Artaxerxes sent the ambassadors back empty-handed, soon followed by 400 Persian cavalry as a diplomatically veiled threat; they were however promptly disarmed and settled in Asia Minor (6, 4, 4–6). How far Herodian's representation of these events is more than fanciful is in any case an open question.

What seems to be the only evidence from the whole of this period for an emissary of high rank conducting negotiations beyond the frontier is contained in a report by Cassius Dio of how in about 170 the Cotini, living somewhere north of the middle Danube, were able to capture and maltreat Taruttienus Paternus, the *ab epistulis Latinis* of Marcus Aurelius, on the pretext that they were going to join in combined operations against the Marcomani (71, 12, 3). It seems evident from this brief report that Paternus had been sent to them to negotiate and was thus exposed to capture. If so, it is another clear indication of the use for external purposes of a court functionary whose role, at least as far as we can grasp it, was normally related to internal correspondence (with officials or Latin-speaking communities in the Empire). It is furthermore not unlikely that, like his Greek equivalent (above), the *ab epistulis Latinis* may normally have had some role in the reception of embassies from Latin-speaking communities. By extension, therefore, he may have been a natural choice to negotiate beyond the frontier.

That serves, however, merely to raise a further problem: in what language did one conduct negotiations with the Cotini, or with any other unsubdued people beyond the frontier? The notion that high-status Romans ever learned to speak any of the Germanic, Celtic, Thracian, or Iranian languages used beyond the frontier in the Eurasian land-mass can be safely dismissed, as can any similar notion relating to the languages of North Africa. The one possible exception here is Punic, attested as a spoken and written language throughout the period concerned.[35] But there is nothing to show that it actually was employed as a vehicle of diplomatic communication, spoken or written. In Mauretania, at least, it is certain, as a whole series of (Latin) inscriptions from Volubilis attests, that third-century governors held repeated negotiations (*colloquia*) with chiefs of the Baquates. One such inscription which dates from A.D. 245 records that a procurator of Mauretania Tingitana had conducted a *conloquium* with Septemazinis, chief (*princeps*) of the *gens* (tribe) of the Baquates "for the sake of establishing peace."[36] Nothing is said about the language of the "colloquium"; we can however safely assume either that an interpreter was employed or that, like the *princeps* of the Zegrenses some decades earlier, Septemazinis had moved into the orbit of the Latin-using Mediterranean world.

Something comparable is clearly attested on the Rhine frontier in the early first century A.D.; chiefs of Cherusci, and indeed an ordinary rank-and-file soldier, are described as having learnt Latin as a result of military service with Rome (Tacitus, *Annals* 2, 9–10; 13). Although it is difficult to imagine that some mechanisms for mutual linguistic understanding were not employed along Rome's frontiers, the available evidence is extraordinarily slight: a soldier of *legio I Adiutrix* at Brigetio in the early third century, described as *interprex Dacorum*, "interpreter of [with?] the Dacians" (*Ann. Épig.* 1947, no. 35); or an "interpreter of [for?]" the procurators in the bilingual (Greek and Aramaic, or even Arabic) region south of Damascus on the edge of the Syrian desert.[37] Such very enigmatic fragments of documentary evidence may be compared with the "chief-interpreter of [with?] the Alani" attested in the Bosporan kingdom,[38] without giving us any clear notion of how significant a function interpretation, on the Roman side, was conceived to be. It would be a relatively safe assumption that the entire Roman system relied on the cultural dominance of the Graeco-Roman world to ensure that words addressed to Roman rulers or governors were in Latin or, failing that, in Greek. In the elaborately staged scene in A.D. 66 when Tiridates, a member of the

---

35. F. Millar, "Local Cultures in the Roman Empire: Latin, Libyan and Punic in Roman Africa," *Journal of Roman Studies* 58 (1968): 126–51 (chapter 12 in this volume).

36. *Inscriptions antiques du Maroc* II, no. 359.

37. R. Cagnat, *Inscriptiones Graecae ad Res Romanas Pertinentes* III (Paris, 1896), no. 1191.

38. Struve, *Corpus Inscriptionum*, no. 1053.

Parthian royal house, came to Rome to receive the crown (diadem) of Armenia from the hands of Nero, seated on a tribunal in the Forum at Rome, an interpreter was employed to translate his words of supplication for the benefit of the crowd (Suetonius, *Nero* 13). But, as we have seen above, it is at least as likely that Tiridates was speaking Greek as Parthian; and in the latter case it would have been unlikely that any qualified interpreter could have been found. It is significant that the person who acted as interpreter on this occasion is described as being of ex-praetor status, that is, a relatively senior senator. Among persons of that class a fluent Greek speaker could easily be found.

Such an event, stage-managed at the centre of the Empire, leaves us entirely in the dark about the normal conduct of low-level exchanges between governors and military personnel on the one side and leaders of unsubdued peoples on the fringes of the Empire on the other. The subject obviously deserves more detailed examination, however fragmentary and enigmatic the evidence would prove. What is rather better known are certain episodes requiring major negotiations involving leading senators, members of the imperial family, or (increasingly) emperors in person. It will be worthwhile, in conclusion, to look at a few of these.

Major negotiations, or campaigns, conducted by senators who were not members of the imperial dynasties hardly outlasted the first century A.D. The tendency to concentrate all major external functions in the hands of the emperor in person is one of the most marked, and most significant, developments in imperial history. However, at the end of Tiberius' reign, for instance, the governor of Syria, Lucius Vitellius, was commissioned to meet King Artabanus of Parthia on the Euphrates to conclude an agreement. The parties are stated to have met in the middle of a bridge over the river, each with an armed escort. Afterwards Herodes Antipas, the tetrarch (effectively a minor king) of Galilee, gave a dinner in a pavilion also constructed in midstream. The proceedings concluded with the dispatch to Tiberius of Artabanus' son Darius as a hostage, accompanied by gifts including a freak, a Jew seven cubits tall (the presentation of freaks and curiosities to the Emperor would be an interesting sidelight on imperial history, worth exploring for itself; compare those sent by an Indian king to Augustus in Strabo, *Geography* 15, 1, 73, 719, cited above).[39] Vitellius then duly sent a report to Tiberius, only to find that Herodes had anticipated him.

Suetonius gives a rather different account of the same episode, stressing that Artabanus crossed to the Roman side of the river and did formal obeisance to the Roman standards and the *imagines* (images) of the emperor. This

---

39. For a collection of some of the evidence, see *ERW*, 139–40.

symbolic procedure, for which, interestingly, the actual presence of the emperor was more and more to substitute itself, is indeed attested on various occasions in the first century.[40]

The last major eastern campaign to be conducted by senators from outside the imperial house belongs to the reign of Nero (54–68). As regards the conduct of diplomacy, we find two senatorial governors in the East in 54 simultaneously sending "messengers" (*nuntii*) to warn Vologaeses of Parthia to keep the peace, provide hostages, and observe the previous *reverentia* of Parthian kings towards the *populus Romanus*. The messengers were in each case military officers, a prefect of a cohort and a centurion (Tacitus, *Annals* 12, 9). Once again the absorption of diplomatic functions within a more general framework is made clear.

Some years later, in 62, when the Parthians launched an invasion of Armenia, where the Romans had installed their nominee as king, we again find the governor of Syria, Domitius Corbulo, sending a centurion as ambassador to upbraid the Parthian king for attacking a king allied to Rome and the Roman auxiliary units which had been sent to support him. Vologaeses replied that he would send ambassadors to Nero: these later returned empty-handed (Tac., *Ann.* 14, 5–7). When a Roman army was then forced to sue for terms, the emissary sent by its commander was again an auxiliary officer (15, 15). The retreat of the Roman forces from Armenia was followed by a Parthian embassy to Nero in Rome, bringing a letter from Vologaeses, ironically stating that his own nominee for the throne of Armenia would be prepared to come to Rome to receive the diadem, but that religious prescriptions prevented him (15, 24). Yet the great campaign into Armenia which Corbulo was then ordered to conduct very rapidly ended in formal negotiations between Corbulo and Vologaeses, conducted by emissaries (again centurions on the Roman side), followed by a formal ceremony at which Tiridates, as the Parthian nominee for the throne of Armenia, laid down his diadem before an *imago* of Nero (15, 24–30), to receive it back in Rome three years later, at the great ceremony already mentioned.

No similar delegation of the conduct of a major campaign occurred later. When relations with Parthia broke down again under Trajan, the Emperor himself went to the East, and our narratives show a number of minor kings from within the Parthian Empire presenting themselves before him in person. Then after two reigns, those of Hadrian (117–38) and Antoninus Pius

---

40. Suetonius, *Cal.* 14. For the use of the imperial image as the object of obeisance by foreign rulers or emissaries, see T. Pekáry, *Das römische Kaiserbildnis in Staat, Kult und Gesellschaft* (Berlin, 1985), 54–55.

(138–61), not marked by major wars, we reach the decisive turning point after which all major wars were conducted by the, or an, emperor; first Marcus Aurelius' co-emperor Lucius Verus, against the Parthians in 162–66, and then Marcus himself, almost continuously on the Danube frontier between the late 160s and his death there in 180. The characteristic shape of foreign relations, as they were to remain to the end of the fourth century, is already visible in Dio's description of Marcus, in his first years in Pannonia, dealing in person with delegations of barbarians from beyond the Danube (71, 11, 1–4):

> Marcus Antoninus remained in Pannonia in order to give audience to the embassies of the barbarians; for many came to him at this time also. Some of them, under the leadership of Battarius, a boy twelve years old, promised an alliance; these received a gift of money and succeeded in restraining Tarbus, a neighbouring chieftain, who had come into Dacia and was demanding money and threatening to make war if he should fail to get it. Others, like the Quadi, asked for peace, which was granted them, both in the hope that they might be detached from the Marcomani, and also because they gave him many horses and cattle and promised to surrender all the deserters and the captives, besides— thirteen thousand at first, and later all the others as well. The right to attend the markets, however, was not granted to them, for fear that the Iazyges and the Marcomani, whom they had sworn not to receive nor to allow to pass through their country, should mingle with them, and passing themselves off for Quadi, should reconnoitre the Roman positions and purchase provisions. Besides these that came to Marcus, many others sent envoys, some by tribes and some by nations, and offered to surrender. Some of them were sent on campaigns elsewhere, as were also the captives and deserters who were fit for service; others received land in Dacia, Pannonia, Moesia, the province of Germany, and in Italy itself.

Very similar descriptions are given by Dio of Commodus' dealings with the barbarian peoples beyond the Danube, when Aurelius' death left him as the emperor in 180. Among them are the Buri, whose representations may later have appeared before the Senate (text to n. 30 above). Dio writes as follows (73, 2–3):

> The Marcomani by reason of the multitude of their people that were perishing and the constant ravaging of their lands no longer had an

abundance of either food or men. At any rate they sent only two of their chief men and two others of inferior rank as envoys to sue for peace. And, although Commodus might easily have destroyed them, yet he made terms with them; for he hated all exertion and was eager for the comforts of the city. In addition to the conditions that his father had imposed upon them, he also demanded that they restore to him the deserters and the captives that they had taken in the meantime, and that they furnish annually a stipulated amount of grain—a demand from which he subsequently released them. Moreover, he obtained some arms from them and soldiers as well, thirteen thousand from the Quadi and a smaller number from the Marcomani; and in return for these he relieved them of the requirement of an annual levy.

Commodus granted peace to the Buri when they sent envoys. Previously he had declined to do so, in spite of their frequent requests, because they were strong, and because it was not peace that they wanted, but the securing of a respite to enable them to make further preparations; but now that they were exhausted he made peace with them, receiving hostages and getting back many captives from the Buri themselves as well as fifteen thousand from the others.

Perhaps equally significant, the image of the emperor receiving the submission of conquered barbarians has an established place in the repertoire of Roman narrative art, as represented above all on the Column of Trajan and the Column of Marcus Aurelius.[41]

Comparable scenes illustrating the personal role of the emperors in negotiating with barbarians or receiving their submission appear repeatedly in our narrative sources, right up to the moment in 375 when Valentinian, spending the winter at Brigetio in Pannonia, died of apoplexy on receiving an insolent answer from an embassy from the Quadi (Ammianus Marcellinus 30, 6). So far as the major issues at least were concerned, the conduct of diplomacy, at all times embedded within the successive political structures of the Roman state, had long since been absorbed by the emperors in person, who themselves had come to function more and more as commanders in the field. This apparent distortion of the nature of government seems wholly irrational, given what we should suppose to have been the needs of a civilian population of some 50 million people. Yet immediately after Hono-

---

41. For this point, see J. F. Matthews in *Reallexikon für Antike und Christentum X* (Stuttgart, 1978), col. 660, art. "Gesandtschaft." See also N. Hannestadt, *Roman Art and Imperial Policy* (Aarhus, 1986), 160–61, 231.

rius and Arcadius, coming to the throne in 395, suddenly abandoned the role of commander in chief in the field, the Empire entered a period of military crisis from which the western part of it never recovered. Mysterious as it is, diplomacy, or its absence, is not the most mysterious feature of the Roman Empire.

CHAPTER ELEVEN

Emperors, Kings, and Subjects:
The Politics of Two-Level Sovereignty*

No one would deny that the Roman Empire was a complex system, incorporating many different geographical zones, ethnic groups, and political formations, or that much of what we might at first want to describe as the "government" of the Empire really involved diplomacy and political relations. But perhaps not enough stress has been laid on one very important aspect of the political structure of the Empire, especially in the earlier period, namely the presence of what one might call a two-level monarchy, in which quite large populations were subject both to local kings and, indirectly, to a distant superior monarch in Rome, the emperor. This chapter is concerned to explore briefly some aspects of the complex diplomatic and symbolic relationships which this structure brought into being. One effect of it was that the public life of the dependent kingdoms was marked by a symbolic language which clearly reflected this dual sovereignty—the power and status of the local king, combined with, and overshadowed by, the unseen presence of the distant emperor. In many very visible respects, the public status of the one would depend on his symbolic association with the other.

This chapter was originally given as a lecture at the conference of the Fédération Internationale des Études Classiques in Québec in August 1994, which was the last occasion on which I had the pleasure of seeing Addi Wasserstein, and when I heard his stimulating paper on non-Hellenised Jews.[1] It was already sadly evident then that his strength was failing. I offer this article now as a small and inadequate tribute to a true scholar. Few people

*First published in Scripta Classica Israelica 15 (Studies in Memory of Abraham Wasserstein I, 1996): 159–73.

1. A. Wasserstein, "Non-Hellenised Jews in the Semi-Hellenised East," SCI 14 (1995): 111–37.

have more fully lived up to the old-fashioned English description of "a scholar and a gentleman."

Dependent Kingdoms in the Early Roman Empire

We will begin with three well-known passages. Firstly, the last sentence of Strabo's *Geography*: "Moreover, kings and dynasts and *dekarchiai* belong to his (the emperor's) portion, and always have done." Strabo is of course referring to the division of the Roman provinces between those of the emperor and those of the Roman people, which he has just described.[2] I hope that it is no longer necessary to point out that the expression "senatorial provinces" is not merely a *mistake* but misconstrues the entire constitution of the early Empire.[3] There is, incidentally, a puzzle here. It is clear enough that Strabo is asserting that kings (*basileis*) and dynasts (*dynastai*—minor rulers without the title of king) belong in the emperor's sphere. A couple of paragraphs earlier he had said that part of Roman territory "is ruled by kings [*basileue-tai*]." Apart from provincial territory proper, he goes on to say, there are free cities, and "there are also dynasts and tribal heads [*phylarchoi*] and priests [*hiereis*] [who are] under them [the Romans]."[4] But what does Strabo mean by *dekarchiai* (δεκαρχίαι)? The text must surely be wrong, for the word itself is very rarely attested, and in any case Strabo should have been speaking of a type of *person*, not of an institution described by an abstract noun. What Strabo actually wrote was surely *tetrarchai* (τετράρχαι). He himself had also referred earlier to the fact that, after the deposition and exile of Archelaus, the son of Herod the Great, his two brothers (Herodes Antipas and Philip) had succeeded, by much cultivation (*therapeia*) of the emperors, in retaining the tetrarchies earlier given to them.[5]

Strabo's allusions to dependent kingdoms and other less prestigious forms of local monarchy are enough to remind us that, if we think of the fully provincial territory of the Roman Empire as it was to be a century later, a very large proportion of it, perhaps 10 per cent, had been, in the early first century, under the rule of subordinate, or intermediate, monarchs. We are dealing with quite a significant aspect of the history of governmental institutions in antiquity.

2. Strabo, *Geography* 17, 3, 25 (840).

3. F. Millar, " 'Senatorial' Provinces: An Institutionalised Ghost," *Ancient World* 20 (1989): 93–97 (= F. Millar, *Rome, the Greek World, and the East* I: *The Roman Republic and the Augustan Revolution*, chap. 13, 314–20).

4. *Geography* 17, 3, 24 (859).

5. *Geography* 16, 2, 46 (765).

The second quotation comes from Suetonius' *Life of Augustus*, and still looks at the kings from the point of view of Rome:[6] "As regards the kingdoms of which he [Augustus] gained control by right of war, he returned them, apart from a few, to the same kings from whom he had taken them, or to external ones. . . . Nor did he treat any of them [the kings] other than as members and parts of the Empire." It is thus assumed by Suetonius, as it had been by Strabo, that from the moment of Actium onwards the disposition of the title of king was in the hands of the emperor. It is this same assumption which lies behind my third quotation, which comes from the Gospel of Luke:[7] "A certain nobleman journeyed to a distant country to get himself a kingdom [*basileia*], and return. . . . But his fellow citizens [*politai*] hated him, and sent an embassy after him, saying 'We do not wish this man to be king over us.'" Although no names are used, and no context is given, the reference is unmistakable. It is to Archelaus, the son of Herod, going to Rome after his father's death, and to the embassy from the Jewish people which followed him, to demand (unsuccessfully at this moment) the ending of Herodian rule, and the attachment of Judaea to provincial territory.[8]

This parable reflects an awareness not only of the power of decision on the part of the distant emperor but of the relation of the Herodian dynasty to the people whom it ruled. Or rather, in this case, different peoples. For in fact it was not only a *Jewish* delegation which followed Archelaus — one which Josephus describes as made up of fifty men, sent "with the consent of the nation"[9] — but also, as we know from Nicolaus, separate embassies from the Greek cities.[10] These too were seeking exclusion from the Herodian kingdom, just as representatives of Gadara had done, unsuccessfully, before Augustus sixteen years before.[11] Two of these Greek cities, Gaza and Hippos, were now, after Herod's death, successful in separating themselves from the kingdom, and were attached to the province of Syria.[12] The subjects of a dependent king could envisage an alternative political situation, *and* knew how to seek it.

6. Suetonius, *Div. Aug.* 48.

7. Luke 19:12–14.

8. See E. Schürer, *History of the Jewish People* I, ed. G. Vermes and F. Millar (1973), 330–35. For a powerful argument for a revised dating of the last phase of Herod's life (winter 4/3 B.C. rather than 5/4 B.C.), see A. Kushnir-Stein, "Another Look at Josephus's Evidence for the Date of Herod's Death," *SCI* 14 (1995): 73–86.

9. Josephus, *Ant.* 17, 11, 1 (300).

10. Nic. Dam., *FGrH* 90, F. 131.

11. Josephus, *Ant.* 15, 2, 3 (354–59).

12. See F. Millar, *The Roman Near East* (1993), 41–43.

These local details are significant only as illustrations of my theme, which is the complexity, and the interest, of the political relations which were created when a kingdom or tetrarchy or *dynasteia* functioned as an element in a wider empire. Firstly, to repeat, the Roman Empire itself was a complex organisation in terms of ideology, constitution, and political structure. In a general sense, it is not misleading to describe it simply as a monarchy. But it was a monarchy which, as seen from the centre, was defined in relation to the institutions of the Roman state, the *res publica*: the Senate, certainly, but not only the Senate. In formal terms, the sovereign body of the early Empire was the Roman people. As the Tabula Siarensis shows, the proper description of the legions which were lost under Varus in A.D. 9 was "an army of the Roman people."[13] Seen from the provinces and the dependent kingdoms, however, the Empire was indeed, to a very large extent, personified by the emperor himself. If we needed any proof of that, it is provided by the city coinages of the early Empire, which give a very prominent place to the name and image of the emperor, and of members of his family. In this respect, as in so many others, the appearance of the first volume of *Roman Provincial Coinage*, covering the period 44 B.C. to A.D. 69, is a landmark in the history of our subject.[14] In actual practice, moreover, so far as kingdoms were concerned, relations to the emperor in person were very important: for instance in the education of royal children at Rome, of which Suetonius also speaks,[15] or in personal appearances by kings at Rome before the emperor, or (occasionally) even before the Senate,[16] or in formal bestowals of a diadem by the emperor in person. Much of the future history of the Empire is summed up in the scene at Rhodes in 30 B.C., when Herod appeared before Octavian without his diadem, argued that his previous loyalty to Antonius should be taken as a sign of his future loyalty to the new emperor, and was

13. *AE* 1984, no. 508; J. González Fernández, *Bronces jurídicos romanos de Andalucía* (1990), no. 11, fr. 1, lines 14–15 (= M. H. Crawford, ed., *Roman Statutes* I [1996], no. 37, lines 14–15 on p. 515): "[T]he fraudulent disaster inflicted on an army of the Roman people has been avenged" (*vindicata frau[dulenta clade] exercitus p. R.*). See F. Millar, "Imperial Ideology in the Tabula Siarensis," in J. González and J. Arce, eds., *Estudios sobre la Tabula Siarensis* (1988), 11–18 (= Millar [n. 3], chap. 15, 350–59).

14. A. Burnett, A. Amandry, and P. Ripollès, *Roman Provincial Coinage* I: *From the Death of Caesar to the Death of Vitellius (44 BC–AD 69)* (1992).

15. Suetonius, *Div. Aug.* 48: "And he raised and educated the sons of many of them together with his own." See, e.g., D. Braund, *Rome and the Friendly King: The Character of the Client Kingship* (1984), chap. 1.

16. See F. Millar, "Emperors, Frontiers and Foreign Relations, 31 BC to AD 378," *Britannia* 13 (1982): 1–23, on p. 4 (chapter 9 in this volume).

duly rewarded with the return of his diadem and confirmation as king of Judaea.[17] Very soon afterwards Herod played a prominent role in escorting Octavian through Palestine to Egypt, and providing supplies for his forces, then in visiting Octavian in Egypt, and finally in escorting him again on the way back, through the Syrian region as far as Antioch.[18] The escorting of the emperor on journeys by kings evidently became an established diplomatic norm; so much so that Suetonius' description of their doing so "in the manner of clients" has been largely responsible for the invention of the misleading modern term "client kings."[19]

It is worth noting that both in receiving Octavian at Ptolemais and (obviously) in going with him as far as Antioch, Herod was playing a very visible political role outside the bounds of his own territory. I do not, however, want to dwell on the case of Herod, partly because it is too well known. But it is worth stressing how strange it is that the three books of Josephus' *Antiquities* (15–18) which describe Herod's reign have played so little part in informing our more general conceptions of the Augustan empire. It is beyond dispute that they depend directly on the later books of the universal history of Nicolaus of Damascus;[20] so we thus have in effect something very close to a 200-page contemporary history of a major dependent kingdom whose affairs repeatedly engaged the emperor's personal attention in the most urgent way. This extensive narrative is thus also, to a significant degree, a history of the early imperial regime.

The political contacts of a dependent king were, however, not only with the emperor in Rome, but with the nearer Roman governors. Again, a complex balance of power was involved. On the one hand dependent kings, in the first century A.D., on occasion provided quite large forces for Roman military operations: for example, when Vespasian advanced into Judaea in A.D. 67, about a third of his forces, some 18,000 men (thus the equivalent of at least three Roman legions), came from the allied kingdoms of Commagene, Emesa, Nabataea, and the domains of Agrippa II.[21]

On the other hand, governors might have to intervene to restore appro-

17. Josephus, *BJ* 1, 20, 1–3 (394–95); *Ant.* 15, 6, 5–7 (183–97).

18. References in Schürer (n. 8), 289.

19. Suetonius, *Div. Aug.* 60: "Kings considered friends and allies . . . often would leave their kingdoms behind and perform (for him) daily chores wearing a toga and without their royal insignia, in the manner of clients, not only in Rome, but also when he was travelling in the provinces" (*Reges amici et socii . . . saepe regnis relictis non Romae modo sed et provincias peragranti cotidiana officia togati ac sine regio insigni more clientium praestiterunt*).

20. See B. Z. Wacholder, *Nicholaus of Damascus* (1962), esp. 62–64.

21. See Millar (n. 12), 72.

priate relations with kings on the fringes of the Empire who were actual
or potential aggressors: we see this, for example, in the famous inscription
of Silvanus Plautius Aelianus from Tibur, which indicates the formal acts of
subservience required of kings, and the role of the Danube as the symbolic
frontier of the Empire: "[H]e led kings, who previously were unknown to
the Roman people or were hostile to it, to our side of the river, which he
guarded, to pay homage to Roman arms"; it also records that Aelianus took
hostages from some of them and describes how he lifted the siege of Chersonesus by the king of the Scythians.[22]

Equally, the governor of the nearest major Roman province might have
to intervene to prevent what seemed to be too close contacts between allied
kings. The most notable example is, of course, the occasion in the early
A.D. 40s when Domitius Marsus, the *legatus* (governor) of Syria, insisted on
the dissolution of a meeting of allied kings called by Agrippa I at Tiberias:
those who attended were Antiochus IV, the last king of Commagene, Samp-
sigeramus of Emesa, Cotys of Armenia Minor, Polemon of Pontus, and
Agrippa's brother, Herod of Chalcis.[23]

When the issue was potentially more serious, the political relations concerned became tripartite, that is to say, king–governor–emperor. Again, there
is a well-known case from Josephus, when Caesennius Paetus, the *legatus* of
Syria, wrote to Vespasian in 72 or 73 to say that he suspected Antiochus IV of
Commagene of connections with Parthia. Vespasian wrote back empower-
ing Paetus to act as he thought best, and the invasion and provincialisation
of Commagene followed.[24]

For the whole period, roughly up to the end of the first century A.D., when
allied kingdoms were a major feature of the structure of the Empire, such
tripartite relations must have been common. We catch a passing glimpse of
such communications in operation, though from the following period, in
Pliny's correspondence with Trajan from Bithynia. Firstly, a messenger from
King Sauromates of the Bosporus arrived in Bithynia with two letters: one
for Pliny, saying that there was an urgent communication for Trajan, to which
Pliny responded by giving the messenger a *diploma* (a permit to use official
wagons) to assist his journey; and, secondly, the letter for Trajan, of which
Pliny learned no more than that it contained news which Trajan needed to
know. Finally, an ambassador (*legatus*) from Sauromates arrived to find Pliny
in Nicaea and stayed for two days before Pliny sent him on en route to Rome.

---

22. *ILS* 982.
23. Josephus, *Ant.* 19, 8, 1 (338–42).
24. Josephus, *BJ* 7, 7, 1–3 (219–43).

Again, there is no indication that Pliny learned anything of the issues at stake between king and emperor.[25]

With this episode, however, we have already passed beyond the period when dependent kingdoms played an important part in the political and military structure of the Empire in the East. For the first and early second centuries had seen a steady tendency, marked by occasional reversals, towards the eradication of dependent kingdoms and their replacement by direct provincial government. Even if we leave out complex minor cases, a summary list of major transformations from kingdom to province would include the following: Cappadocia (A.D. 18), Mauretania (42), Judaea (44), Thrace (46), Armenia Minor (64), Commagene (72 or 73), Emesa (70s?), the territories of Agrippa II (90s?), Nabataea (106). It is thus significant that, of all the major kingdoms which played such a large part in the first century A.D., the kingdom of the Bosporus alone survived until the fourth century. Its potential strategic importance in controlling barbarian movements around the north coast of the Black Sea, was reflected in the fact that by the middle of the second century its kings were receiving a regular annual subsidy from Rome. Thus the narrator in Lucian's *Alexander* records: "There [at Aegiali on the coast of Paphlagonia] I met a party of Bosporans, ambassadors from King Eupator, sailing along the coast on their way to Bithynia to bring back the annual subsidy [*syntaxis*]."[26] It remains unclear in this passing anecdote whether, having reached Bithynia, the ambassadors would have collected the cash there, or merely paid their respects to the governor (like the ambassador from Sauromates to Trajan), before going on to Rome. For what it is worth, the anecdote tends to imply that Bithynia was their actual destination. In that case, not only was tribute revenue from the nearest province being diverted directly to an important allied kingdom, but responsibility for that process rested with the governor. Diplomatic relations, direct or indirect, with the king were clearly part of his duties. The governor of Cappadocia similarly had to keep a watch on the Bosporan kingdom, as well as the kings of various regions in the Caucasus, and in a more active sense than the governor of Bithynia, in that he controlled major forces. Thus, when Arrian, addressing himself to Hadrian, has finished his description of his journey round the coast of the Pontus as far as Dioscurias, where (he says) the *epikrateia* (dominion) of the Romans ends, he continues: "But when I learned that Cotys, the king of the Bosporus called 'Cimmerian,' had died, I made it my concern to describe for you also the coastal voyage as far as the Cimmerian Bosporus,

25. Pliny, *Ep.* 10, 63–64; 67.
26. Lucian, *Alex.* 57.

so that in case you were making plans in relation to the Bosporus you could do so on an informed basis."[27] Both before this point in the work and after it Arrian lists a number of other kings who rule areas around the coast of the Black Sea and indicates which of them have received their kingdoms from the emperor.[28] But the purpose of this chapter is not primarily to look at the relations of kings and emperors but to sketch some of the other relationships to which the combination of provinces and dependent kingdoms gave rise, including those between kings and neighbouring governors.

Inevitably, since our information on Judaea is so superior to that on any other provincial area, it is there that we can see the complex relations of king and governor most clearly. The best illustration of these relations, however, happens to come not from Josephus, but from some of the later chapters of the *Acts of the Apostles*. Paul, probably in the later 50s, is in prison in Caesarea; the new *procurator* of Judaea, Festus, arrives to take up office; after three days he goes up to Jerusalem, and the "high priests" and leading Jews appear before him to renew accusations against Paul. Then, back in Caesarea, Festus holds a hearing at which Paul appears before him and appeals to Caesar. A few days later "Agrippa the king" (Agrippa II, now ruling various territories to the north-east of Judaea), and his sister Berenice arrive in Caesarea to greet Festus. It is implied that it was a routine aspect of diplomacy that he should do so for each new *procurator*. Festus persuades them to join in the hearing. The description of the council which next day heard Paul deserves to be quoted: "On the next day, after Agrippa and Berenice had arrived with great pomp and had taken their seats in the auditorium with tribunes and leading men of the city [Caesarea] and Festus had ordered Paul to be brought in . . ."[29]

In a sense this scene gives us the mirror image of the main theme which I want to stress. For what it shows is the presence and influence of an allied king inside the Roman province bordering his own domains. This was indeed a very extreme case. Agrippa II not only owned a house in Jerusalem but had the right to keep the high priestly robes, to appoint and dismiss the High Priests, and to convene the Sanhedrin.[30] In the years leading up to the Jewish Revolt of 66 Judaea was under a sort of dual local control, both *procurator* and king being under the adjudication of the emperor in Rome.

But what I want to emphasize, as an aspect of the history of government in the ancient world which has been too little studied, is, firstly, the symbolic

27. Arrianus, *Periplus* 17.
28. *Periplus* 11; 18.
29. Acts 25–26.
30. See Schürer (n. 8), 1, 421–22.

presence and real influence of the emperors and the Empire within the allied kingdoms; and, secondly, the complexity of the political—and perhaps one could say also constitutional—structures within those kingdoms. All were of course, by definition, monarchies. But any monarchy, no matter how despotic it may be in intention, has to relate to existing social structures. It has to form marriage alliances either inside or outside its own kingdom, or of course both; it has to recruit a household and a court, which may be made up partly of slaves or freed slaves; it has to recruit an army, and thereby give power to its officers and commanders. It has to raise taxes, which must follow some recognised system of obligations, and cannot be wholly arbitrary. It has to have some definable relations with the various social and political units within its borders. And it is likely to develop some system of symbolisation and self-representation.

To say all this is to say no more than that any established monarchy has to be, in some sense, "constitutional," to operate within established norms. I am thus suggesting that the post-Hellenistic, or sub-Hellenistic, monarchy of the eastern Mediterranean in the early Roman Empire is a proper subject of study in itself, if only because it represented the system within which quite a large part of the Greek-speaking world lived. But, secondly, it is of interest for two particular reasons. One is the implicit or explicit claim on the part of any political unit which defined itself as a Greek city to some degree of diplomatic consideration and respect, to the operation of internal self-government, and to self-representation in a manner which implied a degree of independence. In that sense, the late Hellenistic monarchy of the Roman period continues the pattern of the major monarchies of the Hellenistic period proper, when kings and cities co-existed in a state of tension marked by elaborately polite diplomatic language. The second reason relates to the fact that these monarchies functioned within the shadow of the Empire. Internal relations, and internal systems of self-representation, will have been profoundly affected by that fact, since they had to find a place not only for the king, but for his ultimate superior, the emperor.[31]

It would be easy to go on drawing examples from the history of Judaea —for example, Herod's kingdom, and then that inherited by his grandson, Agrippa I, was profoundly re-structured by his foundation of two Greek cities named after the emperor, Caesarea and Sebaste—not to speak of other Greek cities like "Tiberias" and "Caesarea Panias," as well as minor places

---

31. For other aspects of this complex relationship, see Braund (n. 15), and earlier the very suggestive article by J. Gagé, "L'Empereur romain et les rois: politique et protocole," *Revue Historique* 121 (1959): 221–60.

whose names also reflected the imperial dynasty, and whose status is not entirely clear: "Livias," "Iulias," and so forth. In Caesarea and Sebaste the power
of Rome was explicitly symbolised from the beginning: the main temples
in both cities were dedicated to Augustus, or to Roma and Augustus, as was
that at Caesarea Panias.[32]

There is no need to rehearse these well-known details, which we owe to
the fact that Judaea, alone of all the provinces of the Empire, was the subject of a history (or rather two histories) written by a native of it. It is of
more interest to ask whether we can gain any impression of social, political,
and symbolic structures in other kingdoms, and to consider how far these
reflect the presence of the Empire. Often, our information is only anecdotal:
for instance Tacitus reports, from the year A.D. 17, that after the deaths of
Antiochus of Commagene and Philopator of Cilicia these peoples were in
turmoil, "most preferring Roman rule [*imperium*] and others royal."[33] How
political opinion was expressed in these contexts, we do not know. Each of
these kingdoms, however, contained a number of Greek cities. But we do
gain an impression of how, as in Judaea, direct Roman rule could seem a
desirable alternative to royal authority. Similarly, Cappadocia, until now a
kingdom, became a province in the next year; and whatever the system of
taxation had been under the last king, taxes were deliberately reduced by
the Romans at the moment of the imposition of provincial rule, precisely to
reconcile public opinion.[34] Another perfect, if equally brief and enigmatic,
example of power relations in the shadow of Rome is provided by a further report from Tacitus, under the year 36. The episode relates to the period
of rule on Cilicia by Archelaus II, the son of the recently deceased king of
Cappadocia:[35]

> At about the same time the people of the Cietae, subjected to the rule
> of the Cappadocian Archelaus, because they were forced to undergo a
> census of Roman type, and to endure direct taxation, migrated to the
> heights of the Taurus, and by use of the terrain defended themselves
> against the weak royal troops, until the legionary commander [*legatus*],
> M. Trebellius, despatched by Vitellius, governor of Syria, with 4,000
> legionaries and selected auxiliaries, besieged the two mountains . . .
> which the *barbari* had occupied, and forced them to surrender.

32. Josephus, *BJ*, 1, 21, 1–8 (403–16).

33. Tacitus, *Ann.* 2, 42.

34. Tacitus, *Ann.* 2, 56.

35. Tacitus, *Ann.* 6, 41. See R. D. Sullivan, "The Dynasty of Cappadocia," *ANRW* II.7.2
(1980), 1125–68, on pp. 1167–68.

Such passing reports, though suggestive, are hardly satisfactory. This last one, however, does indicate clearly that a census of a type imitated from the (quite recently instituted) Roman provincial census could be applied within the bounds of a dependent kingdom. But it remains a mere allusion. There is no dependent kingdom other than Judaea from which we have any coherent literary evidence, and it is perhaps only in the Bosporan kingdom that we have enough internal documentary evidence, from the substantial numbers of Greek inscriptions found there, to gain a more nuanced conception of royal rule. The rest of this chapter will be concerned to explore a few relevant aspects of our evidence for this kingdom.

The Bosporan Kingdoms and the Empire

The very remarkable political formation represented by the Bosporan kingdom has perhaps not received the attention from historians of the classical world which it deserves, and it goes without saying that nothing resembling a history of it will be attempted here. Indeed a true internal social history, of the sort which, up to a certain extent, is possible for Judaea, is not in any case attainable in this case. None the less, through allusions in external literary sources, through a very remarkable corpus of inscriptions, through its coins and through archaeology, it is possible to follow in some detail the outlines of its history from the fifth century B.C. to the fourth century A.D.[36] Its extraordinary endurance is all the more remarkable in view of its curious geographical structure, for its main cities straddled the straits of the Cimmerian Bosporus, leading into Lake Maeotis (the Sea of Azov), with Panticapaeum and other cities as far west as Theodosia occupying the eastern promontory of the Crimea, and Phanagoria and other minor cities situated on the opposite side of the straits, on the Taman peninsula. As we will see, in the imperial period the kings also claimed dominion over a large group of peoples living on the east side of Lake Maeotis; and the Greek city of Tanais, at the mouth of the River Tanais (the Don), and situated well over 300 kilometres from Panticapaeum, also formed part of the kingdom. Perhaps surprisingly, the kingdom seems neither to have achieved nor claimed any control of the "Tauroscythians" who occupied most of the Crimea. Even the relatively prominent Greek city of Chersonesus, on the south-west corner of the Crimea, was certainly not an integral part of the kingdom, though from time to time in the imperial period the evidence shows the city to be in alliance with it. As we saw earlier, the governor of Moesia under Nero, Tiberius

36. For a thorough survey, see V. F. Gajdukevic, *Das bosporanische Reich* (1971).

Plautius Silvanus Aelianus, had to intervene to lift the siege of Chersonesus, "which is beyond the Borysthenes (the River Dniepr)," by the king of the Scythians.[37] There is nothing in the text of the inscription to suggest that the Bosporan kingdom played any part.

All the more, therefore, the major Greek cities around the north-west corner of the Euxine, namely Olbia at the mouth of the River Hypanis (the Bug), and Tyras on the River Tyras (the Dniestr), in so far as they belonged to any wider political-military system, were gradually drawn into the orbit of the governors of the province of Moesia. This situation is reflected for instance in the inscription recording that "the city of the Olbiopolitai" had dedicated a bath-house on behalf of Septimius Severus, and all his house, in the governorship of Cosconius Gentianus.[38] But although there are occasional reflections of the presence of Roman soldiers in this area, there was nothing resembling a Roman military occupation of the north-west corner of the Black Sea coast, and the Bosporan kingdom, in spite of its established relation of diplomatic dependence on Rome, remained remarkably isolated, both geographically and strategically. For in the opposite direction also, south-eastwards round the east coast of the Black Sea, was "the dominion of the Romans," as we earlier saw Arrian reporting, some 400 kilometres from Bosporan territory, namely at Dioscurias or Sebastopolis, where there was a Roman fort.[39]

Even if very soon after Arrian's report a Roman fort was established at Pityous, another 75 kilometres north-eastwards up the coast, and although as we saw, Arrian regarded the political circumstances of the Bosporan kingdom as being of great concern to Hadrian, the exposure and isolation of the Bosporan kingdom make its survival and relative stability remarkable.

In terms of our evidence, what is equally remarkable is the extensive corpus of Greek inscriptions from the kingdom, over 1,300 being known so far, of which nearly 900 come from Panticapaeum and its neighbourhood.[40] The inscriptions of the imperial period hint at the complexity of the communal, political, and administrative structure of the kingdom, illustrate the formal status and public honours of the kings, and vividly represent the presence in Bosporan public vocabulary of the Roman emperors, of the wider structure of the Empire, and of the cities of Anatolia, above all those of the Roman province of Pontus and Bithynia, through and to which we have already seen

37. See text to n. 22.

38. B. Latyschev, *Inscriptiones Antiquae Orae Septentrionalis Ponti Euxini* I², 1916, no. 174 (*IGR* I, no. 834).

39. Text to n. 27 above. Arrian, *Periplus*, 10, 3–4; 17, 1–2; see now D. Braund, *Georgia in Antiquity* (1994), 193–94.

40. See V. Struve, *Corpus Inscriptionum Regni Bosporani* (*CIRB*) (1965).

emissaries of the kingdom making their way.[41] The presence of the Roman Empire was to be symbolised from the first century to the early fourth by the fact that the kings were characteristically (and perhaps without exception), to be, like the kings of Judaea, Roman citizens with the Roman three names (*tria nomina*), retaining to the end the Julio-Claudian nomenclature "Tiberius Iulius Rhoemetalces" or "Rhescuporis" and so forth.

All that will be attempted here is to pick out a few examples from the inscriptions of the Bosporan kingdom, to illustrate the symbolic functioning of a system of dual sovereignty, of the local king and the distant, all-powerful emperor. But we will begin with a striking royal letter from Gorgippia, published in the same year, 1965, as Struve's excellent collection of the inscriptions of the kingdom, but too late to be included in it, and remarkably neglected since.[42] It was indeed duly noticed by Louis Robert,[43] but his intention to re-publish it and analyse it fully in a forthcoming *Bulletin* was never fulfilled. By the mid-1990s it had still not gained a place in *Supplementum Epigraphicum Graecum*, or in *L'Année Epigraphique*, until 1994 (as *AE* 1538). As subsequently revised by H. Heinen, the first of the two letters contained in the inscription runs as follows:[44]

King Aspourgos *philorōmaios* [friend of the Romans]
to Pantaleon and Theangelos,
greetings.
Being benevolently disposed towards the city of the Gorgippeis, and wishing to secure for them their rights [*ta dikaia*], since it seemed that in many respects they had been favourable to me, but especially in having preserved themselves, during my journey up [*anabasis*] to Sebastos Autokrator [*Imperator Augustus*], in the most complete absence of disturbance, in accordance with the instructions [*entolai*] given by me, I rule for the future that inheritances [*kleronomiai*] should by right be retained by them according to the kinship law of Eupator. Therefore, by putting

---

41. Text to nn. 25–27.

42. T. V. Blavatatskaya, "Reskripti tsarya Aspurga," *Sovietskaya Archeologia* 10.2 (1965): 197–209. See also S. Yu. Saprykin, " 'Ebratorov zakon o nasledovanii' i yevo znachenie v istorii pontiiskovo tsarstva" ("Eupator's Law on Inheritance," and Its Role in the History of the Pontic Kingdom), *VDI* 197 (1991): 181–97.

43. *Bull. Épig.* 1968, 378.

44. See H. Heinen, "Fehldeutungen der ἀϛάβαϛιϛ und der Politik des bosporanischen Königs Aspurgos," *Hyperboreus* 4 (1998): 340–61; "Zwei Briefe des bosporanischen Königs Aspurgos (*AE* 1994, 1538). Übersehene Berichtigungsvorschläge Günther Klaffenbachs und weitere Beobachtungen," *ZPE* 124 (1999), 133–44, whence *AE* 1998, 1153.

up this decree [*to dogma*] in public, see to it that this judgement of mine becomes known to all. Be well. [Year] 312. 20th of Daisios.

Like the accompanying one, this letter from King Aspourgos (A.D. 10/11–38/9) dates to the summer of 15. As a royal letter to a city, it is thus very close in time to the well-known letter of Artabanus III of Parthia, to Seleucia on the Eulaeus, of A.D. 21.[45] But there is a crucial distinction in the presence here of a two-level monarchy. The date makes it very possible, but by no means certain, that the *Sebastos Autokrator* (*Augustus Imperator*) to whom Aspourgos had "gone up" was the new emperor Tiberius. Aspourgos evidently did not share the doubts felt in Cyprus as to whether the *praenomen* (first name) *Imperator/Autokrator* had actually been assumed.[46] But he may equally be referring to the now deceased *Imperator (Caesar divi filius) Augustus* (Imperator Caesar, son of the divine Caesar, Augustus) and to an earlier voyage. If so, he had failed to incorporate in the letter any reflection of Augustus' recent deification. The form of the name is in fact not fully correct for either emperor.

What is important, however, is on the one hand the very concrete reflection of the dependence of a king like Aspourgos on the distant emperor in Rome. His "going up" thus perfectly mirrored the well-known journeys of the Herodian household to Rome. On the other hand we see Aspourgos' recognition of established rights (granted in this case by the great Mithridates VI Eupator) possessed by the Gorgippeis, and his awareness of the need to address them diplomatically, and to return their goodwill. The letter is thus a reflection of the diplomatic expression both of two-level sovereignty and of the delicate relations of king and city.

In the epigraphy of the Bosporan kingdom over the next three centuries, a double conception of the kings, as monarchs and conquerors on the one hand, and as loyal subjects of Rome on the other, is visible everywhere. For instance, there is a later inscription of King Aspourgos, of the 20s, from Kerch:[47]

The Great King Aspourgos, *philorōmaios*, descendant of King Asandrochos, *philokaisar* [friend of the Caesars] and *philorōmaios*, king of all the Bosporus and Theodosia and the Sindi and Maiti and Taipeii and Toreti,

45. C. B. Welles, *Royal Correspondence in the Hellenistic Period* (1934), no. 75.

46. T. B. Mitford, "A Cypriot Oath of Allegiance to Tiberius," *JRS* 50 (1960): 75–79. See also F. Millar, "Ovid and the *Domus Augusta*: Rome Seen from Tomoi," *JRS* 83 (1993): 1–17, on pp. 16–17 (= Millar [n. 3], chap. 14, 321–49).

47. *CIRB*, no. 40, cf. also no. 39.

Psesi and Tanaiti, who has subjected the Scyths and Tauri, Menestratus
. . . in charge of the island, [honours] his own saviour and benefactor.

Two and a half centuries later, in the 270s, during the reign of King Tiberius
Iulius Teiranes (275/6–278/9), still described as *philokaisar* and *philorōmaios*,
we find an inscription from Panticapaeum which was set up "for the victory and permanence" of the king and his queen, Ailia, and which also gives
a remarkable list of officials of the kingdom, some of them with functions
relating to particular towns or districts: a *lochagos* (military commander); an
official "over the *basileia* [kingdom] and Theodosia"; a man who was both
chiliarches (commander of a thousand) and "over the Aspourgiana"; an *archi-
grammateus* (chief scribe); two former *politarchoi* (civic magistrates); a former
superintendent of accounts.[48] There is no time to explore these details here.
But they give some impression of the complexity of relations between the
king and the different elements of the kingdom.

The Bosporan kings were unique among dependent kings in that they
regularly bore the title "high priest of the Emperors for life" (*archiereus tōn
Sebastōn dia biou*); it appears first in the reign of Cotys I (45/6–68).[49] We do not
know how the king's functions related (for instance) to those of the priest
of the Kaisareion attested in the second century at Phanagoria.[50] But what
is striking and important is that the kings adopted a public role which very
explicitly acknowledged their subordination to a line of superior monarchs.
On the other hand, the Bosporan kings were similar to other kings in that
they themselves received honours from the cities in the nearest Roman province, Pontus and Bithynia. It is indeed a very striking feature of the epigraphy
both of Olbia and of the cities of the Bosporan kingdom that cities and individuals from the northern and north-western regions of Roman Anatolia
play a conspicuous part. In that sense the honours paid to the Bosporan kings
are merely a reflection of those wider economic and diplomatic connections across the Black Sea to which Rostovtzeff called attention in a famous
article.[51] One instance of such honours is a Latin inscription from Panticapaeum naming *Regem Ti(berium) Iu(lium) Sauromaten, amicum Imp(eratoris)
populiq(ue) R(omani) praestantissimum* (King Tiberius Iulius Sauromates, an outstanding friend of the Roman emperor and people) put up by the "C(olonia)

48. *CIRB*, no. 48.

49. See Gajdukevic (n. 36), 343, and W. Blawatsky, "Le culte des empereurs romains au
Bosphore," *Mélanges Piganiol* III (1966), 1541–45.

50. *CIRB*, no. 1050: "having been appointed priest of the Kaisareion (Temple) for life."

51. M. I. Rostovtzeff, "Pontus, Bithynia and the Bosporus," *Pap. Brit. Sch. Athens* 22
(1916–18): 1–22.

I(ulia) F(elix) S(inope)."[52] Sauromates was king from 93/4 to 123/4; the fact
that, as late as this, the Roman people (*populus Romanus*) is also mentioned is
quite striking. Or there is a Greek inscription of 221 put up by the city of
Amastris in Pontus and Bithynia to honour King Tiberius Iulius Rhescuporis
(Rhescuporis III, 210/11–226/7), who is described as "King of the Bosporus
and the surrounding *ethnē* [peoples], *philorōmaios* [friend of the Romans], and
philhellēn [friend of the Hellenes]."[53]

The diplomatics of mutual honour as displayed in the Bosporan inscriptions could be explored endlessly. But the real operations of government
are hardly revealed by the inscriptions (one inscription recording how King
Iulius Tiberius Sauromates rebuilt the walls of Gorgippia is only a partial
exception).[54] Rather more informative is the inscription of 193 from Tanais,
which will date to the reign of Sauromates II, and which celebrates victories against the Sirachi and Scyths, records a dedication by one Zenon "sent
by the king to the *emporion* [trading station]," and refers to sea traffic from
Bithynia.[55]

All that I have wished to suggest in this chapter is that the allied kingdoms of the Roman period represent a significant subject, not just as so-
called client kingdoms, that is, in relation to Rome, but as military, political,
and social groupings of a complex kind, which represent a modest, but not
insignificant, part of human history in the Graeco-Roman period. At one
time there will have been several million people who lived under a form of
two-level monarchy, that is, under their own king, and beyond him under
the distant figure of the emperor. The period of the greatest importance of
these subordinate kingdoms was the first century A.D.; and here we must look
always to the history of Judaea. But the longest-lasting and most interesting of them all was the Bosporan kingdom, which survived until some point
in the fourth century. It may not help the study of it in the modern world
that its territory, on the two sides of the straits, is now divided between two
sovereign states, Ukraine and Russia, though archaeologists from the two
countries are in active collaboration.[56] But, all the same, we can now expect
that this extremely important frontier of the Greek and Roman world will
open up further. While study and exploration of it continues, we can already
contemplate the complex symbolic relations which are embodied in some

52. *CIRB*, no. 46.

53. *CIRB*, no. 54.

54. *CIRB*, no. 1122.

55. *CIRB*, no. 1237.

56. For an overview, see J. G. F. Hind, "Archaeology of the Greeks and Barbarian Peoples
around the Black Sea (1982–1992)," *Archaeological Reports* (1993): 82–112, on pp. 100–109.

of the latest Greek inscriptions from this area, from the early fourth century. For instance, there is the dedication of A.D. 307 put up by the archons of the "Agrippeis" (Phanagoria) and the "Kaisareis" (Panticapaeum) to honour Marcus Aurelius Andronicus, who had formerly been "in charge of the kingdom [*basileia*]."[57] It is striking to see that the Roman *tria nomina*,[58] and the early imperial names of these cities, can still be used. Just as with the city foundations, or re-foundations, by Herod and his descendants, names drawn from the imperial dynasty functioned as prominent symbols of loyalism. In fact, the name "Caesarea" for Panticapaeum otherwise appears in our evidence only on city coins minted under Augustus. "The *dēmos* [people] of the Agrippeis" also appears on such coins,[59] as well as on an inscription of the Augustan period honouring Queen Dynamis *philorōmaios* (9/8 B.C.–A.D. 7/8), and on another fragmentary inscription, probably of the second century.[60] Then, from the year before the dedication to Marcus Aurelius Andronicus, namely 306, there is a dedication from Panticapaeum to "Theos Hypsistos Epekoos" (Supreme God Epēkoos) put up by Sogous, who is described as "in charge of Theodosias," as *sebastognostos* (known to the Emperor), as having been honoured by Diocletian and Maximian, and as having been given the name "Olympianus" in the provincial area.[61] Here again, the distant emperors are made very visibly present in the text. Aurelius Valerius Sogous had built a *proseuchē*, by which we ought perhaps to understand a Jewish synagogue.[62] If so, and if the "Theos Hypsistos" whom Aurelius Valerius Sogous worshipped was the Jewish God, this inscription will serve, like other undoubtedly Jewish ones from the area, to suggest how the Roman Empire had served to make a link between the two best-attested and most interesting of its dependent kingdoms, Judaea and the Bosporus.

57. *CIRB*, no. 1051.

58. See for comparison B. Salway, "What's in a Name? A Survey of Roman Onomastic Practice from *c.* 700 BC to AD 700," *JRS* 84 (1994): 124–45.

59. See Gajdukevic (n. 36), 328, 431; Burnett et al. (n. 14), 334–35, nos. 1936 ("of the Caesareis") and 1935 ("of the Agrippeis").

60. Gajdukevic (n. 36), 477; *CIRB*, no. 979 (Dynamis); 983.

61. *CIRB*, no. 64.

62. This question has of course been long debated and cannot be discussed again here. For the undoubted Jewish presence in the area, see J.-B. Frey, *Corpus Inscriptionum Iudaicarum* I² (1975), nos. 683–91; E. Schürer, *History of the Jewish People* III.1, ed. G. Vermes, F. Millar, and M. D. Goodman (1986), 36–38. For a new Jewish inscription from Phanagoria of A.D. 51, see D. I. Danshin, "Phanagoriiskaya Obschina Yudeev," *VDI* 204 (1993): 59–72, which also presents a general review of the evidence. For Theos Hypsistos, see, e.g., J. Ustinova, "The *Thiasoi* of Theos Hypsistos in Tanais," *History of Religions* 31 (1991): 149–80.

PART II

Society and Culture in the Empire

CHAPTER TWELVE

Local Cultures in the Roman Empire: Libyan, Punic, and Latin in Roman Africa[*]

Introduction

No subject in the history of the Roman Empire has more significance or more pitfalls than that of the local cultures of the provinces. The evidence is in each case, with the exception of Judaea and Egypt, relatively slight, disparate, and ambiguous. But, on the one hand, the subject has very real attractions, which may lead to the building of vast but fragile historical theories, attempting to bring the distinctive culture of an area into a schematic relationship with events such as political movements or the spread of Christianity. On the other, we can never escape the possibility that the denial of the survival of a significant local culture may be falsified by new evidence; even worse, a local culture may have existed in a form which left no written records or datable artefacts.

Yet the problem must be faced, not only for the intrinsic interest which such cultures present, but for the light the enquiry sheds on Graeco-Roman civilization itself. We might conclude for one area that Graeco-Roman culture remained the merest facade, for another that it completely obliterated a native culture. More commonly, we will find a mixture or co-existence of cultures. In such a situation, again, the local element might have been culturally and socially insignificant, or, as it was in Egypt and in Judaea, embodied in a coherent traditional civilization with its own language, literature, customs, religion, and (in Egypt) art forms.

With local languages in particular, we are inevitably driven back to questions both about the role of Latin or Greek in the area and about the status of any evidence in Latin and Greek emanating from it. Was Latin or Greek the language of the towns only, or of the upper classes, or was it wide-

[*]First published in *JRS* 58 (1968): 125–51. The article has not been systematically updated, but occasional, particularly salient, items of subsequent literature have been noted.

spread, with the local language a mere peasant *patois* (a now common view of Punic in Africa)? Or were there linguistic enclaves, like those of the Berber in present-day North Africa? Similarly, when later Christian sources are the only evidence for the survival of a native language—as with Galatian (Celtic), Mysian, Cappadocian, and Isaurian in Asia Minor[1]—what are we to make of the Greek inscriptions or literature from these areas from the preceding centuries? Asia Minor provides further examples of the contradictions inherent in our evidence. For instance, the documents of the Roman colony of Lystra and its territory are in Greek, the majority, and in Latin, while its coin legends purely Latin.[2] There is nothing in the documentary evidence, beyond the appearance of a fair number of native names, to prepare us for the fact that Paul and Barnabas could be hailed as gods in Lycaonian (*Lykaonisti*) within the walls of the town.[3] In Phrygian, by contrast, we have about a hundred inscriptions written in Greek script, all funerary, the great majority accompanying a Greek text, and nearly all of the third century;[4] but the language is not referred to in any literary source until the sixth century.[5] An approximate parallel from another region to the case of Lystra is provided by Tomoi.[6] The inscriptions reveal an absorption of Thracian cults and a significant number of Thracian personal names in the imperial period. But the language is Greek, and they give no hint of what Ovid reveals, that Getic and Sarmatian were spoken there, and Greek often with a heavy Getic accent.[7]

This last point raises a different question relevant to local cultures, namely whether it can be shown that the Greek or Latin of any area was spoken with a distinctive accent or with distinctive verbal or grammatical forms perhaps influenced by a native language. In the two areas whose Latin vocabulary and syntax have been studied, the results are extremely surprising. H. Mihãescu's study of the inscriptions and literary works from the Danubian provinces up to the sixth century revealed no significant linguistic developments not

---

1. See P. Charanis, "Ethnic Changes in the Byzantine Empire in the Seventh Century," *Dumbarton Oaks Papers* 13 (1959): 23.

2. See B. M. Levick, *Roman Colonies in Southern Asia Minor* (1967), 153–54.

3. Acts 14:11.

4. *MAMA* VII, see esp. I–II, XXVII–XXVIII. See O. Haas, *Die phrygischen Sprachdenkmäler* (1966).

5. Charanis (n. 1), 23.

6. See I. Stoian, "La città pontica di Tomis, Saggio storico," *Dacia* 5 (1961): 233; M. Danoff in *RE* Supp. IX (1962), 1397–98; I. Stoian, *Tomitana: contributii epigrafice la istoria cetătii Tomis* (1962).

7. See, e.g., L. P. Wilkinson, *Ovid Recalled* (1955), chap. 10.

common to the other areas of the Empire.[8] This may be compared with the now classic demonstration by Kenneth Jackson that the vast majority of the words which passed from Latin into the Brittonic languages did so with an archaic and conservative phonology distinct from that of the vulgar Latin of the Continent; hence that the type of Latin predominantly spoken in Britain was the correct, "book Latin" of the schools.[9] On the other hand the *graffiti* of Pompeii, for instance, show very substantial variations from "correct" Latin, and reveal that the ordinary Latin of Italians was already before 79 developing forms like those of the Romance languages.[10] So are we to conclude that the population of the Danubian provinces normally spoke their native languages—and for this we have no contemporary local evidence, beyond the fairly widespread appearance of native names[11]—and used the indistinctive, relatively correct language of their Latin inscriptions as a learned language? Or did they speak a true vulgar Latin perhaps with local peculiarities, to which the formal inscriptions of the area offer no guide? That possibility may remind us of how much of the social history of the Roman provinces as we know it is based on the partial and unsatisfactory testimony of formal inscriptions.

The question of whether provincial Latin or Greek might be spoken with a distinctive local pronunciation is baffling precisely because there seems to be remarkably little evidence for such a thing. For instance, Philostratus' *Lives of the Sophists* gives a detailed account of the style and diction of numerous later first- to early third-century sophists, who came from places as far apart as Egypt, Arabia, Syria, Anatolia, Macedonia, Greece, Italy, and Gaul and performed before highly critical audiences in the main centres of Greek culture. Yet there is only one clear reference to a local accent, when Philostratus says of Pausanias of Caesarea in Cappadocia that he orated "with a coarse and heavy accent [*glōtta*], as is the way with the Cappadocians. He would make his consonants collide, would shorten the long syllables and lengthen

8. H. Mihăescu, *Limba latină in provinciile dunărene ale Imperiului roman* (1960), French résumé, pp. 290–91. Compare S. Stati, *Limba latină in inscriptiile din Dacia si Scythia minor* (1961).

9. K. Jackson, *Language and History in Early Britain* (1953), 76–77, esp. 97–98. Compare S. S. Frere, *Britannia: A History of Roman Britain* (1967), 311–12 (3rd ed., 1987, 302–3), and J. Liversedge, *Britain in the Roman Empire* (1968), 315–16.

10. V. Väänänen, *Le Latin vulgaire des inscriptions pompéiennes*[3] (1966).

11. See, e.g., A. Mócsy, *Die Bevölkerung von Pannonien bis zu den Marcommanenkriegen* (1959); Mócsy, "Untersuchungen zur Geschichte der römischen Provinz Moesia Superior," *Acta. Arch. Hung.* 11 (1059): 283; G. Alföldy, *Bevölkerung und Gesellschaft der römischen Provinz Dalmatien* (1965).

the short."[12] Philostratus also says of Apollonius of Tyana as a child "that his accent was Attic, and the sound was not influenced by his origin."[13] The Cappadocian accent is perhaps also reflected in an incident in Gregory of Nyssa's life of Gregorius Thaumaturgus: when a peasant appointed bishop of Comana delivers his first address, an Athenian youth who is present bursts out laughing at "the charmlessness of his speech."[14] Cappadocia apart, it is perhaps the correct interpretation of Dio of Prusa's first Tarsian Oration (38) that he is reproving the people of Tarsos for the peculiar accent with which they spoke Greek. Such evidence amounts to very little, and not much is added to it when one mentions a remark in the *Historia Augusta* about Septimius Severus: "He sounded somewhat African to the end of his life" (*Afrum quiddam usque ad senectutem sonans*).[15] Yet the remark, whether true or false, could hardly have been made if there had been no such thing as an African accent; and the African's striving after correct diction is clearly reflected in a speech by Apuleius at Carthage: "Would any of you condone a single solecism in my speech? Would any of you tolerate one syllable pronounced 'barbarically'?"[16]

I

As a first step, though only as such, the languages of Roman Africa may be considered in isolation from other features of the provincial culture. The supposed remains of "Berber" art[17] (which may seem to the outsider no more than rustic Punic art), and the Punic art of the Roman period—especially the funerary *stēlai* (monuments)—which survived into the third century, and has not yet been the object of any coherent general treatment,[18] may be left aside; so may the cults of Roman Africa,[19] and consequent theses

---

12. Philostratus, *VS* 2, 13 (594).

13. Philostratus, *vita AT* 1, 7.

14. Migne, *PG* XLVI, 937.

15. *HA*, *Sept. Sev.* 19, 9.

16. Apul., *Flor.* 9.

17. See W. H. C. Frend, "The Revival of Berber Art," *Antiquity* 16 (1942): 342; A. Berthier, *Les vestiges du Christianisme antique dans la Numidie centrale* (1943). Cf. G. Camps, *Aux origines de la Berbèrie: monuments et rites funéraires protohistoriques* (1965), 567–68.

18. For examples and recent partial treatments, see, e.g., A. Berthier and R. Charlier, *Le sanctuaire punique d'El Hofra à Constantine* (1955); C. G. Picard, *Catalogue du Musée Alaoui*, n.s. (collections puniques), I (1956); G. Charles-Picard, "Civitas Mactaritana," *Karthago* 8 (1957); for a brief conspectus, G. Picard, *Carthage*, trans. M. Kochan and L. Kochan (1964), chap. 7. See now, however, A. M. Bisi, *Le stele puniche* (1967), esp. 113–14.

19. See the survey by G. Charles-Picard, *Les religions de l'Afrique antique* (1954).

about the connection of Baal and Saturn and of both with the theology of African Christianity.[20] The isolation of one element is not merely a necessary working procedure. The example of the necropolis of Beth She'arim in Judaea/Syria Palestina, where the tombs of leading third-century Rabbis, perhaps of the Patriarch himself, reveal Greek inscriptions and representational decoration,[21] warns us against assuming too readily that different "local" elements in a provincial culture necessarily cohered.

The native languages of Roman Africa were of course Punic, written in a Semitic script which can reasonably be represented in standard Hebrew lettering, and another language too often called "Berber." The term expresses the assumption of a coherent social and linguistic continuum of the native population persisting from pre-Punic times to the present day. But "Berber" is surely an Arabic loan-word from Greek *barbaros*; for Ibn Khaldoun in the fourteenth century says that the name arose because the non-Arabic-speaking population of North Africa spoke a language of unintelligible "ber-ber" noises.[22] In this context the word has no place in our period, and the assumption of a continuum is (see below), though not disprovable, extremely fragile. The non-Punic native language will here have the neutral name "Libyan," a mere label since no ancient literary source names it at all. For convenience the relatively limited evidence for Libyan will be considered first.

As will be attested below, the paradoxical view sometimes argued, that when Augustine talks about *lingua Punica* he means Libyan (or "Berber"), has been shown to have no foundation; and without the supposed testimony of Augustine the literary evidence reduces to at best a couple of oblique references. Sallust says of Lepcis Magna: "[T]he language of this city has just been transformed by intermarriages with the Numidians; its laws and culture are mostly Sidonian."[23] He clearly means to indicate the presence at Lepcis of some language other than Punic. Then there is, if the plural is pressed, a passing hint in Pomponius Mela's summary of the culture of the North African coastline: "[T]he coastline is inhabited by cultivators conforming on the

20. See W. H. C. Frend, *The Donatist Church* (1952), 76–77; cf. M. Leglay, *Saturne Africain: monuments* I–II (1961–66).

21. See the reports by N. Avigad, *Israel Exploration Journal* 5 (1955): 205; 7 (1957): 73, 239; and M. Schwabe and B. Lifshitz, *Beth She'arim II: The Greek Inscriptions* (1967) (Hebrew with English summary). Compare B. Lifshitz, "L'Hellénisation des Juifs de Palestine: à propos des inscriptions de Besara (Beth-Shearim)," *Revue Biblique* 72 (1965): 520.

22. Ibn Khaldoun, *Histoire des Berbères et des dynasties musulmanes de l'Afrique septentrionale*, trans. de Slane, I (1925), 168.

23. Sall., *Bell. Jug.* 78.

whole to our habits except that some use different languages."[24] Finally, it may (or may not) be the same Libyan language to which Augustine refers, when he speaks of the language of the tribes beyond the Roman frontier.[25]

None the less, we have fairly substantial archaeological evidence for a language and script quite distinct from Punic which survived into the Roman period and, as recent discoveries have shown, has left traces all the way from the Atlantic coast to Tripolitania. This may, or may not, be the, or an, ancestor of present-day Berber; the most recent text-book on the latter[26] argues that the connection is as yet unproven. This is not to say that the two languages can be shown to be fundamentally different. It is rather that what we know of Libyan depends solely on parallel Punic, and sometimes Latin, inscriptions; and the vast majority of all the known Libyan inscriptions reveal no more than proper names and a few formulae.[27] On the other hand it is agreed that the signs used on the Libyan inscriptions very closely resemble the script known as *tifinagh* now used by the Tuareg of the Sahara.[28] The precise connection between the two may perhaps never be known.

The Libyan inscriptions are written in twenty-three signs of a rather rigid geometrical form (see Chabot, *RIL*, p. v), normally written in vertical lines beginning in the bottom right-hand corner. Only in the inscriptions of Dougga (*RIL*, nos. 1–2) is the text written horizontally, beginning on the right of the top line, in imitation of Punic. Nos. 1 and 2 have parallel Punic texts; they are exceptional in being building inscriptions, probably contemporary, the former from the well-known mausoleum of Dougga, and the latter from the temple of Masinissa,[29] constructed in the "10th year of Micipsa"—139, or 138 B.C.[30] Apart from those from Dougga, almost all the

24. Mela, *Chorographia* 1, 8, 41.

25. *de civ. dei.* 16, 6.

26. A. Basset, "La langue berbère," in *Handbook of African Languages* I (1952), 47–48.

27. The standard collection and discussion is J.-B. Chabot, *Recueil des inscriptions libyques (RIL)* I (1940–41); see however the excellent earlier discussion by S. Gsell, *Histoire ancienne de l'Afrique du Nord* I³ (1921), 309–10. Compare also J.-G. Février, "Que savons-nous du libyque?," *Revue Africaine* 100 (1956): 263. A more confident linguistic assessment of Libyan is made by O. Rössler, "Die Sprache Numidiens," *Sybaris: Festschrift M. Krahe* (1958), 94. See now L. Galand, "Les études de linguistique berbère de 1954 à 1956," *Annuaire de l'Afrique du Nord* 4 (1965; pub. 1966): 743ff., on pp. 746–49, 750–52.

28. See, e.g., Basset (n. 26), 47.

29. See G. Camps, *Aux origines de la Berbérie: Massinissa ou les débuts de l'histoire (Libyca* 8) (1960), 283–84.

30. J. G. Février, "La constitution municipale de Dougga à l'époque numide," *Mélanges de Carthage (Cahiers de Byrsa* 10) (1964–65), 85.

known Libyan inscriptions (1123 in *RIL*) seem to be from grave *stēlai*, which in form and decoration appear to be of a rustic Punic type; some have parallel Punic texts (*RIL*, p. xiii), for instance *RIL*, no. 31 from the important Libyan-Punic site of Mactar (see below). Though there can be no meaning as yet, or perhaps ever, in the statistical distribution of known texts, it is noticeable that there is a concentration from the Algerian-Tunisian border region south-east of Bône (Hippo). From here come some of the known examples of Libyan-Latin texts, for instance *RIL*, no. 85 and pl. III, V: "Faustus son of Aspernas . . . Lived 75 years." *RIL* no. 145 (= *ILAlg.* 138) has: "Nabdhsen son of Cotuzan of the tribe of Misictrus. Lived 20 years"; the name "Nabdhsen" is recognizable in the Libyan text also. *RIL*, no. 146 (= *ILAlg* 137) would be of exceptional interest if it were certain, instead of probable, that the Libyan text is parallel to the Latin, and not a later addition; for the Latin is of a veteran who was "priest for life" (*flamen perpetuus*) in his city (*civitas*).

The Latin-Libyan bilinguals, of which not all need be noted here, suffice to show, as do the Punic-Libyan inscriptions, that we cannot think in terms of rigid linguistic enclaves; they also exclude the hypothesis, once ventured by W. M. Green,[31] that Libyan was a "secret language" used by the peasantry to baffle strangers. Its use on grave *stēlai*, perhaps its only written use in the Roman period, was probably copied from Punic custom. We cannot hope to deduce from these texts how far, if at all, the language was in daily use.

Recent discoveries, however, have shown that it was known in some sense over the whole length of Latin North Africa. The nine Libyan inscriptions from Morocco known to Chabot are now joined by eighteen more;[32] four of the total are bilingual Latin-Libyan. One of them is thought to date to the third century A.D. The Latin text reads: "Consecrated to the Gods of the Dead. Tacneidir son of Securus from Masaisulae. Lived 45 years."[33]

Libyan inscriptions have also been found in Tripolitania. A preliminary discussion of the thirty-nine known from Ghirza[34] suggests that they were cut on the stonework of mausolea, altars, and buildings in the settlement at a later stage in the existence of these, and that none may be earlier than the

31. W. M. Green (below, n. 40), p. 189.

32. See L. Galand, J. Février, and G. Vajda, *Inscriptions antiques du Maroc* (1966); the Libyan inscriptions (nos. 1–27) are edited by L. Galand, whose introductory discussion (pp. 1–36) is also the most detailed and up-to-date treatment of the Libyan script.

33. Galand (n. 32), no. 1 (pl. I, 1) = *RIL* 882.

34. J. M. Reynolds, O. Brogan, and D. Smith, "Inscriptions in the Libyan Alphabet from Ghirza in Tripolitania," *Antiquity* 32 (1958): 112.

fourth century, and some perhaps much later. See now the full publication of the remains;[35] meanwhile, another preliminary report[36] records three Libyan inscriptions from Bir Bu el-Gherab in the "pre-desert" region of Tripolitania; these were on stone blocks apparently re-used in a building not later than the third century A.D.

Thus the Libyan inscriptions do little more than pose problems. But it seems clear that we are dealing with something more than a few mechanical formulae, perhaps inscribed for ritual or magical purposes; for it is clear at least that some people able to write Latin or Punic could also transliterate their names into Libyan. It was therefore certainly in some sense a "live" alphabet. On the other hand we can hardly be wrong in presuming that it was not in any sense a language of culture, and it remains still to be shown that it was a language in current ordinary use at all. But before reaching firm negative conclusions we have to remember how post-war discoveries, archaeological and documentary, have shown that in Judaea, alongside Aramaic, both Greek and Hebrew were in more common use than had previously been supposed.[37]

II

If we turn to Punic, the situation is quite different. Firstly, there is substantial literary testimony from the imperial period for its survival. The most important evidence is that of Augustine.[38] The view once promulgated that when Augustine speaks of a Punic language he means "Berber"[39] cannot survive the careful study by W. M. Green published in 1951.[40] The two essential

---

35. O. Brogan and D. J. Smith, *Ghirza: A Libyan Settlement in the Roman Period* (1984).

36. By A. di Vita, "Archaeological News," *Libya Antiqua* 1 (1964): 142-2, with pl. LXXXI.

37. See, e.g., A. Díez Macho, "La lengua hablada por Jesucristo," *Oriens Antiquus* 2 (1963): 95. Out of a very extensive subsequent literature, note, as a collection of primary material, H. M. Cotton, W. E. H. Cockle, and F. G. B. Millar, "The Papyrology of the Roman Near East: A Survey," *JRS* 85 (1995): 214–35.

38. Only the barest essentials are given here; compare P. R. L. Brown, "Christianity and Local Culture in Late Roman Africa," *JRS* 58 (1968): 85ff.

39. W. H. C. Frend, "A Note on the Berber Background in the Life of Augustine," *Journ. Theol. Stud.* 43 (1942): 188, and *The Donatist Church* (1950), esp. 57–58; C. Courtois, "S. Augustin et le problème de la survivance de la Punique," *Revue Africaine* 94 (1950): 259; *Les Vandales et l'Afrique* (1955), 126–27.

40. W. M. Green, "Augustine's Use of Punic," *University of California Studies in Semitic Philology* 11 (1952): 179 (I owe this reference to T. D. Barnes). See M. Simon, "Punique ou Berbère? Note sur la situation linguistique dans l'Afrique romaine," *Recherches d'Histoire*

points from the evidence of Augustine are firstly that the Punic language was a Semitic language related to Biblical Hebrew; and, secondly, that it was fairly widespread not only in rural bishoprics but among Augustine's own congregation in Hippo. On the other hand it is clear that it did not rival Latin as a language of culture.[41]

The literary evidence other than that of Augustine stretches from the late first to the sixth century and deserves to be set out in full, in chronological order by the writers:

1. Statius, *Silvae* 4, 5, 45–46 (to Septimius Severus):

   Neither is your speech, nor your dress Punic / yours is no stranger's mind: Italian you are, Italian!

2. Apuleius, *Apologia* 98, 8–9 (on his stepson and opponent Sicinius Pudens):

   He never speaks any other language but Punic, and a bit of Greek he still has from his mother; he cannot speak Latin, nor does he want to. A little while ago you heard, Maximus, the indignity of how my son-in-law, brother of the eloquent young Pontianus, stammered with difficulty isolated broken syllables.

3. Ulpian, *Lib. 2. fideicommissorum* (*Dig.* 32, 11, *pr.*):

   Legacies can be left in any language, not only in Latin or Greek, but also in Punic or Galatian or in another people's tongue (*fideicommissa quocumque sermone relinqui possunt, non solum Latina vel Graeca, sed etiam Punica vel Gallicana vel alterius cuiusque gentis*).

4. Ulpian, *Lib. 48 ad Sabinum* (*Dig.* 45, 1, 1, 6):

   And if someone will pose the question in Latin to be answered in Greek, so long as the answer is appropriate, a legal obligation is created, and conversely. However, there is room for doubt as to whether this applies only to Greek, or also to another language, such as Punic or "Assyrian" (Syriac or Aramaic?) or any other language.

Judeo-Chrétienne (1962): 88; P.-A. Février, "Toujours le Donatisme. À quand l'Afrique?," *Riv. di Stor. e Lett. Religiosa* 2, 2 (1966): 228.

41. The most important passages for the Semitic character of the "lingua Punica" are: *In Ps.* 123, 8; 136, 18; *In Rom. imperf.* 13; *C. Petil.* 2, 239; *Quaest. Hept.* 7, 16; *Loc. Hept.* 1, 24; and for its wide distribution: *Ep.* 66, 2; 84, 2; 108, 14; 209, 2f. *Serm.* 167, 4. All quoted in Green (n. 40).

5. *Epit. de Caes.* 20, 8:

> (Septimius Severus) was sufficiently well educated in Latin letters, competent in conversation in Greek, and more proficient and eloquent in Punic seeing that he grew up in Leptis in the province of Africa.

6. *Historia Augusta, vita Sept. Sev.* 15, 7:

> His sister who had come to visit him could hardly speak Latin and caused the Emperor to blush often on her account . . . he ordered the woman to go back to her homeland.

7. Jerome, *Commentary on Galatians* 2 (Migne, *PL* XXVI, 357):

> The Galatians in addition to the Greek language, spoken all over the Orient, use their own language which is the same as that used by the Treviri in Gaul, and it makes no difference to them if in consequence thereof their language is corrupted, since the Africans too have introduced changes to the Punic language.

8. Procopius, *de bello Vandalico* 2, 10, 20:

> [The Phoenicians] having settled many cities held the whole of Libya up to the Pillars of Heracles; and from then to my time they have been settled there using the language of the Phoenicians.

These texts are of course of very uneven value. Apuleius is trying to discredit his stepson, and the proof that he spoke only Punic is supposed to be his speaking Latin haltingly; and the late biographical passages on Severus have little or no weight in themselves.[42] But the two passages of Ulpian are quite another matter.[43] He is speaking about what is legally permissible in the first passage, and envisaging an exchange of a dubiously binding nature in the second. He is, in other words, talking about the real contemporary world, and it is not an accident that the three languages used as examples are Punic (in both cases), Celtic, and Aramaic or Syriac. It ought to follow, unless Ulpian is making a wild error, that Punic was still used by persons of something more than the lowest social standing and, from the first passage, that it was *written*—though not necessarily (see below) in Semitic script. Jerome compares

---

42. For these points, see T. D. Barnes, "The Family and Career of Septimius Severus," *Historia* 16 (1967): 87ff., on pp. 96–97.

43. So, rightly, R. MacMullen, "Provincial Languages in the Roman Empire," *AJPh* 87 (1966): 1ff.

with those found in Punic changes that have occurred in another living language, Galatian. The passage of Procopius is set in the very dubious context of a legend about the settlement of North Africa, supposedly referred to in an inscription of Phoenician language and lettering at Tigisis; Courtois has argued that the inscription could not have had its supposed contents, and consequently that the people did not understand it (and therefore that in this sentence Procopius refers to Berber).[44] But the argument makes Procopius use *phoinikos* in two different senses in the same passage and proceeds too strictly from what we might presume but cannot know. The sentence is an addition by Procopius himself, who had been in Africa with Belisarius and (especially when combined with Augustine's evidence) should be taken to mean what it says.

The literary evidence may thus provide a framework against which to set the documentary evidence, from coins and inscriptions. The coin evidence is very limited: Punic lettering appears on the coins of a few cities in the early Empire, but disappears in the first half of the first century.[45] The very numerous Punic (or rather neo-Punic) inscriptions of Roman Africa, many with parallel Latin texts, are effectively impossible to survey with confidence, for they have never been assembled in any modern collection.[46] Furthermore, not only in *CIL* VIII but also in the otherwise excellent *Inscriptions of Roman Tripolitania* (*IRT*) (1952) the Punic parallel texts of Latin inscriptions are mentioned but not given. It may be sufficient therefore to start from the conclusion of G. Charles-Picard in his illuminating discussion of the civilization of Roman Africa:[47] extended Punic inscriptions appear roughly up to the beginning of the second century, and brief formulae up to the beginning of the

44. Courtois (n. 39), 267–68. Compare the (not very effective) criticism by Ch. Saumagne, "La survivance du Punique en Afrique aux Ve et VIe siècles après J.C.," *Karthago* 4 (1953): 171ff., on p. 177.

45. L. Müller, *Numismatique de l'ancienne Afrique* II (1861); J. Mrzard, *Corpus Nummorum Numidiae Mauretaniaeque* (1955), e.g., nos. 623–24 (Tingi).

46. The Punic inscriptions of Carthage and its vicinity (only) are contained in the *Corpus Inscriptionum Semiticarum* I (published in fascicules 1881–1962), nos. 166–6068; none appear to be from the Roman period. Others appear sporadically in the *Répertoire d'épigraphie Sémitique* I–VII (1895–1950). Note, however, J. G. Février, "Les découvertes puniques et néopuniques depuis la guerre," *Studi orientali in onore di G. Levi della Vida* I (1956), 274; J. Desanges and S. Lancel, "Bibliographie analytique de l'Afrique antique," *Bulletin d'Archéologie Algérienne* 1 (1962–65) and following issues; and J. Teixidor, "Bulletin d'épigraphie sémitique," *Syria* 44 (1967): 163 (and following issues).

47. G. Charles-Picard, *La civilisation de l'Afrique romaine* (1959), esp. 104, 109, 295.

third. This view is based to a large extent on Charles-Picard's own invaluable work at Mactar,[48] where nearly 130 Punic inscriptions have been found, though far from all published. Among them the latest extended texts have until recently been thought to be the three inscriptions, probably of the first century A.D., on the temple of Hathor Miskar (or Hoter Miscar); the dedicatory inscription on the frieze of the temple runs to forty-seven lines in ten columns.[49] A subsequent discovery, however, has produced two further inscriptions from the temple, one of a mere two lines, but another of eleven columns of three, five, or six lines each. It records the repair of the temple, with the names of thirty-six contributors; eighteen of them appear to have transliterated Latin names. It is suggested by the editors that the occasion cannot have been earlier than the early second century and may well have been considerably later.[50]

At Lepcis Magna, neo-Punic (paralleling Latin texts) appears for the last time under Domitian;[51] similarly, the newly discovered neo-Punic texts from the Wadi El-Amud in Tripolitania appear to date to the first century A.D.[52] But a recently re-published tomb from the Gefara, the now semi-desert coastal plain stretching south-west from Sabratha and Tripoli, has not only splendid rustic relief carvings of scenes from classical mythology, but parallel inscriptions in Latin and neo-Punic. The Latin text runs: "Consecrated to the Gods of the Dead. Quintus Apuleius Maxssimus who is also called Rideus, son of Iuzale, grandson of Iurathe. Lived 90 years. Thanubra his wife and Pudens and Severus and Maximus his most devoted children to their most beloved father (made it) with their own money." It thus illustrates graphically the Romanisation of a prosperous local family, presumably of farmers. More important for the present purpose is the date, which, as the Latin lettering suggests, seems to be the late second century, perhaps even the early third.[53]

48. G. Charles-Picard, *Civitas Mactaritana, Karthago* 8 (1957): esp. 25–26, 42–43, 58–60, 68, 76.

49. Text and translation, with photo, by J.-G. Février, "La grande inscription dédicatoire de Mactar," *Semitica* 6 (1956): 15.

50. J.-G. Février and M. Fantar, "Les nouvelles inscriptions monumentales néopuniques de Mactar," *Karthago* 12 (1963–64; pub. 1965): 43.

51. *IRT*, p. 80, and nos. 318 and 349a.

52. G. Levi della Vida, "Le iscrizione neopuniche di Wadi El-Amud," *Libya Antiqua* 1 (1964): 57; for the setting and date, O. Brogan, "The Roman Remains in the Wadi el-Amud: An Interim Note," *Libya Antiqua* 1 (1964): 47–48. For a collection of the Punic inscriptions of Tripolitania, see G. Levi della Vida and M. G. Amadasi Guzzo, *Iscrizioni puniche della Tripolitania (1927–1967)* (1987).

53. O. Brogan, "Henscir el-Ausāf by Tigi (Tripolitania) and Some Related Tombs in the

The progress of discovery thus begins to indicate that Punic inscriptions which were more than brief formulae were put up at least on occasion up to the end of the second century—and not long after that Latin inscriptions too become substantially less frequent. If that were all, we should be left to ponder the apparent disparity between the disappearance of Punic inscriptions and the evidence of Ulpian, Jerome, Augustine, and Procopius. But from Tripolitania, but so far from there alone, we now have another element in the pattern.

Tripolitania has revealed a number of inscriptions written in Latin lettering but in a language that is not Latin. One comes from Lepcis (*IRT* 826) and one from Zliten on the coast not far to the east of it.[54] But the majority come from the settlements of the Roman period in the (now) "pre-desert" region of the interior. This fact was the starting point for the first attempt at a coherent treatment of these documents, by R. G. Goodchild.[55] He concluded tentatively, firstly, that the language of the documents, though showing definite Punic influence, was more probably basically Libyan; and, secondly, that these inscriptions should be later than the neo-Punic ones of the same area, and should be associated with the establishment of *limitanei* (units of soldiers posted along the border, *limes*) in the area from the early third century onwards; the recurrence of the word TRIBUNUS in the inscriptions, e.g., in *IRT* 886 (Bir ed Dreder), gave definite support to the hypothesis of a military association. Bir ed Dreder, the site of the largest group (nineteen) of these inscriptions, was described subsequently by Goodchild, and still taken to be a settlement of *limitanei* of "Romano-Libyan" culture.[56] Two further examples, from the Wadi Sofeggin and Wadi Zemzem, were published in 1955;[57] and three more, one partially in Latin, from other wadis in 1960.[58] Subsequently, however, G. Levi della Vida showed that at least substantial parts of many of these inscriptions could actually be read as Punic, even if somewhat de-

---

Tunisian Gefara," *Libya Antiqua* 2 (1965): 47, on pp. 54–55, with pls. XVII–XVIII. The neo-Punic text is given in the earlier publication by P. Berger, "Le Mausolée d'El-Amrouni," *Rev. Arch.* 26 (1895): 71.

54. R. Bartoccini, *Africa Italiana* 1 (1927): 232–33. Cf. *IRT* 852.

55. R. G. Goodchild, "The Latino-Libyan Inscriptions of Tripolitania," *Antiquaries Journal* 30 (1950): 135.

56. R. G. Goodchild, "La necropoli romano-libica di Bir ed-Dréder," *Quad. di arch. della Libia* 3 (1954): 91; for the inscriptions, see pp. 100–104.

57. J. M. Reynolds, "Inscriptions of Roman Tripolitania: A Supplement," *PBSR* 23 (1955): 124–25, nos. 20, 24.

58. O. Brogan and J. M. Reynolds, "Seven New Inscriptions from Tripolitania," *PBSR* 28 (1960): 52–53, nos. 5–7.

based Punic.[59] The demonstration seems incontrovertible, and three more such inscriptions published since have been interpreted in the light of it.[60] It thus becomes unnecessary in principle to see these documents as the product of some novel factor in the social development of the hinterland, and to dissociate their authors, in date and otherwise, from those of the neo-Punic inscriptions of the same area.

Furthermore, in a revolutionary reappraisal of the documentary and archaeological evidence from the Tripolitanian hinterland and the forts of the *limes*,[61] A. di Vita has shown, firstly, that an agricultural population of probably mixed Libyan and Punic origin, but of Punic language and culture, was firmly established in the hinterland certainly from the first century A.D. and, at any rate, long before the extension of Roman forts to cover the area from the Severan period onwards; and, secondly, that *limitanei* do not belong in the third century at all. Thus, while acquiring a new viewpoint on these inscriptions, we are deprived of the proposed chronological framework for them. Some certainly seem to be late: that at Zliten mentioned above is a graffito from a late third-century tomb; and the lettering of one (*IRT* 877), from the hill country south-west of Lepcis, is said to be fourth- or fifth-century.

III

Here at last the documentary and the literary evidence begins to come together, in time if not specifically in place. While the main result of this survey must be to reaffirm the extent of our real ignorance about African society, some partial and preliminary conclusions may be drawn.

Firstly, the Libyan alphabet was in use in Roman Africa, and the values of the signs were understood, as were probably the meanings of at least some words. The fact that it is known solely from funerary *stēlai* makes it impossible to say whether or not the language was spoken or, if so, by what sections of the population.

Extended Punic texts, written in neo-Punic script, are very rare both in public inscriptions or on private monuments after the end of the first century A.D., but are not quite unknown, while brief formulae continued to be inscribed until about the end of the second century.

59. G. Levi della Vida, "Sulle iscrizione 'latino-libiche' della Tripolitania," *Oriens Antiquus* 2 (1963): 65, and "Parerga Neopunica," *Oriens Antiquus* 4 (1965): 59.

60. O. Brogan and J. M. Reynolds, "Inscriptions from the Tripolitanian Hinterland," *Libya Antiqua* 1 (1964): 43–44, nos. 3 (partially in Latin), 4, 5.

61. A. di Vita, "Il 'limes' romano di Tripolitania nella sua concretezza archeologica e nella sua realtà storica," *Libya Antiqua* 1 (1964): 65.

There are indications that in Tripolitania at least Punic, in some form, continued to be inscribed in Latin script into the fourth century.

The evidence of what was inscribed in durable form does not, however, allow any conclusions either about what was written in non-durable form (i.e., on parchment or papyrus, or wood?) or as to what language it would have been written in. There is, it is true, not the slightest reason to think that in the Roman period any substantial literary works were written in Punic — which had never been the vehicle of a significant literary culture[62] — or translated into it (as Greek Christian writings were, for instance, into Coptic). None the less, Augustine reveals that acrostic psalms were being composed in both Latin and Punic in his time;[63] were the Punic ones never written down? Ulpian's evidence suggests that legacies (*fideicommissa*) could be written in Punic in the early third century.[64]

The documentary evidence not only cannot by its nature disprove the evidence of Augustine that Punic was widely spoken in Numidia in the late fourth and early fifth centuries; it now offers some trace of confirmation for it. Taken as a whole, the literary and documentary evidence surely makes it reasonable to accept that Punic was a common spoken language throughout the lifetime of Roman Africa.

Such conclusions, however, take us only a small way towards understanding the *place* of Punic in North African society, that is, its social role and its significance vis-à-vis Latin. But even though many of the known Punic inscriptions have never been published, and those that have been are not gathered in an up-to-date collection (which should include parallel Latin, and occasional Libyan, texts), we need not doubt that they would not approach the more than 30,000 Latin inscriptions known from Africa. It cannot be doubted that, as a result of the twin processes of immigration[65] and Romanisation (of which the most vivid single document is the Latin inscrip-

62. The fairly scanty references in ancient sources to books written in Punic in the Carthaginian period are collected by S. Gsell, *Histoire ancienne de l'Afrique du Nord* IV (1920), 212–13.

63. *In Psalm* 118, 32, 8 (*PL* XXXVII, 159–60); see Green (above 41), 185.

64. One may note the bilingual Latin (*IRT* 338) and neo-Punic text from Lepcis Magna dating to A.D. 53, where the Punic translates, with some difficulty, the expression "adopted by will" (*testamento adoptatus*). See G. Levi della Vida, *Rend. Acc. Naz. Lincei* (1949): 400–401, and cf. J.-G. Février, "Textes puniques et néopuniques rélatifs aux testaments," *Semitica* 11 (1961): 5.

65. Especially emphasized recently by L. Teutsch, *Das römische Städtewesen in Nordafrika* (1962).

tion of A.D. 88 from Mactar, giving the *iuvenes* [members of a young men's club] with their Libyan, Punic and Latin names),[66] knowledge of Latin was general throughout the whole area covered by the African provinces; and we cannot define any precise social level at which it remained unknown.[67] But there were still congregations in Augustine's time where Punic was necessary. On the other hand the extensive works of Tertullian and Cyprian, written entirely in Africa, contain not a single reference to Punic. Does the comparison with Augustine suggest a penetration by the church into the lower levels of the population? But even if in the second and third centuries the intellectual and public lives of the educated classes were conducted entirely in Latin, was the same necessarily true of their private lives? Among the documents in the "Cave of Letters" was found the archive of a family from Moab (the "Archive of Babatha"); the documents in it cover the years A.D. 93/4 to 132 and are written in three languages, Nabataean Aramaic, Jewish Aramaic, and Greek.[68] Suppose that—by some chance comparable to the preservation of a Greek papyrus at Thessalonika—a family archive of the second or third, or even the fourth, century were to be discovered at Lepcis or Hadrumetum or Mactar: would it certainly be in Latin alone?

66. See Charles-Picard (n. 48), 77–78.

67. The spread of Latin may be conveniently illustrated by the recent publication of fifty grave *stēlai*, many of distinctly Punic style, from Sétif (Sitifis in Mauretania) dating to the second and third centuries; all have inscriptions in Latin. See P.-A. Février and A. Gaspary, "Le Nécropole orientale de Sétif. Rapport sur les fouilles effectuées de 1959 à 1964," *Bulletin d'archéologie algérienne* 2 (1967): 11.

68. For the publication of these texts, see now N. Lewis, *The Documents from the Bar Kokhba Period in the Cave of Letters: Greek Papyri* (1989); Y. Yadin, J. C. Greenfield, A. Yardeni, and B. A. Levine, *Hebrew, Aramaic and Nabataean-Aramaic Papyri* (2002).

CHAPTER THIRTEEN

P. Herennius Dexippus: The Greek World and the Third-Century Invasions*

In the reign of Claudius, when the Scythians captured Athens and collected all the books in order to burn them, one of them, believed to be clever, prevented them, saying: "[O]ccupied with these, the Romans would not care for war." He said so out of ignorance: had he been aware of the virtues of the Athenians and Romans, how renowned they were both in word and in war, he would not have said so.

—Petrus Patricius

Introduction

The legend of the Scythians and the books of Athens, with Petrus Patricius' comments on it, raises precisely the most crucial question about the culture and society of later antiquity: what was the relationship between the all-pervasive literary culture of the time, with its obsessive and apparently sterile fascination with the classical past, and men's conduct in the world? The question cannot of course be answered. If we wished to stress the positive and vital aspects of imperial Greek culture, we could partly avoid answering it by concentrating on a few figures of real intellectual stature in the second to early fourth century, and thereby pointing to a number of fields in which the Greek Renaissance saw significant, sometimes revolutionary, progress. Ptolemy, Galen, Diophantus, Origen, Plotinus, Porphyry, and Eusebius all in

*First published in *JRS* 59 (1969): 13–29. I was indebted for discussion and comment to a number of friends and colleagues: Professors J. F. Gilliam and H. A. Thompson at the Institute for Advanced Study at Princeton, where I had the pleasure of spending the autumn of 1968; and also Professors Sir R. Syme, T. D. Barnes, J. F. Matthews, A. D. Momigliano, and A. D. E. Cameron.

their different ways marked an epoch in the intellectual history of Europe. Even a man of much lesser originality, Cassius Dio, provided the Byzantine world with its definitive account of the history of Rome. But we can also try, if not to answer the question properly, at least to raise some themes directly relevant to it. Firstly, was constant reference to the classical past predominantly a neutral intellectual exercise, or a means of flight from an oppressive and inglorious present; or had it a real function in providing a frame of reference or a channel of communication, or, even more positively, in actively shaping attitudes to the present? Secondly, how far was there, as well as recurrent reference to incidents from the classical period, any real historical exploration of other areas of the past, remote or more immediate? Thirdly, was the extraordinary stability of educational conventions and cultural forms the reflection and perhaps the product of a real continuity and stability in the lives of the educated classes? Such themes, however partially explored, may provide a standpoint from which to look at the evidence, itself fragmentary, for the life and works of P. Herennius Dexippus, in whom the writing and the making of history momentarily coalesced in 267/8, with the Herulian invasion of Athens.

Past and Present in the Greek Renaissance

Heliodorus, a sophist whom Philostratus calls an "Arab," was sent on an embassy to Caracalla during the German expedition of 213.[1] Called before he was ready into the Emperor's court, he overcame his embarrassment, won favour, and seized the opportunity to ask the Emperor to name a subject for an extempore oration: "And the King said: 'I give you a hearing. Speak on the following subject: Demosthenes, after breaking down before Philip, defends himself from the charge of cowardice.'" No scene embodies more vividly the common culture of the educated classes in the Roman Empire. Heliodorus, if his homeland was the Roman province of Arabia, came from an exotic backwater of the Greek world, which was still seeing a great flowering of its highly original architecture,[2] where Nabataean was still spoken, at least by some,[3] and where distinctive customs prevailed.[4] Alternatively,

1. Philostratus, *Vit. Soph.* 2, 32.

2. See, e.g., C. M. Bennett, "The Nabataeans in Petra," *Archaeology* 15 (1962): 233; P. Parr, "The Beginnings of Hellenisation at Petra," *VIIIᵉ congrès international d'archéologie classique, 1963* (Paris, 1965), 527.

3. See A. Negev, "New Dated Nabataean Graffiti from the Sinai," *IEJ* 17 (1957): 250.

4. See *Digest* 47, 11, 9 (Ulpian, *Lib.* IX *de officio proconsulis*) on *skopelismos* in the province of Arabia.

an *Arabios* might have come from any part of the bilingual (in Aramaic or Syriac, and Greek) area stretching up to the new province of Mesopotamia[5] —which had afforded Septimius Severus the appellation "Arabicus." He confronted an Emperor far from renowned as an intellectual, who came from the Latin-speaking environment of Rome—and at one generation's remove from Emesa in Syria on the one side and on the other from Tripolitania, whose Punic culture was probably not quite extinct at the turn of the second and third centuries.[6] Yet the Roman Emperor of African-Syrian descent can suggest to the "Arab" orator a theme from classical Greek history which has an immediate appositeness to their own situation. Indeed, as Dio of Prusa found on his visit to Olbia,[7] it was those on the fringes of Greek culture who clung with especial tenacity to the common heritage of Greek literature. But even for the rest of the widespread Greek world it was Greek literature which provided the principal bond of common experience. The best-known passages and the major historical incidents could thus serve as a frame of reference for communication. That the purposes for which the frame of reference was used were often essentially empty verbal displays need not be denied; total familiarity with the material was necessary to allow the attention of the audience to be concentrated on the style, gestures, and expression of a speaker, the verbal or historical allusions he introduced, or the coherence with which he sustained the argument of a counter-historical theme. Thus, for example, Polemo delivered orations on the themes "Xenophon refuses to survive Socrates" and "Solon demands that his laws be rescinded after Peisistratus has obtained a bodyguard."[8] Even such orations were expected to have a consistent logic: Ptolemy of Naucratis, for instance, was criticized for an inconsistent argument in his "The Thebans accuse the Messenians of ingratitude because they refused to receive the Theban refugees when Thebes was taken by Alexander."[9]

Reference to the past was an essential element not only in rhetorical display but in those very numerous practical occasions of which an oration, or

5. For the "Arab" culture of the southern part of the area concerned, see R. Dussaud, *La pénétration des Arabes en Syrie avant l'Islam* (Institut français d'archéologie de Beyrouth, Bibliothèque archéologique et historique 59, 1955). For Arabs in Mesopotamia, L. Dillemann, *Haute Mésopotamie et pays adjacents: contribution à la géographie historique de la région, du Ve s. avant l'ère chrétienne au VIe s. de cette ère* (1962), 88–89.

6. F. Millar, "Local Cultures in the Roman Empire: Libyan, Punic and Latin in Roman Africa," *JRS* 58 (1968): 126 (chapter 12 in this volume).

7. *Or.* 36, 9.

8. Philos., *Vit. Soph.* 1, 25 (542).

9. Philos. 2, 15.

orations, formed an integral part. Thus Menander says that in composing a eulogy for a provincial governor "we shall find an example to illustrate this, an old story or one of our own invention, so as not to appear to be dealing in bare facts, in which there is no charm."[10] Moreover, it was the universal assumption of antiquity that historical examples (*exempla*) were no mere verbal adornment, but that their perusal was both an essential element in character training and a primary means of acquiring the political and military skills necessary for public life. It is quite unhistorical to suppose for instance that Valerius Maximus' *Facta et Dicta Memorabilia* (*Memorable facts and deeds*) or Frontinus' *Strategems* were empty literary exercises of no contemporary relevance; it was not for nothing that a Roman senator collected speeches of kings and other leading men from Livy and was executed for it under Domitian.[11] Similarly, Dio of Prusa says to Trajan in his third oration *To a King* (which refers constantly to historical figures, Philip and Alexander in particular): "Since I see, Imperator, you studying the ancients and understanding their wise and precise propositions."[12] The memory of Alexander, whom Trajan envied as he stood on the shores of the Persian Gulf,[13] surely influenced not only him and Caracalla[14] but the overall importance given to the eastern frontier in imperial military policy.

But the selection of relevant models from the past by Roman emperors had inevitably to differ from that made by their Greek subjects. There are traces in Dio of Prusa and in Plutarch of a deliberate effort (which was evidently necessary) to direct attention away from models of military glory in the past and toward those lessons in classical literature which were relevant to the humbler circumstances of the present. Dio, addressing the people of his native city, says:

> Moreover, not only did the Spartans and the Athenians in ancient days
> —and certain other peoples too—through orderly behaviour in civic
> matters have the good fortune to make their cities great and illustrious
> even out of very small and weak beginnings, but such an achievement
> as that is possible also for those of today who wish it. . . . For rest as-

10. Spengel, *Rhet. Gr.* III, 389, trans. D. A. Russels and N. G. Wilson, *Menander Rhetor* (1981), 115–17.

11. Suet., *Dom.* 10; Dio 67, 12, 3–4.

12. Dio Prus., *Or.* 3, 3. Compare *Or.* 18, 9.

13. Dio 68, 29, 1.

14. For references on Caracalla's imitation of Alexander, see F. Millar, *A Study of Cassius Dio* (1964), 151, 158, 214–16. See, however, D. Timpe, "Ein Heiratsplan Kaiser Caracallas," *Hermes* 95 (1967): 470; B. Levick, "Caracalla's Path," *Hommages à M. Renard* (1969), 442.

sured that what is called independence, that nominal possession which comes into being at the pleasure of those who have control and authority, is sometimes impossible to acquire, but the true independence, the kind which men actually achieve, both the individual and the state obtain.[15]

The work which most explicitly and systematically draws the attention of contemporary Greeks to the realities of their situation, Plutarch's *Praecepta rei publicae gerendae* (*Precepts for governing a city*), distinguishes clearly between those lessons from the past which were relevant and those which were delusive:

> Indeed there are many acts of the Greeks of former times by recounting which the statesman can model and correct the character of our contemporaries. . . . By emulating acts like these it is even now possible to resemble our ancestors, but Marathon, the Eurymedon, Plataea, and all the other examples which make the common folk vainly swell with pride and kick up their heels, should be left to the schools of the sophists.[16]

During the second and much of the third centuries the Greeks lived not only under Roman rule but in a profound peace which made the military virtues largely irrelevant: "This is not the right time for such things, you lead your life in a state of peace," as Dio said to the Rhodians.[17] But what would happen if the situation changed, and they once again faced armed invaders before the walls of their cities? Would Marathon and Plataea still belong to the polite irrelevancies of the schoolroom?

Patterns of Greek Historiography in the Second and Third Centuries

The first great achievement of Greek historiography in the imperial period had been the *Jewish Antiquities* of Josephus, integrating in a single narrative the history of the Jewish people from the Creation to the Revolt of A.D. 66. But it remained for a time without detectable influence, until taken up and used in Christian historiography and Byzantine world chronicles. Local histories apart, the pagan historiography of the second and third centuries took broadly three directions: scholarly rewriting of periods of the classical, and

15. Dio Prus., *Or.* 44, 11–12.
16. Plut., *Mor.* 814 B–C.
17. Dio Prus., *Or.* 31, 104.

sometimes the Hellenistic, past; massive compilations of Roman history up to the present; and a remarkably flourishing historiography of the most recent past, chiefly related to the reigns of emperors, or, more specifically, to the wars fought by them. Of the first, the prime example is Arrian's *Anabasis*; there were other lesser works such as the *On the Kings Who Ruled in Syria* with which Athenaeus credits himself.[18] The second produced major works, Appian's vast series on the wars of the Republic, which has never been seriously studied as a whole, and whose originality has been much underestimated by concentration on one element, the Civil Wars; Cassius Dio's *Roman History*, which, ending in A.D. 229, included nearly half a century of his own experience; and the *Chilietēris* (*Thousand years*) of Asinius Quadratus, of which only fragments remain.[19]

Of the writing of contemporary history we have excellent testimony in Lucian's *How to Write History*, provoked by a rash of stylistically derivative (mainly from Thucydides) and factually unreliable accounts of the Parthian campaigns of Lucius Verus; moreover, Lucian says that any other war which occurred would similarly call forth histories to recount it.[20] Thus the sophist Aelius Antipater recorded the "deeds" of Septimius Severus,[21] while Herodian composed his elegant, confused, and uncomprehending account of the emperors from (one must presume) his childhood up to 238; the work itself was perhaps written towards the middle of the third century and suggests an author who remained throughout far from the centre of events.[22]

The violent events of the later third century naturally (though significantly not, so far as we know, in the Latin West)[23] attracted historians of the time. Nicostratus of Trapezus seems to have covered the period 244–60,[24]

18. Athenaeus, *Deipnosoph.* 211 A–D; Jacoby, *FGrH* 166.

19. Jacoby, *FGrH* 97; G. Barbieri, *L'albo senatorio da Settimio Severo à Carino* (1952), no. 59; cf. Millar (n. 14), 62, 192.

20. Lucian, *Quomodo historia scribenda sit* 5. See H. Homeyer, *Lukian, Wie man Geschichte schreiben soll* (1965); cf. G. Avenarius, *Lukians Schrift zur Geschichtsschreibung* (1956).

21. Philos., *Vit. Soph.* 2, 24; see *PIR²* A 137.

22. The best available account of Herodian is the introduction to C. R. Whittaker's excellent Loeb text, vol. I (1969). Beginning in 180, Herodian's work was intended to cover a period of sixty years according to 1, 1, 5 and seventy according to 2, 15, 7. So vague is his knowledge of events that it is tempting to suggest that the phrase "in royal or public service" (1, 2, 5) might refer to minor imperial and *city* office in some province or provinces.

23. On the poverty of the Latin historical tradition in this period, see T. D. Barnes, "The Lost *Kaisergeschichte* and the Latin Historical Tradition," *Bonner Historia-Augusta-Colloquium 1968/69* (1970), 13.

24. Jacoby, *FGrH* 98.

while one Eusebius began with Octavian and went on to the death of Carus; a long surviving fragment (see below) describes the seige of Thessalonica by the Scythians.[25] Others combined the type of scholarly work familiar from the second century with contemporary history. Thus the Suda records an apparently third-century figure: "Ephoros of Cumae, the younger, a historian; wrote the history of Gallienus in 27 books. *History of Corinth*, *On the Aleuades*. Etc."[26] The same combination of scholarly and contemporary history is charmingly exhibited in what Photius records of Praxagoras, a young Athenian contemporary of Constantine.[27] At eighteen he wrote two books on the kings of Athens. At twenty-one he produced two books on Constantine, which went from 306 or before to the victory over Licinius and the foundation of Constantinople. Photius' summary concludes "Praxagoras, although he was a Greek [*Hellēn*] by persuasion, said that the emperor Constantine surpassed all those ruling as kings before him in all virtues and perfection and success." We may safely conclude that the work was published in Constantine's lifetime, and almost certainly very soon after 324. (We shall see below a striking example of Constantine's favour to a member of the pagan intelligentsia of Athens precisely in 326.) Praxagoras then returned to his studies, and at thirty produced six books on Alexander of Macedon. We may profitably compare him with Soterichus, a poet of Diocletian's time, who produced among other works a eulogy of Diocletian and an epic poem on Alexander's capture of Thebes.[28]

A giant beside these figures was Porphyry, who revived the tradition of a universal history embracing both Greece and Rome established by Diodorus and went from the Fall of Troy to the reign of Claudius Gothicus.[29] More significant for the whole vision of society in history were the earliest works of Christian historiography. The *Chronica* of Hippolytus was admittedly no more than a collection of tables in which patriarchs and Roman emperors both found a place.[30] But the *Chronographia* of Sextus (?) Julius Africanus, for all that its author was respectably employed as an architect in the service of Severus Alexander, marks the essential step to the Judaeo-Christian world view of Byzantium. Placing the Creation of the World in 5500 B.C., and devoted essentially to a chronological alignment of Old Testament and classical

---

25. Jacoby, *FGrH* 101.
26. See Jacoby, *FGrH* 212.
27. Photius, *Bib.* 62, *FGrH* 219.
28. Suda (ed. Adler) *Σ* 877.
29. Fragments and discussion of Porphyry's *Chronicle* by Jacoby, *FGrH* 260.
30. Text edited by R. Helm, *GCS* 46 (1965), *Hippolytus Werke, 4ᵉ Band: Die Chronik.*

history, it continued in fact to A.D. 221.[31] Only Porphyry of pagan historians was to bridge the gap thus created by applying his knowledge of Seleucid history to make his revolutionary re-dating of the Book of Daniel.[32]

These writers, however, merely exhibit by contrast the relatively limited nature of conventional pagan historiography in this period. Accepting a restricted set of literary models from the classical period, of whom Thucydides was the most important, it also followed a fairly predictable pattern of choices of subject, which was none the less genuinely responsive to contemporary events. We should hardly be surprised to find that an eminent Athenian of the third century wrote a work on the Diadochi, a universal history up to the reign of Claudius Gothicus, and a detailed account of the barbarian invasions.

Aspects of Society and Culture in Mid-Third-Century Athens

Some time between about 250 and 262/3, Porphyry attended the Platoneia, or dinner to mark the birthday of Plato, given in Athens by his teacher Longinus. We know, from the long quotation by Eusebius[33] from Porphyry's *Lesson in Philology* (*Philologos Akroasis*), one of the subjects of conversation—namely, plagiarism in classical Greek literature. Starting from the historians, Ephorus and Theopompus, and later Herodotus and Hellanicus, they ranged over comedy and tragedy to the poets, and even to Plato himself. The company was distinguished: apart from Longinus and Porphyry, and two men not otherwise known—Prosenes the Peripatetic and Callietes the Stoic—there were Demetrius, the land measurer (Porphyry's teacher according to

---

31. For evidence on his life *PIR*[2] I, 124. There are no editions of the surviving fragments of the *Chronographia* later than Migne, *PG* X, cols. 63–94, and Routh, *Reliquiae Sacrae* II, 138–309. See H. Gelzer, *Sextus Julius Africanus und die byzantinische Chronographie* I–II (1880–98). Note, however, that the biblical chronology is already known to some Hellenistic historians; see B. Z. Wacholder, "Biblical Chronology in the Hellenistic World," *Harvard Theological Review* 61 (1968): 451.

32. Fr. 43 in A. von Harnack, "Porphyrius 'Gegen die Christen,' 15 Bücher: Zeugnisse, Fragmente und Referate," *Abhandlungen der Akademie zu Berlin Philosophisch-Historische Klasse* no. 1 (1916). See A. D. E. Cameron, "The Date of Porphyry's *ΚΑΤΑ ΧΡΙΣΤΙΑΝΩΝ*," *CQ*, n.s., 17 (1967): 382; cf. the general study by M. V. Anastos, "Porphyry's Attack on the Bible," in L. Wallach, ed., *The Classical Tradition: Literary and Historical Studies in Honour of Harry Caplan* (1966), 421; and, for a further fragment, G. Binder in *ZPE* 3 (1968): 81.

33. Euseb., *Praep. Evang.* 10, 3.

Proclus);[34] Apollonius the grammarian, probably another of the teachers of Porphyry;[35] Nicagoras the sophist; and Maior, who, as the Suda records,[36] was from Arabia, a sophist and contemporary of Nicagoras and Apsines. These last two occur together in the final paragraph of Philostratus' *Lives of the Sophists*: "About Nicagoras the Athenian, who was appointed Herald of the Eleusinian Temple, and Apsines the Phoenician and his great achievements of memory and precision I must not write, for I should be distrusted as favouring them too greatly since they are bound to me in friendship."[37]

The area of Syria and Arabia was extraordinarily well represented in the intellectual life of third-century Athens. Apart from Porphyry, from Tyre, and Maior, there was Longinus himself, whose mother (his father is unknown) came from Emesa and was the sister of the sophist Fronto,[38] and Apsines from Gadara, who received consular *insignia* under Maximin.[39] An inscription from the Agora of a dedication to his wife by the city council gives his name more fully, Valerius Apsines.[40] A few decades later there was Callinicus of Petra, who practised rhetoric at Athens and, among other works, wrote an address (*prosphōnētikos logos*) to Gallienus;[41] a rival of his at Athens was another sophist from Petra, Genethlius, a pupil of Minucianus (see below) and Agapetus.[42]

Nicagoras represents a different element at Longinus' table, for he is a native Athenian who comes from a family, or group of families, whose links can be traced, with some conjectures, from the later first century B.C. to the mid-fourth and perhaps the mid-fifth century A.D. As Philostratus indicates, an important aspect of the life of this family, as of other established Athenian families (including that of Dexippus, as we shall see) was office-holding at

34. Proclus, *In rempublicam*, 2, 23, ll. 14–15 Teubner.

35. See E. Hefermehl, *Rh. Mus.* 61 (1906), 299–300.

36. Suda *M* 46.

37. Philos., *Vit. Soph.* 2, 23 (emended Loeb trans.).

38. Suda *Φ* 735.

39. Suda *A* 4735. The text reads "under Maximian," but the correction is obligatory. The suggestion of E. Rohde, *Kleine Schriften* I, 341, n. 1, that all the "Apsines" who flourished in Athens in the third and fourth centuries can be collected in a single family, is unfortunately not viable.

40. J. H. Oliver, *Hesperia* 10 (1941): 260–61; for the family of Apsines' wife, see Oliver, *The Athenian Expounders of the Sacred and Ancestral Law* (1950), 78–79, and E. Kapetanopoulos (n. 65 below).

41. Suda *K* 231. Cf. Cameron (n. 32).

42. Suda *Γ* 132.

Eleusis.[43] It was at Eleusis that Nicagoras put up the following inscription:[44] "Nicagoras the herald of the priests and a sophist holding the chair, descendant of the philosophers Plutarch and Sextus." Plutarch's own works take us back to his great-grandfather, Nicarchus, who witnessed the exactions of Antony's forces before Actium,[45] and his grandfather, one of whose friends had once been a doctor at the court of Antony and Cleopatra in Alexandria.[46] One branch of the family, descending from Plutarch's son Autobulus, evidently remained in Chaeronea, where they still were in the third century.[47] But that which descended through Plutarch's nephew, the philosopher Sextus of Chaeronea, was evidently established in Athens within a few generations. The earlier links in the chain are conjectural,[48] but we reach certainty again with Mnesaeus the father of Nicagoras, and Nicagoras himself who according to the Suda[49] wrote *Lives of Famous Men, On Cleopatra in Troas,* and an embassy speech (*Presbeutikos* [i.e., *Logos*] *to Phillip the Roman Emperor* (so 244–49). His son, Minucianus, is also recorded by the Suda: "son of the sophist Nicagoras, an Athenian, a sophist, born at the time of Gallienus: composed an *Art of Rhetoric* and rhetorical exercises and various speeches."[50] It was he, as mentioned above, who was one of the teachers of Genethlius. Moreover, it seems more than possible that we have some inscriptional evidence of him. A verse on the "Valerian" wall at Athens, whose construction (see below) is now firmly dated to the reign of Probus, mentions its construction by "Illyrius,"[51] Another inscription gives a dedication to Claudius Illyrius,[52] a native Athenian and also proconsul of Achaea, "while Marcus Iunius Minucianus was in charge [of its execution]."[53] Moreover, inscriptions from Epidaurus show as priest of Asclepius in 304 "Mar(cus) Iun(ius), torch-bearer in the mysteries

43. See for this theme M. Rosenbach, *Galliena Augusta: Einzelgötter und Allgott im gallienischen Pantheon* (1958), 15–16.

44. *IG* II[2] 3814 = *Syll.*[3] 845.

45. Plut., *V. Ant.* 68, 4–5.

46. Plut. 28; cf. W. A. Oldfather, "A Friend of Plutarch's Grandfather," *CPh* 19 (1924): 177.

47. See *Syll.*[3] 844 A–B.

48. See O. Schissel, "Die Familie des Minukianos. Ein Beitrag zur Personenkunde des neuplatonischen Athen," *Klio* 21 (1927): 361. Cf. Rosenbach (n. 43), 18–19.

49. Suda *N* 373.

50. Suda *M* 1087.

51. *IG* II[2], 5199, 5200.

52. See *PIR*[2] C 892. The entry requires revision.

53. *IG* II[3], 3689, 3690.

in Eleusis."[54] The coincidence of date (given the new dating of the wall), the apparent coincidence of the family name (*gentilicium*), and the connection with Eleusis, surely make probable the identification of the dedicant to Illyrius with the sophist. The priest at Epidaurus could, it seems, be either Minucianus in old age, or his son, Nicagoras. For, firstly, we have another inscription of a priest at Epidaurus, "M(arcus) [Iun(ius) son of Minucia]nus? Athenian,"[55] and, secondly, there is the famous inscription from the Tombs of the Kings at Thebes:[56]

> (I) the torch-bearer of the most holy mysteries in Eleusis, [Nicagoras] son of Minucianus, an Athenian, having investigated the shafts many years after the times of the divine Plato, on my journey from Athens, was full of admiration and was grateful to the gods, and to the most pious Emperor Constantine who granted me this. Let Plato be gracious to us also here.

The full significance of the visit was not realized until after J. Baillet had published in 1922 the full version of the companion inscription, complete with the date, namely 326:[57] "In the seventh consulate of Constantinus Augustus and the first consulate of Constantius Caesar, the torch-bearer of the [mysteries] in Eleusis Nicagoras son of Minucianus, an Athenian, having investigated the divine shafts, I was full of admiration." The event must surely signify an attempt by Constantine to show favour to, and win the favour of, the established pagan aristocracy of Athens in the period after his victory over Licinius.[58]

Then, addressing the Areopagus in the 340s, Himerius recommended his young son as being descended on his mother's side from Plutarch, Minucianus and (more immediately) Nicagoras.[59] Finally, when Proclus died in 484/5, the archon of Athens was Nicagoras the younger.[60] It is at least a legitimate speculation that the same family was still playing its traditional role.

It is possible, though the merest speculation, that other Athenian descen-

---

54. *IG* IV[2], 428–30.

55. *IG* IV[2], 431.

56. *OGIS* 721.

57. J. Baillet, "Constantin et le dadouque d'Éleusis," *CRAI* (1922): 282.

58. So P. Graindor, "Constantin et le dadouque Nicagoras," *Byzantion* 3 (1926): 209; cf. Schissel (n. 48).

59. Himerius, *Ecl.* 7, 4; cf. *Or.* 23, 21.

60. Marinus, *vita Procli* 36. Cf. P. Graindor, *Chronologie des archontes athéniens sous l'Empire* (1922), 273–74.

dants of Plutarch were the Plutarchus who in 308 held a priesthood at the Asclepieum at Epidaurus,[61] or the Plutarchus son of Nestorius (perhaps identical with, or more likely the son of, the hierophant of Eleusis in 375),[62] the teacher of Proclus.[63] This Plutarchus does not seem to be identical with one whom an inscription of the first half of the fifth century records as having three times managed at great expense the procession in which the sacred ship was conducted up to the Acropolis in the Panathenaea.[64]

The family of Minucianus remains one of the most striking examples of continuity in Athens in the imperial period. As such, it is only surpassed by the family of Honoratiane Polycharmis, a contemporary of Dexippus, who claimed descent from Pericles, Conon, and Alexander (*IG* II², 3679) and whose family tree can in fact be traced for six centuries, from the late third century B.C. to the late third century A.D.[65] But we have other lesser examples from the third century. For instance, the mid-third-century Athenian poet, T. Flavius Glaucus of Marathon, has a family tree whose ramifications lead us back to Sarapion of Chollidae, a friend of Plutarch; Flavius Zoilos of Marathon, a member of the city council (*bouleutēs*) of Athens under Hadrian; and Isaeus, the Syrian sophist whom Pliny heard and who was Hadrian's teacher.[66] Again, an archon of Athens in the middle of the third century was T. Flavius Mondo, son of Philinus, undoubtedly a descendant of a Boeotian family, one of whom, Philinus, was also a friend of Plutarch.[67] Finally, an Athenian inscription of the Constantinian period gives the genealogy of a family which goes back ten generations, to the very end of the first century B.C.[68]

These examples may help to indicate the stability of the world from which Dexippus came, and to hint strongly that that stability was not, in the long term, destroyed by the Herulian invasion. But it is still necessary to collect what we know of the intellectual life of Athens in the period immediately

61. *IG* IV², 436–37.

62. Zosimus 4, 18. See, on the Nestorii, father and grandfather of Plutarch, É. Évrard, *Ant. Class.* 29 (1960): 120–33.

63. Marinus, *vita Procli* 12, 28.

64. *IG* II² 3818. This Plutarchus was a sophist, not a philosopher; see L. Robert, *Hellenica* IV, 4–5.

65. See E. Kapetanopoulos, "Leonides VII of Melite and His Family," *BCH* 92 (1968): 493.

66. See J. H. Oliver, "Two Athenian Poets," *Hesperia* Supp. VIII (1949), 243.

67. See J. H. Olivier, *Hesperia* 2 (1933): 505–6; *Hesperia* 11 (1942): 71–72. For a new inscription of a member of the family, see S. Koumanoudes in Αρχ αιολογικον Δελτ ιον 21, 1 (1966): 143.

68. *IG* II², 2342.

before and after the Herulian invasion. For, although in the state of our evidence we probably cannot answer it, we must pose the question—was the last phase of Dexippus' historical writing the product of a period of the collapse of institutions and of intellectual life? Or, in spite of the undeniable physical destruction and economic decay (see below), did the context of the life of an established office-holding intellectual family in Athens remain recognizably what it had been before?

The evidence cited above, primarily from Porphyry, the Suda, and the inscriptions, abundantly illustrates the intellectual life of Athens around and after the midcentury, and up to the reign of Gallienus—who himself, so the *Historia Augusta* alleges,[69] held the archonship at Athens.[70] Flavius Glaucus will probably have been active after the midcentury, for he dedicates an inscription to his distant cousin, Q. Statius Themistocles of Chollidae, whose father had been an ephebe in 238/9.[71] Porphyry, in his life of Plotinus, adds two further items. Eubulus, the head of the Platonic school at Athens, corresponded with Plotinus during Porphyry's period with him (262/3–267/8); later Porphyry quotes Longinus' opinion of his contemporaries "the successors at Athens, Theodotus and Eubulus."[72] Longinus himself left Athens for Palmyra at some indeterminable date in the 260s. If we come to the period of the invasion itself, Callinicus was certainly active in the 270s (see above), and his rival Genethlius, as the pupil of Minucianus, will presumably still have been teaching in this period.

For the last quarter of the century our evidence is markedly thin. Eunapius mentions,[73] apparently as contemporaries of Porphyry, two prominent rhetoricians in Athens—Paulus (perhaps identifiable with an Egyptian sophist whom the Suda makes a contemporary of Constantine);[74] and Andromachus, a Syrian, who ought to be identifiable with another man mentioned by the Suda: "Andromachus of Neapolis in Syria, a sophist, taught in the ·

---

69. *Vita Gall.* 11, 3: "[Gallienus] was archon in Athens, that is, the supreme magistrate, with his well-known vanity which made him wish simultaneously to be treated as a citizen and take part in all religious rituals"; 11, 5: "[I]n addition he desired to be enrolled among the Areopagites in contempt of the city."

70. For the theme of the "Hellenic revival" under Gallienus, see A. Alföldi, "Die Vorherrschaft der Pannonier im Römerreiche und die Reaktion des Hellenentums unter Gallienus," *50 Jahre Röm.-Germ. Kom.* (1929), II = *Studien zur Geschichte der Weltkrise des 3. Jahrh. nach Christus* (1967), 228; cf. Rosenbach (n. 43).

71. *IG* II², 3704; see Oliver (n. 66).

72. Porph., *Vit. Plot.* 15, 20.

73. Eunap., *Vit. Soph.* 457.

74. Suda *Π* 812.

area of Nicomedia when Diocletian was emperor."[75] It would be a reasonable guess, though no more, that Andromachus went first to Athens, like other Syrians, and moved from there to Diocletian's court at Nicomedia, so before 305. Julian of Cappadocia (whom the Suda makes a contemporary of both Callinicus and Constantine),[76] had among his numerous pupils at Athens Prohaeresius,[77] who was born about 276 or 277;[78] even though he came after associating for a considerable time with Ulpian at Antioch,[79] this can hardly have been later than the first decade of the fourth century, and quite possibly earlier. These fragments of evidence can perhaps be supplemented by another with more definite implications. Libanius, who was born in 314, not only says that from boyhood he had heard tales of the fighting between the schools at Athens[80] but also mentions what was passed on to him by a fellow pupil at Antioch: "[H]e used to tell me, every day so to speak, the things pointed out by older men about Athens and the things happening there, going on and on about some Callinici and Telepolemi and about the force of quite a few other sophists."[81] The passage would surely read oddly if there had been any violent break in the life of the rhetorical schools at Athens between Callinicus' time and the early fourth century.

The Family of Dexippus

We have thus some background against which to set first Dexippus' family, and second his own life and writings. A survey of the family (see Figure 13.1)[82] produces a number of interesting conclusions. First its chronology: his father, P. Herennius Ptolemaeus, was an ephebe under Commodus, and his grandfather, P. Herennius, *hierokēryx* (a sacred herald) about the year 174/5. The father's birth must therefore fall in the period circa 162–75. But Dexippus' sons appear in the ephebe list now dated 254–55,[83] so they must have been born in 235–37. Dexippus' birth is therefore likely to fall in the first decade

75. Suda *A* 2185.

76. Suda *I* 435.

77. Eunap., *Vit. Soph.* 482–83.

78. He was eighty-seven when Eunapius came to Athens about 362/3, *Vit. Soph.* 485, 493.

79. Eunap., *Vit. Soph.* 487.

80. *Or.* 1, 19.

81. Libanius, *Or.* 1, 11.

82. From *IG* II², 3665; *PIR*² H 104; and Rosenbach (n. 43), 23.

83. *IG* II², 2245; see L. Moretti, *Iscrizioni agonistiche greche* (Studi pubblicati dell'Instituto italiano per la storia antica 12, 1953), 202–3.

The Family of Dexippus.

Eudemus   born c. 75/80?
(*IG* II², 3665)

|

Apollonius   born c. 105/110?
"the sophist" (*IG* II², 3665)

|

P. Herennius   born c. 135/40?
ἱεροκῆρυξ *IG* II², 3665; 3666; 1788, l. 39 (c. 174/5); 1792, l. 39
(under Commodus); 1798, l. 16 (c. 180)

|

P. Herennius Ptolemaeus   born c. 162/75
Ephebe under Commodus *IG* II², 2116, l. 11; sophist, κῆρυξ τῆς ἐξ
Ἀρείου πάγου βουλῆς 3666 (Eleusis); 3667; [τὸν π]ολέμαχον καὶ
ἀγωνοθέτην τῶν με[γάλων . . .]ειων 3668; *Syll*³. 877 D (Megara); =?
Ἐρεν. ἱεροκῆρυξ Ἑρμ., II², 1077, l. 42 (209/10)

|

P. HERENNIUS DEXIPPUS   born c. 200/205
IG II², 2931, 3198, 3667, 3669, 3670, 3671

Herennius Ptolemaeus	Herennius Dexippus	Herennia Hermonactia	sons born c. 235/7
IG II², 2245 (254/5), l. 14	*IG* II² (254/5), l. 162	*IG* II², 3670	
ἄρχων ἐφήβων: l. 161	γυμνασιάρχος: l. 177		
γυμνασιάρχος: l. 176	(ἀγωνοθέτης)		
(ἀγωνοθέτης) Ἀσκληπείων:	Ἀντωνείων ἐπὶ		
l. 302 συστρεμμάταρχος	Μά[ρκῳ]: l. 303		
	συστρεμμάταρχος:		
	*IG*², 3670		

of the third century, his father's perhaps about 170, and his grandfather's perhaps 135/40. If so, the great-grandfather, Apollonius "the sophist," may have been born about 105/110, and the great-great-grandfather, Eudemus, perhaps about 75/80. He will thus have reached adulthood about the time that Plutarch's main literary activity began,[84] though, as it happens, no Eudemus is attested among Plutarch's friends.

Thus, like that of Flavius Glaucus, the family can be traced back to the late first century, but not yet forward beyond the middle of the third. Like the family of Minucianus, it shows both a recurrence of sophists in different generations, and a connection with Eleusis; two members hold the post of *hierokēryx*. With Dexippus' father the holding of important posts in Athens begins. He was herald of the Areopagus, by now one of the two principal civil offices of the city, probably involving the presidency of the Areopagus.[85] A fragmentary inscription indicates that he was also *polemarchus* (one of the archons in Athens) and agonothete (president of a festival).

The splendid ephebic inscription of 254/5[86] (the archonship of Flavius Philostratus—"Philostratus of Lemnus") shows Dexippus' two sons occupying a very prominent position, Herennius Ptolemaeus with four, and Herennius Dexippus with two, of the ephebic magistracies and liturgies which mimicked those of the city itself.[87]

The Roman citizenship, the normal concomitant of prominence in a Greek city of the second century, appears (presumably) with the grandfather, P. Herennius; at any rate his descendants have the Roman three names (*tria nomina*) with "Herennius" as the *gentilicium*. It is not possible to suggest the source of the name—unless it goes back in some way to L. Herennius Saturninus, proconsul of Achaea early in Trajan's reign.[88] Dexippus thus came from a family that was firmly established in the public and intellectual life of Athens, though of relatively recent prominence.

Dexippus' Life and Career

If these calculations are not misleading, Dexippus was a man of relatively advanced years, perhaps in his mid-sixties, when he led the Athenians against the Heruli. Eunapius, the continuator of Dexippus' *History* (see below), ap-

---

84. See C. P. Jones, "Towards a Chronology of Plutarch's Works," *JRS* 56 (1966): 61.

85. See D. J. Geagan, *The Athenian Constitution after Sulla* (*Hesperia* Supp. XII, 1967), 41–42.

86. See n. 83.

87. See P. Graindor in *BCH* 39 (1915): 253–54.

88. *PIR²* H, 126.

pears indeed to credit him with a still longer life: speaking of Porphyry, he says, "it so happened that he lived to the times of Gallienus and Claudius, Tacitus, Aurelian, and Probus. At that time there lived also Dexippus who composed an annalistic history [*chronikē historia*], a man full of erudition [*paideia*] and logical power."[89] As will be shown, Dexippus' writing can hardly have been completed before the mid 270s; he may very well, therefore, have lived on into the reign of Probus (276–82).

A number of inscriptions illustrate his role and career in Athens, though none gives dates for specific offices. Three inscriptions give the essentials. In *IG* II², 3670 he appears as having served as "archon *basileus*, eponymous archon, and the most distinguished [*kratistos*] holy priest." The order of the first two items is clearly chronological; the eponymous archonship was in any case the senior post;[90] *kratistos*, which is commonly, but not invariably, used with the names of Areopagites from the second century onwards,[91] may perhaps indicate that Dexippus was an equestrian.[92] The title *hiereus panagēs* seems to be that of a relatively minor priesthood at Eleusis, whose functions are unknown;[93] if so, Dexippus was continuing a family tradition.

Another inscription from Athens (*IG* II², 3198) adds a further function, agonothete of the Great Panathenaic games, and states that he restored the mast and crosspiece of the Sacred Ship, on which the *peplos* (the robe of Athena) was draped when carried in the Panathenaic procession.[94]

The main inscription of Dexippus (*IG* II², 3669) repeats these posts and functions and adds (that he served as) "*panēgyriarchus* and agonothete of the great Panathenian games at his own expense." Here again there is a connection with Eleusis, for the only known function of the *panegyriarchus* was to feed the visitors to the Eleusinian festival.[95] Like his restoration of "the mast and crosspiece of the Sacred Ship," these functions illustrate the familiar liturgical role of the rich magnate in a Greek city.

This inscription comes from a statue base now in the Louvre,[96] which was originally erected in the first half of the second century with an inscription

---

89. Eunap., *Vit. Soph.* 457 = Jacoby, *FGrH* 100 T 2.

90. Geagan (n. 85), 7, 10.

91. Geagan (n. 85), 55.

92. See A. Stein, "Griechische Rangtitel in der römischen Kaiserzeit," *Wiener Studien* 34 (1912): 160.

93. See P. Foucart, *Les mystères d'Éleusis* (1914), 209.

94. So L. Deubner, *Attische Feste*² (1966), 32.

95. Geagan (n. 85), 136.

96. See W. Froehner, *Inscriptions grecques du musée impérial du Louvre* (1865), 220, no. 119; cf. P. Graindor, *Album d'inscriptions attiques d'époque impériale* (1924), 72, no. 105, pl. LXXXIII.

(*IG* II², 3625) honouring one Epictetus, and was re-used for Dexippus; its exact original site does not seem to be recorded. The inscription in honour of Dexippus was put up by his sons "on the request of the council of the Areopagites and the council [*boulē*] of the 750 and the Athenian people."[97] The council of 750 is firmly attested only here; the increased number perhaps indicates a change from annual to permanent membership, and more securely suggests financial stringency and a need for the burden of membership to be spread more widely.[98] There is no indication of date, but we can be certain that it is subsequent to the Herulian invasion, for the poem which follows mentions Dexippus' writing of contemporary history. As we shall see, the earlier of the two works which may be referred to cannot have been completed before about 270. None the less, we could hardly guess from the inscription that Dexippus had ever seen military action. The introductory formula concludes: "to the rhetor and writer on account of his virtue, his sons." Rhetoric was not a new occupation for the family, and it is the novel literary pursuit, the writing of history, rather than the repulse of the Heruli, on which the poem which follows concentrates:

> Mighty in courage, in word, and in counsel are the famous men whom the land of Cecrops has produced, of whom one is Dexippus, who observed and truly recorded the history of long ages. Some events he witnessed himself, some he gathered from books, composing an all-embracing history. O famous man, who, casting wide the scope of his thought, studied the events of long ages! Widespread in Hellas is the fame which the recent reputation of his history has given Dexippus. For this his sons jointly set up this statue representing their father.

We may thus see Dexippus as the product of a well-established Athenian family, which in the previous generation had risen to major office in the city, and was clearly now to be numbered among the most prominent, if it was not indeed the most prominent, of the citizens. At this point, with Dexippus' sons and daughter, we lose sight of the family—unless (as there is no positive reason to suppose) the fourth-century Dexippus, a Neoplatonist and follower of Iamblichus,[99] was a descendant. The historian Dexippus came from a city whose intellectual life was in full flower and was pursued both by the aristocratic local families and by men of learning coming from other parts of the Greek world. By contrast, it is significant that while some men from Athens

97. On the formula κατὰ τὸ ἐπερώτημα, see Geagan (n. 85), 45–46.
98. Geagan (n. 85), 74–75.
99. See A. Busse, "Der Historiker und der Philosoph Dexippus," *Hermes* 23 (1888): 402.

in the third century belonged to the Roman Senate,[100] the family of Dexippus, like that of Minucianus, did not. The rise of provincial and local families into the Roman aristocracy is of course one of the great themes of imperial history. Athens provides examples of a different phenomenon, the maintenance over generations, sometimes over centuries, of a prominent position in the intellectual and political life of the city by families whose members could easily have sought Roman office, but who did not choose to do so. There was a real sense in which Athens remained a capital, not a provincial city; and this fact can hardly have failed to affect the standpoint from which a prominent Athenian wrote history.

Dexippus' Historical Works

The fullest account of Dexippus' writings is given by Photius:[101] "Read, by Dexippus *Events after Alexander* in four books; also read by him another *Historical Summary*, covering the actions up to the reign of the monarchy down to the reign of Claudius; and read by him the *Scythica*." Both of the two last-mentioned works were completed when Dexippus was an elderly man, and it must be probable, though not certain, that it was the least original of his works, the *Events after Alexander* in four books, which was written first. Most of what we know of it comes from the extensive summary by Photius (F 8), which concludes: "[H]e surveys the rest, writing on the whole in agreement with Arrian in many details, as also in these." Arrian's own *Events after Alexander* went down to 321/0 (*FGrH* 156 F II), so we may assume that Dexippus' did likewise. The few fragments (F 31–36) we have of it all, except the first, come from the *Excerpta de sententiis* (*Excerpts on opinions*), and therefore tend to generality. They come from a section in the narrative corresponding to the sixth book of Arrian's work (156 F 9 (13)–(15)), and nearly all derive from a speech by Hyperides. Whether there was in fact any significant Athenian bias in the work we cannot tell. The fragments do suffice, however, to show that this was, as Photius indicates, a work of substantial length, with the normal complement of speeches by leading characters. An unoriginal literary and scholastic composition, it could have been written at any time in Dexippus' adulthood. We may recall that Praxagoras was to complete his six books on Alexander at the age of thirty.

100. Note especially the consular Ulpius Leurus, his son, M. Ulpius Eubiotus Leurus, and grandsons, M. Ulpius Flavius Tisamenus and M. Pupienus Maximus; Barbieri (n. 19), 2119–22. Also Claudius Illyrius, cf. n. 52.

101. Photius, *Bib.* 82 = Jacoby, *FGrH* 100, T 5. *Testimonia* and *Fragmenta* in Jacoby are henceforward cited as T 1, F 1, etc.

The work which Dexippus probably wrote next, the *Historical Summary*, referred to variously as the *Chronikē Historia*, *Chronika*, or *Syvntomon Historikon*, was a considerably more substantial undertaking in twelve books which, as Evagrius notes,[102] began with the mythical period and continued to the reign of Claudius. The *History* did indeed begin with mythical times: the earliest fragment which survives refers to the colonization of Rhodes by the Lacedaimonians driven out by the arrival of the Heraclids (F 9). Here, he was not content, however, with following a single predecessor, but used a variety of sources, thought for himself about the proper means of indicating chronology, and expressed due caution about the early period. All this emerges from a long description of his methods given by his continuator, Eunapius (F 1):

> Dexippus the Athenian arranged his *History* by Athenian archon-years [from the period when archons began], adding in addition the Roman consuls, though the work starts at a point before either existed. The first principle of his *History* was that, in regard to the legendary period, he should leave the question of factual probability to the reader to believe as he thought fit. In the later periods, where there is more evidence, it should be collected and subjected to more rigorous historical examination. Indeed he [also] uses as a strict chronological framework the Olympiads, and for the intervening years, the [Athenian] archons. After a most elegant prooemium he proceeds further and displays the seriousness of the contents, leaving aside and disregarding the too remote and mythical period as being like an out-of-date drug disapproved of by men of understanding. Making his own calculation of Egyptian chronology, and seeking out the earliest and least contaminated source for the history of each people, he sets out the major historians and demonstrates with evidence the falsehoods which each has repeated from another. He collects the material for his *History* from many and various sources, collecting and arranging it like a variety of useful wares in a single shop. Simply sketching and fitting into his narrative all events in history worthy of note, and any individual deeds which have earned especial fame, he brings his work down to the reign of Claudius, that is the first year of the reign, with which it both began and ended (some give Claudius a second year). Then he makes a calculation of Olympiads and consulships and archon-years, making the total a millennium, as if afraid to put an account for too many years before his readers.

102. Evagrius, *Hist. Eccles.* 5, 24 = T 6.

From this it is clear that the structure of the *History* was annalistic, a procedure which caused some difficulty to its author. Almost exactly like Porphyry, he took the mythical period of Greek history as a starting point and related Roman chronology to Greek: in this the work differed fundamentally from the Roman histories of Cassius Dio and Asinius Quadratus, which started from the myths of the foundation of Rome.

The finishing point is given slightly differently by a fragment of Eusebius' *Chronicle* (F 2): "Indeed Dexippus, composing his History down to the 222nd Olympiad, says that in that year Dionysius defeated Alexander." (It is of some interest that the Olympic Games were *held* a year after the Herulian invasion.)

The Herulian invasion itself was at least referred to in the *History*, appearing, as we would expect, in book XII (F 5). It is possible indeed that there was certain concentration on the third century, for a fragment from book X (F 4) refers to the capture of Dyrrachium by some force whose identity is not given; the third century is, as Jacoby assumed, the most probable setting. The possibility of such a concentration is at least not contradicted by the pattern of the other surviving fragments. One (F 10) refers to Alexander, and one (F 11) to the reappearance of the phoenix in the first century A.D.,[103] while a third (F 12) compares the Roman Empire with its predecessors. All the rest refer to events in the third century.

The significance of this distribution is, however, greatly reduced by the fact that all except one of the third-century fragments attributed to the *History* come from the *Historia Augusta*. Against the fact (see below) that the author of the *Historia Augusta* undoubtedly knew something about Dexippus' role in 267/8, we must set his habit, not only of inventing authorities, but of attributing to real ones things which they did not say, or even could not have said.[104] For instance we have *Vita Max.* 33, 2 "when Dexippus, and Arrian and many other Greeks wrote." Apart from two details relating to Severus Alexander (F 13, 14), and one (F 23) on the death of Quintillus, all the fragments concern the events of the year 238. There seems no way even of establishing reasonable guesses as to which, if any, actually come from Dexippus, and for the moment they must be left out of account in trying to reconstruct the *History*.[105]

103. For difficulties about the exact date, see Jacoby on this passage.

104. See R. Syme, *Ammianus and the Historia Augusta* (1968).

105. One may note, however, that further consideration could be given to the arguments of F. Altheim, *Literatur und Geschichte im ausgehenden Altertum* I (1948), 175–92, that Dexippus' *History* is the annalistic source underlying the *HA*'s biographies of the emperors from 240 to 270.

The remaining third-century fragment (F 22) comes from Syncellus' narrative of Decius' operations against the Goths in 250/1, "as Dexippus tells," ending with his death at the Abrittus, and the accession of Gallus and Volusianus "who ruled according to Dexippus for eighteen months having done nothing worthy of note; according to others they ruled for three years, and according to others for two years." The indication of the length of reign may serve to suggest that the quotation is from the *History*. But it raises the question of the relationship between this work and the *Scythica*, which must inevitably have dealt with many of the same events.

Of the *Scythica* we have two brief descriptions. Photius (T 5) completes his list "and also read by him is the *Scythica*, in which he recorded the wars of the Romans and the Scythians against each other and deeds worthy of note." Evagrius (*HE* 5, 24 = T 6) also gives the *Scythica* last, and implies more clearly that the work was written last, or at least came after the *History* in the manuscripts: "[A]nd Dexippus has done much work on these matters, starting from mythical times and stopping at the reign of Claudius the successor of Gallienus; he has encompassed what was done by the Carpi and other barbarian tribes in their attacks on Greece, Thrace and Ionia" (trans. Whitby). We should in fact naturally assume that the *Scythica* is the later work, for it carries on later, at least into the first year of Aurelian. If that is so, then Dexippus, having completed his general history, decided to go over again the history of the Gothic invasions.

It is tempting to find a garbled reference to his starting point in *HA, vita Max. et Balb.* 16, 3 (= T 20): "[U]nder them the Carpi fought against Moesia. This was also the beginning of the Scythian war. At that time occurred the destruction of Histria but, as Dexippus says, of the Histrian community." If this is correct, he began his main narrative with the year 238. At some point (perhaps in the preface?) he seems, on the testimony of Jordanes, to have traced the origin and migrations of the Vandals: "from the stock of the Asdingi, which is eminent among them and stands for a most bellicose nation, as the historian Dexippus relates, who testifies that it took them almost a whole year to travel from the Ocean to our territories due to the gigantic size of the land [in between]."[106]

We have, however, to proceed largely on a priori assumptions to determine which fragments of Dexippus relating to this period come from which of his two major works. When for instance we find an excerpt (F 6) relating

---

106. Jordanes, *Getica* 113 (F 30). See E. Ch. Skrijunskaya, *Iordan o proiskhojdenii i de'aniakh Getov: Getica* (1960).

to Aurelian headed "from the History of *Dexippus*. Book 3," the title of the work as given might suggest that the *History* went on further than our authorities state; only the book number makes the conclusion that this is the *Scythica* secure. None of the other presumed fragments of the *Scythica* (F 24–30) carries any indication of title or book number. However, we can use as a starting point the literary character of F 6 itself, a full description, with speeches by both sides, of negotiations between Aurelian and the Iuthungi; we can reasonably attribute to the same work (rather than to an *Historical Summary* at least F 26—the siege of Philippopolis—which includes Decius' immensely long "letter," which is very much longer than any documentary imperial letter known from this period;[107] and F 28, the Herulian invasion, and Dexippus' own speech to his men. The fact that all the surviving fragments of this work come from the Byzantine Excerpts *de sententiis* (*On opinions*) and *de strategematibus* (*On tactics*) may well give us a distorted picture of the work as a whole. But it remains significant that it was here, not in the *History*, that the excerptors found long accounts of "stratagems" (all from sieges of cities in fact), and substantial speeches replete with interesting sentiments. This impression may be confirmed by Photius' remark on the style of Dexippus (T 5): "Another Thucydides with a certain clarity, but especially in the Scythian histories." A careful examination of the text has in fact shown numerous Thucydidean reminiscences in these fragments.[108] The work was clearly on an ample scale, though we cannot guess at its actual length. It is hardly likely that it could have been finished (even supposing that it did not reach the end of Aurelian's reign) before the mid 270s.

We can thus draw a reasonably confident picture of the development of Dexippus' historical writing. He began with a quite unoriginal work of a traditional type, on Alexander, and followed it with a laboriously compiled chronicle from the mythical Greek past to the end of the reign of Claudius Gothicus. It cannot have been completed less than a couple of years after the repulse of the Heruli; when his sons' poem says: "Some events he witnessed himself, some he gathered from books," the reference *may* be to the *History* alone. At this point he will not have been less than sixty and was probably rather older. We can only assume (especially for lack of information on the end point of the work) that it was his own role in the repulse of the Heruli

107. See F. Millar, "Emperors at Work," *JRS* 57 (1967): 16, n. 100 (chapter 1 in this volume).

108. See F. J. Stein, *Herodianus et Dexippus rerum scriptores quatenus Thucydidem secuti sint* (Diss. Bonn 1957), 10–11.

which prompted him to describe again, more fully, and with all the conventions of Thucydidean historiography the crowded military history of the mid-third century.

The *Scythica*

This is not the place for a re-examination of the evidence for the third-century wars with which Dexippus' *Scythica* was concerned. But the fragments themselves (apart from that on the Herulian invasion, which will be treated separately) do merit a few remarks, for they represent, along with the *Canonical Epistle* of Gregorius Thaumaturgus [109] and the thirteenth Sibylline Oracle,[110] the main contemporary evidence from within the Greek world for the period of the invasions.

If Evagrius' description of it (see above) were our only evidence, we should believe that the *Scythica* dealt solely with the Greek East—Thrace, Greece, and Ionia. The pattern of the surviving fragments almost confirms this. They relate to five episodes, in chronological order: the siege of Marcianopolis (F 25) in perhaps 248; the siege of Philippopolis (F 26–27) in 250/1; the siege of Side in Lycia (F 29), whose date is unknown but which follows F 26 in the Excerpts; the Herulian invasion (F 28); and Aurelian's negotiations with the Iuthungi in Pannonia. Thus only the last takes us outside the Greek area, and there is no indication that events on the Rhine and in Gaul were touched on at all. By contrast, the historian Eusebius did make, in connection with the siege of Thessalonica, a passing reference to the siege of a Gallic city, evidently Tours, and to the Gallic Empire; but even here the impression is of places and events far away and of only marginal interest.[111] With Dexippus, it may be suggested tentatively that we are approaching a "Byzantine" viewpoint, with the inhabitants of the principal Greek areas—the Balkans,

---

109. The text has not been re-edited since Migne, *PG* X, 1019–48, and M. J. Routh, *Reliquiae Sacrae* (1846–48) III, 251–83.

110. J. Geffcken, *Die Oracula Sibyllina* (1902); cf. A. T. Olmstead, "The Mid-Third Century of the Christian Era," *CPh* 37 (1942): 241, 398. See now D. S. Potter, *Prophecy and History in the Crisis of the Roman Empire: A Historical Commentary on the Thirteenth Sibylline Oracle* (1990).

111. Jacoby, *FGrH* 101 F 2: "This I did not hear from the Macedonians themselves; in the case of another siege I learnt of counter-manoeuvering against these fire-bearing missiles when the Celts laid siege to a city called of the Tyrrenians (Etruscans?). And this city (belongs) to the Gallic territory of those inhabiting the west, in the province of Lugdunensis." For the identity of the place, see Jacoby on the passage.

Greece, and Asia Minor—embattled against the barbarian threat. The suggestion gains some substance from the remarkably uniform style and tone of these fragments. In each case the primary protagonists are the barbarians and the inhabitants of a Greek city: the barbarians attack, the inhabitants resist, various stratagems are tried by both sides and finally the barbarians depart. Thus, for instance, the account of the siege of Marcianopolis names and describes in glowing terms the leader of the defenders, Maximus, and recounts the ruses of the inhabitants; it ends "when they [the barbarians] could not hold out any longer, they withdrew without having achieved anything." We happen to have from Jordanes another tradition (not necessarily more truthful) which gives a quite different version: "They assailed Marcianopolis, the famous metropolis of the same land, and after a long siege, having received money from the inhabitants, they withdrew."[112] Very similar phraseology appears at the end of Dexippus' account of the first siege of Philippopolis (F 22, quoted by Syncellus, also recorded the second, and successful, siege).[113] Here he ends "when they were at a loss in every respect, they decided to withdraw" (F 27 (11)), while with the siege of Side (F 29) we have "when the delay turned out to be unprofitable for the Scythians, and there was no hope, they withdrew." Once again, while we are at the mercy of the excerptors, it remains significant that these recurrent themes were there to be found.

The heroes of these episodes are, as stated, the inhabitants of the Greek cities—though, rather surprisingly Dexippus tends to refer to them by ethnic names, "the Mysoi" (F 25 (6)), "the Thracians" (F 27 (11)); the Roman army does not appear. Indeed, we have something more positive than that, a direct statement in the account of the siege of Philippopolis that Decius was afraid of the revolutionary consequences of the people taking too readily to arms, and sent his long "letter" (in fact given by Dexippus in a form like that of a speech) to restrain them: "Decius, the Emperor of the Romans . . . stood in dread of the Thracian force, fearing lest out of it might come some disturbance affecting the stability of the empire" (F 26 (1)).

The two fragments (F 6–7) relating to Aurelian's negotiations with the Iuthungi, which should be dated to 270,[114] have necessarily a quite different focus. Moreover, although most of the long first fragment is taken up with

112. Jordanes, *Getica* 92. See J. Wiesner, *Die Thraker* (1963), 181.

113. On the siege of Philippopolis, see Wiesner (n. 112) and B. Gerov, "Die gotische Invasion in Mösien und Thrakien unter Decius im Lichte der Hortfunde," *Acta Antiqua Philippopolitana: Studia archaeologica* (1963), 127.

114. For the date, see A. Alföldi, "Über die Juthungeneinfälle unter Aurelian," *Studien zur Geschichte der Weltkrise des 3. Jahrh. nach Christus* (1967), 427.

speeches by the barbarian embassy and by Aurelian, both made up substantially of Thucydidean sentiments on the subject of war and peace,[115] there is also a definite factual content. We have (F 6 (2)–(3)) a fine description of the Emperor and his army receiving the embassy; opposite him are "the standards . . . of the selected force." Is this not contemporary evidence for the formation of the "field army," the later *comitatenses*?[116] There are also references to the abandonment of payments to the Iuthungi, and their demands for their restoration; to the barbarian forces, 40,000 horse and 80,000 foot; to the spoils which the Iuthungi had brought from Italy; and to an earlier Roman defeat of 120,000 "Scyths." The second, briefer, fragment contains no speeches but has striking details of Aurelian, after a Vandal embassy, putting the issue of war and peace to his assembled army; the handing over of hostages and the introduction into the Roman army of 2,000 Vandal horse;[117] and the establishment (as was the rule also both in the second and in the fourth century)[118] of a forum where the barbarians were to conduct all trade with the province. Aurelian sends on the main part of the army to Italy and a few days later follows on, "leading the accompanying force which surrounded him [*taxis etairikē*] [*comites?*—or are these the *protectores?*][119] and imperial forces and, from among the allies [barbarians] those who came from the Vandals, and the children given him as hostages." The passage must be admitted (even if the vocabulary is very imprecise) to show more than a little factual knowledge of conditions on the Danube frontier, of the Roman army and of the court.

It therefore raises in perhaps even more acute form than the "Greek" fragments the question, which we cannot answer, of how Dexippus collected his information on contemporary events. The same problem arises with Cassius Dio; but he at least was a senator, largely in Rome and able to use the

---

115. See Stein (n. 108), 48–49.

116. On the problem, for which the evidence is very sparse, R. Grosse, *Römische Militärgeschichte von Gallienus bis zum Beginn der byzantinischen Themenverfassung* (1920), 15–16; D. van Berchem, *L'armée de Dioclétien et la réforme constantinienne* (1952), 103–4. A. H. M. Jones, *The Later Roman Empire* (1964), 52–53.

117. For comparative material, see H. Callies, "Die fremden Truppen im römischen Heer des Prinzipats und die sogenannten nationalen Numeri: Beiträge zur Geschichte des römischen Heeres," *45. Bericht der röm.-germ. Kommission 1964* (1965), 130.

118. See A. Mócsy in *RE* Supp. IX, 690.

119. At this time, however, the title of *protector* seems to have been granted individually to equestrian officers. See Jones (n. 116), 53. Note the evidence in B. Gerov, "La carriera militare di Marciano, generale di Gallieno," *Athenaeum* 43 (1965): 333; T. Nagy, "Die Inschrift des Legionspräfekten P. Ael. Aelianus aus Ulcisia Castra," *Klio* 46 (1965): 339.

common knowledge of events available to all senators.[120] But what sources of information on events in Thrace or Pannonia were open to an Athenian who we have no reason to believe ever left his native city? The text gives no help;[121] and we may therefore pass to the one place where the question does not arise, Athens in 267/8.

The Herulian Invasion

Later literary sources provide only vague and disparate accounts of the Herulian attack on Athens, and none which refers to is earlier than the latter half of the fourth century; a further confusion arises from the fact that the episode apparently came at the very end of Gallienus' reign, and a decisive defeat of the Scythians was achieved only by Claudius.[122] The earliest relevant source, Aurelius Victor, has only a general sentence about attacks on Thrace, Macedonia, Achaea, and Asia Minor under Gallienus;[123] and Ammianus, in a brief digression, is similarly vague.[124] Curiously enough, it is the *Historia Augusta* (which we may now take to date to the last decade of the fourth century)[125] which is not only the earliest source to refer specifically to events at this time in Athens but is the only later source to mention Dexippus by name in his role at this moment: "[W]hile these things were happening the Scythians sailed over the Black Sea and entering (the mouth of) the Danube inflicted many grave disasters on Roman soil. Having learnt of these, Gallienus put Cleodamus and Athenaeus, Byzantines, in charge of restoring and fortifying the cities. . . . And from there they continued to Cyzicus and Asia and overran the whole of Achaia, and were defeated by the Athenians under the generalship of Dexippus, the historian of these times."[126]

Of the later Greek sources, Zosimus, firstly, devotes a single sentence to the ravaging of Greece and capture of Athens by the Scythians in the reign of Gallienus.[127] Then, under Claudius, he describes in considerable detail how Heruli, Peucae, and Goths sailed from near Tyras in 6,000 ships with

120. See Millar (n. 14), 199–73.

121. Unless we include the passing phrase in F 25 (1) on Marcianopolis: "The locals say that the sister of the emperor Trajan gave her name to the city."

122. For more detailed analyses of the sources than that given here, see A. Alföldi in *CAH* XII (1939), 721–23, and J. Straub, *Studien zur Historia Augusta* (1952), 40–41.

123. Aur. Vict., *Caes.* 33, 3; cf. Eutrop. 9, 8, 2 and Oros. 7, 22, 7.

124. Am. Marc. 31, 5, 17.

125. See Syme (n. 104).

126. *Vit. Gall.* 13, 6–8.

127. Zos. 1, 39, 1.

320,000 men, were repulsed from near Tomi and Marcianopolis, and, sailing through the Hellespont, took Thessalonica and ravaged Thessaly and Greece, but without taking any cities.[128] Of Petrus Patricius there remains only the legend quoted at the head of this chapter.[129] Syncellus mentions, in connection with the siege of Thessalonica under Gallienus, that the Greeks manned Thermopylae and built up the walls of Athens and that the Peloponnesians fortified the Isthmus;[130] we need not suppose that they had banished from their minds all memory of Herodotus. A little later, still under the reign of Gallienus, he describes how the Heruli passed through the Hellespont, took Lemnus and Scyrus, burned Athens, Corinth, Sparta, and Argos, and overran Greece—"until the Athenians, having laid an ambush for them in an area of difficult terrain, annihilated most of them."[131] The detail about the Athenian resistance, though it does not name Dexippus, clearly reflects precisely the situation of Dexippus' speech (see below). Finally, Zonaras has, under Valerian and Gallienus, an account of the siege of Thessalonica, the rebuilding of the walls of Athens, and the fortification of the Isthmus.[132] Under Claudius, he recounts another siege of Thessalonica and then the capture of Athens, and reproduces the legend about the books and the Scythian's remark; he continues, "But Kleodēmos the Athenian who had managed to get away, assembled a whole crowd, and attacked them unexpectedly with ships from the sea, killing many, and the survivors fled from there."[133] The name clearly derives in some way from "Cleodamus and Athenaeus, the Byzantines" who appear in the *Historia Augusta*; the description of his activities, however, fits Dexippus, except for the reference to ships: this (see below) fits the imperial fleet, which was in the vicinity. Thus the *Historia Augusta*, Syncellus, and Zonaras all appear to have details which derive, however remotely, from Dexippus' own account. But, for all that, only a hazardous combination can produce a coherent narrative from the later literary sources.

Archaeological evidence, however, yields a clear and definite picture of the effects of the Herulian sack.[134] Extensive burning and destruction of pub-

128. Zos. 1, 42–43.

129. *Exc. Vat.*; 169; *FHG* IV, p. 196, 9 (1) ("anon. continuator of Cassius Dio"); Dio, ed. Boissevain III, 745. For the attribution to Petrus Patricius, see Krumbacher, *Gesch. d. byz. Lit.*, 237–39.

130. Syncellus p. 715, Bonn.

131. Syncellus p. 717, Bonn.

132. Zon. 12, 23.

133. Zon. 12, 26 C–D.

134. The brief summary given here relies on H. A. Thompson, "Athenian Twilight: A.D. 267–600," *JRS* 49 (1959): 61, and A. Franz, "From Paganism to Christianity in the

lic and private buildings in the sack itself was followed in the years up to the 280s by substantial use by the inhabitants themselves of material from existing buildings for constructing a new inner line of defence (the so-called Valerian wall), which surrounded a small area north of the Acropolis, and left even the Agora itself unguarded and deserted; coin evidence shows that the wall was under construction in the reign of Probus (276–82). In this same period we lose almost all evidence of portrait sculpture, grave *stēlai*, lamp manufacture, and the export of sarcophagi; and it is at this point that the long series of ephebe lists comes to an end. A new wave of building did not come until the early fifth century. The old circuit wall, however, was restored about a century after the Herulian invasion.[135]

Thus, however inadequate our literary sources, we cannot doubt that the Athenians in 267/8 faced not a passing scare, but a violent assault on the very being of their city. It was after the capture of the city that Dexippus collected a band of men and prepared a counter-attack. For how he addressed them we have to rely on the version of his speech which he put in his *Scythica* (F 28); it deserves translation as a central document of both the history and the culture of the later third century:

> [A]nd wars are decided by courage rather than numbers. We have no mean force. Two thousand of us have gathered in all, and we have this deserted spot as a base from which to damage the enemy by attacking him in small groups and ambushing him on his way. Once we gain an advantage thus, our forces will swell and we shall strike no small fear into the enemy. If they come against us we shall resist — we have an excellent defence in this rough wooded position. If they assault us from different directions they will be thrown out by fighting against men who are unseen and not fighting like those they have faced before; they will break their line, will not know where to direct their arrows and darts, will miss their aim, and continue to suffer from our attack. We, protected by the wood, will be able to shoot accurately from positions of advantage, and will apply ourselves safely, in minimal danger. As for regular battle, if that is necessary, realize that the greatest dangers call forth the greatest courage, and at the extremity of hope endurance comes more readily. Often the unexpected has happened, when men

---

Temples of Athens," *Dumbarton Oaks Papers* 19 (1965): 185. Note also A. Frantz, "Honours to a Librarian," *Hesperia* 35 (1966): 377, and, for a contemporary coin hoard at Sparta, M. Karamesines-Oekonomidos, Χαριστήριον Α. Κ. Ὀρλάνδου III (1966), 367. See now A. Frantz, *The Athenian Agora* XXIV: *Late Antiquity, AD 267–700* (1988).

135. See A. E. Raubitschek, "Iamblichos at Athens," *Hesperia* 33 (1964): 63.

are forced by circumstances, and fighting for things they love in the hope of revenge. We could not have before us a greater cause for anger, since our families and our city are in the hands of the enemy. Those too, who have been forced against their will to fight alongside the enemy, would, once they realize our approach, join in the attack on them in the hope of freedom.

I learn that the Emperor's fleet is approaching to aid us; joined with them we shall fight nobly. And in addition I think we shall arouse the other Greeks to the same valour. I myself face the same danger and the same misfortune willingly, seeking honour and danger, longing to do noble deeds and fearing to have the honour of the city besmirched in myself. I urge you to realize this: death comes to all men, but to lay down one's life in defence of one's country is the noblest of prizes, which brings eternal fame. If anyone, even after what has been said, is dismayed by the fall of the city and so down-hearted, let him realize that many cities have been taken by a ruse of their enemies . . . [fragmentary]

Fortune too should be on our side. For our cause is just, we resist those who have gratuitously wronged us, and the divine will plays with human affairs in this way, that it most eagerly relieves misfortune and restores the sufferers. It is a noble fate to spread the glory of our city, to be ourselves an example of courage and the love of freedom to the Greeks, and to win among men now and in the future an undying fame, showing by our actions that even in disaster the resolution of Athenians is not broken. Let our watchword in battle be our children and all that is dearest to us, and to save these let us set out together for the conflict, calling on the gods who watch over and aid us.

The speech gives the factual situation quite precisely—Athens taken, 2,000 men, hoping to be joined by more, gathered in an uncultivated part of Attica, no known movement yet on the part of other Greeks, but the imperial fleet in the offing.[136] More significant are (again) the conscious Thucydidean reminiscences,[137] the heavily emphasized Athenian patriotism, and the concluding appeal to the pagan gods. Much of it, of course, might have been little different in tone or sentiment if Dexippus in his youth had composed a school oration, "Miltiades, after the defeat at Marathon, urges the Athenians to re-

---

136. See C. G. Starr, *The Roman Imperial Navy*[2] (1960), 194–95.
137. See Stein (n. 108), 67–68.

sist." But here the same sentiments were called into play in a situation of crushing destruction and real further danger. Dexippus' followers did resist, and the Scyths were driven off.

Greek Resistance to the Third-Century Invasions

It would be fruitless to try to show that the barbarian invaders everywhere met determined popular resistance in the Greek East. Our sources give numerous examples of cities taken, without mentioning such resistance. In particular one might note the case of Pityous, which was first successfully defended against the Scythians by a Roman garrison under Successianus, and then, when he was promoted elsewhere, fell easily.[138] Similarly, the *Canonical Epistle* of Gregorius Thaumaturgus,[139] which probably belongs in the 250s, lays down the procedure for dealing with those who had profited in various ways "at the time of the barbarian invasion," some even actively joining the barbarian forces.

None the less, it is a significant fact which deserves emphasis that we do have more than a little evidence of such resistance. Our earliest relevant case belongs to the second century, the Costoboccan raid on Greece in 170. Pausanias describes how an Olympic victor named Mnesibulus led a force of Elateans against the invaders and was killed.[140] It was probably on this same occasion that, as an inscription records, the free city of Thespiae despatched its own force of volunteers.[141] From the third century we have (to resume) Dexippus' evidence of Marcianopolis and Philippopolis standing siege under Decius, of Side doing likewise, and of Athenian resistance in 267/8. The siege of Thessalonica under Valerian and Gallienus was a famous event commemorated in a variety of sources.[142] Under Claudius, the *Historia Augusta*, for what that is worth, records the repulse of the barbarians from Anchialus and Nico-

138. Zos. 1, 32–33.

139. See n. 108.

140. Pausanias 10, 34, 5 and Frazer, on this passage. Cf. A. von Premerstein in *Klio* 12 (1912): 145–46. I. I. Russu, "Les Costoboces," *Dacia* 3 (1959): 341, and B. Gerov, "Die Krisis in den Ostbalkanländern während der Alleinregierung des Marcus Aurelius," *Acta Antiqua Academiae Scientiarum Hungaricae* 16 (1968): 325.

141. A. Plassart, "Une levée de volontaires Thespiens sous Marc Aurèle," *Mélanges Glotz* II (1932), 731. See esp. C. P. Jones, "The Levy at Thespiae under Marcus Aurelius," *GRBS* 12 (1971): 45.

142. Eusebius, *FGrH* F 101, 1, 2; Amm. Marc. 31, 5, 16; Zos. 1, 29, 2; Syncellus p. 715, Dindorf; Zon. 12, 23.

polis,[143] and Zosimus a similar repulse from Tomi and Marcianopolis;[144] at Tomi we have evidence of the construction or repair of the town walls at this period.[145] Here at any rate, we can gain some conception of the nature of popular resistance by going back to Ovid's description of how when the alarm sounded the population would rush in arms to the walls.[146] But resistance was not confined to those Pontic areas which had throughout their history confronted a barbarian hinterland. Apart from the cases of Athens, Thessalonica, and Side, we have from Miletus evidence of the building of a city wall,[147] and the inscription of an Asiarch named Macarius "averting the attack of man-slaying foes" ([δ]ηίων δ[ῆριν ἀλεξάμενος] ἀνδροφόνων).[148] Miletus seems to have been attacked and not taken.

The building of city walls, often rapidly and enclosing restricted areas, is a common feature of the Empire in the later third century,[149] and does not distinguish between East and West. But it is noteworthy that, if we except the marginal case of Autun which stood siege by the Gallic forces for seven months in 269,[150] there seems to be only one item of evidence from the West showing popular, civilian resistance to barbarian attack in the third century. This is an inscription from Saldae in Africa dedicated by the *iuvenes* (the young men) "because the enemy was driven away from the city walls" (*ob pulsum moenibus hostem*).[151]

This suggestion of an acute disparity between Greek East and Latin West should not be pushed too far; if nothing else, the very paucity of the evidence on either side forbids that. Nor can a sense of history be more than a part of the explanation of such Greek resistance as we find. For all the real and widespread "Roman patriotism" reflected in the Latin literature of the fourth and fifth centuries,[152] the Roman aristocracy, deeply imbued with the traditional

143. *Vita Claud.* 12, 4.

144. Zos. I, 42.

145. See I. Stoian, "La città pontica di Tomis: saggio storico," *Dacia* 5 (1961): 233, see 270–71.

146. Ovid, *Tristia* 4, 1, 71–84.

147. See *Ins. Didyma* no. 159 and comm.; cf. Robert, *Hellenica* 6 (1948): 119–20.

148. *Miletos* I, 9, no. 339a. See Magie, *Roman Rule in Asia Minor* (1950), 1566, n. 28.

149. For examples, see R. MacMullen, *Soldier and Civilian in the Later Roman Empire* (1963), 129, and Magie (n. 148).

150. See P. le Gentilhomme, "Le désastre d'Autun en 269," *REA* 45 (1943): 233.

151. *AE* 1928, 38. Cf. L. Leschi, *Études d'épigraphie, d'archéologie et d'histoire africaines* (1957), 349–50.

152. See F. Paschoud, *Roma Aeterna: études sur le patriotisme romain dans l'Occident latin à l'époque des grandes invasions* (1967).

culture, led no popular resistance to the later barbarian invasions.[153] None the less, we have to face the facts both that the Byzantine world survived against repeated attack in a way that the Latin world did not; and that a profound attachment to the classical Greek past remained fundamental to Byzantine culture.[154] So, with these perspectives in mind, one may venture to suggest that what we find in the third century is not merely that fuller literary evidence happens to reveal more about popular resistance in the Greek East; but rather that the Greek society of the Empire gained self-confidence and coherence precisely from its vigorous literary and intellectual tradition, and its intimate connection with a heroic past.

153. I owed this point to Professor A. D. E. Cameron.

154. N. H. Baynes, "The Hellenistic Civilisation and East Rome," *Byzantine Studies and Other Essays* (1955): 1.

CHAPTER FOURTEEN

The Imperial Cult
and the Persecutions*

To pose the problem of the relevance of the imperial cult to the persecutions, we may begin with a well-known passage from the *Apocalypse*: "And I saw . . . the spirits of those who had been executed for their witness to Jesus and for the word of God, and who did not bow down to worship the beast nor the image of him."[1] The "beast" is Nero, but we, like Cyprian, may understand this as a more general reference to persecution, and to the significance for persecution of the imperial cult. For Cyprian takes up this passage in his *Ad Fortunatum* 12: "He [Saint John] said: they all live and reign with Christ, not only those who were executed, but also all those who persisting in the strength of their faith [*fides*] and their fear of God, did not worship the image of the beast and did not assent to his deathly and sacriligious edicts."

We have now reached a moment when we can begin to understand some of the long-debated problems of the nature of persecution. The basis of that understanding, I believe, must be the article by T. D. Barnes in the *Journal of Roman Studies* 1968 ("Legislation against the Christians"), and the chapter on persecution in his book on Tertullian.[2] We should now accept that there is no good evidence for any general law or edict against Christianity before the reign of Decius. But we also need no longer believe that each cult in the Empire was either a *religio licita* (tolerated religion) or a *religio illicita* (forbidden religion); neither expression, I believe, appears in any ancient source. Nor

---

*First published in *Le culte des souverains*, Entretiens sur l'antiquité classique 19 (Fondation Hardt, 1973), 143–65.

1. *Apoc.* 20, 4.

2. T. D. Barnes, "Legislation Against the Christians," *JRS* 58 (1968): 32; *Tertullian: A Historical and Literary Study* (1971), chap. 9.

need we assume that there were *di publici populi Romani* (official gods of the Roman people), whom all citizens were supposed to worship; for this expression too does not appear in any ancient writer. In short, we can now devote ourselves to the specific evidence as to when, by whom, and for what reasons Christians were persecuted. And only now, when misleading assumptions about the nature of persecution are beginning to be cleared away, does it become profitable to ask what was the significance and the function of the imperial cult in the persecution of the Christians. For it is tempting to suppose, at first, that the imperial cult might supply that general, so to speak "political," explanation of persecution which scholars have often considered necessary. But the answer to the question about the role of the imperial cult in persecution may cast some light also on the wider question of its role within paganism.

But we cannot simply ask, What was the significance of the imperial cult in the persecutions? For the question has no meaning unless we say "significance to whom, and under what circumstances?" At least three different groups are involved: the people in the provinces, who actually initiated the prosecution of Christians; the provincial governors, who heard the cases and were prepared to condemn Christians as such; and the emperors themselves.

If we look first at the pagan population of the provinces, there is ever increasing evidence that the emperor-cult had an important place in public religious life and in private life; and that this place was established very early. An Oxyrhynchus papyrus shows lamplighters swearing by "Caesar, a god from a god" in the "first year of Caesar," 30/29 B.C.[3] In 3 B.C. all the people of Gangra and Phazimon-Neapolis swear loyalty by Augustus himself along with other gods.[4] From the Flavian period onwards the oath was normally taken by the *genius* or *tychē* (fortune) of the living emperor. It is exceptionally interesting for us to see among the Greek papyri from the Judaean desert a document of A.D. 127 in which a Jewish woman and a Jewish man swear by the *tychē* of the Emperor: "I swear by the *tychē* of the Lord Caesar that I have in good faith registered as written above."[5] As time went on the *tychē* came to serve as the personification of the emperor himself: an inscription from

---

3. *P. Oxy.* 1453; see E. Seidl, *Der Eid im römischägyptischen Provinzialrecht* (1933), 10.

4. For the text, see P. Herrmann, *Der römische Kaisereid* (1968), 123–24.

5. For Babatha's oath, see *P. Yadin* 16, lines 33–34, in N. Lewis, *The Documents from the Bar Kokhba Period in the Cave of Letters: Greek Papyri* (1989), 65–70; for the oath by the son of Levi, see *P. Hever* 61, lines 2–3, in H. M. Cotton and A. Yardeni, *Aramaic, Hebrew and Greek Texts from Nahal Hever and Other Sites, The Seiyâl Collection* II (Discoveries in the Judaean Desert XXVII, 1997), pp. 174–80.

Euhippe in Caria records that the city addressed itself in a petition to the *tychē* of Caracalla: "by the great *tychē* of our Lord, the Emperor Antoninus."[6]

Statues of the emperor were everywhere and were the focus of a wide variety of religious, ceremonial, and even legal functions.[7] Oxyrhynchus papyri from the reign of Caracalla, and again from the end of the reign of Constantine, show "bearers of the divine busts and of the Nikē [Victory] which precedes them."[8] The accounts of a temple at Arsinoe in A.D. 215 include a whole range of items such as the celebration of imperial dates, the care of a new statue of Caracalla, or payment to a *rhētōr* for an address before the prefect celebrating an imperial victory.[9] What is most noticeable in all these papyri, however, is the way in which the emperor takes his place among the other gods. Moreover, recent articles by L. Robert and H. W. Pleket show that at least a large proportion of the cult acts directed towards the pagan gods were addressed also to the emperor. Prayers and sacrifices were offered; a *mystikon agōn* (a competition forming part of mystery rites) was performed for Dionysus and Hadrian at Ankyra; *mysteria* (mystery rites) were performed at the temple of Rome and Augustus at Pergamon; the *Sebastophantes* who appears in Bithynian inscriptions will probably have displayed the image of the emperor at the climax of a mystery celebration.[10] Unless we deny the name of "religion" to all pagan cults, our evidence compels us to grant it also to the imperial cult.

But the imperial statue could also receive petitions. In A.D. 267 a man refusing a liturgy writes to the gymnasiarchs of Oxyrhynchus: "I immediately presented to you a petition of appeal to his excellency the *epistrategus* [the equestrian official at the head of an Egyptian district] Aelius Faustus, *ducenarius* [with an annual salary of 200,000 sesterces], and since it was not accepted, I deposited it at the *Sebasteion* there before the divine feet of our Lord, the emperor Gallienus Augustus, to be sent by the guard to the most distinguished prefect."[11] The expression "before the divine feet" gives immediate point to a passage in the *Acta* of Dasius, which relate to the Great

---

6. L. Robert and J. Robert, "La ville d'Euhippé en Carie," *CRAI* (1952): 589; *AE* 1953, 90.

7. For the literary evidence, primarily, see H. Kruse, *Studien zur offiziellen Geltung des Kaiserbildes im römischen Reiche* (1934).

8. *P. Oxy.* 1449, line 2; 1265. Cf. L. Robert, "Recherches Epigraphiques: Inscription d'Athènes," *REA* 62 (1960): 316.

9. *BGU* 362; cf. F. Blumenthal, "Der ägyptische Kaiserkult," *Archiv für Papyrusforschung* 5 (1909–13): 317.

10. L. Robert (n. 8); H. W. Pleket, "An Aspect of the Emperor Cult: Imperial Mysteries," *HThR* 58 (1965): 331.

11. *P. Oxy.* 2130. Other parallels are noted in the commentary.

Persecution; the *legatus* (governor) says to Dasius, "petition the feet of our Lords, the Kings who grant us peace."[12]

Thus both the name of the emperor and the actual statues and images of him played a real part in the life of a provincial pagan community. How did this influence their reactions to the spread of Christianity?

Before we look at the persecutions themselves, two episodes from the reign of Gaius will show how the imperial cult *might* have been used by a pagan community against a dissident group. In Jamnia in Judaea the pagans erected an altar (evidently of Gaius himself) expressly to provoke the Jewish population, who promptly destroyed it. It was the report of this incident, says Philo, which in turn provoked Gaius' plan to set up a golden statue of himself in the Temple.[13] It is also Philo who reports that amid the other outrages in Alexandria in 38, the pagans placed images of Gaius in the synagogues, and in the largest of them a bronze statue of him in a four-horse chariot.[14]

The reign of Gaius of course created quite exceptional circumstances. In general it was accepted that the Jews would not tolerate images and would not be asked to do more than make sacrifices *for* the Emperor in the Temple. But when gentiles began to convert to Christianity, might we not expect that the pagan communities in which they lived would begin to use against them the accusation of not observing the imperial cult? We do at least have in Acts 17:7 a mention of one popular accusation of disloyalty: in Thessalonica the crowd accuses Paul and Silas before the *politarchoi* (the city magistrates), declaring "All these [the Christians] act against the decrees of Caesar, saying that there is another King, Jesus."

After that, it is remarkable how *little* evidence we have of the exact form of the accusations against Christians. We can assume that they were very often accused simply *as* Christians (see I Petr. 4:15–16). But was a reference to the imperial cult never brought in by their accusers? We must confine ourselves here strictly to attested instances of accusations of Christians; the general treatments of the position of Christianity in the apologists are another matter, which we have already discussed.

So if we take the instances attested in reliable sources,[15] the motif of loyalty to the emperor, or specifically of the imperial cult, is brought in *by the*

---

12. R. Knopf, G. Krüger, and G. Ruhbach, *Ausgewählte Martyr-Akten*[4] (1965), no. 23; cf. H. Musurillo, *Acts of the Christian Martyrs* (1972), no. 21.

13. Philo, *Leg. ad Gaium* 200–203.

14. Ibid., 132–35.

15. For the criteria of authenticity in martyr acts, see most recently T. D. Barnes, "Pre-Decian *Acta Martyrum*," *JThS* 19 (1968): 509; cf. also my review of H. Musurillo (n. 12), in *JThS* 24 (1973): 239.

accuser, or by local, as opposed to Roman, officials on only one occasion in the period before the persecution of Decius. In the *Acta Polyrcarpi* 8, 2 the *eirenarch* (police official) and his father try to persuade Polycarp on the way to his trial, "What harm is there for you to say 'the Lord Caesar,' to perform the sacrifices and so forth, and to be saved?"

With the persecutions of Decius, Valerian, and the Tetrarchy the situation changes; for, as we shall see, it is now, for the first time, that imperial commands play an active role in persecution. But in this period we may still ask whether either the accusers of Christians, or local magistrates conducting cases, refer to the imperial cult. One case is the *Acta Pionii* 8; here the *neōkoros* (the temple warden), Polemon, says to Pionius: "[O]ffer sacrifice." When Pionius refuses, he says, "then offer sacrifice at any rate to the Emperor." It is noticeable that the reference to sacrifice to the Emperor is *secondary* to that to the gods in general. In the *Acta Pionii* 18, it is revealed that local pressure *had* made one Christian recant: he had made an offering at the Nemeseion at Smyrna and "had sworn by the *tychē* of the Emperor and by the Nemeseis that he is not a Christian."

After that we have a case concerning a soldier. From Eusebius (*HE* 7, 15) we have the case of Marinus in Caesarea in the early 260s. When he was about to be promoted to the centurionate, a rival accused him, saying "It is forbidden by the ancient laws for him to enjoy a Roman rank since he is a Christian and does not sacrifice to the emperors."

So far as I can discover, that is all the evidence we have which concerns either popular accusations of refusing the imperial cult, or action by *local* magistrates on the same issue. Moreover, the question of the imperial cult does not seem to be brought up at all in accusations of Christians during the Great Persecution under the Tetrarchy. The scarcity of this evidence is partly the result of the form of much of the literary evidence. Detailed descriptions of martyrdoms tend to concentrate on dialogues between martyrs and provincial governors, not on the background to them. But, none the less, the evidence of popular concern about non-observance of the imperial cult is far outweighed by the evidence for popular concern about abandonment of the pagan cults as such, especially local cults. This theme is frequent in the *Acts of the Apostles,* culminating in the great scene about Artemis of Ephesus. In Smyrna a century later what the crowd shouts against Polycarp is, "This is the teacher of Asia, the father of the Christians, *the destroyer of our gods,* the man who instructs many not to sacrifice or do reverence!" And in the anti-Christian movement in Alexandria in 249 a woman named Quinta is dragged to the *eidoleion* (the site of a group of idols of gods) and forced to do reverence (Eus., *HE* 6, 41, 4).

The context in which the question of the imperial cult *does* frequently appear is that of the examination of accused Christians by a Roman provincial governor. But even here it often appears in close conjunction with the wider question of pagan worship in general.

Before we look at the evidence, we may stop to ask what part a provincial governor played in the cults of a province, or in its cult of the emperor in particular. The evidence, which is extremely important for the whole question of what the functions of a governor really were, has never been assembled. But a few items can be mentioned. We may recall first what I mentioned earlier, the orator hired by the temple at Arsinoe to make a speech on the imperial Nikē before the prefect. Then the great inscription from Acraephia in Boeotia shows that the governor was present when the league of Achaeans and Panhellenes took the oath of loyalty to Gaius in 37.[16] More revealing is the letter of a proconsul of Asia to Aphrodisias congratulating the city on the confirmation and extension of its privileges by Severus Alexander. If it is legally possible, he says, "I will gladly come to you and stay in your most splendid city, and sacrifice to your ancestral goddess for the safety and eternal preservation of our lord the emperor Alexander and of our lady the Augusta Mammaea, mother of our lord and of the camps." But, if not, "sacrificing, as is my custom, to the other gods for the Fortune and Safety and eternal preservation" of Alexander and Mammaea, "I will call upon your native [goddess]."[17] But most striking of all is the inscription from Messene showing the quaestor P. Cornelius Scipio, who as *quaestor pro praetore* replaced the praetorian proconsul of Achaea in perhaps A.D. 1–2, carrying out the Caesarea, sacrifices for (or to?) Augustus, and causing the cities to do likewise, sacrificing an ox for the safety of Gaius on his eastern campaign, and giving orders for celebrations and sacrifices in the cities.[18]

Such evidence does give some indication that governors did take part in the cults and festivals of their provinces (indeed the rhetor "Menander" gives the formula specifically for a speech inviting a proconsul to a festival). Moreover, they also took part in the ceremonials of the imperial cult, and in this too participated in the existing local cults.

The governor's close involvement with the cults of the provincial cities comes out most clearly in Pliny's correspondence with Trajan about the

---

17. *REG* 19 (1906): 86; F. F. Abbott and A. C. Johnson, *Municipal Administration in the Roman Empire* (1926), no. 137; J. M. Reynolds, *Aphrodisias and Rome* (1982), no. 48, 174–75.

18. *SEG* XXIII (1968), no. 206; *AE* 1967, no. 458; see J. E. G. Zetzel, "New Light on Gaius Caesar's Eastern Campaigns," *GRBS* 2 (1970): 259.

Christians (*Epist.* 9, 96–97). The issue of the imperial cult does play a role, namely in Pliny's test of those accused who claimed never to have been Christians: "when they had repeated after me a formula of invocation to the gods and had made offerings of incense and wine to your statue [*imago*]." Similarly, the lapsed Christians "all did reverence to your statue and to the images of the gods [*simulacra numinum*]." Trajan's statue (*imago*) is distinguished from the *simulacra numinum*; but yet it is the object of precisely the same ritual observances.

However, it is more important to note that the main point of Pliny's letter concerns *lapsed* Christians; and that the concluding argument of his letter points to the large numbers who were currently lapsing: "[T]here is no doubt that people have begun to throng the temples which had been almost entirely deserted for a long time; the sacred rites which had been allowed to lapse are being performed again. . . . it is easy to learn from this that a great many people could be reformed if they were given an opportunity to repent." Pliny does not identify the temples concerned. There is nothing to indicate that they are those of *Roman* gods, or, still less, of the imperial cult. It is evident in fact that they are the local temples of the Pontic cities. That they should be filled with worshippers is important to Pliny and, by implication, important to Trajan.

The imperial cult thus plays a minor part in this episode. None the less, this is the earliest detailed evidence of the use of the imperial cult as a means either of compelling the submission or of justifying the punishment of Christians. We may note, however, that there is some precedent in what Josephus says of the Jewish *sicarii* (revolutionaries) who were taken prisoner in the early 70s: in spite of the most extreme tortures, he says, not one would acknowledge Caesar as "Lord" (*despotēs*).[19] This is precisely the context in which different aspects of the imperial cult appear in the majority of surviving authentic martyr acts.

So, for instance, the proconsul of Asia says repeatedly to Polycarp, "Swear by the *tychē* of the Emperor." But in the *Acts of Justin* the imperial cult is not mentioned; and in the martyrdoms at Lyon under Marcus Aurelius reported by Eusebius (*HE* 5, 1) what the slaves of the Christians relate under torture is cannibalism and incest; and what the martyrs are urged to do is "to swear by the idols." The imperial cult plays no part. In the *Acts of the Scillitan Martyrs*, however, the test is again to swear by the *genius* of the emperor. Saturninus the *proconsul* says, "we too are religious [*religiosi*] and our religion [*religio*] is simple: we swear by the *genius* of our lord the Emperor and pray for his well-

19. Jos., *BJ* 7, 10, 1 (418–19).

being—which you should do too." The *Acts of Apollon* (or *Apollonius*) as we have them are not authentic; for they are inconsistent with what Eusebius reports of the trial in *HE* 5, 21. But here too the supposed proconsul Perennius says (3), "Swear by the *tychē* of our lord Commodus," and later (7), "Sacrifice to the gods and to the image of the emperor Commodus." In the certainly authentic *Acts of Perpetua and Felicitas*, the procurator acting as a deputy of the proconsul says "sacrifice for the well-being of the emperors." But here we reach a different, and far more important, theme—that of the protection of the emperor by the gods.

We may leave for a moment the proceedings before Roman governors in the persecutions of Decius, Valerian, and the Tetrarchy. For here, unlike the previous occasions, the governor was acting within the terms of immediate imperial instructions. But we can see that up to 249, firstly, Christians were accused simply of being Christians. If other charges were added, they were *flagitia cohaerentia* (associated crimes), cannibalism or incest, rather than non-observance of the imperial cult. But the imperial cult does appear in the tests applied by the provincial governor. It was natural that it should. The letters of Pliny show that the governor took part in and supervised "vows for the safety of the Princeps" on imperial anniversaries (Plin., *Epist.* 10, 35–36, 52–53, 100–101); a passage from the *Apology* of Apuleius indicates that statues of the emperor or emperors were placed on the governor's tribunal.[20] Thus a governor could order a Christian directly to sacrifice to the imperial statue; alternatively, he could demand that the Christian sacrifice, as he did himself, to other gods *for* the emperor; or he could demand an oath by the *genius* or *tychē* of the emperor, a formula which was in daily use in provincial life.

But what of the emperor himself? How significant for him was the Christian's refusal to sacrifice to or for him, or to swear by him? Before we try to answer the question, it is necessary to say something about the nature of imperial government. The emperor was an individual, with a relatively small staff to assist him. Many emperors travelled extensively either in Italy or the provinces or, most frequently, on campaign; the amount of documents taken with them cannot have been large. It is not surprising therefore that the emperor was dependent for information on reports sent to him, or questions brought for decision. He might on occasion initiate the passing of laws or decrees of the Senate, or issue general edicts; but it is essential to emphasize that his pronouncements were far more often made as *responses* to issues brought before him. Most emperors would make these responses in the light of some coherent general principles or policies. But it is necessary to the understand-

20. Apul., *Apol.* 85. Cf. Kruse (n. 7), 79–89.

ing of the function of an emperor, and indeed of the nature of the Roman Empire, that the *application* of any such general principles by an emperor normally depended on the form, nature, and occasion of communications to him by his officials or his subjects.

So, to take the imperial cult, we may read in Suetonius *Aug.* 52: "He would not accept temples in any province unless [built] jointly in the name of Rome as well as of himself." But what this means is what M. P. Charlesworth in a classic article called "An Augustan formula, the refusal of divine honours"[21] —namely, that if a temple or other divine honours were formally *offered* by an embassy, as by Gytheum to Tiberius, or the Alexandrians to Claudius, the offer was refused, or accepted in modified terms. To the examples which Charlesworth could quote we can now add the letter of Claudius to Thasos:[22] "I decline it, judging that a temple is only for the gods." But suppose that no formal offer of a temple or honours were made by such an embassy? Then not only private documents and dedications referred to Augustus as a god, but altars and temples of Augustus appeared too; as we have seen, both Greeks and Romans in Gangra and Phazimon-Neapolis in 3 B.C. swore by the gods and Augustus in the Sebastaeia (temples of Augustus) at the altars of Augustus. Under Augustus, probably in 5 B.C., the city of Samos chose, as ambassadors to the Emperor, Gaius Iulius Amynias who was priest of Augustus, Gaius and Marcus Agrippa, and also several other men described as temple builders of Augustus.[23] There is no reason to suppose that they would have been rebuked if the offices they held had been revealed. An Oxyrhynchus papyrus (vol. XLII, 3020) shows an Alexandrian delegation, probably in 10/9 B.C., addressing Augustus as "Caesar, undefeated hero." And when a delegation from Tarraco reported to Augustus that a palm tree had grown on his altar there, his only reply was to say: "[I]t is obvious how often you use it for sacrificing."[24]

Thus the actual *application* of what we call imperial policy cannot be understood without attending to the real forms of communication to the emperor from his subjects. The same rule applies to the persecutions, and specifically to the question of the significance of the imperial cult in the persecutions.

Various different attitudes might have been adopted by emperors. On the one hand they *might* have insisted positively on the observance of the imperial

21. M. P. Charlesworth, *PBSR* 15 (1939): 1.

22. Chr. Dunant and J. Pouilloux, *Recherches sur l'histoire et les cultes de Thasos* II (1958), no. 179.

23. P. Herrmann, "Inschriften römischer Zeit aus dem Heraion von Samos," *MDAI(A)* 75 (1960): 68, no. 1; the text also in P. Herrmann, *Die römische Kaisereid* (1968), 125–26.

24. Quint., *Inst.* 6, 3, 77.

cult. We may recall the words of Gaius to the Alexandrian Jewish embassy: "So you are the god-haters, the people who do not believe that I am a god— I, who am acknowledged as a god among all other nations by this time, but am denied that title by you."[25] But such an attitude was very rare; of later emperors only Domitian is positively attested as applying the word *deus* to himself.[26] On the other hand, as I have just mentioned, the *fact* of the imperial cult in its very varied forms was accepted by all emperors. It is noticeable that Trajan accepts without comment Pliny's report of supplications to his statue, just as earlier he had accepted Pliny's request to be allowed to put a statue of him, with those of earlier Emperors, in a temple which he was constructing, "although extremely reluctant to receive honours of this kind" (10, 8–9). There is no evidence that any emperors attempted to *prevent* the use of the imperial cult as a test for Christians. Yet they could certainly have done so. It is Trajan, again, who rebukes Pliny for asking if he should hear an accusation of *maiestas* (treason) against Dio of Prusa for placing a statue of the Emperor near the graves of his son and wife—"since you know very well that it is my fixed rule not to gain respect for my name either from people's fears and dread or from charges of treason" (*Epist.* 10, 81–82).

Thirdly the emperors, in so far as they took positive attitudes to persecution, or issued orders for it, might have emphasized other factors and given the reasons for their actions. To find the answer, we must, as I said, determine in what precise ways the issue of persecution came before the emperors, and what pronouncements they issued about it. We may now, I hope, accept that there is no good evidence that any emperor before Decius issued a general edict against Christians; Tertullian's expression *institutum Neronianum* refers not to some sort of legal pronouncement of Nero but to persecution itself. Tacitus, our only detailed account of the events of 64, leaves everything obscure except that Nero's actions depended on the existing hatred of the masses for the Christians, an attitude which both Tacitus himself and Suetonius shared (Tac., *Ann.* 15, 44; Suet., *Nero* 16).

On this occasion Nero was certainly involved personally, though precisely in what way Tacitus does not tell us. After that, up to the Decian persecution, there is no authentic and concrete evidence of imperial pronouncements about the Christians *except* in the form of letters: Trajan to Pliny, Hadrian to Minucius Fundanus, proconsul of Asia (Just., *Apol.* I, 68; Eus., *HE* 4, 9), Antoninus Pius to Larissa, Thessalonica, Athens, and "all the Greeks" (Melito, Fr. ap. Eus., *HE* 4 26, 10); possibly Antoninus Pius or Marcus Aurelius to

25. Philo, *Leg. ad Gaium*, trans. E. M. Smallwood.
26. Suet., *Dom.* 13; cf. Mart. 5, 8, and D. Chr. 45, 1.

the *koinon* (league of cities) of Asia;[27] and Marcus Aurelius to the governor of Lugdunensis (*HE* V 1, 44 and 47). Of these letters all of those addressed to provincial governors were certainly responses; and, in the light of other evidence, those to cities or the *koinon* almost certainly were also.

On the other hand, the alleged "persecutions" of Septimius Severus[28] and Maximin the Thracian[29] do *not* provide any evidence of any specific action by the Emperor himself. If one surveys this evidence, one sees that what Lactantius says about the collection of imperial pronouncements concerning the Christians made by Ulpian in the seventh book of his *De officio proconsulis* (*On the proconsul's duties*) is extremely important: "[H]e collected wicked responses [*rescripta*] of the emperors in order to show what punishments should be inflicted on those who confess themselves to be worshippers of god" (*Inst.* 5, 11, 19). I would suggest that in Ulpian's time there had been *no* imperial pronouncements on the Christians other than *rescripta*—that is, answers to governors, or cities, or leagues of cities.

It is therefore not very significant that our evidence about imperial pronouncements on Christianity up to 249 contains nothing relating to the imperial cult. It is more important to examine the period of positive imperial orders—and of more explicit evidence—from A.D. 249 to 313. The surviving *libelli* (certificates) of the Decian persecution show that the imperial order was for sacrifice "to the gods," as such.[30] The best martyr act of this period, the *Acta of Pionius*, confirms this: Polemon the temple warden says to Pionius, "You certainly know that the edict of the Emperor commands you to sacrifice to the gods." It is only after the refusal of this that he suggests that Pionius sacrifice at least to the Emperor. Other less certainly authentic evidence confirms the terms of the order of Decius.[31] So does a letter of Cyprian

27. Eus., *HE* 4, 13. An alternative text of this letter, which is (in either form) certainly at least partly spurious, in *Cod. Par. Gr.* 450 (*GCS* IX 1, p. 328). For this and what follows, see Barnes (n. 2, 1968), 37–43.

28. See K. H. Schwarte, "Das angebliche Christengesetz des Septimius Severus," *Historia* 12 (1963): 185.

29. See G. W. Clarke, "Some Victims of the Persecution of Maximinus Thrax," *Historia* 15 (1966): 445.

30. See H. Knipfing, "The Libelli of the Decian Persecution," *HThR* 16 (1923): 345.

31. The Latin recension of the *Acts of Carpus, Papylus and Agathonice* (Knopf, Krüger, and Ruhbach [n. 12], no. 2; Musurillo [n. 12], no. 2) is dated specifically to the reign of Decius (paras. 1 and 7), and has (para. 2), "sacrifice to the gods in accordance with the instruction of the Emperor." Cf. the *Acts of Maximus* (Knopf, Krüger, and Ruhbach [n. 12], no. 12), "he sent orders throughout the world that the Christians would withdraw from the living

from 252, which *may*, however, refer to a renewed persecution under Gallus: he refers to "sacrifices which the people are commanded to celebrate in an edict displayed in public."[32]

It is essential to emphasize that what was ordered was sacrifice "to the gods." For A. Alföldi, for instance, has asserted that the imperial cult was important in the persecution of Decius;[33] and it has often been assumed that the gods in question were the "gods of the state" or even the *di publici populi Romani* (official gods of the Roman people).[34] But to understand our evidence in that way is to impose a semi-political interpretation of these events; the essential thing, however, is precisely that the terms used are religious and not political.

From the persecution under Valerian we have three excellent sources of evidence, the letters of Cyprian (*Epist.* 76–81), the *Acta Proconsularia* of his two trials, and the letters of Dionysius of Alexandria, preserved by Eusebius (*HE* 7, 10–11). Between them they show that there were imperial orders for the banning of Christian meetings, the exclusion of Christians from their cemeteries, and the punishment of bishops and presbyters; and also for the punishment of senators, equestrians—and *Caesariani* (imperial employees) who were Christians. But what of the orders for sacrifice? In the *Acta Proconsularia* we find the proconsul of Africa in 257 saying to Cyprian something for which no other source offers a true parallel: "the most holy emperors Valerianus et Gallienus deigned to send me a letter in which they enjoined on those who do not practice Roman religion to respect Roman [religious] ceremonies." After Cyprian's exile, the proconsul of the next year again orders him to "perform the rites" (*caerimoniari*), and on his refusal condemns him as "an enemy . . . of the Roman gods and the holy religious ceremonies [*religiones*]"; nor, he says, have the emperors been able "to recall you . . . to follow their rites."

I must confess that I do not fully understand the significance of these expressions. But what is clear is that they contain no explicit reference to the

---

and true god and sacrifice to idols"; cf. Gregory of Nyssa, *V. Gr. Thaum.* (*PG* XLVI, cols. 893–958), in col. 944.

32. *Epist.* 59, 6. Cf. *Epist.* 57, 1 of the same year forecasting a new persecution, and Eus., *HE* 7, 1 (Dionysius' letter to Hermammon).

33. Alföldi, "Zu den Christenverfolgungen in der Mitte des 3. Jahrhunderts," *Klio* 31 (1938): 323–48 (334); *Studien zur Geschichte der Weltkrise des 3. Jahrhunderts nach Christus* (1967), 285.

34. For example by J. Molthagen, *Der römische Staat und die Christen im zweiten and dritten Jahrhundert* (1970), 63, 79, 93–98.

imperial cult as such. Even clearer is the verbatim record of the trial of Dionysius, bishop of Alexandria, before Aemilianus, who tells Dionysius and his companions that the emperors have given them the chance to save themselves, "if you wish to take the course of nature and prostrate yourselves before the gods who keep their kingdom safe." This is explicitly a documentary record, and it is as clear as possible that the imperial order commanded sacrifice to the gods as such.[35] The imperial cult finds no place here. The concept which *is* present is a quite different one, the protection of the emperors' rule by the gods.

Finally, the connection between the worship of the gods and of the emperors appears in a different form in the martyrdom of Fructuosus and others in 259. Here, again, the *legatus* of Tarraconnensis says that the emperors "enjoined the worship of the gods" (*praeceperunt deos coli*), but continues later "*they* [the gods] are hearkened to, they are feared, they are revered; if the gods are not worshipped, neither are the emperors' countenances revered." If I understand this passage, it exhibits the worship of the emperors as one facet of the worship of the gods in general.

When we come to the "Great" Persecution all our reliable evidence shows that the first imperial order which explicitly commanded a general sacrifice was in the Fourth Edict, of 304, repeated by Maximin in 305–6 and 308–9.[36] So far as our evidence goes, it contained no reference to sacrifice to the emperors.

None the less, even before the Fourth Edict, the test of sacrifice to the gods, and rarely to the emperors, continued to be applied by provincial governors. So in 303 Procopius of Scythopolis is ordered first to sacrifice to the gods, and then, when he refuses, to pour a libation to the four emperors (Eus., *MP* 1, 1). That is, however, the *only* reference to the imperial cult in the short recension of the *Martyrs of Palestine*. In the long recension, preserved in Syriac, there is one other case, also from 303: Alphaeus, a reader and exorcist in the church at Caesarea, is ordered by the governor to sacrifice to the emperors (1, 54).

The emperors are mentioned again in the *Acts of S. Crispina*, when the proconsul explains that it has been ordered by the emperors "that you should sacrifice to all our gods for the well-being [*salus*] of our emperors." The theme is thus exactly the same as that in the trials of Perpetua and Felicitas and of

35. Eus., *HE* 7, 11, 6–11.

36. For the details, see G. E. M. de Ste. Croix, "Aspects of the 'Great' Persecucion," *HThR* 47 (1954): 75.

Dionysius of Alexandria. But here also, as in the *Acta Proconsularia* of Cyprian, the proconsul refers explicitly to the Roman god—"put your head under the yoke of the holy ceremonies [*sacra*] of the Roman gods"; and later says, "we request that with your head bowed you should burn incense in the holy temples to the gods of the Romans." Does *dei Romanorum* here mean specifically the gods of the city of Rome? Or does it mean simply the pagan gods?

What is important about the Great Persecution is that we have a great deal of very explicit evidence about it: for instance, the arguments of a pagan philosopher in favour of persecution, reported by Lactantius (*Inst.* 5, 2); the background of traditional piety expressed by Diocletian and Maximin in their constitutions on incest and on Manicheism;[37] some details of the successive edicts on persecution; the petition of Lycia-Pamphylia to Maximin (*TAM* II 3, 785), and the letter of Maximin to the city of Tyre; and the pronouncements of Galerius, Maximin, Constantine, and Licinius by which persecution was ended. In all this, and in Lactantius' extensive discussion of persecution in the *Divine Institutes* (4, 27; 5, 11; 13–14; 19–24), the imperial cult plays no part at all. Unless we are to reject all our evidence, we must conclude that the Tetrarchic persecutions, like those of the mid-third century, were concerned with the preservation of the pagan cults as such. So Lactantius reports the proclamation of the anonymous pagan philosopher (*Inst.* 5, 2): "Above all the task of the philosopher is to come to the rescue of men who err and recall them back to the right road, that is, to the worship of the gods whose divinity and majesty governs the world."

The evidence for the persecutions is of some importance precisely because it was so rare for the emperor to institute measures which directly and positively affected, or were intended to affect, the whole population of the Empire (even so, of course, the actual carrying out of all the major persecutions was partial and episodic). It had also been very rare, up to this period, for an emperor to express so elaborately and in such detail the reasons for his actions and the attitude to the world which lay behind them. We can see as the culmination of this development the exposition of paganism in Maximin's letter to Tyre in 312.[38] If the imperial cult does not appear prominently in our evidence for the major persecutions, we cannot say it is because our evidence itself is too limited.

Must we then conclude, on the evidence of the persecutions of Chris-

37. *Mos. et Rom. legum collatio* VI 4, 1; XV 3. See J. Vogt, *Zur Religiosität der Christenverfolger im römischen Reich* (1962), 25.

38. Eus., *HE* 9, 7, 3–14.

tians, that the imperial cult was not of any real significance; that, as has been argued so many times, and even in major works on ancient religion,[39] it was a set of formalities, empty of all truly religious content or feeling?

Of course, we shall never know or understand fully the religious experience of pagans in antiquity. By its very nature, our evidence can only tell us about their rituals and cults, about the language they used in literature or private life, or about how they actually behaved in different situations. All that we can say, therefore, is, firstly, that the conception of a human attaining divine status had already long been integral to ancient paganism;[40] and, secondly, that the imperial cult was fully and extensively integrated into the local cults of the provinces, with the consequence that the emperors were the object of the same cult acts as the other gods.

I would like to suggest that it is precisely this integration of the imperial cult into the wider spectrum of pagan cults which is the first reason why it plays only a modest role in the persecutions. The second reason is that, both for the people and, in the end, for the emperors themselves, there was a real fear of the abandonment of the ancient gods, and of the loss of the protection which they extended to the cities and to the Empire as a whole. It was only the men in the middle, the provincial governors and, less often, the magistrates of provincial cities, who, when Christians were brought before them, regularly applied the test of recognition of the imperial cult but, along with that, of the cults of the other gods. The persecutions cannot be explained in political terms, as demands for formal displays of loyalism. They were motivated by feelings which we must call religious; among those religious feelings the worship of the emperor played a real but a minor part. The most important conception which lay behind the persecutions was precisely the one which was to be the foundation of the Christian Empire: that the world was sustained, and the earthly government of it granted, by divine favour. It is thus entirely appropriate that it is in the edict of toleration of Galerius in 311 that an emperor first looks forward to the protection of the Christian god: "[T]he Christians will be obliged to pray to their god for our safety [*salus*] and that of the state, and their own."[41]

39. E.g., K. Latte, *Römische Religionsgeschichte* (1960), 312–26; M. Nilsson, *Geschichte der griechischen Religion* II² (1961), 384–95.

40. Apart from standard works, such as Lily Ross Taylor, *The Divinity of the Roman Emperor* (1931), and Chr. Habicht, *Gottmenschentum und griechische Städte*² (1970), note especially D. M. Pippidi, "Apothéoses imperiales et apothéose de Peregrinos," *Studi e materiali di storia delle religioni* 21 (1947–48): 77, and S. Weinstock, *Divus Julius* (1972), 287–96.

41. Lactantius, *De mort. pers.* 34; Eus., *HE* 8, 17.

CHAPTER FIFTEEN

The World of the Golden Ass*

Those who study and teach the history of the ancient world suffer from a great disadvantage, which we find difficult to admit even to ourselves: in a perfectly literal sense we do not know what we are talking about. Of course, we can dispose of a vast range of accumulated knowledge *about* what we are talking about. We can compile lists of office-holders in the Roman Empire, without our evidence revealing how government worked or even whether it made any impact at all on the ordinary person; we can discuss the statuses of cities and look at the archaeological remains of some of them (or rather some parts of some of them) without having any notion of their social and economic functions, or of whether it made any real difference whether an inhabitant of the Roman provinces lived in a small city or a large village. We can study the remains of temples, the iconography of gods and goddesses, the nature of myth, ritual and sacrifice; but how and in what way did all this provide an important or intelligible context for a peasant in the fields? In the case of religion in particular our attention turns persistently to the exceptional rather than the ordinary, to those aspects which were novel, imported, mystical, or the subject of philosophical speculation. Let me take a precise example from the *Metamorphoses* or *Golden Ass*, Apuleius' brilliant novel of the second century A.D. The exotic aspects of ancient religion which the novel reveals have always attracted attention: the hero's vision of Isis, and

*First published in *JRS* 71 (1981): 63–75, and reprinted in S. J. Hornblower, ed., *Oxford Readings in the Roman Novel* (1999), 247. This chapter represents the almost unaltered text of an Inaugural Lecture given at University College London on 2 March 1981. I am very grateful to Michael Crawford and Nicholas Horsfall for information and discussions on various points.

his conversion to the worship of Isis and Osiris;[1] the band of Syrian priests making their fraudulent way through the Greek countryside;[2] the wicked baker's wife who has abandoned the gods and worships what she says is a single god—in other words, is a Christian.[3] But if we really want to understand how the divine order related to ordinary life in antiquity we should start from an incident a few chapters later (9, 33–34). Strange portents occur in a farm-house: a hen lays a live chicken, blood rises from the floor and wine standing in jars in the wine store begins to boil. The farmer and his friends are reduced to bewilderment: what steps should they take, with how many sacrifices of what sort are they to appease the threats of the heavenly powers? They are *afraid*, just as the pagan world was afraid when too many people began to follow the example of the baker's wife and abandoned sacrifice to the gods.

This story, as Apuleius tells it, has another important characteristic. Rather as in *Wuthering Heights*, the remarkable and fantastic goings-on in Apuleius' novel take place in a solidly realistic background, in this case a farm-house with chickens in the yard, wine jars in store, sheepdogs and sheep. Indeed, I am going to suggest that the realism of tone in the novel may extend beyond purely physical descriptions, to realistic images of social and economic relations, to the framework of communal life in a Roman province, and even, here and there, to the wider context of what it meant to be a subject of the Roman Empire.

I must make clear first how paradoxical this claim is. What we are concerned with is a novel of some 250 pages written in Latin in the second century A.D. by Apuleius, who came from the province of Africa. It is set, however, not in Africa but in central and northern Greece, in the Roman provinces of Achaea and Macedonia.[4] The basic narrative is not original to Apuleius, for it already existed in the form of a longish short story in Greek,

1. *Met.* 11. See esp. J. Gwyn Griffith, *Apuleius of Madauros: The Isis-Book* (*Metamorphoses, Book* XI) (1975).

2. *Met.* 8, 24–29, 10. See F. Cumont, *Les religions orientales dans le paganisme romain*[4] (1929), chap. 5.

3. *Met.* 9, 14. See esp. T. D. Barnes, *Tertullian* (1971), app. 21; M. Simon, "Apulée et le Christianisme," *Mélanges d'histoire des religions offerts à Henri-Charles Puech* (1974), 299.

4. It is quite probable, as argued by G. W. Bowersock, "Zur Geschichte des römischen Thessaliens," *Rh. Mus.* 108 (1965): 277, that Thessaly was transferred from Achaea to Macedonia at the moment of Nero's grant of freedom in 67. As he points out (pp. 285–86), *ILS* 1067 does not imply that Thessaly is within the same province as Athens, Thespiae, and Plataea. But it is in any case clear from Ptolemy, *Geog.* 3, 12, 13–14, and 42 (Müller), that in Pius' reign Thessaly was part of Macedonia; cf. L. Robert, *Hellenica* V, 29–30.

of which one version survives.[5] A brief summary of this story will also give
the main narrative thread of the *Golden Ass*, which uses all the main incidents.
A young man of good family from Patras named Lucius tells the story in the
first person. He had been travelling on business in Thessaly, a region whose
women had a reputation for magical practices.[6] In Hypata he had an affair
with a slave girl, who allowed him to observe her mistress using magic arts
to turn herself into an owl. Lucius asked for the same potion, got the wrong
one, and was turned into an ass instead (keeping his human intellect and
power of observation). When robbers raided the house, they took him away
with them; after various adventures he was rescued, put to work in a mill,
sold at Beroea in Macedonia to some Syrian priests, then in turn to a baker
and a market gardener, was requisitioned by a soldier, and finally bought by
a rich man from Thessalonica. There a lady fell in love with him and insisted
on his making love to her. The master found out and decided to include a
scene of the ass making love to a condemned female prisoner in a public show
which he was about to put on. Just in time before this public degradation, the
ass had been able to apply the formula for release — eating some roses — and
was changed back into human form. At this point the story, which is curiously dull in Greek, reaches a rather fine black-comedy ending. For Lucius,
in human form, rushes back to the lady, only to find that she thinks him
no longer adequately equipped, and has him ignominiously thrown out. He
sets off home, grateful to have escaped from the consequences of his asinine
curiosity.

There is no possible doubt that Apuleius based his novel on a version of
this story; indeed, he explicitly tells the reader that it derived from a Greek
original.[7] However, he has transformed it in various ways. Firstly, he makes
the hero, again called Lucius, come from Corinth, and has the story end there
rather than in Thessalonica. Secondly, he replaces the black-comedy ending by the famous and brilliantly described scene of the release of Lucius
by the goddess Isis and his subsequent conversion. Thirdly, curiosity (*curiositas*), and its improper application to supernatural things, now becomes a

5. I refer to *Lucius or the Ass* preserved in the works of Lucian (most readily available in
the Loeb Lucian, vol. VIII, 47–48), and venture no further on the question of the authorship of this or its relation to the *Metamorphoses* of (?) Lucius of Patras, briefly summarised
by Photius, *Bibl.*, cod. 129. For all these questions, see H. Van Thiel, *Der Eselsroman* I–II
(1971–72).

6. For other allusions, see Bowersock (n. 4), 278.

7. *Met.* 1, 1. See esp. A. Mazzarino, *Le milesia e Apuleio* (1950); H. J. Mason, "Fabula
Graecanica; Apuleius and His Greek Sources," in B. L. Hijmans and R.Th. van der Paardt,
Aspects of Apuleius' Golden Ass (1978), 1. Cf. J. Tatum, *Apuleius and the Golden Ass* (1979).

serious theme running through the novel;[8] at the end the priest of Isis says to Lucius "because you sank to servile pleasures, you have earned the ill reward of your unfortunate *curiositas*" (11, 15). Fourthly, in the Isis scene, and the subsequent conversion, Apuleius *may*—as is generally assumed—be importing into the novel a profound personal experience; and he may even at the end intend to blur the distinction between himself as author, from the African city of Madauros, and Lucius the hero and narrator; for Lucius, who comes from Corinth, has been to Rome to study rhetoric in Latin and finishes up (rather tamely) at the end of the novel as a successful advocate in Rome.[9] Apuleius himself, born in the 120s, had studied in Carthage, then went to Athens to pursue the study of Greek literature and philosophy and at some stage also practised as an advocate in Rome. In a speech before the proconsul of Africa in 162–63, Apuleius boasted that he had written a whole variety of literary works in prose and verse, in both Greek and Latin.[10] In other words the author of the novel and its fictional narrator have crossed the boundary between the Greek- and Latin-speaking worlds in very similar ways but in opposite directions.

So in the novel Apuleius is portraying a young man from a provincial upper-class society closely parallel to his own. He also, of course, knew Athens and very likely Corinth.[11]

But when he describes in the novel the world of the small towns of central and northern Greece, I cannot say whether he is using personal knowledge or imposing his conceptions of what was typical. In any case we must remember the distance between the author and his theme: he is describing in Latin a

8. See esp. S. Lancel, " 'Curiositas' et préoccupations spirituelles chez Apulée," *Rev. Hist. Relig.* 160 (1961): 25; J. Tatum (n. 7), 22–23, 76–77; and esp. A. Wlosok, "Zur Einheit der Metamorphosen des Apuleius," *Philol.* 113 (1969): 68.

9. For the "conversion," see n. 1 and, e.g., A. D. Nock, *Conversion* (1933), chap. 9. For speculations on the autobiographical element, see, e.g., J. Hicter, "Autobiographie dans l'Âne d'or d'Apulée," *Ant. Class.* 13 (1944): 95; 14 (1945): 61. But note the salutary scepticism of J.-C. Fredouille, *Apulée, Metamorphoses Livre XI* (1975).

10. *Flor.* 9, 27–29. There is no need to rehearse here the biographical evidence about him, which is collected in M. Schanz, C. Hosius, and G. Krüger, *Geschichte der römischen Literatur* III³ (1922), 100–102.

11. For his possible knowledge of Corinth and Cenchreae, see, e.g., P. Veyne, "Apulée à Cenchrées," *Rev. Phil.* 39 (1965): 241; H. J. Mason, "Lucius at Corinth," *Phoenix* 25 (1971): 160. For Cenchreae, see now R. Scranton, J. W. Shaw, and L. Ibrahim, *Kenchreai: Eastern Port of Corinth* I: *Topography and Architecture* (1978): esp. 71 on the possible site of the shrine of Isis (Paus. 2, 2, 3). For a collection of evidence on Corinth, J. Wiseman, "Corinth and Rome I: 228 B.C.–A.D. 267," *ANRW* VII.1 (1979), 438.

society which spoke Greek; but, far more important, in narrating the adventures of the ass he is making a fictional journey which descends through all levels of contemporary society. It is therefore a highly self-conscious literary process which has given us some of the very rare representations of lower-class life in the literature of the High Empire. The framework of the existing story is used quite deliberately for social observation: precisely at the point where Lucius as the ass finds himself at the lowest context which he reaches on the economic and social scale—among the wretched slaves working in a mill—he reflects on the opportunities for observation which fortune has granted to him (9, 13):

> Nor was there any comfort for the torments of my existence except that I was sustained by my innate curiosity, in that ignoring my presence they all acted and spoke freely as they wished. Quite rightly the divine author of ancient poetry among the Greeks, wishing to portray a man of the highest wisdom, sang of how he had reached the highest qualities by travelling around many cities and gaining the acquaintance of varied peoples; so I myself give grateful thanks to my ass's shape, in that concealed behind it and tested by various fortunes I was rendered if not very wise, at least more experienced.

It is thus that Apuleius, looking through the eyes of Lucius transformed into an ass, can give his unique description of the slaves toiling in the mill, dressed in a few rags, their half-naked bodies scarred with the marks of beatings, their foreheads branded, their heads half-shaved, their feet in fetters, all of them covered in a fine dust of flour (9, 12). It is undeniable that the novel expresses a rare and distinctive level of sympathy with the working lives of the poor.[12] But that is all; I am not suggesting that Apuleius was a proto-Engels, writing his *Condition of the Working Class in Greece.* If there is a parallel to any work of nineteenth-century literature it is, of course, to Anna Sewell's *Black Beauty,* which by a similar device offers a rather underestimated portrait of the different levels of Victorian society from the point of view of bourgeois sentimentality.

The *Golden Ass* has rightly been called an anti-epic,[13] in which the hero or anti-hero endures a variety of misfortunes before a final liberation from trials. But beyond that there are three original and significant features of its

12. See the interesting if not entirely convincing essay by N. Fick, "Les Metamorphoses d'Apulée et le monde du travail," in J. M. André et al., *Recherches sur les artes à Rome* (1978), 86.

13. See G. Cooper, "Sexual and Ethical Reversal in Apuleius: The *Metamorphoses* as Anti-Epic," in C. Deroux, ed., *Studies in Latin Literature and Roman History* II (1980), 436.

literary character, which are essential to its uses for the historian. Firstly, it is set firmly and unmistakably in the immediate present. The original Greek short story is indeed also set in the Roman Empire. But Apuleius makes Lucius the relative of two real historical persons: Plutarch, who had died in the 120s, and his nephew, the philosopher Sextus of Chaeronea, whom Marcus Aurelius still went to hear when he was emperor after 161.[14]

Secondly, and more important, Apuleius fills out the story with a whole series of separate tales or narratives related by characters in it. One of these, the romance of Amor and Psyche, which is narrated to comfort a young lady captured by the robbers, is quite distinct from the others, for it is set in an imaginary time and place and occupies some fifty printed pages; since it has no obvious literary or thematic connection with the rest of the work, endless displays of ingenuity and erudition have gone into demonstrating that this non-apparent connection really is there.[15] But all the other, much shorter stories which Apuleius has added are set in the same time, place, and social context as the main narrative; all offer at least parallels to, or foreshadowings of, episodes in the main story; and the majority are necessary for explaining its development.[16] It is the combined total of the main story and these nar-

---

14. *Met.* 1, 2; 2, 2–3. For Plutarch and his family, see C. P. Jones, *Plutarch and Rome* (1971), chap. 1. For Marcus still hearing Sextus of Chaeronea while Emperor, Philostratus, *Vit. Soph.* 2, 1; Dio 71, 1, 2. For terminology in the novel implying a setting in the mid-second century, see also n. 19 below.

15. See, e.g., P. Grimal, *Apulée, Metamorphoseis* (IV, 28–VI, 24) (*le conte d'Amour et Psyche*) (1963); G. Binder and R. Merkelbach, eds., *Amor und Psyche* (*Wege der Forschung*, 1968); F. E. Hoevels, *Märchen und Magie in den Metamorphosen des Apuleius von Madaura* (1979), 1: "The enquiry into the meaning of the Amor and Psyche episode (4, 28–26, 24) was and has remained the central question in Apuleius studies to this day."

16. The narrated "real-life" episodes are (1) 1, 5–19, Aristomenes' story, told by himself and set in Hypata; (2) 2, 13–14, the story of Diophanes the Chaldaean at Corinth, told by Lucius' host Milo; (3) 2, 21–30, Thelyphron's story, told by himself and set in Larissa; (4) 4, 9–21, the story of the robber Lamachus and others, told by one of his companions and set in Boeotia; (5) 7, 5–8, the exploits of the pretended robber Haemus, told by himself (in reality, Tlepolemus) and set in Macedonia and Epirus; (6) 8, 1–14, the story of Charite and Tlepolemus, told by one of her slaves; exact setting unclear, but in the same region as the rest; (7) 9, 5–7, the *faber* and his wife; narrator not indicated; (8) 9, 17–21, the decurion Barbarus and his wife's lover, told by an old woman to the baker's wife; (9) 9, 35–38, the fate of the three sons of the *hortulanus'* rich patron, narrator not identified; (10) 10, 2–12, the story of the wicked stepmother, overheard from conversations by the ass, and set somewhere in Thessaly; (11) 10, 23–28, the story of the condemned Corinthian woman; no specific narrator.

rated episodes, some two hundred printed pages of text, which I have called the world of the *Golden Ass*.

But, thirdly, the reason why it is worth exploring this world is the one which I hinted at earlier: that Apuleius clothes his sequence of fantastic episodes in a mass of vivid, concrete, and realistic detail, on physical objects, houses, social structure, economic relations, the political framework of the local communities, and the wider political framework of the Empire. Let me start with an example relating to the emperor. Apuleius borrows from the Greek short story the episode in which the ass, being driven towards their mountain hideout by the robbers, decides to appeal for the Emperor's protection (3, 29). Speaking in Greek of course, he starts off on the words "O Caesar," can manage a loud bray of "O"—but is not equipped to pronounce the rest. Apuleius makes him choose a moment when the robbers are passing by a large village (*vicus*), which is especially full of people because a fair is being held there. Both the short story and the novel offer a very significant image or model of how the emperor was conceived of as an ever present protector. Apuleius adds a revealing presumption about the structure and functioning of social and economic life in the countryside.[17] So, I suggest, we can use the representations in Apuleius in at least three ways: as portrayals of areas of social life which ancient literature usually passes over; as adding colour to patterns which we know already from other, more formal evidence; and—most important—as offering *alternative* models of society to those which we normally accept.

If we combine the main narrative and the stories attached to it into a "world of the *Golden Ass*," we can see that this world of small Greek towns and villages is not at all isolated from a wider context. Lucius himself has been to Rome and returns there at the end; a Chaldaean soothsayer plies his trade in Corinth (2, 12–14); a young man has come from Miletus to see the Olympic games (2, 21); an Egyptian prophet displays his magical skills in Larissa (2, 28); a group of Syrian priests journeys from village to village (8, 24–9, 10). Travel between different regions of the Empire is simply presumed as an aspect of the wider context.

That presumption affects the wider political framework too. The ass is briefly owned by a soldier, who sells him when ordered to go off to Rome with a letter for the emperor (10, 13); letters carried by messenger between governors and emperor were in fact the essential mechanism which allowed a centralized, if passive, government to be carried on. The emperor is invoked

17. For comparative material, see the important article by R. MacMullen, "Market-Days in the Roman Empire," *Phoenix* 24 (1970): 333.

in oaths and prayers (9, 41; 11, 17—along with the Senate, the equestrian order, and the Roman people)—and there is no mistaking the consciousness of the characters that they live in a world with a single ruler,[18] whose name might in principle be used to gain protection. But a real and active intervention by the emperor will only come about in very special circumstances. This is perfectly shown in the false story told to the robbers by a rich young man who arrives at their hideout in disguise to rescue his fiancée. He has to persuade them both that he himself is a famous robber who would add strength to their band and that he has had a convincing piece of bad luck, leading to the destruction of his own band. So he says that he is the renowned robber Haemus whose band had ravaged Macedonia. But by ill-luck a high-ranking *procurator* (financial officer) of the emperor (a *ducenarius*)[19] had lost favour at court and been exiled to the island of Zacynthus—and it was when he, his faithful wife, and their escort of soldiers were staying en route at an inn at Actium that the robbers had happened to attack it and were driven off. They (the robbers) had withdrawn unscathed. But the *procurator's* wife had afterwards gone back to the emperor and successfully petitioned him both for the restoration of her husband and for the despatch of detachments (*vexillationes*) of legions to destroy the band of robbers.

As it happens, we have an inscription from just this period which records that in about 176 detachments of legions from Moesia were sent south to the territory bordering on Macedonia and Thrace to "dislodge" a band of Thracian brigands.[20] But far more important is the implication that, in unim-

---

18. For the theme of the function of the imperial cult in inducing consciousness of belonging to a single political framework, see K. Hopkins, *Conquerors and Slaves* (1978), chap. 5: "Divine Emperors or the Symbolic Unity of the Roman Empire."

19. *Met.* 7, 6: "a procurator of the princeps who filled a ducenariate post" (*procuratorem principis ducenaria perfunctum*). This is only the second recorded usage of the term, the earliest being Suetonius, *Claudius* 24. Documentary uses begin in the reign of Marcus Aurelius with *AE* 1962, 183: "To the rank of a ducenariate procurator" (*ad ducenariae procurationis splendorem*). See *JRS* 53 (1963): 197 (chapter 8 in this volume), and H.-G. Pflaum in *Bonn. Jahrb.* 171 (1971): 349. For the deployment of a fairly new technical term, note also "legal representative of the imperial treasury" (*fisci advocatus*, 7, 10), used ironically of one of the robbers; for its coming into use in Hadrian's reign, see *HA, v. Had.* 20, 6; for the earliest attested case, W. Eck, *RE* Supp. XV, col. 123, s.v. "Iulius" (228a).

20. *AE* 1956, 124, see Pflaum, *Carrières*, no. 181 *bis* (M. Valerius Maximianus): ("put in charge of legionary detachments and sent to the territory between Macedonia and Thracia to get rid of the band of Brisean robbers" (*praeposito vexillationibus et at (sic) detrahendam Briseorum latronum manum in confinio Macedon(iae) et Thrac(iae) ab Imperatore misso*). On the Brisei, see Pflaum, *Carrières*, I, 489.

portant areas like Macedonia and Epirus, only an accident could have stirred the imperial will to action to restore public order; and, more important still, that the mechanism for bringing this about would have been the petition or literally "prayer" (*preces*) of an influential person, answered by the assent, or literally "nod" (*nutus*) of the emperor. Precisely this model of the operations of government was the central theme of *The Emperor in the Roman World.*

If it was only in special circumstances that the emperor would make his distant presence felt, what of the governor of the province—or rather the two proconsular governors of the two provinces—for when Apuleius was writing, probably around 170, Thessaly was part of Macedonia, whose proconsul had his base in Thessalonica?[21] Both he and the proconsul of Achaea, with his seat at Corinth, will have had a few auxiliary units of soldiers.[22] But in the world described by Apuleius neither they nor any other forces perform regular police functions in town or country.[23] Indeed, when the slave girl describes to Lucius the serious dangers of going out at night in Hypata, she says explicitly "nor can the *auxilia* of the governor, far away as they are, rid the city of such carnage."[24] In the scenes set in Thessaly the Roman proconsul never appears in person. But he is mentioned at least in the scene where the ass's current master, a gardener, is riding home from market; a soldier appears, questions him in Latin, and on getting no answer beats him with his stick.[25] Then he starts again in Greek, saying that the ass must be requisi-

21. For the division, see n. 4. The proconsul of Macedonia appears in the last section of *Lucius or the Ass* (54–55).

22. See E. Ritterling, "Military Forces in the Senatorial Provinces," *JRS* 17 (1927): 28; R. K. Sherk, "Roman Imperial Troops in Macedonia and Achaea," *AJPh* 78 (1957): 52 (not considering the evidence from Apuleius); also W. Eck, "Prokonsuln und militärisches Kommando. Folgerungen aus Diplomen für prokonsulare Provinzen," *Heer und Integrationspolitik. Die römischen Militärdiplome als historische Quelle* (Passauer Historische Forschungen 2, 1986), 518–34.

23. In this the novel contrasts clearly with the martyr acts, where Roman soldiers perform an active police role; see G. Lopuszanski, "La police romaine et les Chrétiens," *Ant. Class.* 20 (1951): 5.

24. *Met.* 2, 18.

25. The soldier is described simply as a *miles* but has *vitis* (a staff) with a thickened end (normally thought of as the mark of a centurion); see, e.g., G. Webster, *The Roman Imperial Army*[2] (1979), 132. Exactly the same contradiction confronts us in the grave relief of a *miles* from Corinth; see M. Šašel Kos, *JRS* 68 (1978): 22, who also notes (p. 23) that there are a number of such depictions of soldiers with a *vitis* from Achaea and Macedonia, and suggests (p. 24) some connection with service in the so-called unarmed provinces (*provinciae inermes*).

tioned for transporting the baggage of the governor (*praeses*) from the next village (9, 39). The gardener had evidently not read the *Discourses* of Epictetus, published a few decades earlier; for there the advice is given that in exactly this situation one should give up one's ass promptly when a soldier demands it and avoid a beating.[26] At any rate he knocks down the soldier and makes off. This soldier apparently belongs to a unit which is escorting the governor,[27] and the scene provides a small fictional example of much the most important area of contact and conflict between state and subject in the Roman Empire—that is, the provision of animals, waggons, supplies, and accommodation for passing messengers and officials, or troops on the move. The tensions thus created are reflected in long series of complaints on the one side and of pronouncements by governors and emperors on the other.[28] It is surely significant that in our documentary evidence from outside Egypt far more attention is given to this issue than to that of direct taxation in cash or kind.

In Apuleius' story the gardener is eventually arrested, and the soldier takes the ass and loads him with his baggage, his lance prominently on top to terrify the passers-by. Coming to a small town, the soldier stays not in an inn but in the house of a town councillor (*decurio*, 10, 1)—the right *not* to be forced to accept official travellers was an exceptional privilege.[29] When he sets off for Rome, the soldier sells the ass, which he has acquired for nothing,

26. Epictetus, *Diss.* 4, 1, 79, quoted by M. Rostovtzeff, *The Social and Economic History of the Roman Empire*[2] (1957), chap. 8, n. 37 (also referring to the story of the gardener, the only episode from Apuleius used by Rostovtzeff).

27. It is puzzling that the soldier should be described as a "soldier from a legion" (*miles e legione*; 9, 39). Apuleius might in this case have been misled by the system in Africa, where the *legio III Augusta* provided the staff-soldiers (*beneficiarii*) for the proconsul (Tacitus, *Hist.* 4, 48). On the other hand the soldier's superior officer is described (10, 13) as a *tribunus* (compare the *tribunus* at the head of a *cohors* serving under Caecilius Classicus as proconsul of Baetica, Pliny, *Ep.* 3, 9, 18). *Tribuni* of auxiliary units must have been in command of a *cohors milliaria* (cohort of a thousand men), and what seems to be the same superior officer appears in 10, 1 as *praepositus*: "his *praepositus*, who had the command over a thousand armed people." For comparable usages, see R. E. Smith, "Dux, Praepositus," *ZPE* 36 (1979): 263.

28. See now S. Mitchell, "Requisitioned Transport in the Roman Empire: A New Inscription from Pisidia," *JRS* 66 (1976): 106.

29. For release (*anepistathmeia*) from the obligation of *hospitium* (providing for official travellers and soldiers), see, e.g., R. K. Sherk, *Roman Documents from the Greek East* (1969), no. 57; *FIRA*[2] I, no. 56; 73; *Dig.* 50, 4, 18, 30; 27, 1, 6, 8; F. Millar, *The Emperor in the Roman World* (1977; 2nd ed., 1992), 460–61 (athletes); T. Drew-Bear, W. Eck, and P. Herrmann, "Sacrae Litterae," *Chiron* 7 (1977): 355 (senators).

and pockets the proceeds. As is generally recognized now, nothing could be further from the truth than Rostovtzeff's idea that the army of the imperial period somehow represented an oppressed peasantry.[30] On the contrary, the soldiers were a privileged official class whose presence was feared by ordinary people.

This soldier is represented as being loosely attached to the entourage of the governor as he travels through the province, presumably on his judicial circuit.[31] But no governor appears in person in the story until the final stage at Corinth, the capital (*caput*) of Achaea.[32] In the famous scene in *Acts* set in Corinth we see the proconsul Gallio on his tribunal when Paul is dragged before him and accused. In Apuleius the proconsul is in his house, when one of the victims of a female poisoner, just before death, rushes to the house demanding his protection, and by loud shouts and raising a disturbance among the people, causes the doors to be opened and a hearing granted (10, 28). The proconsul hears the case and condemns the poisoner to the beasts.

Several things are significant in this process. The governor in a provincial city functions under the pressure of crowds following every interesting turn of events. He too may be staying with a local notable, for there is no certain evidence that the Roman state normally owned official residences for governors.[33] Before her execution the woman is brought out of the public prison of Corinth (*de publico carcere* 10, 34), for it was these city prisons which governors normally used (see "Condemnation to Hard Labour in the Roman Empire," chapter 7 in this volume). The governor is dependent on the city in another way too; for the wild beast show in which the woman is to die is one put on by a rich local magnate to celebrate his assumption of the chief office in the city. Apuleius' description perfectly catches the overtones of

30. See Rostovtzeff (n. 26), chap. 11.

31. For the proconsul's assize tour, see G. P. Burton, "Proconsuls, Assizes and the Administration of Justice under the Empire," *JRS* 65 (1975): 92. It is attested that Beroea in Macedonia was an assize centre, and the system probably existed in all proconsular provinces (p. 97). Note that the appointment of *tutores* (guardians) for the children of a man thought to be dead is alluded to in *Met.* 1, 6: "[G]uardians are appointed for your children by decree of the provincial *iuridicus*." No deductions should be drawn from the use of the term *iuridicus*, which simply means the proconsul, as does *dikastēs* in *Lucius or the Ass*, 55.

32. *Met.* 10, 18.

33. The evidence on this puzzling question is very well collected and discussed by R. Egger, *Das Praetorium als Amtssitz und Quartier römischer Spitzenfunktionäre* (1966), without revealing what sort of "residence," owned by whom, was used by proconsuls in the "capitals" of their provinces. See now R. Haensch, *Capita Provinciarum: Statthaltersitze und Provinzialverwaltung in der römischen Kaiserzeit* (1997).

local office-holding; "Thiasus, for that was the name of my owner, a citizen of Corinth, . . . had held the lower offices in succession, as his descent and dignity demanded, and had now been appointed to the quinquennial magistracy; and as, in order to live up to the glory of assuming the *fasces* [insignia of authority], he had promised a gladiatorial show to last three days, he was in the process of making provision for his munificence [*munificentia*]."[34] One of the most curious features of the judicial system of the Empire was that local office-holders, putting on shows at their own expense, could *buy* condemned prisoners from the state and have them exposed to wild beasts for the delectation of large crowds. It was regarded as a remarkable act of benevolence by Marcus Aurelius and Commodus that in 177 they reduced the price which the provincial office-holders had to pay.[35]

We cannot understand the government, such as it was, of the peaceful provinces of the empire if we do not think of the close personal relations which the governor was bound to have with the provincial upper classes and, above all, with those of the city in which he spent most of his time. Exactly for this reason, when the well-born young Lucius from Corinth arrives in Hypata, he is questioned by his host "about our native city and its leading citizens [*primores*] and finally about the governor himself" (1, 26). But in most places the governor was not present (obviously enough); nor—which is perhaps not so obvious—were any forces, officials, or representatives sent by him. The cities ran themselves. Or rather (and this is one of the most vivid impressions left by the novel) they were run by a network of local aristocratic families, whose doings, public and private, were the subject of intense observer participation—approbation, curiosity, indignation, incipient violence—on the part of the lower classes of the towns. The leading families in Apuleius form a social class immediately distinguishable on sight from the rest of the people. Lucius sees a woman arriving in the market-place of Hypata escorted by slaves; her rich dress "proclaimed her a lady [*matrona*]" (2, 2); and the ass at once recognizes the gentle birth (*matronatus*) of a young

34. *Met.* 10, 18. For Corinth, see n. 11 above. The office of *duovir quinquennalis* (one of the pair of annual magistrates elected each five years with the task of taking the census) in the colony is well attested on inscriptions; see, e.g., *Corinth* VIII.2: *Latin Inscriptions*, 157. The assumption that Lucius' first language will have been Greek is fully reflected in the rapidly changing balance of Latin and Greek inscriptions in the second century; see *Corinth* VIII.3: *The Inscriptions, 1926–1950*, 18–19. [Dio], *Or.* 37, 26 (perhaps by Favorinus) records the Hellenisation of the city.

35. For the well-known decree of the Senate (*senatus consultum*) of 177, see J. H. Oliver and R. E. A. Palmer, *Hesperia* 24 (1955): 320. For this interpretation, see Millar (n. 29), 195.

girl captured by the robbers (4, 23). The upper classes have substantial houses in the cities, with households of slaves with carefully differentiated functions (9, 2; 10, 13). They may own landed properties at a distance (10, 4), in one case run by a slave overseer with a staff of slave shepherds (7, 15; 8, 15), and in another by a slave overseer (*vilicus*) who keeps his accounts (*rationes*) in his house (8, 22); alternatively we find a free tenant bringing a leg of venison as a gift to his landlord (8, 31).

The novel, like the pages of Plutarch's *Moralia*, written rather more than half a century earlier,[36] shows how a network of relationships connected the local aristocrats of different Greek cities. Lucius, from Corinth, is portrayed as a relative of Plutarch, from Chaeronea; and the grand lady whom he meets in the market-place of Hypata is a relative of his mother (2, 2–3). He brings with him to Hypata a letter of recommendation from Demeas in Corinth, vouching specifically for his good birth (1, 22–23). On another visit to the market-place he meets a friend with whom he has studied in Athens, and who is now aedile, or market supervisor, in his home town (1, 24).

As Apuleius' description of the magnate from Corinth implies, power and influence in these small provincial towns had become largely hereditary. Hence a group of young men (*iuvenes*) of the best birth were free to terrorize the streets of Hypata by night.[37] Or a poor man could be driven off his lands by "a rich and powerful young neighbour who misused the prestige of his ancestry, was powerful in local politics, and could easily do anything in the town" (9, 35). On the other side rich people could actively avoid local office and responsibility. When a group of robbers reaches Thebes, they ask who are the richest men there and are told of a wealthy money-changer (*nummularius*) who dresses poorly and uses every means to conceal his wealth "for fear of office and public obligations [*munera publica*]" (4, 9). That touches of course on one of the most familiar themes from the city life of antiquity: the extraction of value from the rich not by taxation but by laying on them the obligation to assume expensive functions directly and in person.[38] Here we

---

36. See Jones (n. 14), chap. 5, "Plutarch's Society: *Domi nobiles*."

37. 2, 18. Cf. *Dig.* 48, 19, 28, 3 (Callistratus) on the difficulty for the governor in repressing the disorderly conduct "in some cities" of those "who commonly called themselves 'the young men' [*iuvenes*]."

38. The best analysis of this situation, as it existed in the classical and early Hellenistic Greek city, is provided by P. Veyne, *Le pain et le cirque* (1976), chap. 2, translated as *Bread and Circuses* (1990). The remark of Rostovtzeff (n. 26), chap. 8, n. 41, that there is no adequate treatment of the history of liturgies under the Empire, remains valid. For a useful recent collection of legal evidence, see W. Langhammer, *Die rechtliche und soziale Stellung der*

see the necessary social framework for that process: the man does his best—but everybody in the town knows that his well-guarded house is filled with riches.[39]

The people of the towns might of course follow the doings of the rich with favour and approbation. The young lady captured by the robbers had been engaged to an aristocratic young man "whom the whole city had adopted as its public son [*filius publicus*]," and the engagement had been celebrated by a procession of the family and relatives to make sacrifices at the temples and public buildings.[40] When he heroically rescues her and returns home, "the whole city poured out to see the longed for sight" (7, 13; cf. 8, 2). But favour for one person could quickly turn, in the context of a public ceremonial, into a demonstration against another. So, after the death of a leading citizen in Larissa "by ancestral ritual, as he was one of the *optimates*, the public funeral procession was conducted through the forum." But the dead man's father shouts out that he had been murdered by his wife, and the crowd begins to call for fire and stones (2, 27), just as in another scene the crowd determines to stone a witch to death (1, 10). Again, in a town in Thessaly, an old man goes from the funeral of his younger son to the forum and accuses the elder son of the murder; a regular trial then follows. "By his lamentations he inflamed with such pity and indignation the town council and also the people, that they all shouted that the delays of justice . . . should be set aside and that he should be stoned to death, to provide a communal punishment for a communal wrong." But the magistrates fear that violence will get out of hand, and persuade the council and people that a proper trial should be held. It is conducted in the council chamber (*curia*) with the councillors as jury, and if the charge had been proved the town executioner (*carnifex*) would have carried out the sentence. But it turns out that it was his stepmother who had tried to kill the boy and had only succeeded in giving him an overdose—

"Magistratus Municipales" und der "Decuriones" (1973), 237–38. But see now L. Neesen, "Die Entwicklung der Leistungen und Ämter (*munera et honores*) im römischen Kaiserreich des zweiten bis vierten Jahrhundert," *Historia* 30 (1981): 203.

39. *Met.* 4, 9: "satisfied with a small, albeit sufficiently fortified house, wearing rags and sordid in all other respects, he nestled over his bags of gold [*aureos folles*]." In a very general way the term *aureos folles*, reflecting the custom of storing money in bags, foreshadows the usage which becomes official in the early fourth century, when *follis* becomes a term for a unit of currency. See A. H. M. Jones, "The Origin and Early History of the *Follis*," in *The Roman Economy* (1974), 330; M. H. Crawford, *ANRW* II.2 (1975), 586.

40. *Met.* 4, 26. As regards the remarkable expression *filius publicus*, I owe to Riet van Bremen the perception that the inscriptions of the Greek cities often emphasize the private virtues of members of the leading families as expressed in their public life.

from which (needless to say) he is just waking up. So the stepmother is sent into lifelong exile, and her slave accomplice executed.[41]

These are just the sort of differential penalties for condemned persons of different social status which are well attested in the Roman Empire.[42] But there is a puzzle here, for on the established view only the governor of a province could carry out capital sentences or impose penalties such as exile;[43] and of course as we saw earlier the proconsul of Achaea was doing just that in Corinth. The same problem arises with the famous scene of the mock trial of Lucius in Hypata (3, 2–9). Here, Lucius, before his transformation, comes back late one night from a party, slays (as he thinks) three robbers, is tried next day by the city council and thinks himself near to a death sentence — when it is revealed that the three victims were really inflated bladders blowing about in the wind. Once again the trial, or mock trial, takes place in the context of intense crowd participation, so much so that the people successfully demand that it should be transferred from the forum to the theatre — which was, of course, a normal meeting place in Greek cities.[44]

So Apuleius' novel presents one story in which trial and sentence is carried out by a city council and another in which the whole dramatic point would surely have been lost, if the original readers would have known all along that Lucius' trial could not possibly have been real — that is, if they would have assumed that only the governor could carry out capital sentence. There seem to me to be three possibilities. We can accept that not only the particular course of events but the entire context will have seemed pure fantasy to second-century readers. Or, we can assume that both Apuleius and they

41. *Met.* 10, 6–12. For the sentences, 10, 12: "[T]he stepmother was condemned to perpetual exile, whereas the slave was crucified by means of the *patibulum*." *Patibulum* seems to be used here as a synonym for cross (*crux*); cf. Th. Mommsen, *Römisches Strafrecht* (1899), 920–21 (not discussing this passage), and *RE*, s.v. "Patibulum."

42. See P. Garnsey, *Social Status and Legal Privilege in the Roman Empire* (1970), pt. II.

43. For a statement of the principle, see, e.g., A. N. Sherwin-White, *Roman Society and Roman Law in the New Testament* (1963), 35–36, 75–76. For a survey of the evidence which may cast some doubt on the general assumption that local courts did not and could not carry out capital sentences, see E. Schürer, *History of the Jewish People* II, ed. G. Vermes, F. Millar, and M. Black (1979), 219, n. 80, and D. Nörr, *Imperium und Polis* (1966), 30–31; note *Syll.*³ 799 (Cyzicus, A.D. 38), showing that the city authorities there could impose a sentence of exile from the city.

44. For meetings in the theatre, see J. Colin, "Apulée en Thessalie; fiction ou vérité?," *Latomus* 24 (1965): 330, on p. 342, n. 3; cf. Colin, *Les villes libres de l'Orient gréco-romain et l'envoi au supplice par acclamations populaires* (1965), chap. 3 (assuming that the procedure depends on the freedom of the cities of Thessaly).

knew that the cities of Thessaly were free cities, in which the writ of the proconsul did not run and which had their own capital jurisdiction. But, the trouble is, were they free cities? I can find no clear proof that they were.[45] For that matter it is not possible to state exactly what "freedom" for Greek cities under the Empire meant, or whether it always meant the same thing.[46] In other words, if we switch back to the real world, we find it just as confusing and ambiguous as fiction. Nothing is more illusory than the idea that the real world of the Roman Empire presents us with a clearly defined and intelligible system of public law and administration.

That being so, I should like to try a quite different hypothesis, namely that what the novel represents is Apuleius' assumptions as to how local justice worked in the cities, irrespective of their formal status, when the governor was not there. In the real world too, we must remember, he usually was not; the more privileged communities were visited by the governor of a province once a year; many never saw him at all. We can, of course, find some cases where a prisoner is duly locked up by city officials to await trial by the governor when he comes.[47] But I do suggest that, especially when popular indignation was aroused, it is impossible to imagine that such self-restraint normally operated.

Whatever may have happened in reality, in the world of the novel justice is done and public order maintained, if at all, by self-help. When Lucius disappears, having been turned into an ass, it is reported to the robbers that he is thought guilty of the robbery; his slave has been examined by the magistrates of Hypata under torture, and a group of men has been sent to Corinth to seek him out for punishment (7, 2). When the robbers are finally located, a party sets out from Hypata, catches them, and simply executes them (7, 13). A

---

45. Julius Caesar certainly granted freedom to the Thessalians; see Plut., *Caesar* 48; Appian, *BC* 2, 368. Thereafter the situation is obscure, and neither the existence of Thessalian coins, nor Thessalian votes in the Amphictyonic league (Pausanias 10, 8, 3) nor the adoption of new eras in A.D. 10–11 and again in A.D. 41 necessarily imply grants of freedom — so R. Bernhardt, *Imperium und Eleutheria* (1971), 202, 208. *ILS* 1067, showing P. Pactumeius Clemens, suffect consul in 138, as "*legatus* of the divine Hadrian in Athens, Thespii, Plataeae, as well as in Thessalia" *might* imply the freedom of Thessaly; but the freedom of Plataea is *deduced*, e.g., by Larsen, *ESAR* IV, 447, from its presence on this inscription.

46. Cf. the complex variations discussed by R. Bernhardt, "Die Immunitas der Freistädte," *Historia* 29 (1980): 190 (on freedom from tribute).

47. This pattern is clear in the case of the martyrs of Lyon, Eusebius, *HE* 5, 1, and especially in the martyrdom of Pionius at Smyrna; see Knopf, Krüger, and Ruhbach, *Ausgewählte Märtyrakten*, no. 10; Musurillo, *Acts of the Christian Martyrs*, no. 10.

little later some shepherds arrest a man on suspicion of murder and keep him bound overnight in a hut, intending to take him next day to the magistrates for punishment (7, 26). Similarly, an armed group of local men on horseback arrests the Syrian priests for robbery and takes them back to a prison, apparently located in a mere village (9, 9–10; cf. 9, 4). Even the passing soldiers who arrest the gardener bring him to the local magistrates; he is put in the public prison to await a capital penalty (9, 42).

The world we are looking at is one wholly without policing by any imperial forces, except in one very extreme case. Justice is highly localised. A man who realizes that he will be suspected of murder simply abandons his family, moves to Aetolia, and contracts a new marriage (1, 19). When a group of slaves on an outlying estate hears of the death of their mistress and fears a change of owner, they load all their belongings on pack animals, go on what seems to be a journey of about three days, and settle in a city where they can live without discovery and support themselves (8, 15–23). The cities are not represented as exercising any check on arrivals; when Lucius reaches Hypata, he has to go into an inn to ask which town it is (1, 21). Nor do the towns themselves have any significant police forces. The nearest to that which we meet are the attendants of the market supervisor in Hypata (1, 24–5), and the attendants of the magistrates there who burst into the house where Lucius is, arrest him, and take him to his mock trial; the prosecution is conducted by the prefect of the night watch,[48] who duly claims to have observed the murder while on street patrol. But Lucius had carried his sword to protect himself, and in the several scenes elsewhere in the novel which represent robbers mounting assaults on the town houses of the rich, no organized police force appears. If the attacks are beaten off, as they twice are,[49] it is by self-help from within the house, or from neighbours.

Like the potentially violent crowds which demanded justice in the cities, and the arrests of criminals by armed groups, this self-help is an important aspect of the society represented in the novel. But it is by no means the only area in which the novel presents alternative models of ancient society to those which we normally accept. For instance, one influential modern view represents the typical small town in the Roman provinces as not primarily an economic entity, but rather "a social phenomenon, the result of the predilec-

48. *Met.* 3, 2–3: *nocturnae custodiae praefectus.* The term must translate *nyktostratēgos*, attested on a number of inscriptions from Greek cities; see esp. Jones, *The Greek City*, 212.

49. *Met.* 4, 9–11; 19–21. The realistic and unheroic character of the robbers' tales of defeat is well brought out by P. A. McKay, "*Klephtika*: The Tradition of the Tales of Banditry in Apuleius," *Greece and Rome* 10 (1963): 147.

tion of the wealthier classes for the amenities of urban life."[50] That very important cultural factor is indeed perfectly illustrated in Apuleius: Lucius' rich
female relative in Hypata asks him, "How are you enjoying our native city?
To my knowledge we far excel all other cities in temples, baths, and other
public works. . . . At any rate there is freedom for anyone at leisure, and for
the stranger coming on business a crowd of people like that at Rome" (2, 19).
It is beginning to be recognized, however, that the latter part of that claim is
also important. The economic functions of towns in a pre-industrial society
can be complex and important in aggregate, even if the units of production and exchange are themselves small.[51] It is therefore all the more worth
emphasizing that the towns in Apuleius function, not indeed as centres of
production, but as the focus for organized exchanges of goods and the hiring
of labour. All of this is conducted for cash; whatever else this may be, it is
certainly a fully monetized economy. Admittedly, when the rich accumulate a surplus, they literally just accumulate it in cash. Lucius' miserly host at
Hypata does lend out money against deposits in gold and silver (1, 21); but
the bulk of his money simply rests in a heavily locked storeroom (*horreum*)
in his house. Everyone in the town knows it is there, and the robbers duly
break down the door with axes and take away the money in bags (1, 21; 3,
28). But, otherwise, the cities are the scenes of active exchanges for cash: in
the market-place of Hypata fish is available for sale, and hay for horses can be
bought for cash (1, 24). A man who is by profession a vendor of cheese and related products, travelling throughout Thessaly, Aetolia, and Boeotia, comes
to Hypata, perhaps for the day of a special cheese market, only to find that
a large operator (*negotiator magnarius*) has bought up the entire supply (1, 5).
The poorest free person whom we meet in Apuleius is the market gardener
who works a small patch of land without even a house; none the less, he too
drives the ass to the town each morning to sell his produce to the retailers
(9, 32). The market-places are also the scene of regular auctions; the runaway
slaves can immediately have their animals auctioned for cash (8, 23–25), and
a traveller short of money can find an auctioneer advertising for someone
to be paid in cash for watching a corpse at night (2, 21–23). If all else failed,
one could earn a poor income in cash by portering (*saccaria*, 1, 7), or just beg
for coins at the crossroads (1, 6). No doubt the inns, where you also paid

50. A. H. M. Jones, "The Cities of the Roman Empire," in *The Roman Economy* (1974), 1,
on p. 31.

51. See the valuable article by K. Hopkins, "Economic Growth and Towns in Classical
Antiquity," in P. Abrams and E. A. Wrigley, eds., *Towns in Societies* (1978), 35; the rest of that
volume also presents much relevant material and argument.

in cash (1, 17), did not receive quite as many people as those of Rome. But what is clear is that the towns are represented as providing real concentrations of activity both by way of exchange and in the hire of labour. Crowd reactions, to good or bad news, or the handling of wrongdoers, surely also imply chronic under-employment, and hence the availability of labour for hire. Given the constant exchanges of cash, it is not surprising that the towns have professional money-changers (*nummularii*); when a slave pays a doctor a large sum for a drug, the coins are sealed in a bag, to be checked next day by a money-changer (10, 9).

What is more striking in Apuleius is the level and nature of economic activity outside the towns, firstly in villages (called *pagus, castellum,* or *vicus*), and secondly in the countryside itself. Before I give some examples, I should remind you of how the economic life of the peasantry was described in a very interesting recent article: "The economy of the Roman empire, in spite of its sophistication in some respects, was predominantly a subsistence economy. . . . The bulk of the labour force in the Roman empire, perhaps 80–90 per cent, were primarily peasants who produced most of what they themselves consumed and consumed most of what they produced."[52] The same passage admits, however, that the countryside was affected by the monetary economy, and all I can say in this context is that it is this aspect of rural economic life which the novel puts before us. In the story a village too may have an auctioneer; one of these sells off the ass to a baker from the next village, who is also buying a quantity of corn for cash (9, 10). The baker's neighbour is a fuller (9, 22), and both households conduct their trade in their immediate living quarters, the one with wooden troughs in which flour is sifted (9, 23), the other with wickerwork frames on which cloth is placed for whitening with sulphur (9, 24). In the same village where the ass is sold there is a *faber*, apparently a free man, who works under an *officinator* or owner of a workshop. He works for cash, to buy food; his wife works at wool making (*lanificium*), also for cash, with which they buy oil for lighting (9, 5). When pressed for cash they sell a large jar which is standing in their house (9, 7).

That a household could be a multiple economic unit is also clear elsewhere. The rich young lady with whom the ass is rescued gives him into the care of her slave chief herdsman (*armentarius equiso*), who takes him out to a country property. There the ass is used by the man's wife to turn a mill which grinds corn for the neighbours and earns a cash revenue; the barley meant for the ass's upkeep is also ground in the mill and sold to neighbouring ten-

---

52. K. Hopkins, "Taxes and Trade in the Roman Empire (200 B.C.–A.D. 400)," *JRS* 70 (1980): 101 on p. 104.

ants (7, 15). Released from the mill, the ass is given over to a slave boy whose job is to gather wood in the hills; but once again it turns out that he sells the wood for cash, for use in a next-door household (7, 17–20). I will come back later to this process of gathering from the wild. It is enough to emphasize now that the world portrayed by Apuleius involves cash exchanges for produce right down to the lowest levels. We even find that the slave shepherds in flight ask a goatherd grazing his flock beside the track whether he has milk or cheese for sale (8, 19). The only trace of a subsistence economy in Apuleius is a seasonal one; over the winter the market gardener, having nothing left to sell, lives on overgrown vegetables from his plot which have run to seed (9, 32). In other words all the food-producing operations are specialised, and the products are exchanged for cash. Villages and countryside have small, domestic-scale establishments for processing food or clothes. When we have read Apuleius we might carry away the image not of a subsistence economy but of something more like Alan McFarlane's deliberately provocative description of thirteenth-century England: "a capitalist-market economy without factories."[53]

Direct production for household consumption does appear, but seems to be more characteristic of the *richer* households, which can achieve the necessary variety of production. It is in that context, and only there, that transfers of produce occur which are not for cash, that is, are gifts. So a wealthy neighbour of the market gardener promises him a gift "from his estates" of corn, olive oil, and two jars of wine (9, 33). The same background is implied when Lucius' rich female relative in Hypata sends him as gifts (*xeniola*) a pig, five chickens, and a jar of wine, for use at dinner (2, 11).

In a different context, the tenant (*colonus*) of a rich landlord brings him as a gift (*munus*), a leg of venison—the product, as is explicitly stated, of a hunting expedition (8, 31). With that we come to another side of the ancient economy, and one which is almost wholly neglected. The oft-repeated modern doctrine that agriculture was the fundamental economic activity of the ancient world is of course obviously true but none the less gives a wholly inadequate impression of people's relations to the earth and its products. In the world of Apuleius at least, the people of the countryside are not only agriculturalists; they are also pastoralists whose flocks live in wild country, and for that matter they are hunters and gatherers. To be strict, gathering appears only in the story of the slave boy collecting wood in the hills; but any description of the economy of the ancient world which ignored the gathering

53. MacFarlane, *The Origins of English Individualism* (1978), 196.

of food and other products from the wild would be hopelessly inadequate.[54] Hunting, however, is a fundamental feature of the world in which Apuleius' characters live. Human habitation exists against the backdrop of a landscape in which there are bears (4, 13; 7, 24), wolves (7, 22; 8, 15), boar (8, 4), deer (8, 31), and wild goats (8, 4), not to speak of the unspecified "wild beasts" which the rich man from Corinth has come to collect in Thessaly for his show (10, 18). In consequence the group of shepherds in flight are armed with throwing-spears, heavy hunting spears, arrows, and clubs (8, 16). When force has to be applied against neighbours, a rich household in the country can deploy swords and spears, and call out large and ferocious sheepdogs (9, 36–38). Then again, when the Syrian priests are staying in the house of the leading citizen (*vir primarius*) of a town, the ass is thought to have rabies. The slaves of the household instantly seize spears and axes, until the ass demonstrates by drinking water that he does not have rabies. This town house is also equipped with a stable of horses and a pack of hunting dogs (9, 2).

Nearly all the features which I have tried to isolate in the world of the *Golden Ass* come together in the marvellous mock-heroic story told in the robbers' hideout and added to the main narrative framework by Apuleius (4, 13–22). One group of robbers had gone south into Boeotia; at Plataea they found busy talk of the show which was to be put on by a local notable, Demochares: "[F]or he was a man of distinguished birth, great wealth and eminent liberality, and was preparing public entertainments [*voluptates*] with a splendour worthy of his fortune." He had assembled gladiators, *venatores*, to fight against wild beasts, and condemned criminals (*noxii*) to be eaten by the beasts. The beasts were bears, acquired in three ways: by his own hunting expeditions, by purchase, and by gift from his friends. Unfortunately, in spite of heavy expenditure on upkeep, many of the bears died; their corpses were thrown out on the streets and were seized and eaten by the starving poor.

The robbers therefore skinned one of these deceased bears and put one of their leaders inside it. They took the supposed bear to Demochares and produced a forged letter saying that it was a gift from a friend of his in Thrace who had caught it while hunting. With that they went off, richly rewarded with coins from the store kept in the house—and, in a touch which is typical of the narrative, the people of the town rushed to see the bear and commented with one voice (*consonaque civium voce*) on Demochares' good luck.

---

54. I know of no serious reflection on this fact except J. M. Frayn, "Wild and Cultivated Plants: A Note on the Peasant Economy of Roman Italy," *JRS* 65 (1975): 32 = *Subsistence Farming in Roman Italy* (1979), chap. 4.

At night the robbers came back, and the one disguised as a bear got up from the courtyard, killed the slave janitor, opened the door with his key, and let them in. In the house he showed them the storeroom (*horreum*) filled with silver, which they carried off in coffins taken from a tomb outside the town. But before they could come back for a second load, the household woke up, and the supposed bear was confronted with slaves armed with clubs, spears, and swords, supported by fierce hunting dogs. The story ends with a fine mock-heroic narration of his death—reminding us, if we needed it, that what we are reading is just fiction.

None the less, the novel does offer us a complex and significant portrait of a provincial society: the network of relationships among the provincial aristocracy; the political functions, displays, and generosities of the rich, as acted out in front of their local communities; the crude accumulation of wealth side by side with extreme poverty; an economy which was both monetized on the one hand and gave a large place to hunting in the wild on the other; a world where brigandage was rife, but where society could close ranks to exert force where it was needed, and was fully armed to do so. The forces of the governor were few and far away; to come back to a question which I raised earlier, I suggest that we should not believe for a moment that in the real world the execution of justice on local murderers or robbers was dutifully left to the governor's discretion. The emperor's distant existence was felt by all. But only very special circumstances would bring his forces into action. We should not be surprised, after reading Apuleius, to find that just about this time Thespiae in Boeotia sent a contingent to fight on campaign with Marcus Aurelius,[55] or that when a marauding group of barbarians from the Black Sea reached Boeotia, they were attacked and slaughtered by a local force.[56] We might recall that Apuleius says that the armed group of shepherds in flight needed only a trumpet to resemble a real army (8, 16).[57]

Of course, we must not forget that all this is not only fiction but is a Greek short story transformed and expanded in Latin by a rich and well-born writer from Africa. When he went to Athens, it was not to study the lives of the poor in the Greek countryside but to earn the title which his fellow citizens in Madauros were to give him, "the Platonic philosopher."[58] In

55. See A. Plassart, "Une levée de volontaires Thespiens sous Marc Aurèle," in *Mélanges Glotz* II (1932), 731; and C. P. Jones, "The Levy at Thespiae under Marcus Aurelius," *GRBS* 12 (1971): 45.

56. Pausanias 10, 34, 5.

57. For comparative evidence, note P. A. Brunt, "Did Imperial Rome Disarm Her Subjects?," *Phoenix* 29 (1975): 260.

58. *Ins. lat. d'Alg.* 2115 (Madauros); cf. *PIR*² A 958.

writing his novel, with its exuberant descriptive detail and powerful erotic elements, he was not, in intention, reporting anything, but inventing a world in which to set the adventures of Lucius. But the invented world of fiction may yet represent—perhaps cannot help representing—important features of the real world.[59] For the historian, the *Golden Ass* depicts levels of social and economic life which the vast mass of surviving classical literature simply ignores; it adds depth and perspective to patterns which we know from other evidence, for instance, in portraying the roles played by the local aristocracies, as seen from below. But, above all, it offers us alternative models—of the operations of justice or the nature of economic life outside the towns—to those which we generally accept. The images gained from the novel can be used, in other words, to apply new questions and new hypotheses to the bewildering mass of data which survives from the real world of the Roman Empire.

59. For comparable attempts to use ancient fiction, see, e.g., P. Veyne, "Vie de Trimalcion," *Annales* 16 (1961): 213; A. M. Scarcella, "Les structures socio-économiques du roman de Xénophon d'Éphèse," *REG* 90 (1977): 249. Both the title and the approach adopted in this chapter were suggested by Ivan Morris, *The World of the Shining Prince* (1964), using Murasaki's *The Tale of Genji*.

CHAPTER SIXTEEN

Empire and City, Augustus to Julian: Obligations, Excuses, and Status[*]

Introduction

The early Roman Empire rested on a network of cities, which were capable both of conspicuous expenditure locally, in the form of public buildings, shows, and festivals, and of carrying many of the functions of government; but by the fourth century their capacity to perform these roles had drastically declined. Both the capacity and the decline depended in part on the availability or inavailability of the richer classes to undertake expenditures associated with public offices or with liturgies. These remarks are of course mere common-places. They have become so, in the first place, because precisely these changes were noted, and the issues relating to them consciously formulated, in the fourth century itself. So Libanius writes in his *Funeral Oration* for Julian:[1]

> He showed the same care also in relation to the councils in the cities, which formerly flourished in both numbers and wealth, but by that time had come to nothing, since their members, except for a very few, had switched course, some into military service, some into the Senate. . . . The remainder were all but sunk, and for the majority of them undertaking public services [*to leitourgein*] ended in beggary. Yet who does not know that the vitality of its council is the soul of a city? But Constantius, while in theory aiding the councils, in practice was their enemy, by moving elsewhere men who sought to evade them, and granting illegal exemptions [*ateleiai*].

Three points should be noted here: Libanius assumes an evolution which was, if not universal, at any rate general throughout the Empire; the crisis is

*First published in *JRS* 73 (1983): 76–96.

1. Libanius, *Or.* 18, 146–47. For the general issue also *Or.* 48, 17ff.

regarded as having been caused by the availability of roles or statuses which offered an alternative to the obligations of city councillors; and this availability itself is seen as a product of imperial actions, which (as Libanius goes on to say) Julian had taken steps to reverse.

This chapter has the aim of analysing the main features of the evolution in the relations of city and Empire which lay behind Julian's measures. As regards the three points just made, we certainly cannot *assume* an exactly similar development in all parts of the Empire. The uneven distribution in time and space both of literary and documentary evidence and of the results of excavation clearly rules out any such confident generalisation; it has been argued, for instance, that the cities of North Africa do not show the "decline" in the late Empire which we normally tend to presume.[2] But, as the following pages will illustrate, it is beyond question that evidence which can indeed be located in space and time shows that the tensions and issues described by Libanius were felt in many different parts of the Empire. Much more significant than that, however, is the presupposition that the Empire was a unified system, whose workings at a local level were directly and effectively subject to rulings made by the emperors.

For the fourth century itself it is only necessary to look at any page of the *Codex Theodosianus* to see that the role of emperor included the function of issuing general rules, even if many of their pronouncements were in form replies to office-holders, provincial leagues, or city councils. For the earlier Empire the situation is not so clear: it can be argued that imperial activity typically consisted in the formulation of responses to individual cases.[3] Yet it can also be suggested with some justice that to concentrate on the form or occasion of typical imperial pronouncements is to miss the extent to which these pronouncements did in fact have the function of formulating general rules.[4] Even a response to a particular issue might serve as the basis for a more general ruling by the same emperor, or a later one; or, as is evident throughout the classical juristic writings excerpted in the *Digest*, it might give rise to a general principle or a new, generalised exception to a standing principle. It may be useful to take an example, from Papinian, writing under Septimius Severus:[5]

2. C. Lepelley, *Les cités de l'Afrique romaine au Bas-Empire* I–II (1979–81).

3. F. Millar, *The Emperor in the Roman World* (1977; 2nd ed., 1992), henceforth *ERW*.

4. See the interesting observations, which require further discussion, by J. Bleicken, *Der Regierungsstil des römischen Kaisers eine Antwort auf Fergus Millar* (*Sitzungsberichte der Wissenschaftlichen Gesellschaft an der Johann Wolfgang Goethe-Universität Frankfurt am Main* 18, 5, 1982), and Millar, Afterword, *ERW*².

5. *Dig.* 50, 5, 8, *pr.*

> In the conferment of *honores* [offices] neither being over 70 nor being the father of five children affords exemption. But in Asia those who can claim five children are not compelled to undertake the high priesthood of the province, as our best and greatest *princeps* Severus Augustus ruled in judgement [*decrevit*], and afterwards laid down in a constitution [*constituit*] that this should be the rule in the other provinces.

In this case it is clear that Severus in the first instance made a particular exception for Asia, when judging a dispute about liability, and then generalised it so far as to include all provincial high priesthoods (but without abandoning the overall rule). When others subsequently claimed exemption from *honores* on the grounds of the number of their children, they found their petitions rejected, as for example by Severus Alexander (*CJ* 10, 52, 1). We can thus regard even the giving of individual responses by the emperors as contributing to the formation of a body of rules which were in principle valid throughout the Empire.

Three important characteristics of this system must however be emphasized. Firstly, the body of rules thus created was not so much enforced by any apparatus of government as available for use by interested parties making claims or bringing suits, and then by officials or emperors giving rulings in response. How, to what extent, and to whom the content of the constantly evolving case law of imperial rulings was known in the provinces is a question which—if there were any way of answering it—would be of fundamental importance for the nature of the Empire. Second in importance is the operation of what has been called the "beneficial ideology,"[6] that is, the role of the emperors in dispensing favours, exceptions, and exemptions, usually in response to requests from individuals or groups. It lay in the nature of such a role that the emperors should frequently, but not invariably, assent to such requests. There was thus a clear contradiction between the emperor's function in formulating rules and his role as the dispenser of individual benefits. The tension between rule and exception is fundamental to the nature of imperial law-giving.

Thirdly, imperial law-giving was by no means confined to Roman civil or criminal law; on the contrary, a significant part of the content of our standard sources for "Roman law" involves far wider issues of the social and communal life of the provinces. The *Digest* above all is thus a major document of social history, primarily that of the later second and early third centuries. In par-

---

6. See V. Nutton, "The Beneficial Ideology," in P. D. A. Garnsey and C. R. Whittaker, eds., *Imperialism in the Ancient World* (1978), 209.

ticular, imperial law-giving and rule formulations profoundly affected the framework of provincial city life, and nowhere more so than in the area of the obligation to undertake offices (*honores/archai*) or duties (*munera/leitourgiai*). As Libanius emphasizes in the passage quoted, the availability of men rich enough to undertake "liturgical" functions imposed directly on them as individuals was of crucial importance to city life. It was by this means, and not by the extraction of revenue via taxation, that the cities had been able to deploy for communal advantage the surpluses evident in the second century, to which Libanius looks back.

That being so, it was inevitable that the rules for liability to, or exemption from, offices and functions should also have been of central importance. At the same time the spread of the citizenship, culminating in Caracalla's universal grant, will have given added importance to the closely parallel issues of liability to, or exemption from, *tutela* (guardianship of minors and women) and *cura* (guardianship of cases other than minors and women) under Roman civil law. Thus it was that the earliest work of Roman law written in Greek of which any substantial extracts survive, Herennius Modestinus' "Exemption from *tutela* and *cura*," written perhaps in the 220s,[7] goes beyond its title and deals repeatedly with exemption from city liturgies, as being dependent on almost exactly the same conditions. So, for instance, Modestinus writes "Grammar teachers, sophists, rhetors, and those doctors called *periodeutai* enjoy exemption from the other *leitourgiai*, as they do from *tutela* and *cura*" (*Dig.* 27, 1, 6, 1). Shortly after, he quotes an extract from the enactments of Commodus, paraphrasing a letter of Marcus Aurelius, which gives a vivid impression both of the exercise of the imperial will and of the range of functions from which exemptions might be sought (27, 1, 6, 8):

> In a manner similar to all these cases my most divine father, immediately upon assuming power, confirmed in an edict the existing privileges and exemptions, writing that philosophers, rhetors, grammar teachers, and doctors should be exempt from gymnasiarchies, *agoranomiai* [posts as market supervisor], priesthoods, providing lodgings, buying corn or oil, acting as a judge, going on an embassy, being enrolled in the army against their will, or being forced to undertake any other provincial or other service.

7. Text in O. Lenel, *Palingenesia Iuris Civilis* I, cols. 707–18; for a sketch of some issues relating to the adoption and reception of Roman law in the Greek East, see F. Millar, "Culture grecque et culture latine dans le Haut-Empire: la loi et la foi," in *Les martyrs de Lyon (177), Lyon 20–23 Septembre 1977, Coll. Int. du CNRS 575* (1978), 187.

Modestinus is actually quoting this extract in order to prove by analogy that philosophers were exempt from *cura*, which is not explicitly mentioned. Moreover, in an extract from Antoninus Pius' letter to the *koinon* (league of cities) of Asia, which Modestinus quotes immediately above (*Dig.* 27, 1, 6, 7), philosophers are not listed among the exempt categories. Yet, in fact, from the moment when Flavius Archippus, summoned by Pliny the Younger to act as a *iudex*, began to "claim exemption as a philosopher," apparently with success, no entirely consistent view ever was evolved. The question remained a disputed area of case law, in which exemption could be asserted or denied, or restricted to functions involving personal effort, leaving financial obligations intact.[8]

But even the exemptions granted to the other learned professions required interpretation at a local level, which Modestinus proceeds to supply:

> It is necessary to be clear as to the following, that it is the man who is responsible for teaching or healing in his native city who gains this exemption from liturgies [*aleitourgēsia*]. For if a man who is from Comana acts as a sophist, doctor, or teacher in Neocaesarea, he does not benefit from *aleitourgēsia* among the Comanans. (27, 1, 6, 9)

These extracts, which involve complex issues which need not be discussed further here,[9] are enough to illustrate, firstly, the extension of imperial law-giving beyond the sphere of Roman law proper, and its potential importance in the distribution of functions within any provincial city; and, secondly, the close analogies between *tutela* and *cura* as obligations of Roman private law, offices and burdens imposed for the benefit of a city, and services demanded by the Roman state as such.

In the nature of the case *munera* or *leitourgiai*, personal or financial obligations imposed on individuals, without being actual offices, and performed either for the city or (directly or indirectly) for the Roman state, defied all accurate categorization; the two attempts at classification which survive, by Hermogenianus (*Dig.* 50, 4, 1) and Arcadius Charisius (50, 4, 18), are both no more than ex post facto attempts to describe a complex reality with infinite local variations; and in any case they adopt different principles. Moreover, the distinction between *honores* and *munera*, though never entirely lost (see, e.g.,

8. Pliny, *Ep.* 10, 58; Philostratus, *VS* 1, 8 (Favorinus' unsuccessful case before Hadrian); *Frag. Vat.* 149 (general immunity); *Dig.* 27, 1, 5–7 (exemption from *tutela*; liability for obligations on property); *Dig.* 50, 5, 8, 4 (philosophers, if they teach actively, excused *tutela* and personal duties, not expenditure); *CJ* 10, 42, 6 (Diocletian and Maximian refuse a philosopher exemption from "burdens which are imposed on property").

9. Cf. V. Nutton, "Two Notes on Immunities: *Digest* 27, 1, 6, 10 and 11," *JRS* 61 (1971): 52.

text to n. 46 below), was often little more than a matter of form; as Callistratus put it, *honores* conferred *dignitas* (social standing) and *munera* did not (*Dig.*
50, 4, 14). The important point was that both were liable to involve expenditure—which made them, depending on the circumstances, the privilege or
the burden of the upper classes. G. E. M. de Ste. Croix, in *The Class Struggle
in the Ancient Greek World*, 305, has pointed to the importance of the passage
of Aristotle (*Pol.* 6, 7) in which he recommends precisely the state of affairs
in which public office will involve a liturgical element, so that the poor will
be content to be ruled by the rich.

Thus when Libanius came in 362 to defend one Aristophanes, charged
with evading his obligations as a member of the town council of Corinth,
he spoke quite naturally of Aristophanes "spending on the *leitourgiai* of the
so-called general [*stratēgos*, or in Latin *duovir*, of the colony]." But circumstances had profoundly changed, and Aristophanes had dropped out of his
appointed rank (*taxis*) and, fleeing the life of a city politician, had entered on
that of a soldier. In fact, he had gone to Syria and gained the post of *agens in
rebus* (imperial agent); thus his patron, as Libanius says, had "established him
in the immunity [*adeia*] gained by a rank." [10]

That brings us back to the third crucial feature of what Libanius says in
the *Funeral Oration* about Julian's measures for the cities. For one of the most
important aspects of the way the Empire evolved in the third and fourth centuries is that, on top of all the other conditions of immunity available in the
High Empire (see below), a whole range of official positions and ranks in
the imperial service came to be regarded as conferring a lifelong immunity,
as they had not done before. Since in his major work, referred to above, de
Ste. Croix has claimed that the class struggle offers the most effective explanation of the fall of the Empire, it is important to stress that the divisions
which thus appeared at *this* level of society at any rate were not ones of class;
on the contrary, they were, in the strictest sense, ones of status. The relevant
statuses were acquired by individuals in the course of their lives as a result of
specific official action, bore either a genuine or a nominal relation to actual
office-holding, could be subject to deprivation, and were not transferable to
the next generation. What is more, we see in this period not only the emergence of a set of ranks and statuses with very specific and important social
consequences, but a precise example of something brilliantly analysed some
years ago by David Daube, [11] the formation of concepts by the creation of
abstract nouns from the related verbs, or in this case adjectives. As we shall

10. Libanius, *Or.* 14, 9–12.
11. D. Daube, *Roman Law: Linguistic, Social and Philosophical Aspects* (1969), chap. 1.

see in more detail below, the period from the second to the fourth century saw the emergence, first, of honorific appellations in adjectival form, *egregius, perfectissimus* (for equestrian office-holders), *clarissimus* (for senators), and then of the related nouns denoting formal statuses or ranks, *egregiatus, perfectissimatus, clarissimatus.* As was the case within so many other systems of rank or privilege in the Roman Empire, these ranks, once conceived of as such, could be petitioned for from the emperors; and, as elsewhere, the emperors found themselves simultaneously using these gradations of rank as a framework for the granting of individual exceptions and privileges, and making repeated attempts to impose new rules and limitations on their acquisition and prevent abuse. But before the significance of this linked set of changes can be grasped it is necessary to look at the cities in the early Empire and at a selection of the patterns of obligation and exemption which prevailed in them.

The Cities under the Early Empire: Obligations and Exemptions

Most of the cities on which the early Roman Empire rested were not created by Rome. Colonies (*coloniae*) — and even, in terms of their constitutions, titular colonies — of course were, as were a significant number of newly founded, or refounded, Greek cities.[12] Whether cities designated *municipia* are to be regarded as having been, in a constitutional sense, "created" by a charter (*lex*) issued from Rome, or by the emperor, must remain uncertain.[13] The network of self-governing colonies, *municipia, civitates* (towns with no specific Roman status), or Greek *poleis*, some enjoying various degrees of collective immunity or freedom,[14] which covered the provinces, thus exhibited a considerable variety of constitutions, from the presence or otherwise of an effective popular assembly to the size, function, and method of appointment of their council and the nature and number of their annual offices (*honores/archai*).

12. See the survey by A. H. M. Jones, *The Greek City* (1940), chap. 1.

13. Space does not allow a review of responses, especially in the light of the Tabula Irnitana, to the heretical suggestion in *ERW*, 397–407, 485–86 and app. IV, that *municipia* were not centrally "created" by charter and that the ordinary citizens of "Latin" communities were *peregrini*.

14. Modern work renders our conception of the real content of these terms if anything more complex and obscure than before. See, e.g., L. Bernhardt, *Imperium und Eleutheria* (1971); "Die Immunitas der Freistädte," *Historia* 29 (1980): 190; and "Immunität und Abgabenpflichtigkeit bei römischen Kolonien und Munizipien in den Provinzen," *Historia* 31 (1982): 343.

They varied most of all in the character and distribution of duties or obligations (*munera/leitourgiai*) which were not annual offices and conferred no *dignitas* (see above), but which involved personal effort or expense, or both. None the less, as was stressed earlier (text to n. 3 above), the emperors did issue legal pronouncements which were held to be valid equally for all types of community; consonantly with this, lawyers came to use first *res publica* and later *civitas* as a term to denote any of these communities without distinction.[15] In this general sense it is therefore possible for us also largely to ignore local variations, to focus on the content of imperial rule-giving and hence to think of *honores* and *munera* as having a collective history under the Empire.[16] But although it is to the fact of imperial rule-giving that we owe the possibility of gaining any conception of this history, it is essential to see the entire process not as a one-sided series of pronouncements from the centre of power, but as a constant dialogue of petition and response in which interested individuals and groups sought to gain exceptions for themselves, to have an existing exemption extended to them or to have it generalised. Since an exemption for group A necessarily meant increased burdens for group B, both particular and general claims to exemption were frequently contested by the cities, verbally or in writing, before the emperor. Thus in at least two cases which happen to have survived in our evidence, the process which I have called metaphorically a "dialogue" appears as a quite literal dialogue between the emperor and interested parties. It is in this context of a dynamic interchange between the subject population and the emperor that we can look at some aspects of the wider background of claims and counter-claims over immunities in the cities, before turning to the specific question of Roman ranks and statuses. Handlists of the conditions and categories which conferred immunity are available,[17] and it will only be necessary to pick out a few salient issues.

In a world made up of innumerable local communities, each with its own citizenship, the first question which arose was what factors determined one's citizenship of, or obligations to, a particular place.[18] Hadrian laid down in an

---

15. See A. Mócsy, "Ubique Res Publica," *Acta Antiqua Academiae Scientiarum Hungaricae* 10 (1962): 367; J. Gascou, "L'emploi du terme *respublica* dans l'épigraphie latine d'Afrique," *MEFRA* 91 (1979): 383.

16. See L. Neesen, "Zur Entwicklung der Leistungen und Ämter (munera et honores) im römischen Kaiserreich des zweiten bis vierten Jahrhunderts," *Historia* 30 (1981): 203.

17. See, e.g., W. Langhammer, *Die rechtliche und soziale Stellung der Magistratus Municipales und der Decuriones* (1973): 262–77; Neesen (n. 16), 216–23.

18. For a detailed treatment, see D. Nörr, "Origo," *Tijdschr. v. Rechtsg.* 31 (1963): 525; *RE* Supp. X (1965), 433.

edict (*edictum*) that local citizenship was created by *origo* (birth), manumission (by a citizen of the place), adlection or adoption, while the status of *incola* (non-citizen resident) arose from the establishment of *domicilium* (residence) in a place (*CJ* 10, 40, 7). *Origo* normally meant descent from a male citizen of the town (e.g., *CJ* 10, 39, 3), but there were places which retained the right to claim men's services on the basis of maternal descent;[19] on these grounds, for instance, the Heordaioi in Macedonia brought a case before Caracalla to claim liturgies from the sophist Philiscus. They were apparently successful, although he held a chair of rhetoric in Athens.[20] But if *origo* could give rise to disputes, the problem of the definition of *incolatus* (the status of an *incola*) was insuperable. In the earlier Empire, indeed, the principle that *incolae* were liable to *munera* seems not yet to have been generally established. At any rate a well-known inscription from Aquileia shows that C. Minicius Italus, a prominent equestrian who was prefect of Egypt in 100/1, had petitioned Trajan to allow the town to impose *munera* on *incolae* there.[21] Similarly, in the same period, the colony of Tuder is reported as having gained from its founder (Augustus) the right that *incolae* owning land in its territory should hold all *honores* there, as the colony of Fanum had subsequently "before the emperors."[22] But when the principle of the liability of *incolae* became generally accepted, how was *incolatus* to be defined? The imperial replies in the *Codex Justinianus* show the emperors engaged in a constant process of restatement in answer to the claims of interested parties. Diocletian and Maximian were to lay it down that temporary residence did not make one an *incola*; nor did buying a house, even from the estate of a town councillor there (*CJ* 10, 40, 3–4). "Antoninus" (probably Caracalla) stated, in reply to one Paulinus, that the status of *incola* could be extinguished by moving one's domicile: "It is not to your disadvantage if, while you were an *incola*, you undertook some *munus*, provided that you transferred your domicile before being summoned to other *honores*" (*CJ* 10, 40, 1). This principle, however, in no way affected the claims of one's *origo*; so, for instance, Caracalla replied to a man from Byblos who was resident in Berytus that he was liable to *munera* in both cities (*CJ* 10, 39, 1). What of students living in another city for the sake of their studies? Hadrian laid down a limit of ten years within which students could enjoy

19. E.g., *Dig.* 50, 1, 1, 2. See A. J. Marshall, "Pompey's Organisation of Bithynia: Two Neglected Texts," *JRS* 58 (1968): 103.

20. Philostratus, *VS* 2, 30.

21. *ILS* 1374; R. K. Sherk, *Municipal Decrees of the Roman West* (1979), no. 2.

22. Agennius Urbicus, *de controversiis agrorum*, in *Corpus Agrimensorum Romanorum* I, 1, ed. Thulin, p. 45.

immunity in their place of study. When Severus Alexander replied, quoting this, to a man named Crispus, his words allow us to glimpse the tensions and suspicions to which the system inevitably gave rise: "Nor are those persons themselves who stay in any place for the sake of their studies regarded as having their *domicilium* there—unless after the lapse of ten years they establish residence there, as laid down by a letter of the deified Hadrian—nor is a father who frequently travels there because of a son who is a student. But if it is shown that you have other reasons for *domicilium* in the most splendid *civitas* of the Laodiceans, your deceit will not help you to avoid performing *munera*" (*CJ* 10, 40, 2). By contrast, Diocletian, replying to a group of students from Arabia at Berytus, preferred an age limit of twenty-five (10, 50, 1).

Then there were groups who were permanently established in the area of a city, but were either constitutionally or geographically marginal to it. Here too our evidence provides instances which are clearly located in space and time. A well-known inscription from Tergeste shows that a senator from there, Fabius Severus, had won a case before Antoninus Pius to establish that people from the "attributed" tribes of the Carni and Catuli could be admitted to the town council and thus share the "*munera* of the *decurionatus* [membership of a town council]."[23] Elsewhere the division of *munera* might be at issue between towns and neighbouring large estates.[24] Ulpian, however, sets out the principle that country people should be exempt, on the grounds that *munera* are the obligation of those who enjoy the delights of city life, its forum, baths, spectacles, and festivals (*Dig.* 50, 1, 27, 1). The same thought recurs in Modestinus' Greek work, *Exemption* (*Dig.* 50, 1, 35), and perhaps lies behind the claims made in the famous papyrus record of a case before the prefect of Egypt circa A.D. 250. The issue concerned the resistance by villagers to the imposition of *leitourgiai* by officials of a metropolis; reference is twice made to a ruling by Septimius Severus that villagers (*kōmētai* or *geōrgoi*) were to be exempt.[25]

The gradual spread of imperial estates introduced a further complication. Were the contractors (*conductores*) for the rents of the estates, or the actual tenants (*coloni*), liable to the *munera* of local towns? Or were the claims of the *fiscus* overriding? Our sources of the second and early third centuries give confusing answers. Or, on the contrary, might the local councils be obliged

---

23. *ILS* 8860; Sherk (n. 21), no. 1. For "attribution," see U. Laffi, *Adtributio e contributio* (1966).

24. Agennius Urbicus (n. 22), 45–46.

25. T. C. Skeat and E. P. Wegener, "A Trial before the Prefect of Egypt Appius Sabinus, *c.* 250 A.D.," *JEA* 21 (1935): 224.

to *appoint* superintendents for such estates, as a liturgy, as happened in Panopolis in 298?[26] By A.D. 342 the principle that imperial tenancies overrode
local obligations had re-emerged; as a result it was reported to Constantius
that city councillors in the diocese of Oriens were actively seeking such tenancies as a means of gaining exemption.[27]

Different problems were created by the existence, above all in the Greek
East, of professions which were by their nature peripatetic, or which enjoyed
a prestige which allowed successful individual practitioners to move about
freely, or be attracted to the major cities. Thus, to take an obvious example,
our evidence for Roman grants of exemption from taxation, liturgies, and
the quartering of troops, as made to members of the association (*synodos*) of
stage performers devoted to Dionysus, goes back to a pronouncement by an
unnamed Roman office-holder in the late second century B.C. [28] Very similar
privileges were granted to an association of athletes in Asia by M. Antonius as Triumvir; among other things they had asked for "exemption from
military service, all liturgies, and providing lodgings."[29] It is characteristic
that the exemptions granted cover both the internal life of the cities and
services provided directly for the Roman state. Thereafter the privileges of
the associations of athletes and stage performers, as reaffirmed by successive
emperors, can be traced until the Tetrarchic period.[30]

Similar exemptions, intended to be valid everywhere, and in all categories
of city, were granted under the Empire to members of various learned professions: doctors, rhetors or sophists, grammar teachers. The details, partly
illustrated above (text following n. 7) and often discussed elsewhere, need
not be repeated here. What is important to stress is that imperial rulings and
replies show comparable claims being made by other professional groups, and
being either partially or wholly rejected by the emperors. Philosophers were
not included among the professions for which each city (in Asia) could grant
a specific number of immunities. Their claims for exemption from financial
burdens on their property were also generally rejected; but the emperors did
normally accept that they should have immunity from *munera* involving personal duties.[31] Members of other groups, however, received wholly negative

26. See *ERW*, 180.

27. *CTh* 12, 1, 33. See F. Millar, "The *Privata* from Diocletian to Theodosius," in C. E.
King, ed., *Imperial Revenue, Expenditure and Monetary Policy in the Fourth Century A.D.* (BAR.
Int. Ser. 76, 1980), 125.

28. *IG* VII, 2413–14; R. K. Sherk, *Roman Documents from the Greek East* (1969), no. 44.

29. Sherk (n. 28), no. 57; see *ERW*, 456.

30. *ERW*, 456–63.

31. Text to n. 8 above.

answers: *hydraulae* (players on water organs) (*CJ* 10, 48, 4); *venatores* (hunters) (10, 48, 6); *calculatores* (teachers of arithmetic) (10, 53, 4); doctors not on the list made up by the local council (10, 53, 5); poets (10, 53, 3); *geometrae* (land measurers) and teachers of law (*Frag. Vat.* 150)—unless the latter taught in Rome (*Dig.* 27, 1, 6, 12)—and teachers of *primae litterae* (elementary school) (*Dig.* 50, 4, 11, 4; 5, 2, 8). The emperors thus faced repeated attempts to have immunities extended by analogy to wider groups and (in this area) succeeded in keeping relatively clear boundaries. By contrast, as regards the favoured group, Constantine both reaffirmed their immunities and ordered that salaries should be paid to them "so that they may the more easily train many in liberal studies and the above-mentioned skills" (*CTh* 12, 3, 3; cf. 10, 53, 6).

As regards occupations of more obvious and literal utility, a rather different range of issues arose. It also made some difference whether their functions were purely internal to the cities, involved supplies or services for Rome, or were performed in Rome itself (the latter category will not be considered here). In all cases it was a question of ensuring that groups which had been granted exemptions in respect of useful functions really were devoting their resources to those functions. As regards the purely local aspect, our best evidence is the inscription listing all the names of those registered as *centonarii*, or firemen, at Solva in Noricum in 205.[32] The preceding letter by Severus and Caracalla, probably addressed to the governor of the province, is worth quoting in full; for it provides the perfect illustration of the fact that the imperial rulings of this period, of a type familiar from the *Digest*, could in fact affect even the internal arrangements of small towns in the western provinces:

[Imp(erator) Caes(ar) L(ucius) Sept(imius) Severus] Pert(inax) P(ius) [Aug(ustus) and I]mp(erator) Caes(ar) M(arcus) Aur(elius) Antoninus Pius Aug(ustus) [to . . . ?]. The privileges [*beneficia*] which [on the orders] of the Senate or any emperor have been granted to the associations [*collegia*] of *centonarii* [firemen] ought not to be rashly revoked. [But as for what the laws] enjoin, let it be observed, and let those who you state [are enjoying] their wealth without burden be compelled [to undertake public] obligations [*publica munera*]; nor should the privilege of the associations benefit [either those who] do not practise [that profession] or those who possess resources which are greater than the stated limit. The [legal] remedy is [therefore] to be applied in relation to

32. *FIRA*² I, no. 87; revised text and commentary in E. Weber, *Die römerzeitlichen Inschriften der Steiermark* (1969), no. 149.

[such people], rather than reducing the [fixed] number on their account. Otherwise let [all the others enjoy] an exemption [*vacatio*] which
it is not appropriate to delete from the privileges of the associations.

There followed a list of the ninety-three members of the *collegium*, or association, of *centonarii*, as constituted in the *res publica* of the Solvenses in 205.
Both the general principle and the particular application of the rule are thus
quite clear. Those who possessed the resources adequate for the performance
of *munera publica* must *either* undertake those obligations *or*, if they wished to
enjoy the exemptions granted to the *collegium*, must genuinely practise the
relevant trade or profession. What is more, this exemption was not to apply
beyond a stated limit (*praefinitus modus*) of wealth. This principle closely re-
sembles that which we find in the *Digest*, in an extract from Callistratus' *de
cognitionibus*, written in the Severan period: "Immunity is granted to certain
collegia . . . but it is not given to all those who are co-opted into those associations, but only on the condition that they are [genuine] practitioners. But it
has often been noted that those who [subsequently?] increase their resources
and are capable of undertaking the *munera* of the cities may not enjoy the
privileges granted to the poorer men who are members of the associations"
(*Dig.* 50, 6, 6, 12).
    So far as can be seen, these rulings represent a general and (in intention)
universally applicable intervention in the system of obligations and exemptions within the cities, without there being any direct interest on the part of
the Empire as a governing superstructure. The associations of (for instance)
firemen were therefore regarded as performing services to their cities which
were mutually exclusive alternatives to the general *munera publica*.
    Different considerations applied to the exemptions enjoyed by shipowners
(*navicularii*) and traders (*negotiatores*), for it is clear that these only applied, in
the High Empire, to those who were engaged in bringing supplies to Rome:
"[T]he deified Hadrian stated in a rescript that those enjoy the immunity
associated with seagoing ships who are serving the *annona* [food supply] of
the City" (*Dig.* 50, 6, 6, 5; cf. 50, 5, 2, 3). Here too the question arose of people
who either invested a small proportion of their wealth in ships with the express purpose of avoiding *munera*, or, on becoming wealthier, kept the same
investment in ships in absolute terms (*Dig.* 50, 6, 1; 6, 6, 8–9). A local application of these general principles is visible in a letter written in Greek by
Marcus Aurelius and Lucius Verus, evidently to a Greek city: "There have
been others who on the excuse of belonging to the shipowners or to the
traders in corn or oil for the market of Rome, who are immune, have claimed
to escape *leitourgiai*, although they neither sailed themselves nor had the ma-

jority of their property in shipowning or trade. Let their immunity be removed" (*Dig.* 50, 6, 6, 6).

The principle of the exemption of shipowners was still maintained in the fourth century; Constantine confirmed this in writing to the shipowners of the diocese Oriens in 334, mentioning Constantinople and referring specifically to the *munera*, *honores*, and *tutela* mentioned before (*CTh* 13, 5, 7). Without pursuing the details, it is important to emphasize that claims to exemptions on the one hand, and on the other the determination on the part of the emperors that, *as regards those with sufficient wealth*, that wealth should be devoted *either* to specific services *or* to *munera publica*, forms the background to some aspects of the creation of the so-called caste system in the fourth century.[33] What the emperors of this period were attempting to do was to reinforce the principle just mentioned, that wealth should be devoted *either* to specific services *or* to *munera publica*, by attaching the obligation to fulfil the functions of a shipper specifically to any *property* owned by a shipowner, whether it passed to a son or to anyone else. Hence there emerged the rule that the property of a shipowner should not be alienated to avoid fulfilling the relevant functions—and that, *if it were*, the obligation should fall on the purchaser (*CTh* 13, 6, 1); or (a rule promulgated in the same year, 326) that if a shipowner died intestate and without heir, his property should go to the association (*corpus*) of shipowners (*CJ* 6, 62, 1). Even someone of a "higher dignity" (see below), if he owned a *property* which was liable to the functions of a shipowner, was liable to the obligations in respect of that property (*CTh* 13, 5, 3).

The objective of retaining *resources* for particular functions, above all the *munera* of the cities, quickly emerged when Constantine in 313 defined a new category as performing essential services for the state, namely the Christian clergy, and used immunity from *munera* as their reward. Clerics were to devote their services to the worship of God and to receive the due reward for their labours; hence "I wish them to be constituted once and for all as exempt [*aleitourgētous*] from all *leitourgiai*."[34] Once again a vast case law on the limits and conditions of clerical immunity quickly built up. All that needs to be noted here is that within a few years it proved necessary to *prevent* decurions

---

33. See A. H. M. Jones, "The Caste System in the Later Roman Empire," in *The Roman Economy* (1974), 396. The connection is also made in the detailed and useful article by D. Liebs, "Privilegien und Standeszwang in den Gesetzen Konstantins," *RIDA* 24 (1977): 297.

34. Eusebius, *HE* 10, 7, to the proconsul of Africa, Anullinus, in 313. See T. G. Elliott, "The Tax Exemptions Granted to Clerics by Constantine and Constantius II," *Phoenix* 32 (1978): 326.

(town councillors), or their sons, or simply persons of adequate wealth for undergoing public *munera*, from being enrolled as clerics (*CTh* 16, 2, 3); to impose limits and conditions on ordination; and, "if in doubt as between *civitas* [the relevant city] and *clerici*," to prefer the former. The emperors were in this case, as in so many others, in a self-contradictory posture, wishing to divide resources between functions which were held to be essential but to be mutually exclusive, and thus limiting with one hand the very privilege which they had given with the other. So Constantius in February 361 proclaimed that "our state" (*res publica nostra*) was sustained more by the observance of the Christian religion than by secular efforts, and so justified clerical immunity (*CTh* 16, 2, 16); but in August of the same year he issued rules for the ordination of clerics, involving the reservation for the town council of part of the property of newly appointed presbyters, deacons and sub-deacons (*CTh* 12, 1, 49). That was merely an extreme instance of the process by which those felt to be of service to the state were offered exemptions on which the state itself had constantly to place limits.

Service to the State, Citizenship, and Exemption

As we have seen above (text to n. 28), even under the Republic Rome might grant or confirm a general exemption from liturgies to favoured groups. It might also do so for named individuals who had performed exceptional services, as in the decree of the senate of 78 B.C. rewarding three Greek ship captains, Asclepiades of Clazomenae, Polystratus of Carystus, and Meniscus of Miletus. The Senate decreed, among other things, that as a reward for their services in the "Italian War," they and their descendants should be exempt from liturgies (*aleitourgētoi*) in their native cities, and free of tribute.[35] The grant was thus both a *beneficium* (favour) conferred by the sovereign power and a direct intervention in the functioning of the cities concerned. Some forty years later another Greek *nauarchus* (sea captain), Seleucus of Rhosus, received comparable privileges, with the addition of the Roman citizenship, for himself and his descendants, as a reward for his activities in the Triumviral wars (the privileges he gained are thus relevant to those for ordinary veterans [see following section]). In the surviving text of the inscription the references to citizenship and freedom from tribute are fully preserved, while that to freedom from all liturgies is largely restored.[36] What is clear, however, is

---

35. Sherk (n. 28), no. 22, Greek text l. 12.

36. P. Roussel, "Un Syrien au service de Rome et d'Octave," *Syria* 15 (1934): 33; *IGLS* III, 718; Sherk (n. 28), no. 58, col. II, ll. 22–23.

that any such attendant privileges were listed separately, and therefore were not seen as automatic consequences of the Roman citizenship itself. This distinction was to be of crucial importance for the evolution of the Empire. The fact that it was with the coming of monarchy that the citizenship began to be widely extended to provincials is one aspect of the use of republican institutions, ranks, and privileges by the emperors as the material of patronage.[37] The consequences of individual grants of citizenship to richer provincials, and hence their descendants, might have been disastrous for the working of *honores* and *munera* in the provincial cities. For it might well have been assumed or claimed that the Roman citizenship exempted a man from his local obligations. In fact, it is quite clear that it was so argued, and Augustus' third edict from Cyrene is an emphatic answer to just such claims:[38]

> If any persons from the province of Cyrene are honoured with the [Roman] citizenship, I declare that these must none the less undertake liturgies in their turn within the community of the Greeks, with the exception of those to whom, in accordance with a law or decree of the Senate, exemption from tribute [*aneisphoria*] has been granted along with citizenship by the decision of my father or myself. Furthermore it is my pleasure that those persons to whom exemption from tribute has been given shall be immune [*ateleis*] as regards those properties which they then owned, but as regards subsequent acquisitions they should pay whatever is due.

Once again we see here an implicit rather than explicit correspondence between different forms of exemption, from Roman tribute and from local liturgies. But the key point is the clear refutation of the idea that either or both of these exemptions would follow necessarily on the acquisition of the Roman citizenship. The principle of a dual citizenship (or Cicero's notion that each man has two *patriae*, his home town and Rome)[39] was thus conclusively established, and was to form the social basis of the running of the Empire for three centuries. The spread of the citizenship was to provide a rich harvest of rules and exceptions, petitions and responses, as regards, for instance, the law of inheritance or *patria potestas* (the Roman father's legal authority over his children).[40] But it does not seem ever to have been claimed

37. For this aspect of the ambivalent role of the emperors vis-à-vis the institutions of the Republic, see A. Wallace-Hadrill, "Civilis Princeps: Between Citizen and King," *JRS* 72 (1982): 32, esp. 46–47.

38. *SEG* IX, 8; *FIRA*² I, no. 68, III.

39. Cicero, *de leg.* 2, 5.

40. See, e.g., *ERW*, 483–85.

subsequently that the Roman citizenship affected a man's obligations to his native city. Given the wide extension of individual grants, the existence of the privilege of *latinitas* by which the annual magistrates (or the whole council) of a city automatically became citizens, and above all the evolution in the first century of a system by which discharged auxiliaries were granted the citizenship, the maintenance of the principle of dual citizenship was of fundamental importance.

Veterans and Immunity

But was it in fact true that each of several thousand discharged auxiliaries returning home (or settling elsewhere) each year with a grant of the citizenship was liable to local liturgies? Certainly no such exemption is recorded among the *beneficia* (grants) listed in the *diplomata* (certificates of privileges) given to discharged auxiliaries.[41] But some veterans certainly benefitted from various immunities, and a badly damaged papyrus of the first century records that a veteran recited (presumably in court) an edict of Octavian as Triumvir: he had granted veterans immunity (from tribute?) for all their property, the citizenship for themselves and their families, exemption from further military service and from performing *munera publica*, as well as, among other privileges, that of being neither an ambassador (i.e., one sent by a city), nor *procurator* (?) (financial agent), nor contractor for collecting the tribute.[42] Another veteran, from the *legio X Fretensis*, recorded in A.D. 94 that he had copied from a bronze tablet at the great Caesareum in Alexandria an edict by which Domitian in 88/9 had declared that all veterans and their families were immune from indirect taxes (*vectigalia* and *portoria*) and (probably) that their properties were immune from receiving official travellers.[43] These wide-ranging grants are not fully confirmed by other evidence; but both documents show that, here as elsewhere, it was up to the interested party to produce evidence for privileges or exemptions which he claimed. The exemption from *munera publica* does, however, reappear on a papyrus of 172, in which a veteran settled in the Arsinoite Nome complains that liturgies have been imposed on him in spite of the five-year relief (*anapausis*) granted to them.[44] Other evidence shows that this particular veteran had served in the

---

41. *CIL* XVI; M. M. Roxan, *Roman Military Diplomas, 1954–1977* (1978); *Roman Military Diplomas, 1978–1984* (1985); and *Roman Military Diplomas, 1985–1993* (1994).

42. *BGU* II, no. 628; *CIL* XVI, app. no. 10; S. Daris, *Documenti per la storia dell' esercito romano in Egitto* (1964), no. 100.

43. *ILS* 9059; *CIL* XVI, app. no. 12; Daris (n. 42), no. 104.

44. *BGU* I, no. 180; *Sel. Pap.* II, no. 285; Daris (n. 42), no. 105. See N. Lewis, "Exemption

cohors I Apamenorum, and hence was an ex-auxiliary. But if there was indeed a general five-year exemption for them, this is the only place where we hear of it. Otherwise our evidence from before the Tetrarchy speaks of "veterans," without distinction between legionaries and auxiliaries, and exhibits once again a complex case law which itself reflects the social pressures on a veteran settled among other persons all too eager to share the burden of *munera* with him. They enjoyed an immunity, without (in this evidence) any stated time limit, provided they had served at least twenty years. Those honourably discharged after between five and nineteen years' service earned, says Modestinus, a proportional period of relief from *tutela* (guardianship), as they did from other *politikai leitourgiai* (city liturgies).[45] However, those obligations, such as road repair, which fell on owners of property as such, could not be avoided (*Dig.* 49, 18, 4). The immunity applied in a community where a veteran was an *incola* and was not affected by his voluntarily undertaking an *honor* or *munus* (49, 18, 2, *pr.*). But if a veteran allowed himself to be enrolled in the town council (*ordo*), then he was liable for further *munera* (49, 18, 5, 2). Even here there was a way out, as Severus Alexander said in a reply to one Felicianus: "Veterans, who when they could have protected themselves by the immunity granted to them, have preferred to be made *decuriones* [members of a city council] in their home towns, cannot return to the exemption [*excusatio*] which they have abandoned, unless by a formal rule and agreement for the preservation of their immunity they have accepted [only] a part of that burden" (*CJ* 10, 44, 1). Moreover, as Caracalla replied to one Verinus, those ignominiously discharged were debarred from *honores* but not excused from *munera civilia* (city liturgies) (*CJ* 10, 55, 1). Finally, it did need to be stated that the sons of veterans enjoyed no immunity.[46] It is an important characteristic of the early Empire that, in spite of the obvious presence of a variety of ranks and statuses, the tendencies to inheritance of status, or even individual privileges, were very strictly limited.

From the Tetrarchic period onwards various changes occur in the values attached to the status of veteran, or the situation of being a veteran's son. In principle veterans continued to enjoy immunity, subject to a full period of service; so Diocletian and Maximian replied to a veteran named Carus (*CJ* 10, 55, 2). But in another rescript, to a veteran named Philopator, they refer to the principle that this immunity, after twenty years' service, was confined to sol-

---

from Liturgy in Roman Egypt," *Actes du Xe Congrès Internationale de Papyrologie 1961* (Warsaw, 1964), 69, esp. 72–73.

45. *Dig.* 26, 1, 8, 2–3.

46. *Dig.* 50, 5, 8, 2; *Frag. Vat.* 143 (*tutela*).

diers from legions or *vexillationes* (legionary detachments): "Hence, since you record that you have served in a cohort [of auxiliaries] you understand that it is pointless for you to wish to demand exemption" (10, 55, 3). Yet Valentinian and Valens were later to note that Diocletian himself had made an exception to this rule and had granted immunity to the *cohortales* (soldiers in auxiliary units) of Syria.[47] It is not clear whether it was only to those *cohortales* that Constantine referred when after his victory over Licinius he cancelled the municipal obligations to which "the tyrant" had "most wickedly" exposed them (*CTh* 7, 4, 1). Enough has been said to illustrate the significance of this form of reward for service, and the delicacy (and, for us, obscurity) of the borderlines surrounding it. If Constantine was in any doubt on the point, a group of veterans brought it home to him in a dialogue preserved in the *Codes* (*CTh* 7, 20, 2; *CJ* 12, 46, 1).

> The veterans shouted all together: "Constantine Augustus, what is the point of our having become veterans if we have no *indulgentia*."
>
> Constantine Augustus said: "I ought to be increasing the good fortune of my fellow-veterans more and more, rather than decreasing it."
>
> The veteran Victorinus said: "Let us not be compelled to undertake *munera* or burdens in any place."

Constantine concluded the dialogue with a general confirmation of the veterans' privileges and a reference to the sons of veterans. However, in this area too a shift of attitude had taken place whereby, *if* they had the required property, the sons of veterans were compelled *either* to accept the obligations of a town councillor *or* (*if* physically fit) to join the army.[48] Once again, the nature of the system, in regarding the two desirable forms of service as mutually incompatible, involved the emperors in unresolvable contradictions. Diocletian and Maximian had already expressed the idea of the sons of decurions (and others) fraudulently joining the army to avoid *civilia munera* (city liturgies) (*CJ* 12, 33, 2). By 319 Constantine was requiring men of curial origin (i.e., whose fathers sat on the city council, *curia*) who had been accepted into the army, or into provincial *officia* (the governor's staff), to be returned to their city council. Thereafter the provision was repeated with variations,[49] until Julian, going to some extent against his usual principles, allowed ten years' service to confer immunity.[50] Thus the very privilege which, as the

47. Cf. *CJ* 7, 64, 9; *CTh* 7, 20, 6. For *cohortales* as soldiers, see, e.g., *CTh* 7, 20, 4.

48. *CTh* 7, 22, 2–5; 12, 1, 13; 18; 32; 35 (A.D. 343).

49. *CTh* 7, 22, 1–6; 12, 1, 10–11; 13; 22; 32; 37; 40; 43; 45.

50. *CTh* 12, 1, 56 (the date is 21 December 362, twelve days before the Kalends of January in the consulship of the Emperor and Fl. Sallustius — 363).

veterans had shouted to Constantine, was one of the principal *rewards* of military service became a reason for *preventing* men from entering the army, even in a period of intense military activity on many fronts. Yet there are indications that men were also undergoing a purely nominal military service (*CTh* 12, 1, 40), gaining by influence a supposedly honourable discharge after a short time (12, 1, 43), or finding their way on to the staffs of provincial governors. The relation of civilian service to city obligations presents an even more complex evolution, with even more drastic consequences, than that of military service.

Ranks, Dignities, and Immunity in the First Three Centuries

Like the spread of the citizenship, the rise of men from the provincial cities into equestrian posts and the Senate can be regarded as a fundamental aspect of the early Empire. It can also be assumed without question that under the principle of "absence on public business" (see *Dig.* 4, 6, 32–33), those actually in post at any time will have been excused *honores* and *munera* in their home towns.[51] But, like the citizenship, attachment to one of the two higher *ordines* (the senatorial and equestrians orders) might have carried with it the privilege of life-time exemption, perhaps even extending to the next generation or to successive generations. That it did not in fact do so is one of various indications that statuses under the earlier Empire were more limited in their consequences and far less easily transferable to descendants than we often assume.

Let us take equestrian posts first, confining ourselves to the pre-Tetrarchic period. As mentioned below (n. 51), it is only in the more marginal cases of "absence on public business" that immunity needed actually to be stated; so Paulus writes, "The *comites* [companions] of governors and proconsuls and *procuratores* [financial officials] of Caesar are exempt from *munera* and *honores* and *tutelae*" (*Dig.* 50, 5, 12, 1). For the procurators and other officials themselves it did not need to be explicitly stated. But what permanent privilege, if any, was conferred by either membership in the equestrian order (or nominal possession of a "public horse," if that is a narrower category) or the fact of *having held* equestrian military or civilian posts? No explicit rule is stated anywhere until Carus, Carinus, and Numerianus write in 282, with an unhelpful delicacy and ambiguity: "Those also, who are proved to have acted

51. The principle is specifically related to exemptions in a few relatively marginal cases; see, e.g., Hermogenianus in *Dig.* 27, 1, 41, pr. — 2. Cf. *Frag. Vat.* 131: a *libertus* (freedman) seeing to the affairs of a senator, excused from *tutela*, but not from *munera sordida* (manual liturgies), and *CJ* 5, 62, 13.

as procurators of our possessions, ought to perform *munera civilia* which are appropriate to their dignity" (*CJ* 10, 48, 1). The implication seems clearly to be that there was at that time no general rule exempting former procurators from city *munera*. Much more significant, however, is the fact that the career inscriptions of scores of men of equestrian rank from the High Empire combine city offices, including duovirates and priesthoods, and *munera* such as embassies, with equestrian posts in the imperial service.[52] The issue might seem to be decided in favour of non-exemption but for the possibility that (as Eric Birley argued in a classic article) the city posts normally came first in order of time, and that hence equestrian military officers as a group can be seen as mature ex-holders of municipal posts.[53] Moreover, as in the case of veterans (text following n. 45 above), we have to allow for voluntary acceptance of *honores* or *munera*; so individual cases of the performance of these functions cannot strictly prove that there was no legal exemption. But a considerable volume of evidence, especially from the Greek East,[54] shows that former equestrian office-holders held priesthoods and presidencies of games, spent large sums in their native cities, and in some cases held actual city magistracies; and this strongly suggests the absence not only of a legal exemption but (more important) of any general conception of the incompatibility of the two spheres of activity. Moreover, if the acceptance of city or provincial functions had involved a temporary renunciation of a standing exemption, it would be reasonable to expect that some honorific inscriptions would at least occasionally mention this. The provisional conclusion must be that in the High Empire there was no concept of permanent exemption from city functions either for the possessors of equestrian status (however defined) or for the ex-holders of equestrian military or civilian offices. We may note the contrast between this and the exemption from "plebeian" punishments and forms of judicial torture reported to have been granted by Marcus Aurelius to the sons and grandsons of *eminentissimi* and *perfectissimi*— honorific equestrian statuses to be discussed below.[55]

52. See, e.g., Pflaum, *Carrières*, nos. 1; 3; 5; 7; 11; 13 *bis*; 16; 24 *bis*; 25; 37; 55; 59; 63, etc. From the third century, note esp. Pflaum, no. 319, L. Caecilius Athenaeus, *flamen perpetuus* at Sufetula, whose duovirate there, involving shows (*voluptates*), is commemorated on his inscription (*CIL* VIII, 11340) and clearly followed his equestrian career.

53. "The Equestrian Officers of the Roman Army," in *Roman Britain and the Roman Army* (1953), 133.

54. See F. Quass, "Zur politischen Tätigkeit der munizipalen Aristokratie des griechischen Ostens in der Kaiserzeit," *Historia* 31 (1982): 188, 198–99, for holders of equestrian posts.

55. *CJ* 9, 41, 11 (Diocletian and Maximian); see P. D. A. Garnsey, *Social Status and Legal*

Even in the case of senators, the exemptions attested from the early Empire are strikingly specific and limited. This fact must of course be seen in the light of the restricted number of senators (in principle 600) and the fact that it took time for senatorial status to extend into the upper reaches of provincial society (or rather that of some provinces), in the course of the first three centuries. None the less, it is significant that it had to be stated that a *legatus legionis* (a commander of a legion) was exempt from *tutela* while in office (*Frag. Vat.* 222) and therefore by implication was not exempt *qua* senator as such. Senators were indeed liable, though not while holding office in Rome (*Frag. Vat.* 146), but even then only within the 200th milestone from Rome (*Frag. Vat.* 147) — or the 100th according to Marcianus (*Dig.* 27, 1, 21, 3). This last point, of course, relates to the presumption, which began to be unrealistic in the third century, that senators were in principle resident in Rome; by analogy it may well have been held to affect liability to public functions in provincial cities. Moreover, personal status did certainly affect liability to *tutela*; precisely this is shown by the fact that Modestinus gives as evidence for the fact that *dignitas* did not confer exemption a rescript of Marcus Aurelius and Commodus stating that a senator was obliged to accept the *tutela* of (the children of) persons of senatorial status, but of lower rank within the Senate. Modestinus goes on to say that a person, when made a senator, was released from existing *tutelae* unless the children concerned were of senatorial status (*Dig.* 27, 1, 15, 2–3). Similar presumptions might well have affected liability to the public *munera* of a senator's provincial or Italian home town. But it is highly relevant that this last point is presented simply as a personal *opinion*, on the part of a jurist writing in the early third century. It is essential to remember that what we read in the *Digest* is not the remains of a "code," but of a number of academic legal works, expressing a variety of points of view.

The same is true of the other juristic views preserved in the *Digest* concerning the relation of a senator to his *patria*.[56] These are by no means identical and also show every sign of being personal reflections, or rationalizations, in the face of an evolving reality. So Paulus writes (*Dig.* 1, 9, 11):

> Senators, although they seem to have their *domicilium* in the City [i.e., Rome], none the less are understood to have *domicilium* also in the place of their origin, since their *dignitas* seems to have conferred an addition rather than a change of domicile.

Privilege in the Roman Empire (1970), esp. 142ff., 241ff.; P. A. Brunt, "Evidence Given under Torture in the Principate," *ZSS* 97 (1980): 256, esp. 262.

56. On this problem, see D. Nörr (n. 18); A. Chastagnol, "Le problème du domicile légal des sénateurs romains à l'époque impériale," in *Mél. L. S. Senghor* (1977), 43 (*non vidi*).

The *Sententiae Pauli* expresses a much more general principle and is the only text to relate the question of senatorial domicile to the second, third, and fourth generations (*Dig.* 50, 1, 22, 5):

> Senators and their sons and daughters, wherever born, and likewise their grandsons, [granddaughters], and great-grandsons and great-granddaughters by a son are removed from their [legal] *origo*, even though they retain municipal *dignitas*.

Finally, Hermogenianus, writing in the Tetrarchic period, puts it as follows (*Dig.* 50, 1, 23 *pr.*):

> A man ceases to be a *municeps* [citizen of a *municipium*] on gaining senatorial *dignitas*, as far as regards *munera*; but as regards *honor* [*honores?*] he is regarded as retaining his *origo*.

It will be obvious at once how frail a basis these passages are for any conception of a long-established general principle that senators were legally exempt from *honores* and *munera* in their home towns. By contrast, a surprising volume of epigraphic evidence from the first three centuries shows senators in fact holding regular *honores* and priesthoods, or (in a few cases) being town councillors in their native cities (or others), as well as (less surprisingly) spending large sums by way of munificence.[57] Once again, this cannot prove that a legal exemption was not available, for a sense of obligation to a man's home city might well have prevailed. In this connection it is worth recalling a reply given by Diocletian and Maximian: "A man who enjoys exemption [*vacatio*] from public *munera*, if he freely undertakes any *honor* other than the decurionate, does not, on account of the fact he has been influenced by the needs of his native city, or through eagerness for *gloria* has conceded his public rights, lose the relevant privilege" (*CJ* 10, 44, 2). But here, too, as with equestrians, the absence of any statement on any of the inscriptions to the effect that these senators were not availing themselves of a recognized exemption must create a presumption that none such was known.

Whatever may have been the normal rule in relation to personal *honores* and *munera*, there is no clear evidence that senators enjoyed a general exemption from obligations on property as such. In this connection a well-attested provision, laid down by a decree of the Senate of uncertain date, and attested by inscriptions from three different places, ordained that senators

---

57. See Quass (n. 54), 188–98, and esp. W. Eck, "Die Präsenz senatorischer Familien in den Städten des Imperium Romanum bis zum späten 3. Jahrhundert," *Studien zur antiken Sozialgeschichte: Festschrift F. Vittinghoff* (1980), 283.

were exempt from the *munus* of receiving official travellers against their will. These inscriptions from Paros (in both Latin and Greek), from Phrygia, and from Satala in Lydia, are all copies of a single letter to an unknown addressee written by Severus and Caracalla in Rome at the end of May 204; the emperors firmly remind the addressee of the provisions of the decree of the senate.[58] This exemption itself seems to represent a specific exception to the general rule stated by Ulpian, that the *munus* of receiving official travellers (*hospitium*) was one which lay on properties as such, without regard to the person of the owner.[59] This therefore represents a rather specific area of obligation/exemption, with no necessary implications for the wider question of civic obligations. But the fact that disputes could arise and that the personal rights even of senators could be in need of protection is clear from the fact that the letter of Severus and Caracalla, shorn of its original address (perhaps to a provincial governor) was found worth inscribing by different people (presumably senators or their agents) resident in several different places. We may compare the letter of Valerian and Gallienus to a senator from Smyrna named Iulius Apellas, evidently in reply to complaints from him about some infringement by the local magistrates of his rights in relation to his property there. Almost certainly the issue at stake here too is the reception of *hospites* (official travellers).[60] A century later the issue was still alive: in 361 Constantius wrote to the Senate: "If it is against the will of our senators, let no one stay in their houses by the right of *hospitium*" (*CTh* 7, 8, 1). If this very specific right had to be repeatedly re-stated, we can be reasonably sure, at least, that no general rule exempted senatorial properties as such from local obligations.

The roles performed by senators in their native cities in the first three centuries, and their need to seek imperial protection for the one exemption which is clearly attested, at least from the early third century onwards, illustrate an important truth about the Roman Empire. It is a clear and accepted fact that the Augustan period saw a number of concrete steps to define the senatorial and equestrian orders, partly in terms of a property qualification; to devise for them forms of social and ceremonial precedence, for instance, in the elections and public shows at Rome; and to introduce, in the case of the Senate, a certain element of heritability of status.[61] This meant, strictly speak-

58. T. Drew-Bear, W. Eck, and P. Herrmann, "Sacrae Litterae," *Chiron* 7 (1977): 355.

59. *Dig.* 50, 4, 3, 14. See Eck (n. 57), 379.

60. *CIL* III 412 = *IGR* IV 1404; see *ERW*, 421.

61. On these points, see, e.g., A. H. M. Jones, "The Elections under Augustus," *JRS* 45 (1955): 9 = *Studies in Roman Government and Law* (1960), 27; P. A. Brunt, "The Lex Valeria

ing, no more than that sons of senators had the automatic right to assume the
latus clavus (broad purple stripe worn on the tunic), while their actual membership of the Senate was still dependent on their gaining the quaestorship.
None the less, it was a step towards the creation of a senatorial order (*senato-
rius ordo*). In consonance with this, for instance, the Augustan marriage laws
forbade a senator, or his descendants for three generations, to marry a freedwoman; and the decree of the senate of A.D. 19 from Larinum forbids activity
in the arena to the descendants, down to the third generation, of both senators and equestrians (defined by the right to sit in the equestrian seats).[62] But
these steps were not followed either by a consistent tendency for the two
orders to become hereditary over long periods of time or by further steps
marking off a distinctive status or distinctive privileges. Even in the crucial
area of obligations in the cities, while "absence on public business" necessarily
gave exemption to senators and equestrians, and senators were also held in
some sense to have either their main, or an alternative, domicile in Rome,
men of both orders did in fact hold *honores* and undertake *munera*. Alone of
our legal sources the *Sententiae Pauli*, a text of unknown authorship written
some time in the third century, categorically affirms that senators and their
descendants to the fourth generation were removed from their native *origo*.

Rather than further legal steps to define the two orders, what actually
happened was a gradual process by which honorific appellations came to be
attached, never with complete consistency, to equestrians holding posts of
differing ranks and to senators as such. Following that, the adjectives used
gave rise to the related nouns, and simultaneously to the concept that the
nouns denoted statuses to which legal privileges might be attributed.

The sketch of the evolution of the equestrian status appellations which
follows is not based on a rigorous re-examination of all the sources—which
themselves are the product of the chances of survival. For the earlier period
in particular an impressionistic selection of the evidence, based on the work
of others, will suffice.[63] As regards equestrians, two different scales of honorific appellations appear. One, derived from the level of pay given to different ranks, runs *sexagenarius*, *centenarius*, *ducenarius*, and (very rarely) *trecenarius*

Cornelia," *JRS* 51 (1961): 71; C. Nicolet, "Le cens sénatorial sous la République et sous
Auguste," *JRS* 66 (1976): 20.

62. M. Malavolta, "A proposito del nuovo 'S.C.' da Larino," *Sesta Miscellanea greca e romana*
(1978): 347; *AE* 1978, 145; see also B. Levick, *JRS* 73 (1983): 97ff.

63. For surveys of the evolution of these appellations, see O. Hirschfeld, "Die Rangtiteln
der römischen Kaiserzeit," *Kleine Schriften* (1913), 646; A. Stein, *Der römische Ritterstand* (1922),
47–48; H.-G. Pflaum, "Titulature et rang social durant le Haut-Empire," in C. Nicolet, ed.,
Recherches sur les structures sociales dans l'antiquité (1970), 159.

(denoting a payment of 60,000, 100,000, 200,000, and 300,000 sesterces per annum, respectively).[64] The most commonly attested is *ducenarius*, which also gave rise to related nominal forms or phrases *procuratorem principis ducenaria perfunctum* (a procurator of the princeps who had filled a ducenariate post; Apuleius, *Met.* 7, 6); and *ad ducenariae procurationis splendorem* (to the rank of a ducenariate procurator; *AE* 1962, 183, *codicilli* [letters of appointment] of Marcus Aurelius). In the third century *ducenarius* functions also as a noun to designate a high-ranking procurator (e.g., Eusebius, *HE* 7, 30, 8). Perhaps more significant, *ex ducenariis* (Greek *apo doukēnariōn* [i.e., former *ducenarii*]) appears as a rank or status of former holders of the office (e.g., *AE* 1966, 446).

These terms, as we shall see in the following section, occasionally reappear in the Constantinian period along with those derived from the other scale of status appellations which evolved in the High Empire. This ran as follows:

1. *Eminentissimus* (*exochōtatos* in Greek), apparently reserved for praetorian prefects, and some prefects of the *vigiles* (fire brigades) in the third century, is found in use from Marcus Aurelius (*CIL* IX, 2438) until the middle of Constantine's reign (*CTh* 7, 20, 2, A.D. 320?).

2. *Perfectissimus* (*diasēmotatos*) is used of other high equestrian officials. According to Diocletian and Maximian (*CJ* 9, 41, 11; see text to n. 55 above), it was these two groups whose descendants Marcus Aurelius wished to protect from "plebeian" punishments and tortures. In documents, however, *perfectissimus* is not attested until 201 (*ILS* 1346), used of a prefect of the *annona* (the food supply of the city of Rome). In the course of the third century its use extended to equestrian governors and procurators.[65]

3. *Egregius*, in the form of its (eventual) Greek equivalent, *kratistos*, is used in the later first century of prefects of Egypt (*P. Oxy.* XLV 3240; XLVII 3335) and in the early second of an Idios Logos (a high financial official) (*P. Oxy.* XLVI 3275), and even of a proconsul of Asia (*SEG* XXVIII, 1566). But after the appearance of the other, more honorific, terms, it settled into use for the lower equestrian officials; it is used in this way under Marcus Aurelius (e.g., *ILS* 6885) and thereafter continues through the third century;[66] its last known uses come in the 320s, both in legal sources (*CTh* 6, 22, 1, A.D. 325/6), and in inscriptions.[67]

64. See *JRS* 53 (1963): 197–98 (chapter 8 in this volume).

65. See the list in Pflaum, *Carrières* II, 624.

66. See the list in Pflaum (n. 63), 178–79.

67. *IRT* 467 (Lepcis Magna) of 324–26; see T. D. Barnes, *The New Empire of Diocletian and Constantine* (1982), 168: "curante Cl. Aurel. Generoso v.e., cur. r.p." I owe the reference

Legal sources reveal, furthermore, that by the early fourth century nouns denoting statuses had been derived from both *perfectissimus* and *egregius*. These two nouns, *perfectissimatus* and *egregiatus*, are both attested for the first time in legal sources in the scattered fragments of an extensive imperial reply addressed "to the Bithynians" on 21 July 317. The *Codes* attribute it to Constantine, but it must in fact have been issued by Licinius. All the fragments concern the conditions for admission to higher *dignitates*, and some involve the consequent release from city *munera* (see the following section).

Before we examine the significance of this, it is necessary to look at the parallel evolution in senatorial status appellations. The term *clarissimus* (in Greek *lamprotatos*), which could be used in a variety of contexts, came to be a characteristic appellation for a senator about the beginning of the second century (*TLL*, s.v. "clarus" III); *clarissimus vir*, regularly abbreviated as *c.v.*, was soon followed by *clarissimus puer* (boy) and *clarissima femina/puella* (woman/girl). The corresponding notion of a specific rank or dignity also evolved. An inscription from Ureu in Africa, apparently of the early third century, honours a *c(larissimus) p(uer)*, whose father was an *e(gregius) v(ir)* and who is described as "having gained the *clarissima dignitas*."[68] The same *clarissima dignitas*, Ulpian states, is conferred by senatorial husbands on their wives (*Dig.* 1, 9, 8). Here too, therefore, there evolved the concept of a status or quality, which could be referred to by a nominal phrase. But, perhaps surprisingly, the final shift from *clarissimus* and *clarissima dignitas* to the abstract noun *clarissimatus* was relatively slow in coming. When Constantius, writing from Milan in 354, replied to the town council of Caesena, he still used *clarissima dignitas*: "[B]ut if anyone has acquired the insignia of the *clarissima dignitas*, and if he has not been able to obtain confirmation of the gift granted to him by producing *codicilli* [the letter of appointment], he shall lose the fruit of the *dignitas* he sought" (*CTh* 12, 1, 42).

Clarissimatus is perhaps less well attested precisely because it did not normally belong in the most contentious area, namely the borderline between city and imperial functions, but at a higher level. It first appears in legal sources in the 370s;[69] but Ammianus, writing in the 390s, looks back to the reign of Constantius (337–61), when *duces* (military commanders) were (as they should be) mere *perfectissimi*, and did not (as was known to happen later) gain the *clarissimatus* (Ammianus, 21, 16, 2).

---

to H. Löhken, *Ordines Dignitatum: Untersuchungen zur formalen Konstituierung der spätantiken Führungsschicht* (1982), 131, and n. 102.

    68. J. Peyras and L. Maurin, *Ureu: Municipium Uruensium* (1974), 37, no. 5 = *AE* 1975, 879.

    69. *CTh* 12, 1, 74, 5 (371); *CJ* 12, 1, 11, 1 (377).

It was the two lower "equestrian" grades, the *perfectissimatus* which lasted through the fourth century, and the *egregiatus*, which disappeared almost as soon as attested in legal sources, which stood immediately above the decurionate (i.e., the status of a city councillor, a *decurio*), with its heavy attendant burdens, and afforded a possible escape route from it. But to say that is to assume precisely that change which had evidently happened before 317. For, as we saw, in the first three centuries there is no clear proof either that equestrians as such, or former holders of equestrian posts, enjoyed any general exemption from municipal burdens. At some point, therefore, not only had the two abstract nouns, *perfectissimatus* and *egregiatus*, come into use, but the idea had become accepted that possession of either of these two qualities entitled a man to enjoy precisely that exemption which had previously been conferred only by being "absent on public business" in specific posts. This shift in the conditions for exemption, from actual temporary functions to a formal and permanent status, was a crucial one, with immense consequences. It would be of considerable significance if we could identify some evidence which would even illustrate, if not explain, the process of transition. As it happens, we have such evidence, in the form of a papyrus which has long been known, but seems never to have been fully re-examined since its first publication in 1912.[70] It will be worth-while to present a translation of the bulk of the text, with some comments on the essential points.[71]

P. Oxy. IX 1204: Aurelius Plutarchus

In the consulships of our lords the Emperors Diocletian for the seventh and Maximian for the sixth time, *Augusti* [A.D. 299], to Aurelius Zenagenes, *stratēgos* of the Oxyrhynchite nome, from Aurelius Plutarchus, also called Atactus, *kratistos* [*egregius*] and however he is styled. Since I was nominated to the *dekaprōteia* by Aurelius Demetrianus, *dekaprōtēs*, improperly and in contravention of all the laws, I made an appeal through the agency of my father, Aurelius Sarapammon, also called Dionysius and however he is styled, on the grounds that at that time I was in the Small Oasis for the discharge [*eksphungeusis*] of the soldiers

70. *P. Oxy.* IX 1204; partially quoted by A. H. M. Jones, *The Later Roman Empire* (1964), 70; cf. *ERW*, 289. There is nothing to support the suggestion of J.-M. Carrié, *ZPE* 35 (1979): 221–23, that Aurelius Plutarchus had the rank of *primipilaris* (a centurion who held the senior centurionate of a legion).

71. Dr. J. Rea has kindly re-read the papyrus for me from a photograph and assures me that only minor amendments of the published text are required.

stationed there, on the orders of my lord the *diasēmotatos* [*perfectissimus*] prefect of Egypt, Aelius Publius, and having done all that was required for the appeal, I fled to my lord the *diasēmotatos katholikos* [*perfectissimus rationalis*], Pomponius Domnus, and petitioned him via memoranda, setting these same facts before him. Consequently his Greatness ordered me through his judgement to give notice to the aforesaid person. The relevant part of the judgement runs as follows:

In the consulships of our lords the Emperors Diocletian for the seventh time and Maximian for the sixth time, *Augusti*, on the 14th day before the Kalends of September [19 August 299], in Alexandria in the *sekreton* [private office]: When Plutarchus, *kratistos* [*egregius*], had been called in, Isidorus said: "Plutarchus, *kratistos*, who stands before your Virtue, attempting to find relief from city liturgies [*politikai leitourgiai*], previously petitioned the divine Fortune of our masters, the *Augusti* and *Caesares*, to grant him the dignity of the *kratisteia* [*egregiatus*], and their divine Fortune assented and granted it to him, and it is now in him. He subsequently continued to serve your office, my Lord, and the orders of you great ones. But already, when he was spending time at the Small Oasis, after my lord and your brother, Publius, the *diasēmotatos* [*perfectissimus*] governor, had sent him to discharge the soldiers, a certain Demetrianus, an Oxyrhynchite of the same city, made an attack on him and dared to nominate him to the *dekaprōteia*, being unaware that he had gained a higher dignity [*axiōma*], which probably [*isōs*] relieves him of city liturgies. . . ."

The various parties to the transaction are clear. There are the emperors, who can grant the rank described in Greek by the abstract noun *kratisteia*. Then there is the prefect of Egypt, Aelius Publius, and the *rationalis* (chief financial official) of Egypt, Pomponius Domnus, both given the honorific appellation *perfectissimus*; Domnus receives the petition and hears the case in Alexandria. The town of Oxyrhynchus is seen attempting to discharge the tax-gathering functions laid on it, and other Egyptian towns, by the reform of Septimius Severus a century earlier.[72] One of the existing *dekaprōtoi*, or committee of ten wealthy men with the obligation of collecting (and guaranteeing) the taxes, makes the nomination which is the subject of the appeal. Finally, there is Aurelius Plutarchus himself, who had already conceived the notion that the dignity (*axiōma*) of the *kratisteia/egregiatus* would serve to relieve him of city liturgies. This idea, which he had successfully brought to fruition

72. See A. K. Bowman, *The Town Councils of Roman Egypt* (1972).

(possibly during Diocletian's campaigns and journeys in Egypt in 297–98),[73] was a personal initiative with a clearly defined aim. It is noticeable that his actual service to the administration of Egypt is emphasized but seems not to be regarded as a sufficient condition in itself either for exemption from the *dekaprōteia*, or for the dignity of the *kratisteia/egregiatus*. That is gained independently by a petition, notionally directed to all four *Augusti* and *Caesares*. The favourable response to it confers an abstract quality or status which can be conceived of as inhering "in" him and which confers immunity. Or does it? Plutarchus' advocate, Isidorus, strikes an unexpected note of uncertainty at the end of his submission. It would be invaluable if we could be sure what degree of certainty, uncertainty, suggestion, or persuasion is implied by the word *isōs* (perhaps? probably? surely? fairly? reasonably?) — "the *kratisteia/egregiatus* which *isōs* relieves him of city liturgies."

The importance of *P. Oxy.* 1204 should now be clear. For it is, firstly, the earliest example so far known of the use of an abstract noun formed from *kratistos* = *egregius*, and in fact the earliest such formation attested for any of the status adjectives. It is also, it seems, the only known instance of *kratisteia* in Greek in this sense. More important still, the document contains the earliest known evidence—or, perhaps better, suggestion or implication—that this status as such conferred immunity from city obligations (*politikai leitourgiai*— see text to n. 45 above). More important still, the right thus claimed had been gained by a personal petition to the emperors, and was then quoted, in the man's interest, with some apparent hesitation, by his advocate in court.

Dignitates and Obligations in the Fourth Century

P. Oxy. IX 1204 of A.D. 299 is, of course, no more than a chance item of evidence, which happens to illustrate very clearly a complex process of conceptual and social change relating to status and obligation. Other equally accidental items of papyrus evidence of this period from Egypt seem to indicate that no universal and absolute correlation between status and exemption from city functions had been established. In (probably) 293/4 a *perfectissimus* (*diasēmotatos*) acted as *prytanis* (office-holder) in Oxyrhynchus (*P. Oxy.* XLVI 3297); in probably 322 two men, each described as *diasēmotatos* and one described as *kratistos*, were in charge of public bakeries in the Thebaid (*P. Oxy.* XLIII 3124). Under Constantine two men described as *diasēmotatoi dekaprōtoi* acted as ambassadors of the Sicilian cities to a former *corrector* (special emissary

73. See T. D. Barnes, *Constantine and Eusebius* (1981), 17–18; *The New Empire of Diocletian and Constantine* (1982), 54–55.

appointed to supervise the finances of provincial cities) of Sicily in Rome,[74] while in 346 a *v(ir) p(erfectissimus)* was responsible for the erection of a statue on behalf of the *ordo Spoletinorum* (the town council of Spoletum) (*ILS* 1229). None the less, it is surely of some significance that Lactantius, writing perhaps in about 313/14, speaks of Galerius, after 305, putting to the torture not only *decuriones* (city councillors), but the *primores* (the foremost men) of the cities, that is *egregii* and *perfectissimi viri*, a process which he sees as the removal of *honores*.[75] The implication is clearly that these were ranks whose holders belonged to the cities but were superior to and distinct from the town councillors.

There is no surviving formal statement of this distinction, however, until we come to the extensive document mentioned above (text following n. 67) and addressed by Licinius in 317 "to the Bithynians";[76] it is likely therefore to have been a letter in reply to an embassy from the province, in which his "capital," Nicomedia, lay. It is not unreasonable to imagine that particular tensions had arisen in Bithynia between the claims of the cities and the availability of posts and ranks at court and in the army.

The letter reflects a situation in which various statuses could be granted by letters of appointment (*codicilli*) issued to former holders of various offices (other than *monetarii*, mint officials) and in which, by a consequential development, such *codicilli* could also be acquired by the exercise of influence, without the holding of any relevant office. Licinius' treatment of this aspect recalls many of the aspects of city life discussed above, while also confirming certain new bases for exemption claimed by interested parties:

> But if a town councillor [*decurio*] by exercising influence [*suffragium*] has gained the *dignitas* of the *perfectissimatus* or *ducena* or *centena* [see text to n. 64 above] or *egregiatus*, in the hope of avoiding his *curia* [city council], he shall lose his *codicilli* [letter of appointment] and be restored to his rank, so that, having undergone an examination of his *honores* and *munera civilia*, he may obtain some privilege within the terms of the city law. Nor may a man who, on the basis of *origo* [birth] or *incolatus* [residence] or of owning property there, is [summoned] to the *curia* [city council], be protected by the *dignitas* of the *perfectissimatus* if it has

74. *ILS* 8843, re-edited by L. Moretti, *Inscriptiones Graecae Urbis Romae* I, no. 60.

75. Lactantius, *de mort. pers.* 21, 3. For the date, T. D. Barnes, "Lactantius and Constantine," *JRS* 63 (1973): 29.

76. *CTh* 8, 4, 3 + 10, 7, 1 + 10, 20, 1 (= *CJ* 11, 8, 1) + 12, 1, 5, all with the same dating: *dat(um) XII Kal. Aug. Gallicano et Basso conss.* (issued on 21 July when Augustus Gallienus and Bassus were consuls).

been obtained by influence; the *dignitas* should be removed and he be consigned to the town council. (*CTh* 12, 1, 5)

Subsequent imperial pronouncements continue to assume the existence of a system whereby *codicilli* granting the *perfectissimatus* could be issued (the *egregiatus*, as mentioned above, disappears immediately); the emperors' aim appears as that of limiting the categories of persons eligible and of invalidating *codicilli* gained by influence or bribery.[77] Once again we can see attempts being made to enforce the imperial rules in different regions in the face of individual initiative in acquiring the ranks which would confer exemption. Thus Constantius wrote to the proconsul of Africa in 339: "You have complained that the Senate of the splendid city of Carthage is depleted, and only a few *curiales* remain, while all are buying, at the cost of shameful strains on their resources, the *insignia* of a *dignitas* which is not due to them. So such men shall be deprived of their nominal ranks [*honores imaginarii*] . . . and be subjected to city *munera*" (*CTh* 12, 1, 27). Writing to Caesena in 354, Constantius, before coming to the *clarissima dignitas* (text to n. 68 and following above), had tried a different solution: "If any are found to have been honoured with the rank of *ex praesidibus* [former provincial governors] or of the *perfectissimatus*, they shall, while retaining the *dignitates* which they gained by influence, none the less remain members of their *ordo*, perform *officia curialia* [the duties of a city councillor], and submit to the obligation of the municipal *munera* which they share with you" (*CTh* 12, 1, 42).

That was the other side of the picture. The rulings issued by emperors were open to use not only by those who sought a means of escape but by those in communities all over the Empire who wished to lighten their own burdens by imposing a share of them on others. However, this very reply, intended to assist the town council of Caesena, itself reflects another novelty of the Tetrarchic period, the existence of a category or status of ex-holders of a particular post.

Former Office-Holders, Status, and Exemption

In this area also it seems clear that the general use of honorific terms preceded the attachment of privileges to them. In the course of the third century we can observe on occasion, recorded on inscriptions, terms indicating the fact that a man is classed among the former holders of a particular post: *ex procuratoribus* (*apo epitropōn*) (former procurators); *ex protectoribus* (*apo*

---

77. E.g., *CTh* 6, 38, 1 = *CJ* 12, 32, 1 (Constantine); *CTh* 12, 1, 15 (Constantine, 327); *CTh* 12, 1, 41 (Constantius, 358).

protektorōn) (former protectors, a military rank); and *a ducenariis (apo doukēna-riōn*) (former holders of a ducenariate post).[78] Once again, however, it is not until the Tetrarchic period that we have a specific indication that any formal privileges were attached to such a status. As late as 282, it will be recalled (text to n. 52 above), Carus, Carinus, and Numerianus had laid down that *ex-procuratores* should perform *munera civilia* suitable to their *dignitas*. But a different principle was enunciated, at an uncertain date, by Diocletian; when addressing what was evidently an embassy of *principales* (leading city councillors) from Antioch, he stated: "To certain *dignitates* there has been granted by us *indulgentia* [exemption] from civil and personal *munera*, that is to those who are former *protectores* and former *praepositi* [also a military rank]. Such persons therefore will not be summoned to perform personal or civil *munera*" (*CJ* 10, 48, 2). A few remaining traces of the utterance in Greek by the embassy, preserved in this fragmentary extract from the imperial record of proceedings, are enough to identify this as the second of the two known literal dialogues over obligation and exemption; the implication is clearly that the *principales* had come to object to the exemption claimed by these categories of ex-officers. In this case, as it seems, the emperors had deliberately introduced exemption from civil burdens as a novel means of reward for those in their service. In a sense they were thus merely extending upwards the principle long adopted for ordinary veterans. But in doing so they also created the possibility, as with other ranks, that the *nominal* status of former *protector* or former *praepositus* would be sought by influence or bribery for the sake of the immunity it conferred: "It cannot be tolerated that men should insert themselves into titles of military honour who have neither seen a line of battle nor looked on the standards nor borne arms. So if any have obtained for themselves letters of appointment as former *protectores*, or former *praepositi*, or former *tribuni* [former military tribunes], they shall not enjoy the privilege, which is earned by those who have reached this *honor* by due military service and by undergoing the effort of bearing arms."[79] None the less, Constantine in 314 extended this privilege to persons who had retired from the imperial *cubicula* (bed chambers), from Palatine posts and from the *scrinia* (offices) of the *memoria* (records of decisions), *epistulae* (correspondence), and

78. E.g., "ex protectoribus"; *CIL* III, 7440; VI, 32945; *ILS* 5695 (A.D. 280). Examples of the Greek form (which seems to be more common) in H. J. Mason, *Greek Terms for Roman Institutions* (1974), s.v. ἀπό. Note Bryonianus Lollianus of Side, *doukēnarios, apo epitropōn*, etc. (*AE* 1966, 471); see C. Foss, *ZPE* 26 (1977): 161; J.-M. Carrié, *ZPE* 35 (1979): 213. Note also *AE* 1965, 195, ex p(rimo) p(ilo); *AE* 1966, 429, *apo doukēnariōn; AE* 1972, 579, *apo epitropēs doukēnarias*.

79. *CTh* 7, 21, 1 (either Constantine or Constantius).

libelli (petitions); for these categories alone the privilege of exemption was granted to sons and grandsons, as well as to the men themselves.[80]

This remarkable extension may serve to remind us how very exceptional it was for any of the status distinctions of the imperial period to acquire even a limited hereditary character. But the use of immunity as a reward, or permanent privilege of status, for ex-holders of offices, was soon applied, for instance, to former *comites* ("companions"—a high-status term used in various contexts), *ex praesidibus* (former *praesides*, governors), *ex rationalibus* (former financial officials), and others. Once again, therefore, we see that a form of status designation comes into common use first and has specific privileges attached to it subsequently. This development had two immediate effects. Firstly, we find the emperors trying, exactly as with *clerici* (text to n. 34 and following), to *prevent* town councillors from acquiring the relevant ranks (and with them prospective immunity) until they had fulfilled their local functions.[81] Secondly, as we would expect, men came to acquire *codicilli* giving them the formal or nominal rank of ex-office-holder. So Constantius was to write in 353 to the town council of Carthage:

> All former *comites* and former *praesides*, and the others who, without holding them, have acquired nominal *codicilli* of the implied *dignitates*, if it is proved that they have been of your number, will remain members of your body, and will undertake all the burdens and *honores* which the needs of the town demand, while retaining the titles of the *dignitates* which it is established that they had been granted. (*CTh* 12, 1, 41)

Conclusion

As we saw at the beginning, fourth-century observers were well aware that the altered presuppositions about office in the imperial service and consequent exemption had critically affected the conditions under which the cities functioned. However, Julian's measures, to which Libanius briefly alludes, give, if anything, an indication of how limited were the steps which could now be attempted even by an emperor who was deeply committed to the restoration of the cities.[82] Removing the immunity enjoyed by the Christian

---

80. See *ERW*, 109.

81. E.g., *CTh* 12, 1, 4 (*praesidatus* [the status of the governor, *praeses*], 317); 12, 1, 20 (*procurationes* [procuratorships] and *curae civitatium* [posts as curator of a town], 331); 12, 1, 14 (*honores*, 326 or 353).

82. See, e.g., P. Athanassiadi-Fowden, *Julian and Hellenism: An Intellectual Biography* (1981), 98ff.

clergy was easy.[83] But beyond that his measures were modest and conservative. The immunities enjoyed by chief doctors (*archiatri*) were immediately
confirmed.[84] Moreover, what Libanius (*Or.* 18, 135–45) says about Julian's dis-
missal of the imperial agents called *agentes in rebus* and *curiosi*, who had gained
these posts partly in order to avoid city obligations, does not seem to mean
that they in principle lost their immunity from such obligations; the *Theo-
dosian Code* shows that Julian in fact confirmed the immunity of *agentes in
rebus* who had served three years, or been dismissed in his fourth consulate
(363);[85] he did the same for those who had served for fifteen years in the
scrinia (offices) of the *memoria, epistulae,* and *libelli* (*CTh* 6, 26, 1). We cannot
determine the precise content of his general ruling "that everyone should be
summoned to the council and be enrolled, unless he had valid reason for exemption"[86]—though his own claim to have made the richest former officials
of his finances and of the mint liable for service in the council of Antioch
may serve as an example (*Misop.* 367 D). However, Ammianus represents him
on two separate occasions, at Naissus in 361 (21, 12, 23) and at Ancyra in 362
(22, 9, 12), as giving judgement personally in favour of the city councils and
against individuals trying to escape *munera*, and thus disregarding the claims
of *dignitates, stipendia* (military service), and *origo*. It is striking that his steps
to strengthen the claims of city councils on men's services were seen by Ammianus, in his final summing up, merely as harsh and oppressive (25, 4, 21).

That comment reflects the fact that throughout the imperial period rulings and decisions given by the emperor could have significant effects in
altering the legal framework to which individuals and communities appealed
in contested areas. In this sense the innumerable self-governing cities of the
Empire had always lived within a common framework of rules issued from
the centre. But, equally, the emperor, in issuing his rulings, was subject to
pressures from below, ranging from demands for the settlement of disputes
to requests for individual exceptions and exemptions and for the extension
of existing privileges to cover wider groups. Since ancient cities functioned
not by the imposition of direct taxation but by social, and later legal, pressure
for the performance of expensive *honores* and *munera* by individuals, the con-

83. *CTh* 12, 1, 50 = 13, 1, 4; Sozomenus, *HE* 5, 5, 2; Philostorgius *HE* 7, 4. See Bidez-
Cumont, *Ep.* 54.

84. *CTh* XII, 3, 4; *Ep.* 25b Hertlein = 75b Bidez-Cumont = 31 Loeb. See V. Nutton,
"Archiatri and the Medical Profession in Antiquity," *PBSR* 45 (1977): 191.

85. *CTh* 6, 27, 2. On *agentes in rebus*, see now A. Giardina, *Aspetti della burocrazia nel Basso
Impero* (1977).

86. Libanius, *Or.* 18, 148.

ditions of obligation and exemption were of central importance; and hence
this area was always one in which the emperor's rulings had a vital place.
For a surprisingly long time Roman statuses and the fact of having occupied posts in the service of the Empire did not play much part in providing
the conditions for exemption. But the growth of the imperial service and of
the army meant in the end that the Empire and its constituent cities were
in direct and continuous competition for the same human and financial resources. In that situation the emperors, under pressure both to reward those
in their own service and to protect the interests of the cities, were pursuing aims which were bound to be mutually contradictory. In this delicate
area of conflicting rights, duties, claims, and immunities, various forms of
status, conferred (in principle at least) by the emperor and at least loosely
related to roles in the imperial service, came to represent the key area of dispute. Whether there was a class struggle and, if so, how much it contributed
to the decline of the Empire remain unresolved questions. But *this* area of
conflict was categorically not a matter of class struggle, but of the formal
statuses and privileges available under certain circumstances to members of
the propertied classes. Imperial initiative, in the form of the desire to use
immunity from city obligations as a reward for service, played some part in
the sudden evolution of formal status distinctions, with definite legal consequences, which took place in the late third and early fourth centuries. But it
is surely significant that versions of the status terms themselves had entered
the common stock of honorific vocabulary, typically employed on inscriptions, before legal consequences became attached to them. An earlier stage in
the consciousness of status, as associated with official roles, is perfectly captured in the recently published inscription of a man who in the third century
rose through equestrian posts into the Senate: the inscription retrospectively
attaches the successive status appellations of *egregius, perfectissimus,* and *clarissimus* to the successive stages of his career.[87] But the step from adjectives to
nouns denoting statuses, as abstract qualities which might inhere in a person,
arrived simultaneously with the conception that such a status might confer
immunity from the obligations imposed by a man's native city. It is surely
suggestive that our earliest expression of both of these conceptions is a document which records a petition to the emperors. Aurelius Plutarchus deserves
a small place in history.

87. *AE* 1979, 506.

CHAPTER SEVENTEEN

Italy and the Roman Empire:
Augustus to Constantine*

Italy during the period of the Roman monarchy and Republic has a history; one which offers us enormous challenges and problems, but still a history: the arrival of the Greeks; the flowering of Etruscan civilisation; the "great Rome of the Tarquins"; the Latin League and its dissolution; the Samnite wars; Hannibal's invasion; the Roman conquest and colonisation of northern Italy; the Social War; the Triumviral proscriptions and settlements; and, what is really a part of that story, the veteran colonies of Augustus.[1]

Italy under the Empire has no history. That is to say, it has no narrative history. That ought to be no handicap. Narrative is out of date; what we want is social history, or the *longue durée* of Braudel. But in fact, paradoxically, the absence of a narrative—of any narrative at all which is in any way focused on Italy—has robbed us of historical questions; since there is no narrative history we have been unable to put any coherent questions to such archaeological, epigraphic, and literary evidence as we have, because we do not know what historical evolution it is which we are trying to explain.

*First published in *Phoenix* 40 (1986): 295–318. This chapter represents the expanded text of a lecture given at McMaster University in March 1985 at the conference "Ancient Italy: Eighty Years of Scholarship" held in honour of E. T. Salmon in his eightieth year. I was indebted for advice and comments to Michael Crawford and Brent Shaw. I refer to the *Panegyrics* from Galletier's edition and to W. Eck, *Die staatliche Organisation Italiens in der hohen Kaiserzeit* (Munich, 1979), A. H. M. Jones, *The Later Roman Empire* (Oxford, 1964), and R. K. Sherk, *Municipal Decrees of the Roman West* (*Arethusa* Monographs 2, Buffalo, N.Y., 1970) by author's name. Note now in particular W. Eck, *L'Italia nell'Impero Romano. Stato e amministrazione in epoca imperiale*, 2nd rev. ed. (Bari, 1999).

1. See esp. L. Keppie, *Colonisation and Veteran Settlement in Italy, 47 BC–AD 14* (London, 1983).

Yet a country, or region, with several million inhabitants cannot, in any important sense, have had no history. Nor does it seem feasible that this history, evolving in the centre of a politically unified Mediterranean world, marked by an extraordinary level of urbanisation,[2] of construction in permanent materials, and of public commemoration in written form on stone or bronze,[3] should be wholly beyond our grasp. The most ambitious approach is to survey directly the infinitely varied material available for social history, as Rostovtzeff did in his *Social and Economic History*, and as the late John D'Arms did specifically in relation to Italy.[4]

This chapter will try a different, and more partial, approach. It will ask in what sense and in what forms the Roman imperial state was present in Italy; or, to put it in a different way, in what ways the functioning of the Roman state may have affected the economic and social history of Italy. The question has two interconnected aspects. Firstly, what degree of exchange of human and economic resources took place as between Italy and the imperial system? And, secondly, what forms of authority were exercised in Italy by appointees of the Roman state? At one level the question has often been asked, and the evidence surveyed. It is rather more than a century since Camille Jullian published his admirable monograph on the political transformations of Roman Italy between Augustus and Constantine.[5] More recently Werner Eck has examined the organisation of Italy, and the types of official found in post there, up to the middle of the second century. He concludes, surely rightly, that even in the second half of the second century, with imperial *procuratores* (equestrian financial officials) and senatorial *praefecti alimentorum* (prefects in charge of funds for the support of poor children), *curatores viarum* (officials in charge of roads), *curatores rei publicae* (officials supervising city finances), and *iuridici* (officials performing judicial functions in civil cases in Italy) of the various regions (*regiones*), Italy still exhibits a striking "shortage of government" (*Defizit an Verwaltung*) as against anything that we might expect in a

---

2. For the significance of this, see, e.g., K. Hopkins, "Economic Growth and Towns in Classical Antiquity," in P. Abrams and E. A. Wrigley, eds., *Towns in Societies* (Cambridge, 1978), 35; and his introduction to P. Garnsey, K. Hopkins, and C. R. Whittaker, eds., *Trade in the Ancient Economy* (London, 1983).

3. Note esp. R. MacMullen, "The Epigraphic Habit in the Roman Empire," *AJP* 103 (1982): 233–46.

4. J. H. D'Arms, "Italien," in F. Vittinghoff, ed., *Europäische Wirtschafts- und Sozialgeschichte in der römischen Kaiserzeit* (Stuttgart, 1990), 375–426. I was very grateful to Professor D'Arms for allowing me to see a typescript of this extensive chapter before publication.

5. C. Jullian, *Les transformations politiques de l'Italie sous les Empereurs romains, 43 av. J.-C.– 330 ap. J.-C.* (Paris, 1884).

large territory forming part of a supra-regional Empire. On the other hand, as Brent Shaw pointed out to me, it is not entirely surprising that an administrative structure should have been associated primarily with conquest and tribute, and only came later to grow inwards to cover the homeland of the Empire as well.

The fact that Italy was not treated like a province, and the absence of any obvious reason why it should not be, was in fact duly commented on by at any rate one senator in the early third century, Cassius Dio, whose home city was Nicaea in Bithynia. In the speech which he gives to Maecenas, addressing Augustus, he recommends that governors should be appointed for Italy beyond the 100th milestone from Rome, as for the other areas of the Empire (52, 22, 1); that the two praetorian prefects should command both the praetorian cohorts themselves and the other soldiers in Italy, as well as the imperial slaves and freedmen there (24, 1–4); and that no community or individual should be exempt from direct taxation (28, 6). By implication, that is, Italy should also be taxed.

As regards imperial appointment of senatorial officials to be *curatores* of cities in Italy, or to be *iuridici* of different regions, or, in the third century, *correctores*, it is natural, and not in itself misleading, that we should see all this as preliminaries to the provincialisation of Italy under Diocletian.[6] But that leaves important questions unanswered. What was the nature of the functions which these officials performed? Is "government" in fact an appropriate term for the roles which they fulfilled? Should we give a different description of the functions of the senatorial *correctores* and *consulares* of the various regions of Italy as they were in the earlier fourth century, after Diocletian's reorganisation?

One major innovation which Dio makes Maecenas recommend by implication to Augustus was certainly carried out by Diocletian, that is to say, the extension to Italy of direct taxation. Or at least to part of Italy, as Aurelius Victor records in bafflingly obscure terms. After describing the division of the Empire among the Tetrarchs, with Italy and Africa going to Maximian, Victor says (39, 31): "From this moment on the vast affliction of the *tributa* [direct taxes] was introduced into part of Italy. For, although each of them [the four Emperors] carried out the same functions, and in a restrained manner, in order that the armies and the emperor, who were continually—or (at least) largely—present there, could be supplied, a new set of rules was made for the payment of taxes. This arrangement, which at that time was tol-

---

6. So, e.g., W. Simshäuser, "Untersuchungen zur Entstehung der Provinzialverfassung Italiens," *ANRW* 2.13 (1980), 401–52.

erable, has in our days acquired a destructive character." Writing soon after the middle of the fourth century, Victor slightly blurs two separate developments of the 290s: the introduction of a new general system of taxation by the Tetrarchs, proclaimed in Egypt by the prefect in 297 (*P. CairIsidor* 1 [16 March 297]), and the presence of Maximian, with his army, in northern Italy. The scattered available evidence does indeed suggest that the establishment of the Tetrarchy in 293 meant that Maximian left Gaul to Constantius and moved south to make Milan and Aquileia his primary residences.[7]

With that, two central elements of the Roman state, the court and the army — or rather, by this time, *a* court and *an* army — had so to speak decisively retreated inwards from the frontier zones to impose themselves on northern Italy. This situation, briefly foreshadowed in the barbarian invasions of the 160s, had in fact been recurrent since the middle of the third century, and was subsequently to be perpetuated as a central feature of the political and economic geography of the late Empire.[8] The new situation is perfectly reflected in a panegyrist's description of the meeting of Diocletian and Maximian in Milan in the winter of 290/1 (*Pan.* 3 [11] 8–12). Disregarding the season, Diocletian arrived from the east over the Julian Alps, Maximian from the west over the Cottian Alps. As the news spread through the towns of Italy, all rushed to see the emperors pass, altars were lit, offerings made, and victims slain in sacrifice. The privileged few were admitted to gaze on the emperors, together in the *palatium* in Milan. An embassy arrived from the Senate in Rome, symbolising Milan's acquisition of some of the majesty of the capital city "so that the seat of empire was seen to be that place to which both emperors had come."

The form in which Italy, or part of it, now paid taxes to support court and army can hardly be determined. That court and army *were* supported, in cash and kind, is of course certain. The significance of this obvious fact, however, can only be put into relief if we look at current views of the economic function of the Roman state as such within the wider economy of the Empire. Firstly, it is said, the state minted coins not as a service to economic exchange within its borders, but purely as a means of making its own essential payments.[9] Secondly, it has been argued, the raising of taxes in money in

---

7. T. D. Barnes, *The New Empire of Diocletian and Constantine* (Cambridge, Mass., 1982), 56ff.

8. For army and court in this area, see F. Millar, *The Emperor in the Roman World* (London, 1977; 2nd ed., 1992), 44–45; for the later fourth century and after, see L. Ruggini, *Economia e società nell' "Italia Annonaria"* (Milan, 1961).

9. M. Crawford, "Money and Exchange in the Roman World," *JRS* 60 (1970): 40–48; revised version in his *La moneta in Grecia e a Roma* (Bari, 1982), chap. 5.

the provinces and the transfer of the surplus taxes from the richer provinces to pay troops stationed mainly in poorer, less-developed provinces produced profound effects on inter-regional trade. In consequence the tax-exporting provinces had also to export goods in order to acquire the cash to pay these taxes. In other words the financial operations of the state had significant effects both on the balance of trade within the Empire and on the level of monetisation and long-distance trade.[10]

But where does this picture leave Italy? The answer given does not do justice to a real problem: one of the three spheres of the Empire is defined as "the centre, comprising Italy and the city of Rome, the seat of the Court and of the central government, which, like the armies on the frontiers, consumed a large volume of taxes" (Hopkins 101). As regards Rome itself we need not dispute the point. Even so, it would be worth trying to delimit the nature and extent of the expenditure of imperial tax revenue in cash in the city. The question is not as straightforward as it may seem. We have to presume, rather than being able to prove, that at least some coin from provincial taxation was still physically transported to Rome and stored in the *aerarium* (treasury) in the temple of Saturn, or in the *aerarium militare* (military treasury), which a *diploma* (discharge certificate of an auxiliary soldier) of A.D. 65 now shows to have been an actual structure located on the Capitol.[11]

As regards expenditures made in Rome from taxation revenue, there were public buildings and aqueducts, whether newly built or undergoing repair; there were the *liberalitates* (cash distributions) by the emperors, which occurred erratically, but certainly required the accumulation of very large quantities of coin. There is nothing to indicate that senatorial officials in post in Rome (such as the *curatores* of the aqueducts or of the banks of the Tiber) were paid salaries; but the *apparitores* who attended both them and the magistrates certainly were entitled to pay from the *aerarium* (Frontinus, *de aquae*

10. K. Hopkins, "Taxes and Trade in the Roman Empire (200 BC–AD 400)," *JRS* 70 (1980): 101–25. Note for comparison the calculations by R. W. Goldsmith, "An Estimate of the Size and Structure of the National Produce of the Early Roman Empire," *Review of Income and Wealth* 30.3 (1984): 263–88. I owe this reference to Professor B. W. Frier.

11. See F. Millar, "The Aerarium and Its Officials under the Empire," *JRS* 54 (1964): 33–40 (chapter 4 in this volume); M. Corbier, *L'aerarium Saturni et l'aerarium militare: administration et prosopographie sénatoriale* (Rome, 1974). For the diploma, see S. Dušanić, "A Military Diploma of AD 65," *Germania* 56 (1978): 461–75; *AE* 1978, no. 658. See also M. Corbier, "L'aerarium militare sur le Capitole," *Cahiers die groupe de recherches sur l'armée romaine et les provinces* 3 (1984): 147. The diploma is printed in M. M. Roxan, *Roman Military Diplomas, 1978–84* (London, 1985), no. 1. See also now "Cash Distributions in Rome and Imperial Minting" (chapter 5 in this volume).

ductu 100). But of course the essential recurrent expenditure was that on the pay of the units stationed in Rome, the praetorian cohorts, the urban cohorts, and the *vigiles* (fire brigades).

The imperial state did thus expend a steady flow of money in Rome. It is consonant with this that the (or a) mint was located there.[12] But it is also significant that until the later third century, when mints began to operate in Mediolanum, then moving to Ticinum, and in Aquileia,[13] this was the only mint of any kind in Italy. So *was* Italy outside Rome in fact a zone which received any significant input of state expenditure in cash? Most imperial building in Italy took the form of specific benefactions by individual emperors to specific cities. Beyond that, the emperors very occasionally initiated large-scale building projects, though rarely far from Rome or in areas irrelevant to it: the Claudian and Trajanic harbours at Ostia; Trajan's harbour at Centumcellae; Nero's plan for a canal from Lake Avernus to Ostia. In this last case Suetonius implies that it was at least intended to use convict labour.[14] But in general, however, it should be assumed that the works involved cash payments to contractors using free labour.[15] The same may also have been true of the construction and upkeep of roads: *redemptores* (contractors) are still mentioned in this connection. But in fact, firstly, the question of who normally paid for roads remains remarkably obscure: local communities, the owners of properties bordering a road, or the state, through the *curatores viarum*?[16] In any case in the Empire it was primarily a question of upkeep rather than new construction. Wholly new roads are attested only for

12. For the officials of the *moneta* (mint) in Rome, O. Hirschfeld, *Die kaiserlichen Verwaltungsbeamten bis auf Diocletian*[2] (Berlin, 1905), 181–89; H. Mattingly, *Roman Coins*[2] (London, 1969), 129ff. See also M. Peachin, "The Procurator Monetae," *Numis. Chron.* 146 (1986): 94–106.

13. C. H. V. Sutherland, *The Roman Imperial Coinage* 6 (London, 1967), 5; M. Hendy, "Mint and Fiscal Administration under Diocletian, His Colleagues and His Successors, *AD* 305–24," *JRS* 62 (1972): 75–82; J.-P. Callu, *La politique monétaire des Empereurs romains de 238 à 311* (Paris, 1969); M. H. Crawford, "La zecca di Ticinum," in E. Gabba, ed., *Storia di Pavia* 1 (Milan, 1984), 249–52. See also M. Hendy, *Studies in the Byzantine Monetary Economy, c. 300–1450* (Cambridge, 1985), 378ff.

14. Suet., *Nero* 31; see F. Millar, "Condemnation to Hard Labour in the Roman Empire, from the Julio-Claudians to Constantine," *BSR* 52 (1984): 124–47, esp. at 133 (chapter 7 in this volume).

15. P. A. Brunt, "Free Labour and Public Works at Rome," *JRS* 70 (1980): 81–100.

16. For the evidence, T. Pekáry, *Untersuchungen zu den römischen Reichsstrassen* (Bonn, 1968), chap. 3; H. E. Herzig, "Probleme des römischen Strassenwesens: Untersuchungen zu Geschichte und Recht," *ANRW* 2.1 (1974), 593–648; Eck chap. 2.

Domitian (Statius *Silvae* 4, 3 on the Via Domitiana along the coast of Campania) and above all Trajan, whose extensive programme of road building is celebrated by Galen (ed. Kuhn 10, 633); the Via Traiana and the Via Traiana Nova certainly represented major new projects. In effect, therefore, the normal method of financing road maintenance or construction remains obscure, and it was relatively rare for wholly new roads to be constructed; this aspect of the functioning of the state in Italy, though significant, cannot be assumed to have represented a regular channel for the outflow of state funds.

One very distinctive form of expenditure did relate to Italy and is attested in a wide range of Italian towns. This is, of course, the scheme for *alimenta*, possibly initiated by Nerva and certainly put through by Trajan; it was designed for the upkeep of children, and achieved by the distribution of loan funds, against security in land, which would produce an income for this purpose for each city. It is unnecessary to rehearse again the arguments to show that its purpose was demographic, and that it did not in intention represent a form of investment designed to counteract some supposed general crisis in Italian agriculture.[17] However, even granted this more limited purpose, the scheme was, by the standards of the very slight activity of the state in general, positive and extensive in conception, costing initially perhaps up to 400 million sesterces (roughly the equivalent of two major aqueducts) and benefitting, initially, perhaps between 100,000 and 150,000 children. There are some slight indications that later emperors added further sums to the capital, and Marcus Aurelius certainly issued an edict in which he reaffirmed the central purpose of the scheme, that the population of *iuniores* (young people) in the towns of Italy should increase.[18] But, once again, this scheme, striking though it is, cannot be seen as a major channel for the *recurrent* diffusion of state funds in Italy.

Had there indeed been such a channel, it could only have been through the payment of soldiers in the imperial service.[19] Yet, of course, the almost total absence of imperial forces in Italy under the Principate was precisely one of the most distinctive features of the overall shape of the Roman state. The praetorian and urban cohorts and the *vigiles* were stationed in Rome itself. Under Augustus and Tiberius one praetorian cohort was stationed in

17. I depend here on R. Duncan-Jones, *The Economy of the Roman Empire* (Cambridge, 1982), chap. 7: "Government Subsidies for Population Increase." See also Eck 146–89.

18. Fronto, *Ad M. Antoninum de orationibus* 12, *The Correspondence of Marcus Cornelius Fronto* 2.112, ed. C. R. Haines (London, 1919) (Naber 161; Van Den Hout 154).

19. For a useful collection of the evidence on the economic effects of the presence of units of the army, see L. Wierschowski, *Heer und Wirtschaft. Das römische Heer der Prinzipatszeit als Wirtschaftsfaktor* (Bonn, 1984).

Ostia, to be supplemented, or more probably replaced, by an urban cohort in the reign of Claudius, and then by a cohort of the *vigiles* from Hadrian onwards; a cohort is also said to have been stationed at Puteoli by Claudius. Beyond that, in the Principate, there were only the fleets stationed at Misenum and Ravenna.[20] These forces, of unknown size, but of not less than several thousand men each, will therefore have served as two specific, but isolated, channels through which taxation revenue flowed into Italy.

For the whole of the rest of Italy there is no evidence during the first two centuries A.D. of the establishment of any regular units of the Roman army. No legions and no auxiliary forces were stationed there. The brief and violent irruption of legionary and auxiliary forces from the Rhine and Balkans in 69–70 left no permanent trace. Only under Septimius Severus, as is well known, was a legion, the new *legio II Parthica*, established on the Alban Hills; once again in the immediate neighbourhood of Rome. Whether or not this step was part of the deliberate creation by Severus of a "field army,"[21] at least vexillations of the legion, and possibly on occasion the whole of it, served on campaign with emperors: for instance in 217/18 in Syria, and in 235 with Maximinus, returning from time to time to their base (*RE* XII, 1479ff.).

Over the following century only the most scattered and unsatisfactory evidence reflects the recurrent presence of the imperial court and armies in northern Italy, for instance a concentration of cavalry at Milan in 268,[22] or, later, garrisons protecting the towns of northern Italy against Constantine's advance in 312 (*Pan.* 9 [12] 5–6, 8; 10 [4] 21–22, 25). So far as I can see, however, there is no significant and coherent evidence for what, if any, regular military presence there was in northern Italy from the middle of the third to the middle of the fourth century. Central and southern Italy appear in any case to have remained ungarrisoned.

So, as regards that exchange of wealth which was created by the activities of the state, Italy remained, throughout almost the whole period, a backwater. The Roman state certainly did not *spend* there directly on a year-by-

20. Suet., *Claud.* 25. See R. Meiggs, *Roman Ostia*² (London, 1973), 46, 62–63, 305. For the vigiles in Ostia, see R. Saxer, *Untersuchungen zu den Vexillationen des römischen Kaiserheeres von Augustus bis Diokletian* (*Epigraphische Studien* 1, 1967), 110–15. For the fleets, see C. G. Starr, *The Roman Imperial Navy, 31 BC–AD 324* (London, 1960); D. Kienast, *Untersuchungen zu den Kriegsflotten der römischen Kaiserzeit* (Bonn, 1966); and M. Reddé, *Mare Nostrum: les infrastructures, le dispositif et l'histoire de la marine militaire sous l'empire romain* (Rome, 1986).

21. So, e.g., E. Birley, "Septimius Severus and the Roman Army," *Epigraphische Studien* 8 (1969): 63–82.

22. Zosimus 1.40.1; see R. Grosse, *Römische Militärgeschichte von Gallienus bis zum Beginn der byzantinischen Themenverfassung* (Berlin, 1920), 15ff.

year basis. Nor, of course, did it raise direct taxes. Indirect taxes, in coin, were a different matter. No *portoria* (tolls) seem to have been raised in Italy, except in so far as the *stationes* (posts) for collecting the various regional tolls (such as the *quadragesima Galliarum* [the 2.5 per cent customs duty in the Gallic provinces]) might be situated in its ports. But there was the ancient 5 per cent tax on the value of slaves at the moment of manumission, and another 5 per cent tax on inheritances (*vicesima hereditatium*), instituted by Augustus, as well as the 1 or 1//2 per cent tax on sales (abolished in Italy under Gaius) and the 4 per cent tax on the sale of slaves, attested only in the first century (Eck 111–45). The two 5 per cent taxes were raised by *publicani* (tax farmers), at least until the second century; for the *vicesima hereditatium* there were also, at least in the second and third centuries, imperial *procuratores* related to different regions of Italy. As with almost every variety of official functioning in Italy, there is a fundamental question as to what we should suppose that their functions actually were; and I would suggest that here, as in all cases, we should start from the presumption that the primary role was juridical—hearing accusations and solving disputes. Of this more later. For the moment it may be noted that the *vicesimae* represented one of the relatively few established forms of exchange of value between state and subject attested in Italy: Petronius' *Satyricon*, for instance, almost certainly reflecting first-century Puteoli, three times refers to the payment of the *vicesima* at the moment of manumission, with accounts to be settled with the *vicensimarii* (the collectors of the *vicesima*) (58; 65; 71).

If we are to pursue the baffling question of how to describe the relations between the population of Italy and the Roman state—that is, if we ask what sorts of exchange of any type took place, what if any general rules or individual decisions were imposed there by any central authority, and (above all) how the state exercised force there—taxation, direct or indirect, will not be the only relevant form even of purely financial exchange. The *Satyricon* also reflects another quite different form of exchange, namely the pressure to leave part of one's estate to the emperor (76). There is no need to collect again the scattered evidence for imperial estates, bequeathed to the emperors, or resulting from condemnation and confiscation, which happen to be attested in Italy.[23] It is more relevant that these were felt by Tacitus to have increased since the early first century, and to have led to an extension of the extra-legal powers of those who had charge of them (*Ann.* 4, 6). We should note also the significance of the first part of the *edictum* which Claudius issued

---

23. See D. J. Crawford, "Imperial Estates," in M. I. Finley, ed., *Studies in Roman Property* (Cambridge, 1976), 35–70, esp. 67–69.

from Baiae in 46: the long *controversia* (legal dispute), evidently over boundaries, between the Comenses and Bergalei had revealed that most of the *agri* (fields) and *saltus* (woodland) concerned were imperial property (*mei iuris*). So he had sent one of his *amici* (friends) who was to settle the question of ownership, with the aid of his *procuratores* from that and another (?) *regio*.[24] That there were imperial *procuratores* of estates in an area might be relevant to wider questions of how power was exercised, as we shall see. In this context it will be enough to recall that imperial estates, like private ones, seem normally to have been leased out against a cash rent. We cannot begin to assess the cash income from imperial properties in Italy; but Pliny's income from his property at Tifernum Tiberinum would have paid the salaries of two imperial *procuratores* classed as *ducenarii* (with a salary of 200,000 sesterces per annum) (Pliny, *Ep.* 10, 8).

In an indirect way that fact is also part of the exchange between state and subject. Senators could attend the Senate and occupy magistracies and other positions, of which the majority were unpaid, only as a function of having an independent income based on landed property. The familiar questions of the local origins of senators, of the maintenance into the late Empire of a solid core of senators from Italy, of the spread of senatorial status to the provinces, of how long families might maintain membership over generations — all these questions have a significant financial aspect.[25] Where did the properties of these families lie? Or, to put it in a different way, whose rents supported their unpaid participation in the functioning of the Roman state? If we take a very low estimate and suppose that the average wealth of the 600 senators was no more than twice the minimum requirement of 1 million sesterces, then their combined annual rental income, at 8 per cent of their total property, will have been somewhere in the region of 100 million sesterces.

Provincial senators also were supposed to acquire a substantial holding in Italian land (Pliny, *Ep.* 6, 19; *HA, M. Ant.* 11, 8); but much of this, as Edward Champlin pointed out, will have been, once again, in the suburban area around Rome.[26] The rents paid to senators, whether Italian or provincial, from Italian property, itself entirely untaxed, can thus be seen as an essen-

24. *ILS* 206; see U. Schillinger-Häfele, "Das Edikt des Claudius *CIL* V 5050," *Hermes* 95 (1967): 353–65.

25. For the relationship between the need to maintain an adequate base in property and the relative rarity of the retention of membership in the Senate over more than a few generations, see K. Hopkins, *Death and Renewal* (Cambridge, 1982), chap. 3 (with G. P. Burton). For a systematic survey of the epigraphic evidence for the origins of senators, see S. Panciera, ed., *Epigrafia e ordine senatorio* (Rome, 1982), 9–781.

26. E. Champlin, "The Suburbium of Rome," *AJAH* 7 (1982): 97–117.

tial element in the maintenance of the state. Moreover, from Diocletian onwards, there was some form of direct taxation on at least some Italian land
(text to n. 7 above); and from Constantine onwards there was a tax specifically related to senatorial properties, the *follis* or *collatio glebalis*. Beyond the
bare mention by Zosimus (2, 38) of the institution of this tax by Constantine,
there seems to be no evidence at all even to illustrate its working or effects
in this period in Italy, or anywhere else (Jones 431, n. 51). This aspect, like
so many others, of the history of the Senate between the mid-third and the
mid-fourth centuries, remains wholly mysterious. But, if this new tax was
effectively imposed in Italy, it will have constituted yet another significant
change in the economic relations of Italy to the Roman state.

It is no doubt naive to suppose that the volume of surviving documentation on a particular area of conflict between state and subject will accurately
reflect the real importance of that area. None the less, it does seem significant that we have a far more extensive and explicit dossier of complaints and
disputes over the transport services which the subjects of the Empire were
supposed to provide than, for instance, over direct taxation.[27] In the High
Empire, at least, the issue concerned not a state transport system organised
along particular routes but obligations on the subjects to provide *vehicula*
(waggons) for any official travellers: not merely messengers armed with a *diploma* (a certificate permitting its bearer to demand waggons), but senatorial
and equestrian officials, and soldiers in transit. These obligations were imposed, and the inevitable conflicts arose, in Italy as well. This fact is of course
attested by Claudius' well-known edict, from a copy found in Tegea (*CIL* 3,
7251): "Although I have often attempted to relieve the colonies and *municipia*, not only of Italy but also of the provinces, and the *civitates* [towns with
no specific Roman status] of each province, from the burdens of providing
waggons . . ." The post of *praefectus vehiculorum* (the prefect in charge of the
organisation of this service) had perhaps been created, like the other major
prefectures, by Augustus (Eck 88ff.). If his functions (as usual) remain very
obscure, the question of the obligations imposed on Italy clearly remained
important: hence the much-cited coins of Nerva VEHICULATIONE ITALIAE
REMISSA (the *vehiculatio* of Italy having been remitted) (*BMC Imp.* 3.21, nos.
119–211). Since it is patent that the actual movement of official travellers and
soldiers through Italy to and from Rome cannot in fact have stopped, and
since they presumably did not walk carrying their provisions for the journey,
the reference can only be to an alteration in the terms on which they were

27. See S. Mitchell, "Requisitioned Transport in the Roman Empire: A New Inscription
from Pisidia," *JRS* 66 (1976): 106–31.

entitled to demand transport, accommodation, and services. REMISSA will not necessarily have meant the total abolition of such rights. In the fourth century and later the evidence reveals a vast network of *mansiones* and *stationes* (post-houses and stopping points) at which waggons and horses were supposed to be maintained. But it would still be a mistake to see this *cursus publicus* (as it was now called) purely as a state, or imperial, organisation. In fact, it involved a set of obligations imposed by the state on local communities and was managed normally by persons nominated by the city councils (Jones 830–34 with notes). Again the real nature of the obligations and exchanges involved requires much more examination. The return journey of the Bordeaux pilgrim in A.D. 333, a private traveller, of course, shows him going through a sequence of stopping points called variously *civitates*, *mutationes*, and *mansiones* from Otranto to Capua, Rome, Ariminum, and Mediolanum. But what the journey of an *official* traveller over this route would have involved for the communities he passed through still remains obscure.

The movement of a whole unit, or an army, was a different matter, imposing an immediate large-scale obligation to provide supplies (*annona* or *copiae*). A scatter of inscriptions of equestrian officers shows men assigned to this task, including one who was *praepositus annonae expeditionis felicissimae urbicae* (placed in charge of the food supplies for the most auspicious journey to Rome); the *urbica expeditio* was certainly Septimius Severus' march on Rome in 193.[28] The emperor, whether or not going to or returning from a campaign, will always have had a military escort (at least one praetorian cohort?), so demands for *annona* will have followed.[29]

In Diocletian's new taxation system, so it is often claimed, direct taxation and the provision of supplies for the army were united in a single system, which essentially transformed taxation and payment of troops in coin into an exchange involving the direct provision of taxes in kind for the army. That may be so; but in this case above all the entire question needs re-examination. For the moment we can only return to the evidence that imperial forces will have been stationed in northern Italy, at any rate from the mid-third century onwards. There is nothing whatever, to my knowledge, to indicate that regular units, except for the *legio II Parthica* from Severus onwards, were stationed

28. For these inscriptions, see H.-G. Pflaum, *Les carrières procuratoriennes équestres sous le Haut-Empire Romain* I, 483–84.

29. Note esp. Pliny, *Pan.* 21, contrasting the burdens imposed by journeys of Domitian and of Trajan. Cf. Statius, *Silvae* 4.9.16–19, which Eck (91) is surely wrong (for once) to take as a reference to the *praefectura vehiculorum*. See rather E. Champlin, "Pegasus," *ZPE* 32 (1978): 269–78. On the organisation and supply of imperial journeys, see H. Halfmann, *Itinera Principum* (Stuttgart, 1986), chap. 2.

in central and southern Italy at any time up to the reign of Constantine. This contrast clearly lies behind the allusion in Aurelius Victor to the imposition of taxation on "part" of Italy.

Finally, before turning back to some aspects of Italy under the Principate, it is necessary to consider two great changes of the early fourth century which fundamentally affected, or would have affected, the cities of Italy, as of everywhere else. One of them, in my opinion, never occurred; the other, of considerable importance in my view, has not been given the attention it deserves. The one which never occurred is the general confiscation of city lands—landed property owned by cities—by Constantine or Constantius. It was not often that A. H. M. Jones misunderstood something. But in this case I suggest that he attributed to a specific action by the state what was in fact a perennial effect of private acquisitiveness. The view that city lands were taken away by Constantine is now established doctrine, reappearing specifically, for instance, in Bryan Ward-Perkins' recent book on public construction in Italy from the fourth century to the ninth.[30] That would indeed have been a major change, if it had in reality accompanied the well-known process of the despoliation of temple treasures. But, in fact, the evidence which Jones himself cites makes clear that the lands which Julian set out to restore to the cities had not been taken by any emperor but had been occupied by private persons, in a way which can be easily paralleled from the earlier imperial period.[31] Julian was attempting to strengthen the rights of the cities to their own properties and the income from them, just as he attempted to strengthen their claims to the services of their own citizens.

This latter issue reflects the fundamental change in the relations of state and city which did in reality occur around A.D. 300.[32] In the earlier Em-

---

30. B. Ward-Perkins, *From Classical Antiquity to the Middle Ages: Urban Public Building in Northern and Central Italy, A.D. 300–850* (Oxford, 1984), 22.

31. Jones 732 and n. 44. None of the evidence cited specifically proves the loss of city lands *to the state* by order of Constantine or Constantius; and in particular Libanius, *Or.* 13, 45 and *CJ* 11, 70, 1 show that what was involved was the improper possession of public property by private individuals. *CTh* 10, 3, 1, ordering the recovery and leasing out of *possessiones publicae* (public properties), can be seen in the same context, as can Libanius, *Ep.* 828. Here, it is true that a house to which the city of Tyre was laying claim is said by Libanius to have been granted by an emperor to someone as a reward for his services. But the issue again arose within the context of an instruction by Julian that the cities should recover their property. This same order lies behind Ammianus' brief statement (25.4.15): "[T]he revenues were restored to the cities together with their estates."

32. For what follows, see F. Millar, "Empire and City, Augustus to Julian: Obligations, Excuses and Status," *JRS* 73 (1983): 76–96 (chapter 16 in this volume).

pire neither equestrian rank nor the holding of equestrian office conferred
any permanent immunity from the *honores* (offices) and *munera* (personal
or financial obligations) of a man's native city; the same may even be true,
though this is less certain, of senatorial rank and office. At any rate it is abundantly attested that members of both orders did hold office, discharge functions, and spend money in their cities. Around 300, however, the emperors
came to concede a quite new significance to a variety of ranks in the imperial service (like the *egregiatus* or the *perfectissimatus*) and to the status of ex-
office-holder (*ex protectoribus* and so forth). This significance was precisely that
these ranks and statuses, derived from roles in the imperial service (including sometimes nominal or fictitious service), could now confer a life-long
immunity from the obligations of *curiales* (town councillors) in the cities. In
this respect therefore the so-called caste society of the later Roman Empire
was no such thing. There was instead a running battle, whose preconditions
had been created by the state itself, and which was waged along the frontiers of curial and imperial status. In subsequently trying to prevent *curiales*
from acquiring imperial statuses, the emperors were facing the consequences
of the privileges which they themselves had allowed to be attached to these
statuses. The situation which obtained after 313 with regard to the *clerici* of
the Christian church was exactly analogous. For they too were granted immunity, and it was equally this very fact which then made it necessary for
emperors to try to prevent *curiales* from entering the clergy. From the point
of view of each city, therefore, a gulf had opened up between the declining group of *curiales*, upon whom local obligations could still be imposed,
and those local landholders who had acquired a permanent immunity by real
or fictitious imperial service, or by the possession of an imperial status. It
was this, namely a change in the rules, and not a direct confiscation of resources, which transformed the position of the cities in the fourth century.
The wealth concerned was not removed from the locality by the state, but
the cities were unable to tap it for their communal needs.

In this respect of course the cities of Italy were in no different situation
from those elsewhere. Many different aspects of this complex conflict are reflected, for instance, in the letter which Constantius II wrote to the town
council (*ordo*) of Caesena in Aemilia from Milan in 354 (*CTh* 12, 1, 54). He
begins with nominal ranks gained by influence (*suffragium*):

> If any persons are discovered to have gained the rank of *ex praesidibus*
> [former governors] or the *perfectissimatus*, let them, while retaining the
> *dignitates* [statuses] which they gained by influence, none the less remain
> as members of their town council, let them perform curial duties, and

let them be liable to the duty of performing municipal *munera*, a duty which they share with you. But if anyone has secured the insignia of the *clarissima dignitas* [senatorial status], and has not been able to obtain confirmation of the favour granted to him by producing [the relevant] *codicilli* [letters of appointment], let him lose the benefit of the *dignitas* which he had acquired.

If we go back to the beginning of the Empire, the colonies and municipalities of Italy still formed something like a distinct and privileged political corporation. Augustus could boast of the unprecedented crowds which had come from all over Italy for his election as pontifex maximus (*Res Gestae* 10, 3), and would make appointments to military tribunates on the public recommendation of each town; the group concerned will be those described on inscriptions as *tribuni militum a populo*, all from the Augustan age and all from Italy.[33] As the Tabula Siarensis from Baetica shows, when the Senate passed honours for the deceased Germanicus in December 19, they expressed the wish that the consuls would post up the decree of the Senate with their own edict, and would order the magistrates and ambassadors of the *municipia* and *coloniae* to take copies and send them to the *municipia* and *coloniae* of Italy, and to those *coloniae* which there were in the provinces.[34] By the time Claudius came in 48 to defend to the Senate the idea of accepting senators from Gaul, there had been a slight shift in the terminology used. "But was it a novelty that Divus Augustus, my *avunculus* [great-uncle], and Tiberius Caesar, my *patruus* [uncle], wanted all the flower of the *coloniae* and *municipia* everywhere, provided that they were respectable men and rich, in this Senate house?" (*ILS* 212).

Augustus had also, as Suetonius saw it (*Aug.* 46), populated Italy with twenty-eight colonies (text to n. 1 above), and up to a certain extent given them equal rights and dignity with Rome by allowing the *colonici decuriones* (the town councillors of the colonies) to send in written and sealed votes in the elections for the magistracies in Rome. But no extensive programme of colonial foundation or settlement of veterans was ever attempted again. Only Nero and Vespasian engaged in relatively limited settlements in Campania and southern Italy. Thereafter there were none.[35] This progression, from a

33. Suet., *Aug.* 46; see C. Nicolet, "Tribuni militum a populo," *MEFR* 79 (1967): 29–76.

34. J. González, "Tabula Siarensis, Fortunales Siarenses et Municipia civium Romanorum," *ZPE* 55 (1984): 55–100. The reference is to frag. (b), col. II, ll. 22–26 (p. 76) = M. H. Crawford, ed., *Roman Statutes* I (London, 1996), 518.

35. L. J. F. Keppie, "Colonisation and Veteran Settlement in Italy in the First Century AD," *BSR* 52 (1984): 77–114.

large-scale programme continuing those of Sulla, Caesar, and the Triumvirs, to intermittent minor activity, to total cessation, of course matches the steady decline in legionary recruitment in Italy, on which all studies concur.[36] While Italian recruits for the legions never entirely disappeared, it seems that in the second century regular levies were held in Italy only at moments when new legions were being formed, two under Marcus Aurelius and three under Septimius Severus.[37]

The legions apart, there were also some auxiliary units raised in Italy, the *cohors Apula* and *cohors Campana*, two *cohortes Italicae voluntariorum civium Romanorum*, and some thirty-two *cohortes voluntariorum civium Romanorum*; what proportion of the latter were ever recruited from Italy remains wholly obscure. But, apart from the two or six *cohortes ingenuorum civium Romanorum* raised in Rome in the crises of A.D. 6 and 9, the entire question of these Italian or citizen cohorts awaits clarification.[38] No such problem arises over the urban cohorts, whose soldiers came predominantly from central Italy and to a lesser extent from the North; on our evidence less than 10 per cent of them came from the provinces.[39] A similar pattern prevailed for the praetorian cohorts, at least until Septimius Severus dismissed the existing soldiers and replaced them with men from the provincial armies; he thus, as Dio complains, caused the youth of Italy to turn to banditry, and filled the city with men of barbarian appearance and conduct. Thereafter, through the third century, though Italians were not excluded, the praetorians continued to be recruited primarily from the provincial legions.[40] Valerius Clemens, *natione Italus* (an Italian by birth), who was discharged from the praetorian cohorts in 306, and whose diploma was found near Grosseto, was clearly not typical.[41] He will

36. See G. Forni, *Il reclutamento delle legioni da Augusto a Diocleziano* (Milan, 1953); Forni, "Estrazione etnica e sociale dei soldati delle legioni nei primi tre secoli dell'impero," *ANRW* 2.1 (1974), 339–91; J. C. Mann, *Legionary Recruitment and Veteran Settlement during the Principate* (London, 1983).

37. Note J. C. Mann, "The Raising of New Legions during the Principate," *Hermes* 91 (1963): 483–89.

38. For the available evidence, see M. Speidel, "Citizen Cohorts in the Roman Imperial Army: New Data on the Cohorts Apula, Campana, and III Campestris," *TAPA* 106 (1976): 339–48 (= *Roman Army Studies* I [1984], 91–101).

39. See H. Freis, *Die Cohortes Urbanae* (*Epigraphische Studien* 2, 1967), 50ff.

40. Dio 75.2.4–6. See M. Durry, *Les Cohortes prétoriennes* (Paris, 1938), 247–51; A. Passerini, *Le coorti pretorie* (Rome, 1979), 171–83.

41. M. M. Roxan, *Roman Military Diplomas, 1954–1977* (London, 1978), no. 78. Note also M. Roxan, "The Distribution of Roman Military Diplomas," *Epigraphische Studien* 12 (1981): 265–86.

have left the service just before the coup d'état of Maxentius, whose rule from 306 to 312 was to represent the last imperial régime based on Rome and Italy until the fifth century. What this meant for Italy, in terms of taxation, the raising of forces, and the structure of society, is a question which could and should be pursued.

It should be noted, however, that the patterns of military recruitment have largely been studied through inscriptions, which notoriously decline in numbers in the third century and after. Did the role of northern Italy as a theatre of war in the third century, its provincialisation under Diocletian, the rule there of Maxentius, or the different procedures for recruiting in the fourth century mean that soldiers were again regularly raised there? To my knowledge there has been no study of recruitment by regions in the earlier fourth century, any more than there has of the geographical distribution of the army then. It may have been a sign of the future when the soldiers whom Maximinus used in the 230s for building roads in northern Italy were the "the recruits of his new Italian youth, of the later conscription" (*tirones iuventut(is) novae Italicae suae, dilectus posterior(is)*).[42] The Roman army of the mid-third to mid-fourth century still awaits detailed study.

In the fourth century, as is known, the sons of veterans were legally obliged to serve unless physically disabled. While no such laws can ever have been universally effective, this one did affect at least the future Saint Martin, living at Ticinum (Pavia) (Sulpicius Severus, *Vita S. Martini* 2). In the fourth century also, and possibly earlier, landowners were liable for the production of recruits, while the state could if it wished raise a tax in cash (*aurum tironicum*) instead.[43] Once again, if we knew whether or how early such a system applied in Italy, it would be important for our conception of the relations of state and subject there.

Whatever the uncertainties in this area, we can assume that the demands of the state, in whatever form, will necessarily have been mediated by, or refracted through, the social structures of the individual communities. Thus wherever, as in Italy, there were rich, landowning families with substantial estates, that will have affected how the demands of the state were channelled. We should recall here the important observation from the earlier imperial period contained in the *Corpus Agrimensorum* (1.1, ed. Thulin, 45):

> Some types of *controversiae* [legal disputes] between cities and private persons do not arise readily in Italy, but do so frequently in the provinces, especially in Africa, where private people own estates which are

42. *CIL* 5, 7989 = *ILS* 487; 7990; *AE* 1953, 31; 1979, 256–57.
43. See M. Rostovtzeff, "Συντέλεια Τιρώνων," *JRS* 8 (1918): 26–33; Jones 615–16.

of no lesser extent than the territories of the cities; indeed many own estates which are much larger than city territories. They have a not inconsiderable labouring population on their private estates, and *vici* [villages] round the villa which resemble *municipia*. The cities tend to raise *controversiae* concerning the law of the *territorium*, on the grounds that they claim the right to impose *munera* on such and such a section of land, or to levy a recruit [*tiro*] from a *vicus* or to impose transport services [*vecturae*] or the delivery of supplies [*copiae*].

These and comparable issues will certainly have arisen in Italy, as soon as the state deployed troops there and raised recruits or levied taxes, whether in cash or kind.

One of the most valuable steps that could be taken — and now has been — towards an understanding of imperial Italy would be precisely an edition, with translation and commentary, of the writings of the land surveyors, the *Corpus Agrimensorum*.[44] One of the many things which the works of the *Agrimensores* illustrate is the long-term effect on local property relations, and power structures, of the colonisation programme of the second half of the first century B.C. Even when, as we saw, colonisation itself had ceased, its after-effects did not. These effects included, but were not confined to, major issues such as that of Vespasian's claim on all the *subseciva*, plots of land un-allotted at the moment of foundation of a colony; this led to embassies coming from all over Italy to protest, to a partial concession by Titus, and to a complete withdrawal of the claim by Domitian.[45] Similarly, the allotment to veterans of land in Samnium by Vespasian led quickly to confusion over property rights by the addition and sale of plots and the customary use of natural features or roads to delimit boundaries (*Corpus Agrimensorum* 62, 95). Another fruitful cause of disputes was the preservation of *loca sacra* (sacred plots of land), a duty conspicuously laid down in the *mandata* (codes of instructions) which *legati* (governors in imperial provinces) received from the emperor. But in Italy, as Agennius Urbicus explains, this was not so easily achieved. For the *densitas possessorum* (the density of occupation) meant that much impropriety took place, and *possessores* simply occupied *luci sacri* (sacred groves) which were legally the property of the Roman people, even if located within the borders of colonies or municipalities. This too led to frequent *quaestio* (legal enquiry) as between cities and private people (*Corpus Agrimensorum* 48).

44. See now B. Campbell, *The Writings of the Roman Land Surveyors: Introduction, Text, Translation and Commentary* (JRS Monographs 9, 2000).

45. *Corpus Agrimensorum Romanorum*, 1.1, ed. C. Thulin (Stuttgart, 1971), 41, 96–97.

This brings us to the second question about imperial Italy. How, by whom, and in what ways was power exercised? Did Italy live, in a more specific sense than the provinces, within the decision-making structures of the Roman state, or under the jurisdiction of its magistrates? Or was it the emperor to whom cities and individuals turned? Is the appointment of *consulares* to regions of Italy by Hadrian, of *iuridici* and *correctores* later, or of *curatores* of individual cities, to be seen as the extension of state power, and an intrusion on the autonomy of the cities? What physical force was available either to these senatorial officials or to the cities themselves for the maintenance of order? Or was order in fact not maintained? This last might mean various different things. Local notables might have exercised power in such a way that local organs of communal decision making could not effectively challenge the interests of important individuals; legal sources of the earlier fourth century do indeed reflect the fact that lower courts might be unable to resist the influence of *potentiores* (local potentates).[46] Even earlier, Callistratus applies the concept of being *in vinculis* (being in chains — and hence unable to appear in court) not only to those in *publica custodia* (city prisons) but to anyone oppressed by *latrones* (bandits) or *praedones* (robbers) or *potentior vis* (superior force) (*Dig.* 4, 6, 9); similarly, it was allowable for a man physically detained by *potentiores* to escape to a statue of Caesar (*Dig.* 48, 19, 28, 7). Actual force might, alternatively, have been exercised by employees of the Roman state — that is, since there was no other substantial body of such employees, by the army or by men from the fleets. Or it might have been exerted by the local communities; but what militias, if any, did the cities themselves possess? They certainly might have a prison (*carcer* or *custodia publica*; Millar [note 14] 130–32); and it is striking that the *Corpus Agrimensorum* (once again) states that cities regularly have suburban sites destined for *noxiorum poenae* (punishment of the condemned; 1.1, 47), which must surely mean executions. The implication is confirmed for one Italian colony, Puteoli, by an inscription laying down the duties of the *libitinarius* (undertaker) in relation to executions carried out *publice* (publicly) by the magistrate (*AE* 1971, 88, II.1, 1–14). In both cases the allusion *may* be solely to the execution of slaves; but neither text says so explicitly.

But if the cities had the means, once a criminal had been apprehended, to retain him in custody or carry out his execution, it does not follow that they had either the political will to enforce the law against local *potentiores*, the police resources for the maintenance of public order, or the concentration

---

46. See, e.g., A. Wacke, "Die *potentiores* in den Rechtsquellen. Einfluss und Abwehr gesellschaftlicher Übermacht in der Rechtspflege der Römer," *ANRW* 2.13 (1980), 562–607.

of physical force necessary for confronting groups of bandits. The question of bandits in the Roman Empire has been discussed by Brent Shaw; on the face of it, Italy seems to present a prime case of what he calls the "imperfect control of the central state over the whole geographic regions which were surrounded by its forces but which were inadequately penetrated by its institutions."[47]

For Italy as a whole throughout the period we are confronted by a general question: was legal force exercised by the Roman state, by the cities, by the two in concert, or by neither? Or did there lie, behind the formal apparatus of emperor, courts, magistrates, and imperial officials of various kinds on the one hand, and the cities with their councils and magistrates on the other, some alternative power structures based on patronage, the possession of large properties and groups of slaves, or influence exercised locally, or in Rome, or with the emperor? Some hints as to possible patterns in the exercise of power are, I think, provided by the well-known inscription from Saepinum relating to the movement of flocks. In spite of recent arguments, I still believe that the problem at issue in this document had nothing to do with the taxation of all transhumant flocks. In my view the interests of the *fiscus* (imperial treasury) came in solely because flocks owned by the emperor were among those which used this route.[48] The inscription, from the reign of Marcus Aurelius, contains letters from an imperial freedman to the *a rationibus* (the official in charge of imperial finance); from the *a rationibus* to the praetorian prefects, Bassaeus Rufus and Macrinius Vindex; and from the praetorian prefects to the magistrates of Saepinum. The important feature is that an issue has arisen because the magistrates and *stationarii* (see below) at Saepinum and Bovianum (to whom, presumably, a separate letter was sent) had been descending on the *pastores* (shepherds) driving flocks of sheep, claiming that they were *fugitivi* (runaway slaves), and the animals stolen; in the resultant *tumultus* (disturbances), which it is easy to imagine, sheep, including imperial ones, had got scattered and lost. The praetorian prefects write in threatening terms to the magistrates telling them to leave the *conductores* (lessees) of flocks alone; if not, it might be necessary *cognosci de hoc* (to hold a judicial enquiry on the matter).

Does this exchange imply that communal jurisdiction and public order

47. Brent D. Shaw, "Bandits in the Roman Empire," *Past and Present* 105 (1984): 3–52, at 30.

48. *CIL* 9, 2438; for the different interpretation mentioned, see M. Corbier, "Fiscus and Patrimonium: The Saepinum Inscription and Transhumance in the Abruzzi," *JRS* 73 (1983): 126–31.

throughout Italy were now the concern of the praetorian prefects? One famous anecdote might support this hypothesis, namely Dio's story of Felix
Bulla, the leader of 600 bandits who terrorised Italy for two years under Septimius Severus, evading capture (significantly) by *megalodoria* (munificence);
he rescued two of his men from a local prison by pretending to be a local
magistrate who needed them for a wild-beast show, captured and executed a
centurion, and was finally trapped by a praetorian tribune and interrogated
by the praetorian prefect, Papinian (76, 10). Legal evidence confirms that
Severus laid down that Italy *within* 100 miles from Rome came under the civil
and criminal jurisdiction of the prefect of the city (*Dig.* 1, 12) and outside
that, under the praetorian prefect (*Coll.* 14, 3, 2).

The praetorian prefects, however, clearly could and did warn the local
magistrates to desist from police activities which were damaging to the imperial wealth. Might not the agents of lesser *potentiores* have been able to do
the same? These activities had been reinforced by *stationarii*. Are these to be
seen as a local militia? The whole question needs to be re-examined. It is,
once again, somewhat over a century since the last comprehensive treatment,
R. Cagnat's *De municipalibus et provincialibus militiis* (1880); and a little less since
Henzen published an inscription from near Pisaurum honouring a praetorian
evocatus (a former soldier recalled to service) who in the 240s was operating
with soldiers from the Ravenna fleet *ad latrunculum* (against a brigand), and
surveyed the scattered evidence for the use of official force to maintain order
in Italy.[49] The despatch of praetorian cohorts to deal with specific disorders
is, of course, well known, as at Pollentia under Tiberius, when they were
complemented by a force from the Cottian Alps (Suet., *Tib.* 37), or at Puteoli
under Nero (Tac., *Ann.* 13, 48). It would be much more important to know
whether the *stationes militum* (posts manned by soldiers) which Tiberius is
said to have distributed more intensively in Italy (Suet., *Tib.* 37) represented
the beginning of an established system. In other words might the *stationarii*,
doing what appeared to be their duty in Saepinum and Bovianum, in fact
have been praetorians on police duties? It may be relevant that after the establishment of the *legio II Parthica* at Alba, inscriptions attest two of its soldiers
on police duties elsewhere in Italy, an *optio* [a non-commissioned officer] in
the reign of Severus himself at Luna (*CIL* 11, 1322 = *ILS* 2371), and under
Philip a *stationarius* who made a dedication in the *municipium* of Aveia in the
territory of the Vestini (*ILS* 9087), far from any major road.

There is indeed some indication that throughout the Empire soldiers on

---

49. G. Henzen, "Iscrizione trovata presso la galleria del Furlo," *RömMitt* 2 (1887): 14–20;
CIL 11, 6107 (= *ILS* 509).

police duty came to act in collaboration with, or under the effective orders of, the local magistrates (Millar [note 14] 130–32). If the *stationarii* at Saepinum and Bovianum were not praetorians, the word must be applied here to a strictly local force. But I do not know any certain evidence of that, or indeed any concrete evidence for local militias anywhere in Roman Italy. The question of who, if anyone, in imperial Italy exercised force in the name of the law remains remarkably open.

However, if I am right in saying that the praetorian prefects are intervening to *stop* police operations which were disadvantageous to the interests of the *fiscus*, is that not a model for how things might have worked on a local basis? It is not only that Tacitus, as we saw (text following n. 23 above), noted that when imperial estates were relatively rare in Italy the officials in charge of them were still subject to normal legal processes. Other *potentiores* might imprison people (text to n. 45 above), and cities might find it hard to impose services on large neighbouring estates (text to n. 24 above), or even to recover possession of sacred sites (text following n. 44 above).

When issues arose between city and city, or within a city over public funds or property, or between a city and a private person, especially one who was *potentior*, and if the communal rights could not be enforced, recourse will have been necessary to some outside or higher authority. This is surely, as is now generally recognised, the background to the appointment, from the late first century onwards, of imperial officials for cities and regions in Italy. There is no need to rehearse once again the evidence for *curatores* of individual cities;[50] for the *consulares* briefly introduced by Hadrian (Appian, *BC* 1 38/172; Eck chap. 7); for the *iuridici* and their varied regional distribution, between the reigns of Marcus Aurelius and Aurelian;[51] for the senatorial *correctores* who appear in Italy in the third century, to become the established governors of the regions of Italy after Diocletian, sometimes with the title *consulares*; or

50. See Eck chap. 6; R. Duthoy, "*Curatores rei publicae* en Occident durant le Principat. Recherches préliminaires sur l'apport des sources épigraphiques," *Ancient Society* 10 (1979): 171–238; C. Camodeca, "Ricerche sui *curatores rei publicae*," *ANRW* 2.13 (1980), 453–534. See also G. P. Burton, "*The Curator Rei Publicae*: Towards a Reappraisal," *Chiron* 9 (1979): 465–87. For the prosopography of *curatores*, see esp. F. Jacques, *Les curateurs des cités dans l'Occident romain de Trajan à Gallien, Études Prosopographiques* (Paris 1983). For a detailed discussion of the functions of *curatores*, see the major study by F. Jacques, *Le privilège de liberté: Politique impériale et autonomie municipale dans les cités de l'Occident romain (161–244)* (Collection de l'École française de Rome 76, Paris, 1984).

51. M. Corbier, "Les circonscriptions judiciaires de l'Italie de Marc-Aurèle Aurélien," *MEFR* 85 (1973): 609–90; W. Simshäuser, *Iuridici und Munizipalgerichtsbarkeit in Italien* (Munich, 1973); Eck chap. 7.

for the *vicarii* who appear in the early fourth century.[52] It is more important to see such officials, none of whom commanded any military force, in
the context of the means of redress, or the sources of judicial decision or
arbitration, available to Italian communities and individuals under the Empire. Much, as usual, remains unclear. How far was the jurisdiction of the
praetors in Rome used by individuals in Italy? We would not have expected
the legal procedures current in first-century Puteoli to include the giving
of *vadimonia* (deposits) to appear in the Forum Augustum in Rome, as the
documents from Murecine show that they did.[53] These documents will make
possible a quite new history of the workings of the jurisdiction in Roman
Italy—and in effect show for the first time how what we call "Roman law"
actually operated in the classical period of Roman history.

For communities, although Nero claimed that Italy and the public provinces would henceforth have recourse to the *consulum tribunalia* (the courts of
the consuls) (Tac., *Ann.* 13, 4), the evidence for embassies before the Senate,
or for decrees of the Senate concerning the affairs of individual Italian cities,
is not extensive.[54] But we may note on the one hand the general decree of
the Senate of A.D. 44/6 promoted by Claudius, and fulfilling the Emperor's
care for the *totius Italiae aeternitas* (the survival of the whole of Italy) by for-
bidding the demolition of buildings for their materials—and then the exemption from this provision gained in 56 for Alliatoria Celsilla, the wife of
an *ornatissimus vir* (a most distinguished man), by request to the Senate via
her relatives (*FIRA*² 1, no. 45). On the other hand there is the striking case
recorded by Pliny (*Ep.* 5, 4; 13) where the city of Vicetia brought an action
before the Senate to prevent a praetorian senator from initiating *nundinae*
(market days) on his property; but their *advocatus* (lawyer) failed to appear,
scared off by warnings from his friends as to the danger of opposing, in the
Senate above all, the will of a senator who was now in conflict not so much
about his *nundinae* as his *gratia* (influence), *fama* (reputation), and *dignitas* (dignity). Both issues afford significant hints as to the various forms of influence
which could be exercised by members of the upper classes to secure their
own interests.

52. A. Chastagnol, "L'administration du Diocèse Italien au Bas-Empire," *Historia* 12
(1963): 348–79; Barnes (n. 7), 143–44, 161–65.

53. See, e.g., *AE* 1969–70, 96; 1978, 134, 139. See L. Bove, *Documenti processuali dalle Tabulae Pompeianae di Murecine* (Naples, 1979), 50ff., but above all the essential re-publication by
G. Camodeca, *Tabulae Pompeianae Sulpiciorum (TPSulp.). Edizione critica dell'archivio Puteolano
dei Sulpicii* (Vetera 12, Rome, 1999), with G. Rowe, "Trimalchio's World," *SCI* 20 (2001):
225–45.

54. See R. J. A. Talbert, *The Senate of Imperial Rome* (Princeton, 1984), esp. 384, 417.

We need not doubt that the possibilities of effective recourse to Senate or emperor for Italian communities were profoundly affected by the network of senatorial and equestrian landholding in their territories. Eck has suggested that the relatively slight evidence for embassies from Italian towns might be explained by the functioning of patronage in its place (Eck 15). That is possible, though the extensive evidence for city *patroni* (officially appointed patrons) in Italy does not contain many instances of effective intervention by well-placed patrons from the locality:[55] the two clearest and best-known instances are the request of Minicius Italus to Trajan for the right of Aquileia to impose *munera* on *incolae* (residents) there (*ILS* 1374), and the similar role of a senator from Tergeste, Fabius Severus, in cases on behalf of the city before Antoninus Pius (*ILS* 6680). It is, however, noteworthy that cities and communities in Italy continued into the fourth century to pass honorific decrees appointing *patroni*. When the *ordo* (senate) of Peltruinum passed a decree in 242 that Nummia Varia should be the *patrona praefecturae nostrae* (the patroness of our prefecture), they did so in the hope of being *tuti ac defensi* (safe and protected) as a result (*ILS* 6110 = Sherk 20). So, too, Paestum, in its decrees passed in the reigns of Constantine and Constantius, hoped for the favour of its *patroni* (Sherk 23–25). But the real functioning and significance of that patronage system is not at all clear. Locally, the presence of senatorial landowners may often have limited rather than increased the freedom of action of city councils; how far these and others, as *patroni*, could and did aid their cities in relation to the central powers, remains open to question. When a significant innovation was in question, an Italian community could still, throughout the period, approach the emperor directly. The clearest proof is of course Constantine's reply to Hispellum in the last few years of his reign (*ILS* 705): they had requested to be allowed to give the name "Flavian" to their city; to build there a temple of the *Flavia gens*; and to be able to hold a theatrical and gladiatorial festival separate from that at Volsinii. All this they obtained, without apparent recourse to *patroni* or reference to the *corrector* of Tuscia and Umbria or the *vicarius* of Italy.

The same of course was frequently achieved by provincial cities. The question of the gradual "provincialisation" of Italy is perhaps ultimately of significance not because this expression is itself necessarily misleading, but because it also throws into relief how limited were the functions performed by pro-

---

55. See A. Sofredi, "Il patronato in Italia alle luce delle iscrizioni latine," *Epigraphica* 18 (1956): 157–72; L. Harmand, *Le patronat sur les collectivités publiques* (Paris, 1957); R. Duthoy, "Quelques observations concernant la mention d'un patronat municipal dans les inscriptions," *AntCl* 50 (1981): 295–305.

vincial governors themselves in civilian contexts. *Curatores*, as recent studies by Eck, Camodeca, Burton, and Jacques (above, note 50) all agree, were not in fact there to perform or usurp the functions of cities. Their formal role was to act as a point of recourse when issues arose over the disbursement of city funds or the use of public property. When the magistrates and *decuriones* (town councillors) of Caere wrote in 113 to their *curator* to request his assent to the allocation of a public site for a building, he was elsewhere, and needed only to write a formal letter of assent. But objections might have been made, and he *could* anyway have said no. In that case, of course, there would have been no inscription to record this transaction (*ILS* 5918 = Sherk 51).

Similarly, the *iuridici*, as their title makes clear, were there to give justice (*iura reddere*), as had been Hadrian's *consulares* (*HA, M. Ant.* 11, 6). They, too, were a point of recourse, as is clear above all in the decree of the Senate of the 170s on the price of gladiators.[56] Its provisions were to be enforced on the *lanistae* by the governors; in Transpadana and the *regiones* of Italy the relevant *arbitrium* was a matter for the *praefecti alimentorum*, if present, or a *viae curator*, or, if none were available, a *iuridicus* or prefect of the fleet—in short, any official to whom an interested party could gain access. There were after all only some six *iuridici* throughout Italy. Even where they are recorded as having taken steps in relation to the *annona* of a city,[57] these should not, I suggest, be interpreted as having been administrative measures, for which they had no resources, but legal ones, comparable with the *edictum* of Antistius Rusticus in Antioch in Pisidia in 93, by which those with corn were compelled to put it on the market, under threat of penalties (*AE* 1925, 126). Precisely as with a governor, the single *iuridicus* of a substantial area could in the nature of the case only rule on those issues, disputes, or crises which were brought to his attention. Like the *correctores* who became the established governors, or equivalents of governors, in Italy in the early fourth century, each *iuridicus* functioned in an area containing a population of several hundred thousand people and had no military forces at his disposal. When we come to these fourth-century *correctores*, our knowledge, previously so dependent on formal inscriptions, now derives largely from legal sources. But it still may not be misleading if we see them essentially as judges in both civil and criminal cases. Thus, to take only two instances, Constantine writes in 316 to Hilarianus, *corrector* of Lucania and Bruttii, about the treatment of *decuriones* accused of aiding the falsification of a will (*CTh* 9, 19, 9; *CJ* 9, 22, 2); or to his

56. J. H. Oliver and R. E. A. Palmer, "Minutes of an Act of the Roman Senate," *Hesperia* 24 (1955): 320–49.

57. See, e.g., *ILS* 1118 (Concordia); *CIL* 11, 377 (Ariminum).

predecessor in the previous year about the necessity of retaining cases before his own court and preventing appeals to *vicarii* or praetorian prefects (*CTh* 1, 16, 1).

That was one real change in the government of Italy, the creation of several tiers of jurisdiction. Another, perhaps more significant, was that the issues to be decided now included those relating to the payment of direct taxes. So Constantine laid down to the *consularis* of Aemilia and Liguria in 323 that imperial properties in Italy (*fundi patrimoniales adque enfyteuticarii per Italiam nostram*) were liable for the regular taxes (*canonica*), but were exempt from the *extraordinaria* (*CTh* 11, 16, 2). So too we can see in Italy, but also elsewhere in the Empire, a change whereby the persons who take credit for buildings in cities are not so much local benefactors or magistrates as *curatores* and *correctores*.[58] A prime case is the inscription recording the construction of the temple of Deus Sol in Comum under Diocletian and Maximian: *T(itus) Fl(avius) Post(umus) Titianus v(ir) c(larissimus), corr(ector) Ital(iae), perfecit ac dedicavit, curante Axilio Iuniore v(iro) c(larissimo), curatore* (Titus Flavius Postumus Titianus, a man of senatorial status, *corrector* of Italy, completed and dedicated [the temple], while Auxilius Iunior, the *curator*, a man of senatorial status, was in charge) (*AE* 1919, 52). In this way, in words displayed for every passer-by to read, a new structure of authority and initiative was made visible. More significant still is the inscription recording the reconstruction of the walls of Verona in 265, *iubente sanctissimo Gallieno Aug(usto) n(ostro), insistente Aur(elio) Marcellino v(iro) p(erfectissimo), duc(enario?) duc. (?), curante Iulio Marcellino* (Our most sacred emperor Gallienus giving the order, Aurelius Marcellinus, a most distinguished man of ducenariate status supervising it, [and] Iulius Marcellinus being in charge) (*CIL* 5, 3329). In northern Italy at least, external pressures had now caused the Roman state, in the person of the emperor and his army and its officers, to come much closer to, or collapse inwards onto, a world of self-governing *res publicae* (city-states).

Even now, however, there was another Italy, where the state exercised no more than civil jurisdiction, and where in specific contexts the cities could still look to quite different sources of central authority. For in 289 we find the *decuriones* of Cumae appointing a new priest of the Magna Mater, and having their decision, and the priest's right to wear an armlet and *corona* (wreath) within the bounds of the city, approved in a formal letter by the college of fifteen priests called Quindecemviri Sacris Faciundis in Rome.[59] Diocletian

---

58. See esp. Ward-Perkins (n. 30), chap. 1 and app. 1.

59. *CIL* 10, 3698 = *ILS* 4175 (= F. F. Abbott and A. C. Johnson, *Municipal Administration in the Roman Empire* [Princeton, 1926], no. 149).

and Maximian, with their deep commitment to Roman religious traditions, would no doubt have approved also. But they did not need to be asked.

Imperial Italy still does not have a history. I have, however, attempted to find a number of factors within the overall evolution of the Roman state which might have contributed to social change in Italy. Very little in this is at all clear; but one factor which, in a very general way, is suggestive is the imposition of court and army and taxation in northern Italy in the course of the third century.[60] Elsewhere in Italy the Roman state was present in various very limited ways—the jurisdiction exercised by the few *iuridici* or *correctores*, the need for cities to gain the consent of *curatores* for expenditures, the raising of some indirect taxes, the recruitment of soldiers first for the legions and some citizen cohorts, then (in effect) only for the units in Rome—and in the third century only for the *cohortes urbanae*. In what forms and to what extent taxation and recruitment were imposed on all of Italy in the early fourth century still remains quite uncertain. But there is still nothing to indicate that, apart from those in Rome, and the *legio II Parthica*, substantial forces were stationed there except in the North. Italy thus still presents fundamental puzzles. Firstly, can it really be true that there was no significant exchange of economic and human resources between Italy and the Empire of which it was a part? And, secondly, if the state did not exercise power and physical force there, who did?

60. Between the delivery of this chapter and its revision for publication (both in 1985), and the moment when it actually appeared, a number of important relevant works were published, some of which are noted above. But it was not possible to take account of by far the most significant of them, the papers contained in A. Giardina, ed., *Società romana e impero tardoantico* I–IV (Rome and Bari, 1986), esp. vol. I: *Istituzioni, ceti, economie,* and vol. II: *Roma: politica, economia, paesagio urbano.* Note above all, for its relevance to the central theme of this chapter, A. Giardina, "Le due Italie nella forma tarda dell'impero," I, 1–30, reprinted as chap. 6 of A. Giardina, *L'Italia Romana: storie di un'identità incompiuta* (Rome and Bari, 1997).

CHAPTER EIGHTEEN

*Style Abides**

The publication of the collected papers of a great scholar is a moment for celebration and congratulation, and also for thought. For it is also an explicit invitation to see the writer's work as a whole, as something more than the sum of its parts. In the present case this is exceptionally difficult, for there is something of Syme now in everyone who works on Roman history; but for that very reason we can afford to take his stature as a historian as a pre-supposition and should not shirk the duty of asking what his work has been, what we have learnt from it, what else we should have learnt from it, and how much a record of publication stretching over half a century (and still continuing) has to offer us now.

Thus in this review article the *Roman Papers*, edited with devotion, energy, and infinite labour by Ernst Badian, will form a framework, or starting point, for an attempt to look at Syme's intellectual career, achievement, and influ-ence up to 1970, the year in which he retired from the Camden Chair of Ancient History in Oxford, and the point at which this collection stops. I do not delude myself that my view can be objective, in either personal or intellectual terms.

It must be said at once that we do not have, and now never can have, the complete collection of Syme's papers in chronological order which would alone have made all his work accessible and have formed an appropriate com-

*First published in *JRS* 71 (1981): 144–52 as a review article of Ronald Syme, *Roman Papers* I–II, edited by E. Badian (Oxford, 1979). I am grateful to Tim Barnes, Keith Hopkins, John Matthews, and John Wilkes for comments, criticisms, and corrections. It is almost super-fluous to add that they have no responsibility for the views expressed. An earlier version of this chapter was given at a seminar in the Institute of Classical Studies, London. [Ronald Syme died in 1989; for the best comment on his life and work, see the obituary by G. W. Bowersock in *Proc. Brit. Acad.* 84 (1993): 539.]

panion to his major individual works. Instead the Clarendon Press in 1970 produced *Ten Studies in Tacitus* (now out of print), while in 1971 there appeared *Danubian Papers*, published in Bucharest by the Association internationale d'études du Sud-Est européen. The effect has been firstly to disperse Syme's papers over a disparate series of volumes, and secondly to impose the title *Roman Papers* on the present collection, thus excluding altogether, for instance, "Three English Historians: Gibbon, Macaulay, Toynbee" of 1962 (one of his most revealing papers), and "Thucydides," delivered at the British Academy in 1960, his only excursion into Greek history.

Moreover, this is not a complete collection even of the "Roman" papers up to 1970. Badian states in the introduction (p. xi) that the choice was made by him in consultation with Sir Ronald himself. It is not explained why the idea of a complete collection was rejected, nor what principle of selection was applied. Most unfortunately, the method of selection has operated to reinforce the familiar conception of Syme as the master of political prosopography and to obscure the fundamental importance of Latin literature for the whole of his work, and of military history in the earlier part of it. So his two earliest papers, "Rhine and Danube Legions under Domitian" (1928) and "The *Argonautica* of Valerius Flaccus" are omitted, as are "The Spanish War of Augustus" and "Galatia and Pamphylia under Augustus" (1934), not to speak of his classic chapters on the frontiers in *CAH* X (1934) and XI (1936). The post-war period is much more fully covered—with the significant exception of three papers on Sallust or pseudo-Sallust—but the understanding of Syme's development from a military historian to a political, social, and literary one is helped in these volumes principally by the bibliography up to 1970 given in vol. II, 855–62. These gaps combine with the inevitable omission of papers already reprinted in *Ten Studies* or *Danubian Papers* to give a rather misleading impression of the overall balance of his work.

Nor is it clear why it was thought worthwhile to wait from 1974 to 1979 for the preparation of an index covering both this and the two earlier collections. For it must have been apparent all that time, and indeed earlier, that Syme was not only, as he might have written, "extant," but was writing vigorously. The index on which so much labour has been spent will find its natural place, in expanded form, at the end of a third volume. Thus, for all Badian's devoted labour, for which he deserves our gratitude and sympathy, it must be said that the whole business of collecting Syme's papers has produced sadly unsatisfactory results. The basic fault must lie in the lack of appreciation of an opportunity, and a failure of conception and purpose, in Oxford.

That said, the *Roman Papers* may still afford us the opportunity of discussing his achievement as objectively as we can. For this, some elements of biography are required. Syme was born in Eltham in the North Island of New Zealand in 1903, and in 1921–23 was a student of Classics at Victoria University College in Wellington, becoming a lecturer and temporarily deputy for the professor, at Auckland in 1923. We need not doubt that a good traditional grounding in Classics was available in New Zealand at that time, but it lies in the nature of the case that the level of excellence which he attained must have been very largely a personal achievement; and, in fact, he began the study of Greek only in 1922. The measure of his early attainment is the record of the major Classical prizes in Oxford after Syme came to Oriel College in 1925 to read Literae Humaniores (Ancient History and Philosophy). In 1926 he won the Chancellor's Prize for Latin Prose (turning a passage of Macaulay into Ciceronian prose) and the Gaisford Prize for Greek Prose (putting a section of More's *Utopia* into Platonic prose); in 1927 there followed the Gaisford Prize for Greek Verse (a passage of Morris, *Sigurd the Volsung*, in Homeric hexameters). The facts do not quite support the dramatic picture in the autobiography of Sir Harold Hobson, *Indirect Journey* (1978), 150, of the news bursting in Oriel that the Commoner from New Zealand had won all four major prizes in a single year; but they are still, in the context of the long tradition of prose and verse composition in the major English schools, startling enough. Strange and remote as these arcane art forms may seem now, the facts may serve to emphasize three fundamental aspects of Syme's intellectual career: the conquest of the inner citadel of culture by the outsider; the absolute mastery of Greek and Latin; and the devotion to language and literature, far beyond those of Greece and Rome.

Search as we may, however, we will not find in the Oxford of the late 1920s and 1930s the key to Syme's intellectual biography. But we will find one part of it in the name of the Tutor in Ancient History at Oriel, Marcus Niebuhr Tod, whose *Sidelights on Greek History: Three Lectures on the Light Thrown by Greek Inscriptions on the Life and Thought of the Ancient World* was published in 1932, followed by *Greek Historical Inscriptions* I in 1933. We surely cannot be wrong to see in Syme's work the imprint of Tod's utter devotion and professionalism, his delicacy and precision in the slightly old-fashioned use of language, and above all his use of inscriptions to illuminate the society from which they came.

Tod apart, Oxford at that time housed a number of learned and reputable Roman historians. The most important of them in terms of an intellectual influence, which it becomes increasingly difficult to define (and of which his published work can give no adequate idea), was H. M. Last, then Tutor at St. John's College. The Camden Professor was J. G. C. Anderson, a good and serious student of Tacitus and military history, whom Syme clearly respected. At Brasenose there was Michael Holroyd, whose article on the Jugurthine War in *JRS* 1928 was to be appreciatively quoted in Syme's *Sallust* (1963). At Magdalen College there was H. M. D. Parker, and Syme's first article, on the legions under Domitian (published in 1928, a year after his final undergraduate examination), was in effect a comprehensive rectification of some parts of Parker's *Roman Legions*—and also of Ritterling's great Pauly-Wissowa article, "Legio."

That will give another—and far more important—clue. But for the moment it should be recorded that his remarkable early maturity was recognised in his election in 1929 as Fellow and Tutor in Ancient History at Trinity College, Oxford, where he remained for the decade up to the war, and for four years after it. It is not accidental that, so far as I can find, no "Oxford" autobiography covering those years (Harold Hobson's apart) mentions him. The reason why he was not much in evidence is clear, namely that he was either working or travelling. For it is the fundamental fact of his intellectual biography that the journey, literal and figurative, from New Zealand to Oxford was not enough to satisfy him. As his earliest article shows, he was already deeply imbued with the German scholarship represented in *CIL*, Dessau's *ILS*, Pauly-Wissowa, and the school of *Limesforschung* (frontier studies). What stands out here is a love of detail and of what some might call antiquarian scholarship—but one in which acute observation of the content of documents was informed by a sense of geography, reinforced in the 1930s by many journeys, sometimes on foot, through central and eastern Europe. Yet, as I will try to illustrate more fully later, it has always been Latin literature which has formed his view of what was worth writing about. All the characteristic elements of his work in the 1930s—military history, geography, Latin literature with a dash of prosopography and questions of nomenclature—appear together for instance in "Pollio, Saloninus and Salonae" of 1937; the article is notable also as revealing his earliest observations on bogus names in the *Historia Augusta* (*RP* I, 25).

That brings me to another product of German scholarship, Schulze's *Zur Geschichte lateinischer Eigennamen*, published in 1904, with a second edition in 1933. The formation and sources of the names used to make up the complex nomenclature of the Romans, and above all their uses in tracing origins and parentage, whether in districts of Italy or in the provinces, or as revealing colonial descent—all this has been a fundamental element in Syme's work ever since. Perhaps equally important as an influence were the essays of Richard Heinze on concepts such as *fides*, *pietas*, and *auctoritas*, finally collected in his *Vom Geist des Römertums* of 1938. Reviewing this work in *CR*

1938, 194, Syme makes a revealing comment: "Heinze sought the ancients for themselves, found them in their own social and spiritual context — and did not drag them out of it." It would be difficult to emphasize too strongly the importance in Syme's writing of a fine appreciation of Latin literature and of the deployment of concepts within it — and of finding a means, through the medium of works written in English, of letting them speak for themselves. This may be expressed in writing English sentences which are deliberate paraphrases of ancient ones; but also in a trick of style whose significance has not, I think, been noted, which consists of using such a paraphrased sentence, transferred out of context, to express a thought which a Roman *could* have had about a particular event or set of circumstances (e.g., *Tacitus*, 13 and n. 3).

Finally, the 1930s saw the emerging mastery of the techniques of prosopography, whether in tracing the social and geographical origins of an individual ("Who Was Decidius Saxa?," 1937; *RP* I, 31–41) or his role in a complex series of political events ("The Allegiance of Labienus," 1938; *RP* I, 62–75), or in the analysis of the new class of men brought into the Senate in the last generations of the Republic ("Caesar, the Senate and Italy," 1938; *RP* I, 88–119). With that, of course, we come very close to *The Roman Revolution*, for which various influences, of very diverse natures, were required. One was Friedrich Münzer's *Römische Adelsparteien und Adelsfamilien* of 1920, portraying the changing composition of the Senate, in terms of families, from the Licinian-Sextian rogations of 367 B.C. to what we may call with Syme "the doom of the nobiles" under the Julio-Claudians. The influence — fully acknowledged — is patent in every respect, from the overall theme of the composition of the governing class to the use of "the Free State" ("der Freistaat" in Münzer) as a term for the Republic. We tend to couple the names of Münzer and Matthias Gelzer as the founders of a new style of interpreting Republican political history. Here it will be sufficient to record my impression that it was not so much Gelzer's *Die Nobilität* as Münzer's *Adelsparteien* which formed Syme's underlying conception of Roman political history.

However, while the *Adelsparteien* is a major historical work, it is not *The Roman Revolution*. For that Syme needed to add a number of distinct elements of his own, which I will attempt to indicate below, following no logical order.

One is the (successful) ambition to write a grand historical narrative in high style, in the manner of Gibbon and Macaulay. There were other literary influences too, and it is no accident that — as I think — Stendhal is the only modern author whose name appears in the text (p. 485). It is particularly worth noting what Syme says of Gibbon, Macaulay, and Toynbee in ending his splendid essay in *Emory University Quarterly* 18 (1962): 129–40: "I shall have to confess where my sympathies lie. They lie with the narrative historians Gibbon and Macaulay, not with the saints and thinkers who are eager to use history for our amendment or for our punishment." His criteria for a historical work which will also be a work of literature appear also in passing asides elsewhere; thus in *The Roman Revolution*, 247, on Varro: "The old scholar lacked style, intensity, a guiding idea"; or on Tacitus (in *Tacitus*, 197): "brevity, rapidity, splendour and concentration." *The Roman Revolution*, on rereading, does indeed seem to me a work of art unmatched among major historical works, and one which would still be read as such even if the day were to come when our knowledge of Roman history has been transformed by new evidence, or when we have found wholly new means of interpreting it.

Secondly, *The Roman Revolution* was of course a reaction to the political events of the 1920s and 1930s. As such it is brilliantly illuminated by Momigliano's introduction to the Italian translation of 1962, reprinted in *Terzo Contributo*, 729–37. The reaction to fascism, not least the pompous claims associated with the Mostra Augustea of 1937–38, is obvious throughout: hence chapters entitled "The March on Rome" and "Dux." But Syme himself has pointed to the promulgation of a constitution by the Soviet Union in 1936, a document taken quite seriously by some credulous and high-minded persons. So *The Roman Revolution* would set out to be an opposition history, in total contrast, for instance to Mason Hammond's *The Augustan Principate* of 1933. It hardly matters that, as A. B. Bosworth so admirably showed in *Historia* 1972, the real Asinius Pollio will not actually serve for the role of opposition historian for which Syme cast him. For his truculence was a matter of style and personality, and did not extend to any significant independence from the new régime, to which he accommodated himself just as did so many others.

But if that regime was to be portrayed as the product of an illegal coup d'état carried out by violence, the portrait was to be executed by the use of two techniques of particular importance. First, it was to lose its concentration on the individual major figures, Caesar, Cicero, or Octavian, to cover an infinitely broader canvas of the actions and reactions throughout the period on the part of hundreds of members of the governing class. Moreover, the large-scale transformation of that class, in terms of the social and geographical origins of its members, was to be the major theme; it is summed up perhaps more succinctly than anywhere else in the first two pages of "Roman Senators from Dalmatia" of 1940, reprinted in *Danubian Papers*, 110–21. On the one hand, this was a vast extension of the range of persons brought within the focus of Roman political history. On the other, Syme made, and would still make, no bones about saying that the narrative history which he is writing is that of the upper classes: "The lower classes had no voice in government, no place in history" (476). As he explained once to an audience of students in London, one writes the history of those who have freedom of action, which is not solely or necessarily a matter of social class; and in fact *The Roman Revolution* does acknowledge (e.g., 180–81) that the desires of the soldiery could often thwart the ambitions of the leaders.

Thus Syme could add various elements to a basic conceptual framework provided by Münzer: a sensitivity to the geographical, social, and ethnic character of the various regions of Italy, the Adriatic region, and the West; a detailed use of inscriptional evidence; and the integration of these new elements into a very detailed narrative of revolution, a narrative necessarily based on literary sources. That represents the first of the two new techniques applied; the second concerns the use of the literary sources themselves. In Syme's treatment many of the classic products of Roman literature appear as instruments for the deployment of catchwords and political concepts, or the promulgation of themes of patriotic history or of national regeneration—or alternatively as the expression of opposition to or distance from the regime. In short, the literature of the age is to be seen as the words chosen by men pursuing their course through a troubled and changing period, sometimes perhaps expressing the view of an Italian middle class, whose arrival in Roman public life the revolution was to consolidate; more often perhaps simply evoking whatever themes seemed to be the required ones. In other words the reader was to break down his picture of the "Augustan age," with all its glories, into a mosaic of contrasting testimonies, contemporary and subsequent, which between them reveal the adjustment of Roman society to the fact of monarchy, and the profound ambivalence of that society's relation to it.

The treatment of "Augustan" literature is deeply influenced by the propaganda of the dictatorships (fascist or proletarian) of the interwar years. Perhaps indeed it was too much influenced, in seeing the victory of Actium as prepared and produced by successful propaganda: "[C]reated belief turned the scale of history" (275). But did it? The evidence does not really suggest so. Propaganda, in the form of pamphlets and denunciations of Antonius to the Senate, there certainly was. But who believed it? On the evidence of Plutarch, *Antonius* 58–59, it caused offence and disbelief at Rome. Again, the victory of Actium earned lavish subsequent celebration in literature. But who was writing *before* Actium to celebrate Octavian as the champion of Rome and Italy? Our best contemporary testimony in prose, the last part of Nepos' *Life* of Atticus, shows the firm neutrality maintained by Atticus until his death in March 32, and clearly approved of by Nepos: "Since each of them

(Octavian and Antonius) wished to be *princeps* not only of the city of Rome but of the *orbis terrarum* [whole world]" (*Atticus* 20).

The *Life* of Atticus remains a priceless and still largely unexploited testimony to the realities of late Republican society. *The Roman Revolution* also makes too little of Velleius, ignoring him because of his undoubted mendacity, and thus losing the chance to see the whole process as represented in the loyalist effusions of a man who represented that Italy which the Augustan revolution brought to the fore: the descendant of a very old family from Campania, entering the equestrian service and then the Senate under Augustus, and writing under Tiberius. G. V. Summer, "The Truth about Velleius Paterculus: Prolegomena," *HSCP* 74 (1970): 257–97, and A. J. Woodman, *Velleius Paterculus: The Tiberian Narrative* (1977), 28–45, present a more sympathetic account. But Syme would not have needed to take a *favourable* view, for it is precisely the time-serving loyalism and the carefully designed reticences of Velleius which tell us so much of the inner quality of the regime. However, the fundamental point remains that in this respect, too, *The Roman Revolution* demonstrated a quite new level of intensity and accuracy in making the reader conscious of how what he knows of history is built up of a mass either of reactions and impressions on the part of contemporaries or of the reflections of those reactions and impressions in later authors—who may still, like Tacitus, be writing in a framework created by the revolution.

For all these new and fundamentally important elements *The Roman Revolution* remains also a classic "old-fashioned" political history built on narrative, the accidental outcome of events which might have been otherwise, the actions, intentions, and abilities of the leading actors, and the right and duty of the historian writing now to judge and generalise in his own person. I conclude this section with a quotation from pp. 120–21:

> Such were the resources that Octavian gathered in late summer and autumn of the year. Men and money were the first thing, next the skill and the resolution to use them. An inborn and Roman distrust of theory, an acute sense of the difference between words and facts, a brief acquaintance with Roman political behaviour—that he possessed and that was all he needed. It is a common belief, attested by the existence of political science as an object of academic study, that the arts of government may be learned from books. The revolutionary career of Caesar's heir reveals never a trace of theoretical preoccupations: if it did, it would have been very different and very short.

When *The Roman Revolution* was published in September 1939, the war had already begun. It was to take Syme to Yugoslavia and then, after that, to

Istanbul, where he was "Professor of Classical Philology" from 1942 to 1945. The significance of this long enforced pause in publication cannot now be assessed. It is sufficient to say that he was thirty-six when the war began and forty-two when it ended, and that he published nothing except reviews between "Roman Senators from Dalmatia" in 1940 and "Personal Names in Annals I–VI" in 1949. This was the year in which he succeeded H. M. Last as Camden Professor of Ancient History in Oxford, and we could well discern here a new phase, leading to *Tacitus* in 1958. But it was not in reality a new phase, as he himself made clear in an important passage in *Tacitus*, 545:

> The Revolution at Rome worked itself out in two stages, the one sudden, the other slow. The first act destroyed the Republic in civil war, the second wore down liberty and the aristocracy in the years of peace. Sallust is the child of the one epoch, Tacitus of the other.

The revolution was thus, firstly, a political one, the imposition of a new system of government; and then, as a later consequence, the suppression of the descendants of those families which had embodied the old system and the end of the tradition of political liberty which they represented. Secondly, it was a phase, or two phases, in the history of the Roman governing class. Thirdly, it was something to be summed up in the works of two historians, Tacitus and Sallust, both of whom wrote about that society, and reflected the present in writing about the recent past. Neither went back more than a few decades before the time of his own birth.

Moreover, Tacitus as a political historian permeates *The Roman Revolution* from its opening sentence, and is already present in it also as a representative in himself of the subsequent change in the composition of the governing class: "Tacitus, a knight's son from Italian Transpadana or from the province of Gallia Narbonensis, recaptures in his writings the spirit, the prejudices and the resentment of the Roman aristocracy" (490). The presumption as to origin is that established in the masterly article by Mary L. Gordon, "The *Patria* of Tacitus," *JRS* 26 (1936): 145–51. More important, however, is Syme's clear implication that the two works are to be seen together, as dealing with two phases of a single political, social, and intellectual history.

The history of the governing class, the rise of families over generations, the elucidation of career inscriptions, the patterns of office-holding — all this has of course been Syme's central and enduring preoccupation. Of seventy-odd articles published between 1949 and 1970, a little more than half (but, it should be noted, no more than that) could be classified as prosopography. If Badian really means to say that *all* his work can be summed up as "prosopography" (*RP* I, xii), that seems to me to be simply an aberration. But on the other hand we should not allow the tedium inspired by endless volumes with lists of office-holders to obscure the fact that it has been principally the work of Syme which has shown how the contents of thousands of career inscriptions can be turned into the material of history. "History" here means both the fortunes of families over generations and the role of individuals at specific moments. It also means the study of that very important process by which the elites of many (but not all) provinces gained entry into the equestrian order and then the Senate. In *Colonial Elites* (1958), chap. 1, in "The Greeks under Roman Rule" of 1960 (*RP* II, 566–81), speaking of Popper's *The Open Society and Its Enemies*, and again in 1962, speaking of Toynbee ("Three English Historians: Gibbon, Macaulay, Toynbee"), Syme makes the point that the "open society" of the Roman Empire has failed to win recognition as a major historical phenomenon. The theme is there, its importance is beyond all question; it is worth noting that the once-planned book *The Provincial at Rome* (see *Tacitus*, p. v) had actually been written in draft and was published posthumously in 1999 by Exeter University Press, edited by Anthony Birley.

But if this theme provides one of the central areas of concern in *Tacitus* — which leads by a carefully contrived route (which has baffled some readers) to a focus on Tacitus as a Narbonensian, perhaps from Vaison — it is significant that what was produced was indeed *Tacitus* and not *The Provincial at Rome*. For it is necessary to stress the obvious fact that of Syme's nine books (other than collections) published up to 1981 only *The Roman Revolution*, *Colonial Elites*, and *Some Arval Brethren* do not bear in their titles the names of Latin authors or works: the others are *Tacitus* (1958); *Sallust* (1963); *Ammianus and the Historia Augusta* (1968); *Emperors and Biography: Studies in the Historia Augusta* (1971); *History in Ovid* (1978). I will try to show later just how fundamental is the direction of attention which these titles imply. For the moment they will be enough to suggest that *Tacitus* falls into place not only as a chapter in the history of the Roman governing clan but as a reflection of an enduring concern with the use and meaning of words, with the composition of historical works in Latin, with literary composition set against its social and political background, and with the tensions between that background and men's view of their past.

In a formal sense *Tacitus* must be considered as less successful than *The Roman Revolution*. For one thing, while "style, intensity and a leading idea" are there, the design has proved too complex for many readers to follow (see the many significant points made in Sherwin-White's appreciative review-discussion in *JRS* 1959). None the less, it is the prime example of the combined use of literature and epigraphy to evoke an entire society; and the

richness and diversity of the areas explored and of the thoughts and apho-
risms contained in it make it a treasure-house of methods and approaches,
which still remains not fully exploited. The second reason, in my view, is
that Tacitus himself had failed to find for the *Annales* any unifying theme
from the Julio-Claudian period such as that which informs the *Historiae*—or
at any rate the surviving books on the civil war; *Hist.* 1, 2 does not suggest
to me that the later books would have lived up to the first five. Since, for
all its brilliance and force in individual sections, the *Annales* is reduced by
the absence of a leading idea—and the inappropriate choice of an annalistic
structure—to being overall a shapeless mélange of disparate elements, *Tacitus* must as a consequence pursue divergent paths also, coming back at the
end to the great social change to which Tacitus had of course alluded (*Ann.* 3,
55 and, improving on Claudius, 11, 23–25), but which it took Syme to make
into history.

Syme, needless to say, shows himself aware of this limitation, which he
discusses in a crucial passage which is hardly less illuminating for his own
work than his subject's (*Tacitus*, 444–45):

> Tacitus was aware that large factors operated in history. To describe
> them was not easy. The historian can illustrate social change by means
> of a digression or a speech subsidiary to the annalistic record, but he
> cannot elevate it to the central theme in an exposition that shall em-
> brace not Romans only but the whole empire of Rome. A new form of
> literature would be requisite, not built upon narrative, and not domi-
> nated by the character and attitudes of a few individuals.

It is essential to quote also the footnote which follows at this point:

> That is to say, something more like Rostovtzeff's *Social and Economic
> History of the Roman Empire* (1926). That great work, however, would
> have benefited if the author had properly exploited Tacitus for the social
> history. Many of his generalizations are vague and vulnerable.

Syme has always been conscious of the tension between the wide views and
explanations to which all historians aspire and the need for precision—or,
to put it more simply, the primary claims of truth, and hence of those areas
where truth is possible. For this reason, but not this reason alone, he has
returned constantly to literary texts and epigraphic documents and to the
types of truth which can be extracted from them. G. W. Bowersock was thus
wholly right to quote in the *New York Review of Books* of 6 March 1980, a
passage from "People in Pliny" (*RP* II, 711):

The science (or rather the art) of prosopography has been much in fashion in the recent age, being adduced to reinforce historical studies in the most diverse of periods. Some deprecate. For various reasons. Among them (one surmises), distaste for erudition on a narrow front, to the neglect of broad aspects and the "higher things." Which may cheerfully be conceded. One uses what one has, and there is work to be done. If there be place for censure, it is better visited upon the ignorant and the incompetent.

Here again the voluntary restriction of attention is consciously present. It would be foolish as well as (obviously enough) futile to wish that a silk purse had somehow turned itself into a sow's ear, and that Syme had devoted himself to family structures in Oxyrhynchus, the Roman pottery trade, or the material culture of Pompeii. But, firstly, the very article from which this quotation is taken is itself a prime example of something "broad," namely Syme's profound sense of the geography and the regional character of various parts of the Empire—in this case the Transpadane region (*illa nostra Italia*, "that Italy of ours") from which Pliny came and within which his primary network of relations and patronage operated. We see this quality again in the context of military history in many articles on the Danubian and Balkan areas; as regards North Africa in "Notes sur la légion IIIa Augusta" of 1936 (not reprinted) and especially in "Tacfarinas, the Musulamii and Thubursicu" of 1951 (*RP* I, 218–30); and as regards Spain in "The Conquest of North-West Spain" of 1970 (II, 825–54). "The Lower Danube under Trajan" of 1959 (*Danubian Papers*, 122–34), his only venture into papyrology, is perhaps his clearest demonstration of the combined deployment of a sense of the Latin language, nomenclature, prosopography, literary history, military history, and geography, used in this case to reveal the situation (almost certainly) just before the outbreak of the second Dacian war of 105–6.

Even if we postpone for a moment considering the place of the Greek East in his work, what has been said is enough to indicate two large themes which—I would like to suggest—are directly implied by his work. The first is a history of the Roman imperial army, as deployed over vast areas and in extraordinarily diverse landscapes, from Cumbria (now illuminated by the Vindolanda tablets) to the Rhine and Danube, to the auxiliary units which Arrian visited in the shadow of the Caucasus, to the Tripolitanian *limes*, the units in Egypt which we meet in the Panopolis papyri, or the legions of Ammianus' time garrisoning the cities of Mesopotamia. The other theme, implicit in many pages of *The Roman Revolution* (esp. 82–85) is the history of the cities and communities of pre-Roman and republican Italy, their traditions and identities, cults, constitutions, governing classes, and relations with Rome. For the earlier period, much valuable material is collected in *Popoli e civiltà* 7 (1978); and the theme remains a major one in modern scholarship.

Alternatively, a test of the true worth of a body of historical work is whether its basic procedures and principles can be successfully exported to other areas. As I once suggested, in *JRS* 60 (1970): 216, there could be a Constantinian *Roman Revolution*, analysing the movement of events, the changes in the state, the evolution of ideology and propaganda, and the processes by which innumerable persons adapted themselves to circumstances and used them to their advantage. Eusebius, bishop of Nicomedia, was to prove a *desultor civilium bellorum* (an expert in changing horses in civil wars) to rival anyone in the Augustan age. So, in a way, was "the" Eusebius, as we see in T. D. Barnes, *Constantine and Eusebius* (Harvard, 1981). One could imagine also a comparable treatment of the Greek (or Greek and Persian) world of, say, 350 to 280 B.C., in which the rise of the Macedonian dynasty, the conquests of Alexander, and the establishment of the successor kingdoms would be seen in terms of the fortunes of families and individuals who lived through these profound changes. Badian's brilliant paper on Harpalus in *JHS* 1961 gives an idea of what might be done here at the level of political events. But there are indeed many areas or periods in which it would be worthwhile to replace generalisations with a collective portrait of individuals whose local backgrounds, forebears, careers through time, and descendants can be known, and whose vocabularies, inherited modes of thought, styles of expression, and reactions to their past and present might be understood.

The Greek world in the Roman Empire is one society where these possibilities exist; and one of the most masterly parts of *Tacitus*—namely, chapter 38, "Tacitus and the Greeks"—is designed both to sketch a major historical development of Tacitus' time, the arrival of men from the Greek East in the Senate; and to indicate Tacitus' reaction to it—negative and suspicious, if indeed there is any coherent reaction at all (see esp. 517–19). As noted above, Syme also surveyed the resurgence of the Greek world in "The Greeks under Roman Rule" of 1963 (*RP* II, 566–81). These two studies, by reason both of their range and perceptiveness and of their comparative isolation within his work, may serve to indicate a marked pattern in his output: not, that is, in his areas of attention, but in what he has been prepared to write and publish. To put it more precisely, both the general areas of attention of his published work and the specific topics treated within it have been determined by Latin rather than Greek evidence. In the 1930s, for instance, he gave detailed attention to the historical geography and political-administrative history of Asia Minor in the last century B.C., largely on the basis of Strabo's *Geography*, and wrote a number of studies, published posthumously by Anthony Birley, *Anatolica: Studies in Strabo* (1995). This work, of course, plays its part in chapter 19 of *The Roman Revolution*, "Antonius in the East." But for instance the very important dossier of Seleucus of Rhosos, published by P. Roussel in *Syria* 15 (1934): 33–74, gains only a passing mention (236). It is however a fundamental document for the emergence of the monarchy of Octavian; see *JRS* 63 (1973): 55–58 (= F. Millar, *Rome, the Greek World, and the East* I: *The Roman Republic and the Augustan Revolution*, 253–54). In the rest of *The Roman Revolution* the perspective remains firmly and deliberately Italian. Neither the extensive Greek material in general, nor the Cyrene edicts, published in 1927, nor for instance the very full evidence illustrating Augustus' regime provided by Josephus (esp. *Antiquities* 15–17) plays any major part.

Again, if we are to make any assessment of the quality of the *Historiae* of Tacitus, the question of his predecessors and, in particular, of the "historians who, while the Flavian house was still in power, set out in writing the record of this war" (*Hist.* 2, 101), is all-important. But the section of *Tacitus* on the *Historiae* (i.e., chaps. XII–XVIII), in any case occupying a relatively slight place in the economy of the work, pays no systematic attention to the only narrative of the Civil War of 68–69 which we know to have been written under Vespasian, namely the successive excursuses in the Greek version of Josephus' *Jewish War*, completed between 75 and 79: that is, 4, 440–41; 491–502; 545–49; 585–663 (Vespasian's proclamation and plans); 7, 75–95. Yet here is the "Flavian history" from which Tacitus set out to distance himself.

The dominance of Latin literature in determining the areas of attention to which Syme's own work would be devoted is shown, paradoxically enough, precisely by the chronological range of his prosopographical studies: from the life-time of Cicero to the Antonine age, and then, in close relevance to the *Historia Augusta*, from Severus Alexander to Carinus, and finally—again in relation to the *Historia Augusta* and Ammianus—in the period of the renaissance of Latin literature in the second half of the fourth century. We cannot make any real sense of Syme's prosopographical work if we do not see that its function is to illustrate from documents the backgrounds and careers of the men who wrote and appear in—or (like Glitius Agricola) might have appeared in—the pages of literary works in Latin. It is surely significant that he has never felt moved to discuss the careers of men who were prominent in the later second century, when our major narrative sources are in Greek.

To say that is, of course, to underline at once the fact that what I am describing is Syme's own areas of attention in print. That it has been a choice and not a limitation of sympathy is clearly demonstrated by the books written as doctoral theses under his supervision, and by other books which have followed on these. My *A Study of Cassius Dio* (1964) was consciously an attempt to write one Greek chapter of *The Provincial at Rome*. Something of the same could be said of Glen Bowersock's *Augustus and the Greeks* (1965) and *Greek Sophists in the Roman Empire* (1969), and at a further remove Christopher Jones' *Plutarch and Rome* (1971) and *The Roman World of Dio Chrysostom* (1978).

But the deployment of "Symian" techniques has of course not been confined to the Greek part of the Empire. The tension between social background, literary culture, and public role in Rome forms the central theme of Miriam Griffin's *Seneca: A Philosopher in Politics* (1976), also written originally as a thesis under Syme; for a "provincial at Rome," note also her "The Elder Seneca and Spain," *JRS* 62 (1972): 1–19. Related preoccupations run through John Matthews' *Western Aristocracies and Imperial Court, A.D. 364–425* (1976), written in Oxford and acknowledging Syme's encouragement and influence. The remarkable review-discussion by Patrick Wormald in *JRS* 66 (1976): 217–26, demonstrates how the same themes could be extended into the early Middle Ages. In a very different way, since neither a family background nor a career nor indeed a "biography" in any sense is in question, T. D. Barnes' *Tertullian* (1971), also in origin a thesis begun under Syme, is a striking attempt to see the historical, social, and cultural realities behind the massive theological and polemical works of the first Christian writer from Africa. Finally, and at one remove within the same tradition, E. J. Champlin's *Fronto and Antonine Rome* (1980) moves from the African background to the world of the Roman Senate and the court in the mid-second century.

To list these books as examples of Syme's influence or of the employment of his methods is deliberately to offer a rather different view of his role in the evolution of Roman history as a subject from that normally presumed. I would suggest that, although *The Roman Revolution* is his most complete and formally perfect work, it has not in fact had as much influence in inspiring further work as *Tacitus*. On the one hand, if we see *The Roman Revolution* as a work of "prosopographical" political history, the groundwork had already been laid in the German scholarship of the previous half-century; it is hardly necessary to stress the importance throughout Syme's work of the names not only of Münzer and Gelzer but of H. Dessau, E. Groag, and A. Stein. If, on the other, we see its greatest strength as lying in the use of literary sources to portray the development of situations and attitudes at successive moments, much subsequent writing on republican political history has relentlessly pursued the prosopographical approach, without recreating either the sweep of narrative, or the sense of situation and unresolved possibilities or the analysis of vocabulary as used at particular moments to express (or conceal) men's reactions to events. Nobody, least of all in this context, will forget that powerful and original work, of E. Badian, *Foreign Clientelae* (1958), written as a thesis under Syme, though owing much also to Sherwin-White. But I would like to suggest that the more extensive influence of Syme belongs in a later period, and is owed not to *The Roman Revolution* but to *Tacitus*.

It is perhaps paradoxical to assess Syme's work even partially in terms of influence on others. For he himself has never displayed the slightest interest in the history of scholarship, the development of questions, or the formation of schools of thought. Occasional elegant excursions such as "Roman Historians and Renaissance Politics" (1960; *RP* I, 470–76), or the second chapter of *Colonial Elites* on Spanish America, form no true exception. The "bibliography of the subject" has never interested him, except as embodying clear and concrete discoveries (for instance, Dessau on the *Historia Augusta*), or alternatively large and wordy notions deserving of deflation (so for instance his reactions to Eduard Meyer's conception of Caesar's monarchy and to the effusions of W. Weber on the second century A.D.). In this connection the reviews he wrote in the 1930s and 1940s are a delight: "The book is arid but woolly, dullness unredeemed by exactitude" (on W. Schur, *Das Zeitalter von Marius und Sulla*, in *JRS* 1944). Nor, clearly enough, has the formal analysis of the Roman constitution ever seemed to him much more than a process of inflating words found in our sources to the point where their real meanings are lost or obscured. Here the long review of H. Siber, *Das Führeramt des Augustus* in *JRS* 1946, rightly reprinted in *RP* I, 181–96, is a model: "grave misconceptions about the character of Roman public law and disturbing errors of detail and Latinity." The opposed demonstration of how these things should be done is "Imperator Caesar: A Study in Nomenclature," *Historia* 7 (1958): 172–88 (*RP* I, 361–77)—to my mind his finest single article. To see Syme, as some have, as taking the ideas out of Roman history is seriously misleading. On the contrary, much of his effort has been devoted to mapping out just what concepts the Romans did use—and when, by whom, and to what purpose they were deployed.

It is, however, obviously true that he has always been impatient even of such relatively systematic political thought as any Romans did have, for instance in Cicero's *de re publica*, and has also not been concerned with intellectual history as such (except in the form of historiography) or with religion or philosophy. Nor, in spite of detailed topographical work, and visits to sites to see inscriptions (e.g., *RP* II, 664: Casinum), has his range included architecture or art history, or still less the study of Roman artefacts from the point of view of technology, trade, or standards of living. His work thus represents a conscious restriction of attention by comparison, say, with that of Rostovtzeff: a move away, that is, both from the "higher things" of large historical theories and explanations, and from the "lower" ones of the vast and varied physical and documentary evidence for the life of the ancient world, which Rostovtzeff so avidly explored.

Indeed, it has not perhaps been sufficiently emphasized how firmly and deliberately non-theoretical and non-explanatory his work is. If we follow Syme, we will neither try to form a general theory of revolution nor ask why the Roman revolution occurred. Instead we will ask what occurred, or rather who did or said what at which successive moments. The words, intentions and actions of the actors will be intelligible to those who really understand Latin and Greek, have immersed themselves in the culture of the ancient world, and are prepared for the infinite labour involved. It is, in fact, this which makes it so hard to evolve any effective critique of his major works when one re-reads them. For he does not argue about or explain Roman history and society, nor (with very rare exceptions) expound or justify any particular means of approaching it. He simply selects, constructs, and presents.

Nothing could be further from various contemporary presuppositions: that we should be acutely conscious of the intellectual framework within which our predecessors—and, as far as possible, we ourselves—have approached the ancient world; that we should apply the methods of sociology, anthropology, structuralism, or Marxism (to list some categories which are not mutually exclusive); that we should distance ourselves from the material and attempt to quantify it, or begin by asking about the most basic conditions of a society in the past: its demography, food supplies, average expectation of life, level of material culture. Compared with the dominant styles or schools of historiography since the war, Syme's method is, in a quite literal and objective sense, old-fashioned (as is, of course, most writing on other periods, and nearly all writing on ancient history). On a theoretical level, only Paul Veyne in his highly individual, difficult, and stimulating book of 1971, *Comment on écrit l'histoire*, has argued explicitly that the grandiose pretensions of various schools of history (Marxist history above all) are delusive, and that all that history can offer is curiosity about the past—and praised Syme and others (p. 135) for accepting that history is just history. It is interesting to note, however, in the article by Lawrence Stone, "The Revival of Narrative: Reflections on a New Old History," *Past and Present* 85 (1979): 3–24, the argument that the tide is turning, and that it can now be admitted that events, politics, wars—and in general conscious attitudes and intentions—may be of crucial importance in bringing about social change; note the valuable, but far from conclusive rejoinder by E. J. Hobsbawm in *Past and Present* 86 (1980): 3.

To Syme, I suspect, all such considerations and arguments would seem wholly superfluous. The arena of human action circumscribed and presented by classical Latin literature and by the inscriptions which go with it is accessible to us, and is sufficiently interesting, sufficiently important, and sufficiently intelligible in itself: "One uses what one has, and there is work to be done." The domain is that of conscious human activity and of literary composition within a society of high culture. If in writing about it one can add something to the literature of one's own time, that is the final justification. Hence the last sentence of Tacitus, and the quotation from *Annals* 4, 61 which serves as a footnote to it: "Men and dynasties pass, but style abides"— *meditatio et labor in posterum valescit.*

CHAPTER NINETEEN

A New Approach to the Roman Jurists[*]

Up till a few years ago readers in the (then) Ashmolean Library in Oxford who took down the library's copy of the *Digest* would find themselves experiencing a curious journey in time. For from between the pages there would drop out leaves from German calendars of the early 1920s. If these have now disappeared, the pages themselves still contain scores of minute and precise textual notes in pencil, made by Eduard Fraenkel, whose books came to the library in 1970 after his death. The notes too date to the 1920s, and bore fruit in Fraenkel's article "Zum Texte römischer Juristen," *Hermes* 60 (1925): 415, reprinted in *Kleine Beiträge* II, 417.

Perhaps that was not in fact the last moment at which any established classical scholar took an interest in the textual transmission of the *Digest*, or in the jurists whose works are excerpted there. But no one will deny that such an interest is rare to the point of eccentricity. Yet the majority of these works are the products of men born in the second century, at the height of the outward prosperity and stability of the Empire, when the Latin language and Roman literature were the common possession of more people than ever before, and

---

[*]First published in *JRS* 76 (1986): 272–80 as a review of T. Honoré, *Emperors and Lawyers* (1981) and *Ulpian* (1982). Since so much is said above about the relative inaccessibility of the classical juristic writings as excerpted in Justinian's *Digest*, and the relatively little attention which they have received from students of Latin prose or of Roman history, it is all the more relevant to draw attention here to the publication of *The Digest of Justinian*, Latin text edited by Theodor Mommsen with the aid of Paul Kueger; English translation edited by Alan Watson, I–IV (Philadelphia: University of Pennsylvania Press, 1985). It should be noted also that in the interval Honoré has produced very important, and heavily revised, editions of both works: *Emperors and Lawyers*[2], with a *Palingenesia of Third-Century Imperial Rescripts, 193–305 A.D.* (1994); and *Ulpian: Pioneer of Human Rights* (2002). The review as re-printed here remains that of the first edition of each.

the citizenship was soon to be extended to all. Even Greeks, grudgingly or otherwise, had to acknowledge the significance of all this. "Nowadays, however, the topic of law is of no use [in an *encomium* of a city], since we conduct public affairs by the common laws of the Romans" (*Menander Rhetor*, trans. Russell and Wilson, p. 67). Others took a more positive, if still somewhat ambivalent attitude: "those admirable laws of ours, by which the affairs of all men under Roman rule are governed, and which were neither composed nor can be mastered without toil, being themselves wise, precise, varied, admirable, and in a word very Hellenic." So writes Gregorius, later to be bishop of Neocaesarea in Pontus, on his once projected course of study in Roman law, which he would have pursued at Berytus in about A.D. 230 (*Address to Origen* 7, ed. H. Crouzel, *SC* 148). (For a sketch of the issues relating to the reception of Roman law in the Greek world, see F. Millar, "Culture grecque et culture latine dans le Haut-Empire: la loi et la foi," in *Les martyrs de Lyon (177), Lyon 20–23 Septembre 1977, Coll. Int. du CNRS 575* [1978], 187.)

Not everyone from a Greek background was so hampered by the difficulty of learning Latin, which Gregorius goes on to admit. About 40 per cent of the text of the *Digest*, some 300,000 words, is the work of Domitius Ulpianus from Tyre, a Hellenized Phoenician city which was to become a Roman colony only in the course of his life-time (see F. Millar, "The Phoenician Cities: A Case-Study of Hellenisation," *PCPS* 209 [1983]: 55–71 = *Rome, the Greek World and the East* III: *The Greek World, the Jews and the East*, chap. 2). Whether Ulpian was the descendant of Italian immigrants, or perhaps of a family which had gained the citizenship from Domitius Corbulo, he unmistakably identified himself with the long history of his *patria* (*Dig.* 50, 15, 1 *pr.*).

But he also saw his own avocation as a legal writer not only, like all the other jurists, as the product of a chain of tradition stretching back to the later Republic, but also as a pre-eminent form of *philosophia* (*Dig.* 1, 1, 1, 1):

> The student of *ius* ought first to be aware from where the term *ius* derives. It is indeed called this after *iustitia* [justice]; for, as Celsus elegantly defines it, *ius* is the art of the *bonum* [the good] and the *aequum* [the just]. So whoever will call us *sacerdotes* [priests] will be right to do so. For we worship *iustitia* and profess the knowledge of the *bonum* and the *aequum*, distinguishing the just from the unjust and separating the lawful from the unlawful, seeking to make men good not only by fear of penalties but also by the stimulus of rewards, and thus pursuing, if I am not mistaken, a true *philosophia* rather than a feigned one.

Ulpian thus claims for jurisprudence a pre-eminent place in the intellectual universe of his time; and like his direct contemporary, Cassius Dio (71, 35, 1–2; 77, 19, 1), he found it difficult to resist implications as to the spuriousness of what currently passed as philosophy.

Yet legal writers, so central both to the character of Roman culture and (obviously enough) to the "legacy of Rome," have attracted extraordinarily little attention from classicists, from students of Roman historiography, or even from ancient historians, for whom this gigantic body of material represents, or ought to represent, an almost inexhaustible treasure-house of economic and social history, and of ideologies, conceptions, and attitudes. What proportion of the total of surviving classical Latin prose is represented by the million-odd words of the *Digest*, the earlier rescripts of the *Codex Justinianus*, the other remains of pre-Justinianic legal writing, and by the key text of them all, Gaius' *Institutes*?

Whatever criticisms, either of detail or of overall method, may be levelled at Honoré's work, the fact remains that his studies of the original composition, and the sixth-century excerpting and compilation, of the vast body of Roman legal writing have done for classicists and ancient historians what they have not felt moved to do for themselves. The limited perspective of Latin studies has meant that, for instance, the *Oxford Latin Dictionary* was designed to cover only the period up to about A.D. 200, thus ending just before the writings of Papinian, Ulpian, and Paul. *The Cambridge History of Classical Literature* II: *Latin Literature* (see the review article by R. G. M. Nisbet in *JRS* 73 [1983]: 175) duly exhibits a further profound limitation: not only a stopping point somewhere in the second century, but an overwhelming emphasis on poetry rather than prose (sixty-nine pages for Virgil, nine for Livy). As regards its treatment of the second century, Aulus Gellius, who embodies so much of the scholarly and antiquarian spirit of the age, earns two whole pages. But his much superior contemporary, Pomponius, whose *Enchiridion*, or *Handbook* (Lenel, *Palingenesia Iuris Civilis* II, cols. 44–52), represents the most systematic surviving historical survey both of Roman legal and constitutional institutions and of legal writers, merits not a word (see instead the long essay by Dieter Nörr, "Pomponius oder 'Zum Geschichtsverständnis der römischen Juristen,'" *ANRW* II.15 [1976], 497). But then, nor does their other contemporary, Gaius, the subject of Honoré's adventurous book of 1962; Gaius' *Institutes* is, of course, the only example of Roman legal writing which survives almost complete and does not have to be reconstituted from the excerpts selected, dispersed, abbreviated, perhaps interpolated, and arranged under headings in Justinian's *Digest*—a process most incisively, if again adventurously, studied by Honoré in *Tribonian* (1978), reviewed by Averil Cameron in *JRS* 69 (1979): 199.

It seems extraordinary that the *Digest* itself, whose text is based essentially on a manuscript written very close in time to the original compilation of the work, the Florentine codex of the late sixth or seventh century, should not have earned a place in the indispensable *Texts and Transmission: A Survey of the Latin Classics*, edited by L. D. Reynolds (1983). The only juristic writer who does is Gaius. But it is very significant that this entry, a mere eleven lines, should fall well below the high standard of the rest. Firstly, it is of course correctly reported that the fifth-century palimpsest, the *Codex Veronensis*, which is the main witness to the text, is supplemented by a papyrus, *P. Oxy.* XVII 2103, of the second–third century, and a parchment, *PSI* XI 1182, of the fifth–sixth. But the former of these at least ought to have excited rather more comment. It is very rare indeed for us to have even a fragment of a Latin text which was written within a century or so of the original composition. More important still, the papyrus text (of parts of *Inst.* 4, 57 and 68–72) is fully compatible with the standard text, allowing for the scribal variations common to all types of text; so is the parchment (containing 3, 153–54, with, however, a substantial extra passage on *ercto non cito* [joint, undivided ownership], omitted in the codex from Verona; 3, 167–74; 4, 16–18). The conclusion has to be that the text as we have it, though it has suffered excision, is in essentials the text which was in circulation within a century of writing, which is as close as we are likely to get with any ancient author. For the significance of these papyri, see G. Diósdi, "The Importance of *P. Oxy.* XVII 2103 and *PSI* XI 1182 for the History of Classical Roman Legal Literature," *Proc. XII. Int. Cong. Pap.* (1970): 113.

Secondly (to return to the entry in *Texts and Transmission*), there is no reference at all to the fact that excerpts of Gaius' *Institutes* are also to be found in the *Digest* (parallel passages listed in Lenel, *Palingenesia* I, col. 242). There are certainly variations; but, for instance, the variations between *Inst.* 3, 135–37 and the excerpt of it in *Dig.* 44, 7, 2 are minimal, primarily singulars for plurals, or the tense of a verb. The text, as transmitted through wholly different channels, is substantially the same. Or seems to be; but that of course would raise the question of the textual transmission of the *Digest* itself. If the books of the *Digest* could only have seemed as important to Latinists as Augustan poetry, there would be half a dozen rival editions of each. As it is, we rely on Mommsen's editio minor in the *Corpus Iuris Civilis* (1895), occasionally reverting to his two-volume editio maior of 1870. To the best of my knowledge no text-critical edition of an individual book, or group of books, of the *Digest* has been published since. The situation is different with Gaius' *Insti-*

tutes, transmitted separately. This work has been repeatedly studied; see, for instance, H. L. W. Nelson, *Überlieferung, Aufbau und Stil von Gai Institutiones* (1981). But as for the writers whose works are known through the *Digest*, since Lenel's great *Palingenesia Iuris Civilis* of 1887, which, in reassembling the surviving elements of the works of each of the jurists, itself essentially followed Mommsen's printed text, there have been almost no critical editions of their works taken separately, and treated in the light of characteristic style, choice of words, sources of material, or patterns of thought, as would be the case with almost any author whose works are fortunate enough to be labelled as "literature." The most notable (partial) exception relates to two works of the Tetrarchic period, very probably by the same author; see D. Liebs, *Hermogenians Iuris Epitomae: zum Stand der römischen Iurisprudenz im Zeitalter Diokletians* (1964), and A. Cenderelli, *Ricerche sul "Codex Hermogemanus"* (1965). Otherwise there is the Teubner edition of the texts of the jurists of the early Empire by P. Bremer, *Iurisprudentiae Antehadrianae quae supersunt* II, 1–2 (1898, 1901), or the standard collections of the juristic works preserved entirely, or mainly, outside the *Digest*: Kuschke-Seckel-Keubler, *Iurisprudentia Anteiustiniana* (1908–27), and the indispensable second volume of *Fontes Iuris Romani Antejustiniani*[2] (1940), by S. Riccobono et al. All these major works therefore leave untouched the manuscript tradition, the style, and the composition of the central works of Roman legal science, written in the Severan period and preserved, in so far as they are preserved, in the *Digest*. Detailed studies of any of their individual works remain rare, for instance C. Sanfilippo, *Pauli Decretorum libri tres* (1938), or B. Santalucia, *I "libri opinionum" di Ulpiano* I–II (1971)—but Honoré claims, against Santalucia, that linguistic analysis shows that this work is not by Ulpian.

Honoré has admittedly himself not gone back to the manuscripts and has based his work on the printed text. But, taking that text as his subject matter, he has performed the essential service of treating the jurists as writers of Latin. The methods used have proved acutely controversial, as we shall see, and the results are often highly speculative. But they are presented as such, even if in the excitement of engagement with his massive material, he sometimes claims more certainty than he should. If nothing else, his work must remind us that the authors concerned were not really very good subjects for Justinian's hopelessly self-contradictory scheme for a compilation from which all contradictions would have been removed. For, however close to government many of them stood, the classical jurists had written as academics expressing their own opinions and interpretations within different traditions. Far from being the monolith which Justinian wanted, the *Digest* is in fact a repertoire of varied and mutually contradictory opinions and approaches. Few elements in the history of culture are more remarkable than the fact that this sixth-century repertoire of second–third century legal writing was subsequently made to serve as the basis of medieval and modern civil law.

Honoré's goal has been to rescue at least some of the writers whose works were excerpted in the *Digest* from the off-putting columns of the *Corpus Juris Civilis* and to restore them to life as individuals writing between the later second and the end of the third century. In doing so he has taken one step in their restoration to their real context, in the intellectual culture of the High Empire, the crisis of the Empire, and the Tetrarchy. Not the least of his services is to stress the continuity of jurisprudence which runs through these periods. A further objective has been to bring the imperial rescripts preserved (primarily) in the *Codex Justinianus*, within the same framework. He proposes, that is, to see these rescripts as the compositions of individual jurists, rather than of the emperors who nominally issued them: "to treat the composition of 'imperial' rescripts as a branch of legal practice" (*Emperors and Lawyers*, viii).

The entire project, as also in his *Tribonian*, depends on detailed analyses of style, an area in which the reviewer has no competence. Of the two works here discussed it is *Ulpian* which has raised a controversy of exceptional sharpness among Romanists. It may be sufficient now to indicate what it attempts to do, and what criticisms have been brought against it. It will then be possible to go back to the questions raised by the earlier book. Can it in fact be shown that emperors did not compose the rescripts which they nominally issued? If so, can we really identify those who did compose them? If we can, how does this conclusion bear on the question of the composition of other forms of imperial constitution (*decreta*—judgements in court; *epistulae*—letters, in Latin or Greek; *edicta*—edicts; *orationes*—speeches in the Senate)? If it was the *a libellis* (the grammatically odd term which describes the imperial official in charge of the *libelli*), or later the *magister libellorum*, who composed the answers to private petitions (*libelli*), who composed these other types of document, which might deal with a very similar range of legal issues?

In *Ulpian* Honoré sets out to do the following things. First, to review the known career of Ulpian, from his origins (if not necessarily his actual birth) in Tyre in the 160s to his violent death as praetorian prefect in 223. If too much time is spent struggling to make something of the notoriously treacherous references to Ulpian in the *Historia Augusta*, no great harm is done. Ulpian may (see below) have been *a libellis* in 202–9; he himself on occasion reports having been present (*me adsistente*) at the *consilium* (council) of a praetor in Rome (*Dig.* 4, 2, 9, 3). Nothing else is known for certain until

Severus Alexander in a rescript (*CJ* 8, 37, 4) records him as *Praefectus annonae, iuris consultus, amicus meus* (Prefect of the food supply in Rome, the jurist, my friend), on 31 March 222, some two weeks after his own elevation to the throne. Then Ulpian was briefly praetorian prefect before his death in the next year.

Secondly, Honoré argues, convincingly, that the form of the references to contemporary emperors (Septimius Severus and Caracalla) in Ulpian's work shows that nearly all of his enormous output (217 or 218 *libri* [volumes] in all on Honoré's calculation) belongs in the five-year period 213–17. In my view this has to be accepted: the emperor at the moment of writing is nearly always Caracalla ("Antoninus"), who is often also cited, in a variety of ways, along with his deceased father, Severus (e.g., "the divine Severus and our Emperor" —*divus Severus et imperator noster*; later, Honoré suggests, Caracalla moves to the form: "the Emperor Antoninus together with the divine Severus"—*Imperator Antoninus cum divo Severo*). No later emperor from Ulpian's life-time (Macrinus, Elagabal, or Severus Alexander) is mentioned by name, though Honoré suggests that Ulpian's programme of work in fact continued under the uncertainly legitimate rule of Macrinus in 217.

The notion of so enormous and concentrated a production leads Honoré into a series of wildly ingenious hypotheses about Ulpian's production programme, broken down into units within pre-planned stretches of time. This seems to me not so much improbable or unprovable as not worth the effort. It is enough to know that the bulk of his work bears the marks of being contemporaneous, that it came after the death of Papinian (whom Ulpian cites, alone of all his legal contemporaries, no fewer than 116 times) and that, whenever we date the *Constitutio Antoniniana* (Antoninus's, i.e., Caracalla's, constitution)—and possibly 212 is right after all—Ulpian's careful and massive exposition of Roman law was brought to fruition in the few years which followed it. Alone of the Severan jurists, in the surviving texts Ulpian explicitly refers to Caracalla's universal grant of citizenship (*Dig.* 1, 5, 17): "Those living in the Roman Empire became Roman citizens under the constitution of the emperor Antoninus." The quotation comes from Ulpian's *ad edictum* 22, which on Honoré's scheme was written in 213. That perhaps does not matter so much as the fact that we thus know that Ulpian was writing in the consciousness of this historic step. It is no more than speculation that he wrote for the millions of new Roman citizens (*cives Romani*). But, as we shall see, the inhabitants of at least one provincial city certainly knew, and used, at least one of his works.

Thirdly, Honoré goes on to define the personal characteristics of Ulpian's style, or such features of it as are, in statistical terms, distinctive as against the styles of other legal writers. Since the method is admitted to have a strong subjective element, it may be sufficient here to give an example (p. 54): *proinde* (hence) as a conjunction occurs 212 times in the works of Ulpian, and at the most 4 times in other jurists. The marks of style thus identified are then used (chap. 4) to identify five works attributed to Ulpian which should be regarded as not by him: *Regularum libri* VII; *Regularum liber* I; *Opinionum libri* VI; *Pandectarum liber* I (or X); *Responsorum libri* II.

There then follows a concluding section on Ulpian as a writer, with particular attention to his use of earlier jurists; a sub-section on his imperial sources, that is, his citations of imperial constitutions, neatly demonstrates (p. 236) that such citations are absent from the earlier jurists (e.g., Labeo and Iavolenus) and rise steadily until we reach Ulpian and his contemporaries. It is, of course, what we would expect; but to my knowledge it has not been shown in such clear terms before (though G. Gualandi, *Legislazione imperiale e giurisprudenza* I–II [1963], remains indispensable). In this respect, as in others, Ulpian is broadly in tune with the attitudes of his time. That, of course, will only make it more difficult to assess how far and in what way it matters who actually wrote the private rescripts which were issued as from the emperor. The same issue arises in Honoré's final sub-section on Ulpian as a lawyer: not outstandingly original, admittedly, but with a distinctive sense of proportion and moderation, and also an emphasis on what was *utile* (useful), in stating how legal problems should be resolved. Here particularly, historians need to realize that we are listening to a personal voice and to private opinions. For instance Ulpian writes, in his *de officio proconsulis* (*On the duties of a proconsul*, i.e., a governor of a "public province"), in a way which is in a sense self-contradictory: "Nor is there anything in a province which is not dealt with by him [the proconsul]; but if there is a *fiscalis pecuniaria causa* (a financial case involving the emperor's treasury) which concerns the *procurator principis* (the financial official of the emperor), he would do better not to concern himself with it" (*Dig.* 1, 16, 9 *pr.*). It is not a statement of the *law*, any more than is Ulpian's advice in the same work, of which more later, to observe normal precedence in the matter of the proconsul's entry to his province (1, 16, 4).

In his use of the concept of *utilitas* (utility) Ulpian again, as Honoré shows (p. 247), shares the attitudes of his contemporaries, Papinian and Paul. But he also shares the attitudes of the emperors of his time (or whoever wrote their *epistulae* [letters], as opposed to their replies to *libelli* [petitions]). This clearly appears (p. 244) in Ulpian's own quotation of the letter of Severus and Caracalla on acceptance of gifts (*Dig.* 1, 16, 6, 3): "But the proconsul will be under no obligation to abstain totally from *xenia* [gifts], but should impose a limit, so that he neither captiously refrains altogether nor greedily exceeds a due proportion of gifts. This is a matter on which the deified Severus and Imperator Antoninus laid down the norm most elegantly in a letter, of which the actual words are: 'As regards gifts, hear what we think. There is an old [Greek] proverb "not everything, nor all the time, neither from everyone." For it is truly *inhumanum* to take [gifts] from no one, but to do so without discrimination is most degrading and to take them all is most avaricious.' "

If one takes the broad lines of Honoré's approach, and disregards his enthusiastic pursuit of certainties which must be unreachable (and do not greatly matter), there is very much to be learned, above all in the extension of the range of Latin authors who can be studied and understood as individuals writing in a particular cultural setting. There is also an enormous further gain, a product of these two books taken together. The grandiose and impossible design of Justinian, that the *Digest* should be both a repertoire of the writings of the classical jurists and be edited so as to remove contradictions, led, reasonably enough, to generations of search for the editorial work supposedly done, in short to the wholesale "discovery" of interpolations, duly listed in the *Index Interpolationum*. There are certainly additions, abbreviations, and excisions, not to speak of variants which the texts of Gaius display (see above) quite independently of the work of Justinian's commissioners. But unless *all* of Honoré's statistics as to individual features in the style of the different jurists are to be rejected, the historian can now accept that what we read in the *Digest* does in essence reproduce the actual words of the jurists who wrote in the High Empire, battered but not re-written in the sixth century.

Once again the papyri will offer confirmation that this is indeed so. In 1927, in vol. XVII of *Oxyrhynchus Papyri*, A. S. Hunt published the Greek text of a letter of Severus Alexander to the *koinon* (league of cities) of Bithynia (2104). It was fortunate that for once something relevant escaped him, and that he did not realize that the same letter appears in Greek in *Dig.* 49, 1, 25. He therefore read, independently from the *Digest* text, what is almost exactly the same text, but including the imperial titulature (edited out either by Paulus or the compilers of the *Digest*), with gaps which can be precisely filled from the *Digest* text, and with an extra sentence which the *Digest* omits. In 1975, in *Oxyrhynchus Papyri* XLIII, J. Rea published a second contemporary papyrus copy (3106), with some more of the additional sentence, and a version of the penultimate sentence of the *Digest* which is identical except that it offers *apagoreuō* (I forbid) — that is, the singular, as in the rest of the letter — for the plural *apagoreuomen* (we forbid). Paulus therefore quoted the text verbatim, and Justinian's compilers made no attempt to alter it (e.g., as regards the titles of the officials mentioned in the letter) to fit the conditions of the sixth century. But either Paulus or they abbreviated the imperial title, substituted a plural for a singular, and left out some material at the end. With those limitations, the text appears in the *Corpus Iuris Civilis* exactly in the form in which it circulated in the Roman provinces in the first half of the third century.

It is therefore reasonable to approach the juristic writings excerpted in the *Digest* with a view to style and vocabulary. It would be even more reasonable if the individual authors, or the *Digest* as a whole, had received the textual attention almost guaranteed to anyone who had the sense to write in verse. In default of that, Honoré has shown the way.

Among Roman lawyers the novelty of Honoré's approach has been generally recognized, and his methods and, up to a point, his conclusions broadly accepted by many. See, for instance, Alan Rodger, "Behind the Scenes in Roman Law," *Oxford Journal of Legal Studies* 3 (1983): 382, reviewing *Tribonian, Emperors and Lawyers*, and *Ulpian* as a group. He does note, however, that Honoré's method may not take full account of quotation or paraphrase of jurist A by B, or of the different purposes for which Justinian's compilers may have selected the (relatively limited) extracts of writers other than Ulpian. Honoré's *Ulpian* has also been favourably reviewed by Detlef Liebs, in *Gnomon* 56 (1984): 441, and by P. Birks in *Irish Jurist* 18 (1983, app. 1985): 151–81, the fullest available exposition, and defence, by a third party, of Honoré's methods and results.

None the less, it would be wrong to conceal the fact that enthusiasm and sense of conviction have led him into very detailed arguments and positive assertions which have aroused more than vigorous criticism in juristic circles. Note, for instance, Alan Watson in *TLS*, 16 February 1983, p. 164, "poking fun," as he was later to put it, at the excessive claims, subjectiveness, and biographical/psychological elements in *Ulpian*. The expression quoted comes from a further piece, with a reply by Honoré, in *Rechtshistorisches Journal* 3 (1984): 286–305. The most substantial point here, as in an earlier review by Watson, really concerns the holders of the office *a libellis* under Caracalla (below). The most important critique of Honoré's work known to me, however, is the review of *Ulpian* in *Michigan Law Review* 82 (1984): 856, by B. W. Frier. Its essential point is that the nature of Honoré's stylometric work is itself misconceived: study of style should embrace its overall features (length and structure of sentences, word order, and so forth); to concentrate on individual usages which are *distinctive*, as against other comparable authors (*non*-legal authors, Frier notes, are not adduced for comparison), is to take a very partial and potentially subjective view; it may well relate directly to only a very small percentage of an author's text. Consequently, these features are also poor measures of authenticity or otherwise. Frier's conclusion is that the boldness and subjectivity of his methods and intuitions mean "that much of Honoré's effort was not worthwhile. The book has intermittent flashes of genuine lucidity, even brilliance, but it must always be treated with caution. Would that the matter were otherwise." Essentially similar points are made by W. M. Gordon in *CR* 98 (1984): 232: "[I]t will not be the definitive work on Ulpian, if such a work be possible. If anything it raises more questions than it solves." As regards the methods of stylistic analysis which Honoré chose to employ, it seems clear that we have to conclude that they were not the best ones available.

Chapter 8 of *Ulpian*, "Secretary *a libellis*," takes up the central theme of *Emperors and Lawyers* as a whole, namely the reclaiming for the jurists of the texts of "imperial" private rescripts, issued in reply to *libelli* (petitions). The first thing that might strike one is the placing of this chapter in the book. Ulpian's distinctive style is defined, as we saw, in terms of a vast corpus of writing undertaken in 213–17. Honoré rejects (pp. 139–41) the theory that all or part of the eighty-one-book *ad edictum* was first written under Septimius Severus, that is, before 211, and then revised under Caracalla. On Honoré's view (p. 26) Ulpian had written nothing before 213 except five books of the *ad edictum*, perhaps in early 211, and previous to that a one-book work *de excusationibus* (*On exemptions*) (Lenel, *Palingenesia* II, cols. 899–903). But in fact there are problems here, which deserve more attention than they receive from Honoré. The text of this work *de excusationibus* is in fact entirely made up of a sequence (nos. 123–70) of items in the *Fragmenta Vaticana*, concerned with this topic and written under *imperatores nostri* (our emperors), presumably Severus and Caracalla (198–211). None of them identifies either the author or the title of the work from which they came. Modestinus (*Dig.* 27, 1, 13, 2), does quote Scaevola, Paulus, and Ulpian for a provision found in *FV* 156; and, to complete our confusion, some of the items in *FV* 123–70 reappear verbatim later in *FV* attributed explicitly to Ulpian's *de officio praetoris tutelaris* (*On the duties of the praetor in charge of matters concerning guardianship*) (e.g., *FV* 185 = 240). But this same extract is attributed in *Dig.* 27, I, 7 to the *liber singularis excusationum*.

This long-debated question, which is not within the competence of the reviewer, is mentioned here only to underline a crucial problem. What do we know of Ulpian's standing as a jurist, of any written works of his, or of his literary style, in the period before, or even during, that in which he is claimed to have acted as *a libellis*, namely 202–9? Honoré's identification of Ulpian as the *a libellis* of those years rests on finding stylistic characteristics of Ulpian's works written in 213–17 in the "imperial" rescripts of 202–9. Though there is evidence that Ulpian gave *responsa* (official replies to petitions), and may also have published two books of *responsa*, we know nothing of his training, activity, or standing as a lawyer before 202. We saw earlier how he quotes with approval, and absorbs the attitudes of, a letter of Severus and Caracalla on moderation in accepting gifts. If we are to go in for intellectual biography, might we not ask whether, if Ulpian was *a libellis* in 202–9, it was not there that he learned his characteristic style and approach, which came to be expressed in the next decade in his own independent juristic output?

But do we in fact have secure evidence to show that he was *a libellis* then, or that any other individual, whether a known juristic writer or not, was *a libellis*, or *magister libellorum*, at any other specific period? If we have such evidence, what are the implications of this conclusion for how we read the surviving corpus of Roman law? As regards the legislative activity "of" emperors (i.e., in this case, the innumerable legal rulings issued by them, or in their name, in response to private *libelli*), how much does it matter who composed the actual sentences which made up the private rescripts?

Honoré's basic technique as regards the question of authorship is, as throughout, the identification of distinctive marks of style. In pursuing this objective, he has, however, taken a more basic and fundamental step, whose importance transcends all the individual criticisms concerned with method, overbold hypotheses, or unsound conclusions. It should be stressed first just how extensive and how significant the material concerned is. Apart from later material, continuing to the reign of Justinian himself, the *Codex Justinianus* incorporates, arranged under different headings, about 1,500 imperial constitutions of the period 193 to 305 which show every sign of being addressed to private persons, and nearly 1,000 more which are probably so addressed. In each chapter they are arranged in chronological order, with the name(s) of the emperor or emperors, and nearly always with the consular date, the month and the day. Beyond that, others are preserved in the *Digest* and in pre-Justinianic legal collections and on inscriptions and papyri. A notable feature of this vast material is that nearly half belongs in the period of the Tetrarchy, a concentration which derives in the first instance from the compilation of the *Codex Gregorianus* of 292 and the *Codex Hermogenianus* of 295. Honoré does not draw attention to a very distinctive aspect of the Tetrarchic private rescripts, namely that nearly a third of them are addressed to women. For this material, which surely deserves a place in Women's Studies, see L. Huchthausen, "Herkunft und ökonomische Stellung weiblicher Adressaten von Reskripten des *Codex Iustinianus* (2. und 3. Jh. u. Z.)," *Klio* 56 (1974): 199; "Zu Kaiserlichen Reskripten an weibliche Adressaten aus der Zeit Diokletians (284–305 u. Z.)," *Klio* 58 (1976): 55; the recent book by Jane F. Gardner, *Women in Roman Law and Society* (1986), now provides just the background which is needed to set these rescripts in context. Another notable group of addressees is made up of private soldiers: for these, as regards the period up to Severus Alexander, see J. B. Campbell, *The Emperor and the Roman Army* (1984), chap. 6.

The historical and legal importance of this material is beyond all question. The essential step taken by Honoré has been to reassemble the individual texts in chronological order, and to read them *as* texts, as sets of words and sentences which must in each case have been composed by some individual. They then take their place as part of the legal literature of their time, and potentially (as above) as expressions of the wider Latin culture of the Empire. Like the writings of the jurists, they await the attention of textual critics and (except for Honoré) of students of Latin.

Honoré's conclusions, set out in advance in *JRS* 69 (1979): 51, are that reading in chronological sequence does show significant breaks in style which do not coincide with changes of emperor. The texts, as texts, were therefore composed by persons other than the emperors. Secondly, some though not all of the writers can be identified with known legal writers, or with the writers of known legal works whose authorship is uncertain. The most important suggested identifications are, firstly, Papinian, *a libellis* in 194–202; Ulpian (as above), 202–9; and Hermogenianus (Hermogenes?), 293–95, who duly incorporated "his" rescripts in his *Codex Hermogenianus*, and was also the author of the *Iuris Epitomae*.

Is all this true, and how much does it matter? Firstly, it seems to me beyond dispute that Honoré has shown that not merely the vocabulary but the way of setting out replies and justifying the conclusion to the petitioner changes in significant ways in successive periods. The important result is, once again, that these replies, as preserved in the *Codex Justinianus* and elsewhere, though truncated and abbreviated, do, within the reasonable limits which manuscript transmission itself imposes, represent the words issued by, or in the name of, the emperors. Justinian's compilers, here too, selected what they wanted from texts; but they did not re-write them. The implications with regard to texts far outweigh any possible conclusions as to the role of individuals.

Should we presume that the role of the *a libellis* was of crucial importance in the composition of these texts? The most significant evidence is *Dig.* 20, 5, 12 *pr.*, a passage of Tryphoninus in the eighth book of his *Disputationes*: "[T]he emperor replied, when Papinian was handling the petitions, that a creditor can buy the surety from a debtor." We thus know at least that Papinian did handle the *libelli* for Severus. There is no reliable explicit evidence of this for any other jurist, until we come to Aurelius Arcadius Charisius, whom *Dig.* 1, 11, 1 identifies as *magister libellorum*, before a quotation (of an antiquarian-historical kind) from his *Liber singularis de officio praefecti Praetorio* (*A single book on the duties of the praetorian prefect*). Honoré in his final table of identifications, though not earlier, suggests affinities between Charisius' works (Lenel, *Palingenesia* I, cols. 57–60) and the secretaries no. 17/18 or 19 (280s and early 290s). But D. Liebs in his review article, "Juristen als Sekretäre des römischen Kaiser," *ZSS* 100 (1983): 485, broadly accepting Honoré's results, in this instance goes further, and proposes (pp. 503–4) that Arcadius Charisius is indeed no. 19, secretary in 290–91.

Tryphoninus' allusion certainly suggests that Papinian's handling of the *libelli* was relevant to the content of Severus' reply. But many basic problems remain. Was there in fact regularly only one holder of the office, that is to say, "the" a *libellis* or *magister libellorum*? Another holder of the office, Aelius Coeranus, is attested between 200 and 205 (the inscription is now *I. K Ephesos* VI [1980], no. 2026) in a letter of Caracalla. Perhaps (Honoré, p. 145) he was specifically secretary to the junior Augustus. And as such wrote no rescripts at all? And what of the list of *apokrimata* (rescripts) put up when Severus was in Alexandria in March 200 (Greek texts in *SB* VI 9526)? Was Papinian there, and did he compose *all* private rescripts, including these, or was the job shared out, perhaps according to subject matter or importance? Not all *libelli* concerned matters of Roman law. And what of times when two *Augusti* were functioning in different places? Honoré appears to assume that even in the Tetrarchy there was only one *magister libellorum*, to whose pen all the rescripts of any one period can be attributed. For rather obvious reasons, one *magister libellorum* could only be with one emperor (always Diocletian?) at one place. As T. D. Barnes's extremely useful chronologies of imperial movements under the Tetrarchs show (*The New Empire of Diocletian and Constantine* [1982], 47–64), most private rescripts do emanate from wherever Diocletian was. But some seem to reflect the movements of Maximian. The question remains open. But see now S. Corcoran, *The Empire of the Tetrarchs: Imperial Pronouncements and Government, AD 284–324*[2] (2000), 75–94.

In this period, too, there are problems about how to identify, in personal terms, the origins of the thoughts and attitudes which went into "imperial" pronouncements. Take, for instance, Honoré's secretary no. 17/18 (A.D. 284–87 and 289–90), who, Honoré suggests (p. 115), may have been the compiler of the *Codex Gregorianus*: "A Roman patriot, he firmly rejects institutions foreign to Roman law, such as polygamy, the adoption of brothers, and the public disherison of sons [*apoceryxis*]" (p. 110). But might not the Roman patriot really have been Diocletian himself? Real problems arise when Honoré comes back later to the same secretary (p. 115): "His outlook, with its compound of simplicity, religious feeling, and patriotism, is perhaps best seen in an edict of 295 on incest, composed of course after he had left the office *a libellis*." Never mind that the official was now called *magister libellorum*; the problem is that if a similar "voice" can be heard in *different* forms of imperial pronouncement, the formal connection between office and composition lapses. If the voice is the *criterion* of identity—that is, if no. 17/18 must have been called out of retirement to write this edict (*Coll.* VI, 4, 1), the argument becomes dangerously circular. It is true (and very odd) that we at no time hear of any officials concerned with imperial edicts (and *someone* must have composed, for instance, the preamble of the Prices Edict of 301). But there was certainly a *magister epistolarum*. It would be stretching ingenuity rather far to suggest (not that Honoré does) that no. 17/18 came out of retirement again in 301 to write the letter to the proconsul of Africa about the Manichees who had appeared there (for the date, Barnes, *New Empire*, 55), a missive which embodies a very similar mixture of simplicity, patriotism, conservatism, and attachment to Roman religion (*Coll.* XV, 3, I). At all events, it was not the *magister libellorum* who two years later initiated the Great Persecution.

In spite of these doubts, I am still convinced that Honoré's reading of this mass of rescripts in chronological order does show that different voices and styles made themselves felt at different periods, and have survived not merely the normal processes of transmission but the efforts of Justinian's compilers. I am not as convinced as he is that we understand the process by which these texts were generated at court. The notion of a "draft" is essential to his whole conception: that is to say, an answer was prepared by whoever handled the petitions (*agebat libellos*) and was subsequently assented to by the emperor, perhaps in the form of an actual subscription (*subscriptio*) or authentication. But it is equally possible (for instance) that the emperor himself dictated either the bare substance of a reply (i.e., whether it should be negative or positive) or even a "draft," which was then written up. We do not know, and it is dangerous to import a bureaucratic model from modern procedures.

The notion of "drafts" already prepared for imperial attention, or notional attention, is also central to Honoré's conception of an overlap period between secretaries—that is, that an incoming secretary would find "drafts" already on file, which he would use and adapt for a time until gaining the confidence to write texts which were fully his own. This again is pure hypothesis. It is also one which may bring out all too clearly the dangers of subjectivism, or of pressing the evidence to say what it does not really say, which haunt Honoré's method. See, for instance, Alan Watson's discussion (*Tijdschrift voor*

Rechtsgeschiednis 50 [1982]: 409, on pp. 411–12) of Honoré's argument based on a switch in the course of 213 from the locution *modo si* (only if) (194 to February 213) to *si modo* (if only) (used by secretary no. 5, of late July 213 to 217). Firstly, there is no clear statistical pattern to the use of these phrases in the writings of the putatively relevant authors (Papinian, Ulpian, Arrius Menander), as preserved in the *Digest*. Secondly, the alleged date of this verbal shift does not fit the facts, for *si modo* in fact appears earlier, namely in *CJ* 5, 16, 3 of 4 March 213. Such uncertainties, combined with the purely hypothetical use of drafts, and with the further hypothesis of the use by Secretary B of drafts written by Secretary A, mean, once again, that there is no reason, and no need, to follow Honoré in trying to push the evidence further than it will in fact go.

None the less, Honoré has taken it a long way. If, ideally, the entire work of assembling marks of style should be done again more systematically, without the dangerously subjective bias in favour of picking out *distinctive* marks of style, it has surely been adequately demonstrated that historians and (if they could be persuaded to take an interest) Latinists can feel with confidence that they have before them something very close to the *ipsissima verba* of the great jurists of the classical period. How, and by what persons, or combination of persons, imperial private rescripts were composed, is still a difficult question. But at least one very distinct personality surely emerges from behind the anonymity of the office of *libelli*, namely Honoré's secretary no. 20, Hermogenianus, the major legal systematizer of Diocletian's reign, who "must count as one of the leading Roman lawyers" (*Emperors*, 119). Viewed from a different angle, the vast mass of Tetrarchic rescripts offers a remarkable and largely untapped source for social history.

Honoré's work on private rescripts should lead to further, and improved, stylistic studies of imperial *epistulae*, seen as letters (see, e.g., P. Cugusi, *Evoluzione e forma dell'epistolografia latina* [1983], with a brief glance, chap. 7, at imperial letters); of *edicta* (see M. Benner, *The Emperor Says: Studies in the Rhetorical Style in Edicts of the Early Empire* [1975]) and of *orationes*, above all those in the Senate; R. J. A. Talbert, *The Senate of Imperial Rome* (1984), now provides the necessary framework. All of these were, or could be, forms of legislation. Study of the answers to *libelli* is not enough of itself to rescue the making of law from the unprofessional hands of the emperors. (For a further discussion of this question, see F. Millar, "L'Empereur romain comme décideur," *Du pouvoir dans l'antiquité: mots et réalites*, ed. C. Nicolet [1990], 201, and in the Afterword [pp. 636–52], in *The Emperor in the Roman World*[2] [1992]).

As for the jurists themselves, it is perhaps time for them to be rescued from the exclusive attention of their modern counterparts and studied as figures in the complex cultural landscape of the Empire. For a start, note, for instance, V. S. Ussani, *Valori e storia nella cultura giuridica fra Nerva e Adriano. Studi su Nerazio e Celso* (1979), F. Casavola, *Giuristi Adrianei* (1980), and a whole series of studies in *ANRW* II.15 (1976), including G. Crifò, "Ulpiano. Esperienze e responsabilità del giurista" (pp. 708–85). But beyond the question of what values and ideas, and what methods of expression and argument, the jurists brought to the writing of their extensive works, there remains the wider question of their standing as individuals and of the dissemination and use of their works. Much can still be learned from the late W. Kunkel's admirable book, *Herkunft und soziale Stellung der römischen Juristen*[2] (1967): note for instance his no. 69, M. Cn. Licinius Rufinus, described on an inscription from Thessalonica as *kratistos* (*egregius*) and as *lamprotatos* (*clarissimus*) consular (*hypatikos*) and the greatest expert in law (*empeirotatos nomōn*, equivalent to *iuris peritissimus* in Latin) (*IG* X, 2 [1], no. 142; a new inscription from his native city, Thyatira, now reveals his remarkable career though equestrian and senatorial posts. See F. Millar, "Roman Law in the Greek East: The Dossier of M. Cn. Licinius Rufinus," *JRS* 89 [1999]: 90 = chapter 20 in this volume). The traces of the circulation of juristic works in Latin, as reflected in papyri from Egypt, are also highly suggestive; see in brief R. Cavenaille, *Corpus Papyrorum Latinarum* (1955), nos. 70–101; R. A. Pack, *Greek and Latin Literary Texts from Greco-Roman Egypt* (1965), nos. 2953–93.

The most remarkable evidence for the standing of a jurist and for the use which could be made of his works relates, however, to Ulpian himself. It is an inscription from Ephesos (*JÖAI* 45 [1960]: Beibl: 82, nr. 8; *AE* 1966, 436; now *I. K Ephesos* II [1979], no. 217), containing part of a letter in Greek in which the writer (evidently a proconsul) urges the city to collect and present to him the evidence bearing on its privileges (*dikaiōmata*). Louis Robert, *Rev. Phil.* 41 (1967): 46, quoting an opinion, never to be published, of William Seston, may well have been right to assign the letter (known only from notebooks) to the Tetrarchic period. At all events the proconsul tells the city to put together both "the things said on the basis of ancient *nomoi* [laws]" in the *de officio* of Ulpian and elements from imperial constitutions (*diataxeis*) and the decrees of the Senate. The reference is, beyond all question, to Ulpian's *On the duties of a proconsul*. Ulpian's cautious respect for the social norms of his time comes out nowhere better than in the passage from this work (*Dig.* 1, 16, 4) where he advises a proconsul to take care to arrive first at whichever city in the province has the established precedence: "Certain provinces even observe this custom, that the proconsul should arrive by sea, as in the case of Asia, and indeed to the extent that our Imperator Antoninus Augustus [Caracalla] replied to the request of the Asiani that the proconsul had the obligation to reach Asia by sea and, of the *metropoleis*, to make his arrival first in Ephesos." In Ephesos at least Ulpian's fame was to be secure.

CHAPTER TWENTY

The Greek East and Roman Law:
The Dossier of M. Cn. Licinius Rufinus*

For Tony Honoré, *iuris peritissimus*

Introduction

In A.D. 530 the emperor Justinian gave orders that a commission of lawyers should take the 1,500 *libri* (volumes) containing the works of the classical Roman jurists and condense them into a single work, the *Digesta* or *Pandectae*. His purpose was that the result should be a coherent whole, stripped of repetition and contradiction. Fortunately for us, what they actually produced was something quite different, which belongs to a type which is familiar to all modern students of the ancient world: a source book. For what the commission in fact did was to arrange the work by topics, and under each topic to assemble a series of examples of legal reasoning extracted from the surviving works of classical jurists. Nearly all of these jurists had worked in the Antonine and Severan age, with a few belonging to the period of the Tetrarchy.

It has often been supposed in the modern world that the texts which were thus excerpted and re-arranged really were also mutilated, corrected, or interpolated in pursuit of Justinian's self-contradictory ideal of using the academic products of a major intellectual movement—already three or four centuries in the past—devoted to debating the principles and details of Roman law, but of then reducing them to neat conformity with each other. But in fact no such conformity was achieved. In no real sense is the *Digest* a code of law; on the contrary, it is a collection of varying opinions on points of law. Moreover, modernization of the texts to fit the institutions and the

*First published in *JRS* 89 (1999): 90–108. For very helpful comments, and suggestions I was most indebted to Peter Herrmann, Tony Honoré, Werner Eck, and Greg Woolf, as well as to the Editorial Committee.

public vocabulary of the Justinianic period simply was not carried out. So the texts assembled in the *Digest* reflect with great vividness and accuracy the world of the High Empire of the second and third centuries, with *proconsules* and *procuratores*, *provinciae*, Latin-speaking cities called *civitates* or *res publicae*, and Greek-speaking *poleis*.

The extracts assembled in the *Digest* also kept the names of their original authors, the titles of their works, and very often the book numbering within those works. Moreover, since the jurists had very frequently referred to rulings by past and present emperors, as well as to each other's works, it is possible to arrive at a quite precise chronology of most of the individuals and their works. Thus, to give only the most obvious example, the study of Ulpian by Tony Honoré, whose work is fundamental to everything in this chapter, showed that his truly gigantic output of writing, of which some 300,000 words survive in the *Digest*, was all very largely composed under Caracalla (A.D. 211–17).[1]

Domitius Ulpianus happens also to be one of the very few jurists who alludes explicitly to his own local origins: he came from the ancient Phoenician, and then Greek, city of Tyre, which had become a Roman colony only in his own life-time.[2] In other words, the most fully preserved corpus of Roman juristic writing by a single author, all of it in Latin, was in fact the work of a man who came from a Greek city. We are presented with one of the most profound aspects of that process of integration which Woolf has called "becoming Roman, staying Greek."[3]

Faced with the Justinianic re-arrangement of a vast corpus of earlier academic writing into a massive source book of legal reasoning in Latin, it was an obvious, if extremely labourious, task for a modern scholar to re-assemble the excerpts under the names of their authors and their works (and book numbers), thereby producing by far the largest coherent body of surviving classical Latin prose (along with one work by Herennius Modestinus which had been written in Greek, of which more below). This was the feat per-

1. T. Honoré, *Ulpian* (1982). Note the extensively revised second edition, *Ulpian: Pioneer of Human Rights* (2002).

2. *Dig.* 50, 15, 1 *pr.* (Ulpianus, *libro primo de censibus*). See F. Millar, "The Roman *coloniae* of the Near East: A Study in Cultural Relations," in H. Solin and M. Kajava, eds., *Roman Eastern Policy and Other Studies in Roman History* (1990), chap. 7, on pp. 31–39 (chapter 9 in *Rome, the Greek World, and the East* III: *The Greek World, the Jews and Rome*); Millar, *The Roman Near East, 31 BC–AD 337* (1993), 285–95.

3. G. Woolf, "Becoming Roman, Staying Greek: Culture, Identity and the Civilizing Process in the Roman East," *Proc. Camb. Philol. Soc.* 40 (1994): 116.

formed in Lenel's *Palingenesia*, published in 1889.[4] In it, a mere two pages suffice for the seventeen surviving excerpts of the *Regulae* (*Rules*) (or *Regularum Libri*) of Licinius Rufinus, in twelve or thirteen books. One of the passages quoted, however, serves to date the work, for it too was written under "Imperator Antoninus," most likely "Caracalla" (A.D. 211–17) but possibly "Elagabal" (A.D. 218–22), whose actual name was also "M. Aurelius Antoninus."[5] We also see Licinius Rufinus elsewhere in the *Digest* as one of a number of jurists who consulted the great Iulius Paulus; Paulus' replies to them (or in this case Rufinus' query) were quoted verbatim in his twenty-six books of *Quaestiones* (*On legal problems*).[6] The alleged facts of Paulus' career largely depend on the *Historia Augusta*, but there is no doubt that he was a contemporary of Papinian, and was one of the major jurists of the Severan period, and also gave legal advice at cases heard by the emperor. Although in his case there is no documentary evidence for his origins, and he does not speak of them himself, the form of his name has suggested that he might have come from a provincial family which had acquired the Roman citizenship in the first century and was perhaps from the Greek East.[7]

Nothing in the name of Licinius Rufinus, as preserved in the *Digest*, gives any hint of a particular local origin, still less of roots in the Greek world. So, for instance, in the first edition of the *Prosopographia*, published in 1897, no connection is made between the entry on him, derived from the *Digest*, and that on the "M. Cn. Licinius Rufinus," described as "the *clarissimus consularis* and *amicus* [friend] of the Emperor," who is honoured on two Greek inscriptions from Thyatira in Lydia (nos. 1–2 below).[8]

The subsequent unfolding of a much fuller picture of the professional ex-

4. O. Lenel, *Palingenesia Iuris Civilis: Iuris Consultorum Reliquiae quae Iustiniani Digestis continentur, ceteraque iuris prudentiae civilis fragmenta minora secundum auctores et libros* I–II (1889).

5. Lenel (n. 4), I, cols. 559–62, fr. 12. *Dig.* 24, 1, 41 (Licinius Rufinus, *Regulae*, book 6): "For our Emperor Antoninus ruled that a wife was permitted to donate money to her husband (against the normal rule) on the occasion of his promotion." Note that G. Gualandi, *Legislazione imperiale e giurisprudenza* 1 (1963): 229–30, goes straight from Caracalla to Severus Alexander, attributing no ruling to either Macrinus or "Elagabal."

6. For Paulus' *Quaestiones*, see Lenel (n. 4), I, cols. 1181–1221. For the query from Rufinus, see fr. 1382, *Dig.* 40, 13, 4 (Paulus, *Quaestiones*, book 12): "Licinnius Rufinus to Iulius Paulus . . ." Variation in the spelling of "Licinius" is found also in the contemporary inscriptions; see below.

7. See the important study by W. Kunkel, *Herkunft und soziale Stellung der römischen Juristen*[2] (1967), 244–45. Kunkel (245, n. 507) hints at a Greek origin, and the suggestion is put more positively by H.-G. Pflaum, *Les procurateurs équestres* (1950), 267 and n. 7.

8. *PIR*[1] L 163 (the jurist); 164 (the man from Thyatira).

pertise, the public role, and the career in imperial service of M. Cn. Licinius Rufinus is one small aspect of the way in which, in the nineteenth and twentieth centuries, we have gained an incomparably more detailed and vivid "image," or "representation," of the Roman Empire, as refracted through the epigraphy of the Greek cities. Whether we are talking of the institutions of the imperial cult, of the spread of the Roman citizenship, of the workings of local and provincial government and local self-government, of embassies to emperors and governors, or of equestrian or senatorial office-holding, the Roman—or perhaps better Romano-Greek—Empire presents itself before us now in a way which was hardly imaginable even 100 years ago. All that we almost always lack still is those actual visual representations, in the form of statues, which were put up to honour the dignitaries who were the subject of the language of commemoration, in what Lendon has recently called the "empire of honour."[9]

Literally thousands of individuals can now be (in a metaphorical sense) "seen" through the repetitive and often stereotyped language of honorific inscriptions. But there can be few whose record as now revealed offers us a more powerful conception of the Severan empire than does the dossier of Licinius Rufinus. Thus the relevant volume of the second edition of the *Prosopographia*, published in 1970, already presented a much enriched documentation of his public role, based on inscriptions both from Thyatira (nos. 1–3 below) and from two cities in Macedonia, namely Beroea and Thessalonica (nos. 4–5 below).[10] In particular, it was no. 4 which showed that the Licinius Rufinus of the inscriptions was a jurist, and hence could be identified with the author known from the *Digest*. But now a new and far more detailed inscription from Thyatira (no. 6), published in 1997, in exemplary style, by Herrmann, serves to provide us with a quite new window on the period.[11] The dossier provided below will begin with the longer-known inscriptions from Thyatira, all recently re-edited by Herrmann in *Tituli Asiae Minoris*, in the volume on north-west Lydia,[12] then move to the two texts from Macedonia, and come back finally to the truly remarkable new career inscription from Thyatira. The purpose of the dossier is only to collect and translate the texts as published, and to offer some historical comments, not of course to re-edit the inscriptions.

9. J. Lendon, *Empire of Honour: The Art of Government in the Roman World* (1997).

10. *PIR²* L 236.

11. P. Herrmann, "Die Karriere eines prominenten Juristen aus Thyateira," *Tyche* 12 (1997): 111.

12. *Tituli Asiae Minoris* V. *Tituli Lydiae* 2. *Regio septentrionalis ad occidentem vergens*, ed. P. Herrmann (1989).

The Inscriptions of Licinius Rufinus

1. Thyatira. *TAM* V.2, no. 984 (*IGR* IV, no. 1215).

> Ἀγαθῆι τύχηι.
> Μ. Γν. ⟨Λ⟩ικίν. Ῥουφ[ε]ῖνο[ν],
> [τ]ὸν λαμπρότατον ὑπα⟨τι⟩κόν,
> κτίστην καὶ εὐεργέτην τῆς
> 5 πατρίδος, φίλον τοῦ Σεβ., ⟨Γ.⟩Πε⟨ρ.⟩
> [Α]ὐ⟨ρ.⟩ Ἀλέξανδρος, ἀρχιερε[ὺ]ς
> τοῦ σύνπαντος ⟨ξυ⟩στοῦ διὰ
> ⟨β⟩ίου, ξυστάρχης καὶ ἐπ[ὶ] βαλα-
> νεί⟨ω⟩ν τοῦ Σεβ. καὶ ⟨ἱ⟩ερεὺς το⟨ῦ⟩
> 10 προπάτορος θεοῦ Ἡλίου Πυθί-
> [ο]υ Ἀπόλλωνος ⟨Τ⟩υριμναίου,
> τὸν ἑαυτοῦ καὶ πάσης τῆς πό-
> λεως εὐεργέτην.

To Good Fortune

[To] M. Gn. Licin(ius) Rufinus, the the *clarissimus consularis*, founder and benefactor of his native city, friend of the Emperor, G. Per(elius) Aur(elius) Alexander, High Priest of the whole athletic association for life, official of the association and in charge of the Emperor's baths, and priest of the ancestral god Helios Pythios Apollon Tyrimnaios, [gave honour as] his personal benefactor and that of the whole city.

This inscription reveals a prominent local figure who also enjoys a very high status within the imperial system, as someone who is both consular rank and an *amicus Caesaris* (friend of Caesar). But it neither reflects any specific offices held by the Licinius Rufinus concerned, nor would, as such, serve to identify him with the jurist known from the *Digest*. Nor is there any explicit mention of the date. There is, however, an (approximate) implicit dating, since G. Perelius Aurelius Alexander is recorded in *IGR* IV, no. 1251 = *TAM* V.2, no. 1018, as having been on an embassy on behalf of Thyatira to the emperor M. Aurelius [Antoninus] (erased) Pius Felix Augustus, that is, "Elagabal" (A.D. 218–22). Jones has recently suggested that this man should be identified with the pancratiast named as "Alexander" who is represented on a mosaic from Ostia.[13]

13. C. P. Jones, "The Pancratiasts Helix and Alexander on an Ostian Mosaic," *JRA* 11 (1998): 293.

2. Thyatira. *TAM* V.2, no. 985 (*IGR* IV, no. 1214).

> M. Γν. Λικίνι[ον ʹΡο]υφεῖ-
> νον, τὸν λαμπρότα-
> τον ὑπατικόν, M. Aὐρ.
> Βάσσος, ἱππικὸς ἀπὸ
> 5 χειλιαρχιῶν, τὸν ἑαυ-
> τοῦ εὐεργέτην.

(To) M. Gn. Licinius Rufinus, the *clarissimus consularis*, M. Aurelius Bassus, of equestrian status, ex-*tribunus*, [gave] honour as his personal benefactor.

The inscription adds nothing further to our image of Rufinus (and indeed omits any allusion to his status as *amicus Caesaris*), except in so far as it places him in relation of marked superiority to another man, also evidently from Thyatira, who had also entered imperial service but had remained at a lower level. There is no explicit indication of date, but the expression ἀπὸ χειλιαρ-χιῶν, implying a formal status attaching to ex-holders of the rank of *tribunus militum*, would strongly tend to suggest the third century.[14]

3. Thyatira. *TAM* V.2, no. 986 (*IGR* IV, no. 1216).

> M. Γναῖον Λικίνιον
> ʹΡουφεῖνον, τὸν λαμπρότατον
> ὑπατικόν, φίλον τοῦ
> Σεβαστοῦ, κτίστην
> 5 κ(αὶ) εὐεργέτην τῆς
> πατρίδος
> οἱ βυρσεῖς.

[To] M. Gnaeus Licinius Rufinus, the *clarissimus consularis*, friend of the Emperor, founder and benefactor of his native city, the tanners [gave honour].

The corporation of tanners in Thyatira again stressed Rufinus' role as a local benefactor. The distinctive form of the name, with its two *praenomina*, makes it certain that this is the same person as in 1 and 2. There is no explicit or implicit indication of date.

Two further inscriptions from Thyatira, *TAM* V.2, nos. 987 and 988

14. See F. Millar, "Empire and City, Augustus to Julian: Obligations, Excuses and Status," *JRS* 73 (1983): 76ff., see pp. 90, 94 (chapter 16 in this volume).

(*IGR* IV, nos. 1217 and 1218), honour the son of our Licinius Rufinus, without saying enough to deserve reproduction here.

4. Thessalonica. *IG* X.2(1), no. 142.

Ἀγαθῆι τύχηι.   τον καὶ ἐν-
[. . . .]   πειρότατον
Λικίννιον   10 νόμων ὑ-
Ῥουφεῖνον,   πατικόν,
5 τὸν κράτι-   Κλαύδιος
στον καὶ   Μένων τὸν
λαμπρότα-   εὐεργέτην.

To Good Fortune
[To] Licinius Rufinus, the *egregius* and *clarissimus*, and most versed in the laws, *consularis*, Claudius Menon [gave honour as] his benefactor.

It is this inscription which, while reproducing Rufinus' name in yet a different style and spelling, repeats the representation of his status as a consular, but also adds the crucial description of him as "most versed in the laws" which allows the identification of this man with the jurist known from the *Digest*. Again, while there is no explicit dating, the stemma provided in *IG* X.2(1), under no. 185, shows that Claudius Menon was a high priest (*archiereus*) in the city, and also a *Makedoniarches* (president) and *hierophantes* (priest) of the *koinon* (league of cities) of Macedonia, in the middle of the first half of the third century. The broad chronological setting is thus secure; but what services Licinius Rufinus might have rendered to any individual or institution in Macedonia is left unclear.

Since it is certain that the approximate date is the first half of the third century, the use of the two separate (and formally speaking incompatible) status designations for Licinius Rufinus is of some interest. Here, as in the previous inscriptions, he appears as a ὑπατικός, namely *consularis*, that is someone who has either held the office of consul or has been granted the status of ex-consul by the emperor (but here too, as in no. 2, his status as *amicus Caesaris* does not appear). As a man of consular status, he will necessarily have enjoyed senatorial rank, and hence will have been designated in Latin *vir clarissimus*, of which the established equivalent in Greek was, as here, λαμπρότατος. These two terms go together in all four of the inscriptions so far listed. But in this instance there is an oddity, for Rufinus is described also as κράτιστος. Literally this means simply "most powerful," but more relevantly it was the established equivalent of *egregius*, which by now was the standard status term

used in the mid-second century and after for middle-ranking equestrian officials.[15] So, either this expression is used loosely (which is perfectly possible,
as complete consistency is not to be expected in local honorific texts mirroring the constantly evolving imperial hierarchy), or it is an indication that
Licinius' prominence as an expert in the laws had extended over a period in
which he had risen from equestrian to consular rank. As we will see, the remarkable new inscription listed below as no. 6 attests exactly that. It is the
next inscription, however, which suggests why he will have been honoured
in Macedonia as well as in his native city.

5. Beroea. *Ann. Épig.* 1949, no. 341, from L. Robert, "Un juriste romain
dans une inscription de Beroia," *Hellenica* 5 (1948): 29.

> Ἀγαθῆι τύχηι.
> [Κατὰ τὸ δόξαν τῷ]
> λαμπροτάτῳ συνε-
> δρίῳ, Λικίνιον
> 5 Ῥουφεῖον τὸν ὑ-
> πατικόν, συναγο-
>
> ῥεύσαντα τῇ ἐπαρ-
> χείᾳ περὶ τῆς συντε-
> λείας τῶν Θετταλῶν,
> 10 Δομίτιος Εὐρύδικος,
> ὁ μακεδονιάρχης,
> ἐκ τῶν ἑαυτοῦ.

To Good Fortune

In accordance with the decision of the most distinguished *synedrion*,
to Licinius Rufinus the *consularis*, who has appeared as advocate for
the province in the matter of the *synteleia* [contribution?] of the
Thessalians, Domitios Eurydikos the *Makedoniarches* [gave honour]
out of his own resources.

The general context is therefore the public activity of the *koinon*, or *synedrion*,
of Macedonia, and the specific issue which had arisen will have related to
the fact that at some time in the later second century Thessaly had been de-
tached from the province of Achaea and attached to Macedonia.[16] *Synteleia*
has a variety of meanings,[17] but the most likely point at issue here was surely
the question of the financial contribution which the cities of Thessaly would

15. Millar (n. 14), 90.

16. See J. Deininger, *Die Provinziallandtage der römischen Kaiserzeit* (1965), 91–96; G. W.
Bowersock, "Zur Geschichte des römischen Thessaliens," *RhM* 108 (1965): 277; W. J. Chef,
"The Roman Borders between Achaia and Macedonia," *Chiron* 17 (1987): 135.

17. See M. Corbier, "Cité, territoire et fiscalité," in *Epigrafia: Actes du Colloque international d'épigraphie latine en mémoire d'Attilio Degrassi* (1991), 629, on pp. 640–41, cited by Herrmann (n. 11), 112.

be required to make to the *koinon* of the province in which they now found themselves. The word *synteleia* is used in exactly this context in a letter of Valerian to the city of Philadelphia in Lydia, written from Antioch in Syria in 255, and responding to the city's request to be freed from the *synteleia* made by minor cities to the *metropoleis* towards the expenses of priesthoods and festivals.[18] It is very likely, though it cannot be certain, that the dispute between the Thessalians and the *koinon* of Macedonia had also been heard by an emperor. But it is one of the features of the epigraphic dossier of Licinius Rufinus that no emperor is explicitly named in it. Documents 1 and 3 record that he was an *amicus* of a single emperor, but do not indicate which. The same is true of the remarkable new text representing the public role of Rufinus; but this does, though implicitly rather than explicitly, allow an attempt to date the successive phases of his career.

6. Thyatira. P. Herrmann, "Die Karriere eines prominenten Juristen aus Thyateira," *Tyche* 12 (1997): 111.

>   Ἀγαθῆι τύχηι.
>   Μ. Γναῖον Λικίν. Ῥουφεῖνον,
>   ἱππικόν, σύνβουλον Σεβ., πράξα[ν]-
>   τα τὰς Ἑλληνικὰς ἐπι[σ]τολάς, ἐπὶ
> 5   παιδείας Σεβ., ἐπὶ τῶν καθόλου λό-
>   γων, ἐπὶ τῶν ἀποκριμάτων, στρατη-
>   γὸν Ῥωμαίων, ἡγεμόνα ἐπαρχείας Νο-
>   ρικοῦ, ἱερέα σακερδωτίου Τίτου Τατίου,
>   ἐν τῶι συνβουλίωι τῶν εἴκοσιν [ἀν]-
> 10   δρῶν, ἐπιλεχθέντα φίλον τοῦ Σεβ.,
>   πρεσβεύσαντα πολλάκις πρὸς τοὺς
>   αὐτοκράτορας καὶ πάντα τὰ δίκαια
>   τῆι πατρίδι κατορθώσαντα, τὸν
>   λαμπρότατον ὑπατικόν, διά τε
> 15   ἀφθονίαν τροφῶν καὶ ἔργων πολ-
>   λῶν καὶ μεγάλων κατασκευὰς κοι-
>   νῇ τε καὶ κατὰ ἕνα εὐεργέτην,
>   οἱ κηπουροί.

To Good Fortune
[To] M. Gnaeus Licin(ius) Rufinus, of equestrian rank, *consiliarius* of the Emperor, having handled the Greek letters, *a studiis Augusti*, in

18. *SEG* XVII, no. 528. See F. Millar, *The Emperor in the Roman World*[2] (1992), 390.

charge of the general accounts [*a rationibus?*], in charge of the *apokrimata* [*a libellis?*], praetor of the Romans, governor of the province of
Noricum, priest of the *sacerdotium* of Titus Tatius, in the *consilium* of
the Twenty Men, chosen as *amicus Caesaris*, having acted often as ambassador to the Emperors, and having secured all the rights for his
native city, the *clarissimus consulqris*, and on account of the generosity
of his provision and his construction of many major works both a
communal and an individual benefactor, the gardeners [gave honour].

It should be made clear at once that the remarks which follow, designed to
spell out the significance of this remarkable text, and to suggest some further interpretations, are entirely dependent on the exemplary publication
by Herrmann. What follows makes no attempt to reproduce the details of
his epigraphical commentary, but tries to look at some broad issues which
the text raises. Some detailed issues of vocabulary and technical terminology
will, however, be unavoidable, since one of the prime features of the text
is the style in which it deploys Greek to mirror or represent functions in
the entourage of the emperor. Precisely one of the difficulties is to know,
firstly, whether these functions were themselves stable over successive reigns,
and, secondly, whether they were described in a fixed terminology in Latin.
In almost all respects I will merely attempt to bring out for the English-
language reader the comments made by Herrmann. At one crucial point,
however, namely the translation of ἐπὶ τῶν ἀποκριμάτων, "in charge of the
apokrimata," I will suggest tentatively a different interpretation: not *a responsis*,
but *a libellis*, that is, not the unattested post of secretary in charge of "answers," but *a libellis*, that is, the well-known post of secretary in charge of
petitions. If that were to prove correct, it would take us directly into the
territory brilliantly explored by Tony Honoré, of "Emperors and Lawyers,"
and to the question of whose are the "voices" which are heard in imperial
replies to *libelli* from private persons.[19] At the end, therefore, I will return to
that question, and then (briefly) to the broad issue of "the Greek East and
Roman Law."

This inscription comes from a statue base, discovered in the village of
Selendi, or Akselendi, seventeen kilometres south of the site of Thyatira. It
is likely that it originally stood in the urban centre; even more keenly than
normal, we must regret the disappearance of the statue itself, and with it the

---

19. See T. Honoré, *Emperors and Lawyers*[2] (1994), with my review article on the first edition (1981), "A New Approach to the Roman Jurists," *JRS* 76 (1986): 272ff. (chapter 19 in
this volume).

chance to see how a prominent local figure, who rose high in the imperial service and the Senate, will have been visually represented to his fellow citizens. None the less, even the text, without the statue which it accompanied, gives us a wholly new conception of Rufinus' career.

The Career of Licinius Rufinus

The inscription seems to provide one unambiguous fixed point in time, namely the reference in lines 9–10 to Licinius Rufinus having been a member of the "council of the Twenty Men." For the most natural way to take this, as Herrmann does, is as a reference to the commission of *vigintiviri* appointed by the Senate in A.D. 238 in the face of the invasion of Italy by the forces of the emperor Maximinus.[20] There do not seem to be any other documentary attestations in Greek for the title used for this ad hoc group; the most formal title on a contemporary Latin inscription is *xxvir⟨os⟩ ex senatus consulto r(ei) p(ublicae) curandae* (twenty men [appointed] by a decree of the senate for the preservation of the state), while another inscription, unfortunately fragmentary, refers to the "XX co(n)s(ulares)."[21] But since Lucinius Rufinus was clearly of high senatorial rank at this point, and since there is no indication that the "council" (συμβούλιον) concerned had functioned alongside any emperor (contrast the earlier post of σύμβουλος Σεβαστοῦ [counsellor of the Emperor], recorded in line 3), there seems no alternative to seeing Licinius Rufinus as one of the twenty consulars of 238.

That being so, we should take it as at least a working hypothesis that this detail provides a chronological point of reference for the whole, rather anomalous, career, and explore its implications. Firstly, since the imperial, or non-local, elements in Rufinus' career are clearly set out in chronological order, we have to take it that his selection as the *amicus* of a single emperor, recorded in line 10, belongs in the reign of Gordian III (A.D. 238–44). It will be recalled (text to n. 5 above) that Rufinus wrote his *Regulae* under Caracalla (A.D. 211–17), or possibly Elagabal (A.D. 218–22). So, in reading the inscription, we are looking back at a public career which seems to have covered something like the three decades, A.D. 210–40. If we take the form of the allusion to the emperor, or to successive emperors, seriously, then

20. See K. Dietz, *Senatus contra principem. Untersuchungen zur senatorischen Opposition gegen Kaiser Maximinus* (1980), cited by Herrmann (n. 11), 121.

21. *ILS*, no. 1186 (L. Caesonius Lucillus Macer Rufinianus); *AE* 1903, no. 337 = *ILS*, no. 8979: "[to the companion?] of our [Augusti] who belongs to the council of twenty" [*comiti? Augg.]nn. inter XX cos.*]. Zosimus 1, 14, 2 speaks only of twenty senators.

all of Rufinus' posts fell in the reigns of emperors ruling singly (for the text always uses Σεβ., the abbreviation for Σεβαστός, referring to a single emperor, as opposed to Σεββ. for two, or even Σεβββ., equivalent to "Auggg.," for three). There had been two joint Augusti (Severus and Caracalla) from 198 to 209, and three (with the younger brother, Geta, also) from 209 to 211. We ought therefore to start from the assumption that Rufinus' secretarial posts with (apparently) a single emperor began not earlier than the reign of Caracalla (officially "M. Aurelius Antoninus," and thus probably the "imperator Antoninus" mentioned in Rufinus' *Regulae*). His official career could however have begun later. None of the emperors of the following two decades, Macrinus (217–18), Elagabal, officially also "M. Aurelius Antoninus" (218–22), Severus Alexander (222–35), or Maximinus (235–38), had a co-emperor with the rank of Augustus. These names alone will be enough to suggest the drastically contrasted successive contexts into which Rufinus' "secretarial" and then senatorial functions might have brought him.

The non-imperial, or local, roles attributed to Rufinus in the last part of the inscription (ll. 11–17) firstly take us back to the parallel, but less specific, representations in the other inscriptions from Thyatira (nos. 1–3), in which he is already both a *consularis* and local "founder" and benefactor, and in nos. 1 and 3 is also an *amicus Caesaris*. These latter two inscriptions at any rate should therefore not be earlier than the reign of Gordian III (238–44). The particular local benefactions recorded in no. 6, the supply of provisions and the construction of public works, could of course have belonged to any phase in Rufinus' career. So also, probably, could the repeated embassies to the *Autokratores (Imperatores)*, for this is a less specific term, which might cover appearances before two or three joint *Augusti*, or (for instance) before Macrinus and his son Diadumenianus in 217/18, or before a succession of emperors ruling singly. We may recall the inscription from Ephesus which honours a man who had been on a successful embassy on behalf of his city to Macrinus and Diadumenianus, and also earlier, before Severus and Caracalla and then Caracalla alone, to Rome, Britain, Germany, Sirmium, Nicomedia, Antioch, and Mesopotamia.[22] Though it might seem surprising, such an embassy could even have been undertaken after a man reached senatorial rank, as is clear in the case of the embassy from Philadelphia to Valerian in 255 (text to n. 18 above). Equally, however, some such embassies (which are said to have taken place "often") might have taken place before Rufinus' official career began, and in the period when inscription 6, looking back, can describe him as ἱππικός, "of equestrian rank." The same chronological uncertainties apply to

<hr>

22. *I. K. Ephesos* III, no. 802 (*Ann. Épig.* 1971, no. 455; *SEG* XVII, no. 505).

his appearance as an advocate for the *koinon* of Macedonia. When the inscription (no. 5) recording this was put up in Beroea, he was already a *consularis*; it is possible, but (as Werner Eck suggests to me) unlikely, that his services as advocate will have been at a much earlier stage.

Although there is a clear chronological structure to the representation of Rufinus' imperial career in inscription no. 6, Herrmann rightly notes that some elements are (at best) implicit and are not specifically recorded. His first five posts were equestrian, "secretarial," ones at the side of the emperor. He must then have been adlected to the Senate, presumably *inter aedilicios* (into the status of former aediles), since he then held a praetorship in Rome (ll. 6–7). Although this was of course an honour, it should be noted that in the context of the Severan period it is a surprisingly modest one. In this period, as Eck and Roxan have recently stressed, equestrians holding prominent posts, including specifically "secretarial" posts with the emperor, seem commonly to have entered the Senate with praetorian or even consular status. Examples from among "secretaries" are Aelius Antipater, *ab epistulis Graecis* (in charge of the emperor's Greek correspondence) under Severus, and then attested as a consular governor; P. Aelius Coeranus, *a libellis* (in charge of petitions) under Severus, and suffect consul under Caracalla; and now M. Ulpius Ofellius Theodorus, attested as *a libellis* early in Caracalla's reign, and as a consular governor between 219 and 222. Aelius Coeranus was evidently adlected *inter praetorios* and then made consul; but Philostratus records specifically that Aelius Antipater was "enrolled among the consuls."[23]

Why Licinius Rufinus was adlected at a considerably lower level cannot be known, unless the purpose was precisely that he should use his legal expertise in giving jurisdiction as praetor. After that, at any rate, he went on to a praetorian governorship, of Noricum. The text uses the non-technical term *hēgemon*, the equivalent of *praeses* in Latin. But the formal title will still have been *legatus Augusti pro praetore* (legate of Augustus with praetorian rank) (see, e.g., *ILS*, no. 1194). Herrmann is surely right to find it noteworthy that a person of Rufinus' background had governed an imperial province, and with that had taken command of a legion (the *legio II Italica*). After that, either a suffect consulship or a further adlection *inter consulares* must have followed, though it is not mentioned explicitly either here or in the other inscrip-

---

23. Philostratus, *Vit. Soph.* 2, 24, 2: ὑπάτοις δὲ ἐγγραφείς. See esp. W. Eck and M. M. Roxan, "Zwei Entlassungsurkunden — *tabulae honestae missionis* — für Soldaten der römischen Auxilien," *Archaeologisches Korrespondenzblatt* 28 (1998): 95, 98–99. For M. Ulpius Ofellius Theodorus, see J.-L. Mourges, "Les formules 'rescripsi' 'recognovi' et les étapes de la rédaction des souscriptions impériales sous le Haut-Empire romain," *MEFRA* 107 (1995): 295–98.

tions; for the *vigintiviri* of 238 were certainly all *consulares*;[24] and in any case, in inscription no. 6, as in nos. 1–5, Rufinus is described as ὑπατικός, *consularis*.

The greatest interest must however attach to the five successive "secretarial" posts which Rufinus held in the first half of his career in imperial service. So it may be worthwhile, before looking at these posts in a little more detail, to tabulate the two main phases of Rufinus' remarkable career, and the posts held in each.

EQUESTRIAN POSTS
consiliarius Augusti
ab epistulis Graecis
a studiis Augusti
a rationibus (?)
a libellis (?)

SENATORIAL POSTS
(adlected, *inter aedilicios?*)
praetor
legatus of Noricum
(suffect consul?)
vigintivir
amicus Caesaris

As regards chronology, nothing is certain except that all his posts seem to have been held under an emperor ruling alone (so after 211), and that the vigintivirate belongs (almost certainly) to 238. Working back from 238, we should probably allow two to three years for the legateship of Noricum, followed probably by suffect consulship. Before that, he had been praetor in Rome. What interval should be assumed between the praetorship and the consulship in an entirely non-standard career such as this seems quite uncertain. The normal gap, from *praetor* at age thirty to consul at about forty-two, would put Rufinus' adlection back into the early 220s, and would mean that all of his five equestrian "secretarial" posts had been held in approximately the second decade of the century, or at the latest in early 220s. But we have no idea as to whether there was any norm for how long such a secretarial post would last, or indeed as to whether they would be likely to succeed each other without a break. All that seems certain is that they will all have fallen within the second two decades of the century.

24. Herrmann (n. 11), 120–22, with Dietz (n. 20), 326–27. Note esp. that Herodian 8, 5, 5, speaks of ἄνδρας ὑπατευκότας, "men who had held the consulate" (though he does not mention the figure 20), while *HA, Gord.* 14. 4, speaks of *viginti viri consulares*.

It is necessary to recall here that inscription no. 4, from Thessalonica, describes Rufinus, in unusual style, as τὸν κράτιστον καὶ λαμπρότατον καὶ ἐνπειρότατον νόμων — "the *egregius* and *clarissimus* and most versed in the laws *consularis*." Since, as we have seen (text to n. 15 above), *kratistos/egregius* is an equestrian status designation, this inscription mirrors no. 6, which begins by describing him as *hippikos*, "of equestrian rank," in looking back to a status from which he had since ascended, while mentioning his subsequent consular status also. The way in which the text of inscription no. 4 is expressed might even be thought positively to imply that Rufinus' reputation as a *iurisperitus* did indeed go back to the time when he had been an equestrian. In fact, *iurisperitus* is too weak an equivalent for the superlative of ἐνπειρότατον νόμων — *iuris peritissimus* would be the literal equivalent in Latin, and precisely this superlative form had indeed been used by Cicero in speaking of the great orator Crassus (*Brut.* 39/145). But in any case (text to n. 5 above) it is likely that Rufinus' *Regulae* had been written under Caracalla.

Not much need be said here of the first four of the "secretarial" posts which Rufinus held. The parallel attestations for other holders in this period were conveniently collected by Pflaum in his great work on equestrian careers.[25] We cannot expect to be able to define such posts too precisely, not only because their functions may have been subject to change and re-combination, but because the terminology deployed both in literary and epigraphic mentions will have been subject to variation.

1. *Consiliarius Aug(usti)* — σύμβουλον Σεβ(αστοῦ), line 3 — is well enough attested, for instance in *ILS*, no. 1423 (Pflaum [n. 25], no. 239), from the Severan period. A few decades earlier, M. Aurelius Papirius Dionysius is recorded in Latin (*ILS*, no. 1455) both as *adsumptus in consilium* (appointed to the council) at 60,000 sesterces per annum and as a *centenarius consiliarius* (councillor at 100,000 sesterces per annum), and in Greek (*IGR* I, no. 135) as a σύμβουλος (Pflaum, no. 181). In the middle of the third century a prominent local benefactor from Ancyra, Caecilius Hermianus, with no other attested imperial function, is described in (*OGIS*, no. 549) as δουκ[η]νά[ριο]ν ἐπὶ συμβουλίου τοῦ Σεβ(αστοῦ) — "*ducenarius* in the *consilium Augusti*." Like Licinius Rufinus, he illustrates the close connection between local eminence and imperial roles.

2. *Ab epistulis Graecis*. Described in no. 6 in terms which are not precisely paralleled elsewhere (πράξα[ν]τα τὰς Ἑλληνικὰς ἐπι[σ]τολάς, ll. 3–4), this post is well known, not least from Philostratus' allusion to various

---

25. H.-G. Pflaum, *Les carrières procuratoriennes équestres* I–III (1960–61). For a tabulation of the known holders of "secretarial" posts, see III, 1019–25.

sophists of just this period who held it.[26] A bilingual inscription from Ephesus conveniently provides a Latin and a Greek version of the terminology for both this and the fourth of Rufinus' posts (see under 4 below).

3. Ἐπὶ παιδείας (ll. 4–5). Though there seem to be no bilingual documents formally attesting the equivalence, there is no reason not to accept that this is the Greek for *a studiis Aug(usti)* (a "secretarial" post whose precise role is uncertain), a title which is quite well attested in the second and third centuries.[27]

4. Ἐπὶ τῶν καθόλου λόγων (ll. 5–6). Both functions of, and the relevant vocabulary (Latin or Greek) for, the major financial post, or posts, at the emperor's side are highly unclear. It may suffice to note that there are several different testimonies, literary and epigraphic, using slightly different terminology, for the notion of someone "entrusted with," or "over," οἱ καθόλου λόγοι, "the general accounts."[28] From the later Antonine period an inscription from Ephesus, mentioned above, supplies the parallel terminology, in Latin and Greek, for two of the posts later held by Rufinus: *ab epistulis Graecis et a rationibus Augg.*/τὸν ἐπὶ τῶν Ἑλληνικῶν ἐπιστολῶν καὶ τῶν καθόλου λόγων τῶν μεγίστων αὐτοκρατόρων—"in charge of the Greek letters and the general accounts of the (greatest) emperors."[29] Whether this term had by now been replaced in Latin by *rationalis* is not important in this context.

5. ἐπὶ τῶν ἀποκριμάτων (l. 6). As indicated above (text to n. 19), it is here alone that I would wish to offer a suggestion which is significantly different from that of Herrmann. He proposes as the Latin equivalent *a responsis*, while of course noting (p. 118) that the only (partial) attestation for it belongs to the reign of Claudius—*ad legationes et res[ponsa Graeca?]* (in charge of the embassies and the Greek answers).[30] The term *apokrimata* is also very rarely attested in the titulature of imperial "secretaries," and never along with a Latin equivalent. Herrmann duly notes the only two known cases —C. Stertinius Xenophon, also under Claudius, as ἐπὶ τῶν Ἑλληνικῶν ἀποκριμάτων, "in charge of the Greek *apokrimata*";[31] and the report in the Suda relating to Dionysius of Alexandria, καὶ ἐπὶ τῶν ἐπιστολῶν καὶ πρεσβειῶν ἐγένετο καὶ ἀποκριμάτων, "and he was in charge of the let-

26. Philostratus, *Vit. Soph.* 2, 5 (Alexander of Seleucia, Cilicia); 2, 24 (Antipater of Hierapolis); 2, 33 (Aspasius of Ravenna).

27. Pflaum (n. 25), III, 1022–23.

28. Pflaum (n. 25), III, 1019.

29. *ILS*, no. 1344; *I. K. Ephesos* III, no. 651 (Ti. Claudius Vibianus Tertullus, *PIR²* C 1049).

30. *I. K. Ephesos* VII.1, no. 3042, l. 11 (Ti. Claudius Balbillus, Pflaum [n. 25], no. 15).

31. *Syll.³*, no. 804; Pflaum (n. 25), no. 16.

ters and embassies and *apokrimata*"—some time in the later first or early second century.[32]

Neither of these texts seems to make clear what type of imperial "answer" or "judgement" was implied by the term *apokrima*, and neither relates to the period with which we are concerned. None the less, I would wish to offer the suggestion that what we are concerned with in inscription no. 6 is the post known in Latin as *a libellis* (the post of the secretary in charge of petitions), and later as *magister libellorum*. It must be admitted clearly that no consistent vocabulary describing this function in Greek can be derived from our sources.[33] What seems to be the post in question is recorded in Greek in the inscription of M. Aurelius Papirius Dionysius, found in Rome, as ἐπὶ βιβλειδίων καὶ διαγνώσεω[ν] τοῦ Σεβαστοῦ, "in charge of [the] *libelli* and judicial hearings of the Emperor" (apparently from early in Commodus' reign),[34] while Aelius Coeranus (text to n. 23 above) is described in an inscription from Ephesus as τὴν ἐξή[γησιν] τῶν ἀξιωμάτων πεπισ[τευμένος], "entrusted with the examination of the petitions."[35] The date is the early years of the third century, and the function was being performed for Caracalla as joint Augustus. Both titles, moreover, relate to the petitions themselves (*axiōmata*), not to the imperial answers to them. So also (very inconveniently for the present argument) does what Cassius Dio says in the "speech of Maecenas," when outlining the "secretarial" functions at the emperor's side which should be performed by equestrians: "Moreover, for your judicial work and your letters, to help you attend the decrees of the cities and petitions of private individuals . . . you must have men chosen from the equestrians to be your helpers and assistants."[36] Similarly, Tryphoninus records a rescript being given by Septimius Severus "while Papinian was dealing with *libelli* [petitions]."[37]

Unpromising as the ground may look, we will see that contemporary documentation does provide reasons for believing that *apokrimata* was the

32. Suda, s.v. Διονυσίος, ed. Adler, vol. II, pp. 109–10; Pflaum (n. 25), no. 46.

33. For a thorough examination of the ambiguity of the vocabulary used in this area, and references to recent bibliography, see J.-P. Coriat, *Le prince législateur: la technique législative des Sévères et les méthodes de creation du droit impérial à la fin du Principat* (1997), 81–82.

34. *IGR* I, no. 135 = Moretti, *IGUR* I, no. 59; Pflaum (n. 25), no. 181.

35. *I. K. Ephesos* VI, no. 2026 (*PIR²* A 161).

36. Dio 52, 33, 5: καὶ μέντοι πρὸς τὰς δίκας τάς τε ἐπιστολὰς καὶ τὰ ψμφίσματα τῶν πόλεων τάς τε τῶν ἰδιωτῶν ἀξιώσεις . . . συνεργούς τέ τινας καὶ ὑπηρέτας ἐκ τῶν ἱππέων ἔχε, Loeb trans., with adjustments.

37. *Dig.* 20, 5, 12 *pr.* (Tryphoninus, *libro octavo disputationum* [*Disputations*, book 8]): Rescriptum est ab imperatore libellos agente Papiniano; Pflaum (n. 25), no. 220.

accepted term, or at least an accepted term, in Greek for replies to personal petitions addressed to the emperor. These answers—whether informal statements of the law, or instructions as to appropriate action, or replies to requests—fill the *Codex* of Justinian, and appear also in other legal texts, and are recorded from time to time on inscriptions and papyri. It is also these which, as assembled in vast numbers in the *Codex*, Honoré has brought to life both as examples of composition in Latin and as specimens of legal reasoning issued in the name of the emperor. He has also gone further, however, and by comparing the style of sequences of these private rescripts, when rearranged in chronological order, with the style of juristic works as preserved in the *Digest*, has sought to put names to the holders of the office of *a libellis* in particular periods. In the years with which we are concerned, on Honoré's proposal, the *a libellis* of 194–202 will be Papinian (as in Tryphoninus' reference, text to n. 37 above); that of 203–9 Ulpian; that of 211–13 perhaps Arrius Menander; and that of 223–25 perhaps Herennius Modestinus (see text to nn. 42–49 below).

Licinius Rufinus as *A Libellis*?

If the last of the "secretarial" offices which Licinius Rufinus held was indeed that of *a libellis*, then we might hypothetically be able to explore another possible instance of a connection between the style of imperial rescripts and that of a work preserved, if very scrappily, in the *Digest*. Even if not, we know already, from the inscriptions listed above, that a man from the Greek city of Thyatira in Lydia was both seen as *iuris peritissimus* and held major "secretarial" posts with the emperor; and we also know that he wrote a juristic work in Latin, the *Regulae*.

In fact, the arguments for identifying *apokrimata* as having been in this period at least an accepted term for imperial replies to private petitions (*libelli*, ἀξιώματα in Greek) are quite powerful. They consist above all of the heading of the papyrus text of a series of such answers, delivered by Severus and Caracalla over a three-day period in Alexandria in March A.D. 200. It is headed: "In Alexandria, copies of the *apokrimata* posted in the stoa of the gymnasium, year 8, Phamenoth 18 (and then on the two following days)." Both the form of their promulgation and the nature of the thirteen brief and pointed replies make it certain that these are not letters, but are replies to private petitions (*libelli*).[38] The same usage reappears in court proceedings of the 230s refer-

38. This important document, *P. Col.*, no. 123, was originally published by W. L. Westermann and A. A. Schiller, *Apokrimata: Decisions of Septimius Severus on Legal Matters* (1954), and

ring to an *apokrima* of the same emperors which had also been posted up in Alexandria in their year 8.[39]

This coherent group of imperial replies to petitions represents extremely important evidence for the meaning of the term at the beginning of the third century. It should be stressed that *apokrima* is in itself a neutral term, which does not of itself serve to denote a specific form of imperial reply or decision. Similarly, *rescriptum* (and *rescribere, rescripsit*) can be used of replies either in the form of imperial letters (to office-holders, high-status individuals, the Senate, provincial leagues, or cities) or of the informal replies to petitions (*libelli*, or sometime *preces*) which were posted up wherever the emperor was, to be copied down by interested parties. Equally, it is clear that the term *apokrima* had been used in the first centuries B.C. and A.D. of replies to embassies from Greek cities.[40] By the early third century, however, the responsibility for such imperial letters, issued in Greek, rested with the *ab epistulis Graecis*; but this, as inscription no. 6 shows, was a post which Rufinus had already held. We know that the post of *a libellis* was prominent among the offices in the emperor's entourage, and that it was held by at least one major jurisconsult, Papinian (and, under the title of *magister libellorum*, was to be held later by at least one other, Aurelius Arcadius Charisius).[41] We have also seen that the term *apokrima* is applied to the set of imperial rulings which were unquestionably answers to *libelli*, and which were posted up in Alexandria in A.D. 200. It is therefore a reasonable hypothesis, though it cannot be more, that the last "secretarial" post at the emperor's side which Licinius Rufinus held before being adlected to the Senate was that of *a libellis*.

---

revised by H. C. Youtie and A. A. Schiller, "Second Thoughts on the *Columbia Apokrimata (P. Col.* 123)," *Chron. d'Ég.* 30 (1955): 327, whence the standard text, *SB* VI, no. 9526.

39. *P. Mich.* IX, no. 529, published by E. M. Husselman, *Papyri from Karanis* (3rd series) (*Michigan Papyri*, Vol. IX) (1971), no. 529 (*SB* XIV, no. 11875). Verso line 1: [ἐξ ἀπ]οκριμάτων Θεῶν Σεούν Σεούρου κ[αὶ Ἀντωνίνου]. The text of an *apokrima* follows in lines 40–52, followed by [πρ]οετέθη ἐν Ἀλεξανδρίᾳ (ἔτους) ή Μεχ[είρ . . .].

40. I note only a few examples, based on the computer search kindly carried out for me by Charles Crowther at the Centre for the Study of Ancient Documents in Oxford: *Sardis* VII.1, no. 8, iii, 35; iv, 44; v, 58; x, 105; xi, 25; *I. K. Prusa ad Olympum*, no. 2; J. M. Reynolds, *Aphrodisias and Rome* (1982), no. 8, l. 82; 9, l. 15; *IG* VII, no. 2711, ll. 68, 107; 2712, l. 48.

41. *Dig.* 1, 11, 1 *pr.* (Aurelius Arcadius Charisius, *magister libellorum, libro singulari de officio praefecti praetorio* ["in his one-book work *On the Praetorian Prefect*"]). *PLRE* I, Charisius 2; Honoré (n. 19), 156–62, "Secretary no. 19." See R. Herzog and P. L. Schmitt, *Restauration und Erneuerung: Die lateinische Literatur von 284 bis 374 n. Chr.* (1989), 69–71.

As we have seen (text to n. 23 above), that adlection probably did not take place until some point in the reign of Severus Alexander (A.D. 222–35). It will be worth a moment's further speculation to ask if there might be any basis for identifying Rufinus with any of the *a libellis* whose distinctive style Honoré has discerned in this period. It should be stressed that at all stages the argument is speculative: *apokrimata* may not mean *libelli*; the role of the *a libellis* may not have involved the verbal formulation of the brief texts concerned; the procedure of looking for distinctive marks of style may be unsound, particularly when the object is to compare texts of totally different kinds (extensive academic works on the one hand, and concise rulings in the name of the emperor on the other). Furthermore, in many instances, even after the beginning and end of a hypothetical tenure of the post has been determined on the basis of the style of the replies, there may be no reason to suggest any known jurist as the holder.

In the case of Licinius Rufinus the material for comparison is indeed extremely slight. We know of only one juristic work of his, the *Regulae*, probably written under Caracalla (211–17); and we have fairly strong reasons for identifying the last of his "secretarial" posts as that of *a libellis*, and rather weaker reasons for suggesting that this may have been in the 220s.

If Honoré is right, one *a libellis* was in office from October 223 to October 225, and the very numerous replies to *libelli* issued in this period allow an identification of him as Herennius Modestinus.[42] Whether or not this identification can be proved, Modestinus at any rate was a distinctive and important figure.[43] Firstly, Ulpian records that he himself had replied by letter to an enquiry on a legal point made by Herennius Modestinus, *studiosus meus* (my pupil), writing from Dalmatia (whether this might imply that he was currently occupying a post there need not be decided).[44] Secondly, Modestinus rose at some stage to be *praefectus vigilum* in Rome, in which role he is found as one of a series of *praefecti* who issued extempore judgements (*interlocutiones*) in a property case. The issue dragged on, as is explicitly stated, from the year of the consuls of 226 to that of those of 244. Precisely when Modestinus gave his ruling is not clear. But the Roman inscription which records all this thus provides unique testimony at this point, in the form of the actual words spoken by a known Roman juristic writer:[45]

42. Honoré (n. 19), 101–7, "Secretary no. 8."

43. For the evidence, see *PIR*² H 112.

44. *Dig.* 47, 2, 52, 20.

45. *CIL* VI, no. 266 (remarkably, not in *ILS*); Riccobono, *FIRA*² III, no. 165. The section quoted is lines 19–23.

Si quid est iudicatum, habet suam auctoritatem (si est, ut dixi, iudicatum). Interim apud me nullae probationes exhi[be]ntur, quibus doceantur fullones in-pen[sione]m iu[r]e conveniri.

If any judgement has been given, its authority stands (if, as I say, a judgement has been given). For the moment no proofs are put forward before me by which the *fullones* are shown to be subject to a legitimate demand for payment.

Thirdly, Modestinus was also one of a quite restricted group of jurists who are cited by name in imperial replies to *libelli*. In 239 Gordian III reminded a petitioner sharply that he had already received a ruling on the same point "from Modestinus, a jurisconsult of no insignificant *auctoritas*."[46]

Fourthly, and finally, Modestinus was the author of a considerable body of juristic writing: among other titles, nine books of *Differentiae*, evidently written after 217, single books *de inofficioso testamento, de legatis et fideicommissis*, and *de manumissionibus*, and twelve books of *Pandectae*, also written after Caracalla's death. But his most distinctive contribution to Roman legal literature was to write a book in Greek whose title itself perfectly exemplifies the penetration of Greek by Latin (or pseudo-Latin) loan-words: Παραίτησις ἐπιτροπῆς καὶ κουρατορίας (*On exemption from tutela and cura*, often labelled simply *de excusationibus*).[47] As with all the other juristic works of the period, it survives only in extracts; but, even so, these cover some six large pages in Lenel's *Palingenesia* and show the characteristic traits of Severan jurisprudence: repeated reference both to imperial rulings and to the opinions of other jurists (Paulus, Ulpian, Cervidius Scaevola). It is also very characteristic in treating in parallel, almost without distinction, exemption from *tutela* (guardianship of minors and women) and *cura* (guardianship of cases other than minors and women) within what we would classify as Roman private law on the one hand and exemption from liturgies in provincial cities on the other. It should be recalled that Modestinus, like Licinius Rufinus, was writing in the decades following the moment when the Constitutio Antoniniana had conferred the Roman citizenship, and with it the rules of Roman private law, on (among others) the educated upper classes of the Greek cities. It also incorporates a remarkable series of transliterated Latin, or semi-Latin, words: συνβετερανός, λεγεωνάριος, ἐξκουσατίονες, καλκουλάτορες.

Whether Herennius Modestinus himself came originally from a Latin-

---

46. *CJ* 3, 42, 5: "a non contemnendae auctoritatis iuris consulto."

47. Lenel (n. 4) I, cols. 701–56. The fragments of Modestinus' *de excusationibus*, written in Greek, occupy columns 707–18.

or a Greek-speaking context, it seems impossible to tell. But his example may encourage us to ask what we know of the juristic contribution of Licinius Rufinus. In his case there is no room for doubt that his native city was Thyatira in Lydia, and all of our documentary evidence on his public services and imperial offices is in Greek. His name, with its anomalous double *praenomen* (first name),[48] may suggest that he descended from an Italian family which had settled there earlier. But his own social origins have to be seen as unambiguously Greek.

The few surviving fragments of his one known work, the *Regulae*, show someone who, like Modestinus, is firmly embedded in the scholastic tradition of Roman jurisprudence. In the seventeen fairly brief fragments, he exhibits the same characteristics of Severan jurisprudence as are mentioned above, citing (as we have seen, text to n. 5) a decision of the current emperor, Caracalla, mentioning an opinion of Iulianus (*Iulianus putat*), referring to the *auctoritas* of Aquillius Gallus, and expressing the view that "most have considered" (*plerique existimaverunt*) that there could be a valid sale of a free man, provided that the parties were ignorant of the fact that he was free. In keeping with the nature of the work as indicated by its title, he shows a strong tendency to lay down basic principles: "Any institution [of an heir] which was invalid *ab initio* cannot gain validity subsequently [*ex postfacto*]."[49]

This tendency to state basic principles concisely might be thought to make Rufinus a relatively promising candidate in the context of Honoré's procedure of comparing the verbal, intellectual, and expository styles of juristic works on the one hand and of imperial replies to petitions on the other, in the hope of identifying the real "authors" of the latter. That being so, and given the (very hypothetical) chronology suggested above, and *if* the post which Rufinus held was indeed that of *a libellis*, then the first possibility to examine would be "secretary no. 9," who on Honoré's view was the successor of Modestinus, and who, it is suggested, held office between March 226 and August 229. If the theory, as well as the identification of the private rescripts of this period as those of a single person, is correct, then we have fifty-two or fifty-seven rescripts which (it is proposed) were written by the same man, amounting to some two hundred lines of text, compared with the seventy or so lines quoted in the *Digest* as coming from Rufinus' *Regulae*.[50] Both totals

48. On double *praenomina* in this period, see O. Salomies, *Die römischen Vornamen: Studien zur römischen Namengebung* (1987), 414–18.

49. *Dig.* 50, 17, 210 (Licinius Rufinus, *libro singulo regularum* ["in his one-book work on *Rules*"]): *Quae ab initio inutilis fuit institutio, ex postfacto convalescere non potest.*

50. Honoré (n. 19), 107–9. Honoré's *Palingenesia* of the rescripts in chronological order can be printed out from the disk supplied with the second edition.

are small, especially the second (and, above all, as compared with the vast bulk of Ulpian's writing). But even these relatively modest figures at least serve to underline the scale of the legal reasoning from this period which survives in the form of private rescripts. Having said that, however, it does not seem possible to detect in these rescripts traces of the (very little known) juristic "voice" of Licinius Rufinus.

Alternatively, if we accept the hypothesis that Modestinus was *a libellis* in 223–25, we could look at his (hypothetical) predecessor, Honoré's "secretary no. 7," who, it is suggested, held office from October 222 to October 223. In his case Honoré (of course, writing before there was any reason to identify Licinius Rufinus as one of the *a libellis*) attributed to him ninety-two or ninety-six rescripts, and noted that "a confident note is now sounded, the rescript often beginning with an emphatic statement of the law. . . . Other rescripts open with a pithy statement of principle."[51]

The body of text thus recovered and reassembled in chronological order is thus quite considerable, amounting to some 300 lines when printed out (see n. 50). Even if it were thought not worth pursuing the question of who was the real "author" of these replies, they would still represent evidence for the juristic function performed by, or in the name of, the emperor in the first part of Severus Alexander's reign, and while Domitius Ulpianus was praetorian prefect. Thus a rescript of December 222 lays down that if certain defendants require more strict examination, the provincial governor (*praeses*) "will take care to send the defendants to Domitius Ulpianus, the *praefectus praetorio* and *parens meus*."[52] This same rescript exhibits a characteristic feature of the replies of 222–23, namely specific references to rulings by earlier emperors or the Senate, in this case Antoninus Pius.[53]

This feature appears also in another reply of December 222, where part of the text is unfortunately corrupt:[54]

51. Honoré (n. 19), 98–101. I am very grateful to Tony Honoré for suggesting to me the identification of Licinius Rufinus with "secretary no. 7," and for discussing the issues with me.

52. *CJ* 4, 65, 42.

53. Cf., e.g., *CJ* 8, 10, 2 (*edicto divi Vespasiani et senatus consulto* [by the edict of the divine Vespasian and a decree of the Senate]); 6, 50, 4 (*divo Hadriano placuit* [as seemed right to the divine Hadrian]); 9, 23, 3 (*Senatus consulto et edicto divi Claudii* [by a decree of the Senate and an edict of the divine Claudius]); 4, 1, 2 (*secundum constituta divorum parentum meorum* [according to the rulings of my divine parents]); 9, 22, 2 (*divorum parentum meorum rescriptis* [according to the replies of my divine parents]).

54. *CJ* 4, 52, 2.

> Idem (Imp. Alexander) Eutychiano. Si † ea lege Chreste † servum, sed naturalem filium venumdedit, ut emptor eum manumitteret, quamvis non est manumissus, ex constitutione divorum Marci et Commodi as Aufidium Victorinum liber est.

> Imperator Alexander to Eutychianus. If [. . .] has sold [not?] a slave, but a natural son, on condition that the purchaser will manumit him, even if he has not been manumitted, following the *constitutio* of the Deified Marcus and Commodus to Aufidius Victorinus, he is free.

Whoever wrote this had somewhat compressed the dutiful reference to previous emperors, since Commodus had not been deified. Aufidius Victorinus, however, was an appropriate addressee, praefectus urbi in the later 170s and consul II in 183; he is attested in the correspondence of Fronto, on inscriptions, and in the three references in the *Digest* to other communications addressed to him, by Marcus Aurelius.[55] Once again, we see how profoundly embedded in the Antonine and Severan world the texts of this period collected in Justinian's *Digest* and *Codex* are.

But is there anything beyond the concise and authoritative style revealed in the fragments of Licinius Rufinus' *Regulae* to suggest that he might be "secretary no. 7," in office in 222–23? Essentially, these fragments are too few to form a basis for comparisons of intellectual and verbal style. But it may be worth setting out one of them for comparison with the rescript to Eutychianus quoted above. This is an extract from *Regulae* I, included in the *Digest*:[56]

> Si duobus heredibus institutis servus liber esse iussus sit, si decem heredibus dederit, ab altero ex heredibus venierit et tradius fuerit, pro parte altero ex heredibus, a quo non venierit, dando pecuniam liber erit.

> If, when two heirs have been instituted, it has been laid down [by will] that the slave is to be free, on condition that he gives ten [*aurei*?] to the heirs, but he has been sold and handed over by one of the heirs, by giving money in proportion to the other of the heirs, by whom he has not been sold, he will be free.

The comparison of the two expressions of the law is perhaps suggestive. But it does not seem possible to go beyond that. The identification of this *a libellis* as Licinius Rufinus can be no more than a hypothesis. But if we allow ourselves to entertain this hypothesis, it would follow that Rufinus became *a libellis* some six months after accession of Severus Alexander, and while Ulpian was praetorian prefect. But, while Ulpian was murdered in the summer of 223, Rufinus (on this reconstruction) was rewarded at some point, perhaps in the mid-220s, with adlection to the Senate, though at a surprisingly modest rank, held the praetorship and then a governorship and (it seems) the consulate, and was a member of the twenty-man consular commission which opposed Maximinus in 238.

The latter part of his career thus involved him in quite major convulsions and conflicts. But unless (as is possible) his last equestrian post and his senatorial ones were all compressed into a much shorter period than suggested here—say from the late 220s to the end of the 230s—then we may wonder whether the first four of his important equestrian posts at the emperor's side were held in a continuous sequence, or with intervals, and, in either case, whether the anonymous *Seb(astos)* whom he served was "Caracalla" (211–17) or Macrinus (217–18) or "Elagabal" (218–22), or two of these, or all three. This phase too had involved drastic changes and conflicts, not to speak of the fact that the imperial entourage had been continuously absent from Rome from 214, when Caracalla set out to the East, till 219, when the new emperor Elagabal returned.[57] It is useless to speculate, and also superfluous, since the intellectual and personal career of Licinius Rufinus is in any case of exceptional interest.

Learning Latin, Studying Roman Law

This chapter has been concerned with certain very distinctive external aspects of the complex—and, in historical terms, extremely important—process by which the upper classes of the Greek East "became Roman" while "staying Greek." The end result of this long evolution was to be a Greek-speaking "Roman" Empire ruled from Constantinople; and one of its most remarkable products was to be precisely the compilation of that sixth-century source book of extracts of classical Roman juristic works written (almost entirely) in Latin, the *Digest*.

Inscriptions mirroring the participation of local notables from the Greek cities in the wider Roman world, whether as ambassadors, tax gatherers, soldiers, equestrian civil or military officials, or senators, have transformed our conceptions of the Empire; and, if viewed collectively, they form a "literature" which is comparable in significance to the narrative representations

57. See H. Haufmann, *Itinera Principum* (1986), 223–31.

of Rome and its history by Greek writers like Plutarch, Appian, or Cassius Dio. Greek inscriptions honouring men who became experts in Roman law form a very significant sub-category within this spectrum of public representations, for they imply the acquisition of a specifically Roman expertise, embodied in a scholastic tradition, and only available in Latin.[58] The study of Roman law by Greek-speakers must thus be seen as an exception—but perhaps an exception proving the general rule—to the wider pattern, emphasized recently by Swain, of a powerful linguistic "Hellenism" in the age of the Second Sophistic.[59] A fair number of such inscriptions are known, but by their nature they show us no more than externals—for instance one recording the early death of the young man from Cilicia who had been to Berytus to study "the Ausonian laws."[60] But we lack almost all evidence of the actual process involved in learning first Latin and then Roman law. What sort of thing a "school" of Roman law, in Berytus or in Rome itself, really was, also remains obscure. For a start, we would almost certainly be wrong to think of a single "law school" at Berytus: the *Expositio totius mundi*, in describing the city as it was in the mid-fourth century, speaks of *auditoria legum* (lecture halls of law) in the plural.[61] At any rate it is clear that by the end of the third century it was an established pattern for students from the Greek provinces to go to Berytus to pursue Roman law; one well-known example is provided by the *scholastici* from the province of Arabia who were studying there with a view to becoming lawyers, and to whom Diocletian gave a rescript.[62]

At some point, obviously, Greek students of Roman law had to acquire an advanced knowledge of Latin; but our evidence on the teaching and learning of Latin in the Greek provinces is remarkably poor. The closest that we can come, in the context of the learning of Latin by Greek-speakers for use in a legal context, merely provides us with what we might call text-book material. I refer to the *Fragmentum Dositheanum*, which forms part of a compilation of texts made in A.D. 207, and which preserves the parallel bilingual text of a work on the law of manumission. As Honoré's invaluable study of

58. For an invaluable study by a Roman lawyer, exploiting this and other non-legal evidence for lawyers under the Empire, see the work by Kunkel (n. 7).

59. S. Swain, *Hellenism and Empire: Language, Classicism and Power in the Greek World*, A.D. *50–250* (1996).

60. *AE* 1972, no. 635. For the date (fourth century), see J. F. Gilliam, "A Student at Berytus in an Inscription from Pamphylia," *ZPE* 13 (1974): 147.

61. *Expositio totius mundi et gentium*, ed. J. Rougé (Sources Chrétiennes, 124, 1966), chap. 25.

62. *CJ* 10, 50, 1: "Cum vos adfirmatis liberalibus studiis operam dare, maxime circa professionem iuris, consistendo in civitate Berytorum provinciae Phoenices . . ."

this text shows, the compilation of which it forms a part was intended to provide material for Greek-speaking students of Latin.[63]

We can come rather closer to the experience, attitudes, and aspirations which will have marked the career of a man like Licinius Rufinus, who rose through his learning in Roman law to the very heart of the imperial system, by turning to the autobiographical account of his education by Gregorius from Neocaesarea in Pontus, who was later to be bishop of his native city, to be the subject of a powerful and evocative biography by Gregory of Nyssa, and to achieve lasting fame in the Greek and Russian Orthodox churches as "Gregory the Wonderworker." It was his change of direction, from the pursuit of Roman law to Christianity, by becoming a student of Origen at Caesarea in Syria Palaestina, which was both to give rise to the very important autobiographical record which he left, and to mean that (for present purposes) the record breaks off just when it would have been most illuminating. The narrative comes from the *Address*, the *Prosphōnētikos* (*logos*), in which Gregorius gives thanks to Origen at the end of his studies with him, which seem to have taken place in the 230s.[64] If we suppose that Licinius Rufinus will have been born in about the mid-180s, Gregorius will have been perhaps a quarter of a century younger, born (it is thought) around 212 or 213 (and thus just at the start of Rufinus' career at court, and as a juristic writer).

I have referred to the evidence of Gregorius' *Address* elsewhere,[65] but in this context it is worth spelling it out rather more fully. For there is perhaps no more vivid testimony to the process of acculturation. The account comes from the narration of Gregorius' early experiences, provided as an explana-

---

63. The parallel Latin and Greek text is to be found in G. Goetz, *Corpus Glossariorum Latinorum* III: *Hermeneumata Pseudositheana* (1897), 48–56 and 102–8 (deriving from two separate manuscripts). See A. M. Honoré, "The 'Fragmentum Dositheanum,'" *RIDA* 12 (1965): 301.

64. The best modern treatments of Gregorius' remarkable autobiographical record are to be found in H. Crouzel, ed., *Grégoire le Thaumaturge, remerciment à Origène, suivi de la lettre d'Origène à Grégoire* (Sources Chrétiennes, 148, 1969), whose text is used below, and above all in the review article on this work by J. Modrzejewski (now Mélèze-Modrzejewski), "Grégoire Thaumaturge et le droit romain," *Rev. Hist. Dr. Fr.* 49 (1971): 313. What is said here serves only to bring out in this context the points made by Modrzejewski. For the biographical representation of him by Gregory of Nyssa in the next century, see Migne, *PG* 46, 893–958, with the study by R. van Dam, "Hagiography and History: The Life of Gregory Thaumaturgus," *Classical Antiquity* 1 (1982): 272. Note also the very illuminating treatment of Gregory by R. Lane Fox, *Pagans and Christians* (1986), 516–17.

65. For instance in "Culture grecque et culture latine dans le Haute-Empire: la loi et la foi," in *Les martyrs de Lyon (177), Lyon 20–23 Septembre 1977, Coll. Int. du CNRS* 575 (1978), 187.

tion of how divine providence had brought him from Neocaesarea in Pontus
to Caesarea in Syria Palaestina, from where he had intended to go back to
Berytus (*Address* 5, 48–72).

Gregorius and his brother were born into a pagan family in Neocaesarea,
and were educated by their mother after their father's death. Her first plan
was that, as youths of good birth, they should study with a rhetor (56). But
Gregorius also had a Latin teacher, to whom by divine inspiration there occurred the idea that his pupil should both pursue his Latin studies more am-
bitiously and seek to learn law, perhaps with a view to acting as an advocate
(57–61):

> But, unsleeping as he was, my divine pedagogue and true guardian,
> although my family had not conceived of this idea and nor did I myself
> have the impulse, inspired one of my teachers, who was in any case en-
> trusted with teaching me the Latin language (not with the idea that I
> should reach a high level, but so that I should not be entirely ignorant
> of that language — and he happened to be not unversed in the laws). By
> putting this idea into his head, [my divine guardian] encouraged me
> through him to study the Roman laws thoroughly. . . . [My teacher]
> also added an observation, which turned out in my case the truest of
> all: the study of the laws would be for me the fullest of travelling allow-
> ances (for this was the word which he used), whether I wished to be
> one of the rhetors who compete in the courts, or to follow some other
> way of life.

The way in which the teacher's prediction turned out to be even more accurate than he supposed was that the intention to study the law led Gregorius
to set off for Berytus and Caesarea, to which Origen had moved from Alexandria. Berytus was "a rather more Roman city, and considered as a school of
these laws." Gregorius might have gone to Rome to study, but it was a further accident of circumstances which took him to Berytus instead. For the
governor of Palestine (the *legatus* of Syria Palaestina) had taken Gregorius'
brother-in-law, the brother of his sister, who was also a jurist (νομικός), as a
member of his staff. He was able to send for his wife, and thus it happened
that, just when they (apparently also Gregorius' brother) were about to set
off (apparently for Rome), a soldier arrived with authority to exact transport services, and with *diplomata* (certificates permitting to use the official
means of transport) sufficient to cover several people (69). Thus they travelled to Caesarea, intending then to go the short distance back to Berytus.
But in Caesarea they met Origen, and the whole course of their lives changed
(62–72).

Few passages in our evidence give a better impression of the educational presuppositions of the possessing classes in the Greek East, or of the wider prospects which the Roman Empire offered to them. One could stay at home as an educated local landowner, act as an advocate in the courts, join the staff of a provincial governor, learn Latin, whether to a modest or more profound level, and enter the imperial service as an equestrian or a senator. But there were also now two further possibilities. One had been, in Gregorius's case, quite unexpected: to study with a famous Christian teacher, to become a Christian, and to return home to be a bishop. The other was visualized as a new and challenging direction for intellectual endeavour: the advanced study of Roman law, whether in Berytus or in Rome itself. It is in fact earlier in his *Address* that Gregorius provides a representation of Roman law as a field of study. He begins from the reflection that constant practice in verbal expression is necessary for fluency. But it was another matter when it came to the Roman laws, which were written in Latin:[66]

> On the contrary, a quite different form of study takes a terrible grip on my mind, and binds my mouth and my tongue, if ever I wish to say the least thing in the Greek language—our admirable laws, by which the affairs of all those who are under the rule of the Romans are regulated, which can neither be composed nor studied thoroughly without great labour, being as they are wise and accurate and varied and admirable, and in a word most Hellenic, but expressed and transmitted in the language of the Romans, which is impressive and pretentious and wholly suited to the imperial power—but none the less burdensome for me.

Gregorius appears to mean, in the course of a quite complex train of thought, both that the study of juristic texts in Latin was hard work, though (or because) their intellectual content was at a high—even positively "Hellenic"—level, and also that the attempt to convert this material into Greek caused acute problems of expression. It is of some interest that the latter thought is reflected also in the dedicatory letter which Herennius Modestinus placed at the beginning of his *de excusationibus* (text to n. 47 above), and which—quite against the theoretical intentions of Justinian's grandiose project—was to be preserved verbatim in the *Digest*.[67]

66. *Address* 1.6–7. The text in this section is very defective. I have simply followed Crouzel's text (n. 64), adopted by Modrzejewski (n. 64), 317, except that in the second line as printed I have assumed the suggestion (Crouzel, p. 97, n. 4) to add καί after συνδεῖ.

67. *Dig.* 27. 1, 1 *pr.* (Modestinus *libro primo excusationum*: Ἐρέννιος Μοδεστῖνος Ἐγνατίῳ Δέξτπῳ. Συγγράψας σύγγραμμα, ὡς ἐμοὶ δόκει χρησιμώτατον, ὅπερ παραίτησιν ἐπιτροπῆς καὶ κουρατορίας ὠνόμασα, τοῦτό σοι πέπομφα. Ποιήσομαι δὲ ὡς ἂν οἷος τε ὦ

Herennius Modestinus to Egnatius Dexter. Having composed a work of, it seems to me, the greatest usefulness, which I have entitled *Exemption from tutela and cura*, I have sent it to you. I will, so far as I am able, make the exposition of these matters clear, expressing the legal rules in the language of the Greeks, even though I know that they are regarded as hard to express when subjected to such transformations.

When Gregorius was composing his *Address*, it is likely that Licinius Rufinus will already have reached the summit of senatorial status and influence at Rome, as a *consularis* and *amicus Caesaris*. Gregorius' words may remind us of how arduous and challenging an intellectual journey it was for citizens of Greek cities to master both Latin and Roman law, and then to enter the imperial service, and even, in Rufinus' case, to contribute a work to the corpus of juristic writing in Latin. The inscriptions from Beroea and Thessalonica record between them the role as advocate, and the expertise in Roman law, which could be attributed to a Greek. But those from Thyatira both provide the fullest representation, through the medium of Greek honorific vocabulary, of Rufinus' remarkable Roman career, as an equestrian and then senator, and also assert most emphatically his services to his native city and his fellow citizens.

τὴν περὶ τούτων διδασκαλίαν σαφῆ, ἀφηγούμενος τὰ νόμιμα τῇ τῶν Ἑλλήνων φωνῇ, εἰ καὶ οἶδα δύσφραστα αὐτὰ νομιζόμενα πρὸς τὰς τοιαύτας μεταβολάς). My translation is tentative, and differs somewhat from that in Alan Watson, ed., *The Digest of Justinian* II (1985), 781.

Index

As in Volume One, the index, compiled by the editors, is meant to give some clues and keys to the string of thoughts and ideas developed over the years in Fergus Millar's articles on government, society, and culture in the Roman Empire: names, institutions, events, and dates are all subservient to this principle.